An Introduction to the HUMANITIES

LITERATURE, HISTORICAL DOCUMENTS, AND FINE ART

FOREWORD BY
JANE SMILEY

ScottForesman

EDITORIAL OFFICES: Glenview, Illinois
REGIONAL OFFICES: San Jose, California · Tucker, Georgia
· Glenview, Illinois · Oakland, New Jersey · Dallas, Texas

Authors

Foreword: Jane Smiley, novelist; author of *A Thousand Acres* and *The Greenlanders*.

Introductions: CHAPTER 1: **John L. Foster**, Translator and Professor of English Emeritus, Roosevelt University; author of *Love Songs of the New Kingdom* and *Echoes of Egyptian Voices*. CHAPTER 2: **Jasper Griffin**, Professor of Classical Literature, Oxford University; author of *Homer on Life and Death* and an editor of *The Oxford History of the Classical World*. CHAPTER 3: **Thomas Sheehan**, Professor of Philosophy, Loyola University, Chicago; author of *The First Coming: How the Kingdom of God became Christianity*. CHAPTER 4: **Elizabeth Fernea**, Professor of English and Middle Eastern Studies, University of Texas at Austin; author of *Guests of the Sheik: An Enthnology of an Iraqi Village* and, with her husband Robert Fernea, *The Arab World: Personal Encounters*. CHAPTER 5: **Patrick J. Geary**, Professor of History, UCLA and Director of the UCLA Center for Medieval and Renaissance Studies; author of *Phantoms of Remembrance: Memory and Oblivion at the End of the 1st Millennium*. CHAPTER 6: **David Bevington**, Phyllis Fay Horton Professor in the Humanities, University of Chicago; editor of the *Complete Works of Shakespeare* and the Bantam Shakespeare. CHAPTER 7: **Rhoads Murphey**, Professor of History and Asian Studies, University of Michigan; author of many books on Asia, most recently *A History of Asia*. CHAPTER 8: **Roland Oliver**, Emeritus Professor of African History, University of London; author most recently of *The African Experience*. CHAPTER 9: **Jamake Highwater**, writer and arts advocate; author of many books, including *The Primal Mind: Vision and Reality in Indian America* and the novel *Anpao*. CHAPTER 10: **Peter Gay**, Sterling Professor Emeritus of History, Yale University; author of many books, including *Freud: A Life for Our Time*. CHAPTER 11: **Evelyn Toynton**, essayist; contributor to, among others, *The American Scholar*, *Commentary*, and *The New York Times Book Review*.

Consultants

Neil Anstead, Coordinator of the Humanitas Program, Cleveland Humanities Magnet School, Reseda, California. **Jesus Cardona**, English Teacher, John F. Kennedy High School, San Antonio, Texas. **Anitra Christoffel**, Humanities Teacher, Baldwin Senior High School, Baldwin, New York. **Robert Wayne Johnson**, Social Studies Teacher, Port Charlotte High School, Port Charlotte, Florida. **Mary Price**, World History Teacher, Libertyville High School, Libertyville, Illinois.

Front Cover Design: Margaret Carsello
Front Cover Photos (clockwise from left): Benin bronze head—Foto Marburg/Art Resource, New York; Japanese torii—SEF/Art Resource, New York; Toltec statue—Rene Burri/Magnum Photos; David by Michelangelo—Alinari/Art Resource, New York

ISBN: 0–673–29435–8
Acknowledgments for quoted matter and illustrations are included in the acknowledgments section on pages 600–604. The acknowledgments section is an extension of the copyright page.

56789-DQ-0403020100

Table of Contents

Chapter 3. Judaism and Early Christianity / c. 1000 B.C.–A.D. 550

Chapter 4. Islamic Civilization / 650–1600s

Chapter 5. Medieval Civilization / 700–1450

Chapter 6. The Age of the Renaissance / 1350–1650

Chapter 7. The Asian Civilizations / c. 1000 B.C.– A.D. 1775

Chapter 8. African Civilizations / c. 720 B.C.– A.D. 1816

Chapter 9. Native American Civilizations / c. 600–1890

Chapter 10. The 18th and 19th Centuries / 1687–1897

Chapter 11. The Twentieth Century / 1890–1965

Foreword

JANE SMILEY
Author of A Thousand Acres,
The Greenlanders, *and other works*

I CLEARLY REMEMBER MY FIRST MOMENT OF POLITICAL SELF-consciousness. I was sitting at my fifth grade desk, gazing down upon a page of my social studies textbook, *Our Land and People*. On a small drawing of the United States (not a map, because the well-known outline was floating alone, unconnected to either Mexico or Canada), I could, unassisted, pick out the very spot where I, ten years old, a student at Avery School, a resident of the State of Missouri, happened to be living and breathing at that moment. What incredible luck! Born an American! And living in the middle of the country, surely the most safely American place to be! It could easily have happened otherwise. What I most clearly remember is the sense of myself separating from myself—the "I" that was so busy marveling could be sitting anywhere else in the world (the revelation ran all through my body), could even be sitting in a desk behind the Iron Curtain. And I knew that if I had turned out to be that other person, what I would be feeling, instead of gratitude and pleasure, would be sorrow and envy of that lucky girl me, that student at Avery School, that resident of Missouri and citizen of the United States.

In my private and deeply felt joy, I was a good child of my time. It was 1959, after all, and my entire education had been part of an ideological war that many then assumed would lead to a real war, a nuclear war, unprecedented in its destructive power and the sacrifice to be exacted from civilians like myself. In 1959, the air was full of notions like bomb shelters, nuclear fallout, civil defense, survivability. The point of a nuclear war, it was clear, was not whether we would each live, suffer, or die, but whether enough of us would emerge from our shelters after fourteen days (the half-life of the radiation) with sufficient will to rebuild the victorious United States. Those *Reader's Digest* Condensed

Books that I found on my family's book shelves always depicted the pioneer spirit of the nuclear survivors, their refusal to mourn or look back, their determination to build a United States that was bigger and better than ever.

What in the world might be lost in a nuclear war, what people, cities, ecosystems, natural beauties, architectural wonders, paintings, sculptures, civilizations, traditions, great thoughts, all of these were missing from *Our Land and People* and from every other book I read in school. While our text did not, of course, mention nuclear war, the gist of its argument was that our people inhabited a land that was the acme of human progress and the center of human geography. Other civilizations were worth mentioning only insofar as they foreshadowed or contributed to ours.

My education since those Cold War days has been a welcome surprise, a marvelous discovery of the extent of my ignorance, ignorance that grows everyday, the more I learn what is out there. What you have in this capacious and varied textbook is some of what was missing from my schoolbooks in the Fifties and early Sixties—a record of what in the world there is to be cherished and contemplated, preserved and returned to when people ask themselves why they are alive, what makes us human, and how it is best to live in a world that is mysterious and sometimes frightening.

Is there any duller word than the word *humanities*? *Human* is vulnerable and flawed, forgivable; *humanity* is large and generous; but *humanities* are abstractions of abstractions, dusty dry committee-speak, a word that bores even the person employing it. I suggest, instead, that you think of this book as a collection of minds thinking and voices calling out.

We all have different images of what the mind is. One of my friends always imagines hydraulic pumps churning up thoughts. The English poet, Lord Byron, called it "that fiery particle." I imagine one of those Easter egg dioramas, the thin shell enclosing, not frosting bunnies and ducklings, but a miniature dark universe, sparkling with stars. What I like about the mind is the way it takes the world into itself and seems to light up. All of the minds in this textbook are fully lit up, though each of our own minds may not yet have the capacity to receive all their light. If, for example, we look at the famous painting by Jan van Eyck, *Giovanni Arnolfini and his Bride*, on page 262, our only response might be that Giovanni is rather strange looking, even unattractive, or that the surfaces of the objects in the painting seem remarkably well-defined and smooth, crisper and more real even than a photograph. A little study of the painting, and we discover that each object represents a facet of the marriage, and the painting embodies the hopes of the couple for their future. Many people stop there, their minds partially open to van Eyck's, but if we look further into van Eyck's life and work, if we gaze upon the works of other painters of his time, learn about the materials available to them, if we find out about the lives of Giovanni Arnolfini and his wife Giovanna, if we travel to Bruges where van Eyck lived and look at the sights he looked upon, the painting comes to seem more and more thoughtful, more and more beautiful, more familiar and yet more enigmatic, more worth enjoying again and again. This is because we are experiencing, across thousands of miles and hundreds of years, Jan van Eyck's mind, still present in his painting.

Or, in the same section, we have John Milton writing his *Areopagitica* (see page 276). Even though Milton writes in English and is considered a great stylist, the way he expresses himself is far different from what we are used to, the words and constructions he prefers may seem heavy and dry. How are we to get across the great gulf of boredom between ourselves and his meaning? And why bother? The fact is that freedom of the press from censorship by the government through the licensing of publications is an issue of enormous relevance in our time. The perennial conflict between the government, which prefers not to be closely watched or questioned, and the press, which exercises its freedom with as much irresponsibility as responsibility, has expressed itself as recently as the 1991 Persian Gulf War, when the government successfully restricted press coverage of the war, much to the detriment of Americans' understanding of both its progress and effects. Even more recently, in the coverage of O. J. Simpson's arrest and trial, payments by tabloid journalists to witnesses in the case had the potential of suborning testimony and making the case untriable. But the relevance of the issue is only part of the interest of Milton's piece. His passion about the issue and the sly manner in which he builds his argument reveal not only who he is, but what he had to be careful about. First, he puts himself on the side of God—absolutely necessary in a theocracy—and then he stresses the practical difficulties to the authorities of instituting licensing. He presents the more questionable heart of his argument, that licensing would stifle free inquiry and that free inquiry is desirable, only after the reader has already made some investment in the piece, and he quickly builds upon that investment with open flattery of the authorities — "your own mild and free and humane government." His most important assertion, that truth "may have more shapes than one" and may at first appear "more unsightly and unplausible than many errors," is slipped into the argument only at the end, when the reader has been lulled into a mood of acceptance. In fact, *Areopagitica* is most interesting to an astute reader, not for the substance of its argument, but for what it shows about Milton's effort to criticize the government without appearing to set himself against it, and what that implies about the dangerous times Milton lived in. Times as dangerous as those faced by many writers and journalists in today's theocracies and dictatorships.

But Milton's long sentences and figurative references to works and ideas we are not familiar with are hard. In fact, reading is hard, and finding the author inside his or her work may sometimes seem impossible, but there are three good reasons to make the effort. One is difference. Other minds are exotic. Their strange ideas and modes of logic, their alien experiences and expressions, once we begin to understand them, are refreshing and thought-provoking. They stock our minds with images that we may never have thought of before, that we may find exciting, comforting, intriguing, a refuge from what we see everyday. Another reason to make the effort is similarity. For the paradox of reading is that beyond the exotic is something familiar and recognizable that appeals to us from afar and shows us that we need not feel isolated and alone. Reading is the only sociable activity that avoids appearances—we hear the human voice in the text without seeing the different skin color, the odd dress, the alien body language. Wide reading breaks down prejudice and fear, works against the instinctive human urge to reject the humanity of those who are strange. The last reason, perhaps the least respectable but maybe the most important, is that reading builds upon itself. The more we read the easier and more enjoyable reading becomes, until the lucky day when the pleasure of being quietly swept into a great and difficult book becomes the most complex and delicious pleasure of all, one of the intimate pleasures like friendship and love, and one of the intellectual pleasures, too, like mastering a skill or understanding a concept.

My own education in the humanities commenced rather late in high school, when my class was assigned to read *Crime and Punishment*, by the Russian novelist Feodor Dostoevski. Though I was a good student and an avid reader of young adult fiction, I couldn't make head nor tail of most of the novel. There was a young man named Raskolnikov, said to be a college student, but he lived in a degree of poverty that I found myself literally unable to imagine. For obscure reasons, he seemed to be attacking an old woman with no hair, and stealing things from her, but what the things were and what Raskolnikov intended to do with them I had no idea. I was lost, and I read on automatic pilot, as I often did in high school, hoping that just running my eyes over the words would enable me to bring something to the class discussion (where, I hoped, the other students and the teacher would tell me what was going on). And then Dostoevski introduced Katerina Ivanovna Marmeladova.

Though I had a difficult time picturing the many male characters, as well as sorting through their long Russian names, Katerina Ivanovna was immediately vivid — slender, nervous, excitable, dressed shabbily, and continuously talking in a way that revealed the tumult of her conflicting feelings. Destitute, weakened by tuberculosis, the wife of a hopeless drunkard, Katerina Ivanovna knows that her situation and that of her three children is desperate. She is both terrified and humiliated by the manner in which she is forced to live, particularly because she had grown up as the daughter of a prosperous official. She is fascinating initially because of her shortcomings — anger, snobbishness, ingratitude — but the unfolding narrative reveals the steadfast love she feels for others, especially Sonya, the prostitute who is Dostoevski's heroine. She was not like anyone I knew or had ever met, and yet I recognized her. Her extreme feelings were simultaneously strange and possible to me, because Dostoevski had made her condition the logical outcome of her character and her circumstances. That I was an American girl of the twentieth century and Katerina Ivanovna a woman of the nineteenth century, a Russian woman, too (though the war in Vietnam had eased the megaton threat of the Cold War, the Soviets were still our "enemies") meant nothing. She took up residence in my imagination, compelling, frightening, dramatic. The scene of the funeral dinner Katerina Ivanovna gives in honor of her husband was so clear in my mind that it remains unchanged to this day — a memory I have of something I never saw.

After feeling such strong interest in *Crime and Punishment*, I eagerly sought the same pleasure elsewhere. Of course I found it — literature is full of great books, great characters, great scenes. With Katerina Ivanovna, I had cracked through some barrier between myself and "greatness." I had a handle on some of the complexity of style and plot that had previously bored or intimidated me. My joy in reading grew so intense that I thought I would try writing.

Your introduction to the humanities, then, is really an invitation to an enormous party. The other guests do most of the talking. In pursuing your job of listening and trying to understand, you will find that some of them are uncongenial and off-putting, but you will also find new friends whom you will want to know much better. Enjoy!

The Hall of Two Truths from the
Book of the Dead

Mesopotamia and Egypt

INTRODUCTION by John L. Foster

PORTFOLIO

The Search for Everlasting Life (c. 2000 B.C.)
The epic of Gilgamesh

Babylonian Law (c. 1750 B.C.)
The Hammurabi Code

Egyptian Visions of the Afterlife (1600–1500 B.C.)
The Book of the Dead; The Harper's Song for Inherkhawy

Worship of the Sun (c. 1350 B.C.)
Relief of Akhenaton and his Wife; Akhenaton's Hymn to the Sun

Naturalism in Art: the Amarna Revolution (c. 1353–1336 B.C.)
Statue of Mycerinus and his queen; ceremonial painting of
Sennufer and his wife; Bust of Nefertiti; painting of
Tutankhamen and his wife

Love Songs from the New Kingdom (1300–1100 B.C.)
"My love is one and only, without peer"; "I was simply off to
see Nefrus my friend"; "I think I'll go home and lie very still"

CHAPTER 1 PROJECTS

CHAPTER 1

*Alabaster vase
from Uruk*

c. 3500 B.C.
Settlement of Uruk

Mesopotamia and Egypt

2000 B.C.–1100 B.C.

JOHN L. FOSTER

*Professor of English Emeritus,
Roosevelt University*

This chapter is concerned with the beginnings of historical civilization. The civilizations of Mesopotamia and Egypt developed in two great river valleys, that of the Tigris and Euphrates in Mesopotamia and the Nile in Egypt. It was in these two river valleys that writing was invented and developed, first in ancient Sumer about 3500 B.C. and then in Egypt two or three centuries later. It is this discovery that sets the two lands apart from the other "pre-literate" or "pre-historic" societies; for with the invention of writing, human beings could make records of their lives and actions. They could write down the value of their possessions, or the laws of their land, or the prayers and praises they directed toward their gods. And they could begin to keep records of their common past; for it is this, above all else, which helps unite people into a single group with common goals, beliefs, and heritage. People could now remember the distant past of their ancestors, and they could educate their children to respect and fulfill that heritage.

THE FERTILE LAND

Both Mesopotamia and Egypt are arid lands. Except for a few marshy areas, they are hot, dry, and

Palette of Narmer

Sumerian cylinder seal

c. 3100
Menes unites Upper and Lower Egypt

c. 2750
Gilgamesh king in Uruk

relatively treeless. Civilization could not exist in either except for the rivers that flooded every year, covering the countryside with water, that was rich in natural fertilizers and that left behind a layer of silt in which to grow crops. The people in both lands soon began to make use of these floodwaters. Through the process of irrigation, they dug channels to direct the precious water to their fields, and they formed basins to hold it long after the yearly floods had subsided. In this way they could increase enormously the amount of land under cultivation, thus making possible an abundance of crops and food. In this way surpluses could be stored for lean years and calamities. And indeed, both lands endured agricultural disasters, fields were annihilated and villages were swept away, leaving little trace.

Though both are riverine lands, Egypt was fairly well protected from outside influences (including invasions from other peoples). The

Mediterranean Sea more or less blocked entrance from the north. Seven places of tumbled rock called cataracts prevented easy access to or from the parts of Africa lying to the south. And killing deserts lying both to the east and west of the Nile River valley pretty much prevented approach from these directions. Egypt was safe. These geographical features, plus the regular rhythms of the great Nile flowing north to the sea and the sun rising in the east and setting in the west, gave the ancient Egyptians a sense of security. Partly, as a result of this, the Egyptian outlook tended to be sunny and optimistic.

This was not the case in Mesopotamia. This area included territory from the modern countries of Iran, Iraq, Syria, and Turkey. The great fertile valley of the Tigris and Euphrates rivers was open to all sides, and unfriendly peoples could strike and invade everywhere except the south, where the two rivers flowed into the

Pyramids of Giza

c. 2600
Cheops builds the Great Pyramid

Persian Gulf. And they did. The early history of this area is a tale of almost continuous warfare among the little city-states, which is why so many groups of people contributed to Mesopotamian civilization: Sumerians, Akkadians, Babylonians, Assyrians, and Persians. Life was less certain than in Egypt, and the outlook of the peoples was darker and less optimistic.

The antiquity and the duration of these two civilizations was also important. Sumer, the first phase of the Mesopotamian civilization, became prominent and literate about 3500 B.C.; and by means of the succeeding societies (Akkad, Babylon, Assyria, and Persia) Mesopotamia continued on well into Biblical times. Egypt was united into a single country about 3100 B.C. and continued to function as one well into the classical and Christian eras. The time span of ancient Egypt was about three thousand years. We might compare it to the length of the independent United States, which is

barely 200 years. Most readers are aware of King David of ancient Israel, who ascended the throne about the year 1000 B.C. The major events and stories of ancient Mesopotamia and Egypt all occurred before the reign of David; and it might help us to realize that about 40 percent of recorded human history — almost half — took place *before* King David of Israel.

THE MAKING OF A CIVILIZATION What makes a civilization like the two great early civilizations of Mesopotamia and Egypt? There are several ingredients. There is, first of all, a large number of people living together — in cities and with a sense of community. They must have a sense of place, a common and shared territory (even when they fight over it). They must have enough material resources and wealth to allow the people to eat, gather possessions, raise families, and prosper. There must be some system to govern the people

Detail of the Standard of Ur

Head of Sargon the Great

c. 2650
Sumerian kings established in Ur

c. 2350
Sargon the Great conquers Sumer

(with or without their consent) and to carry out the functions of government; and this all must take place under some form of law, either unwritten or written, like the famous Code of Hammurabi. There must, of course, be writing (for that is how we define historical civilizations) and education to teach the next generation the wisdom and customs of the ancestors. There is a sense of common purpose under a common leader. The leader in both of the Mesopotamian and Egyptian civilizations was a king. There must also be a sense of shared traditions and ideals that have been built up over the centuries. These traditions are the core of the education that the children receive. Finally, there must be a shared sense of the same all-embracing and inclusive divinity (or divinities, since both Mesopotamia and Egypt each had many gods)—a creator who formed the universe and all its creatures, who watches over and cares for the people of that civilization, and who

in his wisdom orders the activities of the world.

In Mesopotamia and Egypt, religion was pervasive. This attitude of the ancient peoples is not only fundamental to understanding their civilizations, it is perhaps the one thing that most distinguishes their ideas from our own. In ancient Sumer, the highest gods were connected with nature. There was the father-god, An, who was god of heaven or the sky; Enlil, the god of the air; Enki, god of water; the mother-goddess, Ninhursag; and Inanna, goddess of love and forerunner of the classical goddess of love, Venus. These were the main gods in a "family" of hundreds of greater and lesser divinities. In Egypt there were also many gods. The primary god was the creator-god, usually called Rê, god of the sun and "father" of the other gods. Others were the falcon-god Horus, the moon-god Thoth, the craftsmen's god Ptah, the goddess of love, Hathor, the mother-goddess Isis, the

Detail from the
Sarcophagus of
Princess Kawit

Detail of tablets
from Nineveh

c. 2133
Middle Kingdom begins in Egypt

c. 2000
The epic of Gilgamesh composed

god of the underworld, Osiris, and many others.

Together these gods, whether in Mesopotamia or in Egypt, controlled the activities of the universe and of human beings. Everything one did was influenced by the gods. The person who was perplexed prayed to them; the person traveling asked them for a safe journey; a young man in love prayed to Hathor for success with his girlfriend and a young woman similarly prayed that her boyfriend would notice her; the priest who tended to a god's work on earth prayed to the god for guidance in his duties; the schoolboy prayed to Thoth for the intelligence to finish his lessons and understand what his teacher was trying to tell him; and the king, the pharaoh of Egypt, also prayed to the great god Rê, whose son he was, to help him govern Egypt wisely. Only once in the long span of early history, and this was in Egypt, did the belief in many gods (polytheism) change.

This came under the reign of King Akhenaton, who believed in one god (monotheism). He ruled about 1350 B.C. His radical belief was not comfortable for the people of Egypt; and after he died, the country returned to its traditional ways of thinking.

Of course, the civilizations of Mesopotamia and Egypt were not completely alike. One contrast is seen in their attitudes toward death. In Mesopotamia death and the grave were dark and forbidding. When persons died, they went to the underworld to live in misery and to eat dust; and they were "shades"—the shadows of their former selves with hardly any energy left. There was an existence after life; but it was pitiful, and people dreaded it. This fear of death can be seen in the great Mesopotamian story of Gilgamesh, the legendary king of Uruk. This poem is the world's first epic, over 1000 years older than the great poems by Homer about the Greek heroes in the war at

Detail of Stela of Hammurabi

Statue of Queen Hatshepsut

c. 1750
Hammurabi becomes king of Babylon

c. 1475
Hatshepsut becomes pharaoh of Egypt

Troy. Gilgamesh had found a friend, Enkidu, who after many adventures with Gilgamesh, died. At this time, Gilgamesh realizes that he too must die some day; and he sets off on a long quest, or adventure, in search of eternal life. He fails, of course; but at the end of the poem, Gilgamesh is allowed to speak for a moment with the dead Enkidu, who gives him an account of life in the underworld. It is ugly and without hope.

In Egypt, on the other hand, we find the idea of a happy afterlife first developed. When Egyptians died, they went in judgment before the god Osiris to find out if they were good or evil. At this time, they declared their innocence, that they were not guilty of any of a long list of deeds or crimes that would have been offensive to the gods and thus considered evil. Then the person's heart was weighed in a balance; and if the good deeds outweighed the bad, the person was sent on to the Field of Reeds to survive forever in happiness in the otherworld. The dying Egyptian faced the afterlife with hope and joy.

ANCIENT WAYS OF LIFE   In these two earliest civilizations the most fundamental duty was to worship and obey the gods, for they controlled all things, including the direction and success of one's life. One should venerate the king, who, in Egypt, was considered divine, and who, in Mesopotamia, was chosen by the gods. One must also be a good citizen, obeying the laws of the land, whether written or, as in Egypt, spoken by the pharaoh. And one must study and honor the lives and actions of the wise men of the past. Both civilizations were conservative—they treasured the accomplishments and wisdom of their ancestors—and "good" to them was the ability to reach the high goals and performance set by "those who have gone before." They were not individualists in our sense of the term; they did

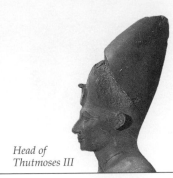

Head of
Thutmoses III

Bas-relief of
Akhenaton

c. 1455
Battle of Megiddo

c. 1350
Akhenaton institutes worship
of the sun god

not seek to be different or original or to accomplish things no one had done before. The civilizations that discovered how one could conserve the traditions of the ancestors—through writing—were content to follow those traditions as best they could. Perfection was in the past, not in some indefinable future.

Very early in Egypt, in the Old Kingdom (c. 2700–2300 B.C.), there developed a kind of moral or ethical code called "The Catalogue of Virtues." In it the deceased person claimed to have done justice, spoken truly, acted rightly, been a fair judge, rescued the weak from the strong, given bread to the hungry, clothed the naked, given those without a boat the means to cross the waters, respected their father, pleased their mother, and even raised their children. In the New Kingdom this recital becomes "The Declaration of Innocence" mentioned on page seven. But most of all the Egyptian tried to follow *ma'at*. This word signifies a combination of truth, justice, and goodness all rolled into one. If we can speak of a "right way" for human beings to act, then *ma'at* was the word for that way.

But we should never get the mistaken impression that life was all seriousness and striving to be good. That could get boring. The idea of how to live certainly included how to enjoy life. People did have private lives, after all; and if they were well off, they would enjoy their great estates, walking the grounds (which were irrigated and thus like great gardens), or fishing and hunting in the marshes that dotted the property; or they would enjoy feasts and banquets, eating and drinking and listening to musicians playing dinner music or to harpers telling stories of the gods or legends of the men and women of old. They took great delight in the trees and flowers of their plantations; and they enjoyed married life and their children. One testimony of this charming private life is the

Head of Rameses II

Winged Bull from Khorsabad

c. 1275	**c. 1250**	**720**
Rameses II defeats Hittites at the battle of Kadesh	Construction of Abu Simbel	Sargon II re-establishes the Akkadian Empire

Egyptian love songs. In them we see the fun and excitement of young men and women falling in love, or being in love, or playing the games of love. And we find that the feelings of these people, who have been dead for over three thousand years, come alive again; we can see what they saw and feel what they felt so long ago. And their feelings about love are no different from ours. There is a direct bond between them and ourselves that shows our common humanity despite the differences of time and place.

The civilizations of both Mesopotamia and Egypt were vital and long-lasting; and they made many discoveries, which we now enjoy and take for granted. They discovered writing, the basis of history. They learned how to live in cities with large populations. They learned how to worship and live with the gods who ruled the universe. They searched out the differences between good and evil and passed their learning on to their chil-

dren. They made great temples and palaces, statues and paintings, and they wrote down their discoveries, their dreams, and their feelings. The civilizations of Mesopotamia and Egypt began the journey that is our history.

The Search for Everlasting Life

The epic of Gilgamesh is one of the oldest poems in the world. Most of it was found in 1850 on twelve clay tablets in the ancient city of Nineveh, in the ruins of the palace library of an Assyrian king, Ashurbanipal, who lived in the seventh century B.C. However, the story of Gilgamesh was already old when Ashurbanipal ruled. He had it translated into his own language from the Babylonian, the language in which it had been composed. In fact, scholars think the story was first written about 2000 B.C. and that it was based on even older stories and legends. This long poem tells of the heroic adventures of Gilgamesh (gil′gə mesh), a legendary king of Uruk (ü′rük), an ancient Sumerian city. The epic tells the story of Gilgamesh's friendship with the wildman Enkidu (en′kē dü). They perform great feats of bravery together and when Enkidu dies, Gilgamesh is heartbroken. He becomes despondent at the prospect of his own death and embarks on a quest for immortality. Although he fails in his quest, he comes to accept the inevitability of old age and death. The following selection is excerpts from the epic of Gilgamesh. It opens with a description of Gilgamesh and his achievements. What does the conception of this hero reveal about Mesopotamian values?

from the epic of Gilgamesh

I WILL PROCLAIM TO THE WORLD THE DEEDS OF GILGAMESH. This was the man to whom all things were known; this was the king who knew the countries of the world. He was wise, he saw mysteries and knew secret things, he brought to us a tale of the days before the flood. He went on a long journey, was weary, worn-out with labor, returning he rested, he engraved on a stone the whole story.

When the gods created Gilgamesh they gave him a perfect body. Shamash the glorious sun endowed him with beauty, Adad the god of the storm endowed him with courage, the great gods made his beauty perfect, surpassing all others, terrifying like a great wild bull. Two thirds they made him god and one third man.

In Uruk he built walls, a great rampart, and the temple of blessed Eanna for the god of the firmament Anu, and for Ishtar the goddess of love. Look at it still today: the outer wall where the cornice runs, it shines with the brilliance of copper; and the inner wall, it has no equal. Touch the threshold, it is ancient. Approach Eanna the dwelling of Ishtar, our lady of love and war, the like of which no latter-day king, no man alive can equal. Climb upon the wall of Uruk; walk along it, I say; regard the foundation terrace and examine the masonry: is it not burnt brick and good? The seven sages laid the foundations.

After the death of his great friend Enkidu, Gilgamesh, afraid of his own death, goes in search of Utnapishtim (**üt nä pesh′tem**), an immortal being, who, along with his family, was spared during a great flood sent by the gods. From him, Gilgamesh hopes to obtain the secret of immortality. Gilgamesh travels throughout the world's wilderness, eventually coming to the sea where he meets Siduri (**si dür′ē**), the goddess of the vine.

BESIDE THE SEA SHE LIVES, THE WOMAN OF THE VINE, THE MAKER of wine; Siduri sits in the garden at the edge of the sea, with the golden bowl and the golden vats that the gods gave her. She is covered with a veil; and where she sits she sees Gilgamesh coming towards her, wearing skins, the flesh of the gods in his body, but despair in his heart, and his face like the face of one who has made a long journey. She looked, and as she scanned the distance she said in her own heart, "Surely this is some felon; where is he going now?" And she barred her gate against him with the cross-bar and shot home the bolt. But Gilgamesh, hearing the sound of the bolt, threw up his head and lodged his foot in the gate; he called to her, "Young woman, maker of wine, why do you bolt your door; what did you see that made you bar your gate? I will break in your door and burst in your gate, for I am Gilgamesh who seized and killed the Bull of Heaven, I killed the watchman of the cedar forest, I overthrew Humbaba who lived in the forest, and I killed the lions in the passes of the mountain."

Then Siduri said to him, "If you are that Gilgamesh who seized and killed the Bull of Heaven, who killed the watchman of the cedar forest, who overthrew Humbaba that lived in the forest, and killed the lions in the passes of the mountain, why are your cheeks so starved and why is your face so drawn? Why is despair in your heart and your face like the face of one who has made a long journey? Yes, why is your face burned from heat and cold, and why do you come here wandering over the pastures in search of the wind?"

Gilgamesh answered her, "And why should not my cheeks be starved and my face drawn? Despair is in my heart and my face is the face of one who has made a long journey, it was burned with heat and with cold. Why should I not wander over the pastures in search of the wind? My friend, my younger brother, he who hunted the wild ass of the wilderness and the panther of the plains, my friend, my younger brother who seized and killed the Bull of Heaven and overthrew Humbaba in the cedar forest, my friend who was very dear to me and who endured dangers beside me, Enkidu my brother, whom I loved, the end of mortality has overtaken him. I wept for him seven days and nights till the worm fastened on him. Because of my brother I am afraid of death, because of my brother I stray through the wilderness and cannot rest. But now, young woman, maker of wine, since I have seen your face do not let me see the face of death which I dread so much."

She answered, "Gilgamesh, where are you hurrying to? You will never find that life for which you are looking. When the gods created man they allotted to him death, but life they retained in their own keeping. As for you, Gilgamesh, fill your belly with good things; day and night, night and day, dance and be merry, feast and rejoice. Let your clothes be fresh, bathe yourself in water, cherish the little child that holds your hand, and make your wife happy in your embrace; for this too is the lot of man."

But Gilgamesh said to Siduri, the young woman, "How can I be silent, how can I rest, when Enkidu whom I love is dust, and I too shall die and be laid in the earth. You live by the sea-shore and look into the heart of it; young woman, tell me now, which is the way to Utnapishtim, the son of Ubara-Tutu? What directions are there for the passage; give me, oh, give me directions. I will cross the Ocean if it is possible; if it is not I will wander still farther in the wilderness." The wine-maker said to him, "Gilgamesh, there is no crossing the Ocean; whoever has come, since the days of old, has not been able to pass that sea. The Sun in his glory crosses the Ocean, but who beside Shamash has ever crossed it? The place and the passage are difficult, and the waters of death are deep which flow between. Gilgamesh, how will you cross the Ocean? When you come to the waters of death what will you do? But Gilgamesh, down in the woods, you will find Urshanabi, the ferryman of Utnapishtim; with him are the holy things, the things of stone. He is fashioning the serpent prow of the boat."

After a fight, Urshanabi (ŭr shä nä´bē) takes Gilgamesh across the Sea of Death and leads him to Utnapishtim's home.

SO UTNAPISHTIM LOOKED AT HIM AND SAID, "WHAT IS YOUR name, you who come here wearing the skins of beasts, with your cheeks starved and your face drawn? Where are you hurrying to now? For what reason have you made this great journey, crossing the seas whose passage is difficult? Tell me the reason for your coming."

He replied, "Gilgamesh is my name. I am from Uruk, from the house of Anu." Then Utnapishtim said to him, "If you are Gilgamesh, why are your cheeks so starved and your face drawn? Why is despair in your heart and your face like the face of one who has made a long journey? Yes, why is your face burned with heat and cold; and why do you come here, wandering over the wilderness in search of the wind?"

Gilgamesh said to him, "Why should not my cheeks be starved and my face drawn? Despair is in my heart and my face is the face of one who has made a long journey. It was burned with heat and with cold. Why should I not wander over the pastures? My friend, my younger brother who seized and killed the Bull of Heaven and overthrew Humbaba in the cedar forest, my friend who was very dear to me and endured dangers beside me, Enkidu, my brother whom I loved, the end of mortality has overtaken him. I wept for him seven days and nights till the worm fastened on him. Because of my brother I am afraid of death; because of my brother I stray through the wilderness. His fate lies heavy upon me. How can I be silent, how can I rest? He is dust and I shall die also and be laid in the earth for ever." Again Gilgamesh said, speaking to Utnapishtim, "It is to see Utnapishtim whom we call the Faraway that I have come on this journey. For this I have wandered over the world, I have crossed many difficult ranges, I have crossed the seas, I have wearied myself with traveling; my joints are aching, and I have lost acquaintance with sleep which is sweet. My clothes were worn out before I came to the house of Siduri. I have killed the bear and hyena, the lion and panther, the tiger, the stag and the ibex, all sorts of wild game and the small creatures of the pastures. I ate their flesh and I wore their skins; and that was how I came to the gate of the young woman, the maker of wine, who barred her gate of pitch and bitumen against me. But from her I had news of the journey; so then I came to Urshanabi the ferryman, and with him I crossed over the waters of death. Oh, father Utnapishtim, you who have entered the assembly of the gods, I wish to question you concerning the living and the dead, how shall I find the life for which I am searching?"

Utnapishtim said, "There is no permanence. Do we build a house to stand for ever, do we seal a contract to hold for all time? Do brothers divide an inheritance to keep for ever, does the flood-time of rivers endure? It is only the nymph of the dragon-fly who sheds her larva and sees the sun in his glory. From the days of old there is no permanence. The sleeping and the dead, how alike they are, they are like a painted death. What is there between the master and the servant when both have fulfilled their doom? when the Anunnaki, the judges, come together, and Mammetun the mother of destinies, together they decree the fates of men. Life and death they allot but the day of death they do not disclose."

THINKING CRITICALLY

1. *Determining Relevant Information* How does the opening of the epic establish Gilgamesh's importance? How is this information relevant to the epic?

2. *Identifying Central Issues* What is the lesson even a great man like Gilgamesh must learn about life?

3. *Linking Past and Present* Are the lessons Gilgamesh learns about mortality still true today? What facets of modern life can you point to which indicate we are still pursuing Gilgamesh's quest for immortality?

WRITER'S PORTFOLIO

1. *Extending the Selection* From your reading of the epic of Gilgamesh, discuss what values you think were celebrated in Mesopotamia.

2. *Examining Key Questions* The Sumerians are believed to have been the first to develop a system of writing. Why is the development of a written language considered a major step in the formation of a civilization?

Babylonian Law

Hammurabi (ham´u rä´bē) was a Babylonian king who ruled in the eighteenth century B.C. It was during his reign that the Babylonians conquered and united the various kingdoms of Mesopotamia into an empire. Hammurabi's code of 300 laws was found in 1901 on a stela, or stone shaft, at Susa, in present-day Iran. This code covers criminal and civil law, economic provisions, and laws regarding families; it also prescribes penalties. These laws provide insight into the everyday life of the Mesopotamians and their views of justice, as well as the structure of Babylonian society. Fifteen of Hammurabi's laws appear below. What do the penalties they provide suggest about Mesopotamian society?

from The Hammurabi Code

IF A MAN'S WIFE IS ACCUSED BY HER HUSBAND, BUT HAS NOT been found lying with another male, she shall swear by the name of God and return into her house.

If a man has been taken captive, and there is food in his house, and his wife forsakes his house, and enters the house of another; then because that woman has not preserved her body, but has entered another house, then that woman shall be prosecuted, and shall be thrown into the water.

If a man has been taken captive, and there is no food in his house, and his wife enters the house of another, then that woman bears no blame.

If a man divorce his spouse who has not borne him children, he shall give to her all the silver of the bride-price, and restore to her the dowry which she brought from the house of her father; and so he shall divorce her.

If a son has struck his father, his hands shall be cut off.

If he has broken the bone of a Freeman, his bone shall be broken.

If he has destroyed the eye of a Plebeian, or broken a bone of a Plebeian, he shall pay one mina of silver.

If he has destroyed the eye of a man's slave, or broken a bone of a man's slave, he shall pay half his value.

If a man has knocked out the teeth of a man of the same rank, his own teeth shall be knocked out.

If a man's slave strike the body of the son of a Freeman, his ear shall be cut off.

If a man has struck an other man in a dispute and wounded him, that man shall swear "I did not strike him knowingly," and he shall pay for the doctor.

If he die of his blows, he shall swear likewise; and if it be the son of a Freeman, he shall pay half a mina of silver.

If a builder has built a house for a man and his work is not strong, and if the house he has built falls in and kills the householder, that builder shall be slain.

If the child of the householder be killed, the child of that builder shall be slain.

If the slave of the householder be killed, he shall give slave for slave to the householder.

THINKING CRITICALLY

1. *Recognizing Values* Who seems to have had the most advantages in this society?

2. *Identifying Assumptions* Do women seem to have more or fewer rights than you expected? How does Mesopotamian law seem to view women?

3. *Linking Past to Present* What is the difference between the philosophy underlying punishment for crimes prescribed here and the philosophy underlying punishment for crimes in the U.S. today?

WRITER'S PORTFOLIO

1. *Extending the Selection* Examine the question of who determines the laws in American society.

2. *Examining Key Questions* Discuss one of the following questions: What is the role of law in society? Why are laws necessary? What is the advantage of having laws written down?

Egyptian Visions of the Afterlife

Egyptians believed very strongly in the afterlife. After death, a person would make the journey to the underworld, where the god Osiris (ō sī′ris), would make the ultimate decision about one's final destination. To prepare for this journey, Egyptians filled their tombs with the necessary items of daily life – such as bowls, cups, furniture, food – and particularly The Book of the Dead, a guide to help the dead on their journey. This book was compiled between 1600 and 1500 B.C., though its individual texts date from much earlier. The "Declaration of Innocence" is a list of all the sins an individual did not commit, to be declaimed upon reaching the Hall of the Two Truths where Osiris's judgment was made. What does this declaration tell you about the types of behavior expected of ancient Egyptians?

"The Declaration of Innocence"

I have not done crimes against people,
I have not mistreated cattle,…
I have not known what should not be known,
I did not begin a day by exacting more than my due,…
I have not blasphemed a god,
I have not robbed the poor.
I have not done what the god abhors,
I have not maligned a servant to his master.
I have not caused pain,
I have not caused tears.
I have not killed,
I have not ordered to kill,
I have not made anyone suffer.
I have not damaged the offerings in the temples,
I have not depleted the loaves of the gods,

I have not stolen the cakes of the dead....
I have not increased nor reduced the measure,...
I have not cheated in the fields.
I have not added to the weight of the balance,
I have not falsified the plummet of the scales.
I have not taken milk from the mouth of children,
I have not deprived cattle of their pasture....
I have not held back water in its season,
I have not dammed a flowing stream,
I have not quenched a needed fire.
I have not neglected the days of meat offerings,
I have not detained cattle belonging to the god,
I have not stopped a god in his procession.
I am pure, I am pure, I am pure, I am pure!

The inner walls of Egyptian tombs were usually decorated with scenes and writing. The Harper's Song for Inherkhawy was found on a tomb wall. The song is an echo of Siduri's advice to Gilgamesh (see page 12): Since no one can be certain what lies beyond death, do not forget to have joy in this world. Does the song reflect "The Declaration of Innocence"?

The Harper's Song for Inherkhawy

I

All who come into being as flesh
    pass on, and have since God walked the earth;
        and young blood mounts to their places.

The busy fluttering souls and bright transfigured spirits
    who people the world below
        and those who shine in the stars with Orion.
They built their mansions, they built their tombs—
    and all men rest in the grave.

So set your home well in the sacred land
    that your good name last because of it;

Care for your works in the realm under God
    that your seat in the West be splendid.

The waters flow north, the wind blows south,
    and each man goes to his hour.

II

So, seize the day! hold holiday!
    Be unwearied, unceasing, alive,
        you and your own true love;
Let not your heart be troubled during your sojourn on earth,
    but seize the day as it passes!

Put incense and sweet oil upon you,
    garlanded flowers at your breast,
While the lady alive in your heart forever
    delights, as she sits beside you....

Let your heart be drunk on the gift of Day
    until that day comes when you anchor.

THINKING CRITICALLY

1. *Drawing Conclusions* How can you tell from the "Declaration of Innocence" that Egypt was a farming society?

2. *Making Inferences* What sacred duties seem to have been required of ancient Egyptians?

3. *Identifying Central Issues* Would someone who is troubled by thoughts of death be more apt to turn to the "Declaration of Innocence," or the Harper's Song, or both? Explain.

WRITER'S PORTFOLIO

1. *Extending the Selection* Write your own "Declaration of Innocence," updating it to reflect modern ethics.

2. *Examining Key Questions* With some exceptions, the literature of the Egyptians (and other ancient cultures) was almost entirely religious. Tell why you think this might have been so.

Worship of the Sun

To us it may seem that the thousands of years of Egyptian dynasties were static. In fact there were constant and quite dramatic changes, especially during the period of the New Kingdom (1554–1070 B.C.). This was an era of intense expansion, cultural development, and religious consolidation. One of the most extraordinary developments was the creation of a new state religion by Amenhotep IV (ä′men hō′tep): the worship of the sun god Aton or Aten. (*Aton* means "disk.") This god was to be worshipped under the sun instead of in a temple, and images of all the other old gods were destroyed. Amenhotep IV changed his name to Akhenaton (äh kə nä′tən) and moved the capital from Thebes to a place he called Akhetaton, and we know as Tel-el-Amarna. The Aton religion

The Royal Family under the rays of the Sun, limestone carving (c. 1350)

seems to have had no moral code, and the threat of punishment for disobedience, so evident in the old Egyptian religion, seems not to have existed. After Akhenaton's death, the cult of Aton was ruthlessly stamped out by the old priesthood. The old gods and goddesses were reinstated, yet Akhenaton's beliefs had made their mark in art and literature. The following selection is part of Akhenaton's Hymn to the Sun, a prayer probably composed by the Pharaoh himself. Akhenaton is pictured above with his queen Nefertiti and their three daughters (they eventually had six). How does the carving reflect the words in Akhenaton's Hymn?

from Akhenaton's Hymn to the Sun

Let your holy Light shine from the height of heaven,
  O living Aton,

source of all life!
From eastern horizon risen and streaming,
    you have flooded the world with your beauty.
You are majestic, awesome, bedazzling, exalted,
        overlord over all earth,
      yet your rays, they touch lightly, compass the lands
          to the limits of all your creation.
There in the Sun, you reach to the farthest of those
    you would gather in for your Son,
        whom you love;
Though you are far, your light is wide upon earth;
    and you shine in the faces of all
        who turn to follow your journeying....

You are the one God,
    shining forth from your possible incarnations
      as Aton, the Living Sun,
Revealed like a king in glory, risen in light,
    now distant, now bending nearby.
You create the numberless things of this world
      from yourself, who are One alone —
    cities, towns, fields, the roadway, the River;
And each eye looks back and beholds you
    to learn from the day's light perfection.
O God, you are in the Sun-disk of Day,
    Over-Seer of all creation
        — your legacy
      passed on to all who shall ever be;
For you fashioned their sight, who perceive your universe,
    that they praise with one voice
        all your labors.

And you are in my heart;
    there is no other who truly knows you
        but for your son, Akhenaton.
May you make him wise with your inmost counsels,
      wise with your power.
That earth may aspire to your godhead,
      its creatures fine as the day you made them.
Once you rose into shining, they lived;
    when you sink to rest, they shall die.

For it is you who are Time itself,
    the span of the world;
        life is by means of you.

Eyes are filled with beauty
        until you go to your rest;
All work is laid aside
        as you sink down the western horizon.

Then shine reborn! Rise splendidly!
        My Lord, let life thrive for the King
Who has kept pace with your every footstep
        since you first measured ground for the world.
Lift up the creatures of earth for your Son
        who came forth from your Body of Fire!

THINKING CRITICALLY

1. *Drawing Conclusions* Who is the son referred to in the hymn? How is this relationship indicated in the carving?

2. *Recognizing Values* In the course of human history, sun worship has flourished in several societies. Why do you think this might be so? What might cause the gradual demise of sun worship in any society?

3. *Linking Past and Present* Has the worship of the sun disappeared in modern societies? What forms does "sun worship" take today?

WRITER'S PORTFOLIO

1. *Extending the Selection* Argue whether Akhenaton was right to institute his new religion. Do you think the worship of Aton was more natural than the worship of a group of gods?

2. *Examining Key Questions* Define the meanings of *theocrat, theocratic,* and *theocracy* and show the etymologies for these words. Tell what these words have to do with ancient Egyptian society.

Naturalism in Art: the Amarna Revolution

The Pharaoh Akhenaton (c. 1353–1336 B.C.) sparked a revolution in art as well as in religion. Amarna (**ä mär⁄nä**) art introduced a realism and naturalness far different from the styles that preceded it. Early Egyptian sculpture and painting tended to be rigidly formal, with stiff poses and idealized features. The sculpture of King Mycerinus and his queen (c. 2500 B.C.), reproduced on page 24, is far from an accurate portrait with very few personal characteristics. In such a traditional posture, the two rulers become types rather than individuals. The same is true of the painting of Sennufer and his wife (c. 1400 B.C.) on page 25, where the pose and the body of the figures are characteristic of Egyptian painting. Sennufer is depicted on the wall of his tomb as part of a burial ritual, not as a portrait. It is this style that Amarna art tried to break from. Just as Akhenaton was introducing a new religion, so he was having his artists depict him and his family in a new fashion, featuring more natural poses and settings, and with their real physical features. This acceptance of naturalism is readily evident in the carving of Akhenaton on page 20, where the long jaw, sagging belly, large thighs and buttocks, and matchstick legs of the Pharaoh are far from ideal. (Modern scholars have speculated that his appearance may have been due to an endocrine disorder.) It is also evident to even greater effect in the bust of his wife Nefertiti (c. 1350 B.C.), on page 113, whose beauty is still radiant more than 3000 years later. While this bust was only a workshop model, a model for apprentice sculptors to follow, the details of her face are far more evident than those of the finished sculpture of Mycerinus's queen. The same is true of the pose of Tutankhamen (**tüt⁄tängk ä⁄mən**) and his queen in the painting from his throne-back (c. 1330 B.C.), that appears on page 113. The king is shown reclining naturally, while the queen rubs scented oil on his arm. The freedom of Amarna art was startling in its day and its natural poses and realistic figures seem all the more striking to us when compared to earlier Egyptian art. Which style seems closer to modern art?

King Mycerinus and his queen c. 2500 B.C.

Sennufer and his wife (c. 1400 B.C.)

THINKING CRITICALLY

1. *Making Comparisons* What differences do you notice in the depictions of Sennufer and Tutankhamen? What about between Mycerinus's queen and the bust of Nefertiti?

2. *Identifying Central Issues* What gives the painting of Tutankhamen a more cultivated and finished look than the painting of Sennufur?

3. *Linking Past and Present* Does public art in America tend to be more natural or more idealized? Do you notice any differences between the style of public murals and the style of public sculpture?

WRITER'S PORTFOLIO

1. *Extending the Selection* Suppose that you are an artist commissioned to paint a mural inside the entrance to your school. What elements would you include that would most accurately reflect the society of your school — its purpose, its beliefs, its hopes, and its ideals? Describe the mural in a paper.

2. *Examining Key Questions* Discuss how our judgment of a society is affected by its artistic works.

Love Songs from the New Kingdom

The poems included here are part of four small collections of love poetry from the time of the Egyptian New Kingdom (c. 1554–1070 B.C.). They were written in hieratic, the cursive form of hieroglyphic writing, and probably were copied by a scribe, who was not the author. That they still speak to us is a tribute, not just to the writers, but to the fundamental commonality of human emotion, especially love. They tell us of a civilization whose people were not always concerned with death, but who knew well the intimate pleasures, and frustrations, of love. Do these poems express a romantic view of love?

My love is one and only, without peer

My love is one and only, without peer,
    lovely above all Egypt's lovely girls.
On the horizon of my seeing,
    see her, rising,
Glistening goddess of the sunrise star
    bright in the forehead of a lucky year.
So there she stands, epitome
    of shining, shedding light.
Her eyebrows, gleaming darkly, marking
    eyes which dance and wander.
Sweet are those lips, which chatter
    (but never a word too much),
And the line of the long neck lovely, dropping
    (since song's notes slide that way)
To young breasts firm in the bouncing light
    which shimmers that blueshadowed sidefall of hair.
And slim are those arms, overtoned with gold,

those fingers which touch like a brush of lotus.
And (ah) how the curve of her back slips gently
  by a whisper of waist to god's plenty below.
(Such thighs as her's pass knowledge
  of loveliness known in the old days.)

I was simply off to see Nefrus my friend

I was simply off to see Nefrus my friend,
Just to sit and chat at her place
  (about men),
When there, hot on his horses, comes Mehy
  (Oh god, I said to myself, It's Mehy!)
Right over the crest of the road
  wheeling along with the boys.

O Mother Hathor, what shall I do?
  Don't let him see me!
  Where can I hide?
Make me a small creeping thing
  to slip by his eye
  (sharp as Horus')
    unseen.
Oh, look at you, feet—
  (this road is a river!)
  you walk me right out of my depth!
Someone, silly heart, is exceedingly ignorant here—
  aren't you a little too easy near Mehy?

If he sees that I see him, I know
  he will know how my heart flutters (Oh,
    Mehy!).
I know I will blurt out,
  "Please take me!"
  (I mustn't).
No, all he would do is brag out my name,
  just one of the many…(I know)…
Mehy would make me just one of the girls
  for all of the boys in the palace.
    (oh Mehy).

I think I'll go home and lie very still,
    feigning terminal illness.
Then the neighbors will all troop over to stare,
    my love, perhaps, among them.
How she'll smile while the specialists
    snarl in their teeth! —

she perfectly well knows what ails me.

THINKING CRITICALLY

1. *Analyzing Cause and Effect* The images in "My love is one and only…" are consistent and combine to produce a central impression of light. List the words that contribute to this central impression, and tell why these images are or are not appropriate to a love poem.

2. *Making Inferences* Why is the speaker in the third poem going to feign terminal illness?

3. *Linking Past and Present* What sort of expressions of love can you find in our society? Are these similar to the Egyptian love songs?

WRITER'S PORTFOLIO

1. *Extending the Selection* Summarize your impressions of what the Egyptians were like from reading these poems. How does this compare with your other impressions?

2. *Examining Key Questions* Discuss whether you think poetry is a type of expression common to all people or a product of civilization.

EXAMINING KEY QUESTIONS

- *What makes a civilization?*
- *How should we live?*

Throughout this chapter, most selections have concluded with a writing project asking you to discuss how the art or literature you have examined provides answers to one of these key questions. The following writing projects will help you draw together what you have learned by examining how several selections illustrate these key questions.

- Analyze the evidence we use to judge a civilization and its success. Compare and contrast the different things that art and literature can tell us about a society. How are they different from what we can learn from historical documents like law codes or archaeological evidence?

- Compare and contrast the attitudes toward life of the Mesopotamians and the Egyptians. Which society seemed to value life more? What do you think may have conditioned these attitudes?

SPEAKING/LISTENING

- Suppose that you could travel back in time to ancient Mesopotamia or Egypt. Give a short presentation to the class telling who of the people you have read about you would like to meet. Tell the other students what you would like to ask this person.

CRAFTING

- Create an Egyptian-style portrait of your class in the two-dimensional pre-Amarna style. Consider carefully how to give each person some identifying characteristic, as each student's pose and features will be similar.

COLLECTING

- Collect advertising images which use Egyptian motifs or elements. When these elements are used, what are they meant to signify? What does this tell you about common assumptions about Egypt?

The Acropolis in Athens

Greece and Rome

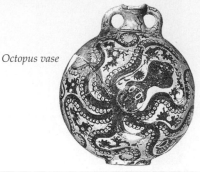
Octopus vase

c. 2500 B.C.
Knossos founded on Crete

Greece and Rome

c. 800 B.C.–A.D. 172

JASPER GRIFFIN
Professor of Classical Literature, Oxford University

The history of the classical world, which lasted roughly from 800 B.C. to A.D. 450, centers on the rise and flourishing of the city-state (in Greek, *polis*) and its eventual defeat and replacement by large-scale kingdoms and empires. In the early period Greece had the good fortune to be on the fringe of the older, developed kingdoms of the Near East, from which it learned much, both practical skills of life and also fine arts: the alphabet was borrowed and adapted from the Semitic peoples of Phoenicia (modern Lebanon and Israel), while in their statues and temples the early Greeks were unmistakably influenced by the Egyptians. But the eastern empires, with their god-kings and powerful priestly classes, could not subjugate a people divided from them and from each other by mountain ranges and the sea.

The Greeks lived in a large number of settlements, physically separate and fiercely independent. Each town had its own coinage and its own calendar. The calendar was shaped by the festivals of the city's gods—there were no weeks with regularly recurring days. Greek religion, like that of all their neighbors, was polytheistic, (although the Hebrews, of whom the Greeks knew almost nothing, were evolving monotheism). There were a number of great gods and goddesses, worshipped

Lion Gate
from Mycene

Detail of
Mycenean
vase relief of
Trojan Horse

1600
Founding of Mycenean city-states

1200
Trojan War

in all Greek states, and arranged in a family, headed by the supreme sky-father Zeus; and there were local divinities—dead men still thought to have power ("heroes"), nymphs in the woods and wild country, minor deities invoked at sowing and reaping, or at marriage, or at starting a journey. These gods gave color and shape to life, and all celebrations were holy days (still in English "holidays"). They were imagined as human in form and emotions, only bigger and stronger; they had love affairs and favorites and enemies. They received sacrifice of the slaughter of animals, whose flesh was then feasted on by the worshippers. There was no priestly class. This religion is nobly expressed in Homer's *Iliad* and *Odyssey*.

In the beginning the cities were ruled by kings, but Greek history opens with most kings losing their supremacy over the other noble families. The poems of the woman poet Sappho, a member of one of the noble families of the island of Lesbos, allow us a glimpse of the color and vividness of an aristocratic society. Strife among the elite families often led to the rise of a demagogic leader, usually a rogue aristocrat who appealed to the common people in his struggle with his rivals. Such men were called "tyrants," a title which their characteristic behavior soon made odious.

THE GOLDEN AGE OF GREECE

The sixth and fifth centuries B.C. were a time of great restlessness both in intellectual and in political affairs. For the first time, eastern empires began to conquer the Greeks in Asia Minor (modern Turkey), and by 500 B.C. the Persian Empire was in control of many of the most important cities, including Ephesus and Miletus, although it allowed a large measure of local rule. Greeks began to reflect: what was it that made them different from non-Greeks? What were the advantages

Vase
painting
of harpist

Romulus
and
Romus,
legendary
founders
of Rome

800
H .ner composes the Iliad and the Odyssey

753
Founding of Rome

and disadvantages of monarchy, aristocracy, and that new thing which was now appearing—democracy? Different peoples obeyed different laws, prayed to different gods; what did that mean for the truth or validity of any of them? Could the old tales of the love affairs of the gods really be true? Were there abstract principles to be found behind the variety of the world, quite different from the stories of Zeus and the other gods? What did it mean that what seemed to be the bones of sea creatures came to light on the tops of hills; had they once been under water?

This ferment of questioning was excited still further by the attempt of the powerful kings of Persia to conquer Greece. It was reasonable to expect their enormous army and fleet to crush the Greek cities, outnumbered and disunited; but the great invasion of 480–479 ended with Athens and Sparta triumphant and the king in flight. Exhilarated by their success, the Athenians felt that it was a vindication

of their democracy—a new thing in the world, much hated and derided by its enemies, at home and abroad. Athens showed an astonishing burst of energy, acquired a much resented "empire" over other Greek states, built the Parthenon and other buildings and statues which since have been regarded as masterpieces, and produced the first scientific historian (Thucydides) and the first works in philosophy and oratory to be seen as classics. "The Funeral Oration of Pericles" from Thucydides gives something of the flavor of that exciting time. So, too, do the new dramatic forms: tragedy and comedy.

Athens embodied a vision: a city with full democracy for all male citizens—political activity for women was a subject for comedies by Aristophanes, and without slave labor, in the absence of machines, there was no civilized life for anybody—with freedom of speech and equality before the law, and with arts and welfare paid

Gold Rhyton

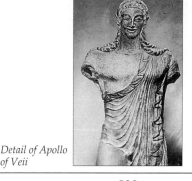

Detail of Apollo
of Veii

559
Cyrus the Great founds Persian Empire

509
Founding of Roman Republic

for by the taxes of the rich and the tribute of the empire. That vision suffered a fearful set-back when Athens fought and eventually lost the Peloponnesian War against the reactionary city of Sparta and her allies (431–404 B.C.). Athens remained democratic, but with her wings clipped; and the execution of Socrates (399) and the loss of the war turned many thinkers, including Socrates' pupil Plato and Plato's pupil Aristotle, against democracy.

The truly innovative period of Greek history is now over. Philosophical thought turns increasingly inward, to the soul of the individual: how is one to secure one's own serenity, irrespective of political or social conditions? The independent city-state is overwhelmed by the world-shaking conquests of Alexander "the Great" of Macedon (356–323 B.C.), a kingdom to the north, Greek in language and to some extent in culture but still a feudal monarchy in the pre-city stage of development. Alexander's triumphs

led to the division of Greece and the vast Persian empire into three or four opulent Macedonian kingdoms.

THE RISE OF ROME   It was during the dissolution of Alexander's empire, that Greece came into contact, and soon into conflict, with the rising power of Rome. Once a kingdom, Rome had long been an aristocratic republic. The great families ran the state and competed with each other for position and power; democracy never caught on at Rome. A hard and aggressive code of morals had as its aims to subordinate the individual to the good of the state — he should be "born not for himself but for the fatherland," as they loved to say; to secure the lasting position and influence of one's family, with no foolish or romantic disregard of its interests; and to prevent any one aristocrat outstripping the rest and endangering the system. An omnipresent pressure of public opinion was

Helmet of Corinthian hoplite

Bust of Socrates

490
Battle of Marathon

399
Death of Socrates

part of the Roman way of life. Rome was a highly warlike society: all the public offices for which ambitious men competed were wholly or partly military, and Roman armies expected to take the field every year. It also, in its early period, produced men of great public spirit, capable of resisting financial and other temptations.

Roman generals gradually conquered Italy and advanced beyond it. Two terrible wars defeated the rival imperial city of Carthage, a Phoenician settlement on the coast of North Africa (264–241 and 218–201 B.C.). In control of the Western Mediterranean, Rome turned to the Greek East. The Greek powers crumpled before the Roman legions, and by 31 B.C. Rome found herself in possession of the whole Greek world, including Egypt, as well as Spain, Gaul (modern France), North Africa, Turkey, Syria, and the southern Balkans. The huge scale of these wars proved incompatible with the old republican system, which insisted on

short-term commands and the equality of all members of the Senate, all interchangeably capable of holding any office or command. The spoils, too, and the temptations were now colossal. Roman grandees became as wealthy as kings, and the old system, resting on voluntary self-restraint and collective morale, buckled under the strain. Roman governors exploited their provinces mercilessly; competition between them reached the point of civil war, with Roman armies marching on Rome herself. We can see an unfettered individualism reflected in the poetry of Catullus.

The end was the victory of one man, Julius Caesar's grand-nephew and adopted son Octavian, who took the name Augustus. The republic lived on in name, but behind a constitutional facade the emperor was firmly in control. The armies took their oath of allegiance to him, and he had a force in Rome, the Praetorian Guard, to overawe, if necessary, the city and the

Head of Alexander

Coin with Hannibal's head

323
Death of Alexander the Great

216
Battle of Cannae

Senate. Months, even, were renamed after Augustus and his father — we still call them July and August. The arts, too, were mobilized. Rome was transformed into a splendid city of marble buildings, colonnades, and fountains; and Virgil wrote the supreme work of Roman Literature, the *Aeneid*, to trace Augustus' Roman Empire back to its mythical origins, with the Trojan hero Aeneas escaping from the sack of Troy.

How were people to live in such a world? Long contact with Greece had made Romans familiar with the tastes, refinements, and vices of the sophisticated society of Greece. Among the rest came philosophy, the study of the right way to live. Roman religion by itself gave little support, being largely a formal, state affair, with far less color and life than the Greek; and even Greek religion was often found rather distant, more aesthetically beautiful than emotionally consoling. Some went in for Oriental cults: the Egyptian

mother goddess Isis, the Iranian soldierly cult of Mithras the Sun, the exotic appeal of Judaism (at this time a proselytizing religion, making many converts). The most successful of such imports was to be Christianity. The upper class struggled to find a way of reconciling service to an emperor with self-respect as a free man. Many found comfort in the pre-packed systems of the philosophers, who analyzed the struggles of the soul and held out hopes of self-mastery and happiness in superiority to temptation.

The characteristic figure of classical antiquity is the citizen. In principle the equal of other citizens, he is subject to laws which are no respecters of persons. The law is independent of the magistrate who administers it; and magistrates are elected, and for a limited period. Conflicts with other citizens are fought out in the law-courts, or by competing for election to the same office. Military service is one of the duties of a citizen; his ideal is a

Ides of March coin

44
Assassination of Julius Caesar

Detail of mosaic portrait of Virgil

8
Death of Virgil

life of civilized leisure. His center is the city, with its rational temples and handsome public buildings. The cities are linked by straight, well-maintained roads. He does not give much thought to sin, nor to immortality. He is concerned with liberty, but not with economic equality. The barbarian is very different. In the tribal society which succeeded when the empire broke down, a man is not a citizen but a member of a tribe; his loyalty is to nothing abstract but to his leader, who has his position by birth and may lose it only by assassination—the coming of the empire was already a step in that direction for Rome. Conflicts are resolved by single combat or by the ordeal; home is the forest or the hills; the gods are worshipped in sacred groves; every man is a warrior as long as he lives.

The emperors promoted worship of themselves, and emperor-worship did provide a framework, both social and intellectual, for the expression of public spirit. Rich men were expected to confer spectacular benefactions on their home towns. The public service provided opportunities for holding office and spending money. Poor citizens passed their time out of their slum houses, enjoying the splendid public buildings and spaces. The armies on the frontiers remained mostly loyal and formidable. The Roman Empire, as we all know, fell; but more striking than its fall is the fact that it lasted so long. Even after the fall of the Western Empire and of Rome itself (410), Byzantium—"New Rome", as it called itself—maintained the Eastern Empire until 1453.

THE CLASSICAL LEGACY The importance of classical culture to our own is enormous. Ancient science was the basis for the new learning of the Renaissance, which struggled free from superstition. The theory that the earth revolves around the sun was put for-

*Detail
of the
Arch of
Titus*

Bust of Trajan

A.D. 69
Year of Four Emperors

96–180
*Roman Empire reaches its height
under the Antonine Emperors*

ward in the third century B.C.; atomic theory, a brilliant guess, was proposed in the fifth century B.C. and accepted by the influential philosophical school of Epicurus; the great philosopher and observer Aristotle made contributions in logic, zoology, political theory, and literary criticism, which remained primary for two thousand years. Architects studied the Roman Vitruvius. Doctors read Hippocrates and Galen—the works of Hippocrates (including the famous oath, which is the first code of medical ethics) were still being reprinted in the 1820s "for the benefit of physicians." In the arts, the achievement of the Greeks was to create the forms within which artists long continued to work. In the Renaissance each European nation in turn emulated classical literature in producing epic poems, tragedies and comedies in verse, pastoral poetry, history, dialogues, romances. Those were the natural forms, because they were the hallowed classical ones. Poets and historians had been brought up on the

Greek and Latin writers, as education consisted primarily of the laborious process of learning to read and write correct Latin prose and verse. In sculpture, the Greeks achieved the perfect representation of the naked body, which was banned by the early Christians and had to be painstakingly relearned during the Renaissance. The great buildings of Greece and Rome, the colonnades and domes and triumphal arches, have left a deep mark on all modern cities and are continually reused by architects. Above all, perhaps, the Greeks and Romans bequeathed two haunting myths. From Rome comes the ideal of a great empire at peace, governed by law, disciplined and austere, preserved from corruption by a high sense of duty. The other vision is that of the Greek ideal city, where life was lived nobly in accordance with reason and beauty and where the arts elevated and civilized a culture of free equals. However great the failures of the Romans and Greeks, these are the lingering visions of these civilizations.

TIME: c. 800 B.C.   PLACE: IONIA

The Death of Hector

Greek tradition attributed the *Iliad* (**il′ē əd**) and the *Odyssey* (**od′ə sē**) to a poet called Homer. Homer (fl. c. 800 B.C.) was probably a bard, or oral poet, from Ionia (**ī ō′nē ə**), an area of Greek settlement on the western coast of what is now Turkey. Around 800 B.C., when the Greek alphabet was first coming into use, these centuries-old oral epics were set down in the form we know today. The *Iliad* tells the story of the ninth year of the siege of Troy, a ten-year-long Greek expedition against the city of Troy that had taken place centuries before Homer's time. The excerpt below is from Book 22 of the *Iliad,* telling of the death of Hector, the greatest Trojan hero and son of the Trojan king, Priam (**prī′əm**). When the excerpt begins, Hector has killed Patroclus (**pə trō′kləs**), the friend of Achilles (**ə kil′ēz**), the greatest of the Greek warriors. Furious over the death of his friend, Achilles routs the Trojans in battle. All the Trojans flee within the walls of the city, leaving Hector standing alone to face Achilles' vengeance. Who is the most responsible for Hector's death?

THEN ACHILLES TURNED TOWARDS TROY. SWIFT, AS A PRIZE-winning chariot horse running all out across the plain, so swift were Achilles' feet and knees. And the old man, Priam, was the first to see him coming. And to Priam he seemed like the star which comes out at harvest time—bright are his rays among the armies of dark night—the star men name the Dog of Orion. Brightest of all, he is but a sign of evil. [Sirius, called the "Dog Star," the brightest star in the sky, was believed to bring pestilence.] Even so the bronze flashed on Achilles' breast as he ran. And the old man moaned, and took his head in his hands and cried to Hector, his son, who was standing before the gates ready to fight with Achilles: "Hector, dear son, do not wait there by yourself for Achilles. He is stronger far than you. Would that the gods loved him as I do. He would quickly enough be food for dogs and birds then. How many of my sons has he killed or sold to the islands oversea."... So he cried pulling at his white hair, but Hector was not to be won over. And his mother Hecuba [hek′yə bə] cried to him, too. "Hector, respect me and pity me if ever I gave you this breast. Fight with Achilles from inside the walls. Do not stand there to face him. Cruel he is and if he kills you I will never have you before me on a bed to sorrow over, dear offshoot of myself, nor will your wife, but he will give you to his dogs far away from us by the Greek ships."

But Hector would not hear them as he waited there for Achilles. And deeply moved, he said to himself: "Alas, if I go inside the gates Polydamas [pol ē däm′əs, Trojan who had earlier advised Hector to retreat into the city] will be the first to say that this is my doing. For he told me to bring the Trojans into the city that terrible night, when Achilles came out. But I would not hear him — how much better if I had! But now that I have brought destruction on us all, blind fool that I was, I cannot face the Trojans and their wives. Some worse man may say: 'Hector, believing too much in himself, undid us all.' They will say that. It will be far better to meet Achilles man to man and kill him and then go in; or be killed by him, in all honor, before the city. Or how would it be to put down my shield and helmet and rest my spear against the wall and go to meet unmatched Achilles and tell him we will give up Helen, and with her all the treasure Paris took from Menelaus, and give the Greeks half of all we have as well? But why do I argue with myself like this? Achilles would have no pity on me but would kill me right away as though I were a woman, if I were unarmed. This is no time for boy and girl talk with him — boy and girl talk under some rock or oak tree. Better fight at once and see on whose side Zeus [züs, chief Greek god] will be."

As he thought so, Achilles came near in his waving helmet, with his great Pelean [pe′lē ən; Peleus was the father of Achilles] spear lifted; and suddenly fear moved Hector and away from the gates under the walls of Troy he ran, with swift-footed Achilles after him. Past the lookout station, and by the wind-waved fig tree away from the wall by the wagon road they went, and past the two springs which feed eddying Xanthus [zan′thəs; one of the rivers near Troy].... By these they ran — a good man in front but a far stronger man at his heels. And the prize they ran for was no bull's skin, or common prize for the swift-footed, but the life of horse-taming Hector.

And all the gods looked on. Then the father of gods and men [Zeus] said: "My heart sorrows for Hector, who has burned many thighs of oxen on the crests of Ida [a mountain near Troy] and in the city. Now think and take counsel, gods. Are we to save him from death or now at last kill him, a good man though he is, at Achilles' hands?"

Then the goddess, flashing-eyed Athene [ə thē′nē, goddess who favors the Greeks], said: "Father, Lord of the bright lightning and the dark cloud, what are you saying? Would you save from death a mortal man whose hour has long been fixed by fate? Do as you will, but know that we other gods are not all with you in this."

And in answer Zeus said: "Take heart, my child. I am not as serious as I seem. Do as your pleasure is and hold back no longer. And down from Olympus [ō lim′pəs, Greek mountain believed to be the home of the gods] Athene went.

Three times around Troy Hector and Achilles ran…. They ran as in a dream where one man cannot escape or overtake another. And how could Hector have escaped so far, if Apollo [ə pol′ō, god who favors the Trojans], for the last time, had not kept up his strength and made swift his knees? And Achilles signed to the other Greeks not to throw their spears at Hector. Three times round Troy they went, but when they came the fourth time to the springs, Zeus lifted up his golden balance and Hector's fate went down; and Phoebus [fē′bəs, "bright"] Apollo left him.

Then Athene came to Achilles and said: "Stand and take breath while I go and make Hector fight with you man to man." And Achilles did so, resting on his great spear. And Athene went to Hector, putting on the form and voice of Dëiphobus [dē′ə fō′bəs], his brother.

"Dear brother," she said, "now let us two meet Achilles' attack together." And Hector answered: "Dëiphobus, you were always dearest to me of my brothers, but now I honor you in my heart even more. You, only, have had the courage to come out here and help me while the others stay inside."

And bright-eyed Athene said: "Truly, my brother, they did all they could, with their prayers, to keep me back — so much they fear Achilles — but now let us fight."

With such words Athene tricked him; and Hector, coming near to Achilles, said: "I will run from you no longer, Achilles, but kill you now or be killed. And let this be our agreement before all the gods as witnesses: if Zeus lets me outlive you and take your life, I will give your body back to the Greeks, after taking your armor. And you will do the same."

But with an angry look Achilles answered: "Talk not to me of agreements, Hector. Between lions and men there is no swearing of oaths. How can wolves and sheep be of one mind? They must hate one another all through. No more of this, but fight your best. For now Pallas [pal′əs] Athene will overcome you by my spear. Now you must pay for all my sorrows for my friends you have killed."

He lifted his far-shadowing spear as he spoke and threw. Hector watched its coming and bent low so that it went over him and fixed itself in the earth. But Athene took it out and gave it back to Achilles without Hector's seeing her. And Hector cried: "So you did not know from Zeus the hour of my death, O godlike Achilles! Did you think your false tongue would make me afraid? Now escape my spear if you can."

And he lifted his far-shadowing spear and threw it and hit Achilles' shield, but the shield turned it back. And Hector saw and cried to Dëiphobus loudly for a long spear. But there was no man there. Then Hector knew all in his heart and said: "Alas! Now the gods have brought me to my death. I thought Dëiphobus was with me, but he is inside the walls and that was Athene who tricked me. Now death is very near me and there is no way of escape. This from of old was the pleasure of Zeus and his son, Apollo, who helped me before, but now my fate has come upon me. At least let me die fighting, to be honored by later men who hear of this."

And he took his sharp sword that hung by his side, a great sword and strong, and sprang on Achilles like an eagle which falls from a cloud on some lamb or hare. But Achilles ran upon him, his heart raging, his breast covered by his shield and the gold feathers of his four-horned helmet waving. As a star comes out among the stars of night, the star of evening, the most beautiful of the stars of heaven, even so came the light from the bronze of his spear as he lifted it in his right hand looking for the place most open for the blow. Now Hector's body was covered with bronze armor, the beautiful armor he had taken from great Patroclus when he killed him; but there was an opening where the collarbones come into the neck; and there, as he came on, Achilles let drive with his spear and straight through the neck went the point. But the bronze-weighted spear did not cut the windpipe, so that Hector still had his voice. Then as he fell in the dust, Achilles gloried over him: "You thought, Hector, you would be safe when you took that armor from Patroclus. Little you thought, you fool, of me, far away among my ships. But now, stronger far, I have come from them and loosed your knees. The Greeks will give him his funeral but throw you to the dogs and birds."

Then Hector, as his breath went from him, prayed: "By your life and knees and parents take the bronze and gold and all the gifts my father and mother will offer you and send my body back so that the Trojans and the Trojans' wives may give me to the fire after my death."

But with an angry look Achilles answered: "Pray me not, dog, by knees or parents. O that I could make myself cut up your flesh and eat it raw myself, for what you have done. There is no man living who can keep the dogs from your head, Hector—no, not though they paid me your weight in gold."

And dying, Hector answered: "I know you for what you are, and knew it before; the heart in your breast is of iron. See that I do not bring the anger of the gods down upon you on the day when Paris and Apollo kill you, strong though you are, at the Scaean [sē′ɑn, one of the gates of Troy] gate."

He ended and death overtook him and his spirit went from him down to the house of Hades [hā′dēz′, god of the dead], crying out sadly against its fate. And after his death Achilles said to him: "Lie dead there; I am ready for my own death whenever Zeus and the other immortals send it."

THINKING CRITICALLY

1. *Identifying Central Issues* Who is most responsible for Hector's death? Is it fate? the gods? Achilles? Hector himself?

2. *Recognizing Values* Hector knows that if he is killed, Troy will fall. Achilles knows that his own death is fated to shortly follow Hector's. With this knowledge, why does each choose to fight?

3. *Linking Past to Present* The attitude of American soldiers to war has varied greatly in this century, from the optimism of World War Two to the pessimism of Vietnam. Yet it has always had little in common with the Greek ideal. Compare Homer's attitudes to war and death to our own. How do the attitudes of American soldiers compare to the attitudes of Hector and Achilles?

WRITER'S PORTFOLIO

1. *Extending the Selection* Write a report of the action of Book 22 of the *Iliad* from the perspective of either a Greek observer standing nearby or a Trojan viewing the events from atop the walls of Troy.

2. *Examining Key Questions* Discuss what ideals were valued in Homer's society? What can you infer about pre-Classical Greek beliefs from their values?

Greek and Roman Sculpture

The development of Greek sculpture was an artistic quest for ideal forms. By around 600 B.C., the major forms of Greek sculpture had all appeared. For the next two centuries, sculptors refined these forms in pursuit of a cultural ideal of human perfection. The most important of these forms was the *kouros* (kür′ōs), or standing youth, a sculpture used in Greek temples. The kouros had the typical form of a young man, with his left foot forward and his fists clenched at his thighs. The figure was always depicted naked, emphasizing the body and its points of motion, particularly the pelvis, knees, and elbows. The kouros was meant to display as accurately as possible the way a body moves. The earliest examples all show the youth standing unnaturally, with his weight evenly divided between both legs. Around 500 B.C., Greek sculptors began experimenting with the more natural, asymmetrical balance known as *contrapposto* (kon′träp pôs′tō; Italian, "counterpoise"). They now showed the kouros with the weight of the body resting on one leg, with the other relaxed, giving a new realism to their sculptural depiction of the body's balance and motion. The statues on page 46 display the three stages in this transformation. The first is represented by the stiffly posed *Kouros of Sounion*. The next stage, the transition to *contrapposto*, is displayed in the *Kritios Boy*, one of the earliest examples of this approach. As Greek sculptors gained experience with *contrapposto*, they began to add more complexity to the kouros figure and his stance. The *Doryphorus* (dō rif′ō rəs) or "Spear-bearer," with its studied weighting of shoulders and hips displaying a truly natural balance of motion and support, represents the climax of this movement. The *Doryphorus* was as near to the goal of naturalness in the depiction of ideal human forms as Greek sculptors could get. The Romans recognized the perfection of this Greek achievement, regularly copying the

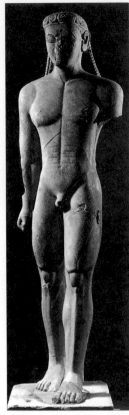

Kouros of Sounion
(c. 600 B.C.)

Kritios Boy
(c. 480 B.C.)

Doryphorus (c. 450–450 B.C.)

Doryphorus and other Greek statues. (Most of our knowledge of Greek sculpture is derived from Roman copies.) Even when not directly copying the Greeks, Roman sculptors adapted Greek forms to their own needs. One type of sculpture that the Romans wanted was the triumphant public image of a leader, such as the *Augustus of Primaporta*, on page 47. For this type of statue, the Greek kouros, with its impersonal perfection, was an appropriate model. The *Augustus of Primaporta* is obviously imitating ideal Greek models. Yet when the Romans employed sculpture for portraiture, this idealism vanished. The portrait bust was immensely popular in Rome and this type shows us vividly two thousand years later how Romans looked. Sculptural portraits like those of the man and woman on page 47

Augustus of Primaporta, c. 20 B.C.

Portrait of a Roman, c. 80 B.C.

Portrait of a Lady, c. A.D. 90

have an attention to realistic detail that the Greek quest for perfection of form did not seek. Why do you think that the Romans might have sought this sort of photographic quality in their portrait busts?

THINKING CRITICALLY

1. *Recognizing Values* Do the faces of the *Kouros of Sounion*, the *Kritios Boy*, and the *Doryphorus* reflect personal qualities? Why do you think that Greek sculptors portrayed the kouros figure in this way?

2. *Making Comparisons* How does the overall effect of the *Doryphorus* differ from that of the *Augustus of Primaporta?*

3. *Linking Past and Present* Many Roman children would have grown up surrounded by sculptural portraits of their ancestors, in something of the same way that modern American children are by photographs, films, or videotapes depicting their families and friends. What are the advantages and disadvantages of exposure to this kind of visual record reflecting one's personal history?

WRITER'S PORTFOLIO

1. *Extending the Selection* Write a brief character sketch in which you describe one of the two Romans depicted in the portrait busts.

2. *Examining Key Questions* What social values are reflected in Greek and Roman sculpture?

The Greek Lyric

Homer is an impersonal poet. He presents his characters and their experiences objectively, rarely intruding his own feelings and judgments into the narrative. During the hundred years after his time, a very different kind of poetry developed as Greek poets adapted hymns and folk songs into short lyric poems that spoke in a very personal voice. One of the earliest and greatest of these Greek lyric poets was Sappho (**saf′ō**), a native of the island of Lesbos (**les′bos**), off the western coast of what is now Turkey. In the dialect of her island, Sappho composed lyrics expressing strong personal feeling, as well as more formal wedding songs. The following selections are a sample of her poems. (Few have survived intact; some exist only as tiny fragments.) Judging by these lyrics, what was important to Sappho?

World
I could not hope
to touch the sky
with my two arms

Wedding Song
Groom, we virgins at your door
will pass the night singing of the love
between you and your bride. Her limbs
are like violets

Wake and call out the young men
your friends, and you can walk the streets
and we shall sleep less tonight than
the bright nightingale

Kleïs

I have a small daughter who is beautiful
like a gold flower. I would not trade
my darling Kleïs[1] for all Lydia[2] or even
for lovely Lesbos.

Then

In golden sandals
dawn like a thief
fell upon me.

Age and Light

Here are fine gifts, children,
O friend, singer on the clear tortoise lyre,

all my flesh is wrinkled with age,
my black hair has faded to white,

my legs can no longer carry me,
once nimble like a fawn's

but what can I do?
It cannot be undone

no more can pink-armed Dawn
not end in darkness on earth,

or keep her love for Tithonos[3]
who must waste away;

yet I love refinement, and beauty and light
are for me the same as desire for the sun.

---

1. Kleïs (klā′əs).
2. Lydia (lid′ē ə), an ancient country famed for its wealth.
3. Dawn...Tithonos (ti thō′nəs). The goddess of dawn, Eos, was said to have loved a mortal man, Tithonus. She made him immortal but not unchanging, so that he wasted away with age but could not die.

To Her Daughter, When Sappho Was Dying

It would be wrong for us. It is not right
for mourning to enter a home of poetry.

Someone, I Tell You

Someone, I tell you
will remember us.

We are oppressed by
fears of oblivion

yet are always saved
by judgment of good men

THINKING CRITICALLY

1. *Making Inferences* What inferences about the role of women in
   the Greece of Sappho's time can you draw from these poems?

2. *Recognizing Values* Was achieving fame as a poet important to
   Sappho? How did her attitude toward her reputation affect her
   feelings about old age and death?

3. *Linking Past and Present* Do Sappho's voice and values seem more
   modern than Homer's? Why or why not?

WRITER'S PORTFOLIO

1. *Extending the Selection* Many of Sappho's lyric fragments make the
   reader wonder about the complete work from which they came. Look
   back over the fragments "World," "Then,"and "To Her Daughter,
   When Sappho Was Dying." Choose one that appeals to you and
   imagine a larger poem suggested by these lines. Then create this
   poem, incorporating the fragment you have selected.

2. *Examining Key Questions* Judging by her poetry, what in Sappho's
   view contributes to the "good life"?

Presocratic Philosophy

For the Greeks, philosophy was the pursuit of knowledge by rational inquiry. The earliest Greek philosophers whose thought has been preserved lived in Ionia (ī ōn′ē ə), an area of Greek settlement on the western coast of what is now Turkey. This group of thinkers included Thales (thā′lēz), Anaximander (an ak′sə man′dėr), Anaximenes (an ak′sim′ə nēz), and Heraclitus (her′ə kli′təs). What little is known about them comes from summaries of their thought by later Greek philosophers, such as Aristotle. Thales appears to have had some knowledge of astronomy, since the Greek historian Herodotus claimed that Thales was able to predict an eclipse of the sun. His pupil Anaximander was the first to attempt to draw a map of the world. Anaximenes, the third of this group, was a friend of Anaximander. Heraclitus, who lived a half-century later than these other thinkers, stressed that all things in the universe constantly undergo change. One of the best known of early Greek philosophers, he became famous for his saying, "You can't step into the same river twice, for fresh waters are ever flowing in upon you." The following excerpts summarize the attempts by these early Greek thinkers to answer the question of what is ultimately real in the universe. (The writer whose name appears at the end of each excerpt is the source of the summary.) Their answers may seem unconvincing today, but modern science has its roots in the speculations of these thinkers. Whose answer seems the most ingenious to you?

Thales

MOST OF THE FIRST PHILOSOPHERS THOUGHT THAT PRINCIPLES in the form of matter were the only principles of all things; for the original source of all existing things, that from which a thing first comes into being and into which it is finally destroyed, the substance persisting but changing in its qualities, this they declare is the element and first principle of existing things, and for this reason they consider that there is no absolute coming to be or passing away, on the ground that such nature is always preserved.... For there must be some natural substance, either one or more than one, from which the other things come into being, while it is preserved. Over the number, however, and the form of this kind of principle they do not all agree; but Thales, the founder of this type of philosophy, says that it is water (and therefore declared that the earth is on water), perhaps taking this supposition from seeing the nature of all things to be moist, and the warm itself coming to be from this and living by this (that from which they come to be the principle of all things) — taking the supposition both from this and from the seeds of all things having a moist nature, water being the natural principle of moist things.

ARISTOTLE

Anaximander

ANAXIMANDER OF MILETUS, THE PUPIL AND FOLLOWER OF Thales, was one of those who maintain that there is one first principle of things, infinite in quantity and extent and capable of motion and change; he was the first to use the term "the infinite" [or "undefined"] for this elemental matter. It is, according to him, neither water or any of the so-called elements [earth, air, water, and fire], but something quite different in its nature; from it arise the heavens and the worlds in them, and to it all things inevitably return. For they must — in the poetical term he uses — make reparation to each other for the injustices they have committed, at the time ordained for them. Anaximander had evidently considered the changes of the four elements into each other, and did not feel that any of them should be regarded as the elemental matter; this, he felt, must be something quite different.

THEOPHRASTUS

Anaximenes

ANAXIMENES OF MILETUS, A COMPANION OF ANAXIMANDER, also says, like him, that the underlying nature is one and infinite, but not undefined as Anaximander said, but definite, for [Anaximenes] identifies it as air; and it differs in its substantial nature by rarity and density. Being made finer it becomes fire, being made thicker it becomes wind, then cloud, then (when thickened still more) water, then earth, then stones; and the rest coming into being through these. He, too, makes motion eternal, and says that change also comes about through it.

THEOPHRASTUS

Heraclitus

THIS WORLD-ORDER DID NONE OF GODS OR MEN MAKE, BUT IT always was and is and shall be: an ever-living fire, kindling in measures and going out in measures.

All things are an equal exchange for fire and fire for all things, as goods for gold and gold for goods.

You cannot step into the same river twice.

THINKING CRITICALLY

1. *Identifying Assumptions* What might have inclined Thales to the view that water was the basic substance from which all things are made?

2. *Recognizing Values* In what way did Anaximander apply almost human characteristics to the elements? Did he seem to regard all matter as in some sense alive?

3. *Linking Past and Present* To the Presocratic philosophers, speculative philosophy and empirical science were one and the same. Yet today, science and philosophy are vastly different disciplines. What do you think is gained by this separation? What is lost?

WRITERS PORTFOLIO

1. *Extending the Selection* Greek tradition listed the four elements — the basic substances of which everything was made — as earth, air, water, and fire. Write a brief essay speculating on why none of the early Greek philosophers selected earth as the primary substance of the universe.

2. *Examining Key Questions* Discuss what common characteristics are shared by the views of ultimate reality expressed by these different philosophers?

Thucydides Depicts Athenian Power

Thucydides (**thü sid′ə dēz′**) (c. 460–c. 399 B.C.) grew up and was educated during the height of Athenian civilization. During this period, under the leadership of the orator and general Pericles (**per′ə klēz′**), the Athenians were undertaking the world's first notable experiment in democratic government. Thucydides studied the new philosophies and sciences and greatly admired the new Athenian democracy. During the second of the bitter wars between Athens and Sparta, Thucydides was exiled from Athens for a military failure. During his exile he observed the conflict and wrote about it, "in the belief that it was going to be a great war and more worth writing about than any of those which had taken place in the past." Thucydides' *History of the Peloponnesian War* is seen as the first modern history because of its narrow scope, its attention to evidence, and its rejection of myth and legend. Thucydides only incorporated events he had witnessed or about which he had obtained reliable accounts, scrupulously avoiding the mythical elements which characterized earlier historians. The scope of the book is the political and military history of the war; it attempts no biography, no cultural history, no civic history. It simply relates and places in context the war and Athenian defeat. To tell this story, Thucydides set up two great contrasts: that between Athens and Sparta; and that between Athenian democracy under Pericles and under his successors. The following two selections from Thucydides' *History of the Peloponnesian War* depict the second of these contrasts. The first selection, excerpts from the Funeral Oration of Pericles, expresses the values of Athens at the height of her powers, during Thucydides' youth. Pericles delivered this speech in 430 B.C. to honor the first dead of the war. In Pericles' view, what ideals characterize Athenian democracy?

Our form of government is not modeled on the constitutions of our neighbors; instead of imitating others we are actually an example to them. So far as the name goes we are called a democracy, because the power rests with the majority instead of a few. But though every citizen has equal rights under the law with respect to his private duties, high standing and honor in the community depend on a man's merit, his achievement in some pursuit, and no one is debarred by poverty and obscurity of birth from contributing what he can to the well-being of the city. We are free people not only in our management of affairs but in our personal tolerance of one another's everyday conduct. We do not get angry at our neighbors for doing as they please or try to inflict on them the petty marks of disapproval which, though harmless, are so unpleasant to experience. While this spirit of tolerance prevails in our private lives, in our public affairs it is fear more than anything else that keeps us law-abiding, obedient to the magistrates of the moment and to the laws, especially those whose purpose is to help the victims of wrongdoing and those unwritten laws which men by common consent are ashamed to transgress....

We strive for distinction but with economy, and for intelligence without the loss of energy. Thus we use wealth to meet the needs of action, not the craving for display, and think it is no disgrace to admit poverty but a real disgrace not to act to escape it. Again we combine the conduct of public and private affairs in the same person and make it possible for others, though absorbed in their work, to gain some insight into politics; for unlike other peoples we judge the man who takes no part in this at all a useless, not just a "quiet" person. Hence we also arrive at sound decisions, not just sound ideas, on policy because we do not believe that action is spoiled by discussion, but by failure to be informed through debate before the necessary action is taken. In fact this is another point in our superiority: we are unusually daring and also unusually disposed to weigh the pros and cons of a proposed undertaking, while with others ignorance brings boldness and second thought brings hesitation. One would not go wrong in saying that the bravest men are those who foresee most clearly the dangerous as well as the pleasurable possibilities and still are not deterred from taking the risk.

Again, so far as generosity goes we are the opposite of most men: we try to win friends not by accepting kindness but by conferring it. We know that the man who does a favor is the firmer friend; he will keep the debt alive out of good will toward the recipient, while the debtor does not feel it so keenly, knowing that a good turn will be put down as payment on his debt, not as a real favor. Our fearless way of serving others rests on the confidence of freedom rather than on the calculations of profit; in this too we are unique.

To sum it all up, I say not only that our city as a whole is a model for all Greece, but that in my opinion there is no other place where the individual can develop independence and self-reliance so easily, so gracefully, and in so many directions.... Athens alone, in our time, is greater than her own fame when the test comes; she alone gives the invader no excuse for annoyance at the quality of the foe who handles him so roughly, and her subjects no ground for complaint that their masters do not deserve to rule them.

> The second selection, excerpts from the Melian (mē′lē ən) Dialogue, reflects Athens after Pericles' death, headed for disaster and defeat. The Melian Dialogue records an episode that took place in 416 B.C. as the Athenians tried to subjugate a weak Spartan colony, the island of Melos (mē′los). The Melians refused to submit and so the Athenians destroyed the town, killed the men, and sold the woman and children into slavery. How does the Athens reflected in the Melian Dialogue contrast with the vision of Pericles?

MELIANS. We cannot quarrel with the reasonableness of a leisurely exchange of views, but the warlike preparations we see already surrounding us, not merely in prospect, have a different look. It is obvious that you have come to sit in judgment on the discussion and that in all probability, if we win the argument on the score of justice and therefore do not give in, the result of our talk will be war, and if we submit it will be slavery.

ATHENIANS. Well, if your purpose in this meeting is to deal in vague conjectures about the future, instead of planning how to save your city on the basis of presentable facts, we may as well stop now. Or, if you accept our conditions, we will continue.

MELIANS. It is natural and forgivable that men in a situation like ours should try many shifts in their speech as well as their thoughts; however the purpose of this meeting is to discuss the preservation of our city and the discussion may proceed along the lines you suggest, if you wish.

ATHENIANS. Well then, we will not spin out a long, wearisome round of speeches, with fine phrases about how righteously we gained our power by destroying the Persians or how this attack was provoked by some wrongs we have suffered; and in return please do not count on convincing us with arguments about your not joining us in the war because you are colonists of the Spartans, or about you never having done us any harm. Let us deal with practical possibilities, the basis of our real intentions on both sides, since you know as well as we do that in their stated arguments and conclusions about justice men are under equal constraints, but when it comes to practice the strong do as they please and the weak acquiesce.

MELIANS. The way it looks to us (and we have no choice, since you have laid it down that we are to ignore justice and talk expediency), you would find it advantageous not to rule out the common good, but to leave open to all who may be in danger an appeal to reason and justice, and the hope of bettering their position by argument, even if they fall short of proof. Actually that is in your own interest, considering that if you fail disastrously others will treat you by your own example.

ATHENIANS. We are not worried about what may happen to our empire, even if it comes to an end. The real danger is not the threat of being beaten by another ruling nation like the Spartans—and after all we are not arguing with the Spartans here—but the possibility that subject states may revolt against their rulers and subjugate them. Anyhow, you can leave that risk for us to deal with. We will state frankly that we are here to further the interests of our empire and that what we are about to say is for the preservation of your city; that is, we want to subdue you with the least effort and leave you unharmed for your sake as well as ours.

MELIANS. But, granting that your power is profitable to you, how can slavery be so to us?

ATHENIANS. In that you have a chance here to submit before you suffer the worst consequences, while we stand to gain by not utterly destroying you.

MELIANS. Would it be acceptable to you if we took no part in the war and remained friendly to you, but neutral to both sides?

ATHENIANS. No, because your hostility is not as dangerous to us as your friendship would be; our subjects would take the friendship as a standing sign of weakness, and the hatred as a sign of our power.

MELIANS. Do your subjects consider it reasonable not to make any distinction between those who are no kin to you and those—mostly your own colonists—who have rebelled against you at one time or another and been reduced to subjection?

ATHENIANS. So far as pleas of justice go they consider that both groups have a case, but that those who elude us owe it to their power, because we are afraid to attack them. That is why, aside from the enlargement of our empire, your subjugation will bring us security: the failure of you, an island and a rather weak one, to win against a sea power would be especially striking.

MELIANS. But, don't you think there is any security in our proposal? Here again, since you have excluded our arguments based on justice and have told us to consider only your advantage, it is incumbent on us to try to show you convincingly where our own interests lie, if it happens that yours lie in the same direction. Now those states that are neutral at present will inevitably join the fight against you when they see what has happened here and become convinced that someday you will attack them too. In short what are you accomplishing by all this except to strengthen your existing enemies and force others, who had never thought of such a thing, to join them?

ATHENIANS. No, you see we are not much afraid of potential enemies on the mainland; they are so used to their freedom that they will procrastinate a long time before putting up a defense against us. Our chief threat is from the islanders, those who are independent like yourselves and also those who are irritated by the constraints of our empire. They are the ones who are most likely to give way to folly and involve themselves and us in dangers that they might have foreseen.

MELIANS. Upon our word, if you are ready to take such extreme risks to maintain your empire, and those who are already your slaves to rid themselves of it, it would be the most contemptible cowardice for us who still have our freedom not to go to any length to avoid slavery....

ATHENIANS. You are showing a gross lack of intelligent thinking if you do not recess this conference now, before it is too late, and come to a more sensible decision. Surely you are not going to give way to shame, the most ruinous impulse one can have when facing a really shameful and foreseeable danger. Often, that is, while men can still foresee what they are being swept into, the thing we call shame, having first overcome their resistance by the power of a seductive word, the work of a mere phrase, lures them on to fall of their own accord into irreparable disaster and incur a new shame, more shameful because brought on by folly, not fortune. If you think carefully you will avoid this error: you will consider it no disgrace to be conquered by the greatest city in

Greece, when she generously offers you the chance to become autonomous tribute-paying allies, and will not make a poor decision out of mere stubbornness when given a choice between war and security. In general those who stand their ground against their equals, behave well towards their superiors, and are decent towards their inferiors, will get along best. Think seriously then after we withdraw and remind yourselves again and again that the issue here is your country: that you have only one and that on this single decision depends its prosperity or its ruin.

THINKING CRITICALLY

1. *Making Comparisons* How do the Athenians depart from Pericles' ideals in their statements in the Melian Dialogue? How do they adhere to them?

2. *Drawing Conclusions* Whose arguments—the Melians' or the Athenians'—do you find most convincing? Explain.

3. *Linking Past and Present* In recent times, the principle underlying the Athenian position in the Melian Dialogue has sometimes been called realpolitik (rā äl′pō li tēk′; German, "real politics"). Realpolitik refers to political policy—particularly foreign policy—that is based on power rather than ideals. Do you think realpolitik should guide the United States in its relations with other countries?

WRITER'S PORTFOLIO

1. *Extending the Selection* Thucydides confesses in his *History* that, "I have found it difficult to remember the precise words used in the speeches which I listened to myself,...so my method has been, while keeping as closely as possible to the general sense of the words that were actually used, to make the speakers say what, in my opinion, was called for in each situation." Do you think this compromises Thucydides as a historian?

2. *Examining Key Questions* What different social values are reflected in the two excerpts? What do you think is Thucydides' point in stressing two different sets of values?

Socrates Refuses to Escape

As a young man, Plato (**plā′tō**) (427–347 B.C.), was transformed through his association with the philosopher Socrates (**sok′rə tēz**) (469–399 B.C.). Socrates wanted to know why things were and in so wishing turned from natural philosophy to the study of the one thing he could know, himself. Socrates would confront people in the Athenian marketplace and question them about right and wrong, good and evil, and all forms of justice. This method of honest and unremitting inquiry won him a following of bright young men, but also the enmity of many Athenians. His self-appointed function was to teach by questioning — the Socratic method. Eventually, Socrates' role as public "gadfly" — a person who goads others to action — made him unpopular. He found himself accused of "corrupting the young" and "refusing to recognize the gods recognized by the State and introducing other new divinities." Tried on these charges before a court of Athenian citizens, he was condemned to drink poison. After Socrates' death, Plato wrote a series of philosophical dialogues in which his former teacher appears in his accustomed role of questioner. The selection below is from the *Crito,* one of the dialogues of Plato, and depicts a debate between Socrates and his friend Crito (**krī′tō**), during Socrates' stay in prison while he awaited execution. What are Crito's reasons for urging Socrates' escape?

CRITO. But, Oh! my beloved Socrates, let me entreat you once more to take my advice and escape. For if you die I shall not only lose a friend who can never be replaced, but there is another evil: people who do not know you and me will believe that I might have saved you if I had been willing to give money, but that I did not care. Now, can there be a worse disgrace than this — that I should be thought to value money more than the life of a friend? For the many will not be persuaded that I wanted you to escape, and that you refused.

SOCRATES. But why, my dear Crito, should we care about the opinion of the many? Good men, and they are the only persons who are worth considering, will think of these things truly as they occurred.

CRITO. But you see, Socrates, that the opinion of the many must be regarded, for what is now happening shows that they can do the greatest evil to any one who has lost their good opinion.

SOCRATES. I only wish, Crito, that they could; for then they could also do the greatest good, and that would be well. But in reality they can do neither; for they cannot either make a man wise or make him foolish; and whatever they do is the result of chance.

CRITO. Well, I will not dispute that with you....

SOCRATES. Then, my friend, we must not regard what the many say of us; but what he, the one man who has understanding of just and unjust, will say, and what the truth will say. And therefore you begin in error when you advise that we should regard the opinion of the many about just and unjust, good and evil, honorable and dishonorable.— "Well," someone will say, "but the many can kill us."

CRITO. Yes, Socrates; that will clearly be the answer.

SOCRATES. That is true: but still I find with surprise that the old argument is, as I conceive, unshaken as ever. And I should like to know whether I may say the same of another proposition—that not life, but a good life, is to be chiefly valued?

CRITO. Yes, that also remains.

SOCRATES. And a good life is equivalent to a just and honorable one—that also holds?

CRITO. Yes, that holds.

SOCRATES. From these premises I proceed to argue the question whether I ought or ought not to try and escape without the consent of the Athenians: and if I am clearly right in escaping, then I will make the attempt; but if not, I will abstain.... Shall we insist on the truth of what was then said, that injustice is always an evil and dishonor to him who acts unjustly? Shall we say so or not?

CRITO. Yes.

SOCRATES. Then we must do no wrong?

CRITO. Certainly not.

SOCRATES. Nor when injured injure in return, as the many imagine; for we must injure no one at all?

CRITO. Clearly not.

SOCRATES. Again, Crito, may we do evil?

CRITO. Surely not, Socrates.

SOCRATES. And what of doing evil in return for evil, which is the morality of the many—is that just or not?

CRITO. Not just.

SOCRATES. For doing evil to another is the same as injuring him?

CRITO. Very true.

SOCRATES. Then I will proceed to the next step, which may be put in the form of a question: ought a man to do what he admits to be right, or ought he to betray the right?

CRITO. He ought to do what he thinks right.

SOCRATES. But if this is true, what is the application? In leaving the prison against the will of the Athenians, do I wrong any? Or rather do I not wrong those whom I ought least to wrong? Do I not desert the principles which were acknowledged by us to be just?

CRITO. I cannot tell, Socrates; for I do not know.

SOCRATES. Then consider the matter in this way: imagine that I am about to play truant (you may call the proceeding by any name you like), and the laws and the government come and interrogate me: "Tell us, Socrates," they say; "what are you about? Are you going by an act of yours to overturn us—the laws, and the whole state, as far as in you lies? Do you imagine that a state can subsist and not be overthrown, in which the decisions of law have no power, but are set aside and overthrown by individuals?" What will be our answer Crito, to these and the like words? Any one, and especially a rhetorician, will have a good deal to say on behalf of the law which requires a sentence to be carried out;—he will argue that this law should not be set aside; and we might reply, "Yes; but the state has injured us and given an unjust sentence." Suppose I say that?

CRITO. Very good, Socrates.

SOCRATES. "And was that our agreement with you?" the laws would reply; "or were you to abide by the sentence of the state?" And if I were to express my astonishment at their words, the laws would probably add: "Answer, Socrates, instead of opening your eyes: you are in the habit of asking and answering questions. Tell us what complaint you have to make against us which justifies you in attempting to destroy us and the state?... Has a philosopher like you failed to discover that our country is more to be valued and higher and holier far than mother or father or any ancestor, and more to be regarded in the eyes of the gods and of men of understanding? Also to be soothed, and gently and reverently entreated when angry, even more than a father, and if not persuaded, obeyed? And when we are punished by her, whether with imprisonment or stripes, the punishment is to be endured in silence." What is the answer we make to this, Crito? Do the laws speak truly, or do they not?

CRITO. I think they do.

SOCRATES. Then the laws will say: "Consider, Socrates, if we are speaking truly that in your present attempt you are going to do us an injury. For, after having brought you into the world, and nurtured and educated you, and given you and every other citizen a share in every good which we had to give, we further proclaim to every Athenian, that if he does not like us when he has come of age and has seen the ways of the city, and made our acquaintance, he may go where he pleases and take his goods with him…. Moreover, you might, if you had liked, have fixed the penalty at banishment in the course of the trial—the state which refuses to let you go now would have let you go then. But you pretended that you preferred death to exile, and that you were not grieved at death. And now you have forgotten these fine sentiments, and pay no respect to us the laws, of whom you are the destroyer; and are doing what only a miserable slave would do, running away and turning your back upon the compacts and agreements which you made as a citizen. And first of all answer this very question: are we right in saying that you agreed to be governed according to us in deed, and not in word only? Is that true or not?" How shall we answer, Crito? Must we not assent?

CRITO. There is no help, Socrates.

THINKING CRITICALLY

1. *Making Inferences* What sort of man is Socrates? Does this make him a philosopher or a wise man?

2. *Recognizing Values* Why does Socrates refuse to escape? What beliefs is he upholding?

3. *Linking Past and Present* What sort of people have taken over Socrates' role as a public gadfly today?

WRITER'S PORTFOLIO

1. *Extending the Selection* Can you think of other reasons for Socrates to escape? Answer them as Socrates would have.

2. *Examining Key Questions* Socrates is generally considered the father of moral philosophy. Examine how the invention of moral philosophy might have changed the way mankind acts.

Epicureanism and Stoicism

Roman philosophy was dominated by Epicureanism and Stoicism, intellectual traditions derived from Greece. Both these schools of thought had originated in Athens around 300 B.C. Epicureanism (ep′ə kyu̇ rē′ə niz′əm) took its name from its founder Epicurus (ep′ə kyu̇r′əs), who suggested that a wise conduct of life was attained by reliance on the evidence of the senses. He rejected the subjective nature of religion and relied on a formula for happiness that pleasure equaled good and vice-versa. However, his definition of pleasure is different from our idea of positive enjoyment. For Epicurus, pleasure meant the absence of pain or grief. Our knowledge of Epicurus's thought comes mainly from the Roman poet Lucretius (lü krē′shəs), who in his long poem *On the Nature of Things* detailed the chief aspects of Epicureanism. Lucretius, born around 100 B.C., ignored the typical career of a high-born Roman and devoted himself to spreading the doctrine of Epicurus. He was particularly concerned to stress its ethical philosophy and counter the impression that Epicureanism meant living only for pleasure. Stoicism (stō′ə siz′əm) was derived from the thought of Zeno (zē′nō) of Cyprus and advocates living a life in accord with nature. For Stoics, nature is controlled by reason, and only acceptance — rather than faith or hope — can bring a satisfying life. Stoics accepted the events of life and death with equanimity, because they had no control over them. They strongly stressed duty and the life of contemplation. Stoicism influenced many great Roman philosophers from the orator Cicero to the statesman and dramatist Seneca, but the most important was the emperor Marcus Aurelius (mär′kəs ô rē′lē əs), whose thoughts on life and duty were collected and published as the *Meditations*. Marcus Aurelius's reign (A.D. 161–180) was characterized by constant wars and insurrection; his life was spent on campaign and it was this isolation which led him to write the personal notebooks which make up the *Meditations*. The first of the following selections is an excerpt from Book 2 of Lucretius's *On the Nature of Things*. What did Lucretius think should guide human behavior?

WHAT JOY IT IS, WHEN OUT AT SEA THE STORMWINDS ARE lashing the waters, to gaze from the shore at the heavy stress some other man is enduring! Not that anyone's afflictions are in themselves a source of delight; but to realize from what troubles you yourself are free is joy indeed. What joy, again, to watch opposing hosts marshaled on the field of battle when you have yourself no part in their peril! But this is the greatest joy of all: to stand aloof in a quiet citadel, stoutly fortified by the teaching of the wise, and to gaze down from that elevation on others wandering aimlessly in a vain search for the way of life; pitting their wits one against another, disputing for precedence, struggling night and day with unstinted effort to scale the pinnacles of wealth and power. O joyless hearts of men! O minds without vision! How dark and dangerous the life in which this tiny span is lived away! Do you not see that nature is clamoring for two things only: a body free from pain, a mind released from worry and fear for the enjoyment of pleasurable sensations?

So we find that the requirements of our bodily nature are few indeed, no more than is necessary to banish pain. To heap pleasure upon pleasure may heighten men's enjoyment at times. But what matter if there are no golden images of youths about the house, holding flaming torches in their right hands to illumine banquets prolonged into the night? What matter if the hall does not sparkle with silver and gleam with gold, and no carved and gilded rafters ring to the music of the lute? Nature does not miss these companies when men recline in company on the soft grass by a running stream under branches of a tall tree and refresh their bodies pleasurably at small expense. Better still if the weather smiles upon them and the season of the year stipples the green herbage with flowers. Burning fevers flee no swifter from your body if you toss under figured counterpanes and coverlets of crimson than if you must lie in rude home-spun.

If our bodies are not profited by treasures or titles or the majesty of kingship, we must go on to admit that neither are our minds.... The fears and anxieties that dog the human breast do not shrink from the clash of arms or the fierce rain of missiles. They stalk unabashed among princes and potentates. They are not awestruck by the gleam of gold or the bright sheen of purple robes.

Can you doubt then that this power rests with reason alone? All life is a struggle in the dark. As children in blank darkness tremble and start at everything, so we in broad daylight are oppressed at times by fears as baseless as those horrors which children imagine coming upon them in the dark. This dread and darkness of the mind cannot be dispelled by the sunbeams, the shining shafts of day, but only by an understanding of the outward form and inner workings of nature.

The second selection is an excerpt from Book 2 of Marcus Aurelius's Meditations. *What did he feel should guide human behavior?*

THIS THING THAT I CALL "MYSELF" IS COMPACT OF FLESH, breath, and reason. Thou art even now in the throes of death; despise therefore the flesh. It is but a little blood, a few bones, a paltry net woven from nerves and veins and arteries. Consider next thy breath. What a trifle it is! A little air, and this forever changing; every minute of every hour we are gasping it forth and sucking it in again!

Only reason is left us. Consider thus: thou art stricken in years; then suffer it not to remain a bond-servant; suffer it not to be puppet-like, hurried hither and thither by impulses that take no thought of thy fellow-man; suffer it not to murmur at destiny in the present or look askance at it in the future....

Let it be thy hourly care to do stoutly what thy hand findeth to do, as becomes a man and a Roman, with carefulness, unaffected dignity, humanity, freedom, and justice. Free thyself from the obsession of all other thoughts; for free thyself thou wilt, if thou but perform every action as though it were the last of thy life, without light-mindedness, without swerving through force of passion from the dictates of reason, without hypocrisy, without self-love, without chafing at destiny. Thou seest how few the things are, that which if a man lays hold of, he is able to live a life which flows in quiet, and is like the existence of the gods; for the gods on their part will require nothing more from him who observes these things....

Let thy every action, word, and thought be that of one who is prepared at any moment to quit this life. For, if the gods exist, to depart from the fellowship of man has no terrors,—for the divine nature is incapable of involving thee in evil. But if they exist not, or existing have no concern of mankind, what profits it to linger in a godless, soul-less universe?...

The measure of man's life is a point, substance a perpetual ebb and flow, sense-perception vague and shadowy, the fabric of his whole body corruptible, the soul past searching out, fortune whirligig, and fame the decision of unreason. In brief, the things of the body are unstable as water; the things of the soul dreams and vapors; life itself a warfare or a sojourning in a strange land. What then shall be our guide and escort? One thing and one only — philosophy. And true philosophy is to observe the celestial part within us, to keep it inviolate and unscathed, above the power of pain and pleasure, doing nothing at hazard, nothing with falsehood, and nothing with hypocrisy; careless whether another do this or that, or no; accepting every vicissitude and every dispensation as coming from that place which was its own home; and at all times awaiting death with cheerfulness, in the sure knowledge that it is but a dissolution of the elements whereof every life is compound. For if to the elements themselves there is no disaster in that they are forever changing each to other, how shall we fear the change and dissolution of all? It is in harmony with nature, and naught that is evil can be in harmony with nature.

THINKING CRITICALLY

1. *Making Inferences* How would Lucretius respond to the idea of fate? What about Marcus Aurelius?

2. *Making Comparisons* When Marcus Aurelius refers to "true philosophy" as our guide in life, does he mean philosophy like that of Socrates and Plato? Is he advocating the Socratic method of searching for perfection?

3. *Linking Past and Present* Modern American society is strongly permeated by the notion that people have a responsibility to help others. Compare this attitude with Lucretius's view that "the greatest joy of all [is] to stand aloof in a quiet citadel, stoutly fortified by the teaching of the wise, and to gaze down from that elevation on others wandering aimlessly in a vain search for the way of life."

WRITER'S PORTFOLIO

1. *Extending the Selection* At the beginning of this excerpt from *On the Nature of Things*, Lucretius gives several images expressing his notion of happiness. Create an image that expresses yours.

2. *Examining Key Questions* Discuss what Lucretius and Marcus Aurelius say should be the guides for a good life.

The Roman Lyric

When Catullus (kə tul′əs) arrived in Rome as a young man, civil war had begun to pull apart the Republican order and its traditional values. He soon began an affair with a faithless woman he called Lesbia. The four years of joy and pain Catullus experienced with Lesbia inspired most of his best-known poetry. In these poems, he overturned former artistic values. Rather than long, serious poems on patriotic themes, he used the themes and forms of the Greek lyric, particularly those of Sappho (pages 49–51), to create brief, intense love poems. Poems which reflected the live-for-today attitude of civil-war Rome. What different feelings did he express for Lesbia?

2

O sparrow that are my sweetheart's pet,
with whom she likes to play, whom to hold in her lap,
to whose pecking to offer her finger-tips
and provoke you to bite sharply
whenever it pleases her, bright-eyed with longing for me,
to engage in some endearing frolic
so that, I fancy, when her fierce passion subsides,
it may prove a diversion for her pain:
to be able to play with you, as does your mistress,
and allay the sad cares of my heart
would be as welcome to me as they say
was to the swift-footed girl[1] that golden apple
which loosed her long-tied girdle.

5

Let us live, my Lesbia, and love,
and value at one penny all
the talk of stern old men.
Suns can set and rise again:

---

1. **girl,** Atalanta, famous for her beauty and swiftness, who finally married a young man who defeated her in a race by throwing a golden apple in her path.

we, when once our brief light has set,
must sleep one never-ending night.
Give me a thousand kisses, then a hundred,
then a second thousand, then a second hundred,
then yet another thousand, then a hundred.
Then, when we have made up many thousands,
we will wreck the count, lest we know it
or any devil have the power to cast an evil eye upon us
when he knows the total of our kisses.

72

You once said, Lesbia, that you belonged to Catullus alone
and wished not to possess even Jove[2] in preference to me.
I cherished you then, not just as an ordinary man a mistress
but as a father cherishes his children and their spouses.
Now I know you: so, though I burn more ardently,
you are much cheaper and slighter in my eyes.
"How so?" you ask. Because such hurt as you have inflicted
forces a lover to love more, but to like less.

-----

2. Jove (jōv), another name for Jupiter, king of the gods in Roman mythology.

THINKING CRITICALLY

1. *Making Inferences* What different feelings did Catullus express toward Lesbia in these poems?

2. *Recognizing Values* How did Catullus argue the importance of living for the moment?

3. *Linking Past and Present* Do you think that Catullus would be surprised by the changing relationship between men and women in contemporary America? Why or why not?

WRITER'S PORTFOLIO

1. *Extending the Selection* Write a comparison between the themes and styles of Catullus and Sappho (pages 49–51).

2. *Examining Key Questions* What attitude toward the values that make human life good is reflected in the poetry of Catullus?

The Death of Turnus

When Octavian (soon to be the emperor Augustus) heard Virgil read his poem the *Georgics* (**jorj´iks**), which celebrates farming, the simple life, and hard work, he felt Virgil was advocating the virtues he wanted to re-instill in Romans. He urged Virgil to write an epic of Roman history. (Octavian actually hoped the poet would write an epic celebrating his victories.) Virgil instead chose to imitate Homer and tell the tale of Aeneas (**i nē´əs**), a member of the royal house of Troy who escapes during the destruction of the city by the Greeks. Aeneas eventually makes his way to Italy, where he founds the colony that became Rome. Virgil's poem, called the *Aeneid* (**i nē´əd**), is in twelve books. The first six mimic Homer's *Odyssey*, telling of Aeneas's trials on his journey to Italy. Books 7–12 imitate the *Iliad* in their depiction of the Trojans' war with the Italian tribes. While Homer is Virgil's model, there are a great many differences in their writing. The *Iliad* is a poem about anger — the anger of Achilles and its consequences. The *Aeneid* is a poem about faithfulness — Aeneas's fidelity to his family and his gods. Achilles chooses his fate, from joining the fight against Troy to killing Hector; but Aeneas is compelled by fate to do things against his will, from fleeing Troy to fighting the Italian hero Turnus. The following selection is from the last section of the *Aeneid*, including the final 65 lines of the poem, depicting Aeneas's duel with Turnus, who leads the Rutulians (**rə tül´ē əns**), a native Italian tribe, in their war against the Trojans. What parallels can you find between this episode and the fight between Achilles and Hector in the *Iliad* (page 40)?

Meanwhile Olympus' king[1] calls out to Juno[2]
as from a golden cloud she scans the battle:
"Wife, how can this day end? What is there left

---

1. Olympus' king, Jupiter, or Jove (**jōv**), the king of the gods.
2. Juno, the wife of Jupiter and queen of the gods; she has been a bitter enemy of Aeneas and the Trojans.

for you to do? You know, and say you know,
that, as a deity, Aeneas is owed
to heaven, that the fates will carry him
high as the stars. What is your plan? What is
the hope that keeps you lingering in these
chill clouds?… Stop at last;
give way to what I now ask: do not let
so great a sorrow gnaw at you in silence;
do not let your sweet lips so often press
your bitter cares on me. This is the end.
You have harassed the Trojans over land
and wave, have kindled brutal war, outraged
Latinus' home,[3] and mingled grief and marriage:
you cannot pass beyond this point." So, Jove;
the goddess, Saturn's daughter,[4] yielding, answered:

"Great Jupiter, it is indeed for this —
my knowing what you wish — that I have left
both Turnus and the earth, unwillingly.
Were it not so, you would not see me now
alone upon my airy throne, enduring
everything;… And now
I yield; detesting wars, I give them up.
And only this — which fates do not forbid —
I beg of you, for Latium, for your
own father's greatness, for the race of Saturn:
when with their happy wedding rites they reach
a peace — so be it — when they both unite
in laws and treaties, do not let the native-
born Latins lose their ancient name, become
Trojans,…let the sons of Rome
be powerful in their Italian courage.
Troy now is fallen; let her name fall, too."

And now Aeneas charges straight at Turnus.
He brandishes a shaft huge as a tree,
and from his savage breast he shouts: "Now what

---

3. Latinus' home. Latinus (la ti′nəs) was king of Latium (lā′sh um), the Trojans' destined
realm in Italy.
4. Saturn's daughter, Juno, daughter of the god Saturn. After being driven from Olympus
by Jupiter, Saturn ruled in Italy.

delay is there? Why, Turnus, do you still
draw back from battle? It is not for us
to race against each other, but to meet
with cruel weapons, hand to hand. Go, change
yourself into all shapes; by courage and
by craft collect whatever help you can;
take wing, if you so would, toward the steep stars
or hide yourself within the hollow earth."
But Turnus shakes his head: "Your burning words,
ferocious Trojan, do not frighten me;
it is the gods alone who terrify me,
and Jupiter, my enemy." He says
no more, but as he looks about he sees
a giant stone, an ancient giant stone
that lay at hand, by chance, upon the plain,
set there as a boundary mark between the fields
to keep the farmers free from border quarrels.
And twice-six chosen men with bodies such
as earth produces now could scarcely lift
that stone upon their shoulders. But the hero,
anxious and running headlong, snatched the boulder;
reaching full height, he hurled it at the Trojan.
But Turnus does not know if it is he
himself who runs or goes or lifts or throws
that massive rock; his knees are weak; his blood
congeals with cold. The stone itself whirls through
the empty void but does not cross all of
the space between; it does not strike a blow.
Just as in dreams of night, when languid rest
has closed our eyes, we seem in vain to wish
to press on down a path, but as we strain,
we falter, weak; our tongues can say nothing,
the body loses its familiar force,
no voice, no word, can follow: so whatever
courage he calls upon to find a way,
the cursed goddess[5] keeps success from Turnus.
Then shifting feelings overtake his heart;
he looks in longing at the Latin ranks
and at the city, and he hesitates,

---

5. cursed goddess, Dira, the bird-winged curse, which Jupiter unleashed against Turnus

afraid; he trembles at the coming spear.
He does not know how he can save himself....

In Turnus' wavering Aeneas sees
his fortune; he holds high the fatal shaft;
he hurls it far with all his body's force.
No boulder ever catapulted from
siege engine sounded so, no thunderbolt
had ever burst with such a roar. The spear
flies on like a black whirlwind, carrying
its dread destruction, ripping through the border
of Turnus' corselet and the outer rim
of Turnus' seven-plated shield; hissing,
it penetrates his thigh. The giant Turnus,
struck, falls to earth; his knees bend under him.
All the Rutulians leap up with a groan,
and all the mountain slopes around re-echo;
tall forests, far and near, return that voice.
Then humble, suppliant, he lifts his eyes
and, stretching out his hand, entreating, cries:
"I have indeed deserved this; I do not
appeal against it; use your chance. But if
there is a thought of a dear parent's grief
that now can touch you, then I beg you, pity
old Daunus[6]—in Anchises[7] you had such
a father—send me back or, if you wish,
send back my lifeless body to my kin.
For you have won, and the Ausonians[8]
have seen me, beaten, stretch my hands; Lavinia[9]
is yours; then do not press your hatred further."

Aeneas stood, ferocious in his armor;
his eyes were restless and he stayed his hand;
and as he hesitated, Turnus' words
began to move him more and more—until
high on the Latin's shoulder he made out

---

6. Daunus (dôn′əs), father of Turnus.
7. Anchises (an ki′sēz), father of Aeneas.
8. Ausonians (ô sōn′ē əns), the Italians.
9. Lavinia (lə vin′ē ə), beloved of Turnus and destined bride of Aeneas.

the luckless belt of Pallas,[10] of the boy
whom Turnus had defeated, wounded, stretched
upon the battlefield, from whom he took
this fatal sign to wear upon his back,
this girdle glittering with familiar studs.
And when his eyes drank in this plunder, this
memorial of brutal grief, Aeneas,
aflame with rage — his wrath was terrible —
cried: "How can you who wear the spoils of my
dear comrade now escape me? It is Pallas
who strikes, who sacrifices you, who takes
this payment from your shameless blood." Relentless,
he sinks his sword into the chest of Turnus.
His limbs fell slack with chill; and with a moan
his life, resentful, fled to shades below.

---

10. **Pallas** (pal′əs), a young friend of Aeneas, slain by Turnus.

THINKING CRITICALLY

1. *Making Comparisons* What similarities and differences are there between Homer's depiction of a duel (on page 40) and Virgil's?

2. *Recognizing Values* While the *Aeneid* ends directly after the death of Turnus, there are two more books after the death of Hector in the *Iliad*, depicting the funeral games of Patroclus and the Trojans' recovery of Hector's body. Why do you think Virgil chooses such a brutally abrupt ending? What is meant by it, that two books of mourning and compassion could not display?

3. *Linking Past and Present* What would be an appropriate subject for a modern American Virgil to undertake for an epic poem?

WRITER'S PORTFOLIO

1. *Extending the Selection* Compare and contrast the actions of the gods in the death of Hector and the death of Turnus.

2. *Examining Key Questions* Discuss what view of ultimate reality emerges in Book 12 of the *Aeneid*.

Roman Arts

The interior of Roman homes was very different from the sort of living arrangements we are used to. They were elaborately laid out, but sparsely furnished; moreover, the decor was a part of the architectural design itself. In the houses of Rome's wealthy classes, there were huge, gorgeous mosaic tile floors and the walls were covered with beautiful paintings. A room's decor would often have a theme from nature or depict some aspect of Roman life, like the theater, in a series of paintings. Many of the paintings gave a *trompe l'oeil* effect (so realistic it creates the illusion that the objects are real). They seemed like windows into the outer world. Some of the best of these paintings show architectural vistas, as in the Cubiculum Boscoreale below, which seem strikingly lifelike in their perspective. Roman paintings and mosaics were rarely used for portraiture, but instead

Cubiculum, or bedchamber, from the Villa Boscoreale at Pompeii 40–30 B.C.

Mosaic of marine life
from Pompeii, c. A.D. 79

concentrated on memorializing daily life and events, as in the mosaic, on page *77*, showing all the kinds of edible fish or *Woman Playing the Kithera*, on page 114, which shows a little girl watching a woman play the instrument. The paintings and mosaics were somewhat like our photographs, telling the tale of how people dressed, went about their day, or entertained themselves. Do you think Romans spent more time indoors or out of doors?

THINKING CRITICALLY

1. *Making Inferences* What does the subject matter of Roman painting indicate about its status as an art form? Do you think it was as highly regarded as sculpture? Why or why not?

2. *Recognizing Values* Do these Roman paintings seem idealized or stylized or do they aim to be faithful reproductions?

3. *Linking Past and Present* How does Roman painting differ from painting today? What does this suggest about the difference in the place of the artist in ancient Rome and in today's world?

WRITER'S PORTFOLIO

1. *Extending the Selection* Using the pictures as your starting point, write a journal entry for a young Roman living in the sort of house that might contain this decor.

2. *Examining Key Questions* Judging by their pictorial art, do you think the Romans were idealists or materialists? Be sure to use examples to defend your thesis.

EXAMINING KEY QUESTIONS

> • *What is ultimately real in the universe?*
> • *How can human beings create a better life on earth?*

Throughout this chapter, most selections have concluded with a writing project asking you to discuss how the art or literature you have examined provides answers to one of these key questions. The following writing projects will help you draw together what you have learned by examining how several selections illustrate these key questions.

• Compare and contrast the conceptions of ultimate reality of the universe found in Homer, the Presocratic philosophers, and Plato. How does Virgil's conception compare with the Greeks'?

• What seem to be the defining notions of the good life in ancient Greece and Rome? Be sure to point out the differences between the Greek and Roman viewpoints and use examples from the texts to support your ideas.

SPEAKING/LISTENING

• Create a talk show with Socrates, Homer, Sappho, and Thucydides as the guests. Some students should choose a role as one of the guests, while others prepare questions to ask as host and audience. Present your show to the rest of the class.

CRAFTING

• Greek art was idealized, while most Roman art aimed for realism. Consider these creative alternatives carefully and then, using any medium you like, create your own image of a man or woman.

COLLECTING

• Collect images of buildings in modern cities which show the influence of Greek and Roman culture. What elements of Greek and Roman architecture show up in modern buildings? What sort of buildings seem to show the most Greek and Roman influence? Why do you think this is?

Christ and the Cross, ivory casket panel, c. A.D. 420

Judaism and Early Christianity

INTRODUCTION by Thomas Sheehan

PORTFOLIO

The Old Testament (c. 1000–200 B.C.)
Genesis Chapters 2–3; Exodus Chapter 19

The New Testament (A.D. 70)
Matthew Chapter 5, "The Sermon on the Mount"

Images of Jesus (200s–400s)
Catacomb wall painting; ivory casket panel;
mosaic of Christus Helios; Byzantine mosaic

The Council of Nicaea (325)
Letter of Eusebius

The Church and Christian Duty (374–397)
Saint Ambrose, "The Duties of the Clergy"

Christianity and Classical Culture (c. 400)
Saint Augustine, *Confessions*; Saint Jerome,
"Jerome's Dream"

Hagia Sophia (537)
Exterior of Hagia Sophia; Interior of Hagia Sophia;
mosaic of the Virgin and Child with Constantine
and Justinian

CHAPTER 3 PROJECTS

Moses crossing the Red Sea

c. 1250 B.C.
The Exodus

CHAPTER 3

Judaism and Early Christianity

1000 B.C.–A.D. 550

THOMAS SHEEHAN

Professor of Philosophy, Loyola University

Imagine yourself, over 1900 years ago, overlooking the city of Jerusalem. It is September of A.D. 70, and this glorious city, the heart of the Jewish faith and hope, is under siege by Titus's terrifying Roman legions, who mean to lay it waste.

Jerusalem and Palestine, long occupied by the Roman Empire, are in fierce revolt. Inside the walls of the Holy City, Jewish revolutionaries of all stripes— peasant rebels driven by poverty and hunger, priests and Zealots inspired by hopes of a coming messiah, all of them armed to the teeth—have risen up against the Roman Empire and proclaimed a final battle "for the liberation of Zion."

The battle goes badly for the rebels. After four months of gory combat, the Romans smash through the city walls, fight their way house-to-house through the narrow streets, and with full fury attack the revolutionaries' last stronghold, their Holy Temple.

Shielding themselves against the defenders' arrows and stones, the Roman legions charge the Temple walls and set fire to the outer gates. The flames burn so hot that the bronze hinges and silver ornaments of the great doors melt as revolutionaries and legionaries fight hand-to-hand in the Temple courtyard. Then suddenly the sacred inner sanctuary bursts into flames. All is lost. As the Jewish historian Josephus later wrote:

"The Temple Mount, everywhere enveloped in flames, seemed to be boiling from its base.... The ground could

Horn of Anointment

Illumination of the Judgment of Solomon

c. 1000
David becomes king of Israel

973
Solomon founds Israelite Empire

not be seen anywhere between the corpses; the soldiers climbed over heaps of bodies as they chased the fugitives."

The few thousand Jews who survived the starvation and the fighting are either butchered outright, sold into slavery, or led away to fight as gladiators in the arenas of the Empire. One of the revolutionaries, Simon, son of Gioras, who had proclaimed himself the messianic "King of the Jews," is taken to Rome, there to be dragged in royal robes and chains in Titus's triumphal procession, then strangled in the Mamartine Prison at the Roman Forum and dumped into a sewer.

Jerusalem, which the Roman author Pliny the Elder had called the most splendid city in the East, lay a smoldering ruin, hardly one stone left on another. One eyewitness to the catastrophe reported that the destruction of the sacred city was so complete "as to leave future visitors no reason to believe the place had ever been inhabited."

The destruction of Jerusalem in A.D. 70 opened up a new era in Western civilization. It marks a turning point

certainly for Judaism, but also for a new sect — Christianity — that had been growing within (and away from) Judaism for some forty years. Let us look at both in turn: first, Judaism and then Christianity and see how their very different paths helped shape the period that this chapter studies.

THE DEVELOPMENT OF JUDAISM

Jewish faith and culture are founded on belief in God not as a harsh and fickle tyrant who might treat human beings with disregard and even contempt, but as the benevolent creator and preserver of the world, who turns over dominion of that world to the splendid creatures called Adam and Eve (see pages 90–93). This belief in the goodness of everything created and in the intrinsic dignity of woman and man, lies (along with other traditions) at the root of Western humanism.

Judaism is founded on the concrete experiences of the ancient Jewish people, especially the following historical events: the Exodus, when Moses lead

Jews leaving
Jerusalem

Pottery
mask of a
Jewish
woman

700
Sennacherib sacks Jerusalem

586
Babylonian exile begins

the Jews out of Egypt around 1250 B.C.; the giving of the *Torah* or law, including what we now call the Ten Commandments, on Mount Sinai soon after the Exodus; the brief but glorious kingdom of David in Palestine and beyond around 1000 B.C.; and the message of the prophets, especially Isaiah, Jeremiah, and Ezekiel, from about 750 to 550 B.C.

Beginning around 725 B.C., a series of foreign empires conquered and occupied the territory once ruled by King David. The destruction of the First Temple and the subsequent exile of the Jewish people to present-day Iraq (the so-called Babylonian Captivity, 586–538 B.C.), marked the lowest and most devastating point. When, under Persian domination, Jews began to return from exile to their former lands, their scholars gathered the people's oral traditions into The Book: the Torah (or Law), the Prophets, and the Sacred Writings. These three groups comprise the Hebrew Scriptures, what has become known as the "Old Testament." The rebuilding of the Temple in Jerusalem under the

priest and scribe Ezra and the leader-reformer Nehemiah gives the period beginning around 450 B.C. the name the "Second Temple" period.

The memory of David's glorious kingdom inspired faithful Jews during the hard centuries of occupation by the Persian, Greek, and (beginning in 63 B.C.) Roman Empires. Many Jews hoped God would restore David's kingdom under a new national and militaristic ruler, the "anointed one" or "messiah."

Other Jews expected not a new earthly kingdom within history, but something radically different: the end of the entire world and the beginning of a "new creation," a "new heaven and a new earth" where God would rule as he did in the very beginning. We call this second hope "apocalyptic," from a Greek word for "revelation": the revelation of God's secret plan to end this world and begin his miraculous and universal kingdom.

When both these hopes were dashed, at least temporarily, in A.D. 70, Judaism began to edge away from revo-

250
*Hebrew scriptures are
translated into Greek*

167
*Judas Maccabeus leads
the Jewish revolt*

lutionary movements and apocalyptic hopes. It turned, instead, to its rich cultural heritage, which scholars began to organize into the Talmud, one of the greatest achievements of religious literature. Between A.D. 70 and 500 Jewish rabbis and teachers, from Palestine to Babylon and beyond, gathered their centuries-old oral teachings into this many-volume work, a collection of teachings and commentaries on the Law given on Mount Sinai.

This magnificent text, whose genesis extends over five centuries, has kept Jewish hopes alive throughout centuries of diaspora and suffering, and continues to inspire Jewish communities worldwide.

THE ORIGINS OF CHRISTIANITY

The destruction of Jerusalem was a turning point for Christianity as well. Born as a movement within Judaism, and nurtured by a form of the apocalyptic hope that inspired first-century Judaism, Christianity by A.D. 70 was turning away from its Jewish origins and direct-ing its preaching of the Gospel of Jesus to the Gentiles (non-Jews) of the Roman Empire.

Jesus probably was born around 5 B.C. and died about A.D. 30. During the last years of his short life he went about Galilee proclaiming a startling new message, that God's reign or "kingdom" did not lie in the future but had already begun in Jesus' preaching and actions. The urgency of this message is captured in a phrase attributed to Jesus in Mark's Gospel, "The time is fulfilled! God's reign is at hand! Change your ways!" (Mark 1:15) Directing his gospel to the poorest members of Jewish society (see "the Sermon on the Mount" on pages 95–99), Jesus taught that God was gathering the destitute and marginalized into the final kingdom. And he lived out this teaching by overturning social custom and eating with the hated outcasts of society — prostitutes, sinners, and tax collectors. He acted with awe-inspiring power and spoke with the authority of an end-of-the-world prophet; and he paid for his ways by being crucified in Jerusalem

Mosaic of Baptism

Gem depicting Crucifixion

A.D. 27	**30**
Jesus baptized by John the Baptist	*Jesus is crucified*

under imperial Roman authority, probably on Friday, April 7, A.D. 30.

However Jesus may have understood himself during his lifetime, soon after his death his followers, without breaking with Judaism, proclaimed that Jesus had been exalted to heaven ("resurrected from the dead") and would soon return in glory to usher in God's final kingdom (the *"parousia"* or "second coming"). The original community of believers, gathered around the fisherman-turned disciple Simon (nicknamed "Peter," the Greek word for the "Rock") regularly visited Temple in Jerusalem where they proclaimed the "good news" or "gospel" about Jesus to their fellow Jews, ate meals together in imitation of their Master's example, and earnestly awaited his return at the dramatic end of the world.

Meanwhile, the community's sense of Jesus' power began to grow. Within ten years of Jesus' death, believers in Antioch, Syria, were calling him the "Christ," (thus earning themselves the title of "Christians"). And before the end of the century he was acknowl-

edged as the divine Son of God, the creative "Word" who had existed with his Father in heaven from all eternity, who had brought the world into existence, and thus was the *Pantocrator* (the Greek for "the almighty ruler"), as well as the final judge of the world at the apocalypse. To symbolize his powers as creator and judge, Christians embellished his image with the first and last letters of the Greek alphabet: Alpha and Omega (see page 116), roughly the equivalent of writing A to Z today.

With that last designation—Jesus as God—Christianity had definitively broken with its parent Judaism. One of the most influential figures in moving Christianity away from orthodox Judaism and in shaping Christian doctrine after Jesus' death was the Jewish-Christian missionary Paul, whose Jewish name was Saul. He began as an early and zealous persecutor of Jesus' followers, but was dramatically converted to the new sect in Damascus, Syria, a few years after the Crucifixion.

Devoting himself to spreading the gospel to the "diaspora," the Jewish

*Statue of
a martyr
and a lion*

*Arch
of Titus*

64
Nero begins persecution of Christians

70
Jerusalem sacked by Romans under Titus

communities outside of Palestine, he traveled throughout present-day Turkey, Greece, and Italy, preaching first to the Jewish synagogues and, if he was rebuffed there, to the non-Jews. Around A.D. 50, Paul, the "Apostle to the Gentiles," was instrumental in convincing Jewish Christians like Simon and James, the brother of Jesus, that Gentile converts did not need to undergo circumcision and become Jews in order to embrace the message of Jesus. That decision, sometimes called the "Council of Jerusalem," marks the official beginning of the separation of the new sect from its Jewish origins.

PERSECUTION AND FINAL VICTORY

Christianity was a way to live as much as it was a doctrine to be believed. In imitation of their Master, Jesus' followers, at least ideally, were intensely moral and passionately devoted to the poor and destitute, and at least in some situations, shared their property and goods in a communistic fashion. These followers believed that Jesus' fate would be their own. On the one hand, they expected (and, indeed, suffered) persecution, especially at the hands of the same Roman Empire that had put Jesus to death. On the other hand, they also expected that the end of the world would come soon and that they, too, would be "resurrected" as Jesus had been. The first believers shared Jewish apocalyptic expectations; they were convinced the end would come in their own lifetime. Perhaps they thought the destruction of Jerusalem was an apocalyptic sign of the soon-to-happen end of the world. In the Book of Revelation, the last book of the "New Testament," John, the evangelist, describes his imaginative vision of that apocalyptic future, a vision of a better world that has become part of the treasury of Western consciousness, both religious and non-religious:

"Then I saw a new heaven and a new earth, for the first heaven and the first earth had passed away, and the sea was no more. And I saw the holy city, New Jerusalem, coming down out of heaven from God, prepared as a bride adorned for her husband. And I heard a

Statue of the
Tetrarchs,
including
Diocletian

Head of
Constantine

285
Diocletian divides the Roman Empire

313
Constantine issues the Edict of Toleration

great voice from the throne saying: 'Behold the dwelling of God is now with men and women. He will dwell with them, and they shall be his people, and God himself will be with them. He will wipe away every tear from their eyes, and death shall be no more, for the former things have passed away.'" (Revelation 21:1–4)

However, as Jesus' return was delayed, and as the original founders of the faith died off (Peter and Paul were martyred by A.D. 70), believers set about the tasks of organizing their sect into a religion. Gospels were written, Christian doctrine began to solidify, church hierarchy came to be established. (See pages 105–107, Ambrose, "The Duties of the Clergy.")

**BECOMING
THE EMPIRE'S
RELIGION**   The crucial turning point, for better or worse, came in A.D. 312. No sooner had the church emerged from the particularly vehement persecution of Emperor Diocletian (from 303 to 305) than rescue appeared on the horizon in

the form of a pagan Roman general, Constantine. On October 28, 312, the rebellious Constantine, marching on Rome from distant Britain, defeated Emperor Maxentius. Two months later (January, 313) he issued the "Edict of Milan" that officially established religious toleration of Christianity.

Twelve years later Emperor Constantine gathered some 300 Christian bishops together at Nicaea in western Asia Minor where, under his tutelage they composed the Nicene Creed and officially declared Jesus to be divine (see pages 102–104). A half-century later — on February 28, 380 — the Emperor Theodosius I declared Christianity the imperial state religion and made the Nicene Creed binding on all Roman citizens. Once freed from persecution and made the state religion, official Christianity was not always so tolerant of those it declared heretics. St. Augustine, when bishop of Hippo in North Africa, justified police-state coercion of the Donatist sect. Repression and even persecution of Jews under Emperor Justinian, the builder of the

*Seal of Alaric
the Visigoth*

*Coin of
Justinian*

476
Visigoths depose Western Roman emperor

529
Enactment of the Justinian Code

Hagia Sophia (see pages 117–120), was not far behind.

With his dedication of the city of Constantinople (now Istanbul, Turkey) as the "new Rome" on May 11, 330, Emperor Constantine I paved the way for the eventual split of the empire into the Byzantine East and the Roman West in 395. Christianity, too, would eventually divide into Eastern and Western branches. The Iconoclasm Controversy (a dispute over the meaning and use of religious images) separated Eastern and Western Christianity for a time in the eighth and ninth centuries. It was a foreshadowing of the full-blown split of the churches in 1054.

Meanwhile, as Constantinople thrived as the capital of the Eastern empire, ancient Rome, beginning in 410, found itself periodically overrun by barbarian invaders. St. Augustine, who had converted to Christianity in 386 within the secure walls of imperial Milan (see pages 108–110), died in Hippo, North Africa, in 430 as the city was besieged by the same Vandal tribe that had sacked Rome two decades ear-lier. For the elite of the Roman empire, the lights went out in the fall of 476 when the last of the Roman emperors, Romulus Augustulus, surrendered the reins of power of the Roman Empire to the barbarian general Odacer.

By 550, Christianity had moved far from its origins, from its hopes in the imminent end of the world and the establishment of God's apocalyptic kingdom. It had become an integral part of the very earthly kingdom of Rome, whose representatives had murdered Christianity's prophetic founder, Jesus of Nazareth, some four centuries earlier. From a small Jewish sect centered on destitute outcasts, through persecuted underground religion, it had finally emerged from the catacombs into the full light of day as the official imperial religion. In the East, its position was secure in the theocratic state of Byzantium. In the West, after the collapse of the traditional Roman Empire, it faced a new and daunting task: to bring to the barbarians of Italy, Gaul, Spain, and Germany the message of the religion that had conquered Rome.

The Old Testament

The Bible is a book sacred to both Jews and Christians. The Jewish Bible contains only the books known to Christians as the Old Testament and according to Jewish usage falls into three divisions: the Law or *Torah* (the first five books), the Prophets, and the Writings. With a few exceptions, the Old Testament was written in Hebrew. The ancient Hebrews were originally nomads, who wandered into Canaan [a region bordering on the Mediterranean in what is now Israel] and then into Egypt. The Bible begins with Genesis, which is excerpted below, meaning "creation" or "birth," and tells how God created the world out of chaos and then created all living things on earth, including man and woman. When the Hebrews had been in Egypt for several generations, the pharaoh became alarmed at their increasing numbers and commanded that every son born to the Hebrews be cast into the Nile. The infant Moses was hidden by his mother in a basket and placed in the reeds along the Nile. He was saved by the pharaoh's daughter, grew up, and one day killed an Egyptian for beating a Hebrew. When this was discovered, Moses fled to Midian [in northwest Arabia] where the Lord spoke to him from a burning bush (Exodus 3:2) and commanded him to lead the people of Israel out of Egypt. Exodus, the second book of the Bible, describes this exodus, or departure, of the Hebrews from Egypt where they had been held in bondage, an event still commemorated by Jews in their annual Passover observance. After Moses had led the Israelites out of Egypt and into the wilderness, God called him to the top of Mount Sinai and gave him the Ten Commandments, which appear below as the second selection. According to Genesis, why does God create mankind?

from Genesis, Chapters 2–3

WHEN THE LORD GOD MADE EARTH AND HEAVEN, THERE WAS neither shrub nor plant growing wild upon the earth, because the Lord God had sent no rain on the earth; nor was there any man to till the ground. A flood used to rise out of the earth and water all the surface of the ground. Then the Lord God formed a man from the dust of the ground and breathed into his nostrils the breath of life. Thus the man became a living creature. Then the Lord God planted a garden in Eden away to the east, and there he put the man whom he had formed. The Lord God made trees spring from the ground, all trees pleasant to look at and good for food; and in the middle of the garden he set the tree of life and the tree of the knowledge of good and evil.

There was a river flowing from Eden to water the garden, and when it left the garden it branched into four streams. The name of the first is Pishon; that is the river which encircles all the land of Havilah, where the gold is. The gold of that land is good; bdellium [a fragrant resin] and cornelians [gemstones] are also to be found there. The name of the second river is Gihon; this is the one which encircles all the land of Cush. The name of the third is Tigris; this is the river which runs east of Asshur. The fourth river is the Euphrates.

The Lord God took the man and put him in the garden of Eden to till it and care for it. He told the man, "You may eat from every tree in the garden, but not from the tree of the knowledge of good and evil; for on the day that you eat from it, you will certainly die." Then the Lord God said, "It is not good for the man to be alone. I will provide a partner for him." So God formed out of the ground all the wild animals and all the birds of heaven. He brought them to the man to see what he would call them, and whatever the man called each living creature, that was its name. Thus the man gave names to all cattle, to the birds of heaven, and to every wild animal; but for the man himself no partner had yet been found. And so the Lord God put the man into a trance, and while he slept, he took one of his ribs and closed the flesh over the place. The Lord God then built up the rib, which he had taken out of the man, into a woman. He brought her to the man, and the man said:

Now this, at last—
bone from my bones,
flesh from my flesh!—
this shall be called woman,
for from man was this taken.

That is why a man leaves his father and mother and is united to his wife, and the two become one flesh. Now they were both naked, the man and his wife, but they had no feeling of shame towards one another.

The serpent was more crafty than any wild creature that the Lord God had made. He said to the woman, "Is it true that God has forbidden you to eat from any tree in the garden?" The woman answered the serpent, "We may eat the fruit of any tree in the garden, except for the tree in the middle of the garden; God has forbidden us either to eat or to touch the fruit of that; if we do, we shall die." The serpent said, "Of course you will not die. God knows that as soon as you eat it, your eyes will be opened and you will be like gods knowing both good and evil." When the woman saw that the fruit of the tree was good to eat, and that it was pleasing to the eye and tempting to contemplate, she took some and ate it. She also gave her husband some and he ate it. Then the eyes of both of them were opened and they discovered that they were naked; so they stitched fig-leaves together and made themselves loincloths.

The man and his wife heard the sound of the Lord God walking in the garden at the time of the evening breeze and hid from the Lord God among the trees of the garden. But the Lord God called to the man and said to him, "Where are you?" He replied, "I heard the sound as you were walking in the garden, and I was afraid because I was naked, and I hid myself." God answered, "Who told you that you were naked? Have you eaten from the tree which I forbade you?" The man said, "The woman you gave me for a companion, she gave me fruit from the tree and I ate it." Then the Lord God said to the woman, "What is this that you have done?" The woman said, "The serpent tricked me, and I ate." Then the Lord God said to the serpent:

> Because you have done this you are accursed
> more than all cattle and all wild creatures.
> On your belly you shall crawl, and dust you shall eat
> all the days of your life.
> I will put enmity between you and the woman,
> between your brood and hers.
> They shall strike at your head,
> and you shall strike at their heel.

To the woman he said:

> I will increase your labor and your groaning,
> and in labor you shall bear children.
> You shall be eager for your husband,
> and he shall be your master.

And to the man he said:

> Because you have listened to your wife
> and have eaten from the tree which I forbade you,
> accursed shall be the ground on your account.
> With labor you shall win your food from it
> all the days of your life.
> It will grow thorns and thistles for you,
> none but wild plants for you to eat.
> You shall gain your bread by the sweat of your brow
> until you return to the ground;
> for from it you were taken.
> Dust you are, to dust you shall return.

---

from Exodus Chapter 19

MOSES WENT UP THE MOUNTAIN OF GOD, AND THE LORD called to him from the mountain and said, "Speak thus to the house of Jacob, and tell this to the sons of Israel: You have seen with your own eyes what I did to Egypt, and how I have carried you on eagles' wings and brought you here to me. If only you will now listen to me and keep my covenant, then out of all peoples you shall become my special possession; for the whole earth is mine. You shall be my kingdom of priests, my holy nation. These are the words you shall speak to the Israelites."

I am the Lord your God who brought you out of Egypt, out of the land of slavery.

You shall have no other god to set against me.

You shall not make a carved image for yourself nor the likeness of anything in the heavens above, or on the earth below, or in the waters under the earth.

You shall not bow down to them or worship them; for I, the Lord your God, am a jealous god. I punish the children for the sins of the fathers to the third and fourth generations of those who hate me. But I keep faith with thousands, with those who love me and keep my commandments.

You shall not make wrong use of the name of the Lord your God; the Lord will not leave unpunished the man who misuses his name.

Remember to keep the sabbath day holy. You have six days to labor and do all your work. But the seventh day is a sabbath of the Lord your

God; that day you shall not do any work, you, your son or your daughter, your slave or your slave-girl, your cattle or the alien within your gates; for in six days the Lord made heaven and earth, the sea, and all that is in them, and on the seventh day he rested. Therefore the Lord blessed the sabbath day and declared it holy.

Honor your father and your mother, that you may live long in the land which the Lord your God is giving you.

You shall not commit murder.

You shall not commit adultery.

You shall not steal.

You shall not give false evidence against your neighbor.

You shall not covet your neighbor's house; you shall not covet your neighbor's wife, his slave, his slave-girl, his ox, his ass, or anything that belongs to him.

THINKING CRITICALLY

1. *Making Inferences* Where in the passage from Genesis is the implication that humans are mortal?

2. *Identifying Central Issues* What do these parts of the Old Testament tell you about God's purpose for humans and about humans' relationship to God?

3. *Linking Past and Present* In Genesis, God places woman under man's control, which many people believe has become a controversial issue in this century. Do you think that religions should become flexible as time passes and societies change? Why or why not?

WRITER'S PORTFOLIO

1. *Extending the Selection* Do you think the punishments that God metes out in Genesis are fair? Why or why not?

2. *Examining Key Questions* Describe the God who appears in these two passages. Is he consistently portrayed in both Genesis and Exodus, or can you detect differences?

The New Testament

According to the New Testament, Jesus was born in Bethlehem in Judea. He was a Jew and in the New Testament is presented as the Messiah of Israel as foretold in the Old Testament. (*Christ* is the Greek translation of the Hebrew word *Messiah*, meaning "anointed" and referring to prophesies of a leader who would deliver the Jews from their enemies.) The New Testament was written in Greek and consists of the four Gospels—Matthew, Mark, Luke, and John—which tell of Jesus' life, teaching and healing, death, and resurrection; the Acts of the Apostles; the twenty-one books of letters from Paul and others; and Revelation. The Gospel according to Matthew is the first Gospel in the New Testament, but not the oldest. The Gospel according to Mark is usually thought to be the first written. Although the first Gospel is called Matthew, it is in fact anonymous. It is so named because one of the sources may have been a collection of the sayings of Jesus made by Matthew, one of Jesus' twelve Apostles or disciples. In the passage from Matthew reprinted here, Jesus is teaching, healing, and preaching in Galilee, a Roman province north of Jerusalem. Crowds have followed him, and he has gone a little away from them. The law that Jesus refers to is the Law of Moses. What patterns can you find in Jesus' style of speaking?

from Matthew, Chapter 5
"The Sermon on the Mount"

WHEN HE SAW THE CROWDS HE WENT UP THE HILL. THERE HE took his seat, and when his disciples had gathered round him he began to address them. And this is the teaching he gave:

"How blest are those who know their need of God;
   the kingdom of Heaven is theirs.
How blest are the sorrowful;
   they shall find consolation.
How blest are those of a gentle spirit;
   they shall have the earth for their possession.

How blest are those who hunger and thirst to see right prevail;
   they shall be satisfied.
How blest are those who show mercy;
   mercy shall be shown to them.
How blest are those whose hearts are pure;
   they shall see God.
How blest are the peacemakers;
   God shall call them his sons.
How blest are those who have suffered persecution for the
cause of right;
   the kingdom of Heaven is theirs....

"Do not suppose that I have come to abolish the Law and the prophets; I did not come to abolish, but to complete. I tell you this: so long as heaven and earth endure, not a letter, not a stroke, will disappear from the Law until all that must happen has happened. If any man therefore sets aside even the least of the Law's demands, and teaches others to do the same, he will have the lowest place in the kingdom of Heaven, whereas anyone who keeps the Law, and teaches others so, will stand high in the kingdom of Heaven.... You have learned that they were told, 'Eye for eye, tooth for tooth.' But what I tell you is this: Do not set yourself against the man who wrongs you. If someone slaps you on the right cheek, turn and offer him your left. If a man wants to sue you for your shirt, let him have your coat as well. If a man in authority makes you go one mile, go with him two. Give when you are asked to give; and do not turn your back on a man who wants to borrow.

"You have learned that they were told, 'Love your neighbor, hate your enemy.' But what I tell you is this: Love your enemies and pray for your persecutors; only so can you be children of your heavenly Father, who makes his sun rise on good and bad alike, and sends the rain on the honest and the dishonest. If you love only those who love you, what reward can you expect? Surely the tax-gatherers do as much as that. And if you greet only your brothers, what is there extraordinary about that? Even the heathen do as much. There must be no limit to your goodness, as your heavenly Father's goodness knows no bounds.

"Be careful not to make a show of your religion before men; if you do, no reward awaits you in your Father's house in heaven.

"Thus, when you do some act of charity, do not announce it with a flourish of trumpets, as the hypocrites do in synagogue and in the streets to win admiration from men. I tell you this: they have their reward already. No; when you do some act of charity, do not let your left hand know what your right is doing; your good deed must be secret, and your Father who sees what is done in secret will reward you.

"Again, when you pray, do not be like the hypocrites; they love to say their prayers standing up in synagogue and at the street-corners, for everyone to see them. I tell you this: they have their reward already. But when you pray, go into a room by yourself, shut the door, and pray to your Father who is there in the secret place; and your Father who sees what is secret will reward you.

"In your prayers do not go babbling on like the heathen, who imagine that the more they say the more likely they are to be heard. Do not imitate them. Your Father knows what your needs are before you ask him....

"Do not store up for yourselves treasure on earth, where it grows rusty and moth-eaten, and thieves break in to steal it. Store up treasure in heaven, where there is no moth and no rust to spoil it, no thieves to break in and steal. For where your treasure is, there will your heart be also.

"The lamp of the body is the eye. If your eyes are sound, you will have light for your whole body; if the eyes are bad, your whole body will be in darkness. If then the only light you have is darkness, the darkness is doubly dark.

"No servant can be the slave of two masters; for either he will hate the first and love the second, or he will be devoted to the first and think nothing of the second. You cannot serve God and Money.

"Therefore I bid you put away anxious thoughts about food and drink to keep you alive, and clothes to cover your body. Surely life is more than food, the body more than clothes. Look at the birds of the air; they do not sow and reap and store in barns, yet your heavenly Father feeds them. You are worth more than the birds! Is there a man of you who by anxious thought can add a foot to his height? And why be anxious about clothes? Consider how the lilies grow in the fields; they do not work, they do not spin; and yet, I tell you, even Solomon in all his splendor was not attired like one of these. But if that is how God clothes the grass in the fields, which is there today, and tomorrow is thrown on the stove, will he not all the more clothe you? How little faith you have! No, do not ask anxiously, 'What are we to eat? What are we to drink? What shall we wear?' All these are things for the heathen to run after, not for you, because your heavenly Father knows that you need them all. Set your mind on God's kingdom and his justice before everything else, and all the rest will come to you as well. So do not be anxious about tomorrow; tomorrow will look after itself. Each day has troubles enough of its own.

"Pass no judgement, and you will not be judged. For as you judge others, so you will yourselves be judged, and whatever measure you deal out to others will be dealt back to you. Why do you look at the speck of sawdust in your brother's eye, with never a thought for the great plank in your own? Or how can you say to your brother, 'Let me take the speck out of your eye,' when all the time there is that plank in your own? You hypocrite! First take the plank out of your own eye, and then you will see clearly to take the speck out of your brother's.

"Do not give dogs what is holy; do not throw your pearls to the pigs: they will only trample on them, and turn and tear you to pieces.

"Ask, and you will receive; seek, and you will find; knock, and the door will be opened. For everyone who asks receives, he who seeks finds, and to him who knocks, the door will be opened.

"Is there a man among you who will offer his son a stone when he asks for bread, or a snake when he asks for fish? If you, then, bad as you are, know how to give your children what is good for them, how much more will your heavenly Father give good things to those who ask him!

"Always treat others as you would like them to treat you: that is the Law and the prophets.

"Enter by the narrow gate. The gate is wide that leads to perdition, there is plenty of room on the road, and many go that way; but the gate that leads to life is small and the road is narrow, and those who find it are few.

"Beware of false prophets, men who come to you dressed up as sheep while underneath they are savage wolves. You will recognize them by the fruits they bear. Can grapes be picked from briars, or figs from thistles? In the same way, a good tree always yields good fruit, and a poor tree bad fruit. A good tree cannot bear bad fruit, or a poor tree good fruit. And when a tree does not yield good fruit it is cut down and burnt. That is why I say you will recognize them by their fruits.

"Not everyone who calls me 'Lord, Lord' will enter the kingdom of Heaven, but only those who do the will of my heavenly Father. When that day comes, many will say to me, 'Lord, Lord, did we not prophesy in your name, cast out devils in your name, and in your name perform many miracles?' Then I will tell them to their face, 'I never knew you; out of my sight, you and your wicked ways!'

"What then of the man who hears these words of mine and acts upon them? He is like a man who had the sense to build his house on rock. The rain came down, the floods rose, the wind blew, and beat upon that house; but it did not fall, because its foundations were on rock. But what of the man who hears these words of mine and does not act upon them? He is like a man who was foolish enough to build his house on sand. The rain came down, the floods rose, the wind blew, and beat upon that house; down it fell with a great crash."

THINKING CRITICALLY

1. *Identifying Central Issues* What is at least one main purpose of this sermon?

2. *Making Inferences* Jesus concludes with a parable, a story that illustrates a moral or point. What is the point of the story about houses?

3. *Linking Past and Present* Reread what Jesus says about food, clothing, and treasures on earth. How would people's lives be different today if they followed this teaching?

WRITER'S PORTFOLIO

1. *Extending the Selection* Choose one of the parts of the "Sermon on the Mount" that has become a well-known saying and write what you think it would mean for modern society if it were heeded.

2. *Examining Key Questions* Describe the ideal Christian as suggested by Jesus' sermon.

Images of Jesus

No one knows what Jesus Christ actually looked like or who first depicted him. Christians, like Jews, at first abstained from religious images. They used symbols such as the fish or dove to represent Jesus and his message. Not until the fourth century did depictions of biblical scenes begin to appear. As there were no records of Jesus' appearance or even descriptions of him, it was left to artists to imagine what he looked like. In the West, Jesus was at first depicted as a youthful and beardless teacher, while Greek depictions in the East showed him as a young bearded man. In reality, it is most likely that Jesus had a beard, as almost all religious Jews wore beards. Some of the earliest depictions of Jesus depict him in Roman allegory, as the Good Shepherd or even a sun god, as in the mosaic of Christus Helios (c. 225) on page 115. A more realistic depiction is the painting of the bust of Jesus (300s), which is on page 116, from the ceiling of the catacomb of Commidilla near Rome. Here he is shown between the Greek letters alpha and omega — the first and last letters of the Greek alphabet — a reference to Revelation 1:8. ("'I am the Alpha and Omega,' says the Lord God, who is and who was and who is to come, the Sovereign.") This figure looks more like a Jewish religious reformer, than a god. The mosaic (c. 313–337), which is on page 116, from the ceiling of the mausoleum of Constantina, daughter of the Emperor Constantine, signals a concept of Jesus as a triumphal figure. In the mosaic, Jesus is shown transferring the responsibility for preaching his message to all the world to Peter, one of the twelve Apostles, and Paul, the Apostle to the Gentiles. With the growth of Christianity as a public religion, depictions of Jesus became a major subject for artists. One wealthy patron had a series of carvings made for his sarcophagus (c. 420), depicting the last days of Jesus' life. The panel shown on page 101 depicts Jesus' crucifixion and the suicide of Judas who, according to the New Testament, betrayed Jesus to the Roman soldiers for thirty pieces of silver (shown at the foot of the tree). Which one of the images conforms the most to your idea of the way Jesus should look?

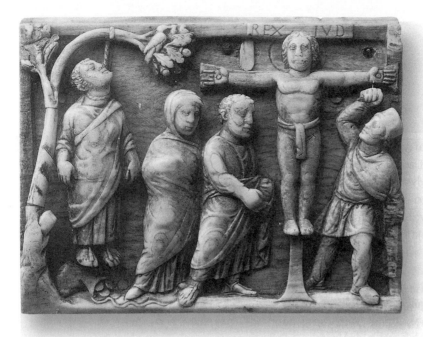

The Crucifixion and the Death of Judas, ivory casket panel, c. A.D. 420

THINKING CRITICALLY

1. *Recognizing Values* What arguments can you think of for refraining from depictions of religious images?

2. *Making Inferences* What do you think lay behind the impulse to depict the figure of Christ? How is he made to seem divine in these images?

3. *Linking Past and Present* Find some recent images of Christ. How do they compare to these? Is there a common perception of how he ought to look?

WRITER'S PORTFOLIO

1. *Extending the Selection* What part do houses of worship, religious images, decorative motifs or symbols, and music play in worship?

2. *Examining Key Questions* How should an artist go about depicting a religious subject? Do you think models should be used or should artists work from their imagination?

The Council of Nicaea

In the fourth, fifth, and sixth centuries, the Christian church was rocked by disputes over matters of doctrine. The first major dispute concerned the nature of Jesus. Was he the son of God or God himself? How was he both man and God? The answers to these complex questions affected worship (how were people to think of Jesus?) and the belief that Jesus Christ could deliver humans from the power of sin. The Arians (named for Arius, a church leader in Alexandria) held that Jesus was not completely divine, a position that not only separated him from God but could lead to polytheism. To deal with these and other questions, the Emperor Constantine convened a council of bishops in Nicaea (nīs ē⁄ə), a city in Asia Minor, now the town of Isnik in Turkey. Out of this council arose the Nicene Creed, which formalized the worship of both God and Jesus Christ as being of the same essence, and defined the chief articles of the Christian faith. The following selection is from a letter of Eusebius, the Bishop of Nicomedia, summarizing the Council and the text of the Nicene Creed. What does the word *consubstantial* seem to mean?

Letter of Eusebius

It is probable, beloved, that you have already learnt from another source, what has been done respecting the ecclesiastical faith in the great Council convened at Nicaea, as common fame usually outruns an accurate report of facts…. We believe in one God, the Father Almighty, Maker of all things, visible and invisible; and in one Lord Jesus Christ, the Word of God, God of God, light of light, life of life, the only begotten Son, the first born of every creature, begotten of the Father before all ages, by whom all things were made; who for our salvation was made flesh and conversed among men; who suffered, and rose again the third day, and ascended to the Father, and will come again with glory to judge the living and the dead. We also believe in one Holy Spirit; believing every one of these to be and subsist, the Father truly the Father, the Son truly the Son, and the Holy Spirit truly the Holy Spirit; as our Lord, when he sent his disciples to preach, said, "Go, and teach all nations, baptizing them in the name of the Father, and of the Son, and of the Holy Ghost." We solemnly affirm that we thus hold and thus think, and have so held formerly, and will hold even unto death, and will always continue in this faith, anathematizing every impious heresy. We testify before Almighty God and our Lord Jesus Christ, that we have believed this sincerely, and from the heart, from the time that we were capable of knowing ourselves, and now also truly think and speak, being prepared to show by sufficient proofs, and to convince your minds, that we have so believed in times past, and have preached accordingly.

Having made this representation of our faith, there was no pretence for contradiction. But our pious emperor himself was the first to declare, that it was extremely well conceived, and that it expressed his own sentiments, exhorting all to assent to, and sign it, that they might unite in its doctrines, with the addition only of the single word consubstantial; which he himself explained by asserting that he did not use the term with reference to corporeal affections, and that the Son did not subsist from the Father, either by division or abscission [the normal separation of leaves from a parent plant], since it was impossible that an immaterial, intellectual and incorporeal nature could admit of any bodily affection; but that it must be understood in a divine and mysterious manner. It was thus that our most wise and religious emperor argued on this subject. But the bishops, taking occasion from the word consubstantial, committed to writing the following form: —

We believe in one God, the Father Almighty, Maker of all things, visible and invisible; and in one Lord Jesus Christ, the Son of God, the only begotten of the Father, that is, of the substance of the Father; God of God, light of light, true God of true God; begotten, not made, consubstantial with the Father, by whom all things were made, both in heaven and in earth; who for us men, and for our salvation, descended, was incarnate, and was made man, and suffered, and rose again the third day; he ascended into heaven, and shall come to judge the living and the dead: And in the Holy Spirit. But the holy, catholic, and apostolic Church of God anathematizes those who affirm that there was a time when the Son was not, or that he was not before he was begotten, or that he was made of things not existing; or who say, that the Son of God was of any other substance or essence, or created, or liable to change or conversion.

When this form was dictated by the prelates, their expressions "of the substance of the Father," and "consubstantial with the father," were not suffered to pass without examination. Hence, therefore, several questions arose, and answers were made, and the sense of these terms was carefully considered. They admitted that the words "of the substance" signified that the Son was of the Father, but not as a part of the Father. We thought it well to assent to this explanation, as conveying the pious doctrine, that the Son was of the Father; but not, however, a part of the Father.

THINKING CRITICALLY

1. *Identifying Central Issues* The creed states that the Son was begotten. How do the words "of the substance of the Father" and "consubstantial" seem to affirm the divinity of Christ?

2. *Making Inferences* What do you think was the Council's purpose in issuing a creed?

3. *Linking Past and Present* Can you think of any modern parallels to the Nicene Council? Are these organized around religion? If not, who are the members?

WRITER'S PORTFOLIO

1. *Extending the Selection* Compare and contrast the two creeds presented in Eusebius's letter. What seems to be the main difference? Is this merely an argument of wording or is there a deeper meaning?

2. *Examining Key Questions* Do you think that a follower of a religion should be guided by a church body or individual conviction and belief?

The Church and Christian Duty

As the Christian Church grew and became the established religion of the Roman Empire, its organization grew also. At first there were local leaders called presbyters or deacons, and worshippers met in houses. Gradually, churches were built, headed by a single leader or bishop, and the presbyters and deacons served under him. As the size of Christian communities increased, so did the responsibilities of a bishop, who might oversee several churches. Eventually a formal hierarchy for accession to that position was established, with candidates for the post of bishop required to proceed through a series of minor offices. Saint Ambrose, however, was an exception. A lawyer and provincial governor, he was acclaimed bishop in 374 by the people of Milan to settle a disputed election — without ever having been baptized into the faith. Ambrose's work as bishop and his large body of writings made him one of the early leaders of the Church. The following passages are excerpts from Ambrose's writings on Christian duty and the Church. What are his views on the relationship between church and state?

I DO NOT THEREFORE CLAIM FOR MYSELF THE GLORY OF THE apostles (for who can do this save those whom the Son of God Himself has chosen?); nor the grace of the prophets, or the virtue of the evangelists, nor the cautious care of the pastors. I only desire to attain to that care and diligence in the sacred writings, which the Apostle [Saint Paul] has placed last among the duties of the saints; and this very thing I desire, so that, in the endeavor to teach, I may be able to learn. For one is the true Master, Who alone has not learnt, what He taught all; but men learn before they teach, and receive from Him what they may hand on to others.

The rule of economy and the authority of self-restraint befits all, and most of all him who stands highest in honor; so that no love for his treasures may seize upon such a man, and that he who rules over free men may never become a slave to money. It is more seemly that in soul he should be superior to treasures, and in willing service be subject to his friends. For humility increases the regard in which one is held…. I think, then, that one should strive to win preferment, especially in the Church, only by good actions and with a right aim; so that there may be no proud conceit, no idle carelessness, no shameful disposition of mind, no unseemly ambition. A plain simplicity of mind is enough for everything, and commends itself quite sufficiently….

The blessedness of individuals must not be estimated at the value of their known wealth, but according to the voice of their conscience within them. For this, as a true and uncorrupted judge of punishments and rewards, decides between the deserts of the innocent and the guilty. The innocent man dies in the strength of his own simplicity, in the full possession of his own will; having a soul filled as it were with marrow. But the sinner, though he has abundance in life, and lives in the midst of luxury, and is redolent with sweet scents, ends his life in the bitterness of his soul, and brings his last day to a close, taking with him none of those good things which he once enjoyed—carrying away nothing with him but the price of his own wickedness….

Is not he unjust who gives the reward before the end of the contest? Therefore the Lord says in the Gospel: "Blessed are the poor in spirit, for theirs is the kingdom of heaven." He said not: "Blessed are the rich," but "the poor." By the divine judgment blessedness begins there whence human misery is supposed to spring…. A reward future and not present,—in heaven not on earth—as He promised shall be given. What further dost thou expect? What further is due? Why dost thou demand the crown with so much haste, before thou dost conquer? Why dost thou desire to shake off the dust and to rest? Why dost thou long to sit at the feast before the course is finished? As yet the people are looking on, the athletes are in the arena, and thou—dost thou already look for ease?

Perhaps thou sayest: Why are the wicked joyous? Why do they live in luxury? Why do they not toil with me? It is because they who have not put down their names to strive for the crown are not bound to undergo the labors of the contest. They who have not gone down into the race-course do not anoint themselves with oil nor get covered with dust. For those whom glory awaits trouble is at hand. The perfumed spectators are wont to look on, not to join in the struggle, nor to endure the sun, the heat, the dust, and the showers. Let the athletes say to them:

Come, strive with us. The spectators will but answer: We sit here not to decide about you, but, if you conquer, will gain the glory of the crown and we shall not.

They, then, who have devoted themselves to pleasures, luxury, robbery, gain, or honors are spectators rather than combatants. They have the profit of labor, but not the fruits of virtue. They love their ease; by cunning and wickedness they heap up riches; but they will pay the penalty of their iniquity, though it be late. Their rest will be in hell, thine, in heaven; their home in the grave, thine in paradise....

The Church belongs to God, therefore it ought not to be assigned to Caesar. For the Temple of God cannot be Caesar's by right.... The emperor is within the Church, not above it.

Who is there can deny that in a matter of faith—in a matter I say of faith—bishops are wont to judge Christian emperors, while emperors are not the judges of bishops.

THINKING CRITICALLY

1. *Making Inferences* What can you infer from Ambrose's writing about the temptations that might have faced the clergy?

2. *Predicting Consequences* Who, according to Ambrose, is to have the final say on matters of faith? How might this pronouncement affect subsequent ages?

3. *Linking Past and Present* Ambrose discusses the perils of wealth for the clergy. Can you think of recent examples of money playing a part in religion?

WRITER'S PORTFOLIO

1. *Extending the Selection* Ambrose says that "humility increases the regard in which one is held." Examine the truth of this statement in the light of current interest in celebrities.

2. *Examining Key Questions* Ambrose refers to "the voice of their conscience within them." *Conscience* comes from the Latin *conscientia*, meaning knowledge or awareness. Discuss what conscience is, where it comes from, and how it conditions our lives.

Christianity and Classical Culture

In the waning years of the Roman Empire, many people struggled with converting to Christianity. These spiritual struggles form the basis of the conversion of many of the Church's most important early leaders. Two of the greatest of the Church fathers, Saint Augustine and Saint Jerome, wrote down the difficulties they experienced in finding their calling. Augustine (o′gəs tēn) (354–430) was born in the Roman province of Numidia, now Algeria, of a Christian mother and a pagan father. When he was a student in Carthage, he read a treatise by Cicero that eventually led him to become a Manichaean. The Manichees or Manichaeans were the followers of Mani, a Persian born in Mesopotamia, who preached a dualistic religion based on the idea of conflict between light or goodness and darkness or chaos. The Manichaeans were vigorous missionaries and claimed that theirs was the true path to salvation. Augustine became a teacher of rhetoric in Rome and Milan, where he became disillusioned with Manichaeanism after an intense study of Plato and hearing Saint Ambrose preach. Ambrose's influence, together with Neoplatonism, which stresses introspection, led him finally to accept Christianity. His spiritual struggles are recounted in his *Confessions*, a selection from which appears below. What kind of physical afflications mirror Augustine's spiritual conflict?

from *The Confessions of Saint Augustine*

MANY YEARS OF MY LIFE HAD PASSED—TWELVE, UNLESS I AM wrong—since I had read Cicero's *Hortensius* at the age of nineteen and it had inspired me to study philosophy. But I still postponed my renunciation of this world's joys, which would have left me free to look for that other happiness, the very search for which, let alone its discovery, I ought to have prized above the discovery of all human treasures and kingdoms or the ability to enjoy all the pleasures of the body at a mere nod of the head. As a youth I had been woefully at fault, particularly in early adolescence. I had prayed to you for chastity and said "Give me chastity and continence, but not yet." For I was afraid that you would answer my prayer at once and cure me too soon of the disease of lust, which I wanted satisfied, not quelled. I had wandered on along the road of vice in the sacrilegious superstition of the Manichees, not because I thought that it was right, but because I preferred it to the Christian belief, which I did not explore as I ought but opposed out of malice....

There was a small garden attached to the house where we [Augustine and his friend Alypius] lodged. We were free to make use of it as well as the rest of the house because our host, the owner of the house, did not live there. I now found myself driven by the tumult in my breast to take refuge in this garden, where no one could interrupt that fierce struggle, in which I was my own contestant, until it came to its conclusion. What the conclusion was to be you knew, O Lord, but I did not. Meanwhile I was beside myself with madness that would bring me sanity. I was dying a death that would bring me life. I knew the evil that was in me, but the good that was soon to be born in me I did not know. So I went out into the garden and Alypius followed at my heels. His presence was no intrusion on my solitude, and how could he leave me in that state? We sat down as far as possible from the house. I was frantic, overcome by violent anger with myself for not accepting your will and entering into your covenant. Yet in my bones I knew that this was what I ought to do. In my heart of hearts I praised it to the skies. And to reach this goal I needed no chariot or ship. I need not even walk as far as I had come from the house to the place where we sat, for to make the journey, and to arrive safely, no more was required than an act of will. But it must be a resolute and whole-hearted act of the will, not some lame wish which I kept turning over and over in my mind, so that it had to wrestle with itself, part of it trying to rise, part falling to the ground.

During this agony of indecision I performed many bodily actions, things which a man cannot always do, even if he wills to do them. If he has lost his limbs, or is bound hand and foot, or if his body is weakened by illness or under some other handicap, there are things which he cannot do. I tore my hair and hammered my forehead with my fists; I locked my fingers and hugged my knees; and I did all this because I made an act of will to do it. But I might have had the will to do it and yet not have done it, if my limbs had been unable to move in compliance with my will. I performed all these actions, in which the will and the power to act are not the same. Yet I did not do that one thing which I should have been far, far better pleased to do than all the rest and could have done at once, as soon as I had the will to do it, because as soon as I had the will to do so, I should have willed it, wholeheartedly. For in this case the power to act was the same as the will. To will it was to do it. Yet I did not do it. My body responded to the slightest wish of my mind by moving its limbs at the least thing from me, and it did so more readily than my mind obeyed itself by assenting to its own great desire, which could be accomplished simply by an act of will.

Why does this strange phenomenon occur? What causes it? O Lord in your mercy give me the right to see, for it may be that the answer to my question lies in the secret punishment of man and in the penitence which casts a deep shadow on the sons of Adam. Why does this strange phenomenon occur? What causes it? The mind gives an order to the body and it's at once obeyed, but when it gives an order to itself, it is resisted. The mind commands the hand to move and is so readily obeyed that the order can scarcely be distinguished from its execution. Yet the mind is mind and the hand is part of the body. But when the mind commands the mind to make an act of will, these two are one and the same and yet the order is not obeyed. Why does this happen? What is the cause of it? The mind orders itself to make an act of will, and it would not give this order unless it willed to do so; yet it does not carry out its own command. But it does not fully will to do this thing and therefore its orders are not fully given. It gives the order only in so far as it wills, and in so far as it does not will the order is not carried out. For the will commands that an act of will should be made, and it gives this command to itself, not to some other will. The reason, then, why the command is not obeyed is that it is not given with the full will. For if the will were full, it would not command itself to be full, since it would be so already. It is therefore no strange phenomenon partly to will to do something and partly to will not to do it. It is a disease of the mind, which does not wholly rise to the heights where it is lifted by the truth, because it is weighed down by habit. So there are two wills in us, because neither by itself is the whole will, and each possesses what the other lacks.

Saint Jerome (c. 347–420) was born to devout Christian parents. He received a superb classical education in Rome and showed great promise as a scholar. While traveling in Antioch, he experienced a vision, recounted below, during which he was accused of favoring Cicero over Christ. After recovering from his experience, Jerome become an ascetic and wandered in the desert. He eventually reconciled himself to his spiritual calling and returned to Rome, where he become one of the most learned of the early Church fathers. He is best known for his translation of the Bible into Latin, known as the Vulgate. How is Jerome's experience similar to Augustine's?

"Saint Jerome's Dream"

MANY YEARS AGO, WHEN FOR THE KINGDOM OF HEAVEN'S sake I had cut myself off from home, parents, sister, relations, and — harder still — from the dainty food to which I had been accustomed: and when I was on my way to Jerusalem to wage my warfare, I still could not bring myself to forego the library which I had formed for myself at Rome with great care and toil. And so, miserable man that I was, I would fast only that I might afterwards read Cicero. After many nights spent in vigil, after floods of tears called from my inmost heart, after the recollection of my past sins, I would once more take up Plautus [Roman comic dramatist]. And when at times I returned to my right mind, and began to read the prophets, their style seemed rude and repellent. I failed to see the light with my blinded eyes; but I attributed the fault not to them, but to the sun. While the old serpent was thus making me his plaything, about the middle of Lent a deep-seated fever fell upon my weakened body, and while it destroyed my rest completely — the story seems hardly credible — it so wasted my unhappy frame that scarcely anything was left of me but skin and bone. Meantime preparations for my funeral went on; my body grew gradually colder, and the warmth of life lingered only in my throbbing breath. Suddenly I was caught up in the spirit and dragged before judgment seat of the Judge; and here the light was so bright, and those who stood around were so radiant, that I cast myself upon the ground and did not dare to look up. Asked who and what I was I replied: "I am a Christian." But He who presided said: "Thou liest, thou art a follower of Cicero and not of Christ. For 'where thy treasure is, there will thy heart be also.'" Instantly I became dumb, and amid the strokes of the lash — for He had ordered me to be scourged — I was tortured more severely still by the fire of conscience, considering with myself that verse, "In the grave who shall give thee thanks?" Yet for all that I began to cry and to bewail myself, saying:

"Have mercy upon me, O Lord: have mercy upon me." Amid the sound of the scourges this cry still made itself heard. At last the bystanders, falling down before the knees of Him who presided, prayed that He would have pity on my youth, and that He would give me space to repent of my error. He might still, they urged, inflict torture on me, should I ever again read the works of the Gentiles. Under the stress of that awful moment I should have been ready to make even still larger promises than these. Accordingly I made an oath and called upon His name, saying: "Lord, if ever again I possess worldly books, or if ever again I read such, I have denied Thee." Dismissed, then, on taking this oath, I returned to the upper world, and, to the surprise of all, I opened upon them eyes so drenched with tears that my distress served to convince even the incredulous. And that this was no sleep nor idle dream, such as those by which we are often mocked, I call to witness the tribunal before which I lay, and the terrible judgment which I feared. May it never, hereafter, be my lot to fall under such an inquisition! I profess that my shoulders were black and blue, that I felt the bruises long after I awoke from my sleep, and that thenceforth, I read the books of God with a zeal greater than I had previously given to the books of men.

THINKING CRITICALLY

1. *Identifying Central Issues* What is the importance of classical literature to Saint Augustine and Saint Jerome?

2. *Recognizing Values* What does Saint Jerome mean when he says, "I would fast only that I might afterwards read Cicero"?

3. *Linking Past and Present* How is this sort of religious fervor viewed today? Is it common for people to go through a spiritual struggle?

WRITER'S PORTFOLIO

1. *Extending the Selection* Compare and contrast Saint Augustine's spiritual struggle with Saint Jerome's.

2. *Examining Key Questions* Why were people more likely to have a spiritual struggle or conversion around A.D. 400 than today? How has our search for God's manifestation changed?

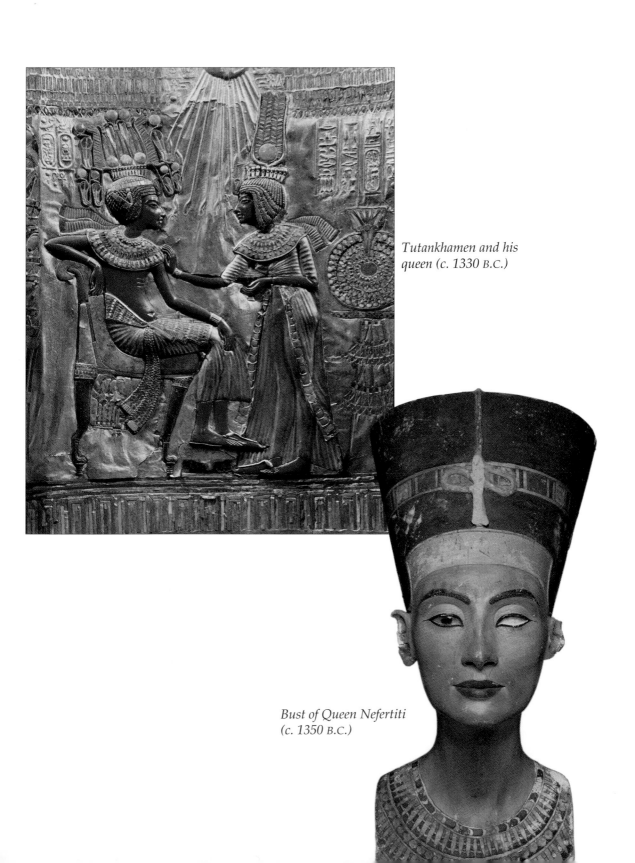

Tutankhamen and his queen (c. 1330 B.C.)

Bust of Queen Nefertiti (c. 1350 B.C.)

(Above)
Woman
with Kithera
(40 – 30 B.C.)

(Below)
Wall painting
from Pompeii
(before A.D. 79)

*Mosaic of Christus
Helios (c. A.D. 225)*

*Catacomb Painting
of Christ (300s)*

*Mosaic of Christ
(c. 313–337)*

Hagia Sophia

Church architecture began to develop during Constantine's reign (A.D. 306–337), though most churches were still based on the plan of the basilica (bə sil′ə kə), a style used for Roman assembly halls. These early Christian basilica churches were rectangular, with a semicircular recess at one end called an apse. The central space was called the nave. Two aisles stretched down either side of the basilica, and the roof was vaulted or pitched and made of wood. During the reign of Justinian (527–565), there was a great fire in Constantinople. This gave him the opportunity to put his stamp on a rebuilt city and build a church that would attest through the ages to his greatness. In 532, Justinian laid the cornerstone for his great church, called in Greek Hagia Sophia (hä′jə sō fē′ə) — Church of the Holy Wisdom. According to legend, an angel revealed the plan of the church to Justinian. The basilica concept was retained because it was the most suitable for a large number of worshippers. However, a magnificent dome, 185 feet over the nave, was needed to provide the splendor suitable to Justinian's plans. Stone cutters, masons,

Hagia Sophia from the South

Interior of Hagia Sophia

Mosaic from Hagia Sophia, showing the Virgin flanked by Justinian and Constantine

carpenters, and iron, bronze, and lead workers were followed by sculptors, mosaicists, marble workers, glass blowers, and gold- and silversmiths. The floors were marble, and columns were of marble and porphyry [an igneous rock imbedded with crystal]. The ceiling of the great dome was covered with mosaics, as was much of the church. The mosaic over the south door, which appears above, shows the Virgin Mary and the Christ Child flanked by Constantine on her left offering his city and Justinian on her right offering his church. Silver lamps hung along the walls at various levels, with oil lamps suspended from the ceiling, giving a rich illumination to the interior at night. Gold and silver objects filled recesses and niches. Procopius, a Greek historian, described it as "[a] spectacle of marvelous beauty, overwhelming to those who see it, but those who know it by hearsay altogether incredible." Earthquakes in subsequent years damaged the dome and the walls of the church, which were repaired. When the Crusaders sacked Constantinople in 1204, most of the religious objects were stolen or destroyed. In 1453, Ottoman Turks conquered Constantinople and renamed it Istanbul. The church was made a mosque and remained so for 500 years, during which time minarets were added and eight large disks, twenty-five feet in diameter, were hung on the walls of the nave. They are inscribed with the names of Allah, Muhammad, and the caliphs. Does Hagia Sophia resemble other churches you have seen?

THINKING CRITICALLY

1. *Analyzing Cause and Effect* Why might a legend of angels be associated with the Hagia Sophia?

2. *Recognizing Values* Is a magnificent place of worship an aid or a distraction to prayer? Does such a place glorify God or its earthly creators?

3. *Linking Past and Present* Describe the architecture of a local church. Does it seem modern or traditional? Is the roof arched, flat, or domed? Of what material is the building made?

WRITER'S PORTFOLIO

1. *Extending the Selection* Do you think the mosaic of the Virgin reflects the piety of Constantine and Justinian or their vanity?

2. *Examining Key Questions* Do holy places such as churches and synagogues make it easier to worship? Why or why not?

EXAMINING KEY QUESTIONS

- *Why be good?*
- *How do humans perceive God?*

Throughout this chapter, most selections have concluded with a writing project asking you to discuss how the art or literature you have examined provides answers to one of these key questions. The following writing projects will help you draw together what you have learned by examining how several selections illustrate these key questions.

- Characterize the moral and ethical teachings of Christianity. Is it an active or passive religion? Is the institution or the individual more important? Is forgiveness a key part of the religious teaching?

- Compare and contrast the different representations of God and Jesus you have read or seen in this chapter. What can you infer about Christianity from its images of the divine?

SPEAKING/LISTENING

- With other students, research and present to the class a report on the life of Jesus. Compare his earthly career to that of other prophets, religious founders, or spiritual leaders.

CRAFTING

- Using any medium you like, create your own portrait of Jesus, based on the impressions of him you take away from reading the "Sermon on the Mount." Try to avoid being influenced by other renditions and concentrate on picturing your own impressions.

COLLECTING

- Collect a series of images which represent Judaism or Christianity in the 20th century. What does this gallery of images tell you about the state of these religions today?

Royal Mosque at Isfahan

Islamic Civilization

Illumination of Muhammad's arrival in Medina

CHAPTER 4

A.D. 622
The Hijra, beginning of Muslim calendar

Islamic Civilization

A.D. 650–1600

ELIZABETH FERNEA

Professor of English and Middle Eastern Studies, University of Texas at Austin

The Arab chroniclers report that in the early ninth century, on summer nights, the famed caliph, Haroun al-Rashid, would take a trusted aide and travel in disguise through the streets of Baghdad. Like all great rulers in history, he wanted to know how things really were among the people of his realm. Poets, storytellers, musicians, and scientists gathered at his court, which became a splendid center of human achievement. This period is known to historians as the Golden Age of Islam, implying, rightly, that Islamic civilization has produced many ages. For over a thousand years, from the seventh century to the nineteenth century, Islamic peoples and cultures ruled and shaped the activities of a large area of the known world. At various times

the Muslim world included Spain, parts of France, India, and Eastern Europe, as well as Arabia, North Africa, and Central Asia. The Arab Abbasid rulers (750–1258) were followed by a number of smaller dynasties, and by the sixteenth century, most of the Muslim world was under the rule of three great empires, Mughal (India), Safavid (Persia), and Ottoman (Turkey). The Ottoman Empire extended into eastern Europe, as far west as modern Algeria, and south across Arabia into Egypt.

THE ORIGIN OF ISLAM

Islamic civilization began in Arabia, in the desert around the cities of Medina and Mecca. A man named Muhammad (mù ham′əd) (c. 570–632) was orphaned at an early

Illumination of Kaaba

Page from the Quran

630
Islam established throughout Arabian peninsula Kaaba in Mecca established as the holiest shrine of Islam

c. 650
Authorized version of the Quran set down

age and raised by his uncle and aunt. He went into the caravan trade, traveled widely, and is reputed to have been interested in Christianity and Judaism. He began to have revelations and soon was proclaiming a monotheistic religion, Islam, which he saw as a return to the original faith of Abraham. (In Arabic, *Islam* means submission to God's will.) This threatened the established leaders of Mecca. Fearing their wrath, in 622 Muhammad and a few disciples fled to the city of Medina. This flight, known as the *Hijra*, marks the beginning of Islam and is commemorated as the first date of the Islamic calendar.

Islam offered a simple but revolutionary message: all members of the faith are equal, irrespective of race, color, social or economic status. However, the faithful must all perform certain duties known as the Five Pillars of Islam: *shahadah* or profession of faith—"There is no god but God; Muhammad is the prophet of God"—which was to be recited; *salat* or regular prayer—to be offered five times daily, as well as in a Friday service; *zakat* or tithe—a percentage of one's annual income paid to the faith for distribution to the poor; *saum* or fasting—not eating, drinking, or smoking between daybreak and sunset during Ramadan, the ninth month of the Muslim calendar, revered as holy as it is the month when the Quran, the Muslim holy text, was revealed to Muhammad; *hajj* or pilgrimage—a religious journey to Mecca, expected of all Muslims who can afford it during their lifetime. Perhaps even more startling, the new faith gave women legal status as persons, with rights to assent to marriage, to divorce, and to inherit. To help level economic differences, Islam also forbade usury, the charging of interest on loans. And, to discourage the development of difference in religious status, Muhammad stated that any Muslim could lead the prayers, including the Friday worship. Thus, there is no Pope in Islam and no clerical hierarchy. Throughout the Islamic world, communities are led by local scholars (*ulama*), many of whom are

Umayyad gold coin

Ivory casket
from Cordoba

661
Umayyad Caliphate established

756
Abd-al-Rahman establishes Muslim court
at Cordoba, Spain

also judges (*qadis*) in religious courts of law.

Muhammad's message — that all people are created equal in the eyes of God — was indeed a threat to the elders. For Mecca in the seventh century was not a desert backwater, but a major international trade center, on the lucrative caravan route from India and China to Europe. It was a time when old shared values were in question and trade was making new people rich beyond belief. Mecca was also a pilgrimage city for many Arabic religious cults. Scores of them offered charms and cures and talismans in exchange for generous contributions to the maintenance and upkeep of their shrines and temples. Muhammad preached against such practices, against idol worship, and against the growing corruption and materialism he saw in Mecca. Most importantly, he preached monotheism, the idea of a single deity, the same conception that had animated Judaism and Christianity.

Muhammad's revelations were written down and are the basis for the Quran, believed by Muslims to be literally the words of God as revealed to Muhammad, the messenger of God. By the time Muhammad died in 632, all of Arabia was loyal to him. Islam was a small but growing new religion that within a century would spread throughout the Middle East and into Spain. By the early days of the eighth century, Muslim armies had reached Spain and driven into France. They were stopped in 732 at Tours, in central France by Charles Martel, an ancestor of Charlemagne.

**THE SPLIT
IN ISLAM**   Muhammad's death was unexpected and since there were no hereditary kingships among the Arabs, conflict arose between those who thought the new leader should be chosen on the basis of blood ties (the old tribal pattern) or on the basis of merit (the new pattern which Muhammad had championed). The majority of the Muslims supported Abu Bakr, one of the Prophet's oldest disciples, and named him Caliph (from

Painting of Persian court poets, including Firdausi

Illustration from the Masnavi

1010
Firdausi completes the Shahnama

1232
Rumi joins Sufi order; begins work on the Masnavi

the Arabic word for successor, *Khalifa*). His supporters became known as the Sunni (sun⁄ē), Arabic for "followers of tradition." A minority supported the Prophet's cousin and son-in-law, Ali. His followers, known as the *Shiah Ali* (Party of Ali) or Shi'ites (shē⁄ītz), referred to Ali as Imam or spiritual leader. In 656, Ali was finally named Caliph by the majority of Muslims, but various factions immediately challenged his leadership and he was assassinated in 661. The Shi'ites then proclaimed Hasan, Ali's son and Muhammad's grandson, both Imam and Caliph. However, he was convinced by the sitting Caliph, Muawiya, who enjoyed the support of the Sunni majority to renounce his claim. His younger brother Hussein then claimed the Caliphate. In 680, he was ambushed and murdered at Karbala, in Iraq, by men in the employ of Muawiya. His death is still commemorated by Shi'ite Muslims with an important annual holy day. The split between Sunnis and Shi'ites continues to this day.

Both Sunnis and Shi'ites see the Quran as the basis for Islam, but differences over interpretation arise and are expressed through different schools of law or rites (four among Sunnis, two among the Shi'ites). This means that a good deal of diversity on matters of religion and social practice is found across the Muslim world. For example, the Malikite school, which is found in North Africa, is often perceived as less conservative than the Hanbalite school, found in Saudi Arabia. In addition to the major sects of Sunnis and Shi'ites, one finds smaller groups within the major groups—such as the Ismailis, which include the Nizaris, the group led by the Aga Khan, among the Shi'ia and the Mutazilites among the Sunnis. And the Sufis, mystics who search for personal union with God, are found among all sects.

For a long time, Christian rulers did not recognize Islam as a separate religion, but simply considered it a Christian heresy. Muslims accept the New Testament, but deny the divinity of Jesus, insisting that only one God

INTRODUCTION **127**

*Tombs of
Mameluke
Sultans*

1250
Mamelukes overthrow Caliphate in Egypt and Syria

exists. However, as Islam grew, it became a real threat to medieval Christianity — in economic, political, and religious terms. Around 1100, European leaders launched a series of wars to try and wrest control of the Holy Land from the Muslims. These Crusades lasted for nearly 200 years and resolved little. Thousands were killed on both sides, as armies fought for control of the Holy Land, but in the end, it remained under Muslim control.

Islamic armies and rulers adopted a live-and-let-live policy that applied not only to Christians and Jews, but to dissenters within their own ranks. Christians and Jews are mentioned in the Quran as "People of the Book," related to Islam, the last of the three Abrahamic religions. In general, Christians and Jews were tolerated and given freedom of worship throughout the great empires: Arab, Mughal, Safavid, and Ottoman. They also had freedom to rule their own communities' legal, religious, and economic activities. Non-Muslims had to pay a special tax and in some areas were not permitted to bear arms; but they were not persecuted, as was the case in reverse in Christian countries. Christianity brooked no dissent, no questioning, no doubts from its believers.

THE FLOWERING OF ISLAMIC CULTURE

Islamic rulers' policy of live-and-let-live, as well as that of unity and diversity led to a flowering of intellectual life, not only in Haroun al-Rashid's Golden Age, but during several periods of Islamic civilization. This was partly due to the cosmopolitan nature of the populations under Islamic rule, who all, living in relative peace together, contributed in different ways to the artistic and scientific as well as the religious development of their times. Arabs, Turks, Persians, Spaniards, Africans, East Indians, Indonesians, and Chinese, who were Muslims, but also Christians and Jews, gathered at the courts of the different rulers. Ibn Batutah, the great fourteenth century traveler who wrote accounts of other lands still read today, was an Arab, but the historian al-Tabari

Miniature
of Sadi

Miniature of Mongol warriors

1257
Sadi publishes the Gulistan

1258
Mongols sack Baghdad

was a native of Persia, now Iran. The poet al-Jahiz was Ethiopian; the philosopher Averröes (Ibn Rushd) was a Spanish Muslim, while Maimonides was a Spanish Jew. Al-Idrisi, who lived in Sicily in the twelfth century, was commissioned by the Norman King, Roger II, to complete a world atlas; his work was based on scores of works by Arab geographers and explorers—one Arab pilot led Vasco da Gama along the East Coast of Africa in the fifteenth century. Ibn Khaldun, who lived in Tunisia in the fourteenth century is considered the father of sociology and historiography. And Ibn al-Haytham, known as Alhazen, an Arab scientist born in Basra, Iraq, wrote his *Book of Optics* in the eleventh century. It is this book on which all modern ideas of perspective are based and which led to the development of that crucial human invention—eyeglasses.

Muslim scholars pioneered areas of medicine, mathematics, astronomy, navigation, horticulture, metallurgy, agriculture, botany, history, and geography. But they began by absorb-

ing the achievements of past civilizations—Mesopotamian, Greek, Roman, Byzantine, ancient Egyptian. The Muslims built on what they were learning from the past: in the eighth century, Arab scholars returned from India with a Hindu invention—a system of numbers to which they added the concept of a cipher, or *zero*. With this "Arabic" numeral system, the mathematical genius al-Khwarizmi developed *algebra*, in the ninth century. Itself an Arabic word, algebra made possible the scientific speculation that is the basis of modern mathematics. For in algebra, the symbols are capable of infinite potential or possibilities. Al Khwarizmi felt this system was an apt concept to apply to the universe itself—a place he said, whose creation by God was an unending, infinitely living process.

The mosques of Islam are a metaphor for the faith, the community ideal, and a tribute to the talents of Muslim architects, artists, and builders. Following Muhammad's abhorrence of idol worship, Muslims forbade any use of the human figure as artistic decora-

Cauldron of Tamerlane

Turkish helmet from siege

1369
Tamerlane becomes king of Samarkand

1453
Constantinople falls to the Turks

tion within a place of worship. Thus, the decoration of mosques is based on the forms of nature (leaves, trees, flowers) and on the elaboration of geometric and abstract designs. Islamic architecture reflected the beliefs of Islam, but also responded to the needs of the faithful and the demands of the climate. Fountains in the courtyards of the mosques provided not only beauty and coolness, but a source of running water in which the faithful performed their ablutions — the ritual washing before prayers. The clusters of arches offered shade from the hot suns of summer. The stone or wood grilles that covered windows discouraged dust and insects while allowing diffused sunshine to fall on the inner court, creating an attractive pattern of light and shade. Brilliant tiles, stonework, and plaster sculpture added texture and beauty to the walls, both inside and outside. In the shaded arcades of the inner court, the faithful could rest and talk after performing prayers.

Poetry has always been a valued art in the Middle East and Asia. A complex and sophisticated oral poetic tradition existed in Arabia before Muhammad, as the *Muallaqat* or great pre-Islamic odes demonstrate. Arabic and Persian are said to be particularly suited to the rhythms of poetry. Arabic, as the language of the holy Quran, has prime place in Islamic civilization. A Muslim may speak Chinese or Turkish or English, but will still know Arabic, for both the Quran and poetry. Poets are both valued for their command of the word and feared for the truths they may reveal.

Politically, Islamic civilization might be called an effort at governance by consensus. The Prophet Muhammad gathered his companions to discuss a course of action, to consider a problem, to mediate a conflict. The idea of the *majlis* or assembly of elders emerged from this, and like the people who gathered to advise the Prophet, many Muslim elders continue to gather in the courts of modern kings. Rule by consensus was the mode of Islamic civilization, although the caliph and eventually the sultan always had the last word.

Signature of Suleiman

Persian miniature of Abbas

1520
Suleiman the Magnificent becomes Ottoman Sultan

1587
Abbas the Great becomes Shah of Persia

When consensus failed, autocratic rule was often found, but the form of the *majlis* remained. Today, some of these *majlis* assemblies have evolved into real parliaments.

From the earliest centuries, the back-bone of Islamic society was agriculture; the invention of the water-wheel, the underground irrigation canal, and cisterns, greatly improved agricultural production. The high quality of manufactured goods — such as tiles, pottery, metalwork, carpets — meant they were in world-wide demand. In the early Middle Ages, Europe provided the raw materials for these manufactures. But by the 18th century, the discovery of the Americas and the Industrial Revolution in Europe began to change the balance of power in the world. Colonial invasions of the Middle East, Asia, Africa, and Latin America reached Muslim lands as well as others. The military technology and manufacturing might that came with the Industrial Revolution in Europe reduced the Islamic empires to inferior states. Once the cultural and economic center of the Mediterranean Sea and the Indian Ocean, admired and envied for learning, economic achievement, and cosmopolitan cities, the Islamic civilization fell under the domination of Western colonialism.

In the two decades after World War II, the Arab countries and many Muslim nations in Asia regained their independence. Today, at the end of the twentieth century, these countries are entering a new period — adapting modern technology and attitudes to fit the ideals of their Islamic heritage. But that heritage is emerging differently in Asia, Africa, and the Arab world, expressing in contemporary terms the diverse histories and ideals of their Muslim civilizations.

The Quran

Born in western Arabia in the oasis town of Mecca (**mek′ə**), the prophet Muhammad (**mō ham′id**) was orphaned at six, raised by relatives, and as a young man traveled with caravan traders to Syria and south Arabia, earning a reputation as a man of integrity, wisdom, and increasing spirituality. About A.D. 610, while in religious retirement on Mt. Hira near Mecca, he received his first revelation from God. For some three years he preached in secret, gaining disciples among his family, servants, and close friends. From 613–622, in obedience to God's wish, he began preaching in public, slowly gaining adherents but arousing also the enmity of the wealthy tribal chiefs of Mecca. Forced by the increasing hostility of the idolatrous Meccans to consider leaving the city of his birth, Muhammad accepted an offer of protection by twelve people from the town of Yathrib, now called Medina, who had earlier become his followers. Muhammad and some 150 followers escaped from Mecca, making a 300-mile journey, known as the *hijra* (**hej′r ə**) or *hegira* ("flight" or "migration"). This journey is still undertaken by Muslims today, as part of their pilgrimage. Both the Muslim calendar and the Muslim era date from the September day in 622, when Muhammad arrived in Medina. Muslims believe that the sacred scriptures of Islam, the Quran (**kô rän′**), were revealed by God to Muhammad through the archangel Gabriel over a period of 23 years — from 610, when Muhammad was 40 years old, to 632, the year of his death. These were set down in a formal book around 650. Of the two excerpts that follow, the excerpt from Chapter 1 was written before the *hijra*, and the one from Chapter 24 was written after it. What benefits has God "the All-Merciful" bestowed on man?

Chapter 1: Al-Fatiha ("The Opening")
In the name of God
Most Gracious, Most Beneficent
All praise be to God,

Who is the Cherisher
And Sustainer of all.
He is indeed, all Compassionate
And Most Merciful
Master of the Day of Judgment.
To You alone, O Lord,
We offer our prayers
And from You alone
We seek all help.
Show us, O Lord,
The right path,
The path of those
Whom You have blessed and not of those
With whom You are wrathful
Nor of those who have chosen to go astray.

Chapter 24: "Light"

In the Name of God, the Compassionate, the Merciful

This is a Chapter which We have revealed and sanctioned, proclaiming in it clear revelations, so that you may take heed.

The adulterer and the adulteress shall each be given a hundred lashes. Let no pity for them cause you to disobey God, if you truly believe in God and the Last Day; and let their punishment be witnessed by a number of believers.

The adulterer may marry only an adulteress or an idolatress; and the adulteress may marry only an adulterer or an idolater. True believers are forbidden such marriages.

Those that defame honorable women and cannot produce four witnesses shall be given eighty lashes. Do not accept their testimony ever after, for they are great transgressors—except that those among them that afterwards repent and mend their ways. God is forgiving and merciful.

If a man accuses his wife but has no witnesses except himself, he shall swear four times by God that his charge is true, calling down upon himself the curse of God if he is lying. But if his wife swears four times by God that his charge is false and calls down His curse upon herself if it be true, she shall receive no punishment....

You that are the true believers, do not walk in Satan's footsteps. He that walks in Satan's footsteps is incited to indecency and evil. But for

God's grace and mercy, none of you would have ever been cleansed of sin. God purifies whom He will; God hears all and knows all.

Let not the rich and honorable among you swear to withhold their gifts from their kindred, the destitute, and those who have fled their homes for the cause of God. Rather let them pardon and forgive. Do you not wish God to forgive you? God is forgiving and merciful.

Those who defame honorable but careless believing women shall be cursed in this world and in the hereafter.

Theirs shall be a woeful punishment on the day when their own tongues, hands, and feet will testify to what they did. On that day God will justly requite them. They shall know that God is the Glorious Truth.

Unclean women are for unclean men, and unclean men for unclean women. But good women are for good men, and good men for good women. These shall be cleared of calumny; they shall be shown forgiveness, and a generous provision shall be made for them.

Believers, do not enter the dwellings of other men until you have asked their owners' permission and wished them peace. That will be best for you. Perchance you will take heed.

If you find no one in them, do not go in till you are given leave. If you are refused admission, it is but right that you should go away. God has knowledge of all your actions.

It shall be no offence for you to seek shelter in empty dwellings. God knows what you reveal and what you hide.

Enjoin believing men to turn their eyes away from temptation and to restrain their carnal desires. This will make their lives purer. God has knowledge of all their actions.

Enjoin believing women to turn their eyes away from temptation and to preserve their chastity; to cover their adornments (except such as are normally displayed); to draw their veils over their bosoms and not to reveal their finery except to their husbands, their fathers, their husbands' fathers, their sons, their step-sons, their sisters' sons, their women-servants, and their slave-girls, male attendants lacking in natural vigor, and children who have no carnal knowledge of women. And let them not stamp their feet when walking so as to reveal their hidden trinkets.

Believers, turn to God in repentance, that you may prosper.

Take in marriage those among you who are single and those of your male and female slaves who are honest. If they are poor, God will enrich them from His own abundance. God is munificent and all-knowing.

Let those who cannot afford to marry live in continence until God shall enrich them from His own bounty. As for those of your slaves who wish to buy their liberty, free them if you find in them any promise and bestow on them a part of the riches which God has given you.

You shall not force your slave-girls into prostitution in order that you may enrich yourselves, if they wish to preserve their chastity. If anyone compels them, God will be forgiving and merciful to them.

We have sent down to you revelations showing you the right path. We have given you an account of those who have gone before you, and an admonition to righteous men.

God is the light of the heavens and the earth. His light may be compared to a niche that enshrines a lamp, the lamp within a crystal of star-like brilliance. It is lit from a blessed olive tree neither eastern nor western. Its very oil would almost shine forth, though no fire touched it. Light upon light; God guides to His own light whom He will.

God speaks in metaphors to men. God has knowledge of all things.

His light is found in temples which God has sanctioned to be built for the remembrance of His name. In them, morning and evening, His praise is sung by men whom neither trade nor profit can divert from remembering Him, from offering prayers, or from giving alms; who dread the day when men's hearts and eyes shall writhe with anguish; who hope that God will requite them for their noblest deeds and lavish His grace upon them. God gives without measure to whom He will.

As for the unbelievers, their works are like a mirage in a desert. The thirsty traveler thinks it is water, but when he comes near he finds that it is nothing. He finds God there, who pays him back in full. Swift is God's reckoning.

Or like darkness on a bottomless ocean spread with clashing billows and overcast with clouds; darkness upon darkness. If he stretches out his hand he can scarcely see it. Indeed the man from whom God withholds His light shall find no light at all.

Do you not see how God is praised by those in the heavens and those on earth? The very birds praise Him as they wing their flight. He notes the prayers and praises of all His creatures, and has knowledge of all their actions.

It is God who has sovereignty over the heavens and the earth. To Him shall all things return.

Do you not see how God drives the clouds, then gathers and piles them up in masses which pour down torrents of rain? From heaven's mountains He sends down the hail, pelting with it whom He will and turning it away from whom He pleases. The flash of His lightning almost snatches off men's eyes.

God makes the night succeed the day; surely in this there is a lesson for clear-sighted men.

God created every beast from water. Some creep upon their bellies, others walk on two legs, and others yet on four. God creates what He pleases. God has power over all things.

We have sent down revelations demonstrating the Truth. God guides whom He will to a straight path.

THINKING CRITICALLY

1. *Making Inferences* What are the fundamental beliefs of Islam, as implied in Chapter 1?

2. *Identifying Assumptions* What reasons does Chapter 24 suggest for the human obligation to glorify God? to obey His word?

3. *Linking Past and Present* In recent years many Arab-American groups have objected strenuously to the portrayal of Muslims in popular books and films. Find and discuss examples of these portrayals. What characterizes them? Are they generally positive or negative?

WRITER'S PORTFOLIO

1. *Extending the Selection* In Chapter 24 of the Quran appear two vivid images: the niche containing a lamp "kindled from a Blessed Tree," and the works of the unbelievers as a "mirage in a spacious plain." Drawing on your own beliefs, create two images, one describing God, one describing unbelievers.

2. *Examining Key Questions* Is the Muslim God presented in the Quran closer to the all-powerful God of the Jewish Old Testament or loving and merciful God of the Christian New Testament?

The Adab

During the rapid expansion of Islam, poetry remained the only real literary form. However, by the beginning of the ninth century, as the Islamic states and empires stabilized, scholars fostered a great revival of learning. These scholars revived the study of Plato and Aristotle and helped preserve the classical legacy the West would not rediscover until the Renaissance. With the growing secularization of learning came a new emphasis on prose literature and, in particular, a unique Arabic literary form known as the *adab*. The *adab* is a literary essay usually comprising poetry, history, grammar, etiquette, morality, as well as anecdotes and quotations. It was a form of didactic literature, which entertained as it educated. The finest practitioner, and indeed the first Arab prose writer of distinction, was al-Jahiz (c. 776– c. 868). Jahiz spent fifty years in Baghdad serving the Abbasid Caliphs as an official writer, while also creating his immensely entertaining books of essays. His most famous work is the seven-volume *Kitab al-hayawan* (Book of Animals), which combined religious and moral teachings with wry anecdotes and an amusingly ironic point of view. Why is evil necessary, according to Jahiz?

Good and evil

I WOULD HAVE YOU KNOW THAT THE WELL-BEING OF THE WORLD, from the beginning to the end, depends on the blending of good and evil, the harmful and the beneficial, the vile and the pleasing, lowliness and loftiness, abundance and scarcity. Pure evil would mean the end of creation. Conversely, if good were undiluted, the testing required of us would be meaningless and there would be no need to take thought. Without thought, wisdom ceases to exist, and when there is no longer scope for choice, discrimination disappears; there is no certainty in the world, no hesitation, no studying and no science, no finding the path of understanding, no way of overcoming an obstacle or gaining an advantage; discomforts are no longer bearable and pleasure no longer gratifying; there can be no rivalry in eloquence, no vying for promotion, and the joys of success and pride in victory are done away with. There can no longer exist the righteous man, secure in the strength of truth, nor the wrongdoer sunk in the humiliation of his error, nor the convinced man, happy in his certainty, nor the sceptic, filled with the weakness of perplexity and the misery of indecision; there is no hope in men's hearts.

Happiness

SOME SAY: "HAPPINESS IN THIS WORLD IS A MATTER ENTIRELY of prosperity, good health, and obscurity." Others hold a different view, saying: "The man endowed with good health and ample means is still left with this dilemma. Either he knows the way of the world or he does not: if he does, then his knowledge makes him speak and act in accordance with what he knows, for knowing and not knowing are two different things, and knowledge not translated into deeds might as well not exist. Words and deeds together constitute the essentials of renown, so that the most likely thing to happen to a man who knows is that his knowledge will lift him out of obscurity; and from then on he is exposed to the onslaughts of men who would not scruple to rob him of his wealth."

Just as knowledge necessarily entails action, so action must take the form either of deeds or of words. Words are only words if there exists someone to whom they are spoken, and deeds are only deeds if there exists someone to whom they are done; it is this that brings the doer out of obscurity and makes him known.

If one of the consequences of knowledge is to attract attention, prosperity is even more likely to make its possessors conspicuous and give rise to intrigues against them. Wealth more than anything leads to backbiting, indebtedness, and treachery; it is highly dangerous for its possessor and most baneful for his kinsfolk.

The more imperfect a man's knowledge is, the less he knows where to find happiness; the more perfect it is, the more it dispels obscurity and brings renown. Those with only a smattering of knowledge and born to mediocrity are unable to understand the advantages of security or the basis of ultimate happiness, and hence cannot see why rich men are averse to notoriety. On the other hand if a man does see why, exactly and completely, then his comprehension must be not intuitive but reasoned; and since he cannot understand this point without also understanding all the learning of his fellow-men, he is certain to emerge from obscurity as a result.

Murder and retaliation

THEY SAY: WE HAVE BEEN ENJOINED TO USE THE SWORD AGAINST a tyrant if the stick does not suffice to deter and punish him, but not wilfully to kill him, our object being merely to prevent his harming us. Should the punishment result in his death, the case is like that of the thief who dies of the amputation of one hand, or the backbiter who succumbs under a scourging. We are enjoined to kill snakes and scorpions in cold blood, even when they are not endangering us, because they belong to a race that can be deadly. But we are only justified in using the sword against a tyrant when he actually threatens us, not when he has his back to us, whereas we may kill snakes and scorpions in both situations — just as an infidel may be killed in any position, whether coming towards us or going away.... We are authorized to kill any kind of animal that causes so much as a scratch, such as mosquitoes, ants, fleas, and lice, and all the more those that wound or kill us. To kill a camel is bad, but good if it is attacking people; to kill a man is forbidden, but lawful when he becomes dangerous.

THINKING CRITICALLY

1. *Identifying Central Issues* How does Jahiz explain the presence of evil in the universe? How does Jahiz justify evil in the universe? Are his conclusions derived from faith or reason?

2. *Making Inferences* What is the general tone of Jahiz's writings? What examples best support your answer?

3. *Linking Past and Present* Do you think Jahiz would be a supporter of capital punishment if he were writing today? Why or why not?

WRITER'S PORTFOLIO

1. *Extending the Selection* Choose a general topic — such as love, table manners, pets, work — and create an essay that incorporates at least three literary elements.

2. *Examining Key Questions* In these three brief excerpts what does Jahiz reveal about himself? About the values of his society?

Islam and the Sciences

Best known by his pen name al-Amiri, the philosopher Abu 'l-Hassan (?–992), like most of his contemporaries, was well-read in the literature of classical Greece. Al-Amiri had access to an astonishing variety of translations from such Greek scientists and philosophers as Galen, Ptolemy, Plato, and Aristotle. These had been available since the early eighth century when an Abbasid caliph had aggressively encouraged such translations. This translation went on vigorously for some 200 years, despite the fears of pious Muslim scholars (the *ulama*) that works about mathematics, astronomy, and medicine (not to mention magic, astrology, and alchemy) were a threat to Islam. The tension between orthodox Islamic believers and determined Muslim scholars is clear in the following excerpt. Al-Amiri takes great pains to justify the exploration of Greek philosophy by asserting that philosophy and Islam are not contradictory, but complementary. The following excerpt is from al-Amiri's book *al-I'lam bi-manaqib al-Islam*. What evidence in the excerpt suggests that al-Amiri was being careful not to offend the ulama?

K NOWLEDGE MEANS THAT ONE GRASPS SOMETHING AS IT IS, without mistake and error. There is the knowledge which belongs to the religious community, and there is philosophical knowledge. The masters of the religious sciences are the recognized philosophers. Every prophet is a philosopher but not every philosopher is a prophet.

The religious sciences consist of three branches. One of them relies on sensual perceptions, namely, the science of the *hadith* [a holy book of the sayings of Muhammad] scholars. The second rests on the intellect, namely the science of the religious philosophers. The third involves both sensual and intellectual perception, namely, the science of the jurists. Linguistics is an instrument serving all three branches....

The philosophical sciences also consist of three branches. One of them rests on sensual perception, namely, natural science. The second rests on the intellect, namely, metaphysics. The third involves both sensual and intellectual perception, namely, mathematics. Logic is an instrument serving all three branches....

Some scholars of the *hadith* have attacked the philosophical sciences on the assumption that they contradict the religious sciences and that all those interested in the philosophical sciences and occupied with their study forfeit this world and the next. In their view, they contain only impressive words and empty phrases, varnished over with deceptive ideas, so as to deceive poor blockheads and lead astray conceited fools. That is not right. Like the religious sciences, the foundations and branches of the philosophical sciences rest on dogmas in harmony with pure reason and confirmed through fully valid proofs. One knows very well that there should be no contradiction between the demands of the true religion and what proofs confirm and reason demands. Hence, he who masters the philosophical sciences is blessed with three advantages. In the first place, he is extremely close to perfect human virtue in that he is familiar with the true reality of things and has the possibility of controlling them. Secondly, he has insight into all that reveals the wisdom with which the Creator has created the various things in the world, and he understands their causes and results and the wonderful order and splendid arrangement they have. Thirdly, he is well versed in the arguments against traditional claims and is in no danger of soiling himself with vain dogmas through a blind belief in authority.

As we remarked, the philosophical sciences consist of three branches, namely, mathematics, natural science, and metaphysics, while logic serves all of them as an instrument.

Exercise and skill in arithmetic are a source of the profoundest joy to human reason. An intelligent person who studies the peculiarities of its parts by themselves and in conjunction with one another can never enjoy them enough and is convinced that the value and importance of arithmetic constitute an inexhaustible wonder. Besides, it is free from contradictions and doubts. Furthermore, one appeals to it as an arbitrator in matters of commerce. God has said: "We have counted and calculated them," and "He has counted everything...."

Natural science deals with sensually perceptible physical objects. All substances in this world can undoubtedly be divided into two parts. Firstly, there are those that were originally created through the perfection of divine omnipotence, for example, the heavenly spheres, the stars and the four elements and, secondly, those that have been brought into existence from them secondarily through divine subjugation. The latter fall into three parts, namely (1) things that develop in the atmosphere, as for example, snow, rain, thunder, lightning, strokes of lightning, and meteors, (2) things that develop in mines [in the interior of the earth] as, for example, gold, silver, iron, copper, quicksilver, and lead, and (3) things that develop between the interior of the earth and the atmosphere, which are classified as plants and animate beings. From natural science some noble crafts have developed, such as, for example, medicine, the culinary art, and the use of dyes and varnishes. Its abundant results and great utility are well attested....

Metaphysics is a science which is exclusively designed for the investigation of the first causes of the emergence of existing things in the world, and furthermore, for the awesome and incontestable knowledge about the nature of the One, the Unique, the Being, which is the aim of all endeavor. The gain of such a blessing is undoubtedly identical with the attainment of eternal bliss. It is absurd to assume that there could be any contradiction between a science leading to such a result and the religious sciences.

THINKING CRITICALLY

1. *Identifying Central Issues* How does al-Amiri justify the study of the philosophical sciences?

2. *Recognizing Values* Al-Amiri suggests that "one man feels drawn to one branch of knowledge, another to another." What branch does al-Amiri seem drawn to? How can you tell?

3. *Linking Past and Present* Al-Amiri is trying to reconcile religion and science in the tenth century. Do you think that scientific knowledge today leads towards or away from religious conviction?

WRITER'S PORTFOLIO

1. *Extending the Selection* Al-Amiri divides science into three branches: natural science, metaphysics, and mathematics. Do you think the modern sciences still fit into these categories? If not create the new categories you think necessary.

2. *Examining Key Questions* How does al-Amiri reconcile the concerns of the religious leaders with the desire of scholars, like himself, to explore the wisdom of the Greeks?

Andalusian Poetry

Between 711 and 718, Arabs and Berbers from North Africa conquered the Iberian peninsula — present-day Spain and Portugal — and renamed it al-Andalus. The North African invaders brought with them not only the Arabic language, the Islamic religion, and Islamic law, but also a long poetic tradition. Over the following five centuries, Andalusian Spain would become one of most sophisticated and opulent states in the world — easily putting its European neighbors to shame. Poetry was a large part of this society, where almost every formal occasion was commemorated in a poem. Most Andalusian poetry is about sensual pleasures — particularly love — and Andalusian poets adopted a rich and decorative language for their intense and florid lyric poems. The three poets in this section — Ibn Hazm (994–1064), Abu'l Hasan (1000s), and Ibn Sara (?–1123) — represent the gamut of Islamic society in Spain. What are the subjects of these poems?

With a Knife
Is there no way I might
Open my heart with a knife
I could slip you in
And close the cut again

Till the end of time
Till the resurrection
You'd be inside
No heart but mine

In the webbing of my heart
You'd live my lifetime
In the tomb's twilight
You'd die when I did
                        Ibn Hazm

The Dove
The surprise of my life:
On a bough between
Isle and river a dove

Cooing, his collar
Pistache green, lapis his breast,
Neck shimmering and maroon

His back and wingtips.
Pupils of ruby, over them eyelids
Of pearl flitted, trimmed with gold,

Black the point
Of his beak, like
The tip of a reed

Dipped in ink. On the arak bough,
His throne, throat now hid
In the fold of a wing, he rested.

But he saw me weep.
Scared by a sob
On the bough he stood,

Spread wings, beat them,
Took as he flew my heart
Away. Where? I know not.

> Abu'l Hasan 'Ali ibn Hisn

Zephyr and Rain
The reason why you seek a cure
In zephyr's breath:
It's brushed with musk

It comes to you perfumed
A message in a letter
From a girl you love

The air tries on
The clothes of all the clouds
And chooses black

It is a rain-charged cloud
It signals to the garden
It weeps to make flowers laugh

Earth needles cloud to cast
The tissue for its mantle off
Cloud with one hand

Threading still the web of rain
Embroiders with the other
The figures of the flowers

Ibn Sara

THINKING CRITICALLY

1. *Drawing Conclusions* Judging by Ibn Hazm's poem "With a Knife," what kind of lover do you think he might have been?

2. *Making Comparisons* Which poet seems to have the most sympathetic view of nature? Which poet seems to you to be the most subtle?

3. *Linking Past and Present* Poets were often powerful figures in the medieval Islamic world, serving as civil servants and advisors to rulers. Do you think the world would be a better place if artists were more prominently represented in government?

WRITER'S PORTFOLIO

1. *Extending the Selection* Rewrite these poems into prose summaries of the author's feelings. What are the authors trying to say?

2. *Examining Key Questions* What is the attitude of these poets toward both nature and human nature? Do they see a connection?

Islamic Design

Islam, like Judaism, practically forbade the creation of religious art. The Christian tradition of portraying Jesus Christ and Biblical scenes has no Islamic counterpart. Instead, Islamic artists devoted themselves to decorating the mosques and tombs with exceptionally intricate patterns and decor. Instead of the West's severe and monochromatic stone, Islamic exterior and interior decorations are marvels of three-dimensional carving in stone, molded stucco, and wood. Moreover, the mosques are covered in colorful glazed tiles assembled into patterns of lustrous gold, deep green and red, brilliant turquoise, and intense cobalt blue. The tiled walls often remind the viewer of the densely patterned backgrounds of the carpets that line the floors, with their stylized arabesques of leaves and flowers, interlacing braidwork, scrollwork bands, and stars, rosettes, and other geometric figures of intricate abstraction. But most notable and significant is the extensive design use of Arabic calligraphy; set against a background of flowers or scrollwork, the calligraphy provides a visual indication of the importance to Islam of the revealed word. While Islamic art may not seem at first as creative or extraordinary as Western sculpture and painting, it shows human ingenuity in all circumstances. The complicated scrollwork is as intricate and artistic as medieval illumination (see page 215), and the tiled

Detail of the Alhambra Palace, Granada, Spain (c. 1300)

niches of the mosques are as inventive and beautiful as any painted altarpieces. The images on pages 147 and 149–150 show the great artistic possibilities of architectural design. What aesthetic principles underlie the Islamic emphasis on abstract design rather than realistic representation?

Detail from the Saadian Tombs, Marrakech, Morocco (1500s)

THINKING CRITICALLY

1. *Making Comparisons* Do you think that, despite the wide geographic spectrum of these pictures, the styles are fairly uniform? Point out similarities and differences.

2. *Recognizing Values* What do these decorative details suggest about the societies that created them?

3. *Linking Past and Present* In the twentieth century we have come to recognize design as an art form, creating textile and design museums. Make a list of items whose design you think is noteworthy. Explain why.

WRITER'S PORTFOLIO

1. *Extending the Selection* The writers who submit pieces to travel magazines often focus on the wonders of a famous building. Using one of the photographs on pages 149–150, pretend you are a travel writer and describe what you see.

2. *Examining Key Questions* What purposes are served by Islamic decorative elements? Are they simply a manifestation of the exuberance of the artists, or do they suggest something about the world Muslims lived in?

Mystical Poetry

As early as the eighth century, some Muslims began to yearn for a closer and more devout relationship with God. The best known of these groups were the Sufis (sü′fēz). Sufis believed in the oneness of the universe and the unknowability of God. A Sufi's life's work was to purify his soul and grow in harmony with nature and all the elements of God's world. Often the effort at purifying one's soul was aided by the repetition of poetry and by frenetic dance rituals. One of Persia's greatest mystical poets was the Sufi shaykh (in Arabic, a religious "master"), Jalal ad-Din Rumi (rü′me) (1207–1273). His greatest work, the *Masnavi* (mäth nä′vē), or "Discourses," is a huge collection of Sufi sermons and fables in verse. Three poems from the *Masnavi* appear below. According to Rumi, what can man really know?

The Song of the Reed
Harken to this Reed forlorn,
Breathing, even since 'twas torn
From its rushy bed, a strain
Of impassioned love and pain.

"The secret of my song, though near,
None can see and none can hear.
O, for a friend to know the sign
And mingle all his soul with mine!

'Tis the flame of Love that fired me,
'Tis the wine of Love inspired me.
Wouldst thou learn how lovers bleed,
Hearken, hearken to the Reed!"

The Mystic Way
Plug thy low sensual ear, which stuffs like cotton
Thy conscience and makes deaf thine inward ear.

*Inlaid ceiling from the Alcazar
Palace, Seville, Spain (1300s)*

*Prayer wall from
the Royal Mosque,
Isfahan, Iran
(c. 1630)*

Ceiling of the Blue Mosque, Istanbul, Turkey (c. 1610)

Three Monarchs, miniature (c. 1630)

Squirrels in a Plane Tree (c. 1600)

Be without ear, without sense, without thought,
And hearken to the call of God, *"Return!"*
Our speech and action is the outer journey,
Our inner journey is above the sky.
The body travels on its dusty way;
The spirit walks, like Jesus, on the sea.

Knowledge Is Power

Knowledge is the seal of the Kingdom of Solomon: the whole
    world is form, and knowledge is its spirit.
Because of this virtue, the creatures of the seas and those of hill
    and plain are helpless before Man.
Of him the pard and the lion are afraid; the crocodile of the
    great river trembles.
From him peri and demon take refuge, each lurks in some
    hiding-place.
Man hath many a secret enemy: the cautious man is wise.
There are hidden beings, evil and good: at every moment their
    blows are falling on the heart.
The pricks of angelic inspiration and satanic temptation come
    from thousands, not only from one.
Wait for your senses to be transmuted, so that you may discern
    these occult presences
And see whose words you have rejected and whom you have
    made your captain.

Perhaps the best loved of Persian poets is Muslil ad-din Sadi (sä′dē) (c. 1208–1293). Sadi was educated in Baghdad and traveled widely. His masterpiece, the *Gulistan* (gül′ə stän), or "Rose Garden," is a combination of verse and prose, extolling wit, piety, and common sense. Nevertheless, Sadi's poems are heavily symbolic and often concerned with a doctrine he summed up as, "Oneness through love, a form of Platonic love in which the love [of] one human spirit for another finally transcends the two people and unites them as one in the love of God." Sadi's subjects in the *Gulistan* include justice, equality, government administration, benevolence, education, love (physical and mystical), contentment, self-restraint, and devout meditations. While Rumi's work was suffused with intense religious emotion and mysticism, Sadi's religious values were grounded in common sense and observations of everyday life. The following four selections are from the *Gulistan*. What is the purpose of the verses?

Story 8

I saw an Arab of the desert who said to his boy: "*O son, on the day of resurrection thou wilt be asked what thou hast gained and not from whom thou art descended*, that is to say, thou wilt be asked what thy merit is and not who thy father was."

> The covering of the Ka'aba which is kissed
> Has not been ennobled by the silkworm.
> It was some days in company with a venerable man
> Wherefore it became respected like himself.

Story 18

I noticed the son of a rich man, sitting on the grave of his father and quarrelling with a dervish-boy, saying: "The sarcophagus of my father's tomb is of stone and its epitaph is elegant. The pavement is of marble, tessellated with turquoise-like bricks. But what resembles thy father's grave? It consists of two contiguous bricks with two handfuls of mud thrown over it." The dervish-boy listened to all this and then observed: "By the time thy father is able to shake off those heavy stones which cover him, mine will have reached paradise."

> An ass with a light burden
> No doubt walks easily.

> A dervish who carries only the load of poverty
> Will also arrive lightly burdened at the gate of death
> Whilst he who lived in happiness, wealth and ease
> Will undoubtedly on all these accounts die hard.
> At all events, a prisoner who escapes from all his bonds
> Is to be considered more happy than an emir taken prisoner.

Admonition 18

Who has power over his foe and does not slay him is his own enemy.

> With a stone in the hand and a snake on a stone
> It is folly to consider and to delay.

Others, however, announce a contrary opinion and say that it is preferable to respite captives because the option of killing or not killing remains; but if they be slain without delay, it is possible that some advantage may be lost, the like of which cannot be again obtained.

> It is quite easy to deprive a man of life.
> When he is slain he cannot be resuscitated again.
> It is a condition of wisdom in the archer to be patient
> Because when the arrow leaves the bow it returns no more.

Maxim 44

Transgression by whomsoever committed is blamable but more so in learned men, because learning is a weapon for combating Satan and, when the possessor of a weapon is made prisoner, his shame will be greater.

> It is better to be an ignorant poor fellow
> Than a learned man who is not abstemious;
> Because the former loses the way by his blindness
> While the latter falls into a well with both eyes open.

THINKING CRITICALLY

1. *Making Inferences* What mystical elements appear in the poems by Rumi?

2. *Drawing Conclusions* How would you summarize the behaviors and attitudes Sadi espouses in his stories? How relevant are Sadi's admonitions and maxims in today's world?

3. *Linking Past and Present* Are children exposed to moral messages like those of the *Gulistan* today? What examples of this can you come up with?

WRITER'S PORTFOLIO

1. *Extending the Selection* Create either an admonition or a maxim in the style of Sadi. End the piece with a poetic excerpt.

2. *Examining Key Questions* What attitudes might Rumi and Sadi consider absolutely imperative if a man is to live a morally good life?

The Philosophy of History

Ibn Khaldun (1332–1406) was a descendant of a prominent Arab family that for generations had lived in Spain but had resettled during the thirteenth century in North Africa. He received a classical education and at the age of 20 was appointed official writer for the Sultan of Morocco. Thereafter, Ibn Khaldun's professional life alternated between politics and scholarship; between worldly adventures — as an official in the courts of Spain, North Africa, and Cairo — and retirement for study and writing; between freedom and occasional prison terms; between esteem for his abilities as a writer, teacher, and magistrate, and hostility to his personal arrogance, ambition, and ruthlessness. Ibn Khaldun's greatest scholarly achievement was a universal history of Islamic civilization (the *Kitab al-'Ibar*) and in particular its introduction — the *Muqaddimah* — written between 1375–1379 during his first retirement from public life. In the *Muqaddimah*, he puts forth a cyclical theory of history and anticipates how many of the then unknown social sciences, such as sociology, anthropology, and economics, would become part of historical scholarship in later centuries. Ibn Khaldun's contribution was less that of the historian than of the historiographer: a philosopher of history who conceives the principles and methodology a historian should utilize. In the following excerpts from the *Muqaddimah*, Ibn Khaldun discusses how history should be studied. Why is it difficult for historians to avoid falsehoods?

IT SHOULD BE KNOWN THAT HISTORY, IN MATTER OF FACT, IS informative about human social organization which itself is identical with world civilization. It deals with such conditions affecting the nature of civilization as, for instance, savagery and sociability, group feelings, and the different ways by which one group of human beings achieves superiority over another. It deals with royal authority and the dynasties that result in this manner and with the various ranks that exist within them. Also with the different kinds of gainful occupations and ways of making a living, with the sciences and crafts that human beings pursue as part of their activities and efforts, and with all the other institutions that originate in civilization through its very nature.

Untruth naturally afflicts historical information. There are various reasons that make this unavoidable. One of them is partisanship for opinions and schools. If the soul is impartial in receiving information, it devotes to that information the share of critical investigation the information deserves, and its truth or untruth thus becomes clear. However, if the soul is infected with partisanship for a particular opinion or sect, it accepts without a moment's hesitation the information that is agreeable to it. Prejudice and partisanship obscure the critical faculty and preclude critical investigation. The result is that falsehoods are accepted and transmitted.

Another reason making untruth unavoidable in historical information is reliance upon transmitters. Many a transmitter does not know the real significance of his observations or of the things he has learned about orally. He transmits the information, attributing to it the significance he assumes or imagines it to have. The result is falsehood.

Another reason is unfounded assumption as to the truth of a thing. This is frequent. It results mostly from reliance upon transmitters.

Another reason is ignorance of how conditions conform with reality. Conditions are affected by ambiguities and artificial distortions. The informant reports the conditions as he saw them, but on account of artificial distortions he himself has not a true picture of them.

Another reason is the fact that people as a rule approach great and high-ranking persons with praise and encomiums. They embellish conditions and spread their fame. The information made public in such cases is not truthful. Human souls long for praise, and people pay great attention to this world and the positions and wealth it offers. As a rule, they feel no desire for virtue and have no special interest in virtuous people.

Another reason making untruth unavoidable—and this one is more powerful than all the reasons previously mentioned—is ignorance of the nature of the various conditions arising in civilization. Every event (or phenomenon), whether (it comes about in connection with some) essence or (as the result of) action, must inevitably possess a nature peculiar to its essence as well as to the accidental conditions that may attach themselves to it. If the student knows the nature of events and the circumstances and requirements in the world of existence, it will help him to distinguish truth from untruth in investigating the historical information critically. This is more effective in critical investigation than any other aspect that may be brought up in connection with it.

Students often happen to accept and transmit absurd information that, in turn, is believed on their authority. Al-Mas'ûdi [Arab historian], for instance, reports such a story about Alexander. Sea monsters prevented Alexander from building Alexandria. He took a wooden container in which a glass box was inserted, and dived in it to the bottom of the sea. There he drew pictures of the devilish monsters he saw. He then had metal effigies of these animals made and set them up opposite the place where building was going on. When the monsters came out and saw the effigies, they fled. Alexander was thus able to complete the building of Alexandria.

It is a long story, made of nonsensical elements which are absurd for various reasons....

There are many similar things [in history books]. Only knowledge of the nature of civilization makes critical investigation of them possible. It is the best and most reliable way to investigate historical information critically and to distinguish truth from falsehood....

On the other hand, to establish the truth and soundness of information about factual happenings, a requirement to consider is the conformity (or lack of conformity of the reported information with general conditions). Therefore, it is necessary to investigate whether it is possible that the (reported facts) could have happened. This is more important than, and has priority over, personality criticism. For the correct notion about something that ought to be can be derived only from (personality criticism), while the correct notion about something that was can be derived from (personality criticism) and external (evidence) by (checking) the conformity (of the historical report with general conditions).

If this is so, the normative method for distinguishing right from wrong in historical information on the grounds of inherent possibility or absurdity is to investigate human social organization, which is identical with civilization. We must distinguish the conditions that attach themselves to the essence of civilization as required by its very nature; the things that are accidental and cannot be counted on; and the things that cannot possibly attach themselves to it. If we do that, we shall have a normative method for distinguishing right from wrong and truth from falsehood in historical information by means of a logical demonstration that admits of no doubts. Then, whenever we hear about certain conditions occurring in civilization, we shall know what to accept and what to declare spurious. We shall have a sound yardstick with the help of which historians may find the path of truth and correctness where their reports are concerned.

Such is the purpose of this first book of our work. [The subject] is in a way an independent science with its own peculiar object—that is, human civilization and social organization. It also has its own peculiar problems—that is, explaining in turn the conditions that attach themselves to the essence of civilization…. We are going to explain such various aspects of civilization that affect human beings in their social organization, as royal authority, gainful occupation, sciences, and crafts, all in the light of various arguments that will show the true nature of the varied knowledge of the elite and the common people, repel misgivings, and remove doubts.

THINKING CRITICALLY

1. *Identifying Assumptions* Early in his introduction, Ibn Khaldun asserts, "Untruth naturally afflicts historical information." According to Ibn Khaldun, what leads to scholarly untruth?

2. *Identifying Central Issues* Ibn Khaldun envisioned the principles underlying his universal history as comprising an original science. Who or what was to be the focus of this science? Do you think it is the appropriate focus?

3. *Linking Past and Present* What might be Ibn Khaldun's attitude toward the recent trend of including previously excluded minorities in the study of history?

WRITER'S PORTFOLIO

1. *Extending the Selection* Research the history of your community through books and by talking to older residents. Describe your community's assets and problems in light of what you learned.

2. *Examining Key Questions* Ibn Khaldun's approach assumes that through close and thorough observation (rather than the traditional speculation of philosophers) one can not only discern patterns in history, but draw lessons from those patterns. What is the value of doing this?

The Mughal Empire

Although Muslims had invaded northern India in the early 700s, the last and greatest Muslim Indian dynasty, that of the Mughals, was founded by Babur ("the Tiger") in 1526 and ended when the British added India to their empire in 1858. Descended from Tamerlane on his father's side, and from Genghis Khan on his mother's, Babur (1483–1530) had one overriding obsession: to reclaim the empire that Tamerlane had once ruled and, in particular, Tamerlane's capital, Samarkand. Although he never achieved that goal, Babur was successful in his forays into India. Operating from his capital city of Kabul in present-day Afghanistan, Babur launched a series of attacks against the many independent Muslim states in northern India. By 1530, the year of his death, Babur had conquered most of these kingdoms. He was not only a valiant warrior but an educated man, a poet, and calligrapher. In his autobiography, the *Babur-nameh*, from which the following selections are excerpted, Babur recounts the events of his life in forthright, matter-of-fact prose. He is a keen observer, his emotions are generally held in check, and his powers of analysis are deep. What in Babur's circumstances might explain his subsequent development into so formidable a general?

IN THE MONTH OF RAMZAN [RAMADAN], IN THE YEAR FOURTEEN hundred and ninety-four, and in the twelfth year of my age, I became King of Fergana.

The country of Fergana is situated on the extreme boundary of the habitable world. It is of small extent, and is surrounded with hills on all sides except the west.

The country abounds in grains and fruits, its grapes and melons are excellent and plentiful, and it is noted for pomegranates and apricots. The people have a way of taking the stones out of the apricot and putting in almonds in their place, which is very pleasant.

It is abundantly supplied with running water, and is extremely pleasant in spring.

There are many gardens overlooking the rivers where tulips and roses grow in great profusion, and there are meadows of clover, sheltered and pleasant, where travelers love to rest. They are called "the mantle of lambskins."

It abounds in birds and beasts of game; its pheasants are so fat that four persons may dine on one and not finish it, and the game and venison are excellent.

It is a good sporting country; the white deer, mountain goat, stag, and hare are found in great plenty, and there is good hunting and hawking.

In the hills are mines of turquoises, and in the valleys people weave cloth of a purple color.

The revenues of Fergana suffice to maintain 4,000 troops.

My father, Omer-Sheikh-Mirza, was a prince of high ambition and magnificent pretensions, and was always bent on some scheme of conquest. He several times led an army against Samarkand, and was repeatedly defeated.

At this time, 1494, the Sultan Muhammad Khan and the Sultan Ahmed Mirza, having taken offense at his conduct, concluded an alliance, and one marched an army from the north, the other from the south, against his dominions.

At this crisis a singular incident occurred. The Fort of Akhsi is situated on a steep precipice, on the edge of which some of its buildings are raised.

On the fourth day of Ramzan, 1494, my father was engaged in feeding his pigeons, when the platform slipped, precipitating him from the top of the rock, and with his pigeons and pigeon-house he took his flight to the other world.

My father was of low stature and was fat. He used to wear his tunic extremely tight, insomuch that as he was wont to contract his waist when he tied the strings; when he let himself out again the strings often burst. He was not particular in food or dress, and wore his turban without folds, allowing the ends to hang down. His generosity was large, and so was his whole soul, yet brave withal and manly. He was only a middling shot with the bow, but had uncommon force with his fists, and never hit a man without knocking him flat to the ground.

He was a humane man, and played a great deal at backgammon.

He had three sons and five daughters. Of the sons, I, Muhammad Babur, was the eldest.

Babur's most significant military triumph occurred in 1526, at Panipat, a town some 50 miles northwest of Delhi. He defeated Ibrahim Lodi, the Sultan of Delhi, gaining control of most of northern India. In the excerpt below, Babur records his thoughts and actions in the days before this decisive and successful battle. What psychological insight into himself and others does Babur evidence in his thoughts and actions?

ON MONDAY, THE 23RD OF JEMADI-UL-AWAL, I HAD MOUNTED TO survey my posts.... At this time, as I have already observed, in consequence of preceding events, a general consternation and alarm prevailed among great and small. There was not a single person who uttered a manly word, nor an individual who delivered a courageous opinion. The Vazîrs, whose duty it was to give good counsel, and the Amîrs who enjoyed the wealth of kingdoms, neither spoke bravely, nor was their counsel or deportment such as became men of firmness. During the whole course of this expedition, Khalîfeh conducted himself admirably, and was unremitting and indefatigable in his endeavors to put everything in the best order. At length, observing the universal discouragement of my troops, and their total want of spirit, I formed my plan. I called an assembly of all the Amîrs and officers, and addressed them:— "Noblemen and soldiers! Every man that comes into the world is subject to dissolution.

"When we are passed away and gone, God only survives, unchangeable. Whoever comes to the feast of life, must, before it is over, drink from the cup of death. He who arrives at the inn of mortality, must one day inevitably take his departure from that house of sorrow — the world. How much better it is to die with honor than to live with infamy!

'With fame, even if I die, I am contented;
Let fame be mine, since my body is Death's.'

The Most High God has been propitious to us, and has now placed us in such a crisis, that if we fall in the field, we die the death of martyrs; if we survive, we rise victorious, the avengers of the cause of God. Let us, then, with one accord, swear on God's holy word, that none of us will even think of turning his face from this warfare, nor desert from the battle and slaughter that ensues, till his soul is separated from his body."

Master and servant, small and great, all with emulation, seizing the blessed Quran in their hands, swore in the form that I had given. My plan succeeded to admiration, and its effects were instantly visible, far and near, on friend and foe.

On Saturday, the 13th of the latter Jemâdi, having dragged forward our guns, and advanced our right, left, and center in battle array, we reached the ground that had been prepared for us. Many tents were already pitched, and they were engaged in pitching others, when news was brought that the enemy's army was in sight. I immediately mounted, and gave orders that every man should, without delay, repair to his post, and that the guns and lines should be properly strengthened....

After this victory I used the epithet *Ghâzi* [a victor over the enemies of the faith], in the imperial titles. On the official account of the victory, below the imperial titles, I wrote the following verses: —

> "For love of the Faith I became a wanderer in the desert,
> I became the antagonist of Pagans and Hindûs,
> I strove to make myself a martyr; —
> Thanks be to the Almighty who has made me a Ghâzi."

THINKING CRITICALLY

1. *Making Comparisons* Often what distinguishes leaders from other men is the complexity of their character. What opposing elements of Babur's character are evident in these two excerpts?

2. *Drawing Conclusions* What specific evidence is there in these excerpts that might explain why Babur was so effective a leader?

3. *Linking Past and Present* How does Babur's autobiography compare to the autobiographies written by leaders today? Do you think they will be read as long as Babur's has? Why or why not?

WRITER'S PORTFOLIO

1. *Extending the Selection* Imagine you were a soldier in Babur's army. Write a letter describing the army before and after Babur's speech.

2. *Examining Key Questions* To what extent were Babur's achievements influenced by geography? by family? by religion?

Mughal Painting

Influenced in the thirteenth century by the pictorial tradition of the Mongol invaders and, later, by the need to illustrate scientific texts on astronomy, botany, zoology, medicine, and mechanical devices, Islamic painters from the eleventh to the seventeenth century began to portray not just animals, but the human figure. Further impetus and legitimacy came when rulers commissioned portraits of themselves, often as illustration for their memoirs. Painting, particularly miniatures, flourished in Persia, and beginning in Babur's reign (1526–1530), many Persian painters were attracted to the Mughal court. Their work became the foundation for the distinctive Mughal painting style, considered among the highest artistic achievements of Muslim civilization. Before the fourteenth century, painted figures were flat rather than dimensional. As representations of both animal and human figures were often in silhouette, they had little individual character. Often, too, figures were placed in stiff poses similar to those in Byzantine mosaic portraits. Later, as examples of Renaissance perspective and shading became available for study, both portraits and landscapes became less formal and more lifelike. The portrait,

Babur Laying a Garden,
(c. 1590)

Babur Laying a Garden, which appears on page 164, was commissioned by his grandson Akbar (1542–1605). Under Akbar's son Jahangir (1569–1627) and grandson Shah Jahan (1592–1666), Mughal painting achieved its extraordinary brilliance. *Three Monarchs*, on page 151, *Squirrels in a Plane Tree*, on page 152, and *Scribe*, on the right, display this brilliance. To what extent are the figures in the paintings individualized?

Scribe, (c. 1625)

THINKING CRITICALLY

1. *Recognizing Values* What can you tell about the people who commissioned *Three Monarchs* and *Babur Laying a Garden*? What did they value?

2. *Making Comparisons* Which of the four pictures best conveys the character and personality of the person portrayed? Which of the four pictures seems the most accessible? Which the most mysterious?

3. *Linking Past and Present* The chief advantage of miniature painting was its portability. Miniature copies of famous paintings or portraits of people were easily accessible and could accompany their owners on travels. What has replaced the miniature in the modern world?

WRITER'S PORTFOLIO

1. *Extending the Selection* Re-create the scene of the picture *Babur Laying a Garden* in a journal entry. Assume that you are one of the eleven characters in the painting and set the scene.

2. *Examining Key Questions* Why do you think that painting achieved its heights in the Islamic world in India and Persia, the two Muslim kingdoms most remote from the Arab Peninsula?

Safavid Persia

The Safavid Persian Empire, centered in modern-day Iran, reached its height under Shah Abbas I (reigned 1588–1629). His patronage of the arts made his capital at Isfahan world-renowned; in fact, many of the mosques, palaces, and gardens that Abbas built still remain today. Abbas encouraged foreign trade, inviting into his empire many foreign merchants and thereby increasing commerce and the general prosperity of his realm. The Safavids had been intermittently fighting with the Ottoman Empire for two centuries and Abbas's desire to overcome his Ottoman enemies led him to invite foreign ambassadors to the capital. He hoped that he could form military alliances and gain access to European military technology. Out of his desire to acquire gunsmiths and troops from Europe, Abbas permitted Roman Catholic religious orders to build monasteries and to carry on missionary work in his empire. One of those early missionaries was Father Simon, a Carmelite monk who travelled to Isfahan in 1604. The following selection is from Father Simon's *A Chronicle of the Carmelites in Persia*. Does he seem an unbiased commentator?

THE COUNTRY WHICH I SAW IS SPARSELY INHABITED, FOR THE most part all flat, with little water and much uncultivated land; while that which is cultivated has a great abundance of all sorts of produce.... The climate is very temperate: last winter there was little cold. In Isfahan, where I was, no snow fell, except for a little at the end of February. The heat of summer is not great: and on account of the clemency of the climate all sleep in the open on the roofs, and those who are sick similarly. The Persians have few doctors, yet there are many old men among them. Their garb is a long garment, different from that of the Turks: they tie shawls round their waists, and almost all of them go clothed in cotton stuffs of various colors in imitation of the king. Their chief food is rice with meat, and they do not use such variety, nor dainties, as in these countries [of Europe]: and they are frugal and satisfied with little food. At their banquets they display great sumptuousness, both in the great quantity of viands, as in the preparation and serving of them. Almost all of them drink wine: they sit and eat on the ground on rich carpets. The houses are of stone, remarkable inside for the great amount of stucco work ornamenting the ceilings and the walls: so they do not employ tapestries. On the street side they have no windows, so that their women should not be seen: and thus the streets are not attractive, nor is the city fine. The Persians are white (skinned), of fair stature, courteous, friendly towards foreigners and tractable: they set store on nobility of birth, which the Turks do not do. They are very ceremonious and use many forms of politeness after their own fashion. There are some of them, who profess to be philosophers and mathematicians, almost all of them to be poets: and they continually have books in their hands. They have many large mosques, where they go to say their prayers, and they allow any nation whatsoever to enter them....

The king, Shah 'Abbâs...is 34 years old...of medium height, rather thin than fat, his face round and small, tanned by the sun, with hardly any beard: very vivacious and alert, so that he is always doing something or other. He is sturdy and healthy, accustomed to much exercise and toil: many times he goes about on foot, and recently he had been forty days on pilgrimage, which he made on foot the whole time. He has extraordinary strength, and with his scimitar can cut a man in two and a sheep with its wool on at a single blow — and the Persian sheep are of large size. He has done many other feats and has found no one to come up to him in them. In his food he is frugal, as also in his dress, and this to set an example to his subjects; and so in public he eats little else than rice, and that cooked in water only. His usual dress is of linen, and very plain: similarly the nobles and others in his realm, following suit, whereas formerly they used to go out dressed in brocade with jewels and other fopperies: and if he see anyone who is overdressed, he takes him to task, especially if it be a soldier. But in private he eats what he likes. He is sagacious in mind, likes fame and to be esteemed: he is courteous in dealing with everyone and at the same time very serious. For he will go through the public streets, eat from what they are selling there and other things, speak at ease freely with the lower classes, cause his subjects to remain sitting while he himself is standing, or will sit down beside this man and that. He says that is how to be a king, and that the King of Spain and other Christians do not get any pleasure out of ruling, because they are obliged to comport themselves with so much pomp and majesty as they do. He causes foreigners to sit down beside him and to eat at his table.... Formerly there was in his service a great favorite of his, employed in removing manure from the stables. The Shah promoted him, and the man got to become very rich. In a chest of porphyry he preserved the patched garments which he had used to shake out the manure and the harness of a mule. The Shah went to his house and wanted to see all the riches he possessed. The man showed him (the Shah) everything. When they came to the chest of porphyry, he said that he did not want to open it, because all that he had exhibited belonged to his Majesty, only what was inside that chest was his own property. Finally he opened it: and the Shah commended him for it. He had kept those articles because he knew the king's temperament. While we were at his Court, he caused the bellies of two of his favorites to be ripped open, because they had behaved improperly to an ordinary woman. From this it comes about that in his country there are so very few murderers and robbers. In all the time I was at Isfahan, i.e. 4 months, there was never a case of homicide. He is very speedy in dispatching business: when he gives audience, which he does at the gate of his palace, he finishes off all the cases that are brought to him. The parties stand present before him, the officers of justice and his own council, with whom he consults when it pleases him. The sentence which he gives is final and is immediately executed.

THINKING CRITICALLY

1. *Identifying Assumptions* What about Persia surprises Father Simon? What can you deduce about Father Simon from this?

2. *Making Inferences* How would you characterize Abbas? Do you think his ruthlessness is a product of his character or his position?

3. *Linking Past and Present* Can you think of any modern equivalents to Abbas? What makes them similar?

WRITER'S PORTFOLIO

1. *Extending the Selection* Do you think Abbas is a generally good or bad leader? What about a popular leader? Why or why not?

2. *Examining Key Questions* Do you think Abbas was a very religious man? Why or why not?

EXAMINING KEY QUESTIONS

- *What is the Islamic community?*
- *What is our religious duty?*

Throughout this chapter, most selections have concluded with a writing project asking you to discuss how the art or literature you have examined provides answers to one of these key questions. The following writing projects will help you draw together what you have learned by examining how several selections illustrate these key questions.

- Throughout this chapter, you have been exposed to the tremendous variety of Muslim experience. Write an essay describing the breadth of the Islamic world and Muslim influence. Stress the number of races and countries included under the Muslim designation.

- Describe your impressions of the Islamic religion and its followers. How does it relate with other religions? Would you describe Islam as an active or passive religion? How open is it to interpretation?

SPEAKING/LISTENING

- Find examples of Sufi music and the muezzin daily call to prayer. Play these for the class and then read the poems of Rumi and Sadi and the opening of the Quran.

CRAFTING

- Create four maps that show the growth of the Islamic world, one for each of the following time periods: eighth century, eleventh century, fourteenth century, and sixteenth century. Indicate the dominant Islamic caliphate or dynasty and its capital.

COLLECTING

- Collect images of Muslims from magazines, newspapers, and the movies. How do Muslims seem to be portrayed in popular culture? Does this seem a fair portrayal to you?

Dante and His Poem
by Domenico da Michelino

Medieval Civilization

Initial from the Lindisfarne Gospels

700
Gospels translated into Anglo-Saxon

Medieval Civilization

700–1450

P A T R I C K   J .   G E A R Y

Director of the UCLA Center for Medieval and Renaissance Studies

During the thousand years that we call the Middle Ages, Europeans forged a new and original civilization from a creative amalgam of Greco-Roman classical culture, Judeo-Christian religion, and Germano-barbaric society. Forging steel requires heat, skill, and force, and the forging of the European civilization demanded passion, learning, and violence. In few periods of history have such sublime expressions of love — religious, romantic, and erotic — combined with such greed, warfare, and hatred.

Although by A.D. 500, the Roman Empire had ceased to be a political reality in Western Europe, Latin remained the language of learning and everywhere Roman philosophy, literature, and law defined civilized culture. Christianity had become not only the official religion, but the clergy had assumed leadership roles in every aspect of urban culture and monasteries had begun to spread through the countryside. The Church, led by aristocratic bishops and world-renouncing monks, taught sin, repentance, and salvation. Descendants of migrating German tribes, whether they came as conquerors, allies, or captives, adopted both the official religion and the Latin culture of the empire while molding its collapsed political

Helmet unearthed at Sutton Hoo

The capture of Jerusalem

900
Beowulf *composed*

1099
Crusaders capture Jerusalem

institutions to fit their warrior-based society.

LIFE IN THE DARK AGES

Warriors fought for treasure, but still more for glory. Young men sought out lords, "gift givers," under whose command they could fight and from whom they expected a share of booty, protection from foes, and an honored place in the banquet hall. This was a life of constant danger and instability for lords and for their followers, as is vividly evoked in "The Wanderer." Roman traditions of government and Christian belief in divine providence, as expressed in Bede's account of Edwin's conversion, offered early medieval society not only stability but meaning in a violent and unpredictable world.

By the year 1000, Christian missionaries and Christian barbarian kings working together spread these values east to Hungary and Poland and north to Scandinavia and distant Iceland. Subsequent generations would take them further still, to the eastern shores of the Mediterranean, to the western coast of Africa, and, by the end of the Middle Ages, to the even more distant shores of the New World.

During the first centuries of the Middle Ages, these cultural heritages existed in an unstable mixture of clashing traditions. A genuine synthesis began to emerge only over the next centuries when European men and women, no longer content to copy the cultural achievements of the past, began to create a distinctive culture.

THE NEW CHRISTIAN SOCIETY

The values of this new society were essentially aristocratic and militaristic. However, from around the year 1000 a new class of warriors joined with the traditional aristocracy to create an elite that was ruled less by counts and kings than by

Charlemagne
weeping

*Illumination
of the murder*

1100
Le Chanson de Roland *composed*

1170
Murder of Thomas à Becket

a rough code of chivalry. For this knightly class, fighting was the highest calling, and mounted combat the supreme expression of personal worth and valor. Noble families, proud of their independence and ancestry, maintained their position through complex kinship networks, mutual defense pacts with other nobles, and control of castles, from which they could dominate the surrounding countryside, drawing their wealth less from pillage and raiding than from the control of the peasants who worked their lands. Safe behind the castle walls, they were by the twelfth century often independent even of counts, dukes, and even kings. This lesser nobility absorbed control of such traditionally public powers as justice, order, and taxation.

For the sons of such nobles preparation for a life of warfare began early, often in the entourage of a maternal uncle or a powerful lord. There boys learned to ride, to handle a heavy sword and shield, to manage a lance on horseback, to swing an axe with deadly accuracy. They also learned more subtle but, equally important lessons about honor, pride, and glory. The legends of King Arthur and his knights, sung by traveling minstrels at the banqueting table on long winter nights, provided models of knightly action. The culmination of this education came in a ceremony of knighting. An adolescent of age sixteen to eighteen received a sword from an older, experienced warrior. No longer a "boy," he now became a "youth," ready to enter the world of fighting for which he had trained.

A "youth" was a noble who had been knighted but who had not married or acquired land either through inheritance or as a reward from a lord for service; and thus he had not yet established his own "house." During this time the knight led the life of a warrior, joining in promising military expeditions and

*Bronze bust
of Frederick*

*Seal from the
Magna Carta*

1190
Death of Frederick Barbarossa

1215
*King John of England signs
the Magna Carta*

amusing himself with tournaments— mock battles that often proved as deadly as the real thing—in which one could win an opponent's horses and armor as well as renown. Drinking, gambling, and lechery were other common activities. This was an extraordinarily dangerous lifestyle, and many youths did not survive to the next stage in a knight's life, that of acquiring land, wife, honor, and his own following of youths.

**THE PLACE
OF WOMEN**   The period between childhood and maturity was no less dangerous for noblewomen than for men. Marriages were the primary forms of alliances between noble houses, and the production of children was essential to the continued prosperity of the family. Thus, daughters were raised as breeders, married at around age sixteen, and expected to produce as many children as possible. Given the primitive state of obstetrics and

nutrition, bearing children was even more dangerous than bearing a lance. Many noblewomen died in childbirth, often literally exhausted by frequent successive births.

In this martial society, the political and economic status of women declined considerably. Because they were considered unable to participate in warfare, women in northern Europe were frequently excluded from inheritance, estate management, courts, and public deliberations. At the same time, however, a growing tradition of "courtliness" glorified the status of aristocratic women in literature and exalted values of romantic love between young knights and older, married noble women. This tradition was playfully summarized by Andreas Capellanus in his "Rules of Courtly Love." Still, for all their martial valor, medieval men feared women and female sexuality. Both secular tradition and Christian teaching portrayed women as headstrong, devious, and

Viking head from the Oseberg Cart

Marco Polo leaving Venice harbor

1220
Elder Edda composed

1271
Marco Polo sets off for China

sexually demanding temptresses often responsible for the corruption and downfall of men.

THE ROLE OF THE CHURCH

The Christian Church not only supported the values of chivalric society, but also worked to transform them. Although monks and bishops were spiritual warriors, most abhorred bloodshed among Christians and sought to limit the violence of aristocratic life. This attitude combined altruistic and selfish motives, since Church property was often the focus of aristocratic greed. During the eleventh century, bishops and popes shifted the goals of warfare from attacks against other Christians to the supposed defense of Christian society. This redirection produced the Crusades, those religious wars of conquest directed against Europe's non-Christian neighbors.

In order to direct noble violence away from Christendom, Pope Urban II in 1095 urged Western knights to use their arms to free the Holy Land from Muslim occupation. In return he promised to absolve them from all of the punishment due for their sins in both this life and the next. The First Crusade was remarkably bloody and remarkably successful. The crusaders took Jerusalem in 1099, slaughtered many of its Muslim and Jewish inhabitants, and established a Christian kingdom in Palestine. For over two centuries bands of western warriors went on armed pilgrimage to defend this precarious kingdom and, after the reconquest of Jerusalem by the Muslim commander Saladin in 1187, to attempt to recapture it. Other such holy wars were directed against the Muslims in Spain, the Slavs in eastern Europe, and even against heretical Christians and political opponents in France and Italy.

THE NEW LEARNING

The religious culture of the Middle Ages meant much more

*Traini painting of
plague victims*

*Illumination
of King Arthur*

1348
Black Death ravages Europe

1375
*Sir Gawain and
the Green Knight composed*

than just the values of crusader warfare. From the later eleventh century, monasteries and cathedrals became centers for study, not only of religious texts, but also of the classics of pagan antiquity. To men such as Peter Abelard, Christian truths combined naturally with the great tradition of Greek and Roman philosophy. These men and women were not ivory tower scholars; rather they were people engaged at once in the pursuit of wisdom and in the concerns of daily life. Abelard could be as passionate in his love of Heloise as he was in his love of philosophy, and she in turn could show herself better at defending the ideal of pure love than her teacher.

In time, the informal schools that developed around influential teachers developed into permanent institutions of higher education, universities. To these great centers, such as Bologna, Paris, and Oxford, came young men from across Europe, eager to obtain the formal training in law, philosophy, theology, and medicine necessary to take positions of leadership in the increasingly sophisticated cities and courts of Europe. Intellectual giants, such as Thomas Aquinas and Roger Bacon, expanded the frontiers of knowledge, both of the divine and the material worlds.

THE EXPANSION OF SECULAR AUTHORITY

Fundamental to the development of universities were the growth of new political institutions, the monarchies of France and England. Between the eleventh and fourteenth centuries, the kings of France combined shrewd marriage strategies, church support, and the exercise of justice through loyal functionaries—many university trained—to expand their authority at the expense of the independent nobility. In England, William the Conqueror and his successors adopted a small, but centralized Anglo-Saxon government

Effigy of Edward

English view of Agincourt

1376
Death of Edward the Black Prince

1415
Battle of Agincourt

and developed it into a powerful royal system of taxation and judicial control. This increasing centralization was checked by the aristocratic reaction that gave rise in 1215 to the Magna Carta, an attempt to turn back the clock to an age of greater noble autonomy.

Expansion of royal authority progressively reduced the warrior aristocracy to the position of subjects or agents of royal control. As the aristocracy lost its autonomy, it retreated into an ever more elaborate imaginary world of chivalry and courtly literature.

**THE WORLD
OF DANTE**   In northern Italy self-governing city states likewise reduced noble families' power and autonomy. In the urban world of Florence, the great poet and humanist Dante Alighieri combined courtly love, medieval Christianity, and civic pride in his poetry. His *Divine Comedy* is the supreme literary expression of the

Middle Ages, a vision of hell, purgatory, and heaven in which the great thinkers, leaders, lovers, and villains of antiquity and the Middle Ages receive rewards or punishments that exemplify their actions in life.

Dante's verbal depiction of the other world, like the visual images created by his contemporary Giotto, are masterful summaries of the medieval culture. For all of their drama, they ultimately present a world that is ordered, rational, and harmonious. In the hundred years that followed the publication of the *Divine Comedy*, plague, warfare, and religious dissent shattered this harmony throughout Europe. The Black Death destroyed over one-quarter of Europe's population; England and France exhausted each other in a century of blood-letting known as the Hundred Years War; and Christianity itself was splintered by rival claims to the papacy and alternative religious traditions. In the face of

*Portrait of
Joan of Arc*

*Portrait of
Henry VII*

1431
Joan of Arc burned at the stake

1485
Battle of Bosworth

these disasters, Europeans began to question the validity of the medieval humanistic synthesis and in particular the way that previous generations had understood the easy continuity between classical antiquity and their own values. Poets, philosophers, and artists began to emphasize the radical difference that separated their world from that of antiquity and to seek a return to the pristine values of Greco-Roman civilization as they understood it. The Renaissance had begun.

Anglo-Saxon Culture

Much of our knowledge about early England comes from two books: the Exeter Book and Bede's *Ecclesiastical History of the English People*. Compiled around 975 at the order of Leofric, the first Bishop of Exeter, the Exeter Book contains much of the surviving writing from the golden era of Old English literature, including "The Wanderer," which appears below. The *Ecclesiastical History of the English People* was written by a scholar, teacher, and monk named Bede (673–735). Born in the Anglo-Saxon kingdom of Northumbria, Bede spent his whole life in monasteries, devoting himself to learning, writing, and teaching; some of his students would help lead the great revival of learning under Charlemagne. His history, an excerpt of which appears on page 182, was completed in 731 and chronicles the history of Britain from the arrival of the Romans in 55 B.C. up to Bede's own day. Both selections provide a somewhat shadowy glimpse into the beginnings of a culture that sprang from Germanic peoples called Angles, Saxons, and Jutes, who invaded Britain's eastern shores after the Roman legions left Britain around A.D. 400. Early churchmen referred to the invaders as a scourge and feared that the teachings of Christianity would be lost. The arrangement of "The Wanderer" on the page in the Exeter Book would seem to indicate that it is prose, but its elegiac mood and language, particularly the pattern of alliteration in the original Old English, mark it as poetry. A narrator's words appear in the second and last paragraphs. What is the mood of the speaker in "The Wanderer"?

---

from "The Wanderer"

"HE WHO IS ALONE OFTEN LIVES TO FIND FAVOR, MILDNESS OF the Lord, even though he has long had to stir with his arms the frost-cold sea, troubled in heart over the water-way, had to tread the tracks of exile. Fully-fixed is his fate."

So spoke the earth-walker, remembering hardships, fierce war-slaughters — the fall of dear kinsmen.

"Often before the day dawned I have had to speak of my cares, alone: there is now none among the living to whom I dare clearly express the thought of my heart. I know indeed that it is a fine custom for a man to lock tight his heart's coffer, keep closed the hoard-case of his mind, whatever his thoughts may be. Words of a weary heart may not withstand fate, nor those of an angry spirit bring help. Therefore men eager for fame shut sorrowful thought up fast in their breast's coffer.

"Thus I, wretched with care, removed from my homeland, far from dear kinsmen, have had to fasten with fetters the thoughts of my heart—ever since the time, many years ago, that I covered my gold-friend in the darkness of the earth; and from there I crossed the woven waves, winter-sad, downcast for want of a hall, sought a giver of treasure—a place, far or near, where I might find one in a mead-hall who should know of my people, or would comfort me friendless, receive me with gladness. He who has experienced it knows how cruel a companion sorrow is to the man who has no beloved protectors. Exile's path awaits him, not twisted gold—frozen thoughts in his heart-case, no joy of earth. He recalls the hall-warriors and the taking of treasure, how in youth his gold-friend made him accustomed to feasting. All delight has gone....

"Therefore the man wise in his heart considers carefully this wall-place and this dark life, remembers the multitude of deadly combats long ago, and speaks these words: 'Where has the horse gone? Where the young warrior? Where is the giver of treasure? What has become of the feasting seats? Where are the joys of the hall? Alas, the bright cup! Alas, the mailed warrior! Alas, the prince's glory! How that time has gone, vanished beneath night's cover, just as if it never had been! The wall, wondrous high, decorated with snake-likenesses, stands now over traces of the beloved company. The ash-spears' might has borne the earls away—weapons greedy for slaughter, Fate the mighty; and storms beat on the stone walls, snow, the herald of winter, falling thick binds the earth when darkness comes and the night-shadow falls, sends harsh hailstones from the north in hatred of men. All earth's kingdom is wretched, the world beneath the skies is changed by the work of the fates. Here wealth is fleeting, here friend is fleeting, here man is fleeting, here woman is fleeting—all this earthly habitation shall be emptied.'"

In the part of Bede's history that appears here, Prince Edwin, after being exiled from Northumbria, has found refuge with Redwald, King of East Anglia. When Ethelfrid, the Northumbrian king, hears of this, he bribes Redwald to kill Edwin. As this passage begins, Edwin, knowing that his friend has agreed to kill him, is alone and brooding. How is Edwin's conversion to Christianity foreshadowed?

---

from the *Ecclesiastical History* of the English People

HE HAD REMAINED A CONSIDERABLE TIME IN SILENCE, GRIEVING and desperate, when suddenly, at dead of night, he saw a man approaching whose face and clothes were strange to him, and whose unexpected arrival caused him considerable alarm. But the stranger came up and greeted him, asking why he was sitting sadly on a stone, watchful and alone, at an hour when everyone else was asleep. Edwin asked what concern it might be of his whether he passed the night indoors or outside. In reply, the man said: "Don't think that I am unaware why you are sad and sleepless and why you are keeping watch alone. I know very well who you are, what your troubles are, and what coming evils you dread. But tell me this: what reward will you give the man who can deliver you from your troubles, and persuade Redwald not to harm you or betray you to death at the hands of your enemies?" Edwin answered that he would give any reward in his power in return for such an outstanding service. Then the other went on: "And what if he also promised that you should become king, defeat your enemies, and enjoy greater power than any of your predecessors who have ever ruled the English nation?" Heartened by these enquiries, Edwin readily promised that, in return for such blessings, he would give ample proofs of his gratitude. The stranger then asked a third question. "If the man who can truthfully foretell such good fortune can also give you better and wiser guidance for your life and salvation than anything known to your parents and kinsfolk, will you promise to obey and follow his salutary advice?" Edwin at once promised that he would faithfully follow the guidance of anyone who could save him out of so many troubles and raise him to a throne. On his assurance, the man who addressed him laid his right hand on Edwin's head, saying: "When you receive this sign, remember this occasion and our conversation, and do not delay the fulfillment of your promise." Hereupon, it is said, he vanished, and Edwin realized that it was not a man but a spirit who had appeared to him.

After his vision, Edwin heard that Redwald's queen had convinced Redwald not to betray Edwin. Moreover, with Redwald's aid, Edwin defeated and killed Ethelfrid and so escaped the plots of his enemy and regained his kingdom. The Paulinus who is referred to was the Bishop of Northumbria.

WHILE KING EDWIN HESITATED TO ACCEPT THE WORD OF GOD AT Paulinus's preaching, he used to sit alone for hours, deliberating what he should do, and what religion he should follow. On one of these occasions, the man of God came to him, and laying his right hand on his head, enquired whether he remembered this sign. The king trembled, and would have fallen at his feet, but Paulinus raised him, and said in a friendly voice: "God has helped you to escape from the hands of the enemies whom you feared, and it is through His bounty that you have received the kingdom that you desired. Remember the third promise that you made, and hesitate no longer. Accept the Faith and keep the commands of Him who has delivered you from all your earthly troubles, and raised you to the glory of an earthly kingdom. If you will henceforward obey His will, which He reveals to you through me, He will save you from the everlasting doom of the wicked, and give you a place in His eternal kingdom in heaven."

When Paulinus had spoken, the king answered that he was both willing and obliged to accept the Faith which he taught, but said that he must discuss the matter with his principal advisers and friends, so that if they were in agreement, they might all be cleansed together in Christ the Fount of Life. Paulinus agreed, and the king kept his promise. He summoned a council of the wise men, and asked each in turn his opinion of this new faith and new God being proclaimed.

Coifi (ko´fe), the High Priest, replied without hesitation: "Your Majesty, let us give careful consideration to this new teaching, for I frankly admit that, in my experience, the religion that we have hitherto professed seems valueless and powerless. None of your subjects has been more devoted to the service of the gods than myself, yet there are many to whom you show greater favor, who receive greater honors, and who are more successful in all their undertakings. Now, if the gods had any power, they would surely have favored myself, who have been more zealous in their service. Therefore, if on examination these new teachings are found to be better and more effectual, let us not hesitate to accept them."

Another of the king's chief men signified his agreement with this prudent argument, and went on to say: "Your Majesty, when we compare the present life of man with that time of which we have no knowledge, it seems to me like the swift flight of a lone sparrow through the banqueting-hall where you sit in the winter months to dine with your thanes and counselors. Inside there is a comforting fire to warm the room; outside, the wintry storms of snow and rain are raging. This sparrow flies swiftly in through one door of the hall, and out through another. While he is inside, he is safe from the winter storms; but after a few moments of comfort, he vanishes from sight into the darkness whence he came. Similarly, man appears on earth for a little while, but we know nothing of what went before this life, and what follows. Therefore if this new teaching can reveal any more certain knowledge, it seems only right that we should follow it."

THINKING CRITICALLY

1. *Recognizing Values* In "The Wanderer," what do the speaker's thoughts on what constitutes a wise man tell you about the Anglo-Saxon world? Are these same attributes apparent in Bede?

2. *Making Comparisons* How is the metaphor of the sparrow flying through the banqueting hall in Bede, similar to the speaker's thoughts about the fate of man in "The Wanderer"?

3. *Linking Past and Present* Both the speaker in "The Wanderer" and Prince Edwin are at times wandering alone and friendless. What modern treatments of these subjects can you think of?

WRITER'S PORTFOLIO

1. *Extending the Selection* Compare and contrast the two writers' purposes in these selections.

2. *Examining Key Questions* What general conclusions can you draw about Anglo-Saxon life, the leaders or rulers in this society, and the status of Christianity?

The Norman Conquest

From the departure of the Romans until the eleventh century, the throne of England was held variously by Danes and Saxons. In 1042, Edward the Confessor became king, but Edward was far from being an Englishman, having spent most of his life in Normandy. Upon ascending the throne, he immediately welcomed his Norman friends and relatives, including his second cousin William, the Duke of Normandy, to the English court. Because Edward and Queen Edith were childless, the succession was doubtful. Before Edward died in January 1066, he advised that Harold, Queen Edith's popular brother, succeed him. Harold was crowned soon after, but William claimed that Edward had promised the throne to him some years earlier. William's claim was supported by the Pope, who excommunicated Harold as William prepared to invade England. On September 28, 1066, William landed with his army on English shores, made camp at Hastings, and waited for Harold and his troops. Harold and two of his brothers were killed at the Battle of Hastings, and the Normans won the battle and the war. William was crowned on Christmas Day 1066. He reigned until 1087. About a decade after the battle, William's half-brother Odo, the Bishop of Bayeux (**bä yô′**) in Normandy, commissioned a tapestry to commemorate the victory. The Bayeux Tapestry depicts the events leading up to the Battle of Hastings, including the death of King Edward, the battle itself, and the death of King Harold on the battlefield. Of the two scenes shown here, the first depicts the crowning of King Harold in 1066 at the palace at Westminster. The legend reads: "Here sits Harold, King of the English." The figure on the left, holding the battle axe, is Harold before he was crowned. Harold sits in the center holding the symbols of his office, the orb and scepter. The Archbishop of Canterbury, Stigant, stands next to Harold holding a maniple. Commoners are shown outside, watching the coronation. The second scene depicts the battle between the Anglo-Saxon infantry and the Norman knights. What do the figures at Harold's coronation represent?

"The Coronation of Harold," from the Bayeux Tapestry (1076) The inscription above Harold's head reads, "Here sits Harold, King of the English."

"The English Shield-wall Withstands Norman Attack," from the Bayeux Tapestry (1076)

THINKING CRITICALLY

1. *Making Comparisons* How do the two scenes differ in effect? How are these effects achieved?

2. *Drawing Conclusions* What tactics did the English use at Hastings? What about the Normans?

3. *Linking Past and Present* Compare the depiction of Harold's coronation to the swearing-in of a contemporary U.S. President. What types of people are present at the inauguration? Where is it held? What part does religion play in the ceremony?

WRITER'S PORTFOLIO

1. *Extending the Selection* Obviously this tapestry could not have been designed or embroidered by eyewitnesses of all the events shown. Describe the possible sources for the more than seventy scenes showing kings, commoners, soldiers, and priests, as well as furniture, and fortifications.

2. *Examining Key Questions* What does the fact that an archbishop is present at Harold's coronation tell you about the relationship between church and state?

The First Crusade

In the Middle Ages, Jerusalem was revered as a holy city by Jews, Christians, and Muslims alike. For centuries, the city, first under the Byzantine Empire, the eastern half of the old Roman Empire, and then under the control of Arab Muslims, had been a place of free pilgrimage for all worshippers. However, as the Seljuk Turks replaced the Arabs as the power in this region in the eleventh century, this freedom to visit the city was threatened. In 1099, the Byzantine Emperor Alexius Comnenus, hoping to regain control of Palestine, which the Empire had lost to the Arabs, asked Pope Urban II for military help. Urban convened the Council of Clermont, in France, in 1095 and in an impassioned address to clergy and commoners, urged the French to help rescue the Eastern Church and "expel the thieves." He promised the remission of many years in purgatory for those who accepted the challenge and marched to the Holy Land. According to those present, a cry immediately went up: "God wills it! God wills it!" For the next two centuries, periodic expeditions were made by Christian armies to force the Muslims from the Holy Land. Usually numbered at eight, the Crusades were far from successful in their goals — only the first Crusade ended with the capture of Jerusalem. But these expeditions did offer Christian knights an opportunity for adventure, wealth, and spiritual redemption. The first Crusaders arrived outside the walls of Jerusalem in June of 1099. It is estimated that the army was made up of 12,000 foot soldiers and 1,200 knights. One of the four divisions of the army was led by Godfrey de Bouillon, Duke of Lower Lorraine, with his brother Baldwin. Baldwin's chaplain was Fulcher (**ful shā**′) of Chartres, who describes the Crusaders' capture of Jerusalem in the account here. How does this account compare to the writings of modern historians?

The seventh of June dawned brightly when
The Franks besieged Jerusalem....

At sight of it, when the Franks saw how difficult it was to storm, they were ordered by our leaders to make wooden ladders by means of which, when these were later on set against the wall, they mounted to the top in a powerful assault and, perhaps with the aid of God, attacked the city.

This done, on the following Sabbath at the command of the chiefs, with trumpets blaring in the clear morning light, in an amazing attack they assailed the city from all sides. When this had continued until the sixth hour of the day and still they were unable to enter over the ladders they had set up because they were too few, they dejectedly gave up the assault. Then a plan was devised and the engineers were ordered to build machines that could be moved up to the walls and, with God's help, thus achieve the result of their hopes. This was done. During this time there was no lack of bread or meat.

But as the location, as mentioned above, lacked water and rivers, our men and their beasts were greatly distressed for want of drinking water. Hence, under the compulsion of necessity, they searched for water far and wide and laboriously brought it for the siege in their leather skins, from a distance of four or five miles. Once the engines were ready, that is the battering rams and the mining devices, they prepared for the assault. Among other contrivances, they fastened together a tower made of small pieces of wood, because large timber was lacking. At night, at a given order, they carried it piece by piece to the most favorable point of the city. And so, in the morning, after preparing the catapults and the other contraptions, they very quickly set it up, fitted together, not far from the wall. This erection they tied fast and bound with leather thongs on the outside, slowly moving it nearer the wall. Then a few daring soldiers at the sound of the trumpet mounted it, and from that position they immediately began to launch stones and arrows. In retaliation against them the Saracens proceeded to defend themselves similarly and with their slings hurled flaring brands soaked in oil and fat and fitted with small torches on the previously mentioned tower and the soldiers on it. Many therefore fighting in this manner on either side met ever-present death.

On the following day, with trumpets resounding, they repeated their actions with greater vigor, breaching the wall in one place with battering rams. In front of the wall defenses two stakes hung, fastened with ropes, that the Saracens had prepared to stop the enemy rushing on them and showering stones. The tower was then moved up to the wall and the ropes that tied the bundles of wood were cut, and from the same wood the Franks fitted together a bridge that they cleverly extended and threw from the tower across the wall.

One stone citadel on the wall was now blazing away, over which our engineers had hurled burning firebrands. The fire was fed by the planks of timber, and the smoke and flame began to issue so that none of the citizen guards could stand there any longer. Presently therefore the Franks entered the city at midday, on the day dedicated to Venus, with bugles blowing and all in an uproar and manfully attacking and crying "Help us, God," and raised a standard on the top of the wall. The heathens, utterly disgraced, all changed their bold stand into a scurrying flight through the alleyways of the city. The more quickly they fled, the more quickly were they driven into flight. Count Raymund, attacking on another side, was unaware of this, and his men too, until they saw the Saracens leap over the top of the wall in front of them. At sight of this, they rushed joyfully as fast as possible to the city and with the rest began to rout and slay the wicked enemy.

Then some Saracens, both Arabs and Ethiopians, fled into the citadel of David, others shut themselves in the temples of the Lord and of Solomon. In the halls of these temples they were fiercely attacked; there was nowhere for them to escape from our warriors. On the top of the temple of Solomon that they had climbed in their flight, many were pierced to death by arrows and wildly hurled down from the wall. In this temple too almost 10,000 were decapitated. If you had been there, you would have seen our feet bespattered to the soles with the blood of the slain. What is there to tell? Not a single life was spared. But they too spared neither women nor children. You would have seen an amazing sight when our squires and the poorest infantry troops, learning of the Saracens' cunning, slit the bellies even of the slain to extract from their bowels the bezants that they had swallowed while alive. After a few days they piled up the bodies in a great heap and burned them in order to find the coins more easily among the burnt ashes....

Then, going to the sepulcher of the Lord and His glorious temple, clerics and laity, chanting in a loud exulting voice the new hymn to the Lord, together joyously visited the sacred places so long yearned for, making offering and humble supplications. O what an hour craved by us all! What a moment to be remembered beyond all others! What an incident above all others desired! Truly craved, since it had always been an object of yearning by all worshippers of the Catholic faith in their innermost yearning heart, that the place in which the Creator of all creatures, God made man, by His manifold compassions for mankind, being born, dying, and being resurrected, conferred the gift of new-born salvation, a place at last cleansed from the contagion of the heathens dwelling therein, long defiled by their superstition, should be restored to its former prestige by the believers and the faithful. And truly memorable and rightly to be remembered, because whatever our Lord Jesus Christ, on earth a man dwelling with men, did and taught, was recalled and brought back to most glorious memory....

> On July fifteenth, it was when
> The day was shining clear and bright
> Jerusalem was taken then
> By Gallic strength, by Frankish might.
> The year was centuries eleven
> Without the one to make it even
> Since Virgin Mary, at His birth,
> Gave us a king to rule the earth.

THINKING CRITICALLY

1. *Identifying Central Assumptions* Does Fulcher's account correspond to any previous assumptions you had about the Crusades? Why or why not?

2. *Recognizing Bias* Do you think Fulcher gives a balanced account of this event? Are the Saracens presented fairly?

3. *Recognizing Values* What does Fulcher's account of the Crusaders visiting the holy places suggest about the quality of their religious faith?

WRITER'S PORTFOLIO

1. *Extending the Selection* Write an objective eyewitness account of this battle as if you were a television news reporter.

2. *Examining Key Questions* How does the combination of piety and slaughter strike you? Describe your feelings toward this Crusade.

Abelard and Heloise

Peter Abelard (1079–1142) was well known as a theologian in Paris during his lifetime. He was born in Brittany, the eldest son of a minor noble family. After studying and teaching for several years, he became *magister scholarium* (head master) at the Cloister School of Notre Dame in Paris in 1113. When he met Heloise (c. 1098–1163), the niece of a canon at Notre Dame, she was considerably younger than Abelard, between fifteen and seventeen years old. In the passage reprinted here, Abelard relates how they fell in love. Although at this time the Church was only beginning to forbid marriage by the clergy, it was assumed that men like Abelard, who was a teacher and theologian, would remain celibate. Heloise subsequently became pregnant, however, and left Paris to stay with Abelard's sister in the country where she gave birth to a boy. Eventually Abelard and Heloise were married secretly, but Fulbert, Heloise's uncle, revealed the secret, causing Abelard to send her to a convent. *Historia calamitatum* is the story of this and many others of Abelard's misfortunes written, when he was abbot of Saint Gildas Monastery, some years after the events described. The letter from Heloise to Abelard, printed on page 194, was written in reply to *Historia calamitatum*. Heloise eventually became an abbess at a convent established by Abelard, and the two were able only to exchange letters for the rest of their lives. How does Abelard contrive to meet Heloise?

Peter Abelard, from *Historia calamitatum*

ALL ON FIRE WITH DESIRE FOR THIS GIRL I SOUGHT AN opportunity of getting to know her through private daily meetings and so more easily winning her over; and with this end in view I came to an arrangement with her uncle, with the help of some of his friends, whereby he should take me into his house, which was very near my school, for whatever sum he liked to ask. As a pretext I said that my household cares were hindering my studies and the expense was more than I could afford. Fulbert dearly loved money, and was moreover always ambitious to further his niece's education in letters, two weaknesses which made it easy for me to gain his consent and obtain my desire: he was all eagerness for my money and confident that his niece would profit from my teaching. This led him to make an urgent request which furthered my love and fell in with my wishes more than I had dared to hope; he gave me complete charge over the girl, so that I could devote all the leisure time left me by my school to teaching her by day and night, and if I found her idle I was to punish her severely. I was amazed by his simplicity—if he had entrusted a tender lamb to a ravening wolf it would not have surprised me more. In handing her over to me to punish as well as to teach, what else was he doing but giving me complete freedom to realize my desires, and providing an opportunity, even if I did not make use of it, for me to bend her to my will by threats and blows if persuasion failed? But there were two special reasons for his freedom from the base suspicion: his love for his niece and my previous reputation for continence.

Need I say more? We were united, first under one roof, then in heart; and so with our lessons as a pretext we abandoned ourselves entirely to love.... Few could have failed to notice something so obvious, in fact no one, I fancy, except the man whose honour was most involved—Heloise's uncle. Several people tried on more than one occasion to draw his attention to it, but he would not believe them; because, as I said, of his boundless love for his niece and my well-known reputation for chastity in my previous life.

Eventually Abelard told Fulbert of the affair and agreed to marry Heloise, provided the marriage was kept secret.

I SET OFF AT ONCE FOR BRITTANY AND BROUGHT BACK MY mistress to make her my wife. But she was strongly opposed to the proposal, and argued hotly against it for two reasons: the risk involved and the disgrace to myself.... What honour could she win, she protested, from a marriage which would dishonour me and humiliate us both? The world would justly exact punishment from her if she removed such a light from its midst. Think of the curses, the loss to the Church and grief of philosophers which would greet such a marriage! Nature had created me for all mankind—it would be a sorry scandal if I should bind myself to a single woman and submit to such base servitude. She absolutely rejected this marriage; it would be nothing but a disgrace and a burden to me....

Heloise then went on to the risks I should run in bringing her back, and argued that the name of mistress instead of wife would be dearer to her and more honourable for me—only love freely given should keep me for her, not the constriction of a marriage tie, and if we had to be parted for a time, we should find the joy of being together all the sweeter the rarer our meetings were. But at last she saw that her attempts to persuade or dissuade me were making no impression on my foolish obstinacy, and she could not bear to offend me; so amidst deep sighs and tears she ended in these words: "We shall both be destroyed. All that is left us is suffering as great as our love has been."

Heloise, Letter to Abelard

YOU KNOW, BELOVED, AS THE WHOLE WORLD KNOWS, HOW much I have lost in you, how at one wretched stroke of fortune that supreme act of flagrant treachery robbed me of my very self in robbing me of you; and how my sorrow for my loss is nothing compared with what I feel for the manner in which I lost you. Surely the greater the cause for grief the greater the need for the help of consolation, and this no one can bring but you; you are the sole cause of my sorrow, and you alone can grant me the grace of consolation. You alone have the power to make me sad, to bring me happiness or comfort; you alone have so great a debt to repay me, particularly now when I have carried out all your orders so implicitly that when I was powerless to oppose you in anything, I found strength at your command to destroy myself. I did more, strange to say—my love rose to such heights of madness that it robbed itself of what it most desired beyond hope of recovery, when immediately at your bidding I changed my clothing along with my mind, in order to prove you the sole possessor of my body and my will alike. God knows I never sought anything in you except yourself. I wanted simply you, nothing of yours. I looked for no marriage-bond, no marriage portion, and it was not my own pleasures and wishes I sought to gratify, as you well know, but yours. The name of wife may be more sacred or more binding, but sweeter for me will always be the words mistress, or, if you will permit me, that of concubine or whore. I believed that the more I humbled myself on your account, the more gratitude I should win from you, and also the less damage I should do to the brightness of your reputation.

You yourself on your own account did not altogether forget this in the letter of consolation I have spoken of which you wrote to a friend; there you thought fit to set out some of the reasons I gave in trying to dissuade you from binding us together in an ill-starred marriage. But you kept silent about most of my arguments for preferring love to wedlock and freedom to chains. God is my witness that if Augustus, Emperor of the whole world, thought fit to honour me with marriage and conferred all the earth on me to possess for ever, it would be dearer and more honourable to me to be called not his Empress but your whore.

For a man's worth does not rest on his wealth or power; these depend on fortune, but worth on his merits. And a woman should realize that if she marries a rich man more readily than a poor one, and desires her husband more for his possessions than for himself, she is offering herself for sale. Certainly any woman who comes to marry through desires of this kind deserves wages, not gratitude, for clearly her mind is on the man's property, not himself, and she would be ready to prostitute herself to a richer man, if she could.

THINKING CRITICALLY

1. *Making Inferences* How would you characterize Abelard ? Does he seem like a good cleric?

2. *Identifying Central Issues* Heloise seemed to believe that Abelard should not marry. What reasons did she give?

3. *Linking Past and Present* If Heloise were alive today, what aspects of the feminist movement would she agree with? What aspects might she disagree with?

WRITER'S PORTFOLIO

1. *Extending the Selection* Discuss the pros and cons of a celibate clergy.

2. *Examining Key Questions* Discuss the importance of love for Abelard and Heloise.

The Great Cathedrals

The revival of building with stone in the twelfth century was marked by the appearance of the great cathedrals, which still dot the landscape of western Europe. In communities emerging from centuries of disorder, these structures served as monuments, not just to God, but also to the prosperity and ingenuity of a city's inhabitants. The building of a cathedral was a lengthy and costly endeavor taken on not by a government, but by all of the city's people, who would support its erection for a period of as much as a century. As the cathedral neared completion it would become the center of city life. Its spires rose high above the rest of the city, the city's government, businesses, and guilds surrounded its walls, and the cathedral bells marked not just the hours, but spread the news of births and deaths through their varied tolling.

To the earliest of these cathedrals, like St. Pierre at Angoulême (1105–1128), we apply the term Romanesque, as they are largely based on Roman building methods and models, using round arches and vaults. The great drawback to these structures was their dark and gloomy interior, as large windows would have weakened the heavy walls that supported the massive roof. Because of the sheer length of time involved in building a cathedral, there is no clear distinction between the building of Romanesque cathedrals and the arrival of Gothic architecture, its more ornate successor. Yet by the thirteenth century, architects were perfecting the techniques that

Exterior of the Cathedral of
St. Pierre at Angoulême

Interior of the Cathedral of St. Pierre at Angoulème

would allow them to create the exquisitely ornamented and light Gothic cathedrals, as exemplified by Chartres Cathedral (1194–1230). Most prominent among these innovations was the flying buttress, which allowed the architects to design larger cathedrals, with spacious interiors. The flying buttress was an exterior column, parallel to the cathedral's outer wall, connected in much the same way the sides of a vault are joined. Rows of flying buttresses were used to shift the great weight of the roof off of the walls, allowing the inclusion of large windows and huge vaulted ceilings.

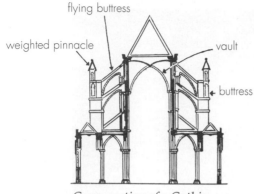

flying buttress

weighted pinnacle

vault

buttress

Cross-section of a Gothic Cathedral showing flying buttresses

With the introduction of light and larger interiors, the architects began to design more and more ornamentation for the cathedral; at the height of Gothic design, even the buttress became more than just a functional support, decorated with beautiful stonework. The cathedrals became lighted jewels, with their beautiful spires, carvings, and stained glass. What do you notice about the basic design of the cathedral?

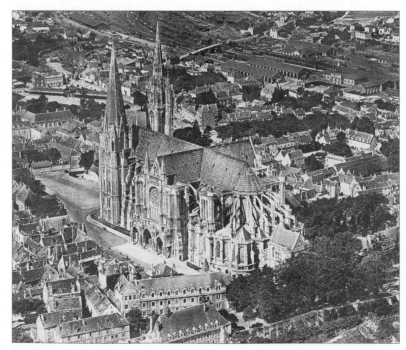

Exterior of Chartres Cathedral

The nave of Chartres Cathedral

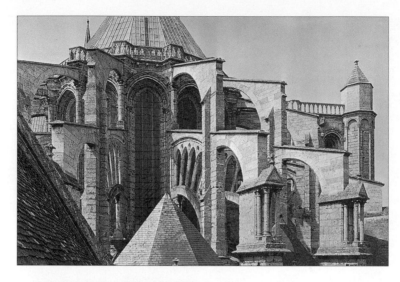

View of buttresses on the apse of Chartres Cathedral

THINKING CRITICALLY

1. *Making Comparisons* How is the interior of Chartres made more appealing than the interior of St. Pierre? What exterior differences may account for this?

2. *Making Inferences* What can you infer about the design of the cathedral? What factors or needs may have conditioned its evolution?

3. *Linking Past and Present* Look at the churches in the area around you. What Romanesque and Gothic elements still persist in religious architecture? What other kinds of buildings seem to use these elements?

WRITER'S PORTFOLIO

1. *Extending the Selection* Do some research on the decoration of the Gothic cathedral and describe the types of intricate ornamentation used by the medieval craftsmen to decorate the cathedral.

2. *Examining Key Questions* Discuss the role of the cathedral as the center of both the secular and spiritual life of a medieval city.

The Art of Love

Courtly love was a medieval code of conduct that began in Provence, a region of southeastern France, and spread to northern France, Spain, Germany, northern Italy, and England. As exemplified in love lyrics composed and sung by poets known as troubadours, this code assumes the (usually) unfulfilled love of a courtier or knight for a noblewoman.Courtly love is expressed in his valorous deeds, romantic songs, and vows of undying devotion. The lady may or may not be married and may or may not return this love. In the twelfth century, Andreas Capellanus, a chaplain at the court of the Count of Champagne, composed a set of rules for love as part of his treatise on love, the *Book on the Art of Loving Honestly*. Although Dante Alighieri (1265–1321) wrote *La Vita Nuova (The New Life)* over a century after Andreas lived, there are still echoes in his work of the ideals of courtly love. *La Vita Nuova* tells of Dante's love for Beatrice (bā′ä trē′chā). Written after her death, it is a collection of thirty-one poems interspersed with a prose narrative that is somewhat auto-biographical. In the whole work, Dante comes to conceive of his idealized love as the beginning of his spiritual growth. Dante's constant use of the number nine comes from it being the square of three, which always refers to the Christian Trinity. What similarities are there between the ideals of Andreas and those of Dante?

Andreas Capellanus, from the *Book on the Art of Loving Honestly*

These are the rules.

   I.   Marriage is no real excuse for not loving.
   II. He who is not jealous cannot love.
   III. No one can be bound by a double love.
   IV. It is well known that love is always increasing or decreasing.
   V.   That which a lover takes against the will of his beloved has no relish.

VIII.   No one should be deprived of love without the very best of reasons.

IX.   No one can love unless he is impelled by the persuasion of love.

XI.   It is not proper to love any woman whom one would be ashamed to seek to marry.

XIII.   When made public love rarely endures.

XIV.   The easy attainment of love makes it of little value; difficulty of attainment makes it prized.

XVII.   A new love puts to flight an old one.

XVIII.   Good character alone makes any man worthy of love.

XIX.   If love diminishes, it quickly fails and rarely revives.

XXI.   Real jealousy always increases the feeling of love.

XXII.   Jealousy, and therefore love, are increased when one suspects his beloved.

XXIV.   Every act of a lover ends in the thought of his beloved.

XXVI.   Love can deny nothing to love.

XXIX.   A man who is vexed by too much passion usually does not love.

XXX.   A true lover is constantly and without intermission possessed by the thought of his beloved.

XXXI.   Nothing forbids one woman being loved by two men or one man by two women.

Dante, from *La Vita Nuova*

I

In the book of my memory, after the first pages, which are almost blank, there is a section headed *Here begins the period of my boyhood.* Beneath this heading I find the words which it is my intention to copy into this smaller book, or if not all, at least their meaning.

II

Nine times the heaven of the light had revolved in its own movement since my birth and had almost returned to the same point when the woman whom my mind beholds in glory first appeared before my eyes. She was called Beatrice by many who did not know what it meant to call her this. She had lived in this world for the length of time in which the heaven of fixed stars had circled one twelfth of a degree towards the East. Thus she had not long passed the beginning of her ninth year when she appeared to me and I was almost at the end of mine when I beheld her. She was dressed in a very noble colour, a decorous and delicate crimson, tied with girdle and trimmed in a manner suited to her tender age. The moment I saw her I say in all truth that the vital spirit, which dwells in the inmost depths of the heart began to tremble so violently that I felt the vibration alarmingly in all my pulses, even the weakest of them. As it trembled, it uttered these words: *Behold a god more powerful than I who comes to rule over me.*

At this point the spirit of the senses which dwells on high in the place to which all our sense precepts are carried, was filled with amazement and, speaking especially to the spirits of vision, made this pronouncement: *Now your source of joy has been revealed.* Whereupon the natural spirit, which dwells where our nourishment is digested, began to weep and, weeping, said: *Woe is me, for I shall often be impeded from now on.* From then on indeed Love ruled over my soul, which was thus wedded to him early in life, and he began to acquire such assurance and mastery over me, owing to the power which my imagination gave him, that I was obliged to fulfil all his wishes perfectly. He often commanded me to go where perhaps I might see this angelic child and so, while I was still a boy, I often went in search of her; and I saw that in all her ways she was so praiseworthy and noble that indeed the words of the poet Homer might have been said of her: 'She did not seem the daughter of a mortal man, but of a god.' Though her image, which was always present in my mind, incited Love to dominate me, its influence was so noble that it never allowed Love to guide me without the faithful counsel of reason, in everything in which such counsel was useful to hear. But, since to dwell on the feelings and actions of such early years might appear to some to be fictitious, I will move on and, omitting many things which might be copied from the master-text from which the foregoing is derived, I come now to words inscribed in my memory under more important headings.

III

When exactly nine years had passed since this gracious being appeared to me, as I have described, it happened that on the last day of this intervening period this marvel appeared before me again, dressed in purest white, walking between two other women of distinguished bearing, both older than herself. As they walked down the street she turned her eyes towards me where I stood in fear and trembling, and with her ineffable courtesy, which is now rewarded in eternal life, she greeted me; and such was the virtue of her greeting that I seemed to experience the height of bliss. It was exactly the ninth hour of day when she gave me her sweet greeting. As this was the first time she had ever spoken to me, I was filled with such joy that, my senses reeling, I had to withdraw from the sight of others. So I returned to the loneliness of my room and began to think about this gracious person. As I thought of her, I fell asleep and a marvellous vision appeared to me. In my room I seemed to see a cloud the colour of fire, and in the cloud a lordly figure, frightening to behold, yet in himself, it seemed to me, he was filled with a marvellous joy. He said many things, of which I understood only a few; among them were the words: *I am your master*. In his arms I seemed to see a naked figure, sleeping, wrapped lightly in a crimson cloth. Gazing intently I saw it was she who had bestowed her greeting on me earlier that day. In one hand the standing figure held a fiery object, and he seemed to say, *Behold your heart*. After a little while I thought he wakened her who slept and prevailed on her to eat the glowing object in his hand. Reluctantly and hesitantly she did so. A few moments later his happiness turned to bitter grief, and, weeping, he gathered the figure in his arms and together they seemed to ascend into the heavens. I felt such anguish at their departure that my light sleep was broken, and I awoke.

THINKING CRITICALLY

1. *Identifying Central Focus* What does Dante say about love and reason and what does this suggest about his feeling for Beatrice?

2. *Making Comparisons* Which of the rules formulated by Andreas seem to apply to Dante in love?

3. *Linking Past and Present* What attributes of Beatrice does Dante admire? Are these attributes in women admired today?

WRITER'S PORTFOLIO

1. *Extending the Selection* Compare and contrast the responses of Heloise and Abelard to Andreas Capellanus's "Rules of Courtly Love."

2. *Examining Key Questions* Does an idealized love contribute to spiritual growth? Why or why not?

Science in an Age of Faith

Roger Bacon (c.1214–1292) is often called the father of English philosophy. He studied at Oxford and the University of Paris and became a Franciscan monk around 1257. Bacon was a learned man, who read with ease the Arabic and Hebrew writings on science and in particular the Greek philosophers. Before joining the Franciscan Order, he had concentrated on studying alchemy and the new science of chemistry and advocating the study of mathematics. Much of his work was forbidden by the Franciscans, who also forbade the publishing of books. Under the protection of Cardinal Foulques, who eventually became Pope Clement IV, Bacon began to write philosophy. In the following excerpt from Bacon's major work, the *Opus maius* or "Greater Work," he affirmed that theology was the supreme art, but that errors occurred in theology because many thinkers lacked learning. He advocated the study of languages — to be able to read classical philosophy — mathematics, and experimental natural science as essential to any thinker, but particularly anyone concerned with theology. Bacon was reaffirming the empirical science of Socrates and Aristotle for the Christian world. After the death of Clement IV in 1268, Bacon's writing and views proved unpopular with his superiors and he spent much of the last years in confinement for espousing "heresies." According to Bacon, what are the two methods of acquiring knowledge?

I NOW WISH TO UNFOLD THE PRINCIPLES OF EXPERIMENTAL science, since without experience nothing can be sufficiently known. For there are two modes of acquiring knowledge, namely, by reasoning and experience. Reasoning draws a conclusion and makes us grant the conclusion, but does not make the conclusion certain, nor does it remove doubt so that the mind may rest on the intuition of truth, unless the mind discovers it by the path of experience; since many have the arguments relating to what can be known, but because they lack experience they neglect the arguments, and neither avoid what is harmful nor follow what is good. For if a man who has never seen fire should prove by adequate reasoning that fire burns and injures things and destroys them, his mind would not be satisfied thereby, nor would he avoid fire, until he placed his hand or some combustible substance in the fire, so that he might prove by experience that which reasoning taught. But when he has had actual experience of combustion his mind is made certain and rests in the full light of truth. Therefore reasoning does not suffice, but experience does.

He therefore who wishes to rejoice without doubt in regard to the truths underlying phenomena must know how to devote himself to experiment. For authors write many statements, and people believe them through reasoning which they formulate without experience. Their reasoning is wholly false. For it is generally believed that the diamond cannot be broken except by goat's blood, and philosophers and theologians misuse this idea. But fracture by means of blood of this kind has never been verified, although the effort has been made; and without that blood it can be broken easily.

This science alone, therefore, knows how to test perfectly what can be done by nature, what by the effort of art, what by trickery, what the incantations, conjurations, invocations, deprecations, sacrifices, that belong to magic, mean and dream of, and what is in them, so that all falsity may be removed and the truth alone of art and nature may be retained. This science alone teaches us how to view the mad acts of magicians, that they may not be ratified but shunned, just as logic considers sophistical reasoning.

This science has three leading characteristics with respect to other sciences. The first is that it investigates by experiment the notable conclusions of all those sciences. For the other sciences know how to discover their principles by experiments, but their conclusions are reached by reasoning drawn from the principles discovered. But if they should have a particular and complete experience of their own conclusions, they must have it with the aid of this noble science. For it is true that mathematics has general experiments as regards its conclusions in its figures and calculations, which also are applied to all sciences and to this kind of experiment, because no science can be known without mathematics. But if we give our attention to particular and complete experiments and such as are attested wholly by the proper method, we must employ the principles of this science which is called experimental. I give as an example the rainbow and phenomena connected with it.

Let the experimenter first, then, examine visible objects, in order that he may find colors arranged as in the phenomena mentioned above and also the same figure…. And further let him observe rowers, and in the drops falling from the raised oars he finds the same colors when the solar rays penetrate drops of this kind. The same phenomenon is seen in water falling from the wheels of a mill; and likewise when one sees on a summer's morning the drops of dew on the grass in the meadow or field, he will observe the colors. Likewise when it is raining, if he stands in a dark place and the rays beyond it pass through the falling rain, the colors will appear in the shadow near by; and frequently at night colors appear around a candle…. Thus in an infinite number of ways colors of this kind appear, which the diligent experimenter knows how to discover.

THINKING CRITICALLY

1. *Recognizing Values* Why does Bacon put so much emphasis on experiment?

2. *Identifying Central Focus* What does Bacon think are the advantages of experimental science?

3. *Linking Past and Present* Bacon suggests that for us to know anything we must have experience of it. Yet today's science is much more complex and elusive than the medieval concern with natural phenomena. How is Bacon's method still applicable today?

WRITER'S PORTFOLIO

1. *Extending the Selection* Bacon uses two examples to illustrate the necessity of experiment — the destructive nature of fire and the breaking of a diamond. Explain the difference between these two examples.

2. *Examining Key Questions* What are some examples of things in this world that are not visible and are incapable of being verified? Does this mean they do not exist? How do these questions help to explain some of the controversies that raged in the medieval church?

Three Interpretations of the Annunciation

Most art in the Middle Ages was created for religious purposes, to teach, to inspire contemplation and prayer, and to aid the worshipper in experiencing spiritual truth. The subjects for medieval art almost always came from the Bible, and one of the most popular scenes was the Annunciation—the announcement by the Angel Gabriel to the Virgin Mary that she will give birth to the Messiah. Giotto di Bondone (c.1266–1337) is generally credited with initiating a sense of realism into Italian painting. Before Giotto (jot′ō), the Byzantine style of icon painting had prevailed, which discouraged individual expression. Giotto, however, favored a naturalism, which seemed almost revolutionary in his lifetime. Earlier painters had aimed at creating a universal figure, rendered in a stark two-dimensional style, while Giotto created figures with individually expressive faces and round, full figures. His fresco (a painting done on moist plaster with water-based pigments) of *The Annunciation*, which appears on page 217, was painted around 1306 and exhibits Giotto's warmth of detail and fullness. Simone Martini (c. 1284–1344) was another painter whose *The Annunciation* (1333) aimed at naturalism. While the background and position of his figures show the influence of Byzantine icons, the clothing and the intensely felt expressions mirror Giotto's fascination with realism and individualism. A painting that reflects the great steps Italian painting took in the years after Giotto is *The*

Simone Martini, The Annunciation *(1333)*

Annunciation (1438) of Fra Angelico (c. 1400–1455), which appears on page 217. Fra Angelico's whole composition looks forward to the accomplishments of the High Renaissance, while his figures look back to Giotto. This painting shows how the stylistic advances of the late Middle Ages became the first steps of the Renaissance. And while these stylistic advances may seem rather minor today, they were as much a revolution in art and depiction in their day as any of the major art movements of this century. In which painting is the tension between the two figures the greatest?

THINKING CRITICALLY

1. *Recognizing Values* Why do you think the Annunciation was a popular theme for painters?

2. *Making Comparisons* How does the overall effect of Fra Angelico's painting differ from the Martini painting?

3. *Linking Past and Present* Obviously the artists have used some background details that correspond to their own periods instead of to biblical settings. What setting might an artist use for a painting of the Annunciation today?

WRITER'S PORTFOLIO

1. *Extending the Selection* Try to imagine that you are a medieval Christian who has seen all three of these paintings. You cannot read, but you know the story of the Annunciation. What might you conclude from these paintings?

2. *Examining Key Questions* Discuss how the three painters interpreted the biblical scene differently. How does this reflect their attitude to the sacred?

A Vision of Hell

Without a doubt, Dante is the major literary figure of the Middle Ages. His epic poem the *Commedia*, or the *Divine Comedy* as it was later called, has come to be considered one of the masterpieces of literature. Divided into three sections, *Inferno, Purgatorio, and Paradiso*, this poem is the story of a journey through the three places of the next world, which in Roman Catholic belief are hell, where the damned are suffering; purgatory, the place where repentant sinners are purified; and heaven, where the righteous are rewarded. The poem is elaborately planned and organized: there are exactly one hundred parts, called cantos; one introductory canto and then thirty-three cantos in each of the three sections. In Italian, the cantos have a complex rhyme scheme, called *terza rima*, in which the first and third lines of each three-line stanza rhyme, and the second line rhymes with the first and third lines of the next stanza. Dante's emphasis on threes reflects the Christian concept of the Trinity, in which God is three persons (Father, Son, and Holy Ghost). The *Commedia* is an allegory, a literary form in which characters and actions represent abstract concepts. It is important to remember that, though Dante himself is the wanderer, he actually represents all humans on a spiritual journey. The figures that appear in the poem, such as the Roman poet Virgil, would have been known to Dante's audience either from literature or history. In Canto I of the *Inferno*, which appears below, Dante begins his journey through hell on Good Friday, the day on which Jesus was crucified. What state does Dante say he was in when he lost his way?

Mɪᴅᴡᴀʏ ɪɴ ᴛʜᴇ ᴊᴏᴜʀɴᴇʏ ᴏғ ᴏᴜʀ ʟɪғᴇ I ғᴏᴜɴᴅ ᴍʏsᴇʟғ ɪɴ ᴀ dark wood, for the straight way was lost. Ah, how hard it is to tell what that wood was, wild, rugged, harsh; the very thought of it renews the fear! It is so bitter that death is hardly more so. But, to treat of the good that I found in it, I will tell of the other things I saw there.

I cannot rightly say how I entered it, I was so full of sleep at the moment I left the true way; but when I had reached the foot of a hill, there at the end of the valley that had pierced my heart with fear, I looked up and saw its shoulders already clad in the rays of the planet that leads men aright by every path. Then fear was somewhat quieted that had continued in the lake of my heart through the night I had passed so piteously. And as he who with laboring breath has escaped from the deep to the shore turns to look back on the dangerous waters, so my mind which was still fleeing turned back to gaze upon the pass that never left anyone alive.

After I had rested my tired body a little I again took up my way across the desert strand, so that the firm foot was always the lower. And behold, near the beginning of the steep, a leopard light-footed and very fleet, covered with a spotted hide! And it did not depart from before my eyes, but did so impede my way that more than once I turned round to go back.

It was the beginning of the morning, and the sun was mounting with the stars that were with it when Divine Love first set those beautiful things in motion, so that the hour of the day and the sweet season gave me cause for good hope of that beast with the gay skin; yet not so much that I did not feel afraid at the sight of a lion that appeared to me and seemed to be coming at me, head high and raging with hunger, so that the air seemed to tremble at it; and a she-wolf, that in her leanness seemed laden with every craving and had already caused many to live in sorrow: she put such heaviness upon me with the fear that came from sight of her that I lost hope of the height. And like one who is eager in winning, but, when the time comes that makes him lose, weeps and is saddened in all his thoughts, such did that peaceless beast make me, as, coming on against me, she pushed me back, little by little, to where the sun is silent.

While I was ruining down to the depth there appeared before me one who seemed faint through long silence. When I saw him in the vast desert, I cried to him, "Have pity on me whatever you are, shade or living man!"

"No, not a living man, though once I was," he answered me, "and my parents were Lombards, both Mantuans by birth. I was born *sub Julio* [when Julius Caesar controlled the Roman Republic], although late, and I lived at Rome under the good Augustus, in the time of the false and lying gods. I was a poet, and I sang of that just son of Anchises [Aeneas, hero of Virgil's epic poem, the *Aeneid*] who came from Troy after proud Ilium was burned. But you, why do you return to so much woe? Why do you not climb the delectable mountain, the source and cause of every happiness?"

"Are you, then, that Virgil, that fount which pours forth so broad a stream of speech?" I answered him, my brow covered with shame. "O glory and light of other poets, may the long study and the great love that have made me search your volume avail me! You are my master and my author. You alone are he from whom I took the fair style that has done me honor. See the beast that has turned me back. Help me against her, famous sage, for she makes my veins and pulses tremble."

"It behooves you to go by another way if you would escape from this wild place," he answered when he saw me weep, "for this beast, the cause of your complaint, lets no man pass her way, but so besets him that she slays him; and she has a nature so vicious and malign that she never sates her greedy appetite and after feeding is hungrier than before…. Therefore I think and deem it best that you should follow me, and I will be your guide and lead you hence through an eternal place, where you shall hear the despairing shrieks and see the ancient tormented spirits who all bewail the second death. Then you shall see those who are content in the fire because they hope to come among the blessed, whensoever that may be; and to these if you would ascend, there shall be a soul worthier than I to guide you; with her I shall leave you at my departing. For the Emperor who reigns there above wills not that I come into His city, because I was rebellious to His law. In all parts is His empire, in that part is His kingdom, there is His city and His lofty seat. Oh, happy he whom He elects thereto!"

And I to him, "Poet, I beseech you, by that God whom you did not know, so that I may escape this ill and worse, lead me whither you said just now, that I may see St. Peter's gate and those whom you term so woeful."

Then he set out, and I followed after him.

In Dante's scheme, hell has nine concentric rings that circle downward, the inner rings being reserved for the worst sinners. In Canto XXVI he reaches the Eighth Circle of hell where those guilty of fraud are punished. Circle Eight has ten divisions, called *Bolgias* ("ditches" or "pouches"). As Dante and Virgil move downward, they pass fortune tellers, grafters, hypocrites, and thieves, until they reach

Bolgia Eight, the place for evil counselors, where Dante sees the Homeric heroes Ulysses and Diomedes. What prompts Ulysses to relate his story?

I WAS STANDING ON THE BRIDGE, HAVING RISEN UP TO SEE, SO that if I had not laid hold of a rock I should have fallen below without a push; and my leader, who saw me so intent, said "Within the fires are the spirits: each swathes himself with that which burns him."

"Master," I replied, "I am the more certain for hearing you, but already I thought it was so, and already I wanted to ask: who is in that fire which comes so divided at its top that it seems to rise from the pyre where Eteocles was laid with his brother?"

He answered me, "Therewithin are tormented Ulysses and Diomedes, and they go together thus under the vengeance as once under the wrath; and in the flame they groan for the ambush of the horse [the Trojan horse] which made the gate by which the noble seed of the Romans went forth...."

After the flame had come where it seemed to my leader the time and place, I heard him speak in this manner: "O you who are two within one fire, if I deserved of you while I lived, if I deserved of you much or little when in the world I wrote the lofty lines, move not; but let the one of you tell where he went, lost, to die"

The greater horn of the ancient flame began to wag, murmuring, like one that is beaten by a wind; then carrying to and fro its tip, as if it were a tongue that spoke, it flung forth a voice and said, "When I departed from Circe, who had detained me more than a year there near Gaeta, before Aeneas had so named it, neither fondness for my son, nor reverence for my aged father, not the due love which would have made Penelope glad, could conquer in me the longing that I had to gain experience of the world, and of human vice and worth. But I put forth on the deep open sea with one vessel only, and with that small company which had not deserted me. The one shore and the other I saw as far as Spain, as far as Morocco, and Sardinia, and the other islands which that sea bathes round. I and my companions were old and slow when we came to that narrow outlet where Hercules set up his markers, that men should not pass beyond. On the right hand I left Seville, on the other I had already left Ceyta. 'O brothers,' I said 'who through a hundred thousand dangers have reached the west, to this so brief vigil of our senses that remains to us, choose not to deny experience, following the sun, of the world that has no people. Consider your origin: you were not made to live as brutes, but to pursue virtue and knowledge.'

"With this little speech I made my companions so keen for the voyage that then I could hardly have held them back. And turning our stern to the morning, we made of our oars wings for the mad flight, always gaining on the left. The night now saw the other pole and all its stars, and ours so low that it did not rise from the ocean floor. Five times the light beneath the moon had been rekindled and as many quenched, since we had entered on the passage of the deep, when there appeared to us a mountain dark in the distance, and to me it seemed the highest I had ever seen. We rejoiced, but soon our joy was turned to grief, for from the new land a whirlwind rose and struck the forepart of the ship. Three times it whirled her round with all the waters, and the fourth time it lifted the stern aloft and plunged the prow below, as pleased Another, till the sea closed over us."

THINKING CRITICALLY

1. *Identifying Central Issues* In order to reach his goal of heaven, Dante must first travel through hell. Why do you think Dante imposed this allegorical journey on his wanderer?

2. *Recognizing Values* The sins of Ulysses and Diomedes are alluded to only briefly and may not seem very serious, yet Dante chose those two figures to represent evil counselors. What does Dante's choice tell you about him and his intended audience?

3. *Linking Past and Present* What three historical figures of the last 100 years would you assign to the flames with other evil counselors?

WRITER'S PORTFOLIO

1. *Extending the Selection* Dante conceives of error as a dark wood. Rewrite the first nine lines using urban images.

2. *Examining Key Questions* Analyze how Dante seems to view the relationship between the sacred and the secular.

Gothic Illumination

The illustrating, or illuminating, of manuscripts was the most important form of painting in northern Europe during the early fifteenth century. Crucial to the development of medieval manuscript illumination was the popularity of devotional books or books of hours. These volumes designed for lay people, not the clergy, contained prayers to be said at the seven canonical hours, periods of the day that called for certain devotions. While most people purchased these books to have their prayers at hand, wealthy aristocrats vied to commission and purchase the most lavish and ornamented copies. Most famous of the book of hours is *Les Très Riches Heures* commissioned by Jean, Duke of Berry (1340–1416). He was a wealthy patron of the arts, a brother of King Charles V, and at one time controlled over a third of France, including the Duchy of Berry. The Duke commissioned illuminations for this volume from the greatest

Brothers Limbourg, October *from*
Les Très Riches Heures *(1416)*

manuscript painters of the day, the Brothers Limbourg. They created twelve illuminations each depicting life during one of the months of the year and containing pictures of the Duke's lavish residences and references to his life. The two illuminations reproduced on pages 215 and 218, depict April and October. *April* pictures the sheltered and luxurious life known to the aristocracy of medieval life, while *October* shows the hard life of the peasantry in contrast to life at the opulent castle of the Louvre in the background. What differences do you note between the dress and expressions of the figures in the two illuminations?

THINKING CRITICALLY

1. *Making Inferences* Do you notice any differences in the way nature is depicted for the peasants versus the nobility?

2. *Making Comparisons* How have the Brothers Limbourg emphasized the hard life of the peasants? How have they emphasized the ease of the nobility?

3. *Linking Past and Present* Do you notice such disparities of life between classes today? Do styles of dress express these differences in modern society?

WRITER'S PORTFOLIO

1. *Extending the Selection* Write an essay describing what a modern book of hours would look like. Be sure to describe not just the pictures of daily life, but also the texts that would be included.

2. *Examining Key Questions* Discuss what you can infer about the relationship between the sacred and the secular from books of hours.

Giotto, The Annunciation *(1306)*

Fra Angelico, The Annuciation *(1438)*

Brothers Limbourg, April
from Les Très Riches Heures *(1416)*

Masaccio, The Holy Trinity with
Virgin, St. John, and Donors *(1427)*

Vermeer, The Allegory of Painting *(1662)*

EXAMINING KEY QUESTIONS

> • What is the relationship between the sacred and
>   the secular?
> • How should we love?

Throughout this chapter, most selections have concluded with a writing
project asking you to discuss how the art or literature you have examined provides answers to one of these key questions. The following
writing projects will help you draw together what you have learned by
examining how several selections illustrate these key questions.

• Compare and contrast the different ideals of love expressed in at least
  two of the following selections: "The Wanderer," Peter Abelard's
  Historia calamitatum, Heloise's "Reply to Abelard," Andreas
  Capellanus's "Rules of Courtly Love," and Dante's *La Vita Nuova.*

• Illustrate the relationship between the sacred and secular in medieval
  culture by using two or more of the following selections: Bede's
  history, the Bayeaux Tapestry, Foucher's chronicle of the First
  Crusade, medieval cathedrals, paintings by Giotto, Simone Martini,
  and Fra Angelico, and Roger Bacon's *Opus maius.*

SPEAKING/LISTENING

• With other students, read "The Wanderer" aloud. Discuss its despairing tone, identifying modern equivalents to its Dark Age imagery and
  references.

CRAFTING

• Using any medium that you like, create a series of images in the style
  of the Bayeux Tapestry that depicts episodes in some event in the history of the community in which you live.

COLLECTING

• Collect a gallery of modern images that reflects contemporary impressions of one or more aspects of the Middle Ages, such as knighthood,
  the Crusades, alchemy, Gothic architecture, courtly love, and so on.

Detail of The Three Magi
(1459–1461) *by Benozzo Gozzoli,*
showing Lorenzo de Medici

The Age of the Renaissance

INTRODUCTION by David Bevington

PORTFOLIO

The Art of the Sonnet (1350–1600)
Petrarch, "The Man of Letters," Sonnets 10 and 17; Louise Labé, Sonnets 8 and 24; William Shakespeare, Sonnets 29 and 73

The Development of Perspective (1400s–1600s)
Masaccio, *The Holy Trinity with Virgin, St. John, and Donors*; Jan van Eyck, *The Madonna and Chancellor Rolin*; Andrea Mantegna, *The Dead Christ*; Jan Vermeer, *Allegory of Painting*

Man and Nature (1480s)
Giovanni Pico Della Mirandola, "Oration on the Dignity of Man"; Leonardo da Vinci, "The Vitruvian Man"

Sculpting David (1432–1501)
Donatello, *David*; Verrocchio, *David*; Michelangelo, *David*

The Rule of Princes (1513 and 1556)
Niccolò Machiavelli, *The Prince*; Charles V, "Instructions to Phillip II, His Son"

The High Renaissance (1510–1514)
Raphael, *The School of Athens* and *Poetry*

The New World (1452–1544)
Christopher Columbus, "Letter to the Spanish Treasurer"; Leardo Map; Agnese Map

The Northern Renaissance (1434–1526)
Jan van Eyck, *Giovanni Arnolfini and His Bride*; Quentin Matsys, *The Banker and His Wife*; Matthias Grünewald, *The Small Crucifixion*

The Reformation (1520)
Martin Luther, "Address to the Christian Nobility of the German Nation"

Mannerism (1586 and 1599)
El Greco, *The Burial of Count Orgaz* and *Saint Martin and the Beggar*

The Heliocentric World (1543 and 1610)
Nicolaus Copernicus, *De revolutionibus orbium coelestium*; Galileo Galilei, *The Sidereal Messenger*; engravings of the Ptolemaic and Copernican universes

The Search for Truth (1637 and 1641)
René Descartes, *The Discourse on Method* and *Meditations on First Philosophy*

The Freedom of the Press (1644)
John Milton, *Areopagitica*

CHAPTER 6 PROJECTS

CHAPTER 6

The Age of the Renaissance

1350–1650

Dome of Florence Cathedral

1436
Dome of the Cathedral of Florence is finished

DAVID BEVINGTON

Phyllis Fay Horton Professor in the Humanities, University of Chicago

Was there really a Renaissance in Europe in the fourteenth, fifteenth, and sixteenth centuries? We should not be too quick to accept such historical generalizations. The term "Renaissance," meaning rebirth, is of nineteenth-century coinage and reflects that age's belief in a progressive view of Western history leading forward to the glories of industrialization, democracy, and scientific innovation in our modern era. Especially in Protestant countries like England, it was tempting to think of the time before the sixteenth-century Reformation as the Dark Ages of Catholic superstition and ignorance. Actually, of course, the Middle Ages saw flourishing periods of arts and learning, as during the reign of Charlemagne (771–814), and during what is often called the twelfth- and thirteenth-century renaissance, when French Gothic architecture reached its perfection and Paris became a center for theological study.

Even if it was not unique, the period we now call the Renaissance nonetheless did experience a quickening of pace and an excited sense of rediscovery that changed the course of Western history. By all accounts, the process began in Italy and moved northward. The Renaissance did not really have a major impact on the Netherlands and northern Germany until the late fifteenth century and on England and Spain until the early sixteenth century. Travel was slow, and

Engraving of Prince Henry

Gutenberg Bible

1439
Prince Henry of Portugal founds naval institute

1454
Gutenberg establishes his printing press

ideas imported from the south had to compete with local habits of thought and expression.

THE BIRTH OF HUMANISM

Francesco Petrarca, or Petrarch (1304–1374), was one of the early Italian so-called humanists. He and other scholarly writers devoted themselves to the study of the language, literature, and architecture of the ancient world, first of classical Rome and then of Greece. Fourteenth-century Italy and especially Rome could, after all, trace a direct lineage back to the Roman empire that had produced Virgil, Ovid, Cicero, Plautus, and many other literary giants. Petrarch and others like him were struck with the importance of rediscovering these ancient writers and of using them as models for an Italian civilization that would then rise above what they took to be the parochial achievements of Italian medieval vernacular culture. Writing in the mid-fourteenth century, Petrarch was indeed a humanist—that is, one committed not only to reviving the glories of classical Rome but more broadly to encouraging those studies that deepen the meaning of human culture. Although it embraced the Christian faith that was so deeply embedded in Western civilization, humanism subtly shifted attention away from theological abstraction to the quality of what it is to be human, to aspire, to yearn for newly discovered knowledge. The Italian humanist Giovanni Pico della Mirandola (1463–1494) was also a Neoplatonist, that is, one of those who sought to reconcile Platonic philosophy with religious thought and especially mysticism. The result was a triumphant affirmation of the perfectibility of human reason under God. Pico's "Oration on the Dignity of Man," 1486, celebrates a human race "constrained by no limits" in pursuing the potential of its own free will. Later humanists pursued philosophical inquiry still further in the direction of what we now recognize as scientific

Portuguese
caravel

1498
Vasco da Gama reaches India

1503–1505
*Leonardo da Vinci paints
the Mona Lisa*

rationalism. Michel de Montaigne (1533–1592), French aristocrat and essayist, gave his contemporaries a strikingly heterodox way of thinking about humanity and its supposed place at the top of the Great Chain of Being. No less unsettling was the startling proposition of the French skeptical philosopher René Descartes (1596–1650): "I think, therefore I am."

THE VISUAL ARTS

The visual and graphic arts followed a similar course of development. Although relatively little painting survived from ancient classical Rome, sculpture was plentifully in evidence even if sometimes badly in need of restoration. Roman sculpture paid impressive tribute to the human body. Even when its subject was nominally religious, in depicting the Roman gods, classical sculpture ennobled the human figure with careful anatomical attention to muscular stance, facial expression, movement, cascading folds of drapery, and the like. Greek vase painting from the sixth century B.C. and later similarly glorified the human shape in motion and often in distinctly secular surroundings.

Masaccio's *The Holy Trinity with Virgin, St. John, and Donors*, painted in about 1427 for a parish church in Florence, expressively captures the way in which Renaissance Italian artists went about representing the human figure and its surroundings in a context that is still devoutly Christian. The fresco painting centers on crucified Christ, behind whom God the Father towers as a timeless icon of divine wisdom. The Virgin Mary and St. John flank the cross at its base, gesturing toward the deeply meaningful image of Christ's sacrifice. At the same time, the painting calls attention not only to the anatomical realism of Christ's suffering body but to the architectural space in which the scene is contained. Perspective drawing, a recent discovery in Renaissance Italian art, accentuates the three-dimensionality of the depiction. The fresco appears to be,

Holbein portrait of Henry VIII

Dürer portrait of Erasmus

1509
Henry VIII becomes king of England

1511
Erasmus publishes The Praise of Folly

as it were, a niche in the church wall where the paintings hung, its perspective art drawing the viewer's eye into the dark recesses at the painting's center. Strikingly, the architecture is neoclassical and Roman in style, with its bold Corinthian columns flanking a Romanesque arch. In the foreground, the donors or patrons add to the sense of secular immediacy. *The Dead Christ* by Mantegna (1431–1506) is similarly conceived: its subject is the mourning of the Virgin Mary for her crucified son, while at the same time the painter is plainly fascinated with a sculpted sense of anatomical form. New techniques in perspective make possible the bold representation of the dead human body from the foot of the space where Christ lies, looking upward along the foreshortened body to the face of one who has suffered the agony of death. Lighting details highlight the folds of the cloth that covers Christ's legs. The holes in Christ's hands and feet, visible as in an anatomy class taught by the great Belgian anatomist

Andreas Vesalius (1514–1564), are no longer symbolically stylized as in much medieval art; they are physically convincing.

In a similar vein, Leonardo da Vinci's "The Vitruvian Man," c. 1487, captures not only a delight in the human body but a sense of its perfect proportions and its ability to mirror ideal geometrical correspondences in the universe that surrounds us. Significantly, the inspiration for this idea, Vitruvius, was an architect of ancient Rome (c. 40 B.C.). With Donatello's and Verrocchio's renditions of *David*, c. 1432 and 1465, we see sculptors turning to biblical subject matter for a study of the human figure. And with Michelangelo's *David*, begun in 1501, we reach a justly famous evocation of what it is to be a human. Northern artists of the fifteenth and sixteenth centuries like Jan van Eyck, Quentin Matsys, and Matthias Grünewald explore ways of combining religious subjects with domestic scenes of marriage or commerce, with loving

Frontispiece of
Luther's Bible

Titian portrait
of Charles V

1517
Martin Luther posts the 95 Theses

1556
Charles V abdicates his throne

landscapes in the background depicting the bustling prosperity of contemporary life in northern cities, and with myriad physical details of the here and now. In Spain, the Cretan-born El Greco shows the arrival in that country in the late sixteenth century of a humanistic focus: his *Saint Martin and the Beggar* takes as its subject an incident in the life of a saint, and yet the painter's interest is in the nearly naked beggar contrasted with the aristocratically dressed young rider and his spirited mount.

Political responses to currents of new thought and expression could take iconoclastic forms. More than any other, Niccolò Machiavelli gave expression to humanistic longings for political stability arising out of the competitive rivalries among fragmented Italian city states. His *The Prince*, 1513, took as its hero Cesare Borgia, the son of one of Italy's most ruthless and immoral popes whose family undertook to establish its rule in central Italy by whatever means nec-

essary. Machiavelli's advice to a prince, "that it is safer to be feared than loved" in the likely event that one must choose between the two, that one must learn to dissemble skillfully, that the mob is easily taken in by appearances, and the like, sounds thoroughly cynical, and yet paradoxically his writing breathes with optimism about the potential of humankind to improve its lot through political manipulation and war. Machiavelli was a hated name, especially in England, where his enemies saw his teaching as atheistic and immoral, but even so his political philosophy was immensely influential (as we can see from Charles V's practical and worldly advice to his son in 1556).

THE SPIRIT OF THE AGE Discovery was the byword of the age. It took the form of exploration across the Atlantic Ocean and to other parts of the world, motivated by a heady mix of commercial greed, human curiosity, and a zealous resolve to convert native populations

Elizabeth I

1558
Elizabeth I becomes Queen of England

1571
Battle of Lepanto

to Christianity. The map of the known world expanded immensely during this era, even if the finding of a westward sea route to China and the rich East Indies remained a will o' the wisp. Columbus thought he had reached "the Indies" in 1492, with the result that native Americans have been known ever since as "Indians." Today we are aware that discovery of the "new world" brought with it ravaging diseases and the beginnings of environmental exploitation, along with appalling massacres of native populations, but in any event the discovery did occur.

The spirit of discovery led also to the invention of printing from movable type by Johannes Gutenberg (1400?–1468), with its almost incalculable influence on a wider readership and improved education. In astronomy, the world had long accepted a model of the universe put forward by Ptolemy of Alexandria in the second century A.D., based on the mathematical work of Hipparchus of Athens in about 130 B.C.

According to Ptolemy, the flat earth stood at the center of nine concentric spheres containing (in order from the center outward) the moon, Mercury, Venus, the sun, Mars, Jupiter, Saturn, the fixed stars on a single plane, and a primum mobile that imparted motion to the whole. Variations were proposed, but no scheme departed from the earth-centered model that put us and our world at the center of God's universe. Hell stood within the earth or beneath it, while heaven, with its nine orders of angels, stood at the top of everything. Life on earth seemed to conform to this hierarchical arrangement, with the king at the apex of the state and the pope at the head of the church; below them, in feudal fashion, nobles ruled over commoners and fathers over their families.

Yet the mathematics of Ptolemaic astronomy proved increasingly cumbersome as more accurate observations were made of movements of the heavenly bodies. The planets especially had a troublesome way of sliding in a

Title page of
Don Quixote

1599
Globe Theater is built

1605
*Cervantes publishes
Part I of Don Quixote*

retrograde direction from time to time, counter to the usual motion of the spheres. These seeming irregularities could be calculated in the mathematical shape of epicycles but were hard to explain until Nicolaus Copernicus presented, in his *De revolutionibus orbium coelestium*, 1543, the challenging hypothesis (proposed in fact in the ancient world by Aristarchus of Samos in the third century B.C. but long forgotten) of a sun-centered system. Resistance to the notion was understandably intense, but the hypothesis did offer a simplified way of accounting for the motions of the planets. Indeed, as Copernicus insisted, the new solar system had a wonderful symmetry of its own. Then, in 1610, Galileo Galilei published the results of his telescopic observations of the irregular surface of the moon and of the existence of moons orbiting around Jupiter, thereby confirming experimentally what Copernicus had proposed in theoretical form. The Catholic Church's opposition was so vociferous

that Galileo was forced to recant his ideas, but the truth of his observations could not long be ignored.

THE REFORMATION

Yet, probably no change during the Renaissance had as great an effect on people's individual lives as the Reformation. Urgings toward reform within the Catholic Church were nothing new; heretical movements in the fourteenth century urged piety, humility, and availability of the Gospels in vernacular tongues. Certainly the Church of Rome was susceptible to corrupt worldliness. When, however, Martin Luther nailed his ninety-five theses to the door of the court church at Wittenberg in 1517 detailing the abuses of indulgences and the like, he forced a break with Rome that was fueled by German nationalism and that soon spread to other countries. Theologically, Lutheranism emphasized human depravity and the absolute need for God's grace; the institutional Church and its sacraments were to an

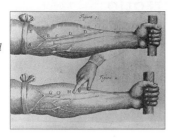

Diagram
of arm and
veins

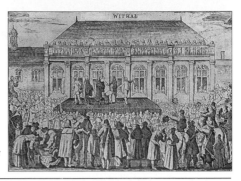

Execution of
Charles I

1628
*William Harvey explains
the circulation of the blood*

1649
Charles I is executed in England

extent demoted to place more of a burden on the individual sinner. John Calvin (1509–1564) in Geneva put even greater stress on predestinate good and evil, and urged the autonomy of individual congregations in place of hierarchical bishoprics. More radical sects called for even greater democracy and for acknowledgment of the individual Christian as the best interpreter of truth. In England, Henry VIII's domestic difficulties in 1529 and following led to a break with Rome and the naming of Henry as head of the English Church. Religious wars were almost incessant from this time onward, culminating among other horrors in a general massacre of Huguenots or French Protestants in 1572. The features of the Reformation that contributed especially to the intellectual currents of the Renaissance were its appeal to individual conscience and authority, its combativeness toward traditional authority, and its nationalism.

The Renaissance came late to England, and never produced a great wealth of painting or sculpture. It did however result in a remarkable flourishing of literature. William Shakespeare (1564–1616) is in some ways the quintessential Renaissance artist, fascinated by a new Machiavellian pragmatism in his history plays, deeply concerned with issues of personal choice in an arena of potentially tragic conflict, wanting to believe in the human readiness to discover a "brave new world." Part of his greatness is the result of a newly discovered capacity of the English language to recapture the greatness of expression that had once belonged to ancient Rome and Greece. Others too, in England, like Edmund Spenser, John Donne, and later John Milton, breathed the excitement of what they perceived to be an age of discovery. Perhaps the best of their achievements rest on the fact that they inherited a vibrant sense of the classical past and yet were able to transform their artistic visions into ones that were expressive of their own time.

The Art of the Sonnet

The poet Francesco Petrarca (1304–1374), generally known as Petrarch (**pē′trärk**), is considered to be the first of the great humanist writers of the Renaissance. While traveling in Avignon, he caught sight of a beautiful married woman named Laura and fell hopelessly in love. Over the next twenty years Petrarch wrote poems to her. He developed a tightly controlled fourteen-line poetic form, called a *sonnet*, to capture and express the intensity of his love. The sonnet's first eight lines (the octave) contain a rhyme scheme of *abbaabba*. These lines present an observation, a problem, or a situation. The last six lines (the sestet), rhyming *cdecde*, bring a resolution or conclusion to the situation. This form proved to be vastly popular with both poets and readers and gave birth to scores of imitators. Two hundred years later Louise Labé (**lwēz lä bā′**) (c. 1524–1566), a French poet, proved to be another master of this form. Although she wrote in the style of Petrarch, her work is sharply set off from that of his many imitators by its honesty of emotion and lyrical intensity. In the 1590s, William Shakespeare (1564–1616) modified the sonnet form and made it his own. The Shakespearean sonnet contains three quatrains, rhyming *abab cdcd efef*, followed by a couplet, *gg*. The quatrains usually present a number of images, observations, or feelings which are brought to a conclusion by the couplet. As with Petrarch and other masters of this verse form, Shakespeare's sonnets are intensely personal, filled with the extremes of emotional life, as well as the contrasting results of sensory experience. The following selections are sonnets by Petrarch, Labé, and Shakespeare, preceded by a selection from Petrarch's "The Man of Letters," an essay describing the poetry of the early Renaissance. Why do you think such a tightly structured verse form would appeal to readers and poets?

Petrarch, "The Man of Letters"

Is it then true that this disease of writing, like other malignant disorders, is, as the Satirist [the Roman poet Lucilius] claims, incurable, and, as I begin to fear, contagious as well? How many, do you reckon, have caught it from me? Within our memory, it was rare enough for people to write verses. But now there is no one who does not write them; few indeed write anything else. Some think that the fault, so far as our contemporaries are concerned, is largely mine. I have heard this from many, but I solemnly declare, as I hope sometime to be granted immunity from the other ills of the soul — for I look for none from this — that I am now at last suddenly awakened for the first time by warning signs to a consciousness that this may perhaps be true; while intent only upon my own welfare, I may have been unwittingly injuring, at the same time, myself and others. I fear that the reproaches of an aged father, who unexpectedly came to me, with a long face and almost in tears, may not be without foundation. "While I," he said, "have always honored your name, see the return you make in compassing the ruin of my only son!" I stood for a time in embarrassed silence, for the age of the man and the expression of his face, which told of great sorrow, went to my heart. Then, recovering myself, I replied, as was quite true, that I was unacquainted with either him or his son. "What matters it," the old man answered, "whether you know him or not? He certainly knows you. I have spent a great deal in providing instruction for him in the civil law, but he declares that he wishes to follow in your footsteps. My fondest hopes have been disappointed, and I presume that he will never be either a lawyer or a poet." At this neither I nor the others present could refrain from laughter, and he went off none the better humored. But now I recognize that this merriment was ill-timed, and that the poor old man deserved our consolation, for his complaints and his reproaches were not ungrounded. Our sons formerly employed themselves in preparing such papers as might be useful to themselves or their friends, relating to family affairs, business, or the wordy din of the courts.

But all this would be nothing if, incredible as it may seem, this subtle poison had not just now begun to show its effects in the Roman Curia [Senate-house] itself. What do you think the lawyers and doctors are up to? Justinian [emperor of Eastern Roman Empire, creator of famous legal code] and Aesculapius [Greek god of healing] have palled upon them. The sick and the litigious cry in vain for their help, for they are deafened by the thunder of Homer's and Virgil's names…. Even carpenters, fullers, and ploughmen leave the implements of their calling to talk of Apollo and the Muses. I cannot say how far the plague, which lately was confined to a few, has now spread.

Petrarch

10

I find no peace and bear no arms for war,
    I fear, I hope; I burn yet shake with chill;
    I fly the Heavens, huddle to earth's floor,
    Embrace the world yet all I grasp is nil.
Love will not close nor shut my prison's door
    Nor claim me his nor leave me to my will;
    He slays me not yet holds me evermore;
    Would have me lifeless yet bound to my ill.
Eyeless I see and tongueless I protest,
    And long to perish while I succor seek;
    Myself I hate and would another woo.
I feed on grief, I laugh with sob-racked breast,
    And death and life alike to me are bleak:
    My lady, thus I am because of you.

17

Life hurries on, a frantic refugee,
    And Death, with great forced marches, follows fast;
    And all the present leagues with all the past
    And all the future to make war on me.
Anticipation joins to memory
    To search my soul with daggers; and at last,
    Did not damnation set me so aghast,
    I'd put an end to thinking, and be free.
The few glad moments that my heart has known
    Return to me; then I foresee in dread
    The winds upgathering against my ways,
Storm in the harbor, and the pilot prone,
    The mast and rigging down; and dark and dead
    The lovely lights whereon I used to gaze.

Louise Labé

8

I live, I die, I burn myself and drown.
I am extremely hot in suffering cold:
my life is soft and harness uncontrolled.

When I am happy, then I ache and frown.
Suddenly I am laughing while I cry
and in my pleasure I endure deep grief:
my joy remains and slips out like a thief.
Suddenly I am blooming and turn dry.
So Love inconstantly leads me in vain
and when I think my sorrow has no end
unthinkingly I find I have no pain.
But when it seems that joy is in my reign
and an ecstatic hour is mine to spend,
He comes and I, in ancient grief, descend.

24

Don't blame me, ladies, if I've loved. No sneers
if I have felt a thousand torches burn,
a thousand wounds, a thousand daggers turn
in me, if I have burnt my life with tears.
Especially, leave my good name alone.
If I have failed, my hurt is very plain.
Don't sharpen razors to increase my pain,
but know that love, whom none of you have known,
needing no Vulcan to excuse your flame,
nor beautiful Adonis for your shame,
can make you fall in love and anywhere.
You will have fewer chances for relief,
your passion will be stronger and more rare,
and so beware of a more shattering grief.

***

William Shakespeare

29

When, in disgrace with Fortune and men's eyes,
I all alone beweep my outcast state,
And trouble deaf heaven with my bootless cries,
And look upon myself and curse my fate,
Wishing me like to one more rich in hope,
Featur'd like him, like him with friends possess'd,
Desiring this man's art and that man's scope,
With what I most enjoy contented least;
Yet in these thoughts myself almost despising,

Haply I think on thee, and then my state,
Like to the lark at break of day arising
From sullen earth, sings hymns at heaven's gate;
    For thy sweet love rememb'red such wealth brings
    That then I scorn to change my state with kings.

73

That time of year thou mayst in me behold
When yellow leaves, or none, or few, do hang
Upon those boughs which shake against the cold,
Bare ruin'd choirs, where late the sweet birds sang.
In me thou see'st the twilight of such day
As after sunset fadeth in the west,
Which by and by black night doth take away,
Death's second self, that seals up all in rest.
In me thou see'st the glowing of such fire
That on the ashes of his youth doth lie,
As the deathbed whereon it must expire,
Consum'd with that which it was nourish'd by.
    This thou perceiv'st, which makes thy love more strong,
    To love that well, which thou must leave ere long.

THINKING CRITICALLY

1. *Recognizing Values* What value does Petrarch place on poetry and poets?

2. *Making Comparisons* Compare and contrast the three poets' ideas about and attitudes towards love.

3. *Linking Past to Present* Find examples of the sonnet form in recent poetry. How has the form changed over the centuries?

WRITER'S PORTFOLIO

1. *Extending the Selection* Write a sonnet of your own, using either the Petrarchan or the Shakespearean form.

2. *Examining Key Questions* How would you characterize these writers' attitudes towards nature and mankind?

The Development
of Perspective

Just as the writers of the Renaissance found forms and techniques to express their new ideas about the place of men and women in the world, so too did the artists discover new means of expression. As notions of the world became more centered on the here-and-now, artists paid closer attention to what this physical world actually looked like and how to re-create it. In painting, one of the ways was through the use of linear perspective. Linear perspective is a drafting technique that gives the illusion that a two-dimensional flat surface is actually three-dimensional. This effect is achieved by using a vanishing point, a point toward which receding parallel lines seem to converge, on the horizon line of the painting. As the artist sketches in figures and objects, all must be seen in accurate relation to the vanishing point; therefore the size and proportion of one figure in relation to all others is more realistic. The later work of the Italian painter Masaccio (**mä zät′chō**) demonstrates the use of linear perspective. In *The Holy Trinity with Virgin, St. John, and Donors* (1427), which appears on page 219, which was painted on the wall of a church in Florence, the sense of three-dimensionality is so vivid that a viewer in the church might believe that the niche has been carved into the wall. Another extraordinary use of perspective is *The Madonna with Chancellor Rolin* (1433) by Jan van Eyck (**yän van īk**), which appears on page 254. Van Eyck painted an interior portrait of the Madonna and the solemn Chancellor, coupled with an exterior view of a garden and

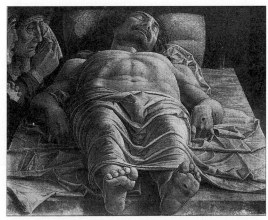

Andrea Mantegna, **The Dead Christ** *(c. 1466)*

city in the background. The eye is drawn towards this exterior by the strong lines and perspective of the tiled floor and the columns. The use of perspective has enriched this portrait of a prominent churchman, by depicting the whole world of the subject. *The Dead Christ* (c. 1466) by Andrea Mantegna (**än dre′ä män te′nyä**), which appears on page 237, is a masterpiece of foreshortening, a technique of perspective in which the lines of a body are compressed in order to appear more real. Here even the wounds on Christ's hands and feet appear strikingly three-dimensional. Two hundred years later, Jan Vermeer (**yän vər mēr′**) a Dutch painter, brought the realistic brilliance of Renaissance painting to its height through his masterful use of perspective and light. *Allegory of Painting* (1662), which appears on page 220, is an example of Vermeer's finest work. The concerns here are even more centered on the here-and-now and a consciousness of the self in this world. In this painting, the artist reflects upon himself and his own personal world while he is working in his studio, just as Vermeer, himself, was doing as he painted. How does the concern with realism affect the spiritual themes of these works?

THINKING CRITICALLY

1. *Recognizing Values* What does a stress on realism and fidelity to nature tell you about the artist and his era?

2. *Drawing Conclusions* It was the custom to include the likeness of the patron or donor in the painting commissioned. Why do you think people would want their portrait included in a religious painting?

3. *Linking Past and Present* Most twentieth century paintings do not employ the technique of linear perspective. Why do you think that painters have for the most part abandoned this technique today?

WRITER'S PORTFOLIO

1. *Extending the Selection* How does Vermeer's painting function as an allegory? What does it tell you about his world and his art?

2. *Examining Key Questions* How did linear perspective help Renaissance painters present a view of the world that was different from the view of earlier times?

Man and Nature

In 1462, an academy was established in Florence for the purpose of studying and discussing the works of the ancient Greeks, particularly those of Plato. This admiration of Plato came to be known as Neoplatonism, a philosophical school combining classical Greek ideals, Christian beliefs, and astrological theories. Those who espoused Neoplatonism believed in the dignity and freedom of humankind, as well as the human ability to take control and transform one's life for the good. Neoplatonic ideals included beauty, goodness, reason, and love; the goal of human life was to know God. One of the members of this academy was Giovanni Pico Della Mirandola (1463–1494), who, although he lived to be only thirty-one, is regarded as one of the most brilliant men of the Italian Renaissance. In his best-known work, "Oration on the Dignity of Man," an excerpt of which appears on page 240, Pico expresses his belief in human dignity and the freedom to choose one's own destiny. Unlike Pico, Leonardo da Vinci (1452–1519) enjoyed a long life, living to be almost seventy. But like Pico, he was one of the great geniuses of his time, expressing his brilliance in everything, from inventing to engineering to painting. Leonardo believed that painters should study the natural world with all their sensory capabilities and not simply imitate the work of earlier painters. It was from this constant study that Leonardo hoped to perceive the ideal forms of nature. In his notebook sketch of a man,

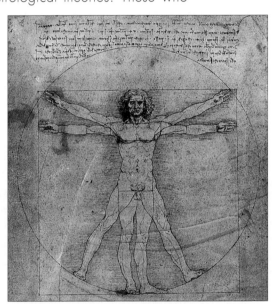

Leonardo da Vinci, notebook sketch "The Vitruvian Man" (c.1487)

commonly known as "The Vitruvian Man," which appears on page 239, Leonardo attempted to depict his belief that there was a universal system of order expressed in the corresponding proportions between the human figure and certain ideal geometric shapes, namely the square and the circle. What common ideal can be found in both Pico's and Leonardo's depictions of man?

NOW THE HIGHEST FATHER, GOD THE ARCHITECT, ACCORDING to the laws of His secret wisdom, built this house of the world, this world which we see, the most sacred temple of His divinity. He adorned the region beyond the heavens with Intelligences, He animated the celestial spheres with eternal souls, and He filled the excrementary and filthy parts of the lower world with a multitude of animals of all kinds. But when His work was finished, the Artisan longed for someone to reflect on the plan of so great a creation, to love its beauty, and to admire its magnitude. When, therefore, everything was completed, as Moses and the Timaeus [a philosophical work of Plato] testify, He began at last to consider the creation of man.... Finally the Great Artisan ordained that man, to whom He could give nothing belonging to himself, should share in common whatever properties had been peculiar to each of the other creatures. He received man, therefore, as a creature of undetermined nature, and placing him in the middle of the universe, said to him: "Neither an established place, nor a form belonging to you alone, nor any special function have We given to you, O Adam, and for this reason, that you may have and possess, according to your desire and judgment, whatever place, whatever form, and whatever functions you shall desire. The nature of other creatures, which has been determined, is confined within the bounds prescribed by Us. You, who are confined by no limits, shall determine for yourself your own nature, in accordance with your own free will, in whose hand I have placed you. I have set you at the center of the world, so that from there you may more easily survey whatever is in the world. We have made you neither heavenly nor earthly, neither mortal nor immortal, so that, more freely and more honorably the molder and maker of yourself, you may fashion yourself in whatever form you shall prefer. You shall be able to descend among the lower forms of being, which are brute beasts; you shall be able to be reborn out of the judgment of your own soul into the higher beings, which are divine.

O sublime generosity of God the Father! O highest and most wonderful felicity of man! To him it was granted to have what he chooses, to be what he wills. At the moment when they are born, beasts bring with them from their mother's womb, as Lucilius [Roman poet] says, whatever they shall possess. From the beginning or soon afterwards, the highest spiritual beings have been what they are to be for all eternity. When man came into life, the Father endowed him with all kinds of seeds and with the germs of every way of life. Whatever seeds each man cultivates will grow and bear fruit in him. If these seeds are vegetative, he will be like a plant; if they are sensitive, he will become like the beasts; if they are rational, he will become like a heavenly creature; if intellectual, he will be an angel and a son of God. And if, content with the lot of no created being, he withdraws into the center of his own oneness, his spirit, made one with God in the solitary darkness of the Father, which is above all things, will surpass all things.

THINKING CRITICALLY

1. *Recognizing Concepts* According to Pico, what is the place of humankind in the universe? What is the most important quality that humans possess?

2. *Identifying Central Issues* What is the key difference between Pico's and Leonardo's concept of man's place in nature? Which side seems more accurate to you?

3. *Linking Past and Present* Humanism, or the belief in the limitless potential of humankind, was a concept that traveled to the new world of the Americas, inspiring the founders of the United States. How do the humanist concepts of Pico relate to the ideals of the founders of the United States?

WRITER'S PORTFOLIO

1. *Extending the Selection* How has Leonardo related man to ideal geometric forms? Do you think his concept is realistic?

2. *Examining Key Questions* Compare and contrast Pico's and Leonardo's images of humankind.

Sculpting David

Renaissance Florence produced some of the most magnificent sculpture of all time. Within a period of seventy years three different statues of David were created — one by Donatello, one by Verrocchio, one by Michelangelo — each suggesting an evolving attitude or feeling about the world, about the place of Florence in that world, and about the role of men and women at this time. In viewing the three Davids, one can see an evolution of self-awareness and strength, of self-confidence and boldness, in the youth who single-handedly slew the giant Goliath and saved his people. The bronze *David* by Donatello (c. 1432) was the first freestanding nude sculpture created in Europe since ancient Greek and Roman times. The life-sized youth stands in the *contrapposto* pose that originated with the ancient Greeks. He wears nothing but military leggings and a shepherd's hat over his long flowing hair. The idealized physical beauty of the youth is elegantly captured in the languid pose. Thirty-three years after Donatello cast his *David*, Verrocchio was commissioned by the Medici to sculpt a bronze David, which echoes the Donatello *David* in many respects. The pose of the life-sized figure is similar at first glance, but Verrocchio's figure is proud of his work and seems posed in triumph over the head of Goliath. In 1501, Michelangelo carved an eighteen-foot David out of marble, which bears little resemblance to his two predecessors. This David towers above his viewers and has an almost idealized beauty and physique. Moreover, this David has yet to fight Goliath and so his defiant pose and gaze seem even more arrogant than Verrocchio's. While Verrocchio's *David* looked confident, Michelangelo's *David* looks defiant, an idealized physique, bristling with energy. Why do you think that David was the character chosen for these statues, created within a 70-year period in Florence?

Donatello, David *(c. 1432)*

Verrocchio,
David *(1465)*

Michelangelo,
David *(1501)*

THINKING CRITICALLY

1. *Making Comparisons* Compare and contrast the stance and the gestures of the three Davids. Which one seems the most realistic to you?

2. *Recognizing Values* How do these sculptures reflect the growth of Florence in the 1400s?

3. *Linking Past to Present* Think about contemporary statues of heroes that are in your city or state. Whom do they depict and what kinds of qualities are reflected in them?

WRITER'S PORTFOLIO

1. *Extending the Selection* Choose one of the Davids and write a character sketch about him. Be sure to include details that describe his emotions and behavior as well as his physical appearance.

2. *Examining Key Questions* How is a changing view of humankind portrayed in each of these statues?

The Rule of Princes

During the Renaissance, Italy was politically quite unstable. It was not in fact a country as we know it today, but rather a collection of city-states, each self-governing and independent to the point of rivalry. Florence, where the Renaissance as we think of it began, was ruled for almost the entire era by the Medici family. Yet, the threat of invasion by the French king or the Holy Roman Emperor always hung over Florence. In 1494, France did invade Florence, and the Medici were ousted from power. During the next eight years chaos reigned, as the new government tried to establish order amidst the reaction of many Florentines to the materialism, corruption, and godlessness of the old regime. Niccolò Machiavelli (1469–1527) was made secretary to the Council of Ten, which was the reigning governing body at this time. But in 1512, the Medici returned and took power once again and Machiavelli was sent into exile. It was during this period that he wrote *The Prince*, the book for which he is famous. While studying the ancient Romans, Machiavelli became intrigued with their ability to put aside questions of morals or right in politics. He came to perceive of idealism and honor as qualities that got in the way of real government. In *The Prince*, Machiavelli set down the qualities of a well-run state as a model to all rulers. In the following excerpts, he discusses how a leader should balance virtue and vice. What are Machiavelli's goals?

Cruelty and Clemency: Is it Better to Be Loved or Feared?

PROCEEDING TO THE OTHER QUALITIES BEFORE NAMED, I SAY that every prince must desire to be considered merciful and not cruel. He must, however, take care not to use this mercifulness. Cesare Borgia [a Renaissance Prince] was considered cruel, but his cruelty had brought order to the Romagna, united it, and reduced it to peace and fealty. A prince, therefore, must not mind incurring the charge of cruelty for the purpose of keeping his subjects united and faithful; for, with a very few examples, he will be more merciful than those who, from excess of tenderness, allow disorders to arise, from whence spring bloodshed and rapine; for these as a rule injure the whole community, while the executions carried out by the prince injure only individuals.... From this arises the question whether it is better to be loved more than feared, or feared more than loved. The reply is, that one ought to be both feared and loved, but as it is difficult for the two to go together, it is much safer to be feared than loved if one of the two has to be wanting. For it may be said of men in general that they are ungrateful, voluble, dissemblers, anxious to avoid danger, and covetous of gain; as long as you benefit them, they are entirely yours; they offer you their blood, their goods, their life, and their children, as I have before said, when the necessity is remote; but when it approaches, they revolt. And the prince who has relied solely on their words, without making other preparations, is ruined; for the friendship which is gained by purchase and not through grandeur and nobility of spirit is bought but not secured, and in a pinch is not to be expended in your service. And men have less scruple in offending one who makes himself loved than one who makes himself feared; for love is held by a chain of obligation which, men being selfish, is broken whenever it serves their purpose; but fear is maintained by a dread of punishment which never fails.

Still, a prince should make himself feared in such a way that if he does not gain love, he at any rate avoids hatred; for fear and the absence of hatred may well go together, and will be always attained by one who abstains from interfering with the property of his citizens and subjects or with their women. And when he is obliged to take the life of any one, let him do so when there is a proper justification and manifest reason for it; but above all he must abstain from taking the property of others, for men forget more easily the death of their father than the loss of their patrimony. Then also pretexts for seizing property are never wanting, and one who begins to live by rapine will always find some reason for taking the goods of others, whereas causes for taking life are rarer and more fleeting.

I conclude, therefore, with regard to being feared and loved, that men love at their own free will, but fear at the will of the prince, and that a wise prince must rely on what is in his power and not on what is in the power of others, and he must only contrive to avoid incurring hatred, as has been explained.

In What Way Princes Must Keep Faith

Hᴏᴡ ʟᴀᴜᴅᴀʙʟᴇ ɪᴛ ɪꜱ ꜰᴏʀ ᴀ ᴘʀɪɴᴄᴇ ᴛᴏ ᴋᴇᴇᴘ ɢᴏᴏᴅ ꜰᴀɪᴛʜ ᴀɴᴅ live with integrity, and not with astuteness, every one knows. Still the experience of our times shows those princes to have done great things who have had little regard for good faith and have been able by astuteness to confuse men's brains have ultimately overcome those who have made loyalty their foundation.

You must know, then, that there are two methods of fighting, the one by law, the other by force: the first method is that of men, the second of beasts; but as the first method is often insufficient, one must have recourse to the second. It is therefore necessary for a prince to know well how to use both the beast and the man. This was covertly taught to rulers by ancient writers, who relate how Achilles and many others of those ancient princes were given to Chiron the centaur to be brought up and educated under his discipline. The parable of this semi-animal, semi-human teacher is meant to indicate that a prince must know how to use both natures, and that the one without the other is not durable.

A prince being thus obliged to know well how to act as a beast must imitate the fox and the lion, for the lion cannot protect himself from traps, and the fox cannot defend himself from wolves. One must therefore be a fox to recognise traps, and a lion to frighten wolves. Those that wish to be only lions do not understand this. Therefore, a prudent ruler ought not to keep faith when by so doing it would be against his interest, and when the reasons which made him bind himself no longer exist. If men were all good, this precept would not be a good one; but as they are bad, and would not observe their faith with you, so you are not bound to keep faith with them. Nor have legitimate grounds ever failed a prince who wished to show colorable excuse for the nonfulfillment of his promise. Of this one could furnish an infinite number of modern examples, and show how many times peace has been broken, and how many promises rendered worthless, by the faithlessness of princes, and those that have been best able to imitate the fox have succeeded best. But it is necessary to be able to disguise this character well, and to be a great feigner and dissembler; and men are so simple and so ready to obey present necessities, that one who deceives will always find those who allow themselves to be deceived.... Let a prince therefore aim at conquering and maintaining the state, and the means will always be judged honorable and praised by every one, for the vulgar is always taken by appearances and the issue of the event; and the world consists only of the vulgar, and the few who are not vulgar are isolated when the many have a rallying point in the prince. A certain prince of the present time, whom it is well not to name, never does anything but preach peace and good faith, but he is really a great enemy to both, and either of them, had he observed them, would have lost him state or reputation on many occasions.

Charles V (1500–1558), the Holy Roman Emperor, ruled the largest European kingdom since the empire of Charlemagne. This kingdom included most of Germany, the Low Countries, Spain, and territories in both the New World and in Italy. But constant wars with France and invasions by the Turks left Charles weary of ruling. In 1556, Charles gave up his crown in favor of his son Phillip, at the same time writing him a letter on the best way to rule his kingdom. An excerpt from this letter appears below. How does Charles's advice differ from Machiavelli's?

I HAVE RESOLVED, MY DEAR SON, TO REMIT TO YOUR HANDS THE sovereignty of my dominions, having told you several times that I had formed this design.... I will not further stress this point, and I think I need not endeavor to exhort you to imitate the conduct which I have adhered to during the course of my life, nearly all of which I have passed in difficult enterprises and laborious employment, in the defence of the empire, in propagating the holy faith of Jesus Christ, and in preserving my peoples in peace and security. I will only say that at the beginning of your reign the two advantages you have — of being my son and of looking like me — will, if I am not mistaken, win for you the love of your subjects; in addition, you on your side must treat them so well that in due course you will have no need of memories of me to assist you in preserving their affection.

Do not imagine, my very dear son, that the pleasure of ruling so many peoples, and the freedom which flatters the feelings of sovereign princes, are not mixed with some bitterness and linked with some trouble. If one knew what goes on in the hearts of princes one would see that the suspicions and uncertainties which agitate those whose conduct is irregular torment them day and night, while those who govern their realms wisely and sensibly are overwhelmed by various worries which give them no rest. And truly, if you weigh in a fair balance, on the one hand, the prerogatives and preeminences of sovereignty, and on the other the work in which it involves you, you will find it a source of grief rather than of joy and delight. But this truth looks so much like a lie that only experience can make it believable....

Remember, the prince is like a mirror exposed to the eyes of all his subjects who continually look to him as a pattern on which to model themselves, and who in consequence without much trouble discover his vices and virtues. No prince, however clever and skillful he may be, can hope to hide his actions and proceedings from them. If during his life he can shut their mouths and prevent them from making his irregularities and excesses public, they will after his death convey the memory of them to posterity. Therefore adhere to so just and orderly a conduct towards your peoples that, seeing the trouble you take to govern them well, they will come to rely entirely on your prudence and take comfort from your valor; and in this way there will grow between you and them a reciprocal love and affection.... It is certain that people submit to the rule of their princes more readily of their own free will than when they are kept in strict bondage, and that one can retain their services better by love than by violence. I admit that the power which rests on a sovereign's gentle kindness is less absolute than that which rests only on fear; but one must also agree that it is more solid and enduring.

THINKING CRITICALLY

1. *Identifying Alternatives* Machiavelli states that the ends or goals of the state are to attain and expand power. Would Charles V agree with this? What other goals might the state have?

2. *Recognizing Values* Why does Machiavelli state that the prince must be like the lion and the fox? What values do these creatures represent?

3. *Linking Past and Present* Machiavelli is often called the father of modern political science. Do politicians in recent times behave according to his theories? Give specific examples.

WRITER'S PORTFOLIO

1. *Extending the Selection* Research a recent political issue and write a letter to the U.S. President advising him how to act, based on Machiavelli's suggestions.

2. *Examining Key Questions* Compare and contrast Charles V's and Machiavelli's views of human nature.

The High Renaissance

Although Florence was the birthplace of the Renaissance, Rome became its cultural center during the papacy of Julius II (1503–1513), who induced the artists Raphael and Michelangelo to come to the Vatican to paint. Michelangelo was asked to paint the ceiling of the Sistine Chapel, while Raphael was asked to decorate several rooms in the Pope's apartment including the Stanza della Segnatura, the Pope's library. Here Raphael painted two vast frescoes, one displaying the Christian tradition through the ceremony of the Mass, the other displaying the classical tradition in what has come to be called the *School of Athens*, which appears on page 253. The latter fresco is a portrait of many of the great thinkers and philosophers of ancient Greece, as well as some of Raphael's own friends and contemporaries. At the center of the painting are two figures, centered under the Roman arches. Plato, the idealist, is on the left; Aristotle, the man of common sense is on the right. Along with Plato on the left are Socrates and other philosophers representing the intuitive, passionate search for truth. With Aristotle on the right are the rational thinkers, those involved with logic, geometry, grammar. Raphael placed himself on the side of Aristotle. (He is in the small group in the foreground, behind Euclid, the geometer who is measuring with a compass.) Also in the foreground, on the left center is a dark, brooding figure, an homage to Michelangelo, painted in the style of the Sistine Chapel. This fresco is very large and carefully planned, and although filled with many people

Raphael, **Poetry** *(1514)*

engaged in various activities, it conveys a balanced, solid feeling. The mood of ancient Athens and the intellectual importance of the classical world are displayed in the temple that surrounds the figures, with the classical statues and reliefs. Classical themes dominated Raphael's work in the Stanza della Segnatura, as he used the themes of classical culture to glorify the new church and its attitude toward learning. The smaller ceiling fresco *Poetry*, which appears on page 251, is a classical allegory of the figure of poetry, depicting the flight of the imagination. The quotation is from Virgil's *Aeneid*, signifying the breath of inspiration. What does Raphael's stress on classical literature and themes for the Pope's library tell us about Renaissance learning?

THINKING CRITICALLY

1. *Making Inferences* Why do you think that Raphael included his own image (and the images of some of his contemporaries) in *The School of Athens*?

2. *Recognizing Values* What do Plato's and Aristotle's gestures in *The School of Athens* indicate?

3. *Linking Past and Present* *The School of Athens* gathers together many of the individuals whose thought shaped the classical world. If you were creating a modern equivalent who would you plan to include in the painting? Make a list of those you would choose.

WRITER'S PORTFOLIO

1. *Extending the Selection* Imagine that you are a painter like Raphael and you have been asked by your village or town to paint a fresco on one wall of the public library. What would your painting look like and who would be depicted in it? Describe your painting and its purpose in several paragraphs.

2. *Examining Key Questions* What view of humanity and the world is suggested by these paintings of Raphael?

Raphael, The School of Athens *(1510)*

Jan van Eyck, Madonna with Chancellor Rolin *(1433)*

Matthias Grünewald, Crucifixion *(1526)*

El Greco, The Burial of Count Orgaz *(1586)*

The New World

With all the focus on the arts and philosophy, it is easy to forget that there were other very practical concerns in Europe during the Renaissance. One of these concerns was finding a new route to the East—to China, India, and the Spice Islands of Southeast Asia. It was hoped that a sea route to the East could replace the arduous overland trading route through Asia and the Middle East. Even with the cost and difficulty of transport, the trade in Eastern spices was vastly profitable as they were critical for meat preservation in European kitchens, which were without refrigeration. Also pepper, cinnamon, nutmeg, ginger, and cloves were used to enhance the flavor of foods and even to create perfumes and medicines. Because there was such a demand for spices, every European country hoped to gain control over this industry which was dominated by the Muslims and the Venetians. One man who believed that there was a new route to the East was Christopher Columbus. Columbus (1451–1506) was a mariner from Genoa, Italy, who dreamed of a route that went west across the Atlantic Ocean. For eight years he tried to convince various monarchs to finance a voyage to the East. Finally, in 1492, Ferdinand and Isabella of Spain agreed to finance such an expedition, furnishing Columbus with three ships and crews. On October 12, 1492, Columbus's fleet reached one of the islands of the Bahamas. Still believing he had arrived in the Indies, Columbus called the people there "Indians." Columbus wrote the following letter to the secretary of the Spanish treasury, detailing what he had seen in this land. A significant product of the explorations was the increase in European knowledge of the world. The Leardo map, which appears on page 258, was created in 1452 and gives a good idea of the geographical knowledge of Europe in the decades before the era of exploration. In the next hundred years the Western Hemisphere would be explored, the Portuguese would sail around Africa to India, and the world would be circumnavigated. The Agnese map, on page 260, from 1544 shows the effect of men like Columbus on the European world view. How does the image of the world change?

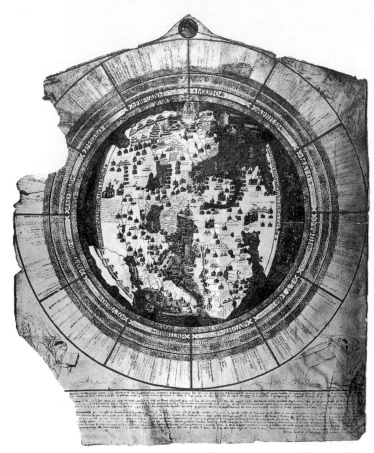

Giovanni Leardo, A Map of the World, *1452*

Sir,—Believing that you will take pleasure in hearing great success which our Lord has granted me in my voyage, I write you this letter, whereby you will learn how in thirty-seven days' time I reached the Indies with the fleet which the most illustrious King and Queen, our Sovereigns, gave to me, where I found very many islands thickly peopled, all of which I took possession without resistance for their Highnesses by proclamation made and with the royal standard unfurled.... They are all most beautiful, of a thousand different shapes, accessible, and covered with trees of a thousand kinds of such great height that they seemed to reach the skies. The nightingale was singing as well as other birds of a thousand different kinds; and that, in

November, the month in which I myself was roaming amongst them. There are palm-trees of six or eight kinds, wonderful in their beautiful variety; but this is the case with all the other trees and fruits and grasses; trees, plants, or fruits filled us with admiration. It contains extraordinary pine groves, and very extensive plains. There is also honey, a great variety of birds, and many different kinds of fruits. In the interior there are many mines of metals and a population innumerable. The inhabitants of this and of all the other islands I have found or gained intelligence of, both men and women, go as naked as they were born, with the exception that some of the women cover one part only with a single leaf of grass or with a piece of cotton, made for the purpose. They have neither iron, nor steel, nor arms, nor are they competent to use them, not that they are not well-formed and of handsome stature, but because they are timid to a surprising degree.

On my reaching the Indies, I took by force, in the first island that I discovered, some of these natives that they might learn our language and give me information in regard to what existed in these parts; and it so happened that they soon understood us and we them, either by words or signs, and they have been very serviceable to us. They are still with me, and, from repeated conversations that I have had with them, I find that they still believe that I come from heaven. And they were the first to say this wherever I went, and the others ran from house to house and to the neighboring villages, crying with a loud voice: "Come, come, and see the people from heaven!" And thus they all, men as well as women, after their minds were at rest about us, came, both large and small, and brought us something to eat and drink, which they gave us with extraordinary kindness.…They assure me that there is another island larger than Espaniola [Hispaniola, a large Caribbean island] in which the inhabitants have no hair. It is extremely rich in gold; and I bring with me Indians taken from these different islands, who will testify to all these things. Finally, and speaking only of what has taken place in this voyage, their Highnesses may see that I shall give them all the gold they require, if they will give me but a little assistance; spices also, and cotton, as much as their Highnesses shall command to be shipped; and mastic, hitherto found only in Greece. I think also I have found rhubarb and cinnamon, and I shall find a thousand other valuable things.

Battista Agnese,
World Map
1543–1544

THINKING CRITICALLY

1. *Identifying Central Issues* What impelled exploration and the voyages of discovery?

2. *Recognizing Values* What attitude does Columbus seem to have toward the people he met?

3. *Linking Past and Present* Compare and contrast these Renaissance maps with world maps today. What features remain constant? What features have changed the most?

WRITER'S PORTFOLIO

1. *Extending the Selection* Imagine that you are the secretary to the Spanish treasury and write a letter of response to Columbus.

2. *Examining Key Questions* How did the Renaissance view of the world change with the discoveries made by Columbus? Where did the people of the Western Hemisphere fit into this view?

The Northern Renaissance

The transition from Gothic to Renaissance painting came later to Northern Europe than it did to Southern Europe. However, Northern Europe was responsible for a development that was to revolutionize painting—oil paints. The Flemish artist Jan van Eyck (yän′ van ik′) (c. 1390–1441) is credited with having perfected the technique of mixing paint pigment with oil, a medium that allowed the artist to have more control over the results, as oil paints take much longer to dry than the older egg-based tempera paints. Oil paints also allowed the artist to capture a wider range of the realistic details of life—vibrant colors, the textures of fabrics from velvet to lace, light reflected on silver mirrors and brass candelabra, intimate moments alone or with others in a household or village. The Northern painters became fascinated with these details of daily life, as did the people who commissioned their portraits from these artists. Portraits, such as Jan van Eyck's *Giovanni Arnolfini and His Bride*, which appears on page 262, or *The Banker and His Wife* by Quentin Matsys (kven′tin mät sīs) (c. 1464–1530), which appears on page 263, show their subjects in their homes with the various possessions that symbolized their status in this world. These portraits would reach their height in the subtle, precise works of Jan Vermeer (yän vər mēr′) (1632–1675), particularly his *Allegory of Painting*, which appears on page 220. While Northern Renaissance painters did not create the vast religious scenes and allegories of their Southern counterparts, Biblical scenes were still of great importance, though they were now depicted with a harsher realism. Van Eyck included a stunning depiction of the Madonna and Child in his portrait of Chancellor Rolin, which appears on page 254, and Matthias Grünewald (mätē′ äs grün′ əvält) (1470–1528) painted what is arguably the first painting of the Crucifixion to emphasize Jesus' intense suffering. Grünewald's painting, which appears on page 255, is an intensely personal expression of feelings that reveal the pain and suffering of Jesus on the cross with those dearest to him in this world. The Southern Renaissance notion of beautiful forms does not seem as important to the Northern painters as the re-creation of surface details to create a particular feeling or effect. And because of the oil paint, the colors in these paintings are as sparkling today as they were five hundred years ago, while many of the Italian frescoes have faded over the years. What factors may have conditioned the differences between Southern and Northern Renaissance paintings?

Jan van Eyck, Giovanni Arnolfini and his Bride *(1434)*

Quentin Matsys,
The Banker and
his Wife *(1514)*

THINKING CRITICALLY

1. *Making Comparisons* Who seemed to commission most of the paintings in the Northern Renaissance? How does this differ from the Southern Renaissance?

2. *Recognizing Values* From these paintings, what do you learn about the values that these people held?

3. *Linking Past and Present* If you were to have your portrait painted today, what objects and people would you want to include in the portrait? Where would you want this portrait to be painted?

WRITER'S PORTFOLIO

1. *Extending the Selection* Choose a person from one of these paintings and develop a short narrative about his or her life. In your story, refer to specific details from the painting.

2. *Examining Key Questions* Do you think the paintings of the Northern Renaissance depict a more or less secularized image of the human world than those of the Southern Renaissance?

The Reformation

Martin Luther (1483–1546) was a monk and university professor in Wittenberg, Germany. A brilliant scholar and theologian, Luther criticized the Church for some of its practices, particularly the sale of indulgences (a purchased absolution for a committed sin). The sale of indulgences had been revived by Pope Julius II in 1503 to raise funds for rebuilding St. Peter's Cathedral in Rome. In October 1517, Luther wrote up his 95 theses, a list of issues to be debated, and hammered them to the door of the cathedral in Wittenberg. Within weeks these were translated from Latin into German and using the new printing presses, distributed throughout Germany. Luther based his objections to Church practices on what he read in the Bible; if the Bible did not literally state that a Church practice was acceptable, Luther rejected it. By studying the ancient scriptures, Luther and other Christian humanists in Northern Europe hoped to find a purer form of Christianity, one that was not colored by the ceremonies, rituals, and dogma of the Roman Church. Luther's simple act, by which he hoped to foster debate on the subject of indulgences, became the first act in a revolution that would divide Europe and plunge it into two centuries of religious wars. The following selection is an excerpt from Luther's *Address to the Christian Nobility of the German Nation*. It is an appeal to temporal authorities to support his revolt against what Luther saw as the corruption of the Roman Church. In what ways was Luther like the Italian humanists?

I HAVE, IN CONFORMITY WITH OUR RESOLVE, PUT TOGETHER some few points concerning the reformation of the Christian estate, with the intent of placing the same before the Christian nobility of the German nation, in case it may please God to help his Church by means of the laity, inasmuch as the clergy, whom this task rather befitted, have become quite careless.... It is not out of mere arrogance and perversity that I, an individual poor man, have taken upon me to address your lordships. The distress and misery that oppress all the Christian estates, more especially in Germany, have led not only myself, but every one else, to cry aloud and to ask for help, and have now forced me too to cry out and to ask if God would give His Spirit to any one to reach a hand to His wretched people. Councils have often put forward some remedy, but it has adroitly been frustrated, and the evils have become worse, through the cunning of certain men. Their malice and wickedness I will now, by the help of God, expose, so that, being known, they may henceforth cease to be so obstructive and injurious.

These Romanists have, with great adroitness, drawn three walls around themselves, with which they have hitherto protected themselves, so that no one could reform them, whereby all Christendom has fallen terribly.

That the Temporal Power Has no Jurisdiction over the Spirituality

It has been devised that the Pope, bishops, priests, and monks are called the *spiritual estate*, princes, lords, artificers, and peasants are the *temporal estates*. This is an artful lie and hypocritical device, but let no one be made afraid by it, and that for this reason: that all Christians are truly of the spiritual estate, and there is no difference among them, save of office alone…. Therefore I say, forasmuch as the temporal power has been ordained by God for the punishment of the bad and the protection of the good, therefore we must let it do its duty throughout the whole Christian body, without respect of persons, whether it strike popes, bishops, priests, monks, nuns, or whoever it may be.

That No One May Interpret the Scriptures but the Pope

The second wall is even more tottering and weak: that they alone pretend to be considered masters of the Scriptures; although they learn nothing of them all their life. They assume authority, and juggle before us with impudent words, saying that the Pope cannot err in matters of faith, whether he be evil or good, albeit they cannot prove it by a single letter…. Therefore it is a wickedly devised fable — and they cannot quote a single letter to confirm it — that it is for the Pope alone to interpret the Scriptures or to confirm the interpretation of them.

That No One May Call a Council but the Pope

The third wall falls of itself, as soon as the first two have fallen; for if the Pope acts contrary to the Scriptures, we are bound to stand by the Scriptures, to punish and to constrain him, according to Christ's commandment, "Moreover, if thy brother shall trespass against thee, go and tell him his fault between thee and him alone; if he shall hear thee, thou hast gained thy brother. But if he will not hear thee, then take with thee one or two more, that in the mouth of two or three witnesses every word may be established. And if he shall neglect to hear the Church, let him be unto thee as a heathen man and a publican."… Therefore when need requires, and the Pope is a cause of offence to Christendom, in these cases whoever can best do so, as a faithful member of the whole body, must do what he can to procure a true free council. This no one can do so well as the temporal authorities….

Let us now consider the matters which should be treated in the councils, and with which popes, cardinals, bishops, and all learned men should occupy themselves day and night, if they love Christ and His Church….

1. It is a distressing and terrible thing to see that the head of Christendom, who boasts of being the vicar of Christ and the successor of St. Peter, lives in a worldly pomp that no king or emperor can equal.

2. What is the use in Christendom of the people called "cardinals"? I will tell you. In Italy and Germany there are many rich convents, endowments, fiefs, and benefices, and as the best way of getting these into the hands of Rome, they created cardinals, and gave them the sees, convents, and prelacies, and thus destroyed the service of God. That is why Italy is almost a desert now.

THINKING CRITICALLY

1. *Expressing Problems* What objections does Luther have to the Roman Church at this time?

2. *Recognizing Values* Does Luther view the individual or the Church as more important to the service of God?

3. *Linking Past and Present* If you disagreed with the practices of a major institution today, how would you go about expressing your views? Would you use any of Luther's methods?

WRITER'S PORTFOLIO

1. *Extending the Selection* Do you think that it is right to judge the practices of the Church based on what is written in the Bible?

2. *Examining Key Questions* What ideals of the Renaissance is Luther emphasizing?

Mannerism

Painters after Raphael were faced with the question of whether to emulate his near-perfection or abandon the serene classicism of High Renaissance art. These painters took Michelangelo's late paintings as their inspiration and began to paint in a style of exaggerated light and color, which aimed for heightened emotional expressiveness. Mannerist painting, as the style came to be known, emphasized the human figure, but depicted it in strained poses and elongated forms, with distorted or unnaturally vivid details. The greatest of the Mannerist painters was the artist known as El Greco or "the Greek." El Greco (1541–1614) was born in Crete, but spent almost twenty years studying painting in Italy, absorbing the lessons of the High Renaissance masters like Raphael and Michelangelo. Around 1575, El Greco went to Spain, where he spent the rest of his life painting in Toledo. During the last quarter of the sixteenth century, Spain underwent a religious reaction against the Reformation begun by Martin Luther in Germany. This Counter Reformation was marked by a return to mysticism and spirituality and El Greco's paintings exemplified this religious fervor. They suggest an intensity of passion and a catharsis

El Greco, **Saint Martin and the Beggar** *(1599)*

found in religion. *The Burial of Count Orgaz*, which appears on page 256, and *Saint Martin and the Beggar*, which appears on page 267, show two sides of El Greco: the one is a monumental altarpiece depicting both heaven and earth, while the other is a simpler portrait of the Roman soldier Martin, sharing his cloak with a poor beggar in winter. Does the style of these paintings seem realistic to you?

THINKING CRITICALLY

1. *Making Comparisons* Compare and contrast the heavenly figures and the earthly figures in *The Burial of Count Orgaz*.

2. *Recognizing Values* From viewing these two paintings, what do you judge to be important human values to El Greco?

3. *Linking Past to Present* El Greco was an artist who developed his own individual painting style. How important is it to have one's own style in the arts today?

WRITER'S PORTFOLIO

1. *Extending the Selection* Write a description of *The Burial of Count Orgaz* for someone who has never seen it or any painting in the style. Try to capture the style and its effect in your prose.

2. *Examining Key Questions* Does the development of Mannerist art seem an extension of Renaissance emphasis on the primacy of man or a reaction against it?

The Heliocentric World

Since the speculations of the earliest Greek philosophers (see pages 52–54), the scientific quest to understand the universe dominated natural philosophy. As early as the third century B.C., the Greek astronomer Aristarchus (ar′i stär′kəs) of Samos proposed that the sun was the center of the universe. His view, however, was rejected in favor of Aristotle's theory that the earth was the center of the universe. In the second century A.D., Ptolemy (tol′ə mē) conceived a geometric model for this earth-centered universe. Around the fixed, motionless earth rotated nine concentric spheres. The spheres contained (in order from the center outward) the moon, Mercury, Venus, the sun, Mars, Jupiter, Saturn, the stars, and the *primum mobile* (Latin for "prime mover"), which gave motion to the whole universe. This theory of the universe was compatible with Church doctrine and it held fast for fifteen centuries. In 1530, while studying ancient Greek texts, the Polish astronomer Nicolaus Copernicus (kō pûr′ni kəs) (1473–1543) rediscovered Aristarchus's theories. He studied and developed the theory of a heliocentric or sun-centered universe for the rest of his life. In 1543, as he lay dying, Copernicus published his theory in *De revolutionibus orbium coelestium*. Later, in the 1600s, the Italian mathematician Galileo (gal′i lē′ō) (1564–1642), using a telescope that he himself built, was able to make the most advanced astronomical observations of his day. He studied the surface of the moon, observed the stars, and saw that the planet Jupiter had moons of its own. Through these observations and further study, Galileo came to believe that Copernicus's theory was correct, at least in terms of the sun being the center of the universe. In 1610, he published *The Sidereal Messenger*, which advocated and built upon Copernican theory. The following selections are excerpts from Copernicus and Galileo and engravings of the Ptolemaic and Copernican universes. How do the engravings compare to what you know of the universe?

Copernicus, from *De revolutionibus orbium coelestium*

FIRST AND ABOVE ALL LIES THE SPHERE OF THE FIXED STARS, containing itself and all things, for that very reason immoveable; in truth the frame of the universe, to which the motion and position of all other stars are referred. Though some men think it to move in some way, we assign another reason why it appears to do so in our theory of the movement of the earth. Of the moving bodies first comes Saturn, who completes his circuit in thirty years. After him, Jupiter, moving in a twelve-year revolution. Then Mars, who revolves biennially. Fourth in order an annual cycle takes place, in which we have said is contained the earth, with the lunar orbit as an epicycle. In the fifth place Venus is carried round in nine months. Then Mercury holds the sixth place, circulating in the space of eighty days. In the middle of all dwells the Sun. Who indeed in this most beautiful temple would place the torch in any other or better place than one whence it can illuminate the whole at the same time? Not ineptly, some call it the lamp of the universe, others its mind, others again its ruler.

Andreas Cellarius,
The Ptolemaic
Universe *(1660)*

Galileo, from *The Sidereal Messenger*

I HAVE BEEN LED TO THAT OPINION WHICH I HAVE EXPRESSED, namely, that I feel sure that the surface of the Moon is not perfectly smooth, free from inequalities and exactly spherical, as a large school of philosophers considers with regard to the Moon and the other heavenly bodies, but that, on the contrary, it is full of inequalities, uneven, full of hollows and protuberances, just like the surface of the Earth itself, which is varied everywhere by lofty mountains and deep valleys.

The appearances from which we may gather these conclusions are of the following nature:—On the fourth or fifth day after new-moon, when the Moon presents itself to us with bright horns, the boundary which divides the part in shadow from the enlightened part does not extend continuously in an ellipse, as would happen in the case of a perfectly spherical body, but it is marked out by an irregular, uneven, and very wavy line....for several bright excrescences, as they may be called, extend beyond the boundary of light and shadow into the dark part, and on the other hand pieces of shadow encroach upon the light—nay, even a great quantity of small blackish spots, altogether separated from the dark part, sprinkle everywhere almost the whole space which is at the time flooded with the Sun's light, with the exception of that part alone which is occupied by the great and ancient spots. I have noticed that the small spots just mentioned have this common characteristic always and in every case, that they have the dark part towards the Sun's position, and on the side away from the Sun they have brighter boundaries, as if they were crowned with shining summits. Now we have an appearance quite similar on the Earth about sunrise, when we behold the valleys, not yet flooded with light, but the mountains surrounding them on the side opposite to the Sun already ablaze with the splendor of his beams; and just as the shadows in the hollows of the Earth diminish in size as the Sun rises higher, so also these spots on the Moon lose their blackness as the illuminated part grows larger and larger. Again, not only are the boundaries of light and shadow in the Moon seen to be uneven and sinuous, but—and this produces still greater astonishment—there appear very many bright points within the darkened portion of the Moon, altogether divided and broken off from the illuminated tract, and separated from it by no inconsiderable interval, which, after a little while, gradually increase in size and brightness, and after an hour or two become joined on to the rest of the main portion, now become somewhat larger; but in the meantime others, one here and another there, shooting up as if growing, are

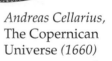

Andreas Cellarius, The Copernican Universe *(1660)*

lighted up within the shaded portion, increase in size, and at last are linked on to the same luminous surface, now still more extended.... Now, is it not the case on the Earth before sunrise, that while the level plain is still in shadow, the peaks of the most lofty mountains are illuminated by the Sun's rays? After a little while does not the light spread further, while the middle and larger parts of those mountains are becoming illuminated; and at length, when the Sun has risen, do not the illuminated parts of the plains and hills join together? The grandeur, however, of such prominences and depressions in the Moon seems to surpass both in magnitude and extent the ruggedness of the Earth's surface.

THINKING CRITICALLY

1. *Identifying Central Issues* Why do you think that the theory that the earth was the center of the universe was believed to be true for fifteen centuries?

2. *Recognizing Values* Look up *empirical* in the dictionary. Do you think that Copernicus and Galileo were empirical scientists? What about their predecessors?

3. *Linking Past to Present* Both Copernicus and Galileo feared presenting their ideas because of the Church. Are similar pressures faced by scientists today?

WRITER'S PORTFOLIO

1. *Extending the Selection* Create a third drawing of the universe, incorporating knowledge we have gained since 1660 and write an essay describing the additions you have made.

2. *Examining Key Questions* How do Copernicus's and Galileo's theories challenge the Renaissance view of man's place in the universe?

The Search for Truth

The Southern Renaissance was exemplified by the revival of classical learning and philosophy. But, as the Renaissance spread throughout Northern Europe, thinkers began to expand upon the classical lessons. At the forefront of the new philosophy was the Frenchman René Descartes (**rə nā′ dā kärt′**) (1596–1650), who is often called the father of modern philosophy. Descartes was a brilliant mathematician and logician, who was fascinated by the way in which human beings acquire knowledge. As a philosopher, he found himself paralyzed by the question of what he could really know; what knowledge could he accept as absolutely true? Descartes began his philosophic quest by trying to find concepts or ideas which he could verify as true and from these foundations construct a philosophic system. Descartes documented this search for truth in his two great works *The Discourse on Method* (1637) and his *Meditations on First Philosophy* (1641), both of which are excerpted below. What types of knowledge does Descartes reject?

---

from *The Discourse on Method*

For a long time I had remarked that it is sometimes requisite in common life to follow opinions which one knows to be most uncertain, exactly as though they were indisputable, as has been said above. But because in this case I wished to give myself entirely to the search after Truth, I thought that it was necessary for me to take an apparently opposite course, and to reject as absolutely false everything as to which I could imagine the least ground of doubt, in order to see if afterwards there remained anything in my belief that was entirely certain. Thus, because our senses sometimes deceive us, I wished to suppose that nothing is just as they cause us to imagine it to be; and because there are men who deceive themselves in their reasoning and fall into paralogisms, even concerning the simplest matters of geometry, and judging that I was as subject to error as was any other, I rejected as false all the reasons formerly accepted by me as demonstrations. And since all the same thoughts and conceptions which we have while awake may also come to us in sleep, without any of them being at that time true, I resolved to assume that everything that ever entered into my mind was no more true than the illusions of my dreams. But immediately afterwards I noticed that whilst I thus wished to think all things false, it was absolutely essential that the "I" who thought this should be somewhat, and remarking that this truth *"I think, therefore I am"* was so certain and so assured that all the most extravagant suppositions brought forward by the sceptics were incapable of shaking it, I came to the conclusion that I could receive it without scruple as the first principle of the Philosophy for which I was seeking.

---

from the *Meditations on First Philosophy*

It is now some years since I detected how many were the false beliefs that I had from my earliest youth admitted as true, and how doubtful was everything I had since constructed on this basis; and from that time I was convinced that I must once and for all seriously undertake to rid myself of all the opinions which I had formerly accepted, and commence to build anew from the foundation, if I wanted to establish any firm and permanent structure in the sciences.

Now for this object it is not necessary that I should show that all of these are false—I shall perhaps never arrive at this end. But inasmuch as reason already persuades me that I ought no less carefully to withhold my assent from matters which are not entirely certain and indubitable than from those which appear to me manifestly to be false, if I am able to find in each one some reason to doubt, this will suffice to justify my rejecting the whole. And for that end it will not be requisite that I should examine each in particular, which would be an endless undertaking; for owing to the fact that the destruction of the foundations of necessity brings with it the downfall of the rest of the edifice, I shall only in the first place attack those principles upon which all my former opinions rested.

All that up to the present time I have accepted as most true and certain I have learned either from the senses or through the senses; but it is sometimes proved to me that these senses are deceptive, and it is wiser not to trust entirely to any thing by which we have once been deceived....

That is possibly why our reasoning is not unjust when we conclude from this that Physics, Astronomy, Medicine, and all other sciences which have as their end the consideration of composite things, are very dubious and uncertain; but that Arithmetic, Geometry, and other sciences of that kind which only treat of things that are very simple and very general, without taking great trouble to ascertain whether they are actually existent or not, contain some measure of certainty and an element of the indubitable. For whether I am awake or asleep, two and three together always form five, and the square can never have more than four sides, and it does not seem possible that truths so clear and apparent can be suspected of any falsity [or uncertainty].

THINKING CRITICALLY

1. *Identifying Central Issues* What is the most important point that Descartes is trying to make?

2. *Recognizing Values* Based on his writing, what human values are most important to Descartes?

3. *Linking Past to Present* Do you think Descartes's ideas about knowledge and truth are still relevant in our thought? Does Descartes seem closer to modern philosophy than to Plato?

WRITER'S PORTFOLIO

1. *Extending the Selection* Using Descartes's method and foundation, write about three things in your life now that you know to be true.

2. *Examining Key Questions* What view of the man and the world do you see reflected in the work of Descartes?

Freedom of the Press

Religious reform led to civil war in England during the seventeenth century. By 1563, the Anglican Church had been officially established as the state religion of England. However, a great many dissenting groups, known generally as Puritans, still opposed the king and his religion. For the next eighty years, these Puritans attempted to use the elected Parliament of England to oppose the king's policies and limit his powers. In the 1640s this became an open civil war. By 1644, the Puritans had gained the upper hand and began to organize a government, known as the Commonwealth. The king, Charles I, would be beheaded in 1649. The great poet John Milton (1608–1674) was a passionate member of the Puritan establishment and he hoped that the new government would allow freedom of the press in England. However, the Parliament enacted new laws restricting printing and Milton responded with his pamphlet *Areopagitica*, arguing the merits and importance of free speech to the new government. Excerpts from *Areopagitica* appear below. Do you think that this essay is a persuasive defense of free speech?

I DENY NOT BUT THAT IT IS OF GREATEST CONCERNMENT IN THE Church and commonwealth to have a vigilant eye how books demean themselves as well as men; and thereafter to confine, imprison, and do sharpest justice on them as malefactors. For books are not absolutely dead things but do contain a potency of life in them to be as active as that soul was whose progeny they are; nay, they do preserve as in a vial the purest efficacy and extraction of that living intellect that bred them. I know they are as lively and as vigorously productive as those fabulous dragon's teeth; and, being sown up and down, may chance to spring up armed men. And yet, on the other hand, unless wariness be used, as good almost kill a man as kill a good book; who kills a man, kills a reasonable creature, God's image; but he who destroys a good book kills reason itself, kills the image of God (as it were) in the eye. Many a man lives a burden to the earth; but a good book is the precious life-blood of a master spirit, embalmed and treasured....

I proceed from the no good it can do to the manifest hurt it causes, in being first the greatest discouragement and affront that can be offered to learning and to learned men.... If therefore ye be loath to dishearten utterly and discontent, not the mercenary crew of false pretenders to learning, but the free and ingenuous sort of such as evidently were born to study and love learning for itself, not for lucre or any other end but the service of God and of truth, and perhaps that lasting fame and perpetuity of praise which God and good men have consented shall be the reward of those whose published labors advance the good of mankind; then know that so far to distrust the judgment and the honesty of one who has never yet offended as not to count him fit to print his mind without a tutor and examiner...is the greatest displeasure and indignity to a free and knowing spirit that can be put upon him....

Truth and understanding are not such wares as to be monopolized and traded in by ticket and statutes and standards. We must not think to make a staple commodity of all the knowledge in the land, to mark and license it like our broadcloth and our woolpacks.... Debtors and delinquents may walk abroad without a keeper, but inoffensive books must not stir forth without a visible jailer in their title. Nor is it to the common people less than a reproach; for if we [are] so jealous over them as that we dare not trust them with an English pamphlet, what do we but censure them for a giddy, vicious and ungrounded people, in such a sick and weak state of faith and discretion as to be able to take nothing down but through the pipe of a licenser? That this is care or love of them we cannot pretend, when in those popish places where the laity are most hated and despised the same strictness is used over them....

Lords and Commons of England, consider what nation it is whereof ye are, and whereof ye are the governors: a nation not so slow and dull, but of a quick, ingenious and piercing spirit, acute to invent, subtle and sinewy to discourse, not beneath the reach of any point the highest that human capacity can soar to.... What could a man require more from a nation so pliant and so prone to seek after knowledge? What wants there to such a towardly and pregnant soil but wise and faithful laborers, to make a knowing people, a nation of prophets, of sages and of worthies?.... What should ye do then, should ye suppress all this flowery crop of knowledge and new light sprung up and yet springing daily in this city? Should ye set an oligarchy of twenty engrossers over it, to bring a famine upon our minds again when we shall know nothing but what is measured to us by their bushel?... If it be desired to know the immediate cause of all this free writing and free speaking, there cannot be assigned a truer cause than your own mild and free and humane government. It is the liberty, Lords and Commons, which your own valorous and happy counsels have purchased us, liberty which is the nurse of all great wits; this is that which has rarefied and enlightened our spirits like the influence of heaven; that is that which has enfranchised, enlarged and lifted up our apprehensions degrees above themselves. Ye cannot make us now less capable, less knowing, less eagerly pursuing of the truth, unless ye first make yourselves (that made us so) less the lovers, less the founders of our true liberty. We can grow ignorant again, brutish, formal and slavish, as you found us; but you then must first become that which ye cannot be— oppressive, arbitrary and tyrannous, as they were from whom ye have freed us.... For who knows not that Truth is strong next to the Almighty? She needs no policies, no stratagems, nor licensings to make her victorious; those are the shifts and the defences that error uses against her power. Give her but room and do not bind her when she sleeps, for then she speaks not true.... Yet it is not impossible that she may have more shapes than one. What else is all that rank of things indifferent wherein Truth may be on this side or the other without being unlike herself?... If it come to prohibiting, there is aught more likely to be prohibited than Truth itself, whose first appearance to our eyes, bleared and dimmed with prejudice and custom, is more unsightly and unplausible than many errors.

THINKING CRITICALLY

1. *Making Comparisons* To what other things does Milton compare censorship?

2. *Recognizing Values* What elements of life do you think are the most important to Milton?

3. *Linking Past to Present* What recent instances do you know of where free speech has been challenged?

WRITER'S PORTFOLIO

1. *Extending the Selection* Using one of the instances from question 3, write an editorial attacking or supporting limits on free speech.

2. *Examining Key Questions* Discuss how Milton was influenced by Renaissance ideals when he wrote his *Areopagitica*.

EXAMINING KEY QUESTIONS

- *What is the nature of man?*
- *What is our image of the world?*

Throughout this chapter, most selections have concluded with a writing project asking you to discuss how the art or literature you have examined provides answers to one of these key questions. The following writing projects will help you draw together what you have learned by examining how several selections illustrate these key questions.

- How did the way human beings viewed themselves change during the period of the Renaissance? Use examples from art, literature, philosophy, and religion to illustrate your thesis.

- The Renaissance was not just a period of cultural change, but one where every aspect of daily life throughout Western Europe changed radically. Write an essay describing the world picture of an educated person of the late Renaissance.

SPEAKING/LISTENING

- Research one of the figures presented in this chapter and give a short report to the class on his or her life. Then, discuss what strikes you most about the way people lived during the Renaissance.

CRAFTING

- Using any medium you like, create your own picture of the world about you and your place in it. Consider very carefully what elements of your life you plan to include, for you could re-create your daily life or you could depict yourself simply as one of millions of people.

DEBATING

- The Florentine humanist Leon Battista Alberti (1404–1472) summed up the spirit of the Renaissance when he declared, "Men can do all things if they will." Divide into two groups, one to defend humanism and one to attack it. Use examples from the Renaissance to prove whether humanism is a profitable or dangerous course for mankind.

The Phoenix Hall in Uji, Japan

The Asian Civilizations

INTRODUCTION by Rhoads Murphey

PORTFOLIO

CHAPTER 7 PROJECTS

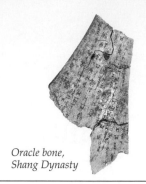

Oracle bone,
Shang Dynasty

1100 B.C.
Chinese produce the first dictionary

CHAPTER 7

The Asian Civilizations

c. 1000 B.C.–A.D.1775

RHOADS MURPHEY

Professor of History, University of Michigan

Civilization, including writing, philosophy, and the arts, has a far longer history in Eastern Asia than in any other part of the world. Such developments were earlier in Mesopotamia and in Egypt, but both of those civilizations had come to an end by Roman times, whereas in Asia the cultures which had emerged in India and China by about 2000 B.C. and in Japan by about A.D. 600 are still vigorous. The great age and the high sophistication of Asian cultures command our attention, but equally important is the fact that the people of these areas constitute about half the world total, as they have for at least the past

4,000 years. Much of our own Western culture has been heavily influenced by earlier developments and advances in Asia, such as paper, printing, and gunpowder in China, and mathematics, steel technology, and medicine in India, while Japanese art and, more recently, modern Japanese technology have also made a profound impact on the West.

All three cultures remain proud of their ancient and modern heritage, and have sometimes succumbed to feelings of intrinsic superiority over other cultures and peoples elsewhere. Haughty Chinese arrogance toward those they called "barbarians," includ-

Copper man, Aryan

Gandharan relief of Buddha

c. 1000
Aryans invade India

c. 1563
Siddhartha (later Buddha) born

ing Westerners, until the present century is well known, and until then Indians also tended to look down on other people, while Japanese assertion of their own unique superiority, as an aspect of Japanese culture, was a basic part of their misguided war against China, Southeast Asia, and the Western powers from 1931 to 1945, a tragedy which Japanese still refer to as their "dark valley." Certainly in the past these Asian cultures have had good reason to feel superior, given their commanding lead over other parts of the world in wealth, power, technology, and sophistication until perhaps the late eighteenth century. But the ascendance of the modern West in all these respects has produced a new kind of world, in which Asians must find a place for themselves, at best as equals. Much Asian pride remains, but with it a realization that although they dominate the world numerically they must find a way to live with other cultures and people who now are as advanced as they are, and in several cases more powerful. What are the bases of Asian pride?

CHINESE CIVILIZATION

China saw the birth of its civilization, including the independent invention of writing, metallurgy, and true cities before 2000 B.C. By about 1600 B.C. the first Chinese dynasty, the Shang, had risen to control much of the north and to produce some of the first masterpieces of Chinese art in bronze and jade. The Shang were succeeded by the Chou (Zhou) (jō) Dynasty (c. 1111–255 B.C.) which continued most of the Shang artistic tradition and saw the emergence of the first Chinese literature, as well as the philosopher Confucius (c. 551–479 B.C.) and his contemporary Lao-tzu (lou′dzu′), the founder of Taoism (dou′iz əm).

China was finally unified politically and culturally by the sweeping conquests of the Ch'in (Qin) (chin) dynasty

Portrait of Confucius

Lion capital from Asoka pillar

c. 551
Confucius born

247
Asoka becomes ruler of India

(221- 206 B.C.) which welded the previous contending states together into the first empire, both north and south. The Ch'in were strict authoritarians and promoted a legalist philosophy, which relied heavily on force, perhaps appropriate for empire-building, but its harsh rule provoked widespread revolt. The Ch'in destroyed most of the records and literature of the past, which is why we have so little of what was written earlier, and hence earned the special hatred of all educated Chinese, for whom the written word and the keeping of records is sacred.

The Han (hän) Dynasty (206 B.C.– A.D. 220) re-established the empire, but under the softening influence of Confucianism, which became in effect the state religion and emphasized responsibility and what Confucius called "human-heartedness." Like all Chinese dynasties, the Han built their cities and temples primarily in wood so that nothing remains except some intriguing clay figures and some fragments of wall painting and valuables from tombs, but these are more than enough to show the great sophistication of Han culture. New samples of Han art continue to be found, befitting the greatest empire of its time, larger and wealthier even than the Roman. The Han also produced the first modern-style histories, romances, and stories. Han rule collapsed by A.D. 220 and various groups from the northern steppe established short-lived kingdoms in the north, while the south was controlled by several Chinese kingdoms. A new Chinese empire was forged by the T'ang (Tang) (täng) (618–907), which saw perhaps the greatest flowering of Chinese culture, especially in poetry. With the Sung (Song) (süng) (960– 1279) China saw the finest period of landscape, bird, flower, and animal painting for which China is still known.

Sung rule was extinguished in 1279 by the brutal Mongol invasion, but superb painting and poetry continued

Jade horse head,
Han Dynasty

*Detail of Haniwa
warrior, late
Tumulus period*

206
Han Dynasty begins in China

c. A.D. 300
Japanese tribes establish themselves on islands

in the unbroken Chinese tradition even under alien rule. Mongol rule was fortunately brief and their control began to break up in the 1350s, less than a century after their triumph, to be replaced ultimately by the Ming Dynasty (1368–1644). It is in the Ming that the full-length novel first appears, really a continuation of printing trends in the Sung, but reaching a much larger audience. Ming novels and stories are as fresh as today's best sellers, and give a picture of a prosperous and sophisticated society. This literature included detective stories, 400 years before their appearance in the West, and a wide range of popular drama and opera. Art continued to follow the Sung styles, stressing the beauty of untamed Nature, with often a tiny human figure in the foreground to emphasize the puny place which people occupied in the larger natural cosmos. The Ming rebuilt the Great Wall along China's northern steppe borders originally constructed by the Ch'in,

and moved the capital to Peking, where they built an impressive complex of palaces, temples, and courtyards which can still be seen largely in their Ming form. Overseas trade and the rise of bourgeois cultures in the cities continued; it was a prosperous, confident time, well reflected in the beauty and elegance of the famous Ming porcelains. Late Ming saw the arrival of Western missionaries and traders all over Asia, who carried back to Europe ample confirmation of Marco Polo's flattering 13th-century account of China as far ahead of the West both materially and culturally.

JAPANESE CIVILIZATION

Japan made a relatively late start in the arts of civilization. The Japanese, who originated in north-central Asia, did not become dominant in the chain of islands that forms Japan until about the second or third century A.D. They were profoundly influenced by earlier devel-

Tomb figure of a camel, T'ang Dynasty

Bugaku mask, Heian

755
Revolt of An Lu-Shan

1000
High point of Heian culture in Japan

oped Korean civilization and through it by China, from which they acquired agriculture, writing, metallurgy, and city-building. Beginning in the sixth and seventh centuries A.D., the Japanese sent successive missions to China in an effort to bring to Japan as much as possible of Chinese civilization, in all of its aspects. This included Buddhism, by then a major religion in China, and the art associated with it, especially in sculpture, but also included Confucianism and the Chinese tradition of learning. Japanese art slowly departed to a degree from the Chinese model, as was only to be expected, but its origins remain clear even now. By about the year 1000, Murasaki Shikibu, a court lady at the elegant capital of Heian (hā′än) (modern Kyoto), had written what is said to be the world's first psychological novel, *The Tale of Genji*, still admired as the masterpiece of Japanese literature. Her contemporary the Lady Sei Shonagon's personal diary, *The Pillow Book*, has survived to give us an extraordinary look at the Heian court.

The Heian order was destroyed by the late twelfth century with the rise of contending warrior groups. The shogun (shō′gun), originally the emperor's military lieutenant, became politically dominant as the real ruler while the emperor remained a largely powerless figurehead. This was the age of the warrior and the bushido (bü′shē dō′) code of the samurai (sam′ü ri), but these tough, spartan fighters took as their talisman, in a very Japanese way, the cherry blossom, whose ethereal beauty is soon demolished by the first heavy rain; just so, the samurai freely gives his life to his feudal lord. Cherry blossoms became a common theme in Japanese art as well, symbolizing life's beauty combined with sadness. This was also the age of feudalism, in a Japan divided among contending groups, each of which tried to ensure the loyalty of its followers (vassals) through oaths of fealty to the

Minamoto Yoritomo

1192
Minamoto becomes Shogun of Japan

lord and the provision of military aid. Such efforts did not however ensure either unity or peace, and the period from the twelfth century to the early seventeenth is marked by constant and increasing warfare.

Nevertheless it is in this period that most samurai became literate, and many wrote poetry in what came to be called the haiku (hī′kü) form, based like so much of Japanese culture on a Chinese original, the 3 or 4-line reflection, usually on the lessons of nature. Buddhism and the Japanese version of the contemplative Chan sect in China, known in Japan as Zen, spread widely and inspired the further development of gardens and temples. Another creation of this time was the No drama, a Zen-inspired blending of dance, chanted lines, costumes, and masks. The rule of the Shogun dissolved into full civil war in the 1570s, but in 1603 the Tokugawa (tō kü gä′wä) Shogunate finally unified the country and kept it under strict feudal control until the 1850s.

Tokugawa art was flamboyantly colorful, especially the painting which covered screens and walls in the shogunal palaces, but always within the limits of good taste. The capital was moved to Edo (ed′ō) (modern Tokyo), and as the merchant group rose to prominence they and the aristocrats supported a lively popular culture there of tea houses, theaters, artists, and geisha houses. Theater now included puppets and kabuki, a more lively form than No. Haiku evolved into a widely popular form, there was a revival of Confucianism, and by about 1750 Edo had become the world's largest city. It was also during the Tokugawa Shogunate, that Japan closed itself off from foreign contact, a ban that would last more than two centuries, preserving the traditional Japanese feudal society well into the second-half of the nineteenth century.

INDIAN CIVILIZATION   Indian civilization

Kublai Khan

Pen drawing
of Akbar

1279
Kublai founds Yuan Dynasty in China

1577
Akbar becomes Mughal Emperor

began earlier even than China's, with the emergence of true cities, writing, metallurgy, and irrigated agriculture in the Indus valley soon after 2500 B.C. But the Indus culture was in decline when invaders or migrants called Aryans moved into India from the steppes of central Asia some time after 1700 B.C. By 1000 B.C. their language, an early version of Sanskrit, the root of the modern tongues of both north India and Europe, had prevailed and they had begun to develop the religion called Hinduism ("Indianism") recorded in Sanskrit texts, a blend of what they brought with them and what they found in India. Hinduism is essentially monotheistic, believing in one supreme god, but as it spread it developed a number of folk-religion gods as aids to the faithful. Indra, his chariot and his great bow, originally a tribal god of thunder, lightning, and war akin to Zeus, to whom many hymns were written, was the principal early deity, yielding later to Siva,

Brahma, and Vishnu as the creators and destroyers. Especially important were Siva Nataraja god of the dance and the harvest and his consort Parvati (later Kali), the god of death. The core of Hinduism has always been the concepts of *dharma* (duty) and *karma* (consequences of one's actions).

Most of India was politically united under the Maurya (mour′ ə) Empire (321–185 B.C.) and its last great emperor Asoka (died c. 232 B.C.) is responsible for most of what Mauryan art has survived—Asoka left beautifully carved stone pillars, to mark his domains and to spread the Buddha's message, along with the first Buddhist temples and surviving sculpture. Sculpture remains the pinnacle of Indian art, at every period in its history, and as Hindu temples were increasingly built of stone (Buddhism having largely been extinguished in India by the thirteenth century) there was new scope for a variety of magnificent architectural styles and for

Screen painting of foreigners in Nagasaki

Jade Screen, Manchu Dynasty

1636
Tokugawa Shogun closes Japan to foreigners

1644
Manchu Dynasty founded in China

sculpted figures. The Gupta (gŭp′tə) Empire (c. 320–c. 500 A.D.) saw a revival of Mauryan grandeur in the north, and produced magnificent sculpture in stone and bronze, while in the south rival kingdoms vied with each other in building splendid stone temples in traditional Hindu style. The poet and playwright Kalidasa, often compared with Shakespeare, lived in fifth century Guptan India as the chief figure in a notable flowering of Sanskrit literature.

More invaders from central Asia, now converted to Islam, poured into India from about the eleventh century. The south resisted them, but the north was ultimately reunified under the Islamic Mughal (mü′gəl) Empire in 1526. The Mughals brought not only a unified political order, but an infusion of Persian culture which profoundly affected Indian painting and architecture. The Mughals dominated India until about 1750, when mounting disarray overcame its ability to rule, and the English East India Company began its growth to ultimate supremacy.

The Chinese Classics

Two Chinese works, *The Analects* of Confucius and the *Tao Te Ching* of Lao tzu have molded the Chinese world view for the last 2500 years. To Confucius (**kən fyü′shəs**) (c. 551–479 B.C.), it was not important to acquire a lofty position in life, but rather to fulfill the responsibilities of one's position well. To show filial piety toward superiors and to set a good example for one's inferiors were life's guiding principles. Confucius believed that the measure of a man is what he contributes to society. For this reason, when he arranged the social order, he placed scholars and priests at the top, farmers second, artisans third, and merchants at the bottom. The following are selections from *The Analects*. What does Confucius mean by harmony?

THE MASTER SAID, TO LEARN AND AT DUE TIMES TO REPEAT what one has learnt, is not that after all a pleasure? That friends should come to one from afar, is this not after all delightful? To remain unsoured even though one's merits are unrecognized by others, is that not after all what is expected of a gentleman?

Master Yu said, In the usages of ritual it is harmony that is prized; the Way of the Former Kings from this got its beauty. Both small matters and great depend upon it. If things go amiss, he who knows the harmony will be able to attune them. But if harmony itself is not modulated by ritual, things will still go amiss.

The Master said, Govern the people by regulations, keep order among them by chastisements, and they will flee from you, and lose all self-respect. Govern them by moral force, keep order among them by ritual and they will keep their self-respect and come to you of their own accord.

The Master said, At fifteen I set my heart upon learning. At thirty, I had planted my feet firm upon the ground. At forty, I no longer suffered from perplexities. At fifty, I knew what were the biddings of Heaven. At sixty, I heard them with docile ear. At seventy, I could follow the dictates of my own heart; for what I desire no longer overstepped the boundaries of right.

The Master said, High office filled by a man of narrow views, ritual performed without reverence, the forms of mourning observed without grief — these are things I cannot bear to see!

The Master said, In the morning, hear the Way; in the evening, die content!

Jan Ch'iu said, It is not that your Way does not commend itself to me, but that it demands powers I do not possess. The Master said, He whose strength gives out collapses during the course of the journey (the Way); but you deliberately draw the line.

The Master said, The wise man delights in water, the Good man delights in mountains. For the wise move; but the Good stay still. The wise are happy; but the Good, secure.

Lao tzu (lou′ tse′) (c. 500s B.C.) respected learning as highly as Confucius, but also emphasized the importance of the senses and instinct. One should flow with the Tao or the way of nature. Flowing with the way of nature provides harmony between opposites and gives Taoism its spiritual force. The following are two chapters from the Lao tzu's *Tao Te Ching*. What is meant by the Tao?

1

The tao that can be told
is not the eternal Tao.
The name that can be named
is not the eternal Name.
The unnamable is the eternally real.
Naming is the origin
of all particular things.
Free from desire, you realize the mystery.
Caught in desire, you see only the manifestations.
Yet mystery and manifestations
arise from the same source.
This source is called darkness.
Darkness within darkness.
The gateway to all understanding.

25

There was something formless and perfect
before the universe was born.
It is serene. Empty.
Solitary. Unchanging.
Infinite. Eternally present.
It is the mother of the universe.
For lack of a better name,
I call it the Tao.

It flows through all things,
inside and outside, and returns
to the origin of all things.
The Tao is great.
The universe is great.
Earth is great.
Man is great.
These are the four great powers.
Man follows the earth.
Earth follows the universe.
The universe follows the Tao.
The Tao follows only itself.

THINKING CRITICALLY

1. *Recognizing Values* What is the purpose of moral force and ritual to Confucius? What is the place of formlessness in Taoism?

2. *Making Comparisons* How can leaders foster unity according to Confucius and Lao tzu? Are their views compatible?

3. *Linking Past and Present* In what parts of contemporary American culture does study of the past and its wisdom play a key role?

WRITER'S PORTFOLIO

1. *Extending the Selection* Examine some aspect of contemporary society — the cult of celebrity or the decline of participation in elections for example — from a Confucian perspective.

2. *Examining Key Questions* What is the right way to live according to Confucius? according to Lao tzu? Are these views compatible?

The Moral Leadership of the Emperor

The Chinese imperial capital was designed as a miniature replica of a great picture of the universe. Through the emperor, it was believed heaven graciously had allowed mankind a glimpse of one of its ultimate secrets. Han rulers were so successful in justifying imperial rule that their theories lasted for two thousand years. They adhered to certain enduring values while adjusting to changing times. They followed the Confucian teaching that if the emperor set a good example, his officials would serve honestly, and his subjects would follow willingly. So long as a ruler continues to set a good example he is said to hold a mandate from heaven. Theoretically this mandate is not absolute, but based on adherence to principle. The emperor is viewed as part of a cosmic totality explained as a trinity of heaven, earth, and man. The two texts, printed below, provide insight into the Han formula. *Huai-nan tzu (The Philosopher of Huai-nan)* was compiled by Taoist scholars of the Han court in 140 B.C. The excerpt here is called "The Moral Power of the Ruler." The second text is written by the famous Confucian scholar, Tung Chung-shu (c. 179– c. 104 B.C.), entitled *Ch'un-ch'iu fan-lu (The Deep Significance of the Spring and Autumn Annals).* What advice is given regarding right?

from the *Huai-nan tzu,* "The Moral Power of the Ruler"

THE POWER TO ACHIEVE SUCCESS OR FAILURE LIES WITH THE ruler. If the measuring-line is true, then the wood will be straight, not because one makes a special effort, but because that which it is "ruled" by makes it so. In the same way if the ruler is sincere and upright, then honest officials will serve in his government and scoundrels will go into hiding, but if the ruler is not upright then evil men will have their way and loyal men will retire to seclusion. Why is it that people often scratch melons or gourds with their fingernails, but never scratch stones or jewels? Because no matter how hard they scratch stones or jewels they can never make an impression. In the same way if the ruler can be made to adhere to right, maintain fairness, and follow a measuring-line, as it were, in measuring high and low, then even though his ministers come to him with evil designs it will be the same as dashing eggs against a rock or throwing fire into water. King Ling loved slim waists and all the women went on diets and starved themselves. The King of Yüeh admired bravery and all the men outdid each other in dangerous feats defying death. From this we may see that he who wields authority can change the customs and transform the manners of his people.

Tung Chung-shu, from *Ch'un-ch'iu fan-lu*

THE RULER IS THE BASIS OF THE STATE. IN ADMINISTERING THE state, nothing is more effective for educating the people than reverence for the basis. If the basis is revered then the ruler may transform the people as though by supernatural power, but if the basis is not revered then the ruler will have nothing by which to lead his people. Then though he employ harsh penalties and severe punishments the people will not follow him. This is to drive the state to ruin, and there is no greater disaster. What do we mean by the basis? Heaven, earth, and man are the basis of all creatures. Heaven gives them birth, earth nourishes them, and man brings them to completion. Heaven provides them at birth with a sense of filial and brotherly love, earth nourishes them with clothing and food, and man completes them with rites and music. The three act together as hands and feet join to complete the body and none can be dispensed with.... If all three are lacking, then the people will become like deer, each person following his own desires, each family possessing its own ways. Fathers cannot employ their sons nor rulers their ministers, and though there be walls and battlements they will be called an "empty city."... But the enlightened and worthy ruler, being of good faith, is strictly attentive to the three bases. His sacrifices are conducted with utmost reverence; he makes offerings to and serves his ancestors; he advances brotherly affection and encourages filial conduct. In this way he serves the basis of Heaven. He personally grasps the plow handle and plows a furrow, plucks the mulberry himself and feeds the silkworms, breaks new ground to increase the grain supply and opens the way for a sufficiency of clothing and food. In this way he serves the basis of earth. He sets up schools for the nobles and in the towns and villages to teach filial piety and brotherly affection, reverence and humility. He enlightens the people with education and moves them with rites and music. Thus he serves the basis of man. If he rightly serves these three, then the people will be like sons and brothers, not daring to be unsubmissive.... This is called a spontaneous reward, and when it comes, though he relinquish his throne, give up his kingdom and depart, the people will take up their children on their backs, follow him, and keep him as their lord, so that he can never leave them....

Those who in ancient times invented writing drew three lines and connected them through the middle, calling the character "king" [王]. The three lines are Heaven, earth, and man, and that which passes through the middle joins the principles of all three. Occupying the center of Heaven, earth, and man, passing through and joining all three—if he is not a king, who can do this?...

Therefore the great concern of the ruler lies in diligently watching over and guarding his heart, that his loves and hates, his angers and joys may be displayed in accordance with right, as the mild and cool, the cold and hot weather come forth in proper season. If the ruler constantly practices this without error, then his emotions will never be at fault, as spring and autumn, winter and summer are never out of order. Then may he form a trinity with Heaven and earth. If he holds these four passions deep within him and does not allow them recklessly to come forth, then may he be called the equal of Heaven.

THINKING CRITICALLY

1. *Recognizing Values* What are the three obligations of the ruler? How does he satisfy them?

2. *Making Comparisons* What do the two selections say will happen to a kingdom if a leader is ineffective?

3. *Linking Past and Present* Do we still expect our leaders to provide moral leadership for the nation? Do you think they ought to provide a good example?

WRITER'S PORTFOLIO

1. *Extending the Selection* Identify and discuss an ideal from one of these texts that could be applied to contemporary American society.

2. *Examining Key Questions* Summarize how a leader should act according to these texts.

Chinese Poetry

Chinese scholars used poetry to reflect both their simplest and most profound and heartfelt thoughts. A theme could be as simple as receiving a gift, or as complex as the morality of war. Frequently themes were based on ancient classics applied to universal concepts such as love, nature, peace, or ethics. The *shih* or lyric form has dominated Chinese literature from ancient times to modern. T'ao Ch'ien (**dou′ chē′en**) (365–427) also called T'ao Yuan-ming, was known as the father of eremitic (reclusive) poetry. T'ao's seclusion, however, belongs to the highest type, that of the mind and spirit. His poetry plainly reflects quietude, rustic simplicity, and nostalgia. "The Peach Blossom Spring" chronicles a flight from the Ch'in (Qin) age of disorder during the reign of the first Chinese emperor, Shih huang-ti (c. 221–207 B.C.). The character or persona whom T'ao created to narrate this poem is a fisherman who accidentally discovers a heavenly serene village of exiles from Ch'in excess. Blessed by political stability, affluence, and imperial patronage, the T'ang (Tang) Dynasty (618–907) was China's most brilliant era of poetic creation. Li Po (**lē bô**) (c. 701–762) and Po Chü-i (**bô jü-ē**) (772–846) are considered among the greatest of all T'ang poets, establishing standards for what became known as China's golden age of literature. While T'ang wars of conquest embellished the history of this age, Li Po's poem "Fighting South of the Ramparts" provides a sober reminder of the question of ethics in territorial expansion. Possibly the best known of all Chinese poets, Li Po was a romantic and imagination is the key to his poetry. Like Confucius, Po Chü-i valued his poems as a method of conveying instruction. He is essentially a serious poet, concentrating on the moral and social value of poetry. In "Watching the Reapers," he expressed his veneration of farmers. During the Sung (Song) Dynasty (960–1279) there was a resurgence of poetry and landscape painting inspired by Taoist attitudes toward nature. The poem by Su Shih (**sü shē**) (1036–1101) addresses nature with words generally reserved in the West for humanist expression. Water symbolizes the arteries of the mountains, and rocks form the bones of heaven and earth. Su's poetry contains the ideals of emancipation and distance from the material world. These ideals reveal the influence of Buddhism which developed in China shortly before Su's time. In the following Chinese poems, what values are expressed?

T'ao Ch'ien

The Peach Blossom Spring

The Ying clan disrupted Heaven's ordinance
and good men withdrew from such a world.
Huang and Ch'i went off to Shang Mountain
And these people too fled into hiding.
Little by little their tracks were obliterated
The paths they followed overgrown at last.
By agreement they set about farming the land
When the sun went down each rested from his toil.
Bamboo and mulberry provided shade enough,
They planted beans and millet, each in season.
From spring silkworms came the long silk thread
On the fall harvest no king's tax was paid.
No sign of traffic on overgrown roads,
Cockcrow and dogsbark within each other's earshot.
Their ritual vessels were of old design,
And no new fashions in the clothes they wore.
Children wandered about singing songs,
Greybeards went paying one another calls.
When grass grew thick they saw the time was mild,
As trees went bare they knew the wind was sharp.
Although they had no calendar to tell,
The four seasons still filled out a year.
Joyous in their ample happiness
They had no need of clever contrivance.
Five hundred years this rare deed stayed hid,
Then one fine day the fay retreat was found.
The pure and the shallow belong to separate worlds:
In a little while they were hidden again.
Let me ask you who are convention-bound,
Can you fathom those outside the dirt and noise?
I want to tread upon the thin thin air
And rise up high to find my own kind.

Li Po

Fighting South of the Ramparts

Last year we were fighting at the source of the Sang-kan[1];
This year we are fighting on the Onion River road.
We have washed our swords in the surf of Parthian seas;
We have pastured our horses among the snows of T'ien
     Shan,
The King's armies have grown grey and old
Fighting ten thousand leagues away from home.
The Huns have no trade but battle and carnage;
They have no fields or ploughlands,
But only wastes where white bones lie among yellow sands.
Where the House of Ch'in built the great wall that was to
     keep away the Tartars.
There, in its turn, the House of Han lit beacons of war.
The beacons are always alight, fighting and marching never
     stop.
Men die in the field, slashing sword to sword;
The horses of the conquered neigh piteously to Heaven.
Crows and hawks peck for human guts,
Carry them in their beaks and hang them on the branches of
     withered trees.
Captains and soldiers are smeared on the bushes and grass;
The General schemed in vain.
Know therefore that the sword is a cursed thing
Which the wise man uses only if he must.

Note of Thanks

The wine of Lu is like amber, the fish of Wên River
Have scales of dark brocade. Noble the spirit
Of these generous clerks in the province of Shan-tung.
With your own hands you brought these things as a present to
     a stranger from afar.
We have found much to agree about and feel regard for one
     another.
The gallons of wine, these two fish are tokens of deep feeling.
See how their gills suck and puff, their fins expand

---

1. **Sang-kan** This and the following place names are meant to reflect the immensity of the Chinese empire and her enemies.

Lashing against the silver dish, as though they would fly away.
I call the boy to clean the board, to wield the frosty blade.
The red entrails fall like flowers, the white flesh like snow.
Reeling I fix my golden saddle, mount and ride for home.

Po Chü-i

Watching the Reapers
Tillers of the soil have few idle months;
In the fifth month their toil is double-fold.
A south-wind visits the fields at night:
Suddenly the hill is covered with yellow corn.
Wives and daughters shoulder baskets of rice;
Youths and boys carry the flasks of wine.
Following after they bring a wage of meat
To the strong reapers toiling on the southern hill,
Whose feet are burned by the hot earth they tread,
Whose backs are scorched by flames of the shining sky.
Tired they toil, caring nothing for the heat,
Grudging the shortness of the long summer day.
A poor woman follows at the reapers' side
With an infant child carried close at her breast.
With her right hand she gleans the fallen grain;
On her left arm a broken basket hangs.
And I today…by virtue of what right
Have I never once tended field or tree?
My government pay is three hundred tons;
At the year's end I have still grain in hand.
Thinking of this, secretly I grew ashamed;
And all day the thought lingered in my head.

Su Shih

At the Heng-ts'ui Pavilion of Fa-hui Monastery
Mornings I see the Wu Mountain recumbent,
Evenings I see the Wu Mountain standing erect.
The Wu Mountain wears more than one face —
Tossing and turning to look its best for you.

A recluse, I rise from my painted pavilion;
Holding everything empty, I see no object before me.
There's only this ridge a thousand paces high,
A barrier and screen from east to west.

Since spring I've had no date of return to my old country.
Who speaks of autumn's sadness? Spring is sadder still.
Having sailed on these placid waters, I long for the Brocade River;
Now, looking at these recumbent green hills, I'm reminded of
      Mount O-mei.

When will the carved railings ever look their best?
Not just the man who leans against railings easily grows old.
A hundred years' flourishing and decay, far more lamentable,
Though I know pools and pavilions will turn to briers and
      brambles.

Wanderers who look for the place where once I've wandered
Need only to come to where the Wu Mountain lies recumbent.

THINKING CRITICALLY

1. *Recognizing Values* Examine each poem. Which echo a Confucian world-view? Which reflect a more Taoist outlook?

2. *Making Inferences* What is the tone of each of these poems? Are they similar to Western poems you have read? Why or why not?

3. *Linking Past and Present* Poets have frequently protested about the pointless barbarity of war. Find some modern war poems and compare them to Li Po's "Fighting South of the Ramparts."

WRITER'S PORTFOLIO

1. *Extending the Selection* Write your own poem, commemorating an experience or event. Try to imitate the tone of one of these four poets.

2. *Examining Key Questions* Are these poets expressing a certain moral viewpoint? What are they attempting to teach?

The Examination System

Po Chü-i was in his twenty-eighth year when he sent a letter to the Supervising Censor in the capital, Chang-an (Xian). Po's letter sought a recommendation to take the civil-service exam based upon his years of study and the quality of his prose and poetry. This exam was first administered in China during the Han Dynasty (206 B.C.– A.D. 220) and was based on the Confucian classics. Only by passing this exam could a candidate ever hope to hold government office or be considered among the scholarly class of society. The self-effacing and fawning terms used in a candidate's letter of application were expected as a show of good manners. The exam questions in Po's time were both cultural and political. One question required him to reconcile the contradiction in two ancient classical texts about the marketing and exchange of products. Another asked the candidate's opinion about a system of price stabilizing called *Harmonizing Purchase*. The exam itself took many days in isolation to complete. Po's letter of application appears below, followed by the last poem Po wrote before taking the exam. What is the tone of Po's letter?

O̲N THIS NEW YEAR'S DAY PO CHÜ-I, A CANDIDATE SENT UP BY his hometown for examination, respectfully sends his page-boy with a letter to your Excellency the Supervising Censor. I know that your Excellency's doors are thronged not only by would-be visitors, but also by the bearers of innumerable letters. But the purpose of those who thus obtrude themselves upon you, numerous though they are, is I believe in every case the same. Their one and only aim is to obtain your Excellency's commendation and patronage. My object is a very different one. The reason that I do not attempt to see you in person and instead am sending you this letter is that I merely wish to furnish you with evidence upon which you may decide for me a point about which I am in doubt....

The ambition of a candidate who has decided to take the Literary Examination, whatever his merits, is naturally to pass successfully and make a name for himself. In this respect I cannot claim to be any exception and for that very reason I have devoted myself unreservedly to the most painstaking study of literature for ten years, and was at last sent up by my home-town for examination.

Among those in like case there are some who have obtained their degree at the first attempt, and their example stirs my ambition and encourages me to push on. But I see that there are others who fail even at a tenth attempt; and this makes me wonder whether I can stay the course and had not better give up....

I am sending you herewith twenty pieces of miscellaneous prose and a hundred poems. I entreat you to recognize the sincerity of my request. The matter is trivial and I am myself of no account. Do not for that reason ignore it, but in a moment of leisure from public business cast a critical eye on these writings. If they justify me in going forward, I beg for one word to that effect; in which case I shall make every effort to polish my dull wits, whip up my nag and forge ahead. If on the other hand you tell me not to stand, then I will give up my plans, retrace my steps and content myself with a life of obscurity.

For days past this conflict has been warring in my breast. I beg for a single word to resolve it. I shall hope for an answer within ten days. If I hear that you have deigned to glance at my shabby productions, I shall be as one "robbed of breath and ravished of his soul." But I must be brief. Chü-i respectfully twice prostrates himself.

> The awninged coaches, the singing and the flutes fill the City
>   with their din;
> One there is, in the midst of them all who "stands facing the
>   corner".
> Sad at midnight when he draws the blind and moonbeams fill
>   the room,
> Weeping at dusk when the green hills make him think of home.
> The spring wind blows the fields, new buds break;
> The light yellow of the willow-branches is wet with a sprinkling
>   of rain.
> My youth is gone, I am almost thirty and know that I have missed
> My last chance in this life to be young and happy in the spring.

Po Chü-i won first-class honors in the exam, which paved the way for him to a successful public career. The following selection was written by Po Chü-i after his name had already appeared on the list of successful candidates. He expresses his sincere hope that he could do justice to the honor of being selected and display the expected humility of a successful candidate. What is Po's mood?

I SWEAR THAT TILL MY DYING DAY I WILL CONTINUE TO REPAY what my lord has done for me, and repay him in this sense: that I will strive to do only what he would wish, that I will further his plans.... I must make all my actions conform to a strict standard and all my writings must inculcate the highest principles. I must make a practice of studying at set times and never be idle or put study aside. As to advancement in the world, I must let it come at its own pace and not go out of my way to force myself on. I have obtained a First Class in the examination and have in so doing made a name for myself; but that is no reason to be puffed up or self-satisfied.

THINKING CRITICALLY

1. *Making Inferences* In the second selection, Po writes that he must not chase after advancement. Why do you think he wrote this? Why do you think he is self-effacing even in a journal?

2. *Making Comparisons* Compare the tone of the Po's writings before and after he took the exams. How are they different? Which words best point out this difference?

3. *Linking Past and Present* Can you think of any modern equivalents to the exams Po took? What does passing these exams allow you to do?

WRITER'S PORTFOLIO

1. *Extending the Selection* Imagine you were one of Po's fellow candidates. Write a letter to a friend telling of Po's success. Think carefully before you write about how a fellow candidate would respond to Po's success.

2. *Examining Key Questions* What does Po's career suggest about the route to success in China?

Chinese Landscape Painting

The Chinese name for landscape painting is *shan-shui*. This word literally means "mountain water pictures." Most Chinese landscape paintings combine these elements together with variations of sheer

cliffs, jagged rocks, and towering waterfalls. Landscape painting emerged at the end of the T'ang (Tang) Dynasty (618–907), and flowered under the Sung (Song) Dynasty (960–1279). The Chinese landscape artist is not as interested in pursuing realism as he is in pursuing spiritual truth. Truth is captured by being in harmony with nature—the main tenet of Taoism. The painting by Chu-jan (c. 975) *Seeking the Tao in the Autumn Mountains* represents this artistic quest. The beauty of the painting comes from the artist's self-conscious attempt to search for harmony and understanding, not from his attempt to be realistic. Although the same can be said for Ma Yuan's (c. 1200) *Bare Willows and Distant Mountains*, which appears on page 321, this painting is far more subtle in its portrayal of the landscape. Shen Chou (jō) (1427–1509) was known not only as a painter, but also a poet. His *Poet on Mountain Top* contains his own poetry in the upper left-hand corner, combining the three

Chu-jan, Seeking the Tao in the Autumn Mountains, *Sung Dynasty*

Shen Chou, Poet on Mountain Top, *Ming Dynasty*

prized arts of landscape, poetry, and calligraphy. The simplicity of the work belies its portrayal of the harmony of the artist with nature. What is the most prominent feature in each of these paintings?

THINKING CRITICALLY

1. *Recognizing Values* What are the perishable or impermanent qualities in each of these scenes?

2. *Drawing Conclusions* How are human beings depicted in these paintings? Is this comparable to humanity's place in Western art?

3. *Linking Past and Present* Chinese artists prepared their spirit before they worked. Do artists still consider their work a spiritual activity?

WRITER'S PORTFOLIO

1. *Extending the Selection* Write a prose description of one of the scenes depicted in these paintings.

2. *Examining Key Questions* What does these artists's view of nature tell you about how humans should live in this world?

Heian Court Life

From the Heian Era (794–1185) emerged Japan's earliest prose literature, much of it written by women. The two best-known works are the great classical novel, *The Tale of Genji* by Lady Murasaki Shikibu (c. 970–c. 1014) and *The Pillow Book* of Sei Shonagon (c. 966–c. 1013). Sei's work is a diary of court life and of her likes, dislikes, and impressions. The term "pillow book" comes from the writing itself. Writers would compose these passages after they retired to their rooms for the evening before falling asleep. The books were kept next to the bed, similar to the way in which one today might keep a book or magazine to read. Sei Shonagon worshipped the imperial family and people of title, and her love of aristocratic life is reflected in her diary. The following two entries from The *Pillow Book* present Sei's unusual method of remembering events. What does Sei find pleasant?

ON THE FIRST DAY OF THE FIRST MONTH

On the first day of the First Month and on the third of the Third I like the sky to be perfectly clear.

On the fifth of the Fifth Month I prefer a cloudy sky.

On the seventh day of the Seventh Month it should also be cloudy; but in the evening it should be clear, so that the moon shines brightly in the sky and one can almost see the shape of the stars.

On the ninth of the Ninth Month there should be a drizzle from early dawn. Then there will be heavy dew on the chrysanthemums, while the floss silk that covers them will be wet through and drenched also with the precious scent of blossoms. Sometimes the rain stops early in the morning, but the sky is still overcast, and it looks as if it may start raining again at any moment. This too I find very pleasant.

IT IS SO STIFLINGLY HOT

It is so stiflingly hot in the Seventh Month that even at night one keeps all the doors and lattices open....

It is dawn and a woman is lying in bed after her lover has taken his leave. She is covered up to her head with a light mauve robe that has a lining of dark violet; the color of both the outside and the lining is fresh and glossy. The woman, who appears to be asleep, wears an unlined orange robe and a dark crimson skirt of stiff silk whose cords hang loosely by her side, as if they have been left untied. Her thick tresses tumble over each other in cascades, and one can imagine how long her hair must be when it falls freely down her back.

Near by another woman's lover is making his way home in the misty dawn. He is wearing loose violet trousers, an orange hunting costume, so lightly colored that one can hardly tell whether it has been dyed or not, a white robe of stiff silk, and a scarlet robe of glossy, beaten silk. His clothes, which are damp from the mist, hang loosely about him. From the dishevelment of his sidelocks one can tell how negligently he must have tucked his hair into his black lacquered headdress when he got up. He wants to return and write his next-morning letter before the dew on the morning glories has had time to vanish; but the path seems endless, and to divert himself he hums "the sprouts in the flax fields."

As he walks along, he passes a house with an open lattice. He is on his way to report for official duty, but cannot help stopping to lift up the blind and peep into the room. It amuses him to think that a man has probably been spending the night here and has only recently got up to leave, just as happened to himself. Perhaps that man too had felt the charm of the dew.

Looking round the room, he notices near the woman's pillow an open fan with a magnolia frame and purple paper; and at the foot of her curtain of state he sees some narrow strips of Michinoku paper and also some other paper of a faded color, either orange-red or maple.

The woman senses that someone is watching her and, looking up from under her bedclothes, sees a gentleman leaning against the wall by the threshold, a smile on his face. She can tell at once that he is the sort of man with whom she need feel no reserve. All the same, she does not want to enter into any familiar relations with him, and she is annoyed that he should have seen her asleep.

"Well, well, Madam," says the man, leaning forward so that the upper part of his body comes behind her curtains, "what a long nap you're having after your morning adieu! You really are a lie-abed!"

"You call me that, Sir," she replied, "only because you're annoyed at having had to get up before the dew had time to settle."

Their conversation may be commonplace, yet I find there is something delightful about the scene.

Now the gentleman leans further forward and, using his own fan, tries to get hold of the fan by the woman's pillow. Fearing his closeness, she moves further back into her curtain enclosure, her heart pounding. The gentleman picks up the magnolia fan and, while examining it, says in a slightly bitter tone, "How standoffish you are!"

But now it is growing light; there is a sound of people's voices, and it looks as if the sun will soon be up. Only a short while ago this same man was hurrying home to write his next-morning letter before the mists had time to clear. Alas, how easily his intentions have been forgotten!

While all this is afoot, the woman's original lover has been busy with his own next-morning letter, and now, quite unexpectedly, the messenger arrives at her house. The letter is attached to a spray of clover, still damp with dew, and the paper gives off a delicious aroma of incense. Because of the new visitor, however, the woman's servants cannot deliver it to her.

Finally it becomes unseemly for the gentleman to stay any longer. As he goes, he is amused to think that a similar scene may be taking place in the house he left earlier that morning.

THINKING CRITICALLY

1. *Making Inferences* What sort of life does Sei seem to live? Does she seem like a happy or sad person?

2. *Recognizing Values* What do you think is the point of Sei's story "It is So Stiflingly Hot"? What is its tone?

3. *Linking Past and Present* One of the compelling qualities of this book is that it is really a gossipy account of the powerful and famous. How does it compare to recent tell-all accounts and biographies?

WRITER'S PORTFOLIO

1. *Extending the Selection* Sei Shonagon loved to make lists. If she were alive today, she might make a list of, for example, the things she disliked most about opening night at the opera. Make your own list of ten things you like or dislike, concentrating on details.

2. *Examining Key Questions* What do you think would be the right way to live according to Sei Shonagon?

Heike Monogatari

The *Heike* (**hā⁄kā**) *Monogatari* ("Tale of the Heike") is an account of the civil wars between two warrior families, the Minamoto and the Taira. In 1156 a dispute over succession to the emperor began a series of struggles between the Minamoto and Taira (or Heike) families that continued until 1185. These wars grasped the imagination of the Japanese people, giving rise to legends of chivalry and daring which have been retold repeatedly in literature. The Taira clan was essentially exterminated in these wars, leaving the Minamoto in control of the central government. Authority rested in the office of Shogun, or supreme military commander — the Emperor was a puppet ruler. The *Heike Monogatari* is the story of the vanquished Taira clan, assembled in the early thirteenth century. The Kamakura period (1185–1333) was characterized by continual warfare and the rise of the powerful military class called the *Samurai*. Because it was essential for these warriors to be highly trained and regimented, they operated under an iron-clad code of conduct called *Bushido*. A samurai was prepared to give his life in defense of his leader or his honor. References to the code recur throughout the *Heike Monogatari*. The following excerpt from the *Heike Monogatari* describes the death of Lord Kiso, a Taira leader. How does Kiso die?

KISO-NO-YOSHINAKA HAD BROUGHT WITH HIM FROM SHINANO two female attendants, Tomoe and Yamabuki. Yamabuki had fallen ill and stayed in the capital. Of the two, Tomoe was especially beautiful, with white skin, long hair, and charming features. She was also a remarkably strong archer, and as a swordsman she was a warrior worth a thousand, ready to confront a demon or god, mounted or on foot. She handled unbroken horses with superb skill; she rode unscathed down perilous descents. Whenever a battle was imminent, Yoshinaka sent her out as his first captain, equipped with strong armor, an oversized sword, and a mighty bow; and she performed more deeds of valor than any of his other warriors. Thus she was now one of the seven who remained after all the others had fled or perished.

There were rumors that Yoshinaka was making for the Tanba Road by way of Nagasaka, and also that he was heading north through the Ryuge Pass. In actuality, he was fleeing toward Seta in the hope of finding Imai no Shiro Kanehira. Kanehira himself had started back toward the capital with furled banner, worried about his master, after having lost all but fifty of his eight hundred defenders at Seta. The two arrived simultaneously at Uchide-no-hama in the vicinity of Otsu, recognized one another from about three hundred and fifty feet away, and galloped together.

Lord Kiso took Kanehira by the hand, "I meant to die at the Rokujo riverbed, but I broke through a swarm of enemies and came away here because I wanted to find you."

"Your words do me great honor," Kanchira said. "I meant to die at Seta, but I have come this far because I was worried about you."

"I see that our karma tie is still intact. My warriors scattered into the mountains and woods after the enemy broke our formations; some of them must still be nearby. Have that furled banner of yours raised!"

More than three hundred riders responded to the unfurling of Imai's banner—men who had fled from the capital or Seta, or who had come from some other place. Yoshinaka was overjoyed. "Why can't we fight one last battle, now that we have a force of this size? Whose is the band I see massed over there?"

"They say the commander is Ichijo no Jiro Tadayori from Kai."

"What is his strength?"

"He is supposed to have six thousand riders."

"Then we are well matched! If we must meet death, let it be by galloping against a worthy foe and falling outnumbered." Yoshinaka rode forward in the lead.

That day, Lord Kiso was attired in a red brocade hitatare, a suit of armor laced with thick Chinese damask, and a horned helmet. At his side, he wore a magnificent oversized sword; high on his back, there rode a quiver containing the few arrows left from his earlier encounters, all fledged with eagle tail feathers. He grasped a rattan-wrapped bow and sat in a gold-edged saddle astride his famous horse Oniashige [Roan Demon], a very stout and brawny animal. Standing in his stirrups, he announced his name in a mighty voice. "You must have heard of Kiso no Kanja in the past; now you see him! I am the Morning Sun Commander Minamoto no Yoshinaka, Director of the Imperial Stables of the Left and Governor of Iyo Province. They tell me you are Ichijo no Jiro from Kai. We are well matched! Cut off my head and show it to Yoritomo!" He galloped forward, shouting.

"The warrior who has just announced his name is their commander-in-Chief," Ichijo no Jiro said. "Wipe out the whole force, men! Get them all, young retainers! Kill them!"

The easterners moved to surround Yoshinaka with their superior numbers, each hoping to be the one to take his head. Yoshinaka's three hundred riders galloped lengthwise, sidewise, zigzag, and crosswise in the midst of the six thousand foes and finally burst through to the rear, only fifty strong.

As the fifty went on their way after having broken free, they came to a defensive position manned by two thousand riders under the command of Toi no Jiro Sanehira. Again, they broke through and went on. Again, they galloped through enemy bands — here four or five hundred, there two or three hundred, or a hundred and forty or fifty, or a hundred — until only five of them were left. Even then, Tomoe remained alive.

"Quickly, now," Lord Kiso said to Tomoe. "You are a woman, so be off with you; go wherever you please. I intend to die in battle, or to kill myself if I am wounded. It would be unseemly to let people say, 'Lord Kiso kept a woman with him during his last battle.'"

Reluctant to flee, Tomoe rode with the others until she could resist no longer. Then she pulled up. "Ah! If only I could find a worthy foe! I would fight a last battle for His Lordship to watch," she thought.

As she sat there, thirty riders came into view, led by Onda no Hachiro Moroshige, a man renowned in Musahi Province for his great strength. Tomoe galloped into their midst, rode up alongside Moroshige, seized him in a powerful grip, pulled him down against the pommel of her saddle, held him motionless, twisted off his head, and threw it away. Afterward, she discarded armor and helmet and fled toward the eastern provinces.

Tezuka no Taro Mitsumori died in battle; Tezuka no Betto fled. Only two horsemen remained, Imai no Shiro Kanehira and Lord Kiso.

"I have never noticed it before, but my armor seems heavy today," Lord Kiso said.

"You are not tired yet, and your horse is still strong. Why should you find a suit of armor heavy? You are discouraged because there is nobody left to fight on our side. But you should think of me as a man worth a thousand ordinary warriors. I will hold off the enemy awhile with my last seven or eight arrows. That place over there is the Awazu Pine Woods: kill yourself among the trees."

As the two rode, whipping their horses, a new band of fifty warriors appeared. "Get into the pine woods. I will hold these enemies at bay," Kanehira said.

"I ought to have perished in the capital. My only reason for fleeing here was that I wanted to die with you. Let's not be killed in different places; let's go down together." Lord Kiso brought his mount alongside Kanehira's, ready to gallop forward.

Kanehira leaped down and took his master's horse by the mouth. "No matter how glorious a warrior's earlier reputation may have been, an ignoble death means eternal disgrace. You are tired; there are no forces following you. If you are isolated by the enemy and dragged down to your death by some fellow's insignificant retainer, people will say, 'So-and-So's retainer killed the famous Lord Kiso, the man known throughout Japan.' I would hate to see that happen. Please, please, go into the pine woods."

"Well, then…" Lord Kiso galloped toward the Awazu Pine Woods.

Kanehira dashed into the fifty riders alone, stood up in his stirrups, and announced his name in a mighty voice. "You must have heard of me long ago; see me now with your own eyes! I am Imai no Shiro Kanehira, aged thirty-three, foster brother to Lord Kiso. The Kamakura Lord Yoritomo himself must know that such a person exists. Kill me and show him my head!" He fired off his remaining eight arrows in a fast and furious barrage that felled eight men on the spot. (It is impossible to say whether or not they were killed.) Then he drew his sword and galloped slashing from place to place, without meeting a man willing to face him. Many were the trophies he amassed! The easterners surrounded him and let fly a hail of arrows, hoping to shoot him down, but none of their shafts found a chink in his armor or penetrated its stout plates, and he remained uninjured.

Lord Kiso galloped toward the Awazu Pine Woods, a lone rider. The shadows were gathering on the twenty-first of the First Month, and a thin film of ice had formed. Unaware that a deep paddy field lay in front of him, he sent his horse plunging into the mire. The animal sank below its head and stayed there, motionless, despite furious flogging with stirrups and whip. Lord Kiso glanced backward, worried about Kanehira, and Ishida no Jiro Tamehisa, who was hard on his heels, drew his bow to the full and sent an arrow thudding into his face. Mortally wounded, he sagged forward with the bowl of his helmet against the horse's neck.

Two of Tamehisa's retainers went up and took Lord Kiso's head. Tamehisa impaled it on the tip of his sword, raised it aloft, and announced in a mighty voice, "Miura no Ishida no Jiro Tamehisa has killed Lord Kiso, the man known throughout Japan!"

Kanehira heard the shout as he battled. "I don't need to fight to protect anyone now. Take a look, easterners! This is how the bravest man in Japan commits suicide!" He put the tip of his sword in his mouth, humped headlong from his horse, and perished, run through. Thus, it turned out that there was no combat worthy of the name at Awazu.

THINKING CRITICALLY

1. *Recognizing Values* Why does Kanehira want Kiso to commit suicide? Do you think Kanehira thought Kiso died appropriately?

2. *Making Inferences* Why does Kiso send Tomoe away? Do you think it is vanity or concern?

3. *Linking Past and Present* What characteristics growing out of the feudal era might you ascribe to Japanese culture? Give examples of how the characteristics you selected are or are not evident in contemporary Japanese society.

WRITER'S PORTFOLIO

1. *Extending the Selection* Write a summary of the death of Kiso from the standpoint of one of Tamehisa's followers.

2. *Examining Key Questions* How should a leader act according to the feudal code exhibited in the *Heike Monogatari*?

No Drama

One of the principal forms of classical Japanese theater, the *No* drama developed from traditional religious festivals in the fourteenth and fifteenth centuries. A highly stylized form of theater, the *No* drama was as much a dance as it was a play. They were staged with little scenery and few props, and performed by all-male casts wearing symbolic masks and magnificent costumes. Most *No* dramas were tragedies, and their authors were actors, as well as playwrights. Their audience was primarily the aristocracy, and the plays were presented as part of dramatic programs that lasted all day. The following *No* play *Hatsuyuki* or *Early Snow* was written by Koparu Zembo Motoyasu (1453–1532). Why is the bird called Early Snow?

SERVANT. I am a servant at the Nyoroku Shrine in the Great Temple of Izumo. My name is Evening Mist. You must know that the Lord Abbot has a daughter, a beautiful lady and gentle as can be. And she keeps a tame bird that was given her a year ago, and because it was a lovely white bird she called it Hatsuyuki, Early Snow; and she loves it dearly.

I have not seen the bird to-day. I think I will go to the bird-cage and have a look at it. (*She goes to the cage.*)

Mercy on us, the bird is not there! Whatever shall I say to my lady? But I shall have to tell her. I think I'll tell her now. Madam, madam, your dear Snow-bird is not here!

LADY. What is that you say? Early Snow is not there? It cannot be true.

It is true. Early Snow has gone! How can that be? How can it be that my pretty one that was so tame should vanish and leave no trace?
Oh bitterness of snows
That melt and disappear!
Now do I understand
The meaning of a midnight dream
That lately broke my rest.
A harbinger it was
Of Hatsuyuki's fate. (*She bursts into tears.*)

CHORUS. Though for such tears and sighs
 There be no cause,
 Yet came her grief so suddenly,
 Her heart's fire is ablaze;
 And all the while
 Never a moment are her long sleeves dry.
 They say that written letters first were traced
 By feet of birds in sand
 Yet Hatsuyuki leaves no testament. *(They mourn.)*

CHORUS. *("kuse" chant, irregular verse accompanied by dancing).*
 How sad to call to mind
 When first it left the breeding-cage
 So fair of form
 And colored white as snow.
 We called it Hatsuyuki, "Year's First Snow."
 And where our mistress walked
 It followed like a shadow at her side.
 But now alas! it is a bird of parting
 Though not in Love's dark lane.

LADY. There's no help now. *(She weeps bitterly.)*

CHORUS. Still there is one way left. Stop weeping, Lady,
 And turn your heart to him who vowed to hear.
 The Lord Amida, if a prayer be said —
 Who knows but he can bring
 Even a bird's soul into Paradise
 And set it on the Lotus Pedestal?

LADY. Evening Mist, are you not sad that Hatsuyuki has gone? But we must not cry any more. Let us call together the noble ladies of this place and for seven days sit with them praying behind barred doors. Go now and do my bidding. *(Evening Mist fetches the noble ladies)*

TWO NOBLE LADIES. *(together).*
 A solemn Mass we sing
 A dirge for the Dead;
 At this hour of heart-cleansing.
 We beat on Buddha's gong. *(They pray.)*
  Namu amida butsu
  Namu nyorai
   Praise to Amida Buddha,
   Praise to Mida our Savior!
 The prayers and gong-beating last for some time and form the central ballet of the play.

CHORUS. *(the bird's soul appears as a white speck in the sky).*

    Look! Look! A cloud in the clear mid-sky!

    But it is not a cloud.

    With pure white wings beating the air

    The Snow-bird comes!

    Flying towards our lady

    Lovingly he hovers,

    Dances before her.

THE BIRD'S SOUL. Drawn by the merit of your prayers and songs.

CHORUS. Straightway he was reborn in Paradise.

    By the pond of Eight Virtues he walks abroad:

    With the Phoenix and Fugan his playtime passing.

    He lodges in the sevenfold summit of the trees of Heaven.

    No hurt shall harm him

    For ever and ever.

    Now like the tasselled doves we loose

    From battlements on holy days

    A little while he flutters;

    Flutters a little while and then is gone

    We know not where.

THINKING CRITICALLY

1. *Recognizing Values* Judging by *Early Snow*, was more emphasis in *No* drama put on the story or the presentation? Explain.

2. *Making Inferences* What is the theme of this play? Does the play seem meant to be a metaphor or for pure aesthetic appreciation?

3. *Linking Past and Present* Can you think of any recent movies or plays which have the aesthetic synthesis of *No* drama? What kind of audience do they reach?

WRITER'S PORTFOLIO

1. *Extending the Selection* By the end of the sixteenth century, *No* drama had been replaced by *Kabuki*. Do some research on *Kabuki* drama. How is it different from *No*? How is it the same?

2. *Examining Key Questions* What does *No* drama suggest about the cultural values of Japanese society?

Haiku

With the advent of the Tokugawa Era (1603–1867), Japan's feudal wars ended and the power of the samurai dwindled. They were replaced in importance by a new merchant class known as *haikai*. The refinements of the feudal aristocracy also began to be replaced by new more popular entertainment. One of the most important of these new arts was *haiku* poetry. Haiku is distinguished by its brevity; it has only seventeen syllables, divided into three lines of five, seven, and five syllables each. These short poems are generally simple descriptions of real scenes or events, with just enough detail to express an emotion to the reader. The greatest haiku poet was Matsuo Basho (1644–1694) who established the conventions of haiku. His school is sometimes called the democratic school because he accepted students from all walks of life from elite samurai to beggars. His most devoted pupil was Mukai Kyorai (1651–1704), who recorded his conversations with the master about haiku. The following selections are three excerpts from the *Kyoraisho*, Basho's talks with Kyorai: the first discussing the inalterability of each word in a well-written haiku; the second showing how the language of haiku should be deliberately suggestive and ambiguous; and the third depicting Basho's technique of linked verse in a haiku about spring's arrival. These are followed by examples of Basho's poetry. What is the subject of each poem?

Mukai Kyorai, *Kyoraisho*

The departing spring
With the men of Omi
Have I lamented.

The Master said, "Shohaku criticized this poem on the grounds that I might just as well have said "Tamba" instead of "Omi," or "departing year" instead of "departing spring." How does this criticism strike you?" Kyorai replied, "Shohaku's criticism completely misses the mark. What could be more natural than to regret the passing of the spring, when the waters of the Lake of Omi are veiled so enchantingly in mist? Besides, it is especially fitting in a poem written by one like yourself who is living by the lake." The Master said, "Yes, the poets of old loved spring in this province almost as much as in Kyoto." Kyorai, deeply struck by these words, continued, "If you were in Omi at the close of the year, why should you regret its passing? Or, if you were in Tamba at the end of spring, you would not be likely to have such feelings. What truth there is in the poetry of a man who has been genuinely stirred by some sight of nature!" The Master said, "Kyorai, you are a person with whom I can talk about poetry." He was very pleased.

> The tips of the crags —
> Here too is someone,
> Guest of the moon.

Kyorai said, "Shado thinks that the last line should be 'monkey of the moon,' but I think that 'guest' is better." The Master said, "How can he suggest such a word as 'monkey'? What had you in mind when you wrote the poem?" Kyorai answered, "One night, when I was walking in the mountains by the light of the harvest moon, composing poetry as I went along, I noticed another poet standing by the crags." The Master said, "How much more interesting a poem it would be if by the lines 'Here too is someone, guest of the moon' you meant yourself. You must be the subject of the verse."

> Somber and tall
> The forest of oaks

> In and out
> Through the little gate
> To the cherry blossoms.

When the former verse was given, I thought how difficult it would be to add a verse about cherry blossoms without destroying the image of the forest of oaks. When I asked the Master to add such a verse, this was how he did it.

Very soon they die—
      but of that there is no sign
            in the locust cry.

On a moor: from things
      detached completely—
            how the skylark sings!

To bird and butterfly
      it is unknown, this flower here:
            the autumn sky.

Summer grass:
      of stalwart warriors' splendid dreams
            the aftermath.

THINKING CRITICALLY

1. *Making Inferences* In the third selection from the *Kyoraisho*, how is Basho able to add his verse without destroying the image?

2. *Recognizing Values* Characterize the images that Basho uses in his haiku. Are they drawn from the court or the countryside?

3. *Linking Past and Present* Basho's school of poetry was known as the democratic school because he accepted anyone with talent. Is poetry a democratic art today or is it elitist? Explain.

WRITER'S PORTFOLIO

1. *Extending the Selection* Write your own haiku on a natural subject. Remember to use seventeen syllables, divided into three lines of five, seven, and five. Also try to capture an element of permanence and an element of change in your poem.

2. *Examining Key Questions* Are these haiku purely impressionistic or do any of them offer insights on moral questions? Explain.

Japanese Art

One of the finest schools of Japanese court painting was the Kano (kä´nō). Founded by Kano Motonobu (c. 1476–1559), it was modeled after Chinese ink-painting, though with bolder lines and a new element of decorative patterning. Motonobu's grandson, Kano Eitoku (1543–1590), was the greatest painter of this school. Eitoku, whose *Crane and Pine Tree* appears on page 322, principally

Suzuki Harunobu, Visiting a Shrine on a Rainy Night *(after 1765)*

painted landscapes, easily recognized for their golden colors—he often employed gold-leaf in his painting—and the ease and energy of his subjects. Throughout the feudal wars and into the Tokugawa shogunate, Kano painting was the dominant school of painting in Japan. Kano Eitoku's grandson would become the first official painter of the Tokugawa. However, as the feudal wars ended, the immense changes in Japanese society also affected artistic styles. The large-scale, colorful Kano style gave way to a new, intimate, small-scale popular art, known as *Ukiyo-e* (ü´ki´yō´ye). *Ukiyo-e* is the Japanese word for "pictures of the floating world" and is a euphemism for the entertainment quarter of Edo, where the style first developed and from which many of its subjects were drawn. This style brought a new emphasis on the everyday, urban world. *Ukiyo-e* artists were also the first to exploit the wood-block medium, which enabled them to use bright colors and to produce images for mass consumption.

Ma Yuan, Bare Willows and Distant Mountains *(after 950)*

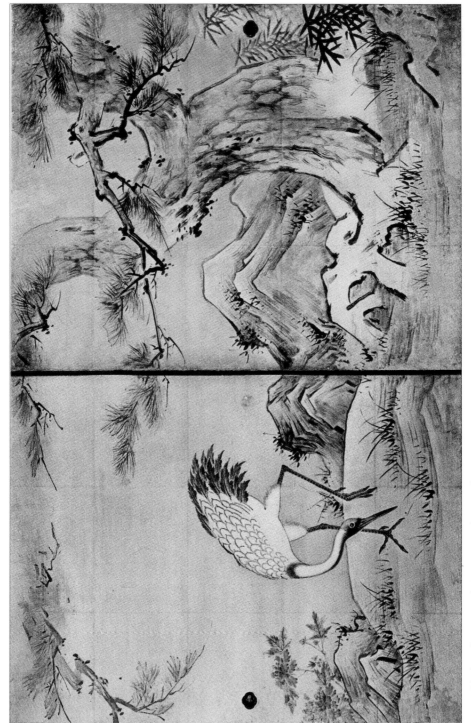

Kano Eitoku, Crane and Pine Tree (c. 1566)

Okumura Masanobu, Interior of a Tea-House (c. 1740)

Siva Nataraja, bronze (1300s)

The two *ukiyo-e* artists represented here, Okumura Musunobu (1691–1768), whose *Interior of a Tea-House* appears on page 323, and Suzuki Harunobu (1725–1770), whose *Visiting a Shrine on a Rainy Night* appears on page 320 were the first to introduce polychromatic wood-block printing. *Ukiyo-e* art is a demonstration of the growth of the middle-class and the fading of the aristocracy under the Tokugawa shogunate. Which picture seems the most influenced by Chinese painting?

THINKING CRITICALLY

1. *Recognizing Values* What are the subjects of the two *ukiyo-e* wood-block prints? How would you characterize these subjects?

2. *Making Comparisons* Do you think the *ukiyo-e* art is more compelling than the Kano? Which type of art do you think would have more favor in the Western world?

3. *Linking Past and Present* Generally, the subjects of wood-block prints were events from urban life or a scene from a *kabuki* play or Japanese novel. What would you select as a subject for a print today? Describe your scene.

WRITER'S PORTFOLIO

1. *Extending the Selection* Write a narrative description of one of the scenes in these three pictures. Consider carefully before choosing your narrator.

2. *Examining Key Questions* What inferences can you make about how life changed in Japan from the sixteenth to the eighteenth centuries from viewing these pictures?

The *Mahabharata*

The nomadic people who began invading northern India around 1500 B.C. made two important contributions to Indian literature. The first was their language, which was the ancestor of Sanskrit, the classical language of India. The second was their traditional religious poetry, known as the *Vedas*. More familiar than the Vedas to the ordinary person, however, were two epic tales, the *Ramayana*, the story of King Rama and his beautiful and virtuous wife, Sita, and the *Mahabharata*, the story of a great civil war between the five Pandava brothers and their royal cousins, the 99 Kaurava brothers. This epic contains almost 100,000 Sanskrit verses, approximately seven times the length of the *Iliad* and the Odyssey combined. Ethics in Hindu tradition are based on the concepts of *karma*, the idea that people's actions create their fate; and *dharma*, the duty of virtuous action. These twin concepts shape the Hindu religion and the actions of the characters in the *Mahabharata*. The virtues being promoted are very clearly isolated in the story of Yudhishthira (**yu dish′ti ra**), the oldest of the Pandavas. The excerpt from the epic which appears below, is from the end of the story. The Pandavas, Yudhishthira and his four brothers, have defeated their cousins and are now headed toward the sacred mountain, Meru. They are accompanied by Draupadi, the woman to whom all five brothers are married, and a dog, regarded by Hindus as an unclean animal. What causes Draupadi and four of the brothers to fall?

THEY GATHERED TOGETHER THEIR INNER FORCES AND ENTERED into a yogic state and set out for the north. They saw the great Himalayan mountain and went beyond it until they saw the ocean of sand, and they gazed down upon mount Meru, the ultimate mountain. As they were all moving along quickly, absorbed in their yoga, Draupadi lost her yogic concentration and fell to the ground. When the mighty Bhima saw that she had fallen, he spoke to Yudhishthira, the king of dharma, about her, saying, "The princess Draupadi never did anything against dharma; then what has caused her to fall to the ground?" Yudhishthira replied, "Draupadi was greatly partial to Arjuna (among us, her five husbands); and now she has experienced the fruit of that partiality." When Yudhishthira the son of Dharma had said this, he went on, never glancing at her, for he concentrated his mind; he was the very soul of dharma, a bull among men.

Then the wise Sahadeva fell to the ground, and when Bhima saw that he had fallen he said to the king (Yudhishthira), "This man was always eager to serve us all, with no thought for himself; why has he fallen to the ground?" Yudhishthira said, "He did not think that anyone was as wise as he was. This flaw in his character has caused the prince to fall." And when he had said this, Yudhishthira left Sahadeva behind and went on with his brothers, and with the dog.

When the warrior Nakula saw that Draupadi and Sahadeva had fallen, he was tormented, for he loved his family, and he himself fell to the ground. And when the handsome hero Nakula had fallen, Bhima spoke to the king again, saying, "This man, my brother, Nakula, never violated dharma, and always did what he said he would do; and he was the handsomest man in the world. But now he has fallen to the ground!" When Bhima had said this about Nakula, Yudhishthira, the soul of dharma, the most intelligent of all men, replied: "His philosophy was, 'There is no one as handsome as me; I am the best, the only one.' This thought stuck in his mind, and so Nakula had fallen. Come along, Bhima, Wolf-belly. Whatever is fated for anyone, that is what he must, inevitably, experience."

But when Arjuna, the Pandava who rode on a white horse, the killer of enemy heroes, saw that they had fallen, he himself fell to the ground after them, overcome by grief. And when that tiger among men, the seed of Indra, hard to withstand, had fallen and was dying, Bhima said to the king, "I cannot recall anything that this noble man ever did wrong, particularly on purpose. To whom, then, did he do some harm that has caused him to fall to the ground?" Yudhishthira replied, "Arjuna said, "I will burn up my enemies in a single day." But, though he was proud of his heroism, he did not do this; and so he has fallen. He despised all (the other) archers; but a man who wishes for greatness must do what he says he will do."

Having said this, the king went forth; and Bhima fell. As he fell, Bhima said to Yudhishthira, the king of dharma, "Your highness! Look! I, whom you love, have fallen! What has caused me to fall? Tell me, if you know." And Yudhishthira replied, "You ate too much, and boasted about your vital energy, and despised your enemy. That is why you have fallen to the ground." And when he had said this, the great-armed Yudhishthira went on, never looking down. Only the dog followed him—the dog that I have already told you about quite a lot.

Then Indra [the major Hindu deity, god of the wind] came to Yudhishthira in his chariot, making heaven and earth reverberate everywhere, and he said to him, "Get in." But Yudhishthira, the king of dharma, had seen all his brothers fallen, and burning with grief he said to Indra, the thousand-eyed, "My brothers have all fallen here; let them come with me. I do not want to go to heaven without my brothers. And the delicate princess (Draupadi), who deserves to be happy—let her come with us. Give your permission, O lord of the gods."

"You will see all your brothers and your sons, who have reached heaven before you, together with Draupadi." said Indra. "Don't be sad. They have cast off their human bodies and gone; but you will go to heaven with this body; this is certain." Then Yudhishthira said, "O lord of all that has been and is to be, this dog has been devoted to me constantly. Let him come with me; for my heart is incapable of cruelty." "Today, great king, you have become immortal, like me," said Indra, "and you have won complete glory and great fame, and all the joys of heaven. Abandon this dog; there is no cruelty in this." "Noble god, god of a thousand eyes," said Yudhishthira, "it is hard for one who is noble to commit an ignoble act like this. I do not want to achieve glory if I must do it by abandoning someone who has been devoted to me."

"But there is no place for dog-owners in heaven," said Indra, "for the evil spirits called Overpowered-by-anger carry off their sacrificial merit (that would earn them a place in heaven). And so, king of dharma, you should think before you act; abandon this dog; there is no cruelty in this." Yudhishthira said, "People say that to abandon one who is devoted to you is a bottomless evil equal to murdering a Brahmin. Therefore, great Indra, I will never, in any way, abandon him now in order to achieve my own happiness." Indra said, "The evil spirits called Overpowered-by-anger carry off what has been offered, sacrificed, and given as an oblation into the fire, if it is left uncovered and a dog has looked at it. Therefore you must abandon this dog, and by abandoning the dog you will win the world of the gods. By abandoning your brothers, and even your darling Draupadi, you reached this world by your own heroic action; how is it then that you will not abandon this dog? Perhaps, having abandoned everything, you have now lost your mind."

Yudhishthira said, "There is no such thing as either union or separation for mortals when they are dead; this is common knowledge. I could not keep them alive, and so I abandoned them—but (I would not abandon) those who are alive. Handing over someone who has come to you for refuge; killing a woman; confiscating the property of a Brahmin; and betraying a friend; these four acts, Indra, are equalled by the act of abandoning someone who is devoted to you; this is what I think."

When he heard these words spoken by the king of dharma, the god (who had been there in the form of the dog) took his own form, Dharma [Hindu god of justice, father of Yudhishthira]. He was satisfied with king Yudhishthira, and spoke to him with smooth words of praise: "Great king, you are well born, with the good conduct and intelligence of your father, and with compassion for all creatures. You abandoned the celestial chariot, for you insisted, 'This dog is devoted to me.' Because of this, great king, there is no one your equal in heaven. And because of this, you have won the undying worlds, won the supreme way of heaven, and won them with your own body."

THINKING CRITICALLY

1. *Making Inferences* The violation of what different virtues causes the fall of Draupadi and each of Yudhishthira's four brothers?

2. *Recognizing Values* Why does Yudhishthira leave his wife and brothers, but refuse to leave the dog? What does Yudhishthira equate the act of abandoning the dog to?

3. *Linking Past and Present* Which aspects of Indian ethics seem the least like contemporary American values?

WRITER'S PORTFOLIO

1. *Extending the Selection* Compare and contrast the concepts behind the fall of Draupadi and Yudhishthira's four brothers with the biblical fall of man (see pages 90–93). What can you infer about the ethics and the attitudes toward fate of these religions?

2. *Examining Key Questions* How do the concepts of dharma and karma serve as a guide in life?

The *Bhagavad Gita*

The most famous part of the *Mahabharata* is the *Bhagavad Gita* (bug′ə vəd gē′tə) or "Song of the Lord." It is a philosophical dialogue, between Arjuna, Yudhishthira's brother and the leader of the Pandava army, and Krishna, the Hindu god who serves as his charioteer, which takes place with the armies of the Kauravas and the Pandavas arrayed for battle. Arjuna is expected to blow his horn beginning this apocalyptic battle, but hesitates at this decisive moment, fearing that to undertake the slaughter of his kinsmen for worldly gain must be sinful. Krishna reassures him with a long discourse in eighteen chapters in which he explains that a disinterested performance of duty involves no desire and hence no sin. What does Arjuna see that causes him to hesitate?

THEN ARJUNA SAW IN BOTH ARMIES FATHERS, GRANDFATHERS, sons, grandsons; fathers of wives, uncles, masters; brothers, companions and friends.

When Arjuna thus saw his kinsmen face to face in both lines of battle, he was overcome by grief and despair and thus he spoke with a sinking heart.

ARJUNA. When I see all my kinsmen, Krishna, who have come here on this field of battle,

Life goes from my limbs and they sink, and my mouth is sear and dry; a trembling overcomes my body, and my hair shudders in horror;

My great bow Gandiva falls from my hands, and the skin over my flesh is burning; I am no longer able to stand, because my mind is whirling and wandering.

And I see forebodings of evil, Krishna. I cannot foresee any glory if I kill my own kinsmen in the sacrifice of battle.

Because I have no wish for victory, Krishna, nor for a kingdom, nor for its pleasures. How can we want a kingdom, Govinda [epithet for Krishna], or its pleasures or even life, when those for whom we want a kingdom, and its pleasures, and the joys of life, are here in this field of battle about to give up their wealth and their life?

Facing us in the field of battle are teachers, fathers and sons; grandsons, grandfathers, wives' brothers; mothers' brothers and fathers of wives.

These I do not wish to slay, even if I myself am slain. Not even for the kingdom of the three worlds: how much less for a kingdom of the earth!…

Thus spoke Arjuna in the field of battle, and letting fall his bow and arrows he sank down in his chariot, his soul overcome by despair and grief.

Then arose the Spirit of Krishna and spoke to Arjuna, his friend, who with eyes filled with tears, thus had sunk into despair and grief.

KRISHNA. Whence this lifeless dejection, Arjuna, in this hour, the hour of trial? Strong men know not despair, Arjuna, for this wins neither heaven nor earth….

Thy tears are for those beyond tears; and are thy words words of wisdom? The wise grieve not for those who live; and they grieve not for those who die — for life and death shall pass away.

Because we all have been for all time: I, and thou, and those kings of men. And we all shall be for all time, we all for ever and ever.

If any man thinks he slays, and if another thinks he is slain, neither knows the ways of truth. The Eternal in man cannot kill: the Eternal in man cannot die.

He is never born, and he never dies. He is in Eternity: he is for evermore. Never-born and eternal, beyond times gone or to come, he does not die when the body dies.

When a man knows him as never-born, everlasting, never-changing, beyond all destruction, how can that man kill a man, or cause another to kill?

As a man leaves an old garment and puts on one that is new, the Spirit leaves his mortal body and wanders on to one that is new.

Weapons cannot hurt the Spirit and fire can never burn him. Untouched is he by drenching waters, and winds, the Spirit is everlasting, omnipresent, never-changing, never-moving, ever One.

Invisible is he to mortal eyes, beyond thought and beyond change. Know that he is, and cease from sorrow.

But if he were born again and again, and again and again he were to die, even then, victorious man, cease thou from sorrow.

For all things born in truth must die, and out of death in truth comes life. Face to face with what must be, cease thou from sorrow.

Invisible before birth are all beings and after death invisible again. They are seen between two unseens. Why in this truth find sorrow?

One sees him in a vision of wonder, and another gives us words of his wonder. There is one who hears of his wonder; but he hears and knows him not.

The Spirit that is in all beings is immortal in them all: for the death of what cannot die, cease thou to sorrow.

Think thou also of thy duty and do not waver. There is no greater good for a warrior than to fight in righteous war.

There is a war that opens the doors of heaven, Arjuna! Happy the warriors whose fate is to fight such war.

But to forgo this fight for righteousness is to forgo thy duty and honor: is to fall into transgression.

Men will tell of thy dishonor both now and in times to come. And to a man who is in honor, dishonor is more than death....

In death thy glory in heaven, in victory thy glory on earth. Arise therefore, Arjuna, with thy soul ready to fight.

Prepare for war with peace in thy soul. Be in peace in pleasure and pain, in gain and in loss, in victory or in the loss of a battle. In this peace there is no sin.

THINKING CRITICALLY

1. *Understanding Concepts* According to Krishna, why is it impossible to kill or be killed?

2. *Recognizing Values* Do you think Krishna's argument that Arjuna should fight because it is a warrior's duty is a valid one? Is it a validation of war or only of *dharma*?

3. *Linking Past and Present* How is the concept of karma generally employed in today's world? Do you think this new age definition is in opposition to Hindu belief? Why or why not?

WRITER'S PORTFOLIO

1. *Extending the Selection* Write a rejoinder to Krishna in the form of Arjuna's answer to him. Refute as many of his arguments as you can.

2. *Examining Key Questions* How do Hindus regard fate? Do they believe in predestination?

The Treasury of Well-Turned Verse

Sanskrit, much like Latin during the Middle Ages, was a language used for literature and learning. It was never spoken informally and so remained free from the constant evolution most languages undergo. As an expression of this formality, Sanskrit poetry followed rigid guidelines, that tested the poet's ability to draw the maximum meaning out of each word, rather than his lyrical inventiveness. Vidyakara was a Buddhist monk, who around A.D. 1100 compiled an anthology of classical Sanskrit poetry, including over two hundred poets, going back as far as the eighth century. This *Treasury of Well-Turned Verse* contained *subhasitas* or "well-turned verses," lyric poems which aim to convey a mood or emotion by suggestion. These lyric poets took advantage of the inflections of formal Sanskrit to create puns and acute images. Their goal was to manipulate the language to express their meaning. The following verses are taken from Vidyakara's anthology. What subjects do these poems cover?

Summer
The embrace of fawn-eyed damsels
just bathed and moist with sandal paste,
their hair decked out with new-born flowers,
slowly makes love rise again,
whose strength had withered in the summer beams.

The Rains
Rich is he who drinks his bride's red-lotus lip
in a roof pavilion screened by mats against the rain,
their amorous murmurs mingling with the sound of moorhens
wakened in their baskets by the driving downpour.

Autumn

The sun gives sharp pain
like a low man newly rich.
The deer drops his horns
like a thankless friend.
The waters grow lucid
like a saint's pious thought;
and the mud is squeezed dry
like a poor man who keeps a mistress.

Late Winter

The cold beauty of the moonlight fades as though
from lack of luck in love;
for no more is it met by laughter of the waterlilies;
its darling moonstone, overlaid by frost,
no longer sweats with yearning;
nor is it welcomed by the eyes of lovers
between their bouts of love.

The Blossoming of Love

The speed of the dance has shaken loose
the circled blade of palmleaf, which escapes,
as from Love's quiver, from the slender maiden's ear
that, goldened with saffron paste to steal our hearts,
is like the stem, bent in a graceful loop,
of the waterlily flower of her eye.

A Lover Separated from his Mistress

If my absent bride were but a pond,
her eyes the waterlilies and her face the lotus,
her brows the rippling waves, her arms the lotus stems;
then might I dive into the water of her loveliness
and cool of limb escape the mortal pain
exacted by the flaming fire of love.

Sunset

The Darkness wears the guise of rising smoke
and the sky is filled with opening stars for sparks
as the sun descends into the sunset fire.
As his loves, the lotuses, bow down in grief,

lamenting with the cry of struggling bees,
the goddess of the day turns west and joins him in his death.

The Moon
The East has borne the Moon.
Love dances and the nymphs of the directions laugh,
while the wind scatters holiday powder,
the pollen of waterlilies, through heaven's court.

THINKING CRITICALLY

1. *Making Inferences* Do you think that Vidyakara's collection of poetry was for all people or was it written mostly for the nobility? Cite some verses to defend your answer.

2. *Recognizing Values* Do these poems read like formal or informal verse? Explain.

3. *Linking Past and Present* Does the way in which love is expressed in these poems resemble modern romantic songs? Why or why not?

WRITER'S PORTFOLIO

1. *Extending the Selection* Look up the meaning of the phrase "pathetic fallacy" in the Handbook of Cultural Terms. Do these lyric poems fit that criticism? Why or why not?

2. *Examining Key Questions* Nature is the essential subject of Indian lyric poetry. How does the Indian poet's response to nature compare to Chinese poetry (pages 296–300) or Japanese haiku (pages 317–319)?

Indian Sculpture

India's most inspiring art form has always been its sculpture. Sculpture developed as decoration for the massive temples and palaces built by India's ancient dynasties. The Sunga dynasty dominated northern India during the first century B.C. and their sculpture, such as the warrior figure at right, imitated wood carving with relief figures hardly emerging from the stone block. The arm resting on the warrior's chest is the only attempt to show movement. During the fourth century A.D., a Western influence can be observed in Mathura sculpture. The Mathura region is sometimes called an open door between East and West because it is where most Western invasions ended and traditional Indian culture began. Greek influences included a tendency toward more elegant and vertical shapes, and a more mature style of religious expression. The serenity and composure of the Mathura Buddha on page 337, however, completely reflects Indian spirituality. It was during the eighth century that sculpture took on the representational characteristics usually associated with Indian sculpture: free-standing, *contrapposto* figures, surrounded by religious symbols. The Avalokitesvara Padmapani, Buddhism's most popular deity, on page 337, shows the beginnings of this development which would lead to the dancing figures of later

Figure of a warrior from Bharhut, Sunga period

*Standing Buddha from
Mathura, Gupta period
(A.D. 400s)*

*Avalokitesvara Padmapani
from Nalanda (c. 800)*

centuries. Avalokitesvara is a figure who combines both female and male attributes, lending itself to the soft contours of this style. In his left hand he holds a lotus, representing rebirth. By the twelfth and thirteenth centuries complete freedom of movement had emerged. The bronze Siva Nataraja, which appears on page 324, is a magnificent reflection of this energetic movement. This statue represents Siva, the third of Hinduism's trinity of gods, as the Nataraja, the "Lord of the Dance." Siva's symbolism reveals many Hindu beliefs. He stands atop a small figure, Apasmara, who symbolizes ego and ignorance, conquered through the dance. The snake around the lower-right arm represents the conquest of ego, and Siva's power over nature. The gesture of the lower-right hand is one of reassurance and protection for his worshippers. The gesture of the left hand pointing toward the upraised foot is one of salvation or the escape from illusion. The fire he holds in his uplifted left hand as well as the circle of flames represent the cycle of destruction leading to creation. The Siva Nataraja represents the height of Indian sculpture before the Mughal invasion brought Islam and a suppression of Hindu artistic expression. What quality does each of the sculptures convey?

THINKING CRITICALLY

1. *Recognizing Values* What are the subjects of these sculptures? What traditional values do they express?

2. *Making Inferences* How did the poses of the sculpted figures evolve over the centuries?

3. *Linking Past and Present* Art is a reflection of a society. Looking at these sculptures, it is obvious religion was important to Indians. Pick a major twentieth-century American artist and examine what their subject matter can tell you about what is important in our society.

WRITER'S PORTFOLIO

1. *Extending the Selection* If you were to create a portrait of yourself, what symbolic objects would you include? Describe your portrait and what it contains.

2. *Examining Key Questions* Do you think the religious symbols add to or subtract from the effect of the sculptures? Explain.

EXAMINING KEY QUESTIONS

- *How should a leader act?*
- *What is the right way to live?*

Throughout this chapter, most selections have concluded with a writing project asking you to discuss how the art or literature you have examined provides answers to one of these key questions. The following writing projects will help you draw together what you have learned by examining how several selections illustrate these key questions.

- Compare and contrast the spiritual beliefs of the Chinese, Japanese, and Indians. Are any of these peoples fatalists? Is harmony a tenet of their beliefs?

- Compare and contrast what you have learned about the Chinese, Japanese, and Indian codes of behavior. How should a leader act? How should a follower act?

SPEAKING/LISTENING

- Give a performance of the Japanese *No* drama *Early Snow*. Research carefully the costumes and choreography of *No* and then try to create your own version of this ancient art.

CRAFTING

- Research the geography and population of Asia. Make a map of Asia showing all the countries which are part of Asian culture. What percentage of the world's land mass does Asia represent? of the world's population? of the world's Gross National Product?

COLLECTING

- Collect recent art and literature which have been influenced by Asian themes. Begin with the work of the American painters James McNeill Whistler and Mary Cassatt and the poet Ezra Pound. What other examples can you find? How have their mediums been affected by the Asian influence?

Kushite Site, Ancient Sudan

African Civilizations

INTRODUCTION by Roland Oliver

PORTFOLIO

The Conquest of Upper Egypt (c. 720 B.C.)
The Piankhi Stele

Traditional Folk Tales
"How the World Changed"; Baila tale

Trickster Tales
"Why Kwaku Ananse runs when he is on the water";
"Edju and the Two Friends"

An Epic of Old Mali (A.D. 1200s)
The *Sundiata*

Traditional African Poetry
"The Ancestors"; "Death"; "Sadness of Life"; "The Beloved";
Bagirmi Love Song; Zulu Love Song

The Kingdom of Mali (1324)
al-Omari, "Travels"

African Masks (after 1500)
Benin ivory mask; Luba *Kifwebe* mask; Wee nature-spirit mask;
Kono war mask; Jokwe *Mbweso* mask

Life in Benin (1789)
Olaudah Equiano, *The Interesting Narrative of the Life
of Olaudah Equiano*

The Zulu Empire (1816)
Thomas Mofolo, *Chaka*

CHAPTER 8 PROJECTS

Statue of King Shabaqo, pharaoh of 25th Dynasty

CHAPTER 8

African Civilizations

c. 720 B.C.–A.D. 1816

c. 720 B.C.
Piankhi, King of Kush, conquers Egypt, founds 25th Dynasty

ROLAND OLIVER

Professor Emeritus of African History, University of London

We are all, in a sense, the children of Africa. It was there, in the high grasslands that stretch from Ethiopia southwards to the Cape of Good Hope, that our remote ancestors began to diverge from the chimpanzees, who are our nearest primate relatives. The earliest among them have been identified from about four million years ago. Around two and a half million years ago some of them began to chip stone to make sharp-edged tools for woodworking, skinning, and butchery, and so to leave abundant and indelible evidence of their presence and distribution. During the first million years or so of their tool-making history, our ancestors remained in the high savannas of eastern Africa, which they shared with much larger populations of grazing and browsing animals and with the carnivores who were their fellow predators. At first, it seems, they were little more than scavengers, who used their skills in butchery to clean up the refuse left by the larger carnivores. Gradually, as their tools and their means of communication improved, they became independent hunters. Between one and two million years ago, they began to colonize other environments, starting in northern Africa and western Asia, and spreading outwards from there. But throughout the hunting and gathering phase of our history, which has dominated all but the last ten thousand years of our existence, the highlands of eastern Africa, with their uniquely dense concentrations of wild game,

*Relief of
Kushite
Queen*

Asante Mask

600
Kushite pharaohs transfer capital back to Meroë

A.D. 400
Kingdom of Ghana founded

remained at the very center of human endeavor, deeply influencing the development of our bodies, our minds, our powers of imagination and communication.

THE ADVENT OF FARMING

It was the slow evolution from intensive gathering to deliberate and selective sowing and planting, accomplished in most of the world between about fifteen and five thousand years ago, which at last shifted mankind's preferred habitat from the plains and savannas to the river valleys with their deep soils and flowing water. In the valley of the upper Nile, wild grains were being reaped with stone sickles more than fifteen thousand years ago. From about ten thousand years ago until about five thousand years ago, the southern Sahara and the Sudanic belt to the south of it experienced a period of wet climate, during which rivers and lakes filled up, and former hunting populations settled beside them to exploit the fish and the waterfowl.

Meanwhile, the northern third of Africa, from the Mediterranean coast to the middle of the Sahara, was sharing in the transition to food production initiated in the Fertile Crescent of western Asia. This centered upon the sowing of wheat and barley, the planting of vegetables, and the breeding of domestic animals, especially cattle, sheep, goats, pigs, and donkeys, soon to be followed by horses and camels. In the unique conditions of the lower Nile valley, with its rich deposits of fertile silt carried down by the annual flood, the transition to food production soon brought about a population explosion, which was confined by the surrounding deserts into a narrow, green ribbon on either side of the river. Five to six thousand years ago, the population of Egypt had already reached an almost suburban density, with perhaps two million people settled on the twelve thousand square miles of flood plain. The process of political centralization under local dynasties had begun. The practice of building in mud-brick had been

1054
Beginning of Muslim conquest of West Africa

imported from Mesopotamia. Precision tools were now made of copper rather than stone. Carpentry had reached a pitch of accuracy that could be used for the making of elegant furniture or the building of seagoing ships. Seals and property marks were paving the way for pictographic writing. Five thousand years ago, the local rulers were united under a single dynasty of pharaohs, rich and powerful enough to embark on monumental architecture for palaces, tombs, and temples. In the course of the next three thousand years, Egyptian kingship achieved an elaboration and a durability without parallel in any continent, and it grew from a set of underlying ideas that were common to much of Africa. The pharaoh was a god-king. His most important subjects were his god-bearing mother and the sister-wife who would bear the successor-god. The passing generations were marked by the growing line of temple-tombs of the predecessor-gods, his ancestors. These were no mere memorial monuments, but cult centers believed to

enjoy special access to the unseen world and its wisdom.

Between 3000 B.C. and 1000 B.C. the population of Egypt is thought to have quadrupled, from about two million to about eight million, and it is probable that during these two thousand years Egypt supported as many people as the rest of Africa put together. The desert latitudes to the east and west were occupied only sparsely by pastoralists, and in the rest of North Africa only the Tunisian plain saw the development of a Bronze Age agriculture among the Numidian people, later to become the peasant subjects of Carthage and then of Rome. South of the Sahara and north of the equatorial forest, small communities of two or three hundred people proliferated slowly in the areas best suited to Stone Age food production. In nearly all of Africa below the equator, people continued to live by hunting and gathering and in groups of twenty or thirty individuals. Only in the valley of the upper Nile directly to the south of Egypt did there emerge a substantial

Wagadou-Bida Carving

Detail of an engraving of Timbuktu

1076
Ghana destroyed by West Africans

1100
Timbuktu founded

---

kingdom, that of Kush, where a Nubian state founded in the third millennium B.C. succumbed to Egyptian colonization in the second millennium, to re-emerge in independence during the first. It was as king of Kush that Piankhi (pē äng′kē) conquered Egypt in the eighth century B.C. and founded the Twenty-Fifth Dynasty of pharaohs. Driven out of Egypt a century later, Piankhi's successors retreated to Kush, where they ruled in Egyptian style for another thousand years. Kush thus formed a cultural bridge between the civilization of Bronze Age Egypt and that of the Iron Age of sub-Saharan Africa.

THE IMPACT OF IRON-WORKING

More than anything else, it was the discovery and spread of iron working which created the patterns of settlement and daily life that survived in the rural areas of Africa until quite recent times. Though more difficult to smelt than copper, iron was plentiful enough to supply the tools and weapons of ordi-nary people. With iron axes and hoes, land could be cleared and cultivated, houses built and thatched, stockades erected, canoes hollowed out from tree-trunks; while smaller tools like needles, knives, razors, chisels, and fishing tackle served many daily needs much better than their stone equivalents. Iron spears were useful not only for fighting but for protection against wild animals and for the hunting that continued to supply an important part of the diet. In many parts of Africa iron tools and weapons constituted almost the only items of storable wealth. It is no wonder that the various practices of smelting and smithing were surrounded by ritual and secrecy, and that kings and other potentates laid claim to skill in the craft.

While we do not yet know precisely where iron working was first practiced in Africa, it is clear that the broad direction of its spread was from north to south and that it took about one thousand years to spread from the southern fringes of the Sahara to the coastlands of southern Africa. In West

*Benin plaque
of Oba and
attendants*

*Dogon
equestrian
sculpture*

1170
Eweka becomes first Oba of Benin

1235
Sundiata creates Mali Empire

Africa the earliest known center of an Iron Age culture was situated on and around the Jos plateau of northern Nigeria, where its remains are characterized by the presence of a marvelous tradition of pottery sculptures of people and animals, called after the type-site at Nok. The sites yielding Nok sculptures have been dated from about 600 B.C. to about A.D. 300. The human figurines are thought to be connected with a cult of ancestors and to have been kept in shrines in family compounds. The Nok tradition may well have been the prototype for later traditions of sculpture, some of it cast in bronze, which were practiced around Ife and Benin and other centers in southern Nigeria from about A.D. 1000 onwards.

Another manifestation of the early Iron Age in West Africa is to be seen in the agglomeration of mud-built, walled towns around Old Jenne in the south of modern Mali, where thirty to forty small towns came into existence almost simultaneously about two thousand years ago, the inhabitants of

which sallied forth by day to practice farming and fishing around the flood-plain of the upper Niger. Such towns became a characteristic feature of West Africa. They spread at approximately the same period right across the sub-Saharan savanna from the Senegal to Lake Chad, and into the forest fringes to the south. Most West Africans lived in towns, and the town, with its surrounding countryside, was the basic unit of government. From time to time military leaders arose, who united groups of towns into larger kingdoms or empires. Such were the empires of Ghana, Mali, and Songhay (sŏng′gī′), which succeeded each other in the western Sudan between about A.D. 1000 and 1600. Sundiata (sün′dē′ə tä) was the warlord who, in the early thirteenth century A.D., built up the nucleus of the Mali empire by successive conquests, beginning with a victory over Sumaoro (sü mä′ōr ō) of Soso at the battle of Krina. His successors ruled for more than two centuries over an empire which stretched from the great bend of the Niger to the

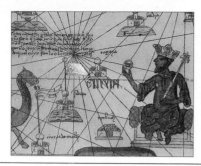

Detail of map, showing Mansa Musa

Detail of carving of an ibis hunter

1307
Mansa Musa expands Mali Empire
by subjugating Songhay Empire

1440
Ewuare the Great rules Benin

upper Senegal and controlled the rich gold mines of the western Sudan. Later rulers adopted Islam and several of them, including Mansa Musa, made the pilgrimage to Mecca, and astonished the people of Cairo by lavish displays of wealth.

South of the equator, the coming of the Iron Age was even more revolutionary than in West Africa, for it seems likely that here the earliest iron-using farmers formed a new and rapidly expanding population, speaking a set of closely related languages known collectively as Bantu, which moved into country hitherto occupied mainly by hunters and gatherers, who were soon outnumbered and gradually absorbed by the newcomers. Comparative linguists are agreed that the Bantu languages must have originated in the southeastern corner of West Africa, and that their speakers must have expanded both southeastwards through the Congo forest and eastwards around the forest's northern fringe. In the western half of Bantu Africa, in and around the Congo basin,

settlement patterns and life-style were reminiscent of the southern, forested parts of West Africa. Most people lived in large, concentrated villages, ruled by "big men," in which specialist artisans practiced as weavers, woodcarvers, and metal workers and produced many of the finest art objects in the whole continent.

Eastern Bantu Africa had, in contrast, a very different flavor, in which pastoral influences emanating from Ethiopia and the Nilotic Sudan were powerful. People lived dispersed in patriarchal families around the corrals housing their livestock. Wealth accumulated in herds of cattle rather than hoards of metal. Representational art was avoided in favor of the geometrical designs employed in pottery and basketwork. Where herders and cultivators lived side by side, rich cattle owners leased out a part of their stock in twos and threes to their farming neighbors and so gained political power. Pasturage demanded larger areas than agriculture, and competition for it led to warfare and the

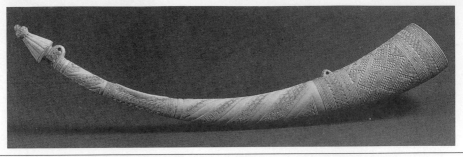

Congo oliphant

1490
*Portuguese missionaries convert
the ruler of the Congo*

enlargement of political units. The densest agricultural populations grew up in pockets of well-watered land, in the foothills of the high mountains or in the rainbelts adjoining the ocean coast and the large lakes. The largest and longest lasting kingdom on the eastern side of Africa grew up in the Ethiopian highlands to the north of the Bantu sphere, where Christianity took root in the fourth century A.D. In the surrounding lowlands Islam became the religion of the pastoral Somali and also of the harbor towns which grew up along the Indian Ocean coast. Inland, belief systems centered around the cult of ancestors, who were revered as links in the chain leading back through time to the Creator God.

THE ARRIVAL
OF EUROPEANS

By the time of its first contacts with Europe, in the late fifteenth and early sixteenth century, sub-Saharan Africa had long been a continent of Iron Age farmers, numerous enough and well enough armed to repel any attempts at invasion and

conquest that could have been mounted at that period. Europeans could trade with Africa round its coasts, buying the gold, the ivory, and the slaves brought down to them at their seaside warehouses, but they could not penetrate inland. Nevertheless, Africa was still, as a whole, very lightly populated and its political communities were mostly very small. A handful of states and kingdoms, headed by Egypt, Morocco, Ethiopia, Songhay, and the Congo, may have had more than a million subjects. Twenty or thirty others may have numbered more than 100,000. But the great majority of African states probably had between 5,000 and 15,000 people, and their rulers knew most of their subjects by sight. Such states tended to form in clusters of twenty or thirty among peoples speaking mutually intelligible dialects and observing similar customs. They intermarried with each other, but they also fought each other, taking booty and capturing prisoners whom they used and traded as slaves, not only to

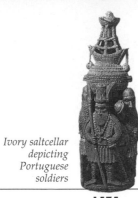

Ivory saltcellar depicting Portuguese soldiers

Engraving of Chaka

1575
Portuguese begin conquest of Angola

1818
Chaka founds Zulu Empire

Europeans and other foreigners, but also on the internal African networks, which crisscrossed the continent, using camels and donkeys, canoes and human porters.

By the nineteenth century the technological gap between Africa and the industrialized world had grown much wider, and it had become inevitable that, one way or another, external influences would break in. No one could prevent the importation into Africa of industrial Europe's mass-produced firearms. So armed, the coastal peoples, the Egyptians, the Ethiopians, the Swahili-Arabs of the Zanzibar coast, the Boer frontiersmen of the Cape Colony, the Chokwe of Angola, and many others, moved into the interior regions to hunt out the ivory, confident in their ability to shoot down any opposition. When the European powers at the end of the century decided upon partition, they found an Africa destabilized and demoralized, which could offer little resistance to their incursion. There followed seventy to eighty years of colonial rule, which reduced its ten thousand or so political units to about forty, which was the indispensable condition of any fundamental modernization. It also did something to prepare a tiny elite of educated Africans to take over these colonies as independent nation states capable of survival in the modern world. But the cost to the traditional languages and cultures of Africa has been high.

The Conquest of Upper Egypt

Around 3100 B.C., Egypt was united into a powerful kingdom. For more than two thousand years, the Egyptian pharaohs expanded their control of the region and were worshipped as gods within their kingdom. By the eighth century B.C., Egyptian power had waned and the country became vulnerable to attack by outside forces. Around 720 B.C., Piankhi (**pē änk′ē**), King of Kush, a powerful desert kingdom, invaded Egypt from the southwest. His goal was not to sack the cities of Egypt, but to bring the whole Nile Valley under his control as a new pharaoh. After conquering Memphis, just south of Cairo on the Nile, Piankhi assumed the role of Pharaoh and inaugurated the XXV Dynasty in Egypt, adapting all the traditional Egyptian symbols, rituals, and gods. After his victory, Piankhi had the following account of his invasion and the capture of Memphis engraved on a granite stela in Napata, the capital of Kush. Why does Piankhi not sack Memphis?

THEN HIS MAJESTY SENT AN ARMY TO EGYPT, CHARGING THEM earnestly: "[Delay] not [day nor] night, as at a game of draughts; fight ye on sight. Force battle upon him from afar. 'Thou knowest that Amon is the god who has sent us.'"

Then they threw themselves upon their bellies before his majesty (saying): "It is thy name which endues us with might, and thy counsel is the mooring-post of thy army; thy bread is in our bellies on every march, thy beer quenches our thirst. It is thy valor that giveth us might, and there is strength at the remembrance of thy name; no army prevails whose commander is a coward. Where is thy equal therein? Thou art a victorious king, achieving with his hands, chief of the work of war."

They sailed downstream, they arrived at Thebes, they did according to all that his majesty had said…. They found many ships coming upstream bearing soldiers, sailors, and commanders; every valiant man of the Northland, equipped with weapons of war, to fight against the army of his majesty. Then there was made a great slaughter among them, whose number was unknown. Their troops and their ships were captured, and brought as living captives to the place where his majesty was.

When day broke, at early morning, his majesty reached Memphis. When he had landed on the north of it, he found that the water had approached to the walls, the ships mooring at [the walls of] Memphis. Then his majesty saw that it was strong, and that the wall was raised a new rampart, and battlements manned with mighty men. There was found no way of attacking it. Every man told his opinion among the army of his majesty, according to every rule of war. Every man said: "Let us besiege it—; lo, its troops are numerous." Others said: "Let a causeway be made against it; let us elevate the ground to its walls. Let us bind together a tower; let us erect masts and make the spars into a bridge to it. We will divide it on this (plan) on every side of it, on the high ground and—on the north of it, in order to elevate the ground at its walls, that we may find a way for our feet."

Then his majesty was enraged against it like a panther; he said: "I swear, as Re loves me, as my father, Amon [who fashioned me], favors me, this shall befall it, according to the command of Amon.... I will take it like a flood of water. I have commanded." Then he sent forth his fleet and his army to assault the harbor of Memphis; they brought to him every ferry-boat, every [cargo]-boat; every [transport], and the ships, as many as there were, which had moored in the harbor of Memphis, with the bow-rope fastened among its houses. [There was not] a citizen who wept, among all the soldiers of his majesty.

His majesty himself came to line up the ships, as many as there were. His majesty commanded his army: "Forward against it! Mount the walls! Penetrate the houses over the river. If one of you gets through upon the wall, let him not halt before it, [so that] the [hostile] troops may not repulse you. It were vile that we should close up the South, should land [in] the North and lay siege in 'Balances of the Two Lands.'"

Then Memphis was taken as by a flood of water, a multitude of people were slain therein, and brought others as living captives to the place where his majesty was.

Now afterward, when it dawned, and the second day came, his majesty sent people into it, protecting the temples of the god. He, the holy of holies of the gods, offered to the community of gods of Hatkeptah (Memphis), cleansed Memphis with natron and incense, installed the priests in their places....

His majesty proceeded to the house of [Ptah], his purification was performed in the Dewat-chamber, and every custom that is practiced upon a king was fulfilled upon him. He entered into the temple, and a great oblation was made for his father, "Ptah-South-of-His-Wall" consisting of bulls, calves, fowl, and everything good. His majesty proceeded to his house....

When the land brightened, very early in the morning, his majesty proceeded eastward, and an offering was made for Atum in Khereha, the divine ennead (a group of gods) in the house of the ennead, the cavern and the gods dwelling in it; consisting of bulls, calves, and fowl; that they might give life, prosperity, and health to the King of Upper and Lower Egypt, Piankhi, living forever.

THINKING CRITICALLY

1. *Understanding the Action* How did Piankhi capture Memphis?

2. *Drawing Conclusions* What did Piankhi do to anoint himself Pharaoh? What did these steps signify?

3. *Making Inferences* Why do you think Piankhi was able to set himself up as a new pharaoh in Egypt? Why did the Egyptians accept him?

WRITER'S PORTFOLIO

1. *Extending the Lesson* Write a news story reporting on Piankhi's conquest of Upper Egypt. Report as many details as you can.

2. *Examining Key Questions* What does the Kushite conquest of Egypt tell you about the importance of Egypt in African development?

African Folk Tales

African folk tales are a rich source of wisdom and tradition. Centuries of advice, humor, and beliefs are wrapped up in these oral entertainments. African folk tales discuss almost every facet of tribal life and are as varied as the tribes of the continent. "How the World Changed" is a tale from Liberia, that explains the origins of night and day and the different human races. The Baila tale, from Zambia, is a parable of how we should act in our lives. What is the tone of these tales?

How the World Changed

MELEKA (GOD) MADE THE WORLD AND THE MOON AND THE sun. The sun shone all the time, for Meleka considered that constant light would benefit men and beasts. Therefore, there was no night. For every man there was a woman. There were no white or brown or yellow people, there was only a single race of noble and pure-black men. In those days men and animals were friends and wandered freely in the forest eating fruit and nuts and green foods. Caves and houses were not needed, for when a man or a beast was tired he simply lay down to sleep where he was. Men possessed no spears and animals had no claws.

Little children left their parents whenever they pleased, wandering for months and years in foreign places. This was a source of worry and grief to men and animals, for they loved their children well. Sometimes children wandered away and were never seen again. The mothers and fathers wept in sorrow and appealed to Meleka for aid.

Meleka then took away the sun. All the men and animals were alarmed as they could not understand what the darkness was. Families grouped together in defense against unknown terrors: children roaming far away called pitifully for their parents.

After a time, Meleka caused the sun to shine again. Everyone was happy again; children who had been returning home began to wander about again. Meleka decided to divide time into nights and days to encourage the little ones to go back home and not to stray too far from their parents. In common protection against the night, men and animals united in a single friendly clan and lived together under a giant cotton tree. This tree was the only shelter they could find. They took good care of the tree for it was the only home they had. All of the animals and men loved one another and it was a happy home.

One day the son of a man discovered a piece of fire discarded by Lightning Bug. He played with it. Being a normal child with mischief in his head, he waited until no one was watching, then carried fire to the foot of the cotton tree. The giant tree had already been badly burnt before the animals and men saw and smelled the smoke.

A great cry of despair rose up from the animals. They stood about in fear, helplessly watching fire consume their home in a roaring, smoking blaze. After many hours the tree groaned, cracked and came crashing down to earth amid a shower of bright red sparks. The men and animals fled in all directions.

"It is finished!" cried the animals. "We have been betrayed by man. We agreed to live in peace beneath the cotton tree, but man is wicked. We will not stay any longer. There is war between us!"

Most of the animals fled far into the forest where they made their homes in caves and thickets. Men built houses of mud and thatch and their tribe multiplied. A few brave or foolish animals, such as dogs, goats, or cows, decided to live with them.

On the other side of a mountain there was a certain pond which Meleka had used as a painting bowl. His colors had settled to the bottom of the pond, leaving the water looking clear and sweet. A group of naughty children bathed there. Their swimming and splashing stirred up Meleka's colors and the children were astonished to see their skins change color from lustrous black to white, brown and yellow. In great alarm they rushed from the pond and washed themselves in a stream, but the colors were fixed and would not be washed off.

Baila Tale

SHE WAS AN OLD WOMAN OF A FAMILY WITH A LONG genealogy. Leza Shikakunamo—"The Besetting One"—had stretched out his hand against her family. He slew her mother and her father while she was yet a child; and in the course of the years all connected with her perished. She said to herself, "Surely, I shall keep those who sit on my thighs"—but no, even they, the children of her children, were taken from her. She became withered with age, and it seemed to her that she herself was at last to be taken. But no, a change came over her: she grew younger. Then came into her heart a desperate resolution to find God and ask the meaning of it all. Somewhere up there in the sky must be His dwelling: if only she could reach it!

So she began to travel, going through country after country, nation after nation, always with the thought in her mind: "I shall come to where the earth ends, and there, where the earth and sky touch, I shall find a road to God, and I shall ask him, 'What have I done to Thee that Thou afflictest me in this manner?'"

The old woman never found where the earth ends, but, though disappointed, she did not give up her search. As she passed through the different countries the people asked her, "What have you come for, old woman?"

And her answer would be, "I am seeking Leza."

"Seeking Leza! For what?"

"My brothers, you ask me! Here in the nations is there one who suffers as I have suffered?"

And they would ask again, "How have you suffered?"

"In this way, I am alone. As you see me, a solitary old woman: that is how I am!"

And they answered again, "Yes, we see. That is how you are! Bereaved of friends and kindred? In what do you differ from others? Leza Shikakunamo sits on the back of every one of us, and we cannot shake him off!"

She never obtained her desire; she died of a broken heart.

THINKING CRITICALLY

1. *Making Comparisons* Compare and contrast the gods in these folk tales. Are Meleka and Leza Shikakunamo similar figures?

2. *Recognizing Values* When reading these folk tales, how are you as a reader linked to the African tradition?

3. *Linking Past to Present* What kinds of stories do you hear told today? Are there any that you would consider folk tales?

WRITER'S PORTFOLIO

1. *Extending the Lesson* Write a folk tale of your own describing the origin of something or creating a parable of wisdom.

2. *Examining Key Questions* How does the African folk tale help to create a sense of community within a cultural group?

Trickster Tales

The clever trickster who lives by his wits is one of the oldest and most prevalent mythological figures in the world. In Africa, he took as many forms as there are different tribes or languages. Two of the most prominent were Kwaku Ananse the spider, known throughout West Africa, but especially to the Ashanti of Ghana, and Edju, one of the Orisha, the gods of the Yoruba people from Nigeria. This figure represents the worst of human nature: selfishness, greed, irrationality, disorder, and dissent. The trickster is a cunning and clever figure, yet, as often as not, his cunning is ineffective and he is punished for his ways or suffers because of his foolishness. In the following stories, Kwaku Ananse is taught a lesson by a crocodile, and Edju wreaks havoc in two friends' lives. What seem to be the trickster's motives?

Why Kwaku Ananse runs when he is on the water

Kwaku Ananse, the Spider, went and said to Okraman, the Dog, "Dog, let us join in play." The Dog said, "What kind of play?" The Spider replied, "The binding-binding game; you bind me first, then I, too, shall bind you, but when you hear me say, 'Wui!' then you leave off." The Dog said, "No, you tie me up first." The Spider said, "Take yourself off, when your elder is telling you something, do you argue about it?" The Dog said, "Well, let it remain (as you wish)." The Spider said, "Come and tie me up." The Dog took his rope-creeper and bound up the Spider. And he took him up on his head, saying he was going to sell him that he might get something to eat. When Ananse heard that, he raised a lament and said: "I, Ananse Akuamoa, I have not even got a proper kind of beast to sell me. Only this fool of a Dog, he is going to sell me. Whom can I get to save me? O, Path, save me!"

Ananse could only cry and cry. The Dog carried him until he reached some stream. Now, Odenkyem, the Crocodile, heard the Spider crying. When he came, he asked the Dog what was the matter. The Dog threw Ananse down, and ran away, and the Crocodile loosed Ananse.

And Ananse said, "Father, what kind of thing can I give you to show how grateful I am?" The Crocodile said, "We do not desire anything at all." Ananse said, "If you have children, then tomorrow I shall come and dress their hair for them very becomingly."

The Crocodile said, "I have heard." Ananse came home; he said, "Aso, go and seek palm-nuts and onions, for tomorrow I am going to kill and bring back a crocodile that we may have a soup stew to eat." Aso went and got some, and the Spider sharpened his knife and mashed *eto*, and took it to the stream. He said, "Father Crocodile, the Water-animal, I am coming to reward you." And he took the pounded yams and put them in the water. The Crocodile came, and he was about to take the pounded yams to eat, when the Spider took his knife and cut at him, *gya*! but he did not get him (properly) and he went off. Ananse returned home. Aso asked him, saying, "Where is that animal?" Ananse said, "Take yourself off; a person comes off a journey, and hasn't even got his breath back, and you begin to bother him with questions." Aso said, "I have seen that you did not get him." Ananse did not say anything. Next morning, very early, Aso said she was going to the stream. When she got there, there was the Crocodile lying on the river bank, and the blue-bottle-flies were buzzing round him. Aso returned home and told her husband. Ananse said, "Now you see how a certain medicine I have, acts; when I kill meat (one day), not until things become visible, the next day, do I go and fetch it, but nevertheless I congratulate you on seeing it." Ananse cut a stick and took it with him to the stream there, and there he came across the Crocodile. He poked at it with the stick, saying, "Crocodile, are you dead? Crocodile, are you dead?" and he turned it over and over. And the Crocodile lay still, but he was not dead. When Ananse was about to take his hand to touch it, the Crocodile suddenly snapped him kua! Ananse struggled, petere! petere! and found a way to escape. That is why, when the Spider passes on the water, he hastens along; he is afraid that the Crocodile will come to catch him again.

Edju and the Two Friends

ONCE UPON A TIME, OLORUN FIRST CREATED ENJA, OR MORTAL man, and, after that, Edju, the god. Once there were a pair of friends. When they went out they were always dressed alike. Everyone said, "These two men are the best of friends." Edju saw them and said, "These men are very dear to each other. I will make them differ and that will be a fine beginning for a very big Idja [lawsuit]." The fields of these friends adjoined. A path ran between and separated them. Edju used to walk on it of a morning and then wore a "filla" or black cap.

Now, when Edju wanted to start this quarrel, he made himself a cap of green, black, red, and white cloth, which showed a different color from whatever side it was looked at. He put it on one morning on his walk abroad. Then he took his tobacco pipe and put it, not, as usual, in his mouth, but at the nape of his neck, as if he were smoking at the back of his head. And then he took his staff as usual, but, this time, carried it upside down, that is to say, so that it hung, not over his breast in front, but over his shoulder behind. Both the friends were at work in their fields. They looked up for a second. Edju called out, "Good morning!" They gave him the same and went on with their toil.

Then they went home together. One said to the other, "The old man (Edju) went the opposite road through the fields today. I noticed that by his pipe and his stick." The other said, "You're wrong. He went the same way as usual, I saw it by the way his feet were going." The first said, "It's a lie; I saw his pipe and his staff much too plainly; and, besides, he had on a white instead of a black cap." The second one retorted, "You must be blind or asleep; his cap was red." His friend said, "Then you must already have had some palm-wine this morning, if you could see neither the color of his cap, nor the way he was walking." The other one answered him, "I haven't even seen a drop this morning, but you must be crazed." The other man said, "You are making up lies to annoy me." Then the other one said, "Liar yourself! And not for the first time by a good deal." One of them drew his knife and went for the other who got a wound. He also drew his knife and cut his assailant. They both ran away bleeding to the town. The folk saw them and said, "Both these friends have been attacked. There will be war." One of them said, "No, this liar is no friend of mine." And the other one, "Don't believe a single word of his. When he opens his mouth, the lies swarm from it."

Meanwhile, Edju had gone to the King of the town. He said to the King, "Just ask the two friends what is the matter with them! They have cut each other's heads about with knives and are bleeding." The King said, "What, the two friends, who always wear clothes alike have been quarreling? Let them be summoned!" So it was done. The King asked them, "You are both in sad case. What made you fall out?" They both said, " We could not agree as to what it was that went through our fields this morning." Then the King asked, "How many people went along your footpath?" "It was a man who goes the same way everyday. Today he went in another direction, wearing a white cap instead of a black one," said one of the friends. "He lies," shouted the other; "the old man had on a red cap and walked along in the usual direction!" Then the King asked, "Who knows this old man?" Edju said, "It is I. These two fellows quarreled because I so willed it." Edju pulled out his cap and said, "I put on this cap, red on one side, white on the other, green in front, and black behind. I stuck my pipe in my nape. So my steps went one way while I was looking another. The two friends couldn't help quarreling. I made them do it. Sowing dissension is my chief delight."

THINKING CRITICALLY

1. *Making Comparisons* Compare and contrast Kwaku Ananse and Edju. Which one seems more redeemable?

2. *Recognizing Motives* Why does Kwaku Ananse try to trick the crocodile? Why does Edju trick the friends?

3. *Linking Past to Present* Can you think of any modern equivalents to the trickster?

WRITER'S PORTFOLIO

1. *Extending the Lesson* Write a brief story, describing an encounter between Kwaku Ananse and Edju.

2. *Examining Key Questions* What does the figure of the trickster represent in these African cultures?

An Epic of Old Mali

The tradition of oral literature thrived throughout African history, particularly as practiced and transmitted by the griots. A griot (**grē′ō**) was a combination of a poet, historian, troubadour, and court jester. In a land without written language the role of the griot was critical to the history and literature of the country; he committed anything of importance to memory: battles, laws, genealogies, stories. The role of the griot was so important to the society that he was often the friend and counselor of the king. One of the great works created by a griot is the *Sundiata*, the story of the king who founded the Empire of Mali, which dominated West Africa from the thirteenth to the sixteenth century. The epic tells of the war between Sundiata (**sün′dē′ə tā**) and Soumaoro, King of Sosso, for control of Mali. The following selection depicts their great battle as well as a war of words fought by the kings on the eve of the battle. What is the griot's role in this history?

U<small>P TILL THAT TIME, S</small>UNDIATA <small>AND</small> S<small>OUMAORO HAD FOUGHT</small> each other without a declaration of war. One does not wage war without saying why it is being waged. Those fighting should make a declaration of their grievances to begin with. Just as a sorcerer ought not to attack someone without taking him to task for some evil deed, so a king should not wage war without saying why he is taking up arms.

Soumaoro advanced as far as Krina, near the village of Dayala on the Niger and decided to assert his rights before joining battle. Soumaoro knew that Sundiata was also a sorcerer, so, instead of sending an embassy, he committed his words to one of his owls. The night bird came and perched on the roof of Djata's [Sundiata's lieutenant] tent and spoke. The son of Sogolon [Sundiata] in his turn sent his owl to Soumaoro. Here is the dialogue of the sorcerer kings:

"Stop, young man. Henceforth I am the king of Mali. If you want peace, return to where you came from," said Soumaoro.

"I am coming back, Soumaoro, to recapture my kingdom. If you want peace you will make amends to my allies and return to Sosso where you are the king."

"I am king of Mali by force of arms. My rights have been established by conquest."

"Then I will take Mali from you by force of arms and chase you from my kingdom."

"Know, then, that I am the wild yam of the rocks: nothing will make me leave Mali."

"Know, then, that I have in my camp seven master smiths who will shatter the rocks. Then, yam, I will eat you."

"I am the poisonous mushroom that makes the fearless vomit."

"As for me, I am the ravenous cock, the poison does not matter to me."

"Behave yourself, little boy, or you will burn your foot, for I am the red-hot cinder."

"But me, I am the rain that extinguishes the cinder; I am the boisterous torrent that will carry you off."

"I am the mighty silk-cotton tree that looks from on high on the tops of other trees."

"And I, I am the strangling creeper that climbs to the top of the forest giant."

"Enough of this argument. You shall not have Mali."

"Know that there is not room for two kings on the same skin, Soumaoro; you will let me have your place."

Thus Sundiata and Soumaoro spoke together. After the war of mouths, swords had to decide the issue....

Several oxen were slaughtered and that evening Balla Fasséké, in front of the whole army, called to mind the history of old Mali. He praised Sundiata, seated amidst his lieutenants, in this manner:

"Now I address myself to you, Maghan Sundiata. I speak to you king of Mali, to whom dethroned monarchs flock. The time foretold to you by the jinn is now coming. But listen to what your ancestors did, so that you will know what you have to do.

"Bilali, the second of the name, conquered old Mali. Latal Kalabi conquered the country between the Niger and the Sankarani. By going to Mecca, Lahibatoul Kalabi, of illustrious memory, brought divine blessing upon Mali. Mamadi Kani made warriors out of hunters and bestowed armed strength upon Mali. His son Bamari Tagnokelin, the vindictive king, terrorized Mali with this army, but Maghan Kon Fatta, also called Naré Maghan, to whom you owe your being, made peace prevail and happy mothers yielded Mali a populous youth.

"You are the son of Naré Baghan, but you are also the son of your mother Sogolon, the buffalo-woman, before whom powerless sorcerers shrank in fear. You have the strength and majesty of the lion, you have the might of the buffalo.

"I have told you what future generations will learn about your ancestors, but what will we be able to relate to our sons so that your memory will stay alive, what will we have to teach our sons about you? What unprecedented exploits, what unheard of feats? by what distinguished actions will our sons be brought to regret not having lived in the time of Sundiata?

"Griots are men of the spoken word, and by the spoken word we give life to the gestures of kings. But words are nothing but words; power lies in deeds. Be a man of action; do not answer me any more with your mouth, but tomorrow, on the plain of Krina, show me what you would have me recount to coming generations. Tomorrow allow me to sing the 'Song of the Vultures' over the bodies of the thousands of Sossos whom your sword will have laid low before evening.…"

The sun had risen on the other side of the river and already lit the whole plain. Sundiata's troops deployed from the edge of the river across the plain, but Soumaoro's army was so big that other sofas [infantry] remaining in Krina had ascended the ramparts to see the battle. Soumaoro was already distinguishable in the distance by his tall headdress, and the wings of his enormous army brushed the river on one side and the hills on the other. As at Negué-boria, Sundiata did not deploy all his forces. The bowmen of Wagadou and the Djallonkés stood at the rear ready to spill out on the left towards the hills as the battle spread. Fakoli Koroma and Kamandjan were in the front line with Sundiata and his cavalry.

With his powerful voice Sundiata cried "An gnewa [forward]." The order was repeated from tribe to tribe and the army started off. Soumaoro stood on the right with his cavalry.

Djata and his cavalry charged with great dash but they were stopped by the horsemen of Diaghan and a struggle to the death began. Tabon Wana and the archers of Wagadou stretched out their lines towards the hills and the battle spread over the entire plain, while an unrelenting sun climbed in the sky. The horses of Mema were extremely agile, and they reared forward with their fore hooves raised and swooped down on the horsemen of Diaghan, who rolled on the ground trampled under the horses' hooves. Presently the men of Diaghan gave ground and fell back towards the rear. The enemy center was broken.

It was then that Manding Bory galloped up to announce to Sundiata that Soumaoro, having thrown in all his reserve, had swept down on Fakoli and his smiths. Obviously Soumaoro was bent on punishing his nephew. Already overwhelmed by the numbers, Fakoli's men were beginning to give ground. The battle was not yet won.

His eyes red with anger, Sundiata pulled his cavalry over to the left in the direction of the hills where Fakoli was valiantly enduring his uncle's blows. But wherever the son of the buffalo passed, death rejoiced. Sundiata's presence restored the balance momentarily, but Soumaoro's sofas were too numerous all the same. Sogolon's son looked for Soumaoro and caught sight of him in the middle of the fray. Sundiata struck out right and left and the Sossos scrambled out of his way. The king of Sosso, who did not want Sundiata to get near him, retreated far behind his men, but Sundiata followed him with his eyes. He stopped and bent his bow. The arrow flew and grazed Soumaoro on the shoulder. The cock's spur no more than scratched him, but the effect was immediate and Soumaoro felt his powers leave him. His eyes met Sundiata's. Now trembling like a man in the grip of a fever, the vanquished Soumaoro looked up towards the sun. A great black bird flew over above the fray and he understood. It was a bird of misfortune.

The king of Sosso let out a great cry and, turning his horse's head, he took to flight. The Sossos saw the king and fled in their turn. It was a rout. Death hovered over the great plain and blood poured out of a thousand wounds.

THINKING CRITICALLY

1. *Making Comparisons* Compare and contrast the verbal battle and the military battle between Sundiata and Soumaoro.

2. *Recognizing Values* The night before the battle why does the griot recite the list of ancestors and their great deeds for Sundiata?

3. *Linking Past to Present* Argue for or against the following statement: The role of tradition is very important in my life.

WRITER'S PORTFOLIO

1. *Extending the Lesson* Does the *Sundiata* read like an oral history?

2. *Examining Key Questions* What links the world that can be seen with the one that can't be seen in this account?

Traditional African Poetry

The tradition of oral poetry in Africa is a vast and wonderful heritage. In lands with no written language, memory and recitation played critical roles in the preservation of literature. Poetry, stories, and proverbs were passed along from one voice to another, from one generation to the next. Africa is a vast continent with many nations and many languages and its poetry reflects this diversity. The following selection of poems reflects only a tiny part of the cultural diversity. These poems were not created by a single poet as in Western culture, but instead over the years they were changed, adapted, updated, so that, in a way, all of the persons who have recited these poems are poets. The images are the building blocks of this poetry, and you will find images that are special and exotic as well as those that are everyday and familiar. But they are always surprising and always satisfying. To whom is each poem addressed?

The Ancestors
The days have passed;
we are a wandering camp
brighter days before us
perhaps.

Light fades
night becomes darker.
Hunger tomorrow.

God is angry
the elders have gone
Their bones are far
their souls wander.
Where are their souls?

The passing wind
knows it perhaps.

Their bones are far
their souls wander.
Are they far away,
are they quite close?
Do they want sacrifice,
do they want blood?
Are they far,
are they near?

The passing wind
the spirit that whirls the leaf
knows it perhaps.

(Hottentot)

Death

There is no needle without piercing point.
There is no razor without trenchant blade.
Death comes to us in many forms.

With our feet we walk the goat's earth.
With our hands we touch God's sky.
Some future day in the heat of noon,
I shall be carried shoulder high
through the village of the dead.
When I die, don't bury me under forest trees,
I fear their thorns.
When I die, don't bury me under forest trees.
I fear the dripping water.
Bury me under the great shade trees in the market,
I want to hear the drums beating
I want to feel the dancers' feet.

(Kuba)

Sadness of Life

The beautiful playing field has fallen to ruins.
The beautiful pleasure ground has fallen to ruins.
Dense forest has reverted to savanna,
our beautiful town has become grassland,
our beautiful home is nothing but grassland.

May the gravedigger not bury me.
Let him bury my feet, let him leave bare my chest,
let my people come and see my face,
let them come and look at my eyes.

The drum does not beat for joy.
"Sadness of Life" "Sadness of Life" sounds the drum.
The drum only sounds for sadness of life.

(Ewe)

The Beloved
Diko,
of light skin, of smooth hair and long;
her smell is sweet and gentle
she never stinks of fish
she never breathes sweat
like gatherers of dry wood.
She has no bald patch on her head
like those who carry heavy loads.
Her teeth are white
her eyes are like
those of a new born fawn
that delights in the milk
that flows for the first
time from the antelope's udder.
Neither her heel nor her palm
are rough; but sweet to touch
like liver; or better still
the fluffy down of kapok.

(Fulani)

Love Song
I painted my eyes with black antimony
I girded myself with amulets.

I will satisfy my desire,
you my slender boy.
I walk behind the wall.

I have covered my bosom.
I shall knead coloured clay
I shall paint the house of my friend,
O my slender boy.
I shall take my piece of silver
I will buy silk.
I will gird myself with amulets
I will satisfy my desire
the horn of antimony in my hand,
Oh my slender boy!

(Bagirmi)

Love Song
The body perishes, the heart stays young.
The platter wears away with serving food.
No log retains its bark when old,
No lover peaceful while the rival weeps.

(Zulu)

THINKING CRITICALLY

1. *Making Comparisons* Compare and contrast the attitudes toward tradition and the past in these poems.

2. *Recognizing Values* How is the spirit of community reflected in these poems?

3. *Linking Past to Present* Compare and contrast recent poets and poetry to these traditional poems. Do poems still serve the same purpose?

WRITER'S PORTFOLIO

1. *Extending the Lesson* Choose one of the poems and update and alter it to speak with your voice. Read these living poems aloud in class.

2. *Examining Key Questions* How are the worlds of the seen and the unseen linked in these poems?

The Kingdom of Mali

The Empire of Mali, founded by Sundiata Keita, was the most powerful force in West Africa for two centuries. One of the main reasons that Mali enjoyed such economic success was because of its vigorous trade with other countries. Mali was the home of a skillful and powerful merchant class, most of whom were Muslim. These merchants had access to the huge European market through their trade in North Africa and Egypt. Europeans were eager for gold, and Mali possessed rich supplies of that metal. The greatest King of Mali was Mansa Musa (reigned 1312–1337), who expanded Sundiata's kingdom and solidified its trade. In 1324 he made the traditional Muslim pilgrimage to Mecca, passing through Cairo, where the Egyptians were astonished by the Malians' wealth. The following accounts of Mansa Musa's pilgrimage and of his kingdom were written by a Muslim writer named al-Omari. Although al-Omari had not actually been in Cairo at the time of the emperor's visit, he heard the details of the story from a member of the court at Cairo, who had greeted the pilgrims upon their arrival. Why does Mansa Musa finally bow before the Sultan?

Mansa Musa Arrives in Cairo

"WHEN I WENT OUT TO GREET HIM IN THE NAME OF THE glorious Sultan el Malik en Nasir of Egypt," he told me, "he gave the warmest of welcomes and treated me with the most careful politeness. But he would talk to me only through an interpreter [that is, his spokesman or linguist] although he could speak perfect Arabic. He carried his imperial treasure in many pieces of gold, worked or otherwise.

"I suggested that he should go up to the palace and meet the Sultan [of Egypt]. But he refused, saying: 'I came for the pilgrimage, and for nothing else, and I do not wish to mix up my pilgrimage with anything else.' He argued about this. However, I well understood that the meeting was repugnant to him because he was loath to kiss the ground before the

Sultan or to kiss his hand. I went on insisting and he went on making excuses. But imperial protocol obliged me to present him, and I did not leave him until he had agreed. When he came into the Sultan's presence we asked him to kiss the ground. But he refused and continued to refuse, saying: 'However can this be?' Then a wise man of his suite whispered several words to him that I could not understand. 'Very well,' he thereupon declared, 'I will prostrate myself before Allah who created me and brought me into the world.' Having done so he moved towards the Sultan. The latter rose for a moment to welcome him and asked him to sit beside him: then they had a long conversation. After Sultan Musa had left the palace the Sultan of Cairo sent him gifts of clothing for himself, his courtiers and all those who were with him; saddled and bridled horses for himself and his chief officers....

Let me add that gold in Egypt had enjoyed a high rate of exchange up to the moment of their arrival. The gold *mitqal* that year had not fallen below twenty-five drachmas. But from that day [of their arrival] onward, its value dwindled; the exchange was ruined, and even now it has not recovered. The *mitqal* scarcely touches twenty-two drachmas. That is how it has been for twelve years from that time, because of the great amounts of gold they brought to Egypt and spent there.

The Empire of Mali

THE KING OF THIS COUNTRY IS KNOWN TO THE PEOPLE OF EGYPT as the king of Tekrur [roughly, inland Senegal]; but he himself becomes indignant when he is called thus, since Tekrur is only one of the countries of his empire. The title he prefers is that of lord of Mali, the largest of his states; it is the name by which he is most known. He is the most important of the Muslim Negro kings; his land is the largest, his army the most numerous; he is the king who is the most powerful, the richest, the most fortunate, and the most feared by his enemies and the most able to do good to those around him....

The sultan of this country has sway over the land of the "desert of native gold," whence they bring him gold every year. The inhabitants of that land are savage pagans whom the sultan would subject to him if he wished. But the sovereigns of this kingdom have learned by experience that whenever one of them has conquered one of these gold towns, established Islam there and sounded the call to prayer, the harvest of gold dwindles and falls to nothing, meanwhile it grows and expands in neighboring pagan countries. When experience had confirmed them in this observation, they left the gold country in the hands of its pagan inhabitants, and contented themselves with assuring their obedience and paying tribute.

The sultan of this kingdom presides in his palace on a great balcony called *bembe* where he has a great seat of ebony that is like a throne fit for a large and tall person: on either side it is flanked by elephant tusks turned towards each other. His arms stand near him, being all of gold: sabre, lance, quiver, bow and arrows. He wears wide trousers of a kind which he alone may wear. Behind him there stand about a score of Turkish or other pages which are bought for him in Cairo: one of them, at his left, holds a silk umbrella surmounted by a dome and a bird of gold: the bird has the figure of a falcon. His officers are seated in a circle about him, in two rows, one to the right and one to the left; beyond them sit the chief commanders of his cavalry. In front of him there is a person who never leaves him and who is his executioner; also another who serves as intermediary [that is, official spokesman] between the sovereign and his subjects, and who is named the herald. In front of them again, there are drummers. Others dance before their sovereign, who enjoys this, and make him laugh. Two banners are spread behind him. Before him they keep two saddled and bridled horses in case he should wish to ride.

THINKING CRITICALLY

1. *Identifying Cause and Effect* Why do Mansa Musa and his people bring so much gold with them on the pilgrimage? What is its effect in Cairo?

2. *Recognizing Values* Why does Mansa Musa refuse to speak in Arabic or to kiss the ground or the hand of the Sultan of Egypt?

3. *Linking Past to Present* Do people still make pilgrimages today? Where do they go?

WRITER'S PORTFOLIO

1. *Extending the Lesson* Write a description of Mansa Musa's encounter with the Egyptian official, as it appeared to one of the Malians.

2. *Examining Key Questions* Do you think Mali's conversion to Islam helped it become an economic power?

African Masks

Of all the African art forms the mask is probably the one that most immediately brings to mind the continent of its origin. The pervasive use of the mask in African cultures has left an artistic legacy, which alternately startles, terrifies, and charms its viewers. No one knows how far back the history of masks goes since most were made of organic materials such as wood and bone that decayed over a period of time. However, they are the richest African art form, capturing an array of emotions and moods and using a wide variety of materials and styles. The following sampling of masks is from widely separated regions in Africa and from over a long period of time. The oldest of them is the ivory mask from the west African Kingdom of Benin, on page 421, made in the early 1500s. This mask depicts the king of Benin, wearing a headdress or crown that includes tiny carved figures of Portuguese soldiers, the first European explorers to come to Benin. This mask was meant to be worn on the belt of the king.

Luba Kifwebe *mask, 16 inches*

The Wee mask from the Ivory Coast, on page 421, is a nature spirit mask, but an untamed and threatening spirit, with its hooded eyes and headdress of leopard's teeth. The mask, on page 422, from what is now Angola is used for ceremonial initiation rites. It is made of fibrous bark and woven material, painted red and white. The mask from the Luba in the Katanga Province, which appears on the preceding page, is black and white and was used for celebrations and funerals. The Kono mask, from Guinea is a war mask made of wood with animal teeth and aluminum eyes. It is given offerings before battles and it rules over the division of the spoils of war. How do you think the use of such masks began?

THINKING CRITICALLY

1. *Making Judgements* Which of the masks do you like the best? Which do you like the least? Give reasons why.

2. *Recognizing Values* From observing these masks, what values do you think were most important to these people?

3. *Linking Past to Present* When do we use masks today? What is the pupose for which they are used?

WRITER'S PORTFOLIO

1. *Extending the Lesson* Choose one of these masks and write a detailed description of it. Be as clear and specific as possible in your description.

2. *Examining Key Questions* How is the individual linked to tradition through the use of masks such as these?

Kono War mask,
11 inches

Life in Benin

Although African culture can be traced back thousands of years in time, the first book known by an African writer was not written until 1790. This book was titled *The Interesting Narrative of the Life of Olaudah Equiano or Gustavus Vassa, the African.* Equiano, the son of a West African tribal elder, was kidnapped by his own countrymen and sold into slavery when he was eleven years old. In Jamaica, Equiano was fortunate enough to have a master who cared about him. He was allowed to travel with his master as well as obtain some education. Eventually when Equiano was freed, he went to England where he became an active member in the abolitionist movement, speaking out against the cruelty of British slave owners in Jamaica. At this time he also wrote his narrative, describing life in Benin as well as arguing for the abandonment of the slave trade in favor of free trade with Africa, based on its wealth of natural resources. His book was published with the help of his many British friends and it became extremely popular in England as well as in America. The following selection from Equiano's book describes life in Benin, before he was kidnapped. How would you charcterize life in Benin?

As OUR MANNERS ARE SIMPLE OUR LUXURIES ARE FEW. THE dress of both sexes is nearly the same. It generally consists of a long piece of calico or muslin, wrapped loosely round the body somewhat in the form of a highland plaid. This is usually dyed blue, which is our favorite color. It is extracted from a berry and is brighter and richer than any I have seen in Europe. Besides this our women of distinction wear golden ornaments, which they dispose with some profusion on their arms and legs. When our women are not employed with the men in tillage, their usual occupation is spinning and weaving cotton, which they afterwards dye and make into garments. They also manufacture earthen vessels, of which we have many kinds. Among the best are tobacco pipes, made after the same fashion and used in the same manner, as those in Turkey.

Our manner of living is entirely plain, for as yet the natives are unacquainted with those refinements in cookery which debauch the taste: bullocks, goats, and poultry supply the greatest part of their food. These constitute likewise the principal wealth of the country and the chief articles of its commerce. The flesh is usually stewed in a pan; to make it savory we sometimes use also pepper and other spices, and we have salt made of wood ashes. Our vegetables are mostly plantains, eadas, yams, beans, and Indian corn. The head of the family usually eats alone; his wives and slaves have also their separate tables. Before we taste food we always wash our hands: indeed our cleanliness on all occasions is extreme, but on this it is an indispensable ceremony. After washing, libation is made by pouring out a small portion of the drink on the floor, and tossing a small quantity of the food in a certain place for the spirits of departed relations, which the natives suppose to preside over their conduct and guard them from evil. They are totally unacquainted with strong or spirituous liquors, and their principal beverage is palm wine. This is got from a tree of that name by tapping it at the top and fastening a large gourd to it, and sometimes one tree will yield three or four gallons in a night. When just drawn it is of a most delicious sweetness, but in a few days it acquires a tartish and more spirituous flavor, though I never saw anyone intoxicated by it. The same tree also produces nuts and oil. Our principal luxury is in perfumes; one sort of these is an odiferous wood of delicious fragrance, the other a kind of earth, a small portion of which thrown into the fire diffuses a more powerful odor. We beat this wood into powder and mix it with palm oil, with which both men and women perfume themselves.

In our buildings we study convenience rather than ornament. Each master of a family has a large square piece of ground, surrounded with a moat or fence or enclosed with a wall made of red earth tempered, which when dry is as hard as brick. Within this are his houses to accommodate his family and slaves, which if numerous frequently present the appearance of a village. In the middle stands the principal building, appropriated to the sole use of the master and consisting of two apartments, in one of which he sits in the day with his family. The other is left apart for the reception of his friends. He has besides these a distinct apartment in which he sleeps, together with his male children. On each side are the apartments of his wives, who have also their separate day and night houses. The habitations of the slaves and their families are distributed throughout the rest of the enclosure. These houses never exceed one story in height: they are always built of wood or stakes driven into the ground, crossed with wattles, and neatly plastered within and without. The roof is thatched with reeds. Our day-houses are left open at the sides, but those in which we sleep are always covered, and plastered in the inside with a composition mixed with cow-dung to keep off the different insects which annoy us during the night. The walls and floors also of these are generally covered with mats. Our beds consist of a platform raised three or four feet from the ground, on which are laid skins and different parts of a sponge tree call plantain. Our covering is calico or muslin, the same as our dress. The usual seats are a few logs of wood, but we have benches, which are generally perfumed to accommodate strangers: these compose the greater part of our household furniture. Houses so constructed and furnished require but little skill to erect them. Every man is a sufficient architect for the purpose. The whole neighborhood afford their unanimous assistance in building them and in return receive and expect no other recompense than a feast....

Our land is uncommonly rich and fruitful, and produces all kinds of vegetables in great abundance. We have plenty of Indian corn, and vast quantities of cotton and tobacco. Our pineapples grow without culture; they are about the size of the largest sugar-loaf and finely flavored. We have also spices of different kinds, particularly pepper, and a variety of delicious fruits which I have never seen in Europe, together with gums of various kinds and honey in abundance. All our industry is exerted to improve those blessings of nature. Agriculture is our chief employment, and everyone, even the children and women, are engaged in it. Thus we are all habituated to labor from our earliest years. Everyone contributes something to the common stock, and as we are unacquainted with idleness we have no beggars.

Our tillage is exercized in a large plain or common, some hours walk from our dwellings, and all the neighbours resort thither in a body. They use no beasts of husbandry, and their only instruments are hoes, axes, shovels, and beaks, or pointed iron to dig with. Sometimes we are visited by locusts, which come in large clouds so as to darken the air and destroy our harvest. This however happens rarely, but when it does a famine is produced by it. I remember an instance or two wherein this happened. This common is often the theater of war, and therefore when our people go out to till their land they not only go in a body but generally take their arms with them for fear of a surprise, and when they apprehend an invasion they guard the avenues to their dwellings by driving sticks into the ground, which are so sharp at one end as to pierce the foot and are generally dipped in poison. From what I can recollect of these battles, they appear to have been irruptions of one little state or district on the other to obtain prisoners or booty....

As to religion, the natives believe that there is one Creator of all things and that he lives in the sun and is girded round with a belt that he may never eat or drink; but according to some he smokes a pipe, which is our own favorite luxury. They believe he governs events, especially our deaths or captivity, but as for the doctrine of eternity, I do not remember to have ever heard of it: some however believe in the transmigration of souls in a certain degree. Those spirits which are not transmigrated, such as their dear friends or relations, they believe always attend them and guard them from the bad spirits or their foes. For this reason they always, before eating, as I have observed, put some small portion of the meat and some of their drink on the ground for them, and they often make oblations of the blood of beasts or fowls at their graves.

CRITICALLY THINKING

1. *Identifying Central Issues* What allows the villagers to live harmoniously?

2. *Recognizing Values* What beliefs do these people have about God and the afterlife? How do their lives reflect these beliefs?

3. *Linking Past to Present* What lessons drawn from Equiano's account of Benin village life might have applicability to contemporary American society?

WRITER'S PORTFOLIO

1. *Extending the Lesson* Having read Equiano's description of life in Benin, write a description of your life and people, considering some of the same factors he covers.

2. *Examining Key Questions* How is a spirit of community reflected in this selection?

The Zulu Empire

The story of Chaka (c. 1787–1828), the founder of the Zulu empire in southern Africa, was retold by Thomas Mofolo (1876–1948), considered by many to be the first great African novelist of the twentieth century. When Chaka was a child, he and his mother were driven out of their home and village because of jealousy and pettiness resulting from his illegitimate birth. But he grew into a powerful warrior, and soon a powerful military leader, eventually becoming the Zulu chieftain in 1816. He transformed the Zulu army by introducing new weapons and strategies. His army became the most powerful in the region, devastating every village in its path. Revenge against those who taunted him and his mother when he was a child and the quest for ever more power seemed to be the forces motivating Chaka. However, as Mofolo tells the story, witchcraft and sorcery also play a part in Chaka's rise to power. In the following selection from Mofolo's work, the sorcerer Isanusi agrees to give Chaka endless power, if he kills his wife Noliwe. What arguments does Isanusi use to persuade Chaka?

THE MONTHS FOR REFLECTION APPOINTED BY ISANUSI CAME TO an end, and Chaka's decision was not altered; he stood where he did before…. All the same Chaka continued to visit Noliwe and she became pregnant. And now she longed for Chaka's love, and always wept if she could not see him.

And Chaka loved Noliwe in return; she was the one person we could imagine Chaka as loving, as if he loved any woman with sincerity. All that is good, all that is beautiful, all that a true wife can give her husband, Chaka would have got from Noliwe if from any one. And although he was bartering her away in this fashion and was planning to kill her, yet his conscience troubled him, and gave him no rest, telling him always that he had descended from the level of a man. But because of the chieftainship he smothered his conscience and pressed on, bearing death on his shoulders….

The evening of that day Isanusi arrived and he broached the question: "How is it with thee Chaka? Hast thou decided to live with Noliwe as thy wife as was determined by Dingiswayo [Noliwe's father, the Zulu chieftain] and his tribe and also by thee, or hast thou determined to win the chieftainship?"

"I, Chaka, know not how to make my tongue say two different things. What I have said I have said, Isanusi." Isanusi remained silent for a long while and gazed on the ground.

And then Isanusi said: "Think well, Chaka. What has been done by my servants can be undone, but that which I will do through the blood of Noliwe, thy wife, even I cannot undo. What will be done will be done for ever. Therefore a man must understand what he doth while there is yet time, lest afterwards he repent and it is of no avail. When I departed from thee I told thee that today we would teach thee the innermost secrets of witchcraft, and so it is; for we are witch-doctors mightier than all others. If thou dost determine to win the chieftainship, thou wilt become a different man and be like unto the chiefs of our country. But I will ask thee yet again and do thou answer speaking the truth that is in thy heart and fear nothing, fear not even that I shall weary thee again to no purpose. Which doest thou choose, Noliwe or the chieftainship?"

And Chaka answered, "The chieftainship."

"Thou art a man of understanding, Chaka; truly there are not many like unto thee for knowing the times. For there is a time in the life of man which, if it pass him and leave him, then fortune has passed him by, such fortune as he will never see again until he comes to lie in the cold earth. But if he give heed to the time and perceive it, he can win a happiness that will never again elude him. One such time was when I found thee asleep under the bush: if thou hadst not chosen manhood then, where wouldst thou have been?" (And Chaka said to himself, "Indeed where should I have been?")

"Today is another such time. Thou hast known how to choose the path along which thou wilt walk and the way in which thou wilt live on earth, and when thou diest thy kingdom will be without limits. And greatest of all, thy fame and the glory of thy reign — thou wilt find it all there increased tenfold among thy fathers when thou comest to them, and it will be for ever and ever; for there is no death: there men live for ever according as they have lived here on earth." Isanusi was again silent for a long while and then he drew Chaka to him and they went outside where he looked up at the sky and pointed to the stars: "The number of thy warriors will soon be greater than the multitudinous stars thou seest in the heavens. Among the tribes thou wilt shine as doth the sun when no clouds cover it, before which when it riseth the stars disappear. And before thee, too, the tribes will indeed disappear when thou appearest, for the blood of Noliwe will bring to thee untold riches."

The reader can imagine what were the thoughts of Chaka when he was promised such fame and such glory, and was promised them by the one whom he knew to speak the truth in all things....

The next day Chaka, after he returned from watching his regiments drill, found that Isanusi and his attendants were no longer there but had gone to procure medicines from the veld and the bush. He entered Noliwe's hut and found her alone with her servant girl, and at once when he saw her he discovered that she had a beautiful brown color, her skin was smooth and shining, and her beauty was overpowering. There was a look of tenderness in her sparkling eyes. Her voice, when she spoke to Chaka her beloved, far surpassed in his ears the war songs and praises which he had persuaded himself were so beautiful. The tone of her voice was beautifully pitched, clear yet soft, and full of sincerity without guile or deceit. But above all, her eyes, which so clearly said, "I am thine, Chaka, my whole self is thine, in life and in death." At that moment her beauty made him dumb, so that he could not speak, but stood there powerless. He rubbed his eyes and looked away, and when he looked at Noliwe again he found that her beauty was greater than ever; it was a beauty befitting the woman so dearly loved by him and who had been chosen out by him to show to men the perfection of womanhood. In Chaka's mind a whirlwind seemed to spring up, a mighty tempest shook him and the dust flew; then he went. When Isanusi returned he said to him, even before Chaka spoke: "Thou art a man indeed, Chaka. I saw the confusion of thy thoughts when thou didst look upon Noliwe, but thou holdest to thy manhood like a chief, for a chief should not vary his purposes from day to day."

As Chaka's day approached Noliwe sickened, for she was pregnant, and she was suffering from her burden, although her pregnancy was not yet so advanced that people would take notice. On the evening before Chaka was to go down to the pool, Chaka went to her, taking with him a long needle of the kind used for sewing grain baskets. He found her sitting alone with only her handmaiden, in order to be quiet, and as he entered the handmaiden went out. There was a fire of wood burning and its flames provided a bright light which lit up the hut.

Chaka approached her; he fondled and kissed her and then asked what ailed her. Noliwe answered, "Chaka, my lord, thy brow frowns and thy voice soundeth strained and sorrowful. What hath vexed thee?" Chaka said that nothing had vexed him except that he had been angered by some scoundrel during the drill of his warriors. They continued thus, speaking together happily and exchanging kisses, when suddenly Chaka pressed his strong hand down upon Noliwe's mouth and pierced her with the needle under the armpit. Then he turned her on her side and raised up the part that had been pierced so that the blood might flow back into the wound. When Noliwe was on the point of death her eyelids fluttered a few times and she said: "Chaka, my beloved, thou who art now my father, who art Jobe, who art Dingiswayo, who art…." the brief candle of her life went out, and her pure spirit fled and went to Dingiswayo, to the place of glory above. When Chaka saw her eyelids flutter, he was terrified; he began to tremble, and then he fled. When Noliwe was quite dead, Chaka felt within himself something like a heavy stone falling, falling, till it rested on his heart.

He fled outside, but his eyes were dim and he saw nothing, save only the face of Noliwe on the point of death, when her eyelids had fluttered. His ears were stopped, and he heard nothing save only Noliwe's last cry. When he recovered he found himself with Isanusi in the hut and Isanusi was saying words of praise: "Now thy name hath been enrolled among the number of our chiefs, even the great and the mighty."

THINKING CRITICALLY

1. *Making Comparisons* Compare and contrast the characters of Chaka, Noliwe, and Isanusi.

2. *Recognizing Values* Why does Chaka make the decision that he does? What are his alternatives?

3. *Linking Past to Present* Can you think of any recent examples of people choosing between love and power? Is it comparable to choosing between family and career?

WRITER'S PORTFOLIO

1. *Extending the Lesson* Choose one of the characters – Chaka, Noliwe, or Isanusi and retell this episode from their point of view.

2. *Examining Key Questions* What links the world of the seen with the world of the unseen in this story? How does this link occur?

EXAMINING KEY QUESTIONS

- *What links the individual and tradition?*
- *How are we a part of nature?*

Throughout this chapter, most selections have concluded with a writing project asking you to discuss how the art or literature you have examined provides answers to one of these key questions. The following writing projects will help you draw together what you have learned by examining how several selections illustrate these key questions.

- Using selections from the chapter discuss the role of nature in traditional African cultures. Was it a major influence on their way of life? What is the relationship between the physical world and the spiritual?

- Illustrate the relationship between the individual and tradition in African cultures by comparing the folk tales and poetry to the *Sundiata* and Equiano's description of life in Benin. How was the past incorporated into everyday life?

SPEAKING/LISTENING

- Divide into groups and create short plays from one of the folk tales or trickster tales and then perform them for the other groups in the class.

CRAFTING

- Create your own African-style mask. Decide what kind of mask you want and then design it to represent its use.

COLLECTING

- Collect images from as many different African tribes as you can. How much difference do you notice between the tribes? Do you think referring to them as African cultures fails to represent their diversity?

*Masked dancers,
Pacific Northwest*

Native American Civilizations

*Statue of
"Maize God"*

CHAPTER 9

Native American Civilizations

c. 600–1890

c. 1500 B.C.
*Maya develop agriculture and begin
worship of the corn goddess*

JAMAKE HIGHWATER
Writer and Arts Advocate

When Christopher Columbus stumbled upon the Western Hemisphere that is now known as the Americas, his extraordinary encounter with the native people of that hitherto unknown land was entirely unexpected. What Columbus found in the Western Hemisphere was something far more fabulous than he could possibly have realized in his era. He discovered a marvelous and unique world entirely unknown to Europeans, Asians, and Africans. On that momentous day, Columbus unknowingly encountered a world as different from Europe as an astronaut might discover on a planet in a distant galaxy. He came face to face with an alien people who did not know that white men like Columbus existed. And, likewise, Europeans did not realize that the peoples of the Americas existed. They had been living in completely different worlds for countless centuries. And the only clue to the possible existence of the Americas was found in the ancient legends of the seafaring Vikings of Greenland: stories dating from about the year 1000. These ancient tales were accounts of the adventures of a Viking leader named Leif Ericson, who apparently encountered Native Americans when he sailed to Newfoundland off the far eastern coast of Canada, landing in the Americas almost 500 years before the voyage of Columbus. The Vikings did not stay, but the Spaniards stayed on, and with the subsequent

*Great
Serpent
Mound*

c. 700
Adena people erect barrow mounds

invasions by the French, English, Russians, Portuguese and Dutch, Europeans claimed the Americas as their own.

It has taken nearly 500 years for us fully to realize what Leif Ericson and Christopher Columbus found: a holy land not unlike the holy lands of many other peoples of the world. Only now do we fully understand that the Americas have witnessed a long succession of brilliant and fascinating civilizations, creating worlds as marvelous and almost as technically advanced as the greatest of African, European, and Asian societies.

THE EARLIEST AMERICANS

The early ancestors of the people that Columbus called Indians found their way from northeastern Asia into the vast American continents, at a time when no other human beings inhabited that wonderful world of deep forests, great rivers, and enormous, prehistoric mammals. Scholars also tell us that it was Indians, not people from outer space or Egyptians or Phoenicians, as was speculated by Europeans,who invented the complex technologies, elaborate social structures, brilliant arts, culture, architecture, and ingenious agriculture of the Americas. They did not know they had left their Asiatic homeland or that they had quite literally walked into the Americas. They were simply searching for food, hunting the huge beasts of the Ice Age into a perilous new landscape. What they found was a huge sea of ice engulfing much of Siberia, Alaska, and Canada. The ice had frozen so much of the earth's water that the sea level had fallen 300 feet, exposing a windy and cold thousand-mile-wide landbridge across the Bering Strait between Asia and North America.

From a cultural point of view, what is most astounding about this migration to the Americas is that it apparently took place during the Stone Age, before the invention of the wheel and the domestication of beasts of burden. In the Americas they discovered no horses or camels. While both animals had originated in America, they

Inca silver alpaca

Mimbres pot depicting bat

c. 400
Inca establish themselves on the Pacific coast
of South America

c. 200
Mogollon settle Southwest

migrated to other parts of the world and became extinct in the western hemisphere. As the glaciers of the Ice Ages melted and the ocean rose, the landbridge was flooded, and all contact with the Asian world from which they had come was terminated until October 1492, when Indians renewed contact with the other peoples of the world. As we know from history, it has not been a very happy or compassionate reunion.

Once Indians were isolated from all the other peoples of the world, they had to develop for themselves every aspect of their culture and technology, for Native Americans came to their new world with very little in the way of cultural baggage. This occurred before the evolution of any of our modern Asian or European languages, even before the development of agriculture. They had no metal tools and relied entirely on implements chipped from stone and bone. They knew nothing of weaving or basketmaking, and they had not yet invented any form of pottery. Even the oldest animal friend of human beings—

the dog—was apparently not yet domesticated when Indians came to the Americas. And, for this reason, they had to invent just about everything for themselves. As a result, the extraordinary cultures they eventually created have little in common with the other cultures of the world.

Of course, there are many similarities between all the peoples of the world, but there are also many differences that we need to celebrate. There are even vast differences between various Indian tribes, for Indians, like Europeans, are many *different* peoples who simply share a common heritage and certain geographical boundaries. For instance, the language of the Blackfeet Indians of the northern plains of the United States and Canada is as different from the language of the Pueblo Indians of New Mexico as English is different from Chinese. In this way, the term "Indians" includes a great many people of different characteristics and cultures. This is not to say that among all human beings there are not many important cultural similari-

Detail of Keller figurine from Cahokia

Detail of Tula figures

c. A.D. 700
Cahokia founded in Mississippi River Valley

c. 1000
Rise of Toltec and Aztec cultures

ties. For instance, the Indian peoples of Mexico and Central America and the high Andes Mountains of South America built pyramids and temples somewhat like the pyramids and temples of Egypt and the Near East. They had villages and great cities; they had families and children. They experienced happiness and sorrow. They suffered pain and torment. They buried their dead and worshipped the Almighty in elaborate ceremonies. But the similarity between various peoples ends at a very basic level. From there on, what we find are fascinating *differences*, which are the basis of what we mean by the word *culture*.

Indians and Europeans have completely different ideas about some very basic things, such as what we really mean when we use words like *time* and *god* and *nature* and *morality*. In the days before Columbus, Indians had entirely different calendars from the calendars of Europe, Asia, and Africa. They had a completely different form of writing, though only the Central American Maya Indians (and, perhaps their fore-

bears, the Olmec Indians) developed an elaborate, written language. Many Indian tribes also had an exceptionally compassionate and respectful attitude about their relationship to other animals and to the earth itself, an attitude quite different from European viewpoints about the place of humans in the natural world. Out of this unique Native American mentality came several distinctive kinds of art, with forms and images that still astound us for their complexity and amaze us for their technical refinement and artistic beauty.

CIVILIZATION IN THE AMERICAS

Though Europeans often spoke of Indians as "savages," the native peoples of the Americas were anything but primitive. For instance, Teotihuacán, the most ancient city of the Americas, located in the Valley of Mexico, had a population of approximately 150,000 people, making it more populous than the Athens of Plato and Aristotle (c. 350 B.C.). The massive pyramids of Teotihuacán are staggering architectural achievements.

Detail of Codex
Mendoza

Aztec drawing
of Montezuma
and Cortés

1325
Aztecs found Tenochtitlán

1521
Cortés captures Tenochtitlán, ending Aztec rule

The city of Teotihuacán sprang up in the inhospitable high desert of central Mexico about 50 B.C. Over a humble earthen mound, the famous Pyramid of the Sun was constructed in one complex and continuous effort. An almost unbelievable achievement given the fact that it was constructed by workers who did not have the use of wheeled vehicles or beasts of burden. It is broader at the base than the great pyramid of Cheops in Egypt. The core of the pyramid is composed of more than 1,175,000 cubic meters of sun-dried brick and rubble.

Even today, nobody knows what the people of Teotihuacán called themselves; what language they spoke, what gods they believed in, under exactly what kind of political system they lived, or why, after years of peace and progress, they were suddenly attacked and defeated around A.D. 700, when they completely vanished from history. The mystery of the rise of their civilization and their mysterious decline is the kind of puzzle that surrounds most of the great Native American cultures that once existed along the Mississippi and Ohio river valleys, in central and coastal Mexico, in the tropics of Central America, and in the high Andes of South America. Virtually all of these societies had disappeared long before Europeans found their way to the Americas, leaving behind only their extraordinary monuments and artifacts.

Spanish explorers and profiteers eagerly sailed to the Americas, following in the footsteps of Columbus, and between 1519 and 1521, Hernán Cortés conquered the Aztec people of Mexico, who had long ruled over a vast empire. What the Spaniards found in Mexico amazed them, for these were clearly not the humble villages that Columbus had found in the Caribbean. This was a great civilization with a long history and a powerful ruler; a society with a huge, well-trained army; a place of magnificent temples dedicated to gods unknown to Europeans; a great city that was more impressive than any capital in fifteenth century Spain, England, France, or Italy; a majestic metropolis with wide avenues

Woodcut of
Potosí mine

Wampum belt

1545
Discovery of the silver mine at Potosí

c. 1570
League of the Iroquois founded

filled with strolling princes whose great riches came from prosperous gold and silver mines; an enormous settlement surrounded by boundless fields abundant with crops, impeccably cultivated with a highly refined agricultural knowledge. Yet the Aztec Indians, who ruled Mexico at the time of the Spanish invasion, were puzzled by the ruined monuments just forty miles from their capital—the place called Teotihuacán. They had no more idea than the Spaniards about who had built that vast city in their midst. It was already a ruin in the fourteenth century, when the Aztecs seized power in the Valley of Mexico, just 200 years before the Spanish invasion.

The Mexican pyramids at Teotihuacán had been constructed by a mysterious people, who created their metropolis centuries before the Aztecs rose to power in the Valley of Mexico. Today we know scarcely any more about the builders of Teotihuacán than the Aztecs did at the time of the Spanish invasion. We do know, however, that the Aztec people were

not the most culturally accomplished tribe of Mexico. To the contrary, in many ways they were the least remarkable of a long succession of incredible societies that flourished, built temples and pyramids, assembled armies and worshipped their gods until they vanished from history. In fact, the tribes encountered by the Spaniards, like the Aztecs of Mexico and the Inca people of the South American Andes, invented very little of their own cultures; many of their most outstanding achievements were the legacy of far older civilizations that had disappeared long before Columbus arrived in the Americas. And for all the technical mastery of Aztec and Inca societies, these Indian empires were every bit as aggressive, greedy, and brutal as the Spanish invaders under the fierce and arrogant conquistadors, Hernán Cortés and Francisco Pizarro.

HUNTING AND GATHERING CULTURES Though we are always fascinated by peoples who build great empires, it is

Arrival of English at Roanoke

Sioux painting

1585
Founding of Roanoke Colony

c. 1700
Plains Indians acquire horses

important to realize that not all of the tribes of the Americas were city builders. Many Indians developed equally complex, but less monumental cultures based on hunting and gathering. Other tribes, such as those of the forested northeast and arid southwest of North America, created small agricultural communities where they practiced intricate religious rituals in the charge of a highly organized priesthood. An elaborate community life developed around various kinds of permanent structures — sacred underground chambers, thatched and bark longhouses, adobe apartment complexes — rudimentary forms of architecture by comparison to the buildings of the Aztec, Maya, and Inca worlds. Yet, these hunting and farming tribes invented political systems that greatly impressed the founding fathers of the United States because of their respect for every member of their communities.

Among the largely nomadic pre-Columbian hunters of the Great Plains and the Great Lakes, communities gathered only during particular seasons, since the food supply provided by hunting was not sufficient to sustain a village population. These wandering bands of hunters did not have the community incentive to create a communal culture; so they developed highly personal traditions, with religious ceremonies carried out not by an organized priesthood (as is the case in the northeast, southwest, and northwest areas of North America), but conducted by individual hunters and their small family groups. They carried their religion and their entire culture with them as they followed the herds through the seasons. They personally owned their sacred symbols and their ritual objects, passing them down from generation to generation.

NATIVE AMERICANS TODAY It is customary to speak of Native Americans in the past tense, as if they once existed but are now extinct. To the contrary, Indian culture is very much alive throughout the Americas. It can be

Lithograph of Sequoia and his alphabet

Sioux Chief Big Foot lies dead in the snow

1821
Sequoia creates Cherokee alphabet

1890
Battle of Wounded Knee

found in the modern literature and painting, music and dance of Indian artists of all the Americas. The Indian past is alive; and so is the Indian future.

What distinguishes Indian culture is its ideas about reality. Like most of the tribal peoples of the world, Indians do not live in the same world that Europeans live in. They do not believe that they and they alone have all the answers to all the important questions that people ask about their origins and their destinies. Tribal people live in a world of many possibilities. They do not live in a universe, but in a cosmos far larger—a place called a *multiverse*. And for those who live in a multiverse there are many different realities, and so there are many different ways of creating a house, a family, a work of art, a religion, a political system, and a civilization. Culture is a reflection of the many different realities in which human beings have always lived their various lives. And in the many worlds found among the Indians of the Americas, we can vividly see the end-less possibilities of human beings in a boundless and miraculous multiverse.

Pre-Columbian Art

The great Maya civilization dominated the southern part of Central America, particularly Guatemala, Honduras, and the Yucatán peninsula of Mexico. The Maya were extraordinarily advanced in the sciences and the arts. The Palenque cylinder, which appears on page 423, is from the classical Maya period (300–900), discovered at the seventh-century Mayan site at Palenque. It depicts the head of the Mayan sun god held between the jaws of the earth monster. It is a little over 45 inches high and was one of many found; it may have been an architectural decoration or possibly an incense burner. The Olmec people lived along the coast of the Gulf of Mexico in what is now Mexico and were among the earliest civilizations in Central America (founded c. 1100 B.C.). The stone brazier or incense burner, which appears at left, depicts the god of fire, a very ancient deity named Huehueteotl (wā wā tā′otl). He is usually shown with crossed legs, a wrinkled face, and two circular earplugs. Representations of this deity in a similar attitude have been found in central Mexico dating from around 500 B.C. The vessel on his head was to hold live coals. The Inca were the dominant civilization on the western coast of South America. The puma was regarded as a symbol of strength and power by the Inca, and the capital city of Cuzco was

Brazier representing the god of fire, Olmec

designed in the shape of a puma. The Inca *kero*, or wooden ceremonial goblet, which appears below, was made in the shape of a puma's head. A silver band surrounds the throat, and a solid gold snake rests at his left jaw. The Aztecs ruled central Mexico from around 1200 until the time of the Spanish conquest. A fierce and warlike people, they borrowed heavily from older civilizations such as the Maya. The Aztec mask on page 423 is the front part of a human skull inlaid with turquoise and lignite. The eyes are of iron pyrite, and red shell is inserted in the nose. The pieces are glued in place with a vegetable pitch. The mask represented Tezcatlipoca (**tesh kat⁄lē pō⁄kä**), a god of night associated with evil and death. What feelings about the world are conveyed by these images?

Kero *representing the Puma god, Inca*

THINKING CRITICALLY

1. *Making Inferences* All of these images represent deities. What can you infer about the beliefs of these peoples from the images of their gods?

2. *Recognizing Values* Compare and contrast the style of these pieces. Which seems the most realistic? the most abstract? the most spiritual? the most beautiful?

3. *Linking Past and Present* Images of skulls have a significant role in the observance of the "Day of the Dead" in Hispanic communities. Do some research on this festival. How is the use of this imagery like and unlike that of the image of Tezcatlipoca?

WRITER'S PORTFOLIO

1. *Extending the Selection* What questions and ideas do these images inspire? Write a series of questions to ask the artists, who made these images.

2. *Examining Key Questions* What do these images tell you about how these cultures imagined their relationship with the spiritual world?

The Inca Empire

The Inca were descended from a group of people who settled in the Valley of Cuzco in the southern part of Peru in South America. (The name *Inca* also referred to their rulers.) When the Spaniard Francisco Pizarro and his followers arrived in Peru in 1532, the Inca ruled an empire that stretched from central Chile north to Ecuador. They were highly skilled in architecture, engineering, weaving, and metal-working, but had no written language. The first grammar in Quechua (kech′wä), a language still spoken by people of the Andes Mountains, was not published until 1595. Much of what we know about the Inca comes from Spanish accounts or from archaeology. The most important textual source for early Inca history is the *Royal Commentaries* written by Garcilaso de la Vega (1539–1616). Born in Peru, the son of an Inca princess and a Spanish soldier, he grew up hearing the ancient legends and stories told by his mother's friends and relatives. Although he lived a disappointed life, caught between two cultures, Garcilaso was able to use his Spanish education to record the vanishing history of the Inca. The temple of the Sun, which Garcilaso refers to in this excerpt, was dedicated to Inti, the sun god, and was part of a compound of six buildings in the capital of Cuzco. Most of the buildings were stripped of their gold by the Spanish invaders. The city of Cuzco is in the Andes, 11,000 feet above sea level. How does Manco Cápac, the first Inca, turn an ancient fable about the sun to his own advantage?

ONE OF THE CHIEF IDOLS OF THE INCA KINGS AND THEIR subjects was the imperial city of Cuzco which the Indians worshipped as a sacred thing because of its foundation by the first Inca Manco Cápac, the innumerable victories it had brought in his conquests, and its position as the home and court of the Incas, who were regarded as gods. This veneration was so great that it was displayed even in very small things: if two Indians of equal rank met on the road, one going towards Cuzco and one coming from it, the latter was saluted and greeted by the other as his superior, simply because he had been in the city, and the respect was the greater if he were a resident in it and greater still if he was born there. Likewise seeds, vegetables, or anything else taken from Cuzco to other places was preferred, even if not of better quality because whatever came from Cuzco was deemed superior to the product of other regions and provinces. It may be deduced to what extent this distinction was applied in things of greater moment. Such was the veneration which the kings held the city that they ennobled it with splendid houses and palaces, which many of them had built for themselves, as we shall see in describing some of the buildings. Among these was the house and temple of the Sun, to which they devoted special attention, adorning it with incredible riches, to which each Inca added so as to excel his predecessor....

It is built of smooth masonry, very level and smooth. The high altar (I use the term to make myself clear, though the Indians did not, of course, have altars) was at the east end. The roof was of wood and very lofty so that there would be plenty of air. It was covered with thatch: they had no tiles. All four walls of the temple were covered from top to bottom with plates and slabs of gold. Over what we have called the high altar they had the image of the Sun on a gold plate twice the thickness of the rest of the wall-plates. The image showed him with a round face and beams and flames of fire all in one piece, just as he is usually depicted by painters. It was so large that it stretched over the whole of that side of the temple from wall to wall. The Incas had no other idols of their own or of any other people in the temple with the image of the Sun, for they did not worship any other gods except the Sun, though some say otherwise.

On both sides of the image of the Sun were the bodies of the dead kings in order of antiquity as children of the Sun and embalmed so that they appeared to be alive, though it is not known how this was done. They sat on golden chairs placed on the golden daises they had used. Their faces were towards the people....

Among other famous temples dedicated to the Sun in Peru, which might have rivalled that of Cuzco in their wealth of gold and silver, there was one on the island called Titicaca. The island gave its name to the lake called Titicaca in which it stands, about two shots of an arquebus [a primitive musket] from the shore. It is five or six thousand paces round, and is said to have been the place where the Sun placed his two children, male and female, when he sent them down to earth to instruct and teach the barbarous savages who then dwelt there how to live like human beings. To this fable they add another relating to more ancient times: they say that after the deluge the rays of the Sun were seen on that island and on that lake before any other place. The lake is seventy or eighty fathoms deep in places and is eighty leagues round. Padre Blas Valera writes that it has much loadstone and says that this is why boats cannot sail on its waters: of this I can say nothing.

The first Inca Manco Cápac, taking advantage of this ancient fable, and of his own shrewdness and inventive wit, saw that the Indians believed this and regarded the lake and island as sacred places, so he made up the second fable that he and his wife were children of the Sun and that their father had placed them on that island so that they should go about the land teaching the people, as was described at length at the beginning of this history. The Inca, *amautas* [priests], the philosophers, and wise men of the state, reduced the first fable to the second, applying it as a prefiguration or prophecy, so to speak. They said that the fact that the Sun had cast its first rays on that island to illuminate the world was a sign and promise that he would place his first two children there to teach and illuminate the natives, and to draw them out of their primitive savagery, as the Inca kings later did. With these and other inventions made for their own benefit, the Incas induced the remaining Indians to believe they were children of the Sun and confirmed it by the good they did. Because of the fables the Incas and all the peoples of their empire regarded the island as a sacred place, and therefore ordered a very rich temple to be built on it, completely lined with gold plates, and dedicated to the Sun. Here all the provinces subdued by the Incas offered up a great quantity of gold, silver, and precious stones every year as a thank offering for the two benefits he had conferred on them at this spot. The temple had the same service as the one in Cuzco. There was such a store of gold and silver offerings on the island, apart from what was worked for the use of the temple, that the accounts given of it by the Indians are rather to be wondered at than believed. Padre Blas Valera, speaking of the wealth of the temple, and the quantity of treasure left over from it and stored there, says that the Indian colonists (called *mítmac*) who live in Copacabana assured him that the quantity of gold and silver left over was enough to have made another temple from foundation to roof without using any other material.

Apart from the temple and its decorations, the Inca kings greatly honored the island as being the first place trodden by their forebears when they came down from the sky, as they said. They flattened the island as much as possible, removing the rocks, and made terraces which they covered with good fertile soil brought from a distance so as to bear maize, for the whole of that region is too cold for growing maize. On these terraces they sowed the seeds and by dint of great care grew a few cobs which were sent to the Inca as sacred objects. He took them to the temple of the Sun and sent them to the chosen virgins in Cuzco, and ordered them to be taken to other temples and convents throughout the kingdom, in some years to some and in other years to others, so that all might enjoy the grain sent from heaven. It was sown in the gardens of the temples of the Sun and houses of the virgins where these existed and the crop was divided among the peoples of the provinces. A few grains were cast in the granaries of the Sun and of the king and in the municipal barns, so that its divine power would protect, increase, and preserve from corruption the grain gathered there for the general subsistence. Any Indian who could get a grain of that maize or any seed to cast in his barn thought he would never want for bread for his whole life, so great was their superstition in any matter relating to the Incas.

THINKING CRITICALLY

1. *Drawing Conclusions* What does the story about the maize tell you about the Inca way of life?

2. *Making Inferences* Since the Inca had no written language, what do you think were Garcilaso's sources for his *Commentaries*?

3. *Linking Past and Present* The island of Titicaca was sacred as the birthplace of the Inca. How are important or sacred places commemorated in modern America?

WRITER'S PORTFOLIO

1. *Extending the Selection* With what other cultures do the Inca share the deluge tradition, the worship of a sun god, or the veneration of a sacred place? Why do you think these traditions are common to so many peoples and cultures?

2. *Examining Key Questions* How was the spirit world revealed to the Inca?

The Aztec Universe

The Aztecs believed that four worlds or suns had existed and had been destroyed before the present universe. At the end of the first sun, all people were destroyed by jaguars. At the end of the second sun, the world was destroyed by hurricanes. The third sun ended in a rain of fire, and the fourth sun ended in a flood, survived by only one man and one woman. Today's world, the world of the fifth sun, is commemorated in an extraordinary monument known as the Calendar Stone. Carved out of basalt in the late fifteenth century, the stone is almost twelve feet across. The face in the inner circle has been identified either as Tonatiuh (tō′nä tē′ü), the fifth sun, or Tlaltecuhtli (tläl′tē küt′lē), the earth monster. The tongue is in the form of a sacrificial knife. There

Aztec Calendar Stone

Diagram of the Aztec Calendar Stone

were many gods and spirits in the Aztec pantheon and most were worshipped by human sacrifice. On either side of the face are claws holding human hearts. Dates when the previous suns were destroyed are in the four rectangular panels. Twenty symbols in the narrow band surrounding the claws and four dates contain hieroglyphs of the days of the Aztec calendar. Eight solar rays and other glyphs make up the next band. The outer band contains two fire serpents at the bottom; their open jaws are at the bottom and their tails at the top. The rest of the band depicts the stars and planets. What impressions of Aztec civilization are conveyed by the Calendar Stone?

THINKING CRITICALLY

1. *Identifying Central Issues* What do the Aztec beliefs about the four worlds reveal about their view of the universe in general?

2. *Making Inferences* Based on the symbolism of the calendar stone, how would you describe the Aztecs? Were they a passive culture? Did they believe that life was sacred? that fate was benevolent?

3. *Linking Past and Present* The Aztec believed that the world or at least life on it, was cyclically destroyed and reborn. Do you think history and science can support this sort of viewpoint today?

WRITER'S PORTFOLIO

1. *Extending the Selection* Do you think the Calendar Stone helped the Aztecs make sense of their world? How?

2. *Examining Key Questions* Does it seem that the Aztecs tried to live in harmony with nature? Why or why not?

The Creation of the World

The two creation stories here, though both of Native American origin, are quite different from each other. The Navajo story describes how the *Diné*, the name the Navajo use for themselves, were created. In the first world lived the insect people, who ascended through the second and third worlds and were living in the fourth world when the gods or Holy People appeared. The *Diné Bahane*, from which the first excerpt comes, decribes how humans were created and ascended to the earth's surface from the many worlds below. From what are man and woman formed?

It is also said that late in the autumn of that year the newcomers heard a distant voice calling to them from far in the east. They listened and waited, listened and waited. Until soon they heard the voice again, nearer and louder than before. They continued to listen and wait, listen and wait, until they heard the voice a third time, all the nearer and all the louder.

Continuing to listen, they heard the voice again, even louder than the last time, and so close now that it seemed directly upon them. A moment later they found themselves standing among four mysterious beings. They had never seen such creatures anywhere before. For they were looking at those who would eventually become known as *Haashch'ééh dine'é.*

In the language of *Bilagáana* the White Man, that name means Holy People. For they are people unlike the earth-surfaced people who come into the world today, live on the ground for a while, die at a ripe old age, and then move on. These are intelligent people who can perform magic. They do not know the pain of being mortal. They are people who can travel far by following the path of the rainbow. And they can travel swiftly by following the path of the sunray. They can make the winds and the thunderbolts work for them so that the earth is theirs to control when they so wish....

Without speaking the Holy People made signs to those who were gathered there, as if to give them instructions. But the exiles could not understand their gestures. So they stood by helplessly and watched.

And after the gods had left, the people talked about that mysterious visit for the rest of that day and all night long, trying to determine what it meant.

As for the gods, they repeated their visit four days in a row. But on the fourth day, *Bits'íís lizhin* the Black Body remained after the other three departed. And when he was alone with the onlookers, he spoke to them in their own language. This is what he said:

"You do not seem to understand the Holy People," he said.

"So I will explain what they want you to know.

"They want more people to be created in this world. But they want intelligent people, created in their likeness, not in yours.

"You have bodies like theirs, true enough.

"But you have the teeth of beasts! You have the mouths of beasts! You have the feet of beasts! You have the claws of beasts!

"The new creatures are to have hands like ours. They are to have feet like ours. They are to have mouths like ours and teeth like ours. They must learn to think ahead, as we do.

"What is more, you are unclean!

"You smell bad.

"So you are instructed to cleanse yourselves before we return twelve days from now."

That is what *Bits'íís lizhin* the Black Body said to the insect people who had emerged from the first world to the second, from the second world to the third, and from the third world to the fourth where they now lived.

Accordingly, on the morning of the twelfth day the people bathed carefully. The women dried themselves with yellow corn meal. The men dried themselves with white corn meal.

Soon after they had bathed, they again heard the distant voice coming from far in the east.

They listened and waited as before, listened and waited. Until soon they heard the voice as before, nearer and louder this time. They continued to listen and wait, listen and wait, until they heard the voice a third time as before, all the nearer and all the louder.

Continuing to listen as before, they heard the voice again, even louder than the last time, and so close now that it seemed directly upon them, exactly as it had seemed before. And as before they found themselves standing among the same four *Haashch'ééh din'é*, or Holy People as *Bilagáana* the White Man might wish to call them.

Bits'íís dootl'izh the Blue Body and *Bits'íís lizhin* the Black Body each carried a sacred buckskin. *Bits'íís ligaii* the White Body carried two ears of corn.

One ear of corn was yellow. The other ear was white. Each ear was completely covered at the end with grains, just as sacred ears of corn are covered in our own world now.

Proceeding silently, the gods laid one buckskin on the ground, careful that its head faced the west. Upon this skin they placed the two ears of corn, being just as careful that the tips of each pointed east. Over the corn they spread the other buckskin, making sure that its head faced east.

Under the white ear they put the feather of a white eagle.

And under the yellow ear they put the feather of a yellow eagle.

Then they told the onlooking people to stand at a distance.

So that the wind could enter.

Then from the east *Nílch'i ligai* the White Wind blew between the buckskins. And while the wind thus blew, each of the Holy People came and walked four times around the objects they had placed so carefully on the ground.

As they walked, the eagle feathers, whose tips protruded slightly from between the two buckskins, moved slightly.

Just slightly.

So that only those who watched carefully were able to notice.

And when the Holy People had finished walking, they lifted the topmost buckskin.

And lo! the ears of corn had disappeared.

In their place there lay a man and there lay a woman.

The white ear of corn had been transformed into our most ancient male ancestor. And the yellow ear of corn had been transformed into our most ancient female ancestor.

It was the wind that had given them life: the very wind that gives us our breath as we go about our daily affairs here in the world we ourselves live in!

When this wind ceases to blow inside of us, we become speechless. Then we die.

In the skin at the tips of our fingers we can see the trail of that life-giving wind.

Look carefully at your own fingertips.

There you will see where the wind blew when it created your most ancient ancestors out of two ears of corn, it is said.

The Cherokee creation story "How the World was Made," excerpted below, describes the formation of the earth and explains some of the characteristics of the seasons and animals. How is it like and unlike the Navajo account?

THE EARTH IS A GREAT ISLAND FLOATING IN A SEA OF WATER, and suspended at each of the four cardinal points by a cord hanging down from the sky vault, which is of solid rock. When the world grows old and worn out, the people will die and the cords will break and let the earth sink down into the ocean, and all will be water again. The Indians are afraid of this.

When all was water, the animals were above in Galûn'lati, beyond the arch; but it was very much crowded, and they were wanting more room. They wondered what was below the water, and at last Dâyuni'si, "Beaver's Grandchild," the little Water-beetle, offered to go and see if it could learn. It darted in every direction over the surface of the water, but could find no firm place to rest. Then it dived to the bottom and came up with some soft mud, which began to grow and spread on every side until it became the island which we call the earth. It was afterward fastened to the sky with four cords, but no one remembers who did this.

At first the earth was flat and very soft and wet. The animals were anxious to get down, and sent out different birds to see if it was yet dry, but they found no place to alight and came back again to Galûn'lati. At last it seemed to be time, and they sent out the Buzzard and told him to go and make ready for them. This was the Great Buzzard, the father of all the buzzards we see now. He flew all over the earth, low down near the ground, as it was still soft. When he reached the Cherokee country, he was very tired, and his wings began to flap and strike the ground, and wherever they struck the earth there was a valley, and where they turned up again there was a mountain. When the animals above saw this, they were afraid that the whole world would be mountains, so they called him back, but the Cherokee country remains full of mountains to this day.

When the earth was dry and the animals came down, it was still dark, so they got the sun and set it in a track to go every day across the island from east to west, just overhead.... Every day the sun goes along under this arch, and returns at night on the upper side to the starting place.

When the animals and plants were first made—we do not know by whom—they were told to watch and keep awake for seven nights, just as young men now fast and keep awake when they pray to their medicine. They tried to do this, and nearly all were awake through the first night, but the next night several dropped off to sleep, and the third night others were asleep, and then others, until, on the seventh night, of all the animals only the owl, the panther, and one or two more were still awake. To these were given the power to see and to go about in the dark, and to make prey of the birds and animals which must sleep at night. Of the trees only the cedar, the pine, the spruce, the holly, and the laurel were awake to the end, and to them it was given to be always green and to be greatest for medicine, but to the others it was said: "Because you have not endured to the end you shall lose your hair every winter."

Men came after the animals and plants. At first there were only a brother and sister until he struck her with a fish and told her to multiply, and so it was. In seven days a child was born to her, and thereafter every seven days another, and they increased very fast until there was danger that the world could not keep them. Then it was made that a woman should have only one child a year, and it has been so ever since.

THINKING CRITICALLY

1. *Making Comparisons* Compare and contrast the Navajo story of the creation of the first people with the account in Genesis of the creation of Adam and Eve (see page 90).

2. *Making Inferences* What place is assigned to humans in the Navajo world? in the Cherokee?

3. *Linking Past and Present* Environmentalists often credit Native American tradition with a respectful attitude toward nature. What evidence in these creation stories supports this view?

WRITER'S PORTFOLIO

1. *Extending the Selection* Create a myth to explain some phenomena such as gravity, tornadoes, landslides, drought, or the phases of the moon.

2. *Examining Key Questions* From these tales, what can you infer about the Navajo and Cherokee relationship with nature?

The League of the Iroquois

Founded around 1570, the League of the Iroquois was a confederacy of tribes that ruled over the area that is now New York State. The League was initially composed of five nations — the Mohawk, Oneida, Seneca, Cayuga, and Onondaga. The government of the League was in the hands of a ruling council composed of 50 principal chiefs, or sachems (**sā′chəmz**), who met in council each fall. In 1754, when Benjamin Franklin was pleading the cause of political union of the American colonies, he offered the League of the Iroquois as an example of a successful confederation. In the following reading, the traditional founder of the Iroquois League, Deganiwidah (**de′gä nä wē′dä**) outlines the principles that were to guide the Iroquois sachems in council. How is a council declared open?

I AM DEGANIWIDAH, AND WITH THE FIVE NATION [IROQUOIS] confederate lords I plant the Tree of the Great Peace... I name the tree the Tree of the Great Long Leaves. Under the shade of this Tree of the Great Peace we spread the soft white feather down of the globe thistle as seats for you, Atoharho [traditional name for the premier chief of the Onondaga, who served as head of the Iroquis council] and your cousin lords. There shall you sit and watch the council fire of the confederacy of the Five Nations. Roots have spread out from the Tree, and the name of these roots is the Great White Roots of Peace. If any man of any nation shall show a desire to obey the laws of the Great Peace, they shall trace the roots to their source, and they shall be welcomed to take shelter beneath the Tree of the Long Leaves. The smoke of the confederate council fires shall pierce the sky so that all nations may discover the central council fire of the Great Peace. I, Deganiwidah, and the confederate lords now uproot the tallest pine tree and into the cavity thereby made we cast all weapons of war. Into the depths of the earth, down into the deep underearth currents of water flowing into unknown regions, we cast all weapons of war. We bury them from sight forever and plant again the Tree.

We do now crown you with the sacred emblem of the antlers, the sign of your lordship. You shall now become a mentor of the people of the Five Nations. The thickness of your skin will be seven spans, for you will be proof against anger, offensive action, and criticism. With endless patience you shall carry out your duty, and your firmness will be tempered with compassion for your people. Neither anger nor fear shall find lodgment in your mind, and all your words and actions shall be tempered with calm deliberation. In your official acts, self-interest shall be cast aside. You shall look and listen to the welfare of the whole people, and have always in view, not only the present but the coming generations—the unborn of the future Nation.

The Onondaga lords shall open each council by expressing their gratitude to their cousin lords, and greeting them, and they shall make an address and offer thanks to the earth where men dwell, to the streams of water, the pools, the springs, the lakes, to the maize and the fruits, to the medicinal herbs and the trees, to the forest trees for their usefulness, to the animals that serve as food and who offer their pelts as clothing, to the great winds and the lesser winds, to the Thunderers, and the Sun, the mighty warrior, to the moon, to the messengers of the Great Spirit who dwells in the skies above, who gives all things useful to men, who is the source and ruler of health and life.

Then shall the Onondaga lords declare the council open.

THINKING CRITICALLY

1. *Recognizing Values* What standards of personal conduct did Deganiwidah establish for the Iroquois leaders?

2. *Making Inferences* Why does Deganiwidah compare the League of the Iroquois to a tree? Is this an appropriate image?

3. *Linking Past and Present* Do you think Deganiwidah's ideals would be of value to modern governments? Why or why not?

WRITER'S PORTFOLIO

1. *Extending the Selection* Compare and contrast the Preamble of the U.S. Constitution to Deganiwidah's goals for the Iroquois.

2. *Examining Key Questions* What attitude toward the natural world is embodied in the ceremonies surrounding the Iroquois council?

Indian Prayers and Songs

Traditional Indian prayers and songs express a reverence for nature and a deep understanding of the cycles of life. They are frequently related to growing up or to death, though sometimes they express other themes, such as in the Inca song below, which is about love. The songs and prayers are akin to both poems and religious texts like hymns or psalms. Like western poems they express emotions and desires, and like hymns and psalms they tell of humanity's place in the world and spiritual beliefs. The power which was invested in language and the centrality of nature in the Indian way of life are both obvious from this oral literature. What was the purpose of each poem?

Prayer

Father, Great Spirit, behold this boy! Your ways he shall see!

Sioux

Song

In an accessible place
you will sleep.
At midnight
I will come.

Inca

Song

Our mother of the growing fields, our mother of the streams,
will have pity upon us.
For to whom do we belong? Whose seeds are we? To our
mother alone do we belong.

Cágaba

Song

The world is rolling around for all young people, so let's
    not love our life too much, hold ourselves back from
    dying.
   Tlingit

Prayer to the Deceased

Naked you came from Earth the Mother. Naked you return
    to her. May a good wind be your road.
                            Omaha

Prayer to a Dead Buck

In the future that we may continue to hold each other with
    the turquoise hand
Now that you may return to the place from which you came
In the future as time goes on that I may rely on you for food
To the home of the dawn you are starting to return
With the jet hoofs you are starting to return
By means of the zigzag lightning you are starting to return
By the evening twilight your legs are yellow
That way you are starting to return
By the white of dawn your buttocks are white and that way
    you are starting to return
A dark tail is in your tail and that way you are starting to
    return
A haze is in your fur and that way you are starting to return
A growing vegetation is in your ears and that way you are
    starting to return
A mixture of beautiful flowers and water is in your intestines
    and that way you are starting to return
May turquoise be in your liver and abalone shell the parti-
    tion between your heart and intestines and that way
    you are starting to return
May red shell be your lungs and white shell be your wind-
    pipe and that way you are starting to return
May dark wind and straight lightning be your speech and
    that way you are starting to return
There you have returned within the interior of the jet basket
    in the midst of the beautiful flower pollens

Beautifully you have arrived home
Beautifully may you and I both continue to live
From this day may you lead the other game along the trails,
    that I may hunt.
Because I have obeyed all the restrictions laid down by your
    god in hunting and skinning you
Therefore I ask for this luck: that I may continue to have
    good luck in hunting you.
Navajo

THINKING CRITICALLY

1. *Recognizing Values* Are these poems a form of self-expression? Why or why not?

2. *Making Inferences* What is the mood of "Prayer to a Dead Buck"? What is the point of the poem?

3. *Linking Past and Present* The Indian ideal of living in harmony with nature is increasingly challenged by the industrial and commercial needs of the modern world. What ways can you think of to preserve our natural heritage?

WRITER'S PORTFOLIO

1. *Extending the Selections* Observe some aspect of nature and write a brief description of it in prose or poetry. Try to go beyond a physical details and convey the essence of what you have observed.

2. *Examining Key Questions* What do these prayers and songs reveal about the Native Americans's relationship to the natural world?

Sioux History

In 1926 a folklorist recorded the type of oral history known as a "winter count" from an Oglala Sioux named Ben Kindle. The writer Barry Lopez has defined a winter count as follows: "Among several tribes of the northern plains, the passage of time from one summer to the next was marked by noting a single memorable event. The sequence of such memories, recorded pictographically on a buffalo robe or spoken aloud, was called a winter count." Ben Kindle had received his winter count from his grandfather, Afraid-of-Soldier. It recorded events dating back to 1759, serving as an aid to memory by encapsulating in a few words an episode that would then be further elaborated to summon up a portion of the tribal past. The following are a sampling of events from Ben Kindle's winter count and a cloth painting of a Dakota Sioux winter count. (The literal translations of the Sioux phrases are followed by commentary from the folklorist who recorded this winter count.) How do Ben Kindle's winter count and the painting compare?

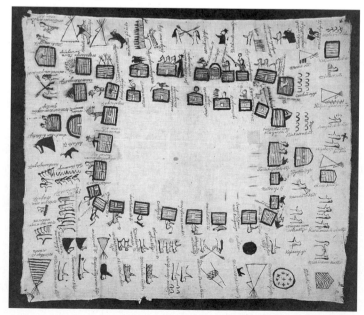

Winter Count
Painting,
Dakota Sioux

1767   Both sides / in company with / they go off.
The Crow Indians are at peace with the Sioux and the two live together, also the Sioux are at peace with the Shawnee and they live together. When the Crow and Pawnee fight together, they find that there are Sioux on both sides, and so they make peace.

1768   White or clear speakers (those whose language is understandable; that is, those in the same tribe) / they fight against each other.
The first civil war among the Sioux Indians: the Standing Rock Indians and the Cheyenne fight against the Oglala and the Rosebud.

1770   God / to see in vision, or dream of in sleep / woman / a / she goes crazy.
A woman has been accustomed to go to lonely places for visions and then come back and tell the people where to go for buffalo or when the enemy is coming. One morning she cannot speak, she does not know anything and soon she dies.

1771   Mandans / they are burned out.
Hostile Indians dig a trench down by the creek and the Sioux are unable to drive them away. So they build fires all about the trench and the enemy have to escape in the night.

1772   Carriers of wood on the back / three / coming to them they kill them. (The Sioux phrase used here always means that an enemy coming there from a great distance commits the deed. It implies a killer journeying there to do it.)
The Sioux make a new camp and the Crows hide in the timber and kill three old women sent after wood as they are returning with the wood on their backs.

1773   Dogs / even / eyes / they are inflamed.
Even the dogs got snow-blindness this winter because there was a heavy fall of snow and they had to move camp constantly to escape attack by hostile Indians.

1782   They break out with a rash.
The first epidemic of measles.

1784   Soldiers / many / they freeze to death.
White soldiers were encamped by the creek and Indians came down the creek and shot them and ran away. It was so cold that all the white men were frozen to death.

1785   Oglalas / cedar / they took.

The Sioux came west after cedar to use as medicine. "'Fraid for the Thunder" is the name of cedar smoke because if men have passed through its smoke, the lightning will not strike them in a thunderstorm. They also burn cedar for the sick.

1792   Woman / a / white / they see.

Once three Indians had gone after a buffalo and were returning with the meat tied to the saddles. They looked up toward a hill just at sunset and saw a woman in white looking toward the sun. They ran back to camp, and before dawn twelve young men went out to investigate and saw the woman in white at sunrise looking toward the sun. They believed this to be a spirit warning them of the approach of an enemy and moved camp.

THINKING CRITICALLY

1. *Making Comparisons* Compare and contrast Ben Kindle's Winter Count with the Dakota painting. Do they record the same sort of events? Which seems more explicit?

2. *Drawing Conclusions* Does violence between the Sioux and their enemies seem to have been on the level of periodic full-scale wars or of continual raiding by individuals or small groups?

3. *Linking Past and Present* The compressed style of historical narrative represented by a winter count is familiar today in journalistic headlines. Gather samples of different types of newspapers and magazines and examine how their approach to this capsule form of historical writing varies.

WRITER'S PORTFOLIO

1. *Extending the Selection* Create a "winter count" for some community to which you belong — for example, your family or school — expressing the history of the past five years.

2. *Examining Key Questions* How important do you think visions were to the Sioux?

North American Indian Art

The art included here reflects the range of both religious beliefs and cultural forms of the Native American tribes. The false face mask, made of basswood and trimmed with horsehair, was carved sometime between the middle and the end of the nineteenth century by an Onondaga (on´on dä´ga) artist, a member of one of the Iroquois tribes of New York. Wood masks or false faces are part of the Iroquois religion and represent spirits who have the power to heal. They would be worn by men portraying these spirits in curative rituals. This mask is meant to portray the pain of a spirit Hadúigona, known as the Great Doctor, whose face was struck by a mountain. The sculptures of the Salmon People, which appear on page 424, were carved by the Tlingit people of the Pacific Northwest. For these tribes, salmon were not only the main source of food, but also represented the cyclical nature of life and death. According to tradition the salmon were people who annually changed their human forms for those of fish in order to migrate upstream. After dying, their bones floated back to sea and were once more transformed the next year. Both sculptures portray the same idea: the one on the left is half fish and half human; the one on the right shows a human emerging from the jaws of a fish. The Yankton are a Sioux people of western Minnesota. The figure, which appears on page 416,

The Great Doctor,
Iroquois False Face mask

represents a tree dweller, one of a race of forest spirits who live in tree stumps and confuse hunters's minds. All of the Pueblo Indians of the Southwest believed in the supernatural figure of the kachina. The Kachinas were ancestral spirits who served as intermediaries between the Pueblo and their gods. Dancers would impersonate these figures at rituals. Kachinas were also carved into figures and dolls, as means of religious instruction. The kachina figure below was carved by a Hopi from Arizona and represents a butterfly maiden. How do these images link the natural world and the world of spirits?

Kachina figure, Hopi

THINKING CRITICALLY

1. *Making Comparisons* Compare and contrast the Hopi and the Sioux spirit figures. From the way they are represented, what do you think were their characteristics?

2. *Making Inferences* How is the otherworldly aspect of the false face represented? Why do you think this style was chosen?

3. *Linking Past and Present* The Iroquois employed art in curative rituals. How is art used therapeutically today?

WRITER'S PORTFOLIO

1. *Extending the Selection* Create a short folk tale describing an encounter with a being like the Sioux tree dweller.

2. *Examining Key Questions* Do these images suggest that Indians viewed the spirit world as transcendent (that is, completely outside of human experience)? Why or why not?

Tree dweller effigy, Yankton Sioux wood carving

Wounded Knee

On December 29, 1890, more than 200 Sioux women, children, and men were massacred by United States troops near Wounded Knee Creek in southwestern South Dakota. Charles Eastman (1858–1939) was a Santee Sioux and a government doctor on the Pine Ridge Reservation at the time, and in the following excerpt from his autobiography, *From the Deep Woods to Civilization*, he recounts the events leading up to and following that fateful day. The "religious craze" he mentions in the first line is a reference to the Ghost Dance movement which sprang up first in 1869 and again in the late nineteenth century among groups of Indians in the West. Its belief that the dead would return to restore the Indian lands and ways of life attracted many Plains Indian peoples, and early in 1890 the movement reached the Teton Sioux. When some of the Sioux performed certain rites and dances, white settlers became alarmed, and troops intervened. Many Sioux then left the reservation but were pursued by troops and on December 28 were surrounded near Wounded Knee Creek. They surrendered the next day, but when a dispute arose, a shot was fired and a Seventh Cavalry trooper fell. Immediately U.S. soldiers began firing on the Indians. What does Eastman say would have happened to the "religious craze" eventually?

A RELIGIOUS CRAZE SUCH AS THAT OF 1890–91 WAS A THING foreign to the Indian philosophy. I recalled that a hundred years before, on the overthrow of the Algonquin nations, a somewhat similar faith was evolved by the astute Delaware prophet, brother to Tecumseh. It meant that the last hope of race entity had departed, and my people were groping blindly after spiritual relief in their bewilderment and misery. I believe that the first prophets of the "Red Christ" were innocent enough and that the people generally were sincere, but there were doubtless some who went into it for self-advertisement, and who introduced new and fantastic features to attract the crowd.

I scarcely knew at the time, but gradually learned afterward, that the Sioux had many grievances and causes for profound discontent, which lay back of and were more or less closely related to the ghost dance craze and the prevailing restlessness and excitement. Rations had been cut from time to time; the people were insufficiently fed, and their protests and appeals were disregarded. Never was more ruthless fraud and graft practiced upon a defenseless people than upon these poor natives by the politicians! Never were there more worthless "scraps of paper" anywhere in the world than many of the Indian treaties and Government documents! Sickness was prevalent and the death rate alarming, especially among the children. Trouble from all these causes had for some time been developing, but might have been checked by humane and conciliatory measures. The "Messiah craze" in itself was scarcely a source of danger, and one might almost as well call upon the army to suppress Billy Sunday [popular evangelist of the early twentieth century] and his hysterical followers. Other tribes than the Sioux who adopted the new religion were let alone, and the craze died a natural death in the course of a few months.

At this juncture came the startling news from Fort Yates, some two hundred and fifty miles to the north of us, that Sitting Bull had been killed by Indian police while resisting arrest, and a number of his men with him, as well as several of the police. We next heard that the remnant of his band had fled in our direction, and soon afterward, that they had been joined by Big Foot's band from the western part of Cheyenne River agency, which lay directly in their road. United States troops continued to gather at strategic points, and of course the press seized upon the opportunity to enlarge upon the strained situation and predict an "Indian uprising." The reporters were among us, and managed to secure much "news" that no one else ever heard of. Border towns were fortified and cowboys and militia gathered in readiness to protect them against the "red devils." Certain classes of the frontier population industriously fomented the excitement for what there was in it for them, since much money is apt to be spent at such times. As for the poor Indians, they were quite as badly scared as the whites and perhaps with more reason.

Three days later, we learned that Big Foot's band of ghost dancers from the Cheyenne River reservation north of us was approaching the agency, and that Major Whiteside was in command of troops with orders to intercept them.

Late that afternoon, the Seventh Cavalry under Colonel Forsythe was called to the saddle and rode off toward Wounded Knee Creek, eighteen miles away.

The morning of December 29th was sunny and pleasant. We were all straining our ears toward Wounded Knee, and about the middle of the forenoon we distinctly heard the reports of the Hotchkiss guns.

At dusk, the Seventh Cavalry returned with their twenty-five dead and I believe thirty-four wounded, most of them by their own comrades, who had encircled the Indians, while few of the latter had guns. A majority of the thirty or more Indian wounded were women and children, including babies in arms.

In spite of all our efforts, we lost the greater part of them, but a few recovered, including several children who had lost all their relatives and who were adopted into kind Christian families.

On the day following the Wounded Knee massacre there was a blizzard, in the midst of which I was ordered out with several Indian police, to look for a policeman who was reported to have been wounded and left some two miles from the agency. We did not find him. On the third day it cleared, and the ground was covered with an inch or two of fresh snow. We had feared that some of the Indian wounded might have been left on the field, and a number of us volunteered to go and see. I was placed in charge of the expedition of about a hundred civilians, ten or fifteen of whom were white men. We were supplied with wagons in which to convey any of whom we might find still alive. Of course a photographer and several reporters were of the party.

Fully three miles from the scene of the massacre we found the body of a woman completely covered with a blanket of snow, and from this point on we found them scattered along as they had been relentlessly hunted down and slaughtered while fleeing for their lives. Some of our people discovered relatives or friends among the dead, and there was much wailing and mourning. When we reached the spot where the Indian camp had stood, among the fragments of burned tents and other belongings we saw the frozen bodies lying close together or piled one upon another. I counted eighty bodies of men who had been in the council and who were almost as helpless as the women and babes when the deadly fire began, for nearly all their guns had been taken from them. A reckless and desperate young Indian fired the first shot when the search for weapons was well under way, and immediately the troops opened fire from all sides, killing not only unarmed men, women, and children, but their own comrades who stood opposite them, for the camp was entirely surrounded.

It took all of my nerve to keep my composure in the face of this spectacle, and of the excitement and grief of my Indian companions, nearly every one of whom was crying aloud or singing his death song. The white men became very nervous, but I set them to examining and uncovering every body to see if one were living. Although they had been lying untended in the snow and cold for two days and nights, a number had survived. Among them I found a baby of about a year old warmly wrapped and entirely unhurt. I brought her in, and she was afterward adopted and educated by an army officer. One man who was severely wounded begged me to fill his pipe. When we brought him into the chapel he was welcomed by his wife and daughters with cries of joy, but he died a day or two later.

Under a wagon I discovered an old woman, totally blind and entirely helpless. A few had managed to crawl away to some place of shelter, and we found in a log store near by several who were badly hurt and others who had died after reaching there.

All this was a severe ordeal for one who had so lately put all his faith in the Christian love and lofty ideals of the white man. Yet I passed no hasty judgment, and was thankful that I might be of some service and relieve even a small part of the suffering. An appeal published in a Boston paper brought us liberal supplies of much needed clothing, and linen for dressings. We worked on.

THINKING CRITICALLY

1. *Recognizing Values* Why does Eastman say the Ghost Dances began? What does he say was the best way to deal with them?

2. *Making Inferences* Does Eastman blame anyone for the terrible sequence of events? What are his reasons?

3. *Linking Past and Present* In 1968 during the Vietnam War, American soldiers killed hundreds of unarmed civilians in the village of My Lai. What do you think causes massacres such as My Lai and Wounded Knee?

WRITER'S PORTFOLIO

1. *Extending the Selection* Pretend you were one of the reporters and compose a sensational account of Wounded Knee.

2. *Examining Key Questions* What was the importance of the Ghost Dance religion to the Sioux? What was its importance to Eastman?

Benin ivory mask,
9 inches

Wee nature-spirit mask,
17 inches

Jokwe Mbweso mask, 24 inches

*Mosaic inlaid over human skull,
representing Texcatlipoca, Aztec*

*Palenque cylinder representing
the sun god, Maya*

Salmon People, Tlingit wood carving

EXAMINING KEY QUESTIONS

> • *How do we live in harmony with nature?*
> • *How do we encounter the spirit world?*

Throughout this chapter, most selections have concluded with a writing project asking you to discuss how the art or literature you have examined provides answers to one of these key questions. The following writing projects will help you draw together what you have learned by examining how several selections illustrate these key questions.

• Using selections from the chapter discuss the role of nature in Native American civilizations. Do you notice any differences between North and South or Meso-American civilizations' attitudes towards nature?

• How much was the spirit world a part of everyday life in the Native American civilizations? What roles did spirits or spirit worship play?

SPEAKING/LISTENING

• With other students, do a choral reading of "Prayer to a Dead Buck."

CRAFTING

• Create a drawing of the scenes from the *Diné Bahane* or the Cherokee "How the World was Made." Use your imagination to depict the figures within it.

COLLECTING

• Collect images of the Battle of Wounded Knee. You should be able to find photographs and drawings. How do they compare to Charles Eastman's account (see page 417)?

Traveller Looking over a
Sea of Fog *(c. 1815)*
by Caspar David Friedrich

The 18th and 19th Centuries

Engraving of Newton

1687
Isaac Newton publishes the Principia

CHAPTER 10

The 18th and 19th Centuries

1687–1897

PETER GAY

Sterling Professor Emeritus of History, Yale University

The word "revolution" has been bandied about so freely that it is in danger of losing all its force. But it accurately describes the eighteenth and nineteenth centuries: the world in 1900 was vastly different from that in 1700. This is not to say that earlier centuries were static. The Reformation of the sixteenth century had shattered whatever religious unity, already fragile, Europe possessed. The nation-state that emerged from the old feudal and dynastic arrangements took long to mature, but it manifested itself half a century after Luther and Calvin with the emergence of coherent territories in France, Spain, and England. Then came another upheaval, the scientific revolution, sparked near the beginning of the seventeenth century by Kepler, advanced by Galileo and other giants, and culminating in the work of Sir Isaac Newton.

NEWTON AND THE PHILOSOPHES

Newton is a bridge from the seventeenth to the eighteenth century. His fundamental work, the *Principia Mathematica*, which established the laws of gravitation and of motion, generalizations that affected all science for the centuries ahead, was published in 1687; his *Opticks*, only marginally less path-

Coronation medal for George I

Print from L'Encyclopédie showing a blast furnace

1714
Hanoverian Succession in England

1751
Encyclopédie published

breaking, in 1704. His ability to record his findings in precise, if difficult, mathematical language gave Newton all the greater authority. What mattered even more than Newton's theories—and they mattered a great deal—and what made him in the words of Voltaire (poet, dramatist, historian, wit, philosopher) the greatest man who ever lived, was his method of investigation. It is called empiricism: a way of establishing theories, based upon proof and experience rather than the construction of grandiose philosophical systems that depend on verbal ingenuity alone. What raised Newton into the incomparable model he became was that he combined the gift for making connections with the gift for observation.

In central respects, the Enlightenment, the eighteenth century intellectual movement that accepted reason as the supreme authority in matters of opinion, belief, or conduct, was a working out of Newton's method; the

age produced more than one aspirant to Newton's mantle aiming to become a Newton of the mind or of the state. The *philosophes*—a French word for an international family of philosophical reformers—did not agree on everything, but Newton was their god. Some, indeed, had no other. Although they covered a wide spectrum in religious and political convictions, all were confident that the traditional religions dominating Western civilization, notably dominant Protestantism and Catholicism, rested on invalid assumptions, incredible assertions, and falsified history. Worse, these superstitions were, to the *philosophes'* minds, the source of wars and persecutions.

In politics, the *philosophes* differed widely, some supporting enlightened absolute rulers, who would launch and superintend reforms or parliamentary government which gave the public a share. The *philosophes*, who distrusted beneficent authoritarianism, opted for liberalism; a handful—the controver-

Engraving of the taking of Quebec

Engraving of the first manned ascent

1759
British take Quebec from the French

1783
Montgolfier brothers fly the first balloon

sial political thinker, educational reformer, novelist, and dreamer from Geneva, Jean Jacques Rousseau, counts among them—envisioned a kind of democracy. Some, like Voltaire, that keen observer and meddler in politics, were relativists, advocating the kind of government most suitable to each society. But they agreed in demanding an end to arbitrary power and to cruel punishments, the right at least of the educated to determine their own destiny, freedom to express opinions, and an efficient and humane way of dealing with social problems. The hope for a science of society that would permit their favorite form of government, whatever it was, to solve these problems was widespread among them.

Voltaire's tough-minded realism is a reminder that the *philosophes* were much more than idealistic coffee-house reformers. Two major misconceptions have obscured our view of the men and women of the Enlightenment. They have been called faint-hearted optimists and extreme rationalists. But their hopes for humanity, though grand, were not unlimited and were controlled by an awareness of the misery that was then, and would long be, most people's lot. More significant is the notion that they were so enamored of reason that they had no sense of passion or imagination. We must distinguish between the kind of rationalism that fostered the ambitious philosophical systems of the seventeenth century, which the *philosophes* derided, and the rationalism that, like Newton's theories, was always based the solid ground of experience and verified its propositions with experiment and reflection.

THE FRENCH REVOLUTION If the Enlightenment was the working out of Newton's thought, was the French Revolution the working out of the Enlightenment? Almost from the start, some historians have argued that it was. Certainly in

Jacobin medal

Tintern Abbey

1789
The French Revolution begins

1798
Wordsworth and Coleridge publish Lyrical Ballads

their search for heroes, the rhetoricians of the Revolution, as full of talk as of action, freely resorted to eighteenth-century and classical texts. At the same time, these borrowings were used by all political sects. Ideas mattered, but so did hard realities: the virtual bankruptcy of the French state, the growing rumblings against the privileged nobility and clergy, the need in late 1788 to summon the Estates-General to advise King Louis XVI in his governmental and fiscal crisis. No simple verdict can be offered on the impact of ideas on the revolutionary leadership, nor judgment on the Revolution itself. It brought instability and war, it killed (at times indiscriminately) those denounced as enemies of the state, but it also put ordinary people on the political map and spread progressive ideas across Europe. Whatever else one may say, the French Revolution spectacularly inaugurated modern politics.

Restless times did not start with the Revolution and did not end

with it. Napoleon, both the child and the gravedigger of the Revolution, left a complicated legacy. He redrew the map of the continent, introduced legal innovations in the countries he conquered—many of them repealed after his fall, but remaining as a goad and a threat—and put an end to that anachronistic entity, the Holy Roman Empire, which Voltaire once maliciously said was neither holy, nor Roman, nor an empire. After Napoleon's definitive defeat in 1815, his shadow lingered on. States anxious to restore the situation as it had existed before 1789 brought the old regime back to France and everywhere censored political ideas they deemed subversive, particularly nationalism.

ROMANTICISM   While one cannot, then, simply call the Revolution and the Napoleonic empire a direct consequence of the Enlightenment, the Romantic decades, roughly dating

Sketch of
Napoleon
crowning
himself by
David

Painting of
Beethoven

1804
Napoleon becomes Emperor of France

1824
Beethoven composes his Ninth Symphony

from the end of the eighteenth century to the 1830s, were indeed such a response. It was complex: many Romantics were political conservatives, others revolutionary; most of them were religious; a few, like Shelley, were proud to be atheists. But generally, the British, French, and German Romantics and their allies elsewhere were intent on repairing what they believed to be the damage the *philosophes* had wrought. We have seen that the Enlightenment was a persistent attempt to discredit religion. And this, many Romantics believed, had deprived humanity of the awe before the glorious beauties of nature or the comforting mercies of God.

Religious preoccupations, though, were not the Romantics' sole hallmark. In their poems, their novels, their paintings, their music—it was the age of Beethoven—they defied traditional styles and, as true individualists, followed (as they might have said) their own star. And there was one domain in

which their influence was both radical and widespread: love. The term "romantic love" has been vulgarized as much as the term "revolution." But to the Romantics, its meaning was plain. They looked for a union at once spiritual and physical that rejected the time-honored financial arrangements binding families together through marriages in a kind of commercial treaty, or the pride of status that decried marriages between "unsuitable" partners. The Romantic ideal of love as the only force that should govern had to be sanitized before it could become the ideal of many among the middle classes—few Romantics, after all, believed in lifelong fidelity and lifelong marriages. But this ideal did spread, especially in the United States and Britain, eventually reaching the more conservative societies like France and Germany.

THE NEW SCIENCES While the Romantics and their followers concentrated on the

Victoria's drawing of herself

Engraving of fighting at the Berlin barricades

1837
Victoria becomes queen of England

1848
The Year of Revolution

salience of feeling in poetry as in marriage, the nineteenth century also moved in a very different direction in the sciences. Not surprisingly, the Romantics had a view of scientific thinking that could only retard discoveries. They spoke grandly of nature as a mysterious, quasi-divine force that deserved to be adored rather than analyzed. But by mid-century, scientists had taken the opposite tack. After decades of the most patient, most meticulous observations and experimentation, Charles Darwin developed his famous—or notorious—theory of evolution which by attacking Biblical creation, indirectly undermined the place of God. Here indeed was a legitimate heir to Newton! And with great discoveries in physics and chemistry, the relation of science to technology, and with that to society, grew ever more intimate. The work of the French chemist Louis Pasteur is exemplary in this regard. His epoch-making studies of molecules and of bacteria permitted

remedial action against diseases that had made milk unsafe to drink, ruined French wine crops, and killed thousands with infectious ailments. Science was on the march, another reason why the nineteenth century deserves to be called a revolutionary age.

There were other unsettling developments. Buoyed by growing self-confidence, middle-class populations, especially in the United States, Britain, and France, made increasing claims to participation in government. Yet, few of the liberals, who led in demanding a drastic widening of the suffrage and a government in which they would have a say, were democrats, as few believed that the "lesser" orders, the working class and the peasantry, were educated enough to join the active citizenry. And liberalism, which gathered momentum through the decades despite fierce (and in some countries like Germany, largely successful) resistance, had an economic as well as a political agenda, demanding an end to state tutelage,

Engraving
of 54th
Massachusetts
storming
Fort Wagner

Engraving
of the
Proclamation
at Versailles

1861
American Civil War begins

1871
German Empire is declared

freeing trade from regulations (which could mean opposition to legislation protecting working men and women), and expansion of European economic power to continents like Africa.

But the "masses" also had champions, notably in the socialist ideas and movements led by a divergent group of theorists and politicians. Of these, it was Karl Marx who would have the greatest influence, though not until after his death in 1883. Marx held that all history had been a history of class struggles, which would end in a revolution in which the proletariat would take power from the bourgeoisie and, being the largest and hence universal class, would bring the class struggle to an end. Such ideas made the nineteenth century a bubbling cauldron.

NATIONALISM   The century was revolutionary, finally, in that it witnessed the triumph of many nationalistic aspirations. The feeling of belonging to a

nation—of being French or American, and therefore of course superior to those of other nationalities—is not new. But it could not be translated into political institutions until more traditional types of government had been exploded or at least heavily modified. The nineteenth century saw two major national powers emerge—Germany and Italy—while nationalist fervor mounted elsewhere. The creation of the German Empire in January 1871, though, shows that the success of nationalist demands, which called for the gathering of all German-speaking people under a single political umbrella, was not complete. The Hohenzollern dynasty, which had ruled over Prussia since it was recognized as a state in 1701, now supplied the emperors of the new state; millions of German-speakers, like Austrians, were excluded; many thousands continued to consider themselves Bavarians or Saxons. But national feeling intensified with the passage of

The Valkyries

1876
Der Ring des Nibelungen *by*
Richard Wagner is first performed

1879
Thomas Edison invents the light bulb

time and especially with the fear of
enemies — always a force for unity.
And so, by the end of the century,
nation states stood against one
another, bound together by alliances,
but also clashing overseas over imperi-
alistic acquisitions or at home as they
viewed their neighbors with suspicion.
High culture — painting, music, the
drama, the novel — remained international, but in such an atmosphere,
peace, for all the pacific implications of
international trade and natural science,
remained precarious and was shattered by the catastrophic war of 1914,
properly called World War I.

The Enlightenment

Isaac Newton (1642–1727) was undoubtedly the most famous scientist and thinker of his time and the central figure in the scientific revolution which culminated in the Enlightenment of the eighteenth century. His first work was the revolutionary *Principia Mathematica* (1687), which established the laws of gravitation and motion, and more particularly that the entire physical universe is subject to the same laws of gravity and motion as we observe on earth. It was Newton's ability to subject his observations to the rigors of mathematical proofs which gave his theories such weight. Newton was the first empirical scientist and his celebration of reason and logic was the catalyst for the Enlightenment. The following selection is an excerpt from the Preface of the *Principia*. What is Newton's purpose in the *Principia*?

SINCE THE ANCIENTS…ESTEEMED THE SCIENCE OF MECHANICS of greatest importance in the investigation of natural things, and the moderns, rejecting substantial forms and occult qualities, have endeavored to subject the phenomena of nature to the laws of mathematics, I have in this treatise cultivated mathematics as far as it relates to philosophy. The ancients considered mechanics in a twofold respect; as rational, which proceeds accurately by demonstration, and practical. To practical mechanics all the manual arts belong, from which mechanics took its name. But as artificers do not work with perfect accuracy, it comes to pass that mechanics is so distinguished from geometry that what is perfectly accurate is called geometrical; what is less so, is called mechanical. However, the errors are not in the art, but in the artificers. He that works with less accuracy is an imperfect mechanic; and if any could work with perfect accuracy, he would be the most perfect mechanic of all, for the description of right lines and circles, upon which geometry is founded, belongs to mechanics. Geometry does not teach us to draw these lines, but requires them to be drawn, for it requires that the learners should first be taught to describe these accurately before he enters upon geometry, then it shows how by these operations problems may be solved. To describe right lines and circles are problems, but not geometrical problems. The solution of these problems is required from mechanics, and by geometry the use of them, when so solved is shown; and it is the glory of geometry that from those few principles, brought from without, it is able to produce so many things. Therefore geometry is founded in a mechanical practice, and it is nothing but that part of universal mechanics which accurately proposes and demonstrates the art of measuring. But since the manual arts are chiefly employed in the moving of bodies, it happens that geometry is commonly referred to their magnitude, and mechanics to their motion. In this sense rational mechanics will be the science of motions resulting from any forces whatsoever, and of the forces required to produce any motions, accurately proposed and demonstrated. This part of mechanics, as far as it extended to the five powers which relate to manual arts, was cultivated by the ancients, who considered gravity (it not being a manual power) no otherwise than in moving weights by those powers. But I consider philosophy rather than arts and write not concerning manual but natural powers, and considering chiefly those things which relate to gravity, levity, elastic force, the resistance of fluids, and the like forces, whether attractive or impulsive; and therefore I offer this work as the mathematical principles of philosophy, for the whole burden of philosophy seems to consist in this — from the phenomena of motions to investigate the forces of nature, and then from these forces to demonstrate the other phenomena…. I wish we could derive the rest of the phenomena of Nature by the same kind of reasoning from mechanical principles, for I am induced by many reasons to suspect that they may all depend upon certain forces by which the particles of bodies, by some causes hitherto unknown, are either mutually impelled towards one another, and cohere in regular figures, or are repelled and recede from one another. These forces being unknown, philosophers have hitherto attempted the search of Nature in vain; but I hope the principles here laid down will afford some light either to this or some truer method of philosophy.

The Enlightenment was a broadly based intellectual movement with the avowed goal of applying reason to society for human betterment. The leading lights of this movement were known as the *philosophes*, though they were more like social activists than traditional philosophers. They claimed to speak on behalf of all who were oppressed by tyranny and blighted by ignorance, and their goal was to create a world where reason was the only sovereign. The bible of the *philosophes* was the *Encyclopédie* (1751–1772) edited by Denis Diderot. This compendium of human knowledge had articles by all the leading *philosophes*, including Voltaire, Montesquieu, and Rousseau, and its twenty-eight volumes represented the largest publishing venture in history up to that time. The following selection from the *Encyclopédie* is Diderot's definition of a *philosophe*. What does Diderot suggest is the method of a philosopher?

THERE IS NOTHING WHICH COSTS LESS TO ACQUIRE NOWADAYS than the name of *Philosopher*; an obscure and retired life, some outward signs of wisdom, with a little reading, suffice to attach this name to persons who enjoy the honor without meriting it.

Others in whom freedom of thought takes the place of reasoning, regard themselves as the only true philosophers, because they have dared to overturn the consecrated limits placed by religion, and have broken the fetters which faith laid upon their reason. Proud of having gotten rid of the prejudices of education, in the matter of religion, they look upon others with scorn as feeble souls, servile and pusillanimous spirits, who allow themselves to be frightened by the consequences to which irreligion leads, and who, not daring to emerge for an instant from the circle of established verities, nor to proceed along unaccustomed paths, sink to sleep under the yoke of superstition. But one ought to have a more adequate idea of the philosopher, and here is the character which we give him:

Other men make up their minds to act without thinking, nor are they conscious of the causes which move them, not even knowing that such exist. The philosopher, on the contrary, distinguishes the causes to what extent he may, and often anticipates them, and knowingly surrenders himself to them. In this manner he avoids objects that may cause him sensations that are not conducive to his well being or his rational existence, and seeks those which may excite in him affections agreeable with the state in which he finds himself. Reason is in the estimation of the philosopher what grace is to the Christian. Grace determines the Christian's action; reason the philosopher's.

Other men are carried away by their passions, so that the acts which they produce do not proceed from reflection. These are the men who move in darkness; while the philosopher, even in his passions, moves only after reflection. He marches at night, but a torch goes on ahead.

The philosopher forms his principles upon an infinity of individual observations. The people adopt the principle without a thought of the observations which have produced it, believing that the maxim exists, so to speak, of itself; but the philosopher takes the maxim at its source, he examines its origin, he knows its real value, and only makes use of it, if it seems to him satisfactory.

Truth is not for the philosopher a mistress who vitiates his imagination, and whom he believes to find everywhere. He contents himself with being able to discover it wherever he may chance to find it. He does not confound it with its semblance; but takes for true that which is true, for false that which is false, for doubtful that which is doubtful, and for probable that which is only probable. He does more — and this is the great perfection of philosophy; that when he has no real grounds for passing judgment, he knows how to remain undetermined.

The philosopher is then an honest man, actuated in everything by reason.

THINKING CRITICALLY

1. *Making Comparisons* How do Diderot's descriptions of a philosopher parallel Newton's explanation of his method?

2. *Making Inferences* Diderot says that the philosopher "marches at night, but a torch goes on ahead." Explain this metaphor.

3. *Linking Past and Present* Do you think that philosophers are still "actuated in everything by reason" today?

WRITER'S PORTFOLIO

1. *Extending the Selection* Look up how a philosopher is defined in a modern dictionary. How does this definition compare to Diderot's? What can you learn from the changes?

2. *Examining Key Questions* What are Newton and Diderot presenting as the highest authority? Do you think they are right?

Philosophy of the State

Born in Geneva, Switzerland, Jean Jacques Rousseau (**zhän zhäk rü sō′**) (1712–1778) was poor and ill-educated, and often lived on the edge of poverty. In 1744, he went to live in Paris and became known to most of the influential *philosophes*. He worked on Diderot's *Enyclopédie* and begin to write the political tracts that keep his name alive today. His major work is *The Social Contract* (1762), excerpted below, in which Rousseau lays out his ideas of how to create a society in which private interest is subordinated to the common good. He argues that this is done by all the people of a state vesting their rights into a collective entity known as the "general will." From this subordination comes the real freedom of a just and equitable state. Rousseau called this subordination the "social contract." Why does Rousseau say man is everywhere in chains?

MAN IS BORN FREE; AND EVERYWHERE HE IS IN CHAINS. ONE thinks himself the master of others, and still remains a greater slave than they. How did this change come about? I do not know. What can make it legitimate? That question I think I can answer.

If I took into account only force, and the effects derived from it, I should say: "As long as a people is compelled to obey, and obeys, it does well; as soon as it can shake off the yoke, and shakes it off, it does still better; for, regaining its liberty by the same right as took it away, either it is justified in resuming it, or there was no justification for those who took it away." But the social order is a sacred right which is the basis of all other rights. Nevertheless, this right does not come from nature, and must therefore by founded on conventions....

The problem is to find a form of association which will defend and protect with the whole common force the person and goods of each associate, and in which each, while uniting himself with all, may still obey himself alone, and remain as free as before. This is the fundamental problem of which the *Social Contract* provides the solution.

If we discard from the social compact what is not of its essence, we shall find that it reduces itself to the following terms:

Each of us puts his person and all his power in common under the supreme direction of the general will, and, in our corporate capacity, we receive each member as an indivisible part of the whole.

At once, in place of the individual personality of each contracting party, this act of association creates a moral and collective body, composed of as many members as the assembly contains voters, and receiving from this act its unity, its common identity, its life, and its will. This public person, so formed by the union of all other persons, formerly took the name of *city*, and now takes that of *Republic* or *body politic*; it is called by its members *State* when passive, *Sovereign* when active, and *Power* when compared with others like itself....

The passage from the state of nature to the civil state produces a very remarkable change in man, by substituting justice for instinct in his conduct, and giving his actions the morality they had formerly lacked. Then only, when the voice of duty takes the place of physical impulses and right of appetite, does man, who so far had considered only himself, find that he is forced to act on different principles, and to consult his reason before listening to his inclinations. Although, in this state, he deprives himself of some advantages which he got from nature, he gains in return others so great, his faculties are so stimulated and developed, his ideas so extended, his feelings so ennobled, and his whole soul so uplifted, that, did not the abuses of this new condition often degrade him below that which he left, he would be bound to bless continually the happy moment which took him from it forever, and, instead of a stupid and unimaginative animal, made him an intelligent being and a man.

Let us draw up the whole account in terms easily commensurable. What man loses by the social contract is his natural liberty and an unlimited right to everything he tries to get and succeeds in getting; what he gains is civil liberty and the proprietorship of all he possesses. If we are to avoid mistakes in weighing one against the other, we must clearly distinguish natural liberty, which is bounded only by the strength of the individual, from civil liberty, which is limited by the general will; and possession, which is merely the effect of force or the right of the first occupier, from property, which can be founded only on a positive title.... By the social compact we have given the body politic existence and life; we have now by legislation to give it movement and will....

Conventions and laws are therefore needed to join rights to duties and refer justice to its object. In the state of nature, where everything is common, I owe nothing to him whom I have promised nothing; I recognize as belonging to others only what is of no use to me. In the state of society all rights are fixed by law, and the case becomes different.

When I say that the object of laws is always general, I mean that law considers subjects *en masse* and actions in the abstract, and never a particular person or action. Thus the law may indeed decree that there shall be privileges, but cannot confer them on anybody by name…. On this view, we at once see that it can no longer be asked whose business it is to make laws, since they are acts of the general will; nor whether the law can be unjust, since no one is unjust to himself; nor how we can be both free and subject to the laws, since they are but registers of our wills.

We see further that, as the law unites universality of will with universality of object, what a man, whoever he be, commands of his own motion cannot be a law; and even what the Sovereign commands with regard to a particular matter is no nearer being a law, but is a decree, an act, not of sovereignty, but of magistracy.

I therefore give the name "Republic" to every State that is governed by laws, no matter what the form of its administration may be: for only in such a case does the public interest govern, and the *res publica* rank as a *reality*.

THINKING CRITICALLY

1. *Drawing Conclusions* Why would an individual want to submit to the general will?

2. *Identifying Central Issues* What is the difference between natural liberty and civil liberty?

3. *Linking Past and Present* Is Rousseau's famous paradox in the first sentence as true today as it was when he wrote it?

WRITER'S PORTFOLIO

1. *Extending the Selection* Rousseau says that when laws are "acts of the general will," it can no longer be asked "…whether the law can be unjust, since no one is unjust to himself." What flaws can you find in this theory?

2. *Examining Key Questions* Do you think Rousseau is inciting people to a revolution? Why or why not?

The French Revolution

During the summer of 1789, a number of dramatic events took place in France. A financial crisis in preceding years, caused by military expenditures and the refusal of the aristocracy to pay any taxes, had grown desperate. The year before King Louis XVI had called a meeting of the Estates General, a legislative body that had not met since 1614. This body was made up of representatives from three groups: the clergy, the nobility, and commoners, known as the Third Estate. The delegates representing the Third Estate came armed with grievances and reform proposals, including demands for a jury system and equitable taxes. On June 17, after weeks of deadlock, the Third Estate took a decisive step, declaring themselves a National Assembly, with rights to legislate in the public interest. They were locked out of their chamber, but they vowed not to disband until they had given France a constitution. The standoff between the National Assembly and the aristocratic monarchy spread to the streets. On July 14, an angry mob stormed the ancient fortress of the Bastille, and while this event had little political significance, it was of enormous symbolic importance. It was the baptism by blood of the French Revolution. Riots and looting occurred all across France, further undermining the monarchy. On August 26, the National Assembly issued the "Declaration of the Rights of Man and the Citizen," which is excerpted below. Based on the American Bill of Rights, this declaration eliminated in one stroke the archaic social class system of France and gave equality to every citizen. For the next two years, the National Assembly attempted to govern the nation, while writing a constitution, which it presented to the nation in September of 1791. Does the "Declaration" seem like a revolutionary document?

THE REPRESENTATIVES OF THE FRENCH PEOPLE, CONSTITUTED AS a National Assembly, considering that ignorance, forgetfulness, or contempt of the rights of man are the sole causes of public misery and the corruption of governments, have resolved to set forth in a solemn declaration the natural, inalienable, and sacred rights of man, in order that this declaration, constantly before all the members of the social body, may remind them continually of their rights and their duties:

I. Men are born and remain free and equal in rights. Social distinctions can be founded only upon common utility.

II. The aim of all political association is the conservation of the natural and inproscribable rights of man. These rights are liberty, property, security, and resistance to oppression.

III. The principle of all sovereignty resides essentially in the nation. No body, no individual, can exercise any authority which does not expressly emanate from it....

VI. Law is the expression of the general will. All citizens have the right to assist personally, or by their representatives, in its formation. It should be the same for all, whether it protects or punishes. All citizens, being equal in the eyes of the law, are equally admissible to all dignities, places, and public employments according to their capacity, and without distinctions other than their virtue and talents....

VII. No man can be accused, arrested, or detained except in cases determined by law....

X. No one should be disturbed because of his opinions, even in religion, provided their manifestation does not disturb public order as established by law.

XI. The free communication of thoughts and opinions is one of the most precious rights of man; thus every citizen can speak, write, and publish freely; but in cases determined by law he shall be responsible for the abuse of this liberty....

With its work done, the National Assembly was replaced by an elected Legislative Assembly. But this constitutional order would last barely ten months. The Legislative Assembly fought a disastrous war against Austria, which caused even further economic deterioration. In August 1792, the constitution was suspended and a National Convention was elected to create a republic. They immediately abolished the monarchy and after order had been restored, they condemned the king to death. He was guillotined on January 21, 1793, an event commemorated by Jean Paul Marat, a tremendously popular radical, in his newspaper article "Le Tyran Puni" ("The Punished Tyrant"), excerpted below. The Revolution had entered its climactic phase, a time of passions and terror. How does Marat justify the beheading of Louis XVI?

THE TYRANT'S HEAD HAD JUST FALLEN BENEATH THE BLADE OF the law. By the same act the foundations of monarchy among us have been overthrown: now at last I believe in the republic.

How vain were the fears which the dethroned despot's henchmen sought to arouse in us concerning the consequences of his death, in the hope of saving him from execution! To be sure, the precautions taken to keep order were impressive and were dictated by prudence, but they proved superfluous. All along the route from the Temple to the scaffold public wrath could be trusted to stand guard. Not a voice was heard during the execution to ask that the king be spared, not a voice was raised on behalf of the man who once decided the destinies of France; all about him profound silence reigned until his head was displayed to the people, when everywhere shouts rose up, "Long live the nation!" "Long live the republic!"

The rest of the day was perfectly calm. For the first time since the [massacre of the] Federation, the people seemed to be moved by serene joy; it was as if they had just witnessed a religious ceremony and were at last released from the burden of oppression which had weighed down upon them for so long, and they were imbued with the feeling of brotherhood. Every heart opened itself to the hope of a happier future.

The execution of Louis XVI is one of those memorable events which begin a new era in the history of nations. It will have a prodigious influence upon the fate of the despots of Europe and of the peoples who have not yet broken their shackles.

The National Convention no doubt showed its greatness when it sentenced to death the tyrant of France, but it obeyed the will of the nation. The way in which the people observed the punishment of their former master raised them even above their representatives, for you may be sure that the feelings of the citizens of Paris and the *fédérés* [provincial delegates] are shared by the citizens in every department.

Far from disturbing the peace of the state, the execution of Louis XVI will serve only to strengthen it by restraining, through terror, the enemies inside and outside the country. It will also give the nation new energy and strength to repel the ferocious hordes of foreign satellites who dare to bear arms against her; for there is no better means of driving them back. Our present position is one in which we must triumph or perish. "We have just landed upon the Isle of Liberty, and we have burned the ship which brought us here."

> By the middle of 1793, France was at war with most of the nations in Europe and the domestic situation was chaotic. On August 23, 1793, the National Convention essentially conscripted the entire nation into the army. They created the first modern national army and it swept France's enemies from the field by sheer numbers and determination. In September, though, the "Law of Suspects," excerpted below, was passed, which essentially suspended individual rights and allowed massive abuse of government power. This began the famous Reign of Terror, in which, between September 1793 and July 1794, over 300,000 people were arrested and 17,000 executed, with many thousands more dying in prison. What do you think were the immediate consequences of the "Law of Suspects"?

1. Immediately after the publication of the present decree, all suspected persons within the territory of the Republic and still at liberty shall be placed in custody.

2. The following are deemed suspected persons: 1st, those who, by their conduct, associations, talk, or writings have shown themselves partisans of tyranny or federalism and enemies of liberty; 2nd, those who are unable to justify their means of existence and the performance of their civic duties; 3rd, those to whom certificates of patriotism have been refused; 4th, public functionaries suspended or dismissed from their positions by the National Convention or by its commissioners; 5th, those former nobles, husbands, wives, fathers, mothers, sons or daughters, brothers or sisters and agents of the *émigrés* [aristocrats and other opponents of the Revolution who fled France], who have not steadily manifested their devotion to the Revolution; 6th, those who have emigrated during the interval between 1 July, 1789, and the publication of the decree of 30 March–8 April, 1792, even though they may have returned to France within the period established by said decree or prior thereto.

3. The Watch Committees…are charged with drafting, each in its own *arrondissement* [district], a list of suspected persons and with issuing warrants of arrest against them.

4. The members of the committee may order the arrest of any individual if seven are present, but only by absolute majority of votes.

The National Convention was dominated by two men, Maximilien Robespierre and Georges Danton. On February 5, 1794, Robespierre delivered a speech, excerpted below, in which he described the aims of the Revolution and justified the Reign of Terror. The Terror eventually engulfed its own progenitors; in April and July, 1794, Danton and Robespierre, respectively, were sent to the guillotine and in October 1795, the National Convention was dissolved. It was replaced by a Legislative Assembly, which in turn appointed a five-member Directory to rule the nation. The Directory imposed order and ruled for four years by suppressing opposition and withholding elections. In 1799, they were ousted by a coup and replaced by a consulate headed by the conquering general Napoleon Bonaparte. He would govern France alone first as Consul, then after 1804 as Emperor. The Revolution was over. Is Robespierre employing reason in his speech to support his arguments?

It is time to mark clearly the aim of the Revolution and the end toward which we wish to move; it is time to take stock of ourselves, of the obstacles which we still face, and of the means which we ought to adopt to attain our objectives....

What is the goal for which we strive? A peaceful enjoyment of liberty and equality, the rule of that eternal justice whose laws are engraved, not upon marble or stone, but in the hearts of all men....

In our country we wish to substitute morality for egotism, probity for honor, principles for conventions, duties for etiquette, the empire of reason for the tyranny of customs, contempt for vice for contempt for misfortune, pride for insolence, the love of honor for the love of money; that is to say, all the virtues and miracles of the Republic for all the vices and snobbishness of the monarchy.

We wish in a word to fulfill the requirements of nature, to accomplish the destiny of mankind, to make good the promises of philosophy...that France, hitherto illustrious among slave states, may eclipse the glory of all free peoples that have existed, become the model of all nations.... That is our ambition; that is our aim.

What kind of government can realize these marvels? Only a democratic government.... But to found and to consolidate among us this democracy, to realize the peaceable rule of constitutional laws, it is necessary to conclude the war of liberty against tyranny and to pass successfully through the storms of revolution. Such is the aim of the revolutionary system which you have set up....

Now what is the fundamental principle of democratic, or popular government—that is to say, the essential mainspring upon which it depends and which makes it function? It is virtue: I mean public virtue,…that virtue which is nothing else but love of fatherland and its laws….

The splendor of the goal of the French Revolution is simultaneously the source of our strength and of our weakness: our strength, because it gives us an ascendancy of truth over falsehood, and of public rights over private interests; our weakness, because it rallies against us all vicious men, all those who in their hearts seek to despoil the people….

If the basis of popular government in time of peace is virtue, the basis of popular government in time of revolution is both virtue and terror: virtue without which terror is murderous, terror without which virtue is powerless. Terror is nothing else than swift, severe, indomitable justice; it flows, then, from virtue.

THINKING CRITICALLY

1. *Making Comparisons* How does the "Law of Suspects" compare to the original "Declaration of the Rights of Man"? Which of these does Marat's editorial seem closer too? What about Robespierre's speech?

2. *Analyzing Cause and Effect* How does Marat justify the beheading of Louis XVI, and what effect does he say it will have?

3. *Linking Past and Present* How do you think the United States should react to oppressive governments in other parts of the world? Should citizens be encouraged to revolt? Why or why not?

WRITER'S PORTFOLIO

1. *Extending the Selection* Robespierre was a fanatical believer in Rousseau's ideas. Does Robespierre's speech echo Rousseau's sentiments (see pages 440–442)? Why or why not?

2. *Examining Key Questions* Do you think the French Revolution was necessary to reform the nation or was less radical reform a better option? Explain.

The Rights of Women

Mary Wollstonecraft (1759–1797) was a champion of women's rights. In 1792, she published *A Vindication of the Rights of Woman*, an appeal for education and greater independence for women. Her views on women's rights were shaped in part by an unhappy childhood with an alcoholic father who abused his wife and five children. Because the family moved frequently, Wollstonecraft's formal schooling was often interrupted, but she discovered that she had a gift for writing. After opening a school and then working as a governess in Ireland, she went to London and began to write reviews, novels, and works on education and politics. *A Vindication of the Rights of Woman*, excerpted below, was a publishing sensation and provoked attacks on Wollstonecraft herself because of her outspoken views and unorthodox lifestyle — she had a daughter outside of wedlock. What is Wollstonecraft's goal for women?

To ACCOUNT FOR, AND EXCUSE THE TYRANNY OF MAN, MANY ingenious arguments have been brought forward to prove, that the two sexes, in the acquirement of virtue, ought to aim at attaining a very different character: or, to speak explicitly, women are not allowed to have sufficient strength of mind to acquire what really deserves the name of virtue. Yet it should seem, allowing them to have souls, that there is but one way appointed by providence to lead *mankind* to either virtue or happiness.

If then women are not a swarm of ephemeron [short-lived] triflers, why should they be kept in ignorance under the specious name of innocence? Men complain, and with reason, of the follies and caprices of our sex, when they do not keenly satirize our headstrong passions and grovelling vices. Behold, I should answer, the natural effect of ignorance! The mind will ever be unstable that has only prejudices to rest on, and the current will run with destructive fury when there are no barriers to break its force. Women are told from their infancy, and taught by the example of their mothers, that a little knowledge of human weakness, justly termed cunning, softness of temper, *outward* obedience, and a scrupulous attention to a puerile kind of propriety, will obtain for them the protection of man; and should they be beautiful, every thing else is needless, for at least twenty years of their lives....

The most perfect education, in my opinion, is such an exercise of the understanding as is best calculated to strengthen the body and form the heart. Or, in other words, to enable the individual to attain such habits of virtue as will render it independent. In fact, it is a farce to call any being virtuous whose virtues do not result from the exercise of its own reason. This was Rousseau's opinion respecting men. I extend it to women, and confidently assert, that they have been drawn out of their sphere by false refinement, and not by an endeavor to acquire masculine qualities. Still the regal homage which they receive is so intoxicating, that till the manners of the times are changed, and formed on more reasonable principles, it may be impossible to convince them, that the illegitimate power, which they obtain by degrading themselves, is a curse, and that they must return to nature and equality, if they wish to secure the placid satisfaction that unsophisticated affections impart....

Many are the causes that, in the present corrupt state of society, contribute to enslave women by cramping their understandings and sharpening their senses. One, perhaps, that silently does more mischief than all the rest, is their disregard of order.

To do everything in an orderly manner, is a most important precept, which women, who, generally speaking, receive only a disorderly kind of education, seldom attend to with that degree of exactness that men, who from their infancy are broken into method, observe. This negligent kind of guesswork, for what other epithet can be used to point out the random exertions of a sort of instinctive common sense, never brought to the test of reason prevents their generalizing matters of fact, so they do today what they did yesterday, merely because they did it yesterday....

Let us examine this question. Rousseau declares, that a woman should never, for a moment feel herself independent, that she should be governed by fear to exercise her *natural* cunning, and made a coquettish slave in order to render her a more alluring object of desire, a *sweeter* companion to man, whenever he chooses to relax himself. He carries the arguments, which he pretends to draw from the indications of nature, still further, and insinuates that truth and fortitude, the cornerstones of all human virtue, shall be cultivated with certain restrictions, because with respect to the female character, obedience is the grand lesson which ought to be impressed with unrelenting rigor.

What nonsense! When will a great man arise with sufficient strength of mind to puff away the fumes which pride and sensuality have thus spread over the subject! If women are by nature inferior to men, their virtues must be the same in quality, if not in degree, or virtue is a relative idea; consequently, their conduct should be founded on the same principles and have the same aim.

Connected with man as daughters, wives, and mothers, their moral character may be estimated by their manner of fulfilling those simple duties; but the end, the grand end of their exertions should be to unfold their own faculties, and acquire the dignity of conscious virtue. They may try to render their road pleasant; but ought never to forget, in common with man, that life yields not the felicity which can satisfy an immortal soul. I do not mean to insinuate, that either sex should be so lost, in abstract reflections or distant views, as to forget the affections and duties that lie before them, and are in truth, the means appointed to produce the fruit of life; on the contrary, I would warmly recommend them, even while I assert, that they afford most satisfaction when they are considered in their true subordinate light.

THINKING CRITICALLY

1. *Identifying Central Issues* What social reforms does Wollstonecraft advocate?

2. *Analyzing Cause and Effect* Wollstonecraft criticizes women for their "disregard of order" and for degrading themselves. What does she say are the causes of these two faults?

3. *Linking Past and Present* Some recent surveys have shown that girls think boys don't like it when girls are smarter in class and that boys are called on to answer questions more than girls are in class. Link these findings to Wollstonecraft's views.

WRITER'S PORTFOLIO

1. *Extending the Selection* Write a letter to Mary Wollstonecraft telling her of the progress in the fight for women's rights.

2. *Examining Key Questions* Is reason or passion guiding Wollstonecraft's argument about women's rights?

The Problem of Population

Thomas Malthus (1766–1834), a clergyman and a pioneering writer on economics, was a contemporary of the English liberals and social reformers who believed that human progress was inevitable and continuous and that humans were better off when unfettered by government. Malthus disagreed and argued that disease, starvation, and poverty are the inevitable results if population growth is not controlled. His *Essay on the Principle of Population* was first published anonymously in 1798 and advocated moral restraint as an additional check on population. Malthus's ideas were decried by reform-minded liberals and hailed by conservatives, who could now blame many of society's problems on those poor who had large families. Although Malthus was not as unfeeling as his work might indicate, he believed that the facts pointed to the conclusion that unless there were checks on population, the number of people living in misery would only increase. In this excerpt from his *Essay on the Principle of Population*, how does Malthus classify the two checks on population?

THE PRINCIPAL OBJECT OF THE PRESENT ESSAY IS TO EXAMINE the effects of the constant tendency of all animated life to increase beyond the nourishment prepared for it.

It is observed by Dr. Franklin, that there is no bound to the prolific nature of plants or animals, but what is made by their crowding and interfering with each other's means of subsistence....

This is incontrovertibly true. Through the animal and vegetable kingdoms, nature has scattered the seeds of life abroad with the most profuse and liberal hand; but has been comparatively sparing in the room and the nourishment necessary to rear them. The germs of existence contained in this earth, if they could freely develop themselves, would fill millions of worlds in the course of a few thousand years. Necessity, that imperious, all-pervading law of nature, restrains them within the prescribed bounds. The race of plants and the race of animals shrink under this great restrictive law; and man cannot by any efforts of reason escape from it.

In plants and irrational animals, the view of the subject is simple. They are all impelled by a powerful instinct to the increase of their species; and this instinct is interrupted by no doubts about providing for their offspring. Wherever therefore there is liberty, the power of increase is exerted; and the superabundant effects are repressed afterwards by want of room and nourishment.

The effects of this check on man are more complicated. Impelled to the increase of his species by an equally powerful instinct, reason interrupts his career, and asks him whether he may not bring beings into the world, for whom he cannot provide the means of support. If he attend to this natural suggestion, the restriction too frequently produces vice. If he hears it not, the human race will be constantly endeavoring to increase beyond the means of subsistence. But as, by that law of our nature which makes food necessary to the life of man, population can never actually increase beyond the lowest nourishment capable of supporting it, a strong check on population, from the difficulty of acquiring food, must be constantly in operation....

The ultimate check to population appears then to be a want of food, arising necessarily from the different ratios according to which population and food increase. But this ultimate check is never the immediate check, except in cases of actual famine.

The immediate check may be stated to consist in all those customs, and all those diseases, which seem to be generated by a scarcity of the means of subsistence; and all those causes, independent of this scarcity, whether of a moral or physical nature, which tend prematurely to weaken and destroy the human frame.

These checks to population, which are constantly operating with more or less force in every society, and keep down the number to the level of the means of subsistence, may be classed under two general heads — the preventive, and the positive checks.

The preventive check, as far as it is voluntary, is peculiar to man, and arises from that distinctive superiority in his reasoning faculties, which enables him to calculate distant consequences. The checks to the indefinite increase of plants and irrational animals are all either positive, or if preventive, involuntary. But man cannot look around him, and see the distress which frequently presses upon those who have large families; he cannot contemplate his present possessions or earnings, which he now nearly consumes himself, and calculate the amount of each share, when with very little addition they must be divided, perhaps, among seven or eight, without feeling a doubt whether, if he follow the bent of his inclinations, he may be able to support the offspring which he will probably bring into the world. In a state of equality, if such can exist, this would be the simple question. In the present state of society other considerations occur. Will he not lower his rank in life, and be obliged to give up in great measure his former habits? Does any mode of employment present itself by which he may reasonably hope to maintain a family? Will he not at any rate subject himself to greater difficulties, and more severe labor, than in his single state? Will he not be unable to transmit to his children the same advantages of education and improvement that he had himself possessed? Does he even feel secure that, should he have a large family, his utmost exertions can save them from rags and squalid poverty, and their consequent degradation in the community? And may he not be reduced to the grating necessity of forfeiting his independence, and of being obliged to the sparing hand of Charity for support?

THINKING CRITICALLY

1. *Analyzing Cause and Effect* According to Malthus, what part does reason play in the check of population?

2. *Drawing Conclusions* Would you label Malthus an optimist or a pessimist? Support your answer.

3. *Linking Past and Present* In 1994, the United Nations held a population conference in Cairo. What were the major issues and proposed solutions? Were they similar to Malthus's ideas?

WRITER'S PORTFOLIO

1. *Extending the Selection* In 1750, the world's population is estimated to have been about 700 million, while in 1994 it is estimated to be about 5.7 billion. What factors can you point to that have allowed the food supply to keep pace with population growth?

2. *Examining Key Questions* Is Malthus advocating reason as an answer to the problem of population? Why or why not?

Landscape Painting

Romantic artists abandoned the idealizing tendencies of Renaissance and Neoclassical artists, in favor of emotion and spontaneity. Nature was a source of endless beauty, mystery, and inspiration and landscape painting proved a prevalent vehicle of these artists's feelings. The greatest landscape artists of the nineteenth century were two English painters, John Constable and J.M.W. Turner. Constable (1776–1837) was concerned with light and atmosphere, making cloud studies in oil accompanied by notes on the date and the time of day. In his most famous painting, *The Hay Wain*, which appears on page 489, the farmer and his wagon seem almost overpowered by the sky and nature. Constable's landscape paintings have an almost religious scale and mystery. J. M. W. Turner (1775–1851), like Constable, studied at the Royal Academy of Arts in London. Turner began as a watercolorist, but he turned to painting landscapes in oil. When the Houses of Parliament burned in 1834, he sat nearby making sketches. The final painting, which appears on page 490, is so suffused with smoke and fire that the solid objects seem to melt away. Caspar David Friedrich (1774–1840) was one of the finest

German Romantic artists. His *Monastery Graveyard in the Snow* is in many ways unlike what viewers expect in a landscape painting. Here there is a sense of stillness and cold, and the leafless trees and ruined abbey seem more symbolic than real. Friedrich's landscape is one of heightened senses and emotions, where the landscape is a more human than a divine object. Also very different were the American landscape painters. To them nature was

Caspar David Friedrich, Monastery Graveyard in the Snow *(1817)*

capable of having a moral effect since it declared God's glory, but Thomas Cole (1801–1848), an American artist born in England, was also well aware of the effect of humans on nature. Cole is credited with founding the Hudson River School, a group of nineteenth-century landscape artists who painted many scenes in and around the Catskill Mountains in New York. In *Genesee Scenery: Landscape with Waterfall* Cole has combined sky, rocks, water, and trees to convey both a sense of the age of the earth and of the majesty of God's creation. Which of these Romantic paintings seems the most realistic to you?

Thomas Cole, Genesee Scenery: Landscape with Waterfall *(1847)*

THINKING CRITICALLY

1. *Making Comparisons* Which one of these paintings most appeals to you and why?

2. *Making Inferences* What does Turner's painting convey to you that a more realistic depiction (or a photograph) might not?

3. *Linking Past and Present* Do you think people's thoughts and opinions about nature have changed since the Romantic period?

WRITER'S PORTFOLIO

1. *Extending the Selection* Contrast European and American landscape painting in this chapter with the Chinese landscape painting on page 304. What are the chief differences? similarities?

2. *Examining Key Questions* Why do you think there was such a prevalence of landscape painting during the Romantic era?

English Romanticism

The Romantic movement encompassed many different approaches to art, music, and literature and to politics, religion, and society. Romantic writers found inspiration in nature, praised beauty, and expressed joy in living, along with a melancholy view of the decay and death of beauty and life. Most Romantics were intent on creating a new way of interpreting reality. They turned away from the supreme confidence in reason of the Enlightenment to focus on discovering underlying truths, often disregarding social conventions in favor of a broad humanitarianism. Above all, they extolled the power of imagination. Percy Shelley (1792–1822) was one of the greatest Romantic poets. He was a rebellious nonconformist, who was thrown out of university for advocating atheism. His great prose work on poetry, *A Defense of Poetry*, part of which is included here, was written in 1821 in response to an ironic essay by Shelley's friend Thomas Love Peacock in which Peacock, himself a poet, concluded that poetry is useless in a scientific age. The sonnet which follows, "Lift Not the Painted Veil," is in many ways a metaphor for the view of the Romantic poet that Shelley expounded in *A Defense of Poetry*. John Keats (1795–1821), another major English Romantic poet, was concerned more with strong images than with abstract ideas in his poetry. Keats's love of nature was only equaled by his passion for beauty in art and literature. He wrote most of his greatest poetry in 1819, but "On First Looking into Chapman's Homer" was written in 1816 when Keats's former teacher introduced him to a translation of Homer by George Chapman. After they read through the night, Keats walked home at dawn and composed this sonnet, which he sent to his teacher that morning. In his essay, what does Shelley say is "the great instrument of moral good"?

Percy Shelley, *A Defense of Poetry*

A POEM IS THE VERY IMAGE OF LIFE EXPRESSED IN ITS ETERNAL truth. There is this difference between a story and a poem, that a story is a catalogue of detached facts, which have no other bond of connection than time, place, circumstance, cause and effect; the other is the creation of actions according to the unchangeable forms of human nature, as existing in the mind of the creator, which is itself the image of all other minds. The one is partial, and applies only to a definite period of time, and a certain combination of events which can never again recur; the other is universal, and contains within itself the germ of a relation to whatever motives or actions have a place in the possible varieties of human nature. Time, which destroys the beauty and the use of the story of particular facts, stripped of the poetry which should invest them, augments that of Poetry, and for ever develops new and wonderful applications of the eternal truth which it contains. Hence epitomes have been called the moths of just history, they eat out the poetry of it. The story of particular facts is as a mirror which obscures and distorts that which should be beautiful: Poetry is a mirror which makes beautiful that which is distorted....

It awakens and enlarges the mind itself by rendering it the receptacle of a thousand unapprehended combinations of thought. Poetry lifts the veil from the hidden beauty of the world, and makes familiar objects be as if they were not familiar; it reproduces all that it represents, and the impersonations clothed in its Elysian [paradisal] light stand thenceforward in the minds of those who have once contemplated them, as memorials of that gentle and exalted content which extends itself over all thoughts and actions with which it coexists. The great secret of morals is Love; or a going out of our own nature, and an identification of ourselves with the beautiful which exists in thought, action or person, not our own. A man, to be greatly good, must imagine intensely and comprehensively; he must put himself in the place of another and of many others; the pains and pleasures of his species must become his own. The great instrument of moral good is the imagination, and poetry administers to the effect by acting upon the cause. Poetry enlarges the circumference of the imagination by replenishing it with thoughts of ever new delight, which have the power of attracting and assimilating to their own nature all other thoughts, and which form new intervals and interstices whose void for ever craves fresh food. Poetry strengthens that faculty which is the organ of the moral nature of man, in the same manner as exercise strengthens a limb....

For the literature of England, an energetic development of the national will, has arisen as it were from a new birth. In spite of the low-thoughted envy which would undervalue contemporary merit, our own will be a memorable age in intellectual achievements, and we live among such philosophers and poets as surpass beyond comparison any who have appeared since the last national struggle for civil and religious liberty. The most unfailing herald, companion, and follower of the awakening of a great people to work a beneficial change in opinion or institution, is Poetry. At such periods there is an accumulation of the power of communicating and receiving intense and impassioned conceptions respecting man and nature. The persons in whom this power resides, may often, as far as regards many portions of their nature, have little apparent correspondence with that spirit of good of which they are the ministers. But even whilst they deny and abjure, they are yet compelled to serve the Power which is seated upon the throne of their own soul. It is impossible to read the compositions of the most celebrated writers of the present day without being startled with the electric life which burns within their words. They measure the circumference and sound the depths of human nature with a comprehensive and all-penetrating spirit, and they are themselves perhaps the most sincerely astonished at its manifestations, for it is less their spirit than the spirit of the age. Poets are the hierophants of an unapprehended inspiration, the mirrors of the gigantic shadows which futurity casts upon the present, the words which express what they understand not; the trumpets which sing to battle, and feel not what they inspire; the influence which is moved not, but moves. Poets are the unacknowledged legislators of the World.

Percy Shelley, "Sonnet"

Lift not the painted veil which those who live
Call Life: though unreal shapes be pictured there,
And it but mimic all we would believe
With colors idly spread, — behind, lurk Fear
And Hope, twin Destinies; who ever weave
Their shadows, o'er the chasm, sightless and drear.
I knew one who had lifted it — he sought,
For his lost heart was tender, things to love,
But found them not, alas! nor was there aught
The world contains, the which he could approve.
Through the unheeding many he did move,
A splendor among shadows, a bright blot
Upon this gloomy scene, a Spirit that strove
For truth, and like the Preacher found it not.

John Keats, "On First Looking into Chapman's Homer"

Much have I travell'd in the realms of gold,
    And many goodly states and kingdoms seen;
    Round many western islands have I been
Which bards in fealty to Apollo hold.
Oft of one wide expanse had I been told
    That deep-brow'd Homer ruled as his demesne;
    Yet did I never breathe its pure serene
Till I heard Chapman speak out loud and bold:
Then felt I like some watcher of the skies
    When a new planet swims into his ken;
Or like stout Cortez when with eagle eyes
    He star'd at the Pacific—and all his men
Look'd at each other with a wild surmise—
    Silent, upon a peak in Darien.

THINKING CRITICALLY

1. *Recognizing Values* What does Shelley mean when he says that "poets are the unacknowledged legislators of the World"?

2. *Identifying Central Issues* To what does Keats compare his experience of reading Chapman's Homer? Do you think they are appropriate comparisons?

3. *Linking Past and Present* Who do you think has the power in today's world which Shelley assigned to poets? What does that say about our time versus Shelley's?

WRITER'S PORTFOLIO

1. *Extending the Selection* Keats's sonnet is about a personal discovery. Write a description of an event which changed your way of thinking.

2. *Examining Key Questions* Do you think Shelley and Keats are favoring reason or passion? Give examples.

Modern Warfare

Carl von Clausewitz (**kärl fən klou′zə vits**) (1780–1831) was a Prussian military officer who served with distinction in the Napoleonic wars. After the defeat of Napoleon at Waterloo, Clausewitz became head of the Prussian War College, where he spent twelve years working on his study of modern warfare, *On War.* Although incomplete at his death, *On War* has exerted tremendous influence on the political objectives of war, as well as on military strategy and tactics in the years since it was written. Particularly important have been Clausewitz's concepts of absolute war and the idea of war as a political activity. Absolute or total war calls for an army to attack an enemy nation's people and property in every way possible, as well as suggesting that a nation's entire resources and population should be mobilized for a war. Most influential of all was Clausewitz's suggestion that war is a political act and is controlled more by politicians than generals. In the following excerpt from *On War,* how does Clausewitz express the relationship between war and politics?

UP TO NOW WE HAVE CONSIDERED THE INCOMPATIBILITY between war and every other human interest, individual or social—a difference that derives from human nature, and that therefore no philosophy can resolve. We have examined this incompatibility from various angles so that none of its conflicting elements should be missed. Now we must seek out the unity into which these contradictory elements combine in real life, which they do by partly neutralizing one another. We might have posited that unity to begin with, if it had not been necessary to emphasize the contradictions with all possible clarity and to consider the different elements separately. This unity lies in *the concept that war is only a branch of political activity; that it is in no sense autonomous.*

It is, of course, well-known that the only source of war is politics— the intercourse of governments and peoples; but it is apt to be assumed that war suspends that intercourse and replaces it by a wholly different condition, ruled by no law but its own.

We maintain, on the contrary, that war is simply a continuation of political intercourse, with the addition of other means. We deliberately use the phrase "with the addition of other means" because we also want to make it clear that war in itself does not suspend political intercourse or change it into something entirely different. In essentials, that intercourse continues, irrespective of the means it employs. The main lines along which military events progress, and to which they are restricted, are political lines that continue throughout the war into the subsequent peace. How could it be otherwise? Do political relations between peoples and between their governments stop when diplomatic notes are no longer exchanged? Is war not just another expression of their thoughts, another form of speech or writing? Its grammar, indeed, may be its own, but not its logic.

If that is so, then war cannot be divorced from political life; and whenever this occurs in our thinking about war, the many links that connect the two elements are destroyed and we are left with something pointless and devoid of sense.

This conception would be ineluctable even if war were total war, the pure element of enmity unleashed. All the factors that go to make up war and determine its salient features—the strength and allies of each antagonist, the character of the peoples and their governments, and so forth, all the elements listed in the first chapter of Book 1—are these not all political, so closely connected with political activity that it is impossible to separate the two? But it is yet more vital to bear all this in mind when studying actual practice. We will then find that war does not advance relentlessly toward the absolute, as theory would demand. Being incomplete and self-contradictory, it cannot follow its own laws, but has to be treated as a part of some other whole; the name of which is policy.

In making use of war, policy evades all rigorous conclusions proceeding from the nature of war, bothers little about ultimate possibilities, and concerns itself only with immediate probabilities. Although this introduces a high degree of uncertainty into the whole business, turning it into a kind of game, each government is confident that it can outdo its opponent in skill and acumen.

So policy converts the overwhelmingly destructive element of war into a mere instrument. It changes the terrible battle-sword that a man needs both hands and his entire strength to wield, and with which he strikes home once and no more, into a light, handy rapier—sometimes just a foil for the exchange of thrusts, feints, and parries.

Thus the contradictions in which war involves that naturally timid creature, man, are resolved; if this is the solution we choose to accept.

If war is part of policy, policy will determine its character. As policy becomes more ambitious and vigorous, so will war, and this may reach the point where war attains its absolute form. If we look at war in this light, we do not need to lose sight of this absolute: on the contrary, we must constantly bear it in mind.

Only if war is looked at in this way does its unit reappear; only then can we see that all wars are things of the *same* nature; and this alone will provide the right criteria for conceiving and judging great designs.

In the last decade of the eighteenth century, when that remarkable change in the art of war took place, when the best armies saw part of their doctrine become ineffective and military victories occurred on a scale that up to then had been inconceivable, it seemed that all mistakes had been military mistakes. It became evident that the art of war, long accustomed to a narrow range of possibilities, had been surprised by options that lay beyond this range, but that certainly did not go against the nature of war itself.

But is it true that the real shock was military rather than political? To put it in the terms of our argument, was the disaster due to the effect of policy on war, or was policy itself at fault?

Clearly the tremendous effects of the French Revolution abroad were caused not so much by new military methods and concepts as by radical changes in policies and administration, by the new character of government, altered conditions of the French people, and the like.

Not until statesmen had at last perceived the nature of the forces that had emerged in France, and had grasped that new political conditions now obtained in Europe, could they foresee the broad effect all this would have on war; and only in that way could they appreciate the scale of the means that would have to be employed, and how best to apply them.

In short, we can say that twenty years of revolutionary triumph were mainly due to the mistaken policies of France's enemies.

It is true that these mistakes became apparent only in the course of the wars, which thoroughly disappointed all political expectations that had been placed on them. But the trouble was not that the statesmen had ignored the soldiers' views. The military art on which the politicians relied was part of a world they thought was real — a branch of current statecraft, a familiar tool that had been in use for many years. But *that* form of war naturally shared in the errors of policy, and therefore could provide no corrective. It is true that war itself has undergone significant changes in character and methods, changes that have brought it closer to its absolute form. But these changes did not come about because the French government freed itself, so to speak, from the harness of policy; they were caused by the new political conditions which the French Revolution created both in France and in Europe as a whole, conditions that set in motion new means and new forces, and have thus made possible a degree of energy in war that otherwise would have been inconceivable.

It follows that the transformation of the art of war resulted from the transformation of politics. So far from suggesting that the two could be disassociated from each other, these changes are a strong proof of their indissoluble connection.

Once again: war is an instrument of policy. It must necessarily bear the character of policy and measure by its standards. The conduct of war, in its great outlines, is therefore policy itself, which takes up the sword in place of the pen, but does not on that account cease to think according to its own laws.

THINKING CRITICALLY

1. *Analyzing Cause and Effect* What reasons does Clausewitz give for France's victories in the 1790s?

2. *Making Inferences* Why does Clausewitz say that war is not autonomous from politics? Do you agree?

3. *Linking Past and Present* Do you think the Persian Gulf War of 1992 fits Clausewitz's definition of war as a "continuation of political intercourse"? Why or why not?

WRITER'S PORTFOLIO

1. *Extending the Selection* Clausewitz states, "In making use of war, policy...bothers little about ultimate possibilities, and concerns itself only with immediate probabilities." Does this statement still hold true?

2. *Examining Key Questions* Do you think war is a necessary part of international relations or has the concept become outmoded in the twentieth century? Why or why not?

German Romanticism

The two finest German Romantic poets were Johann Wolfgang von Goethe (gėr′tə) (1749–1832) and Heinrich Heine (hī′nə) (1797–1856). Goethe is one of the giants of world literature, whose novels and plays, as well as his poems, have had a profound effect on modern civilization. His finest lyric poems predate the English Romantics and are part of the German *Sturm und Drang* (Storm and Stress) literary movement. These lyric poems concentrate on strong imagery, which conveys an emotion or state of mind. Two of Goethe's *Sturm und Drang* poems appear below. In them Goethe expresses a highly charged vision of nature. How do these poems convey an appeal to the senses?

Johann Wolfgang von Goethe

On the Lake

And fresh nourishment, new blood
I suck from a world so free;
Nature, how gracious and how good,
Her breast she gives to me.
The ripples buoying up our boat
Keep rhythm to the oars,
And mountains up to heaven float
In cloud to meet our course.

Eyes, my eyes, why abject now?
Golden dreams, are you returning?
Dream, though gold, away with you:
Life is here and loving too.

Over the ripples twinkling
Star on hovering star,
Soft mists drink the circled
Towering world afar;

Dawn wind fans the shaded
Inlet with its wing,
And in the water mirrored
The fruit is ripening.

Autumn Feeling
More fatly greening climb
The trellis, you, vine leaf
Up to my window!
Gush, denser, berries
Twine, and ripen
Shining fuller, faster!
Last gaze of sun
Broods you, maternal;
Of tender sky the fruiting
Fullness wafts around you;
Cooled you are, by the moon
Magic, a friendly breath,
And from these eyes,
Of ever quickening Love, ah,
Upon you falls a dew, the tumid
Brimming tears.

Heine was part of the later German Romantic movement, which took Goethe and the English Romantics as inspiration. In his poems, Heine strove to simplify his language and capture the essence of his experiences. He was particularly fascinated by German folklore and often used folk ballads as the forms for his poems. "The Loreley," which appears below, is based on the folk legend of a woman who lures sailors to their deaths on the Rhine river. "The Silesian Weavers," which also appears below, tells the story of the German weavers who revolted against their working conditions in 1844. This poem is Heine's expression of sympathy for their plight. How do the emotions conveyed by these two poems differ?

Heinrich Heine

The Loreley
I do not know what haunts me,
What saddened my mind all day;

An age-old tale confounds me,
A spell I cannot allay.

The air is cool and in twilight
The Rhine's dark waters flow;
The peak of the mountain in highlight
Reflects the evening glow.

There sits a lovely maiden
Above, so wondrous fair,
With shining jewels laden,
She combs her golden hair.

It falls through her comb in a shower,
And over the valley rings
A song of mysterious power
That lovely maiden sings.

The boatman in his small skiff is
Seized by turbulent love,
No longer he marks where the cliff is,
He looks to the mountain above.

I think the waves must fling him
Against the reefs nearby,
And that did with her singing
The lovely Loreley.

The Silesian Weavers

No tears they shed from eyes of doom,
Gnashing their teeth they sit at the loom:
"A shroud for Germany we weave
With a triple curse — and no reprieve!
    We are weaving, we are weaving!

"A curse on the God to whom we prayed,
Who left us hungry, cold, and dismayed;
We trusted and waited and hoped in vain,
He duped and fooled us again and again —
    We are weaving, we are weaving!

"A curse on the King of the rich, whose ear
was deaf to our grief and blind to our tear,
Who took the last penny out of our purse
And had us shot like mangy curs.
     We are weaving, we are weaving!

"A curse on the fatherland, where apace
Grow the wealth of the rich, and our shame and disgrace
Where every bud is felled by a blight,
Where rot and decay feed the parasite—
     We are weaving, we are weaving.

"The loom groans with the shuttle's flight,
We are busy weaving by day and by night—
A shroud for Old Germany we weave
With a triple curse—and no reprieve!
     We are weaving, we are weaving!"

THINKING CRITICALLY

1. *Making Comparisons* How do Goethe's and Heine's presentations of nature differ? Which one appeals more to you?

2. *Making Inferences* What Romantic elements can you identify in these poems? How would you contrast them with those in the Shelley and Keats poems on pages 459–460?

3. *Linking Past and Present* Heine wrote "The Silesian Weavers" to express sympathy for the weavers' plight. In what ways do artists express their political sentiments today?

WRITER'S PORTFOLIO

1. *Extending the Selection* Is the theme of "The Silesian Weavers" valid today or is it important chiefly for historical and literary reasons?

2. *Examining Key Questions* Are Goethe and Heine expressing a reasoned or impassioned vision of nature? Give examples.

Imperialism

During the 1840s, there was a revival of British interest in acquiring overseas territory. Many business and government leaders thought that new colonies would solve the problems caused by shrinking European markets and rapid population growth. In 1843 Charles Buller, a member of Parliament, gave a speech in the House of Commons advocating colonization. In the following excerpts from his speech, what does Buller say England will gain from colonization?

I THINK, SIR, THAT WE CANNOT CONTEMPLATE THE CONDITIONS of this country without coming to the conclusion that there is a permanent cause of suffering in the constant accumulation of capital and the constant increase of population within the same restricted field of employment. Every year adds its profits to the amount of capital previously accumulated; and certainly leaves the population considerably larger at its close than at its commencement. This fresh amount both of capital and population have to be employed; and if no further space for their employment be provided, they must compete for a share of the previous amount of profits and wages....

I propose that you should investigate the efficacy of colonization as a remedy against the distress of the country.... I propose colonization as subsidiary to free trade; as an additional mode of carrying out the same principles and attaining the same object. You advocates of free trade wish to bring food to the people. I suggest to you at the same time to take your people to the food. You wish to get fresh markets by removing the barriers which now keep you from those that exist throughout the world....

But the whole, nay the main advantage of colonization, is not secured by that mere removal of the laborer from the crowded mother country.... His absence is only the first relief which he affords you. You take him hence to place him on a fertile soil, from which a very small amount of labor will suffice to raise the food which he wants. He soon finds that by applying his spare time and energies to raising additional food, or some article of trade or material of manufacture, he can obtain that which he can exchange for luxuries of which he never dreamed at home. He raises some article of export and appears in your market as a customer. He who a few years ago added nothing to the wealth of the country, but received all from charity…comes, after providing his own food, to purchase from you a better quality and a larger quantity of the clothing, and other manufactures which he used to take as a dole, and to give employment and offer food to those on whose energies he was a burden before….

It seems a paradox to assert that removing a portion of your population enables a country to support more inhabitants than it could before; and that the place of every man who quits his country because he cannot get a subsistence may speedily be filled up by another whom that very removal will enable to subsist there in comfort. But the assertion is as true as it is strange.

After 1860, the nations of Western Europe competed with each other in a mad scramble to capture control of colonies in Africa. Britain did this by enacting treaties with the local rulers, which enabled them to set up free trade and to stamp out the African slave trade. The following selection, a treaty between the King of Mellella and the British government enacted in 1877, is an example of one of these agreements. Is England attempting to curtail competition?

1.   The export of slaves to foreign countries is forever abolished in my territory.

2.   No European or other person whatever shall be permitted to reside in my territories or those of my heirs or successors for the purpose of carrying on in any way the traffic in slaves; and no houses, stores, or buildings of any kind whatsoever shall be erected for the purpose of the slave trade.

3.   If at any time it shall appear that the slave trade is being carried on through or from any part of my territories, the slave trade may be put down by force.

4.   The subjects of Her Britannic Majesty and all white foreigners may always trade freely with my people. I, for myself, my heirs or successors, pledge myself to show no favor and to give no privilege to the ships and trade of other countries which I do not show to those of Great Britain….

6. Should any British or other foreign vessel, being aground in the river, apply to me for assistance, I promise to render her all help in my power, provided I am fairly paid for my trouble.

7. Should the ships be attacked by pirates or plunderers, I promise assistance by sending my people with arms, and doing all in my power to punish the robbers.

8. If at any time a naval officer of Great Britain shall require guides or armed people from myself to accompany the said officer against pirates or other enemies of the Queen of Great Britain, I faithfully promise to provide them.

9. I declare that no human being shall be sacrificed on account of religious or other ceremonies, and that I will prevent the barbarous practice of murdering prisoners of war.

10. Missionaries or other ministers of the Gospel are to be allowed to reside in my territory for the purpose of instructing the people in all useful occupations.

11. And, in consideration of these engagements, all past offences of the King of Mellella against the Queen of Great Britain are hereby forgiven.

THINKING CRITICALLY

1. *Identifying Central Issues* Is Buller's idea of removing a laborer from England and placing him in a colony a sensible one?

2. *Drawing Conclusions* The treaty between Britain and the King of Mellella explicitly states the obligations of the King. What do you think were the obligations of Britain?

3. *Linking Past and Present* What remnants of colonialism are still in place today? Why do you think they remain?

WRITER'S PORTFOLIO

1. *Extending the Selection* Assume that you were a member of Parliament when Buller presented his proposal. Compose a diary entry expressing your opinion of his remarks.

2. *Examining Key Questions* Do you think that Buller's speech is a reasoned justification of imperialism? Why or why not?

Communism

As Europe became more industrialized in the nineteenth century, the major nations — Britain, Germany, France, Russia, Italy, and the Austro-Hungarian empire — grew in economic power. The capitalistic system enabled private individuals to amass huge fortunes, often to the social, political, and economic detriment of the workers hired to produce goods and services. In 1848, Karl Marx (1818–1883) and his colleague, Friedrich Engels (1820–1895) published *The Communist Manifesto* in which they outlined a wide-ranging program for reform, predicted the overthrow of the ruling bourgeoisie (the middle class property owners and business people) by the proletariat (the workers), and advocated a classless society. Their ideas influenced whole generations of European intellectuals, most particularly the Russian radicals under Nikolai Lenin (1870–1924), who led the Russian revolution in 1917. In the following selection from *The Communist Manifesto*, Marx and Engels describe the economic situation that they believe will lead to revolution. How do Marx and Engels sum up communism?

A SPECTER IS HAUNTING EUROPE — THE SPECTER OF Communism. All the Powers of old Europe have entered into a holy alliance to exorcise this specter; Pope and Czar, Metternich [Austrian Prime Minister] and Guizot [French Prime Minister], French Radicals, and German police-spies.

Where is the party in opposition that has not been decried as communistic by its opponents in power? Where the Opposition that has not hurled back the branding reproach of Communism against the more advanced opposition parties, as well as against its revolutionary adversaries?

Two things result from this fact:

I. Communism is already acknowledged by all European Powers to be itself a Power.

II. It is high time that Communists should openly, in the face of the whole world, publish their views, their aims, their tendencies, and meet this nursery tale of the specter of Communism with a Manifesto of the party itself....

The history of all hitherto existing society is the history of class struggles.

Freeman and slave, patrician and plebeian, lord and serf, guild-master and journeyman, in a word, oppressor and oppressed, stood in constant opposition to one another, carried on uninterrupted, now hidden, now open fight, a fight that each time ended, either in a revolutionary re-constitution of society at large, or in the common ruin of the contending classes.

In the earlier epochs of history we find almost everywhere a complicated arrangement of society into various orders, a manifold gradation of social rank. In ancient Rome we have patricians, knights, plebeians, slaves; in the middle ages, feudal lords, vassals, guild-masters, journeymen, apprentices, serfs; in almost all of these classes, again, subordinate gradations.

The modern bourgeois society that has sprouted from the ruins of feudal society, has not done away with class antagonisms. It has but established new classes, new conditions of oppression, new forms of struggle in place of the old ones.

Our epoch, the epoch of the bourgeoisie, possesses, however, this distinctive feature: it has simplified the class antagonisms. Society as a whole is more and more splitting up into two great hostile camps, into two great classes directly facing each other: Bourgeoisie and Proletariat.

But the weapons with which the bourgeoisie felled feudalism are now turned against the bourgeoisie itself. Not only has the bourgeoisie forged the weapons that bring death to itself; it has also called into existence the men who are to wield those weapons—the modern working-class—the proletarians.

In proportion as the bourgeoisie, i.e., capital, is developed, in the same proportion is the proletariat, the modern working-class, developed, a class of laborers who live only so long as they find work, and who find work only so long as their labor increases capital. These laborers, who must sell themselves piecemeal, are a commodity, like every other article of commerce and are consequently exposed to all the vicissitudes of competition, to all the fluctuations of the market....

The lower strata of the middle class—the small trades-people, shopkeepers and retired tradesmen generally, the handicraftsmen and peasants—all these sink gradually into the proletariat, partly because their diminutive capital does not suffice for the scale on which Modern Industry is carried on, and is swamped in the competition with the large capitalists, partly because their specialized skill is rendered worthless by new methods of production. Thus the proletariat is recruited from all classes of the population....

But with the development of industry the proletariat not only increases in number; it becomes concentrated in greater masses, its strength grows and it feels that strength more. The various interests and conditions of life within the ranks of the proletariat are more and more equalized, in proportion as machinery obliterates all distinctions of labor, and nearly everywhere reduces wages to the same low level....

The proletarian is without property; his relation to his wife and children has no longer anything in common with the bourgeois family relations; modern industrial labor, modern subjection to capital, the same in England as in France, in America as in Germany, has stripped him of every trace of national character. Law, morality, religion, are to him so many bourgeois prejudices, behind which lurk in ambush just as many bourgeois interests.

The modern laborer, on the contrary, instead of rising with the progress of industry, sinks deeper and deeper below the conditions of existence of his own class. He becomes a pauper, and pauperism develops more rapidly than population and wealth. And here it becomes evident that the bourgeoisie is unfit any longer to be the ruling class in society, and to impose its conditions of existence upon society as an over-riding law. It is unfit to rule, because it is incompetent to assure an existence to its slave within his slavery, because it cannot help letting him sink into such a state that it has to feed him, instead of being fed by him. Society can no longer live under this bourgeoisie; in other words, its existence is no longer compatible with society....

The theory of the Communists may be summed up in the single sentence: Abolition of private property....

If the proletariat during its contest with the bourgeoisie is compelled, by the force of circumstances, to organize itself as a class, if, by means of a revolution, it makes itself the ruling class, and, as such, sweeps away by force the old conditions of production, then it will, along with these conditions, have swept away the conditions for the existence of class antagonism, and of classes generally, and will thereby have abolished its own supremacy as a class.

In place of the old bourgeois society, with its classes and class antagonisms, we shall have an association in which the free development of each is the condition for the free development of all....

In short, the Communists everywhere support every revolutionary movement against the existing social and political order of things.

In all these movements they bring to the front, as the leading question in each, the property question, no matter what its degree of development at the time.

Finally, they labor everywhere for the union and agreement of the democratic parties of all countries.

The Communists disdain to conceal their views and aims. They openly declare that their ends can be attained only by the forcible overthrow of all existing social conditions. Let the ruling classes tremble at a Communistic revolution. The proletarians have nothing to lose but their chains. They have a world to win.

Working men of all countries, unite!

THINKING CRITICALLY

1. *Analyzing Cause and Effect* Why, according to Marx and Engels, does the "lower strata of the middle class...sink gradually into the proletariat"?

2. *Making Inferences* How do Marx and Engels say that the bourgeoisie originated? What will cause its downfall?

3. *Linking Past and Present* Marx and Engels say that "the modern laborer...becomes a pauper" and that the bourgeoisie "cannot help letting him sink into such a state that it has to feed him, instead of being fed by him." Do you see any evidence of this in modern society? Explain.

WRITER'S PORTFOLIO

1. *Extending the Selection* How does what you just read compare to your previous impressions of communism? How did they differ? Why do you think they differed?

2. *Examining Key Questions* What is the best way of changing a political system? Is violent revolution a first or last resort? What are the advantages and disadvantages of violent and peaceful means of changing a political system?

Opening of Japan

In 1636, the Japanese Shogun Ieyasu had enacted the Closed Country Edict, which effectively excluded foreigners from Japan for more than two centuries. In 1852, U.S. President Millard Fillmore commissioned Commodore Matthew Perry (1794–1858) as a special diplomatic envoy charged with negotiating a treaty with Japan. Perry was to gain protection for American seamen shipwrecked in Japan, secure a fuel depot, and open at least one

Americans Landing at Yokohama, Japanese print (1853)

Japanese port to American commerce. On July 8, 1853, Perry's squadron of two steam frigates and two sloops swept into Tokyo Bay and dropped anchor. Six days later amid much pomp and pageantry, the two sides met formally for a brief period. Perry presented the American demands and announced that he would return with a larger fleet to receive Japan's reply. At this time, the Japanese were still ruled by a shogun (or warlord), and they realized they could not maintain their seclusion when threatened by modern ships and guns. When Perry returned to Tokyo Bay on February 12, 1854, he found Japanese officials more receptive and an agreement was signed on March 31, 1854. The shogunate promised to take care of stranded American sailors and allowed two ports to serve as trading and fueling stations. The following selections are a partial list of the gifts exchanged between the Japanese and Americans and two paintings showing how each culture depicted the other. Whose gifts seem more concerned with private life? Whose with public life?

Commodore Perry meeting the Imperial Commissioners at Yokohama, American drawing (1853)

For the Emperor, from the U.S. President

Miniature steam engine, 1/4 size, with track, tender, and car.

2 telegraph sets, with batteries, three miles of wire, gutta percha [rubber-like insulation] wire, and insulators.

1 Francis' copper lifeboat.

1 surfboat of copper.

Collection of agricultural implements.

Audubon's Birds, in nine vols.

Natural History of the State of New York, 16 vols.

Annals of Congress, 4 vols.

Laws and Documents of the State of New York.

Journal of the Senate and Assembly of New York.

Lighthouse Reports, 2 vols.

Bancroft's History of the United States, 4 vols.

Farmers' Guide, 2 vols.

1 series of United States Coast Survey Charts.

Morris, *Engineering.*

Silver-topped dressing case.

8 yards scarlet broadcloth, and scarlet velvet.

Series of United States standard yard, gallon, bushel, balances and weights.

Quarter cask of Madeira [wine].

Barrel of whiskey.

Box of champagne and cherry cordial and maraschino.

3 boxes of fine tea.

Maps of several states and four large lithographs.

Telescope and stand, in box.

Sheet-iron stove.

An assortment of fine perfumery.

5 Hall rifles.

3 Maynard muskets.

12 cavalry swords.

6 artillery swords.

1 carbine.

20 Army pistols in a box.

For the Government of the United States of America from the Emperor and Commissioners

1 gold lacquered writing
   apparatus.
1 gold lacquered paper box.
1 gold lacquered book case.
1 lacquered writing table.
1 censer [incense-burner] of
   bronze.
1 flower holder and stand.
2 braziers [charcoal burners].
10 pieces fine red pongee [silk].

10 pieces white pongee.
5 pieces flowered crape [silk].
5 pieces red dyed figured crape.
4 boxes assorted sea-shells,
   100 in each.
1 box of branch coral and feather
   in silver.
1 lacquered chow-chow
   [preserved fruit] box.
1 box, set of three, lacquered
   goblets.
7 boxes cups and spoons and
   goblet cut from conch shells.

THINKING CRITICALLY

1. *Making Comparisons* What aspects of American life are reflected in the gifts brought by Perry? What aspects of Japanese culture do the Japanese gifts represent?

2. *Making Inferences* From the lists of gifts, how would you characterize nineteenth-century Japanese and Americans? Do these characterizations resemble more recent stereotypes?

3. *Linking Past and Present* Discussing the Japanese attack on Pearl Harbor, Admiral Isoroku Yamamoto wrote: "I wanted to return Commodore Perry's visit." Yet others think that the Japanese have paid back Perry's visit in kind in recent years. What are they referring to and do you agree with this sentiment?

WRITER'S PORTFOLIO

1. *Extending the Selection* If you were going to meet people from a new culture today, what items would you take to represent America. Create a list of items and give reasons why you chose them.

2. *Examining Key Questions* What do you think was the main reason behind the U.S. interest in Japan? Explain.

Evolution

In the mid-nineteenth century, Charles Darwin (1809–1882) formulated a major scientific theory. The theory stated that all complex organisms developed from simple forms through the operation of natural causes. This theory of evolution was based on the work of earlier scientists, on that of Darwin's contemporaries, and on his own observations as a naturalist. Darwin was an eager observer of nature and from 1831 to 1836 was the naturalist aboard the H.M.S. *Beagle*, which sailed along the coast of South America and among the Galapagos Islands. He collected and classified plant, fish, and animal specimens and in 1839 published his *Journal of Researches into the Geology and Natural History of the various countries visited by the H.M.S.* Beagle. After his return to England, Darwin continued his studies of plants and animals and began to experiment with pigeon breeding. By 1844 he had formulated his famous theory of natural selection, which says that the most adaptable individuals survive. Darwin's basic point in his theory is that each species gives birth to more individuals than can survive, so that those who are most efficient and adaptable succeed in the struggle for survival. Hence the famous formulation — "the survival of the fittest." In 1859 Darwin published *On the Origin of Species by Means of Natural Selection*, which explained his theory, followed in 1871 by *The Descent of Man*, which provided the scientific evidence and application for his theory. Excerpts from both works appear below. What is the main point of Darwin's argument?

---

from *On the Origin of Species,* "Conclusion"

I HAVE NOW RECAPITULATED THE FACTS AND CONSIDERATIONS which have thoroughly convinced me that species have been modified, during a long course of descent. This has been effected chiefly through the natural selection of numerous successive, slight, favorable variations; aided in an important manner by the inherited effects of the use and disuse of parts; and in an unimportant manner; that is, in relation to adaptive structures, whether past or present, by the direct action of external conditions, and by variations which seem to us in our ignorance to arise spontaneously. It appears that I formerly underrated the frequency and value of these latter forms of variation, as leading to permanent modifications of structure independently of natural selection. But as my conclusions have lately been much misrepresented, and it has been stated that I attribute the modification of species exclusively to natural selection, I may be permitted to remark that in the first edition of this work, and subsequently, I placed in the most conspicuous position — namely, at the close of the Introduction — the following words: "I am convinced that natural selection has been the main but not the exclusive means of modification."…

I see no good reason why the views given in this volume should shock the religious feelings of any one. It is satisfactory, as showing how transient such impressions are, to remember that the greatest discovery ever made by man, namely, the law of the attraction of gravity, was also attacked by [the philosopher and mathematician] Leibnitz, "as subversive of natural, and inferentially of revealed, religion." A celebrated author and divine has written to me that "he has gradually learnt to see that it is just as noble a conception of the Deity to believe that He created a few original forms capable of self-development into other and needful forms, as to believe that He required a fresh act of creation to supply the voids caused by the action of His laws."…

It is interesting to contemplate a tangled bank, clothed with many plants of many kinds, with birds singing on the bushes, with various insects flitting about, and with worms crawling through the damp earth, and to reflect that these elaborately constructed forms, so different from each other, and dependent upon each other in so complex a manner, have all been produced by laws acting around us. These laws, taken in the largest sense, being Growth with Reproduction; Inheritance which is almost implied by reproduction; Variability from the indirect and direct action of the conditions of life, and from use and disuse; a Ratio of Increase so high as to lead to a Struggle for Life, and as a consequence to Natural Selection, entailing Divergence of Character and the Extinction of less-improved forms. Thus, from the war of nature, from famine and death, the most exalted object which we are capable of conceiving, namely, the production of higher animals, directly follows. There is grandeur in this view of life, with its several powers, having been originally breathed by the Creator into a few forms or into one; and that, whilst this planet has gone cycling on according to the fixed law of gravity, from so simple a being endless forms most beautiful and most wonderful have been, and are being evolved.

---

from *The Descent of Man,* "General Summary"

THE MAIN CONCLUSION HERE ARRIVED AT, AND NOW HELD BY many naturalists who are competent to form a sound judgment, is that man is descended from some less highly organized form. The grounds upon which this conclusion rests will never be shaken, for the close similarity between man and the lower animals in embryonic development, as well as in innumerable points of structure and constitution, both of high and of the most trifling importance — the rudiments which he retains, and the abnormal reversions to which he is occasionally liable — are facts which cannot be disputed. They have long been known, but until recently they told us nothing with respect to the origin of man. Now when viewed by the light of our knowledge of the whole organic world, their meaning is unmistakable. The great principle of evolution stands up clear and firm, when these groups or facts are considered in connection with others, such as the mutual affinities of the members of the same group, their geographical distribution in past and present times, and their geological succession. It is incredible that all these facts should speak falsely. He who is not content to look, like a savage, at the phenomena of nature as disconnected, cannot any longer believe that man is the work of a separate act of creation. He will be forced to admit that the close resemblance of the embryo of man to that, for instance, of a dog — the construction of his skull, limbs, and the whole frame on the same plan with that of other mammals, independently of the uses to which the parts may be put — the occasional reappearance of various structures, for instance of several muscles, which man does not normally possess, but which are common to the Quadrumana [non-human primates] — and a crowd of analogous facts — all points in the plainest manner to the conclusion that man is the co-descendant with other mammals of a common progenitor....

The main conclusion arrived at in this work, namely, that man is descended from some lowly organized form, will, I regret to think, be highly distasteful to many. But there can hardly be a doubt that we are descended from barbarians. The astonishment which I felt on first seeing a party of Fuegians [South American natives] on a wild and broken shore will never be forgotten by me, for the reflection at once rushed into my mind—such were our ancestors.... He who has seen a savage in his native land will not feel much shame, if forced to acknowledge that the blood of some more humble creature flows in his veins.... Man may be excused for feeling some pride at having risen, though not through his own exertions, to the very summit of the organic scale.... But we are not here concerned with hopes or fears, only with the truth as far as our reason permits us to discover it; and I have given the evidence to the best of my ability. We must, however, acknowledge, as it seems to me, that man with all his noble qualities, with sympathy which feels for the most debased, with benevolence which extends not only to other men but to the humblest living creature, with his god-like intellect which has penetrated into the movements and constitutions of the solar system—with all these exalted powers—Man still bears in his bodily frame the indelible stamp of his lowly origin.

THINKING CRITICALLY

1. *Identifying Central Issues* Why did Darwin's theory of natural selection cause such an uproar? Why does he quote the letter at the end of the "Conclusion" to *On the Origin of Species*?

2. *Making Inferences* Many people during Darwin's time began to apply his ideas about natural selection to social, political, and economic matters. How could this application be used to justify imperialism?

3. *Linking Past and Present* Is Darwin's theory of natural selection still contentious today? Why or why not?

WRITER'S PORTFOLIO

1. *Extending the Selection* Write a letter to the editor of a Victorian newspaper attacking or defending Darwin's theory. Be sure to take opposition views into account.

2. *Examining Key Questions* Darwin's theory has been called the final triumph of reason. Why do you think this was said? What was reason triumphing over?

Impressionism

In 1874 French painters Claude Monet, Paul Cézanne, and others formed a group called Artists' Cooperative Society of Painters, Sculptors, Engravers, etc., with the aim of holding their own exhibitions. The artists taking part in the exhibitions varied over the years, but their purpose was to gain an audience for their work, known as Impressionism, which had been rejected by the Paris Salon because of its departure from traditional techniques and approaches to subject matter. The term Impressionism, which was at first meant derisively, was taken from *Impression: Sunrise* by Claude Monet (**klōd mō nā′**) (1840–1926), which appears on page 491. In general, the Impressionists painted directly from the scenes before them rather than sketching and then completing their painting in a studio, rearranging objects and figures for compositional effect. Whether painting landscapes or interior scenes, they were interested in

Eduard Manet, A Bar at the Folies Bergère *(1881)*

capturing the effects of light on color, often to the dismay of their detractors, who objected to violet tree branches, yellow skies, and forms that seemed to dissolve. *Impression: Sunrise* is a view of the French port city of Le Havre, where Monet spent much of his childhood. Desperately poor throughout most of his life, he was able to buy a house in Giverny in his later years, where he concentrated on a series of paintings of his gardens. Although Eduard Manet (ā dwar′ ma nā′) (1832–1883) did not participate in the eight Impressionist exhibitions, he was nevertheless a part of the movement. *A Bar at the Folies Bergère*, which appears on page 483, was his last major painting. In this interior of a nightclub, the barmaid is painted in a relatively straightforward manner, but Manet draws us into the painting with the Impressionistic reflections of the crowd in the mirror. He captures a dazzling array of light and action in the mirror, beginning with the barmaid's customer in the top right. Paul Cézanne (sā zan′) (1839–1906) lived much of his life in Provence where he was born, but played a major role in organizing the Impressionist movement. *Mont Sainte-Victoire*, which appears on page 492, is one of a series of paintings of this scene near his home. He is renowned for his use of warm light, and his late paintings were immensely influential on early twentieth century artists. Mary Cassatt (kə sat′) (1844–1926) was born into a wealthy Philadelphia family but spent most of her life in France. She exhibited with the Impressionists on four occasions. She is best known for painting interiors, mostly of women and children. Her style of unsentimental portraiture was heavily influenced by the flat-perspective of Japanese woodcuts (see page 476). *The Bath*, which appears on

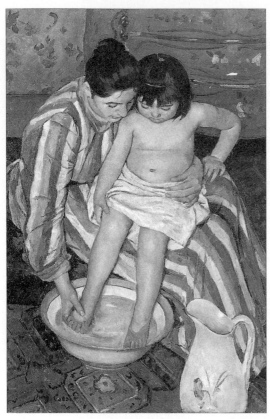

Mary Cassatt, The Bath *(1891)*

page 484, is a marvel of interior light and color. Vincent van Gogh (van gō) (1853–1890) was born in Holland and was influenced by the Impressionists, although he developed a unique style quite unlike any of the other painters. He moved to Arles in 1888 where he painted *The Night Cafe*, which appears on page 492, of which he wrote: "I have tried...to express the powers of darkness in a low drink-shop...." He has come to be one of the most renowned and popular painters in the world. What is the source of light in each of these paintings?

THINKING CRITICALLY

1. *Making Comparisons* How would you compare the Impressionists' use of light to that of the nineteenth-century landscape painters? (See page 455.) What seem to be the fundamental differences in the methods of painting?

2. *Making Inferences* What sort of interiors have Manet, Cassatt, and van Gogh painted? Do you think these would have been the subjects for earlier painters? Why or why not?

3. *Linking Past and Present* Impressionist paintings have been immensely popular in modern America. Why do you think these century-old paintings have such widespread appeal?

WRITER'S PORTFOLIO

1. *Extending the Selection* How can you account for the fact that the works of painters are very often scorned or ignored during their lifetimes while their work may subsequently command millions of dollars long after their death?

2. *Examining Key Questions* Do you think the Impressionist painters reflect a belief in reason or passion? Explain.

The New Sculpture

Auguste Rodin (ō güst′ rô dan′) (1840–1917) was an innovative sculptor whose realistic work often baffled or angered the critics. He sculpted in a highly expressive style, with strong emotion and physical realism as its hallmarks. *The Thinker*, one of the most famous works of sculpture ever created, was originally intended as a part of the double doors for the Museum of Decorative Arts in Paris, Rodin's first public commission. The theme was to be *The Gates of Hell*, based on Dante's *Inferno*, and *The Thinker* was to have gazed downward at the Purgatorial figures below. Much of the work for the doors was completed and resulted in the modeling and casting of a number of individual works, but the doors remained unfinished. Another public

Auguste Rodin,
The Thinker
(1879–1889)

Auguste Rodin, **The Burghers of Calais** *(1884–1886)*

commission was Rodin's depiction of *The Burghers of Calais,* medieval city leaders who had surrendered the keys to Calais and their selves to the English during the Hundred Years War — their lives were eventually spared. Rodin concentrated on depicting the emotion of these men making a sacrifice to save their city. In 1891 Rodin was commissioned to create a monument to Honoré de Balzac, the great French novelist. Rodin examined daguerreotypes of the author and read Balzac's novels before beginning the project, but the nude sculpture he created offended the commissioners. Rodin, angry at the rejection of his work, simply placed a cloak around his nude figure and resubmitted it. This cloaked figure, which appears on page 488, is still displayed in Paris. Which of the three sculptures seems the least realistic?

THINKING CRITICALLY

1. *Making Comparisons* Look back at the figures on pages 46–47 and 243–244. What are the similarities and differences between these and Rodin's work?

2. *Drawing Conclusions* What emotion does *The Thinker* convey to you? What about *Balzac*?

3. *Linking Past and Present* These three sculptures of Rodin were all part of public monuments. What do recent public monuments look like? Are they in innovative styles like Rodin's were?

WRITER'S PORTFOLIO

1. *Extending the Selection* Greek sculpture was based on achievement of an ideal form. What do you think is the expressive ideal behind Rodin's work?

2. *Examining Key Questions* Do you think Rodin's sculptures are guided by reason or passion? Why?

Auguste Rodin, Balzac *(1892–1897)*

John Constable, The Hay Wain (1821)

J.M.W. Turner, Burning of the Houses of Parliament (*c. 1835*)

Claude Monet, Impression: Sunrise (1872)

Paul Cézanne, Mont Sainte-Victoire *(1885)*

Vincent van Gogh, The Night Cafe *(1888)*

EXAMINING KEY QUESTIONS

- *Is reason or passion a better guide?*
- *Is revolution necessary?*

Throughout this chapter, most selections have concluded with a writing project asking you to discuss how the art or literature you have examined provides answers to one of these key questions. The following writing projects will help you draw together what you have learned by examining how several selections illustrate these key questions.

- The debate between reason and passion was a key part of the intellectual and artistic movements of the eighteenth and nineteenth centuries. Which do you think had a greater overall effect on social, political, intellectual, and artistic events of these centuries?

- Why was revolution such an important factor of the eighteenth and nineteenth centuries? In the end was it a force for good or did it cause more misery than it cured? Use examples from the chapter to prove your thesis.

SPEAKING/LISTENING

- With a group of students, create a dialogue among Charles Darwin, Charles Buller, Mary Wollstonecraft, Jean Jacques Rousseau, Thomas Malthus, and Karl Marx on the future of mankind. Then, each student should choose one character and present the dialogue to the class.

CRAFTING

- Study a natural scene and then create your own Romantic landscape. Try hard to capture the spirit and power of nature, as well as your own sense of its importance.

COLLECTING

- Collect images of world cultures in the eighteenth and nineteenth centuries. Was there much change during these centuries in the cultures? What can you infer about those that changed the most?

Detail of Guernica (1937)
by Pablo Picasso

The Twentieth Century

Robie House

CHAPTER 11

1909
*Frank Lloyd Wright
builds Robie House*

The Twentieth Century

1890–1965

EVELYN TOYNTON
Essayist

"The past was devoted to answers, the modern period confines itself to questions." While no single generalization can sum up the spirit of a century, that statement by the American critic Irving Howe aptly describes much of the intellectual and artistic activity of the past hundred years.

However much nineteenth century painters and writers rebelled against the conventions of their day and rejected the certainties of their predecessors, they were still engaged in the quest for a higher, universal truth, something fixed and permanent. And although their work had become increasingly subjective, with the individual consciousness at its center, they still had a vital sense of their connection to the world around them, whether the life of nature or the society in which they lived. In their art, they struggled towards a vision of harmony and completeness, believing that such a harmony was present, in however hidden a form, and that it was their role to discover and express it.

TWENTIETH CENTURY ART

In Western art of the twentieth century, the search for completeness and harmony was largely abandoned. The works that have come to be seen as the most representative of the time are notable for their fragmentation, dissonance, and sense of alienation from the world — the feeling that the narrator or central figure in a work of literature, for example, is profoundly alone, unable to connect with the world

Louis Raemakers's *cartoon* Harvest Is Ripe

Albert Einstein

1914
World War I begins

1915
Einstein offers the General Theory of Relativity

in any meaningful way, even the way of defiance and rebellion. The real, if troubled, hopefulness of the nineteenth century was replaced by a spirit of doubt and disillusionment. "Things fall apart; the centre cannot hold," wrote the great Irish poet William Butler Yeats; "Mere anarchy is loosed upon the world...." This sense of disintegration, of the breakdown of spiritual and moral order, became pervasive, although it sometimes found ironic rather than gloomy expression.

Many reasons have been cited for this phenomenon: the weakening of religious faith; the violent social upheavals that destroyed people's sense of community; the increasingly urbanized, man-made environments in which people lived, surrounded by machines rather than nature. And some commentators have pointed to the influence of intellectual concepts like Albert Einstein's theory of relativity, which shattered the old, comforting belief in the stability of time and space.

In fact, by the time the theory of relativity entered into the public con-

sciousness in 1919, the writers and artists of the early twentieth century had already subverted traditional notions of space and time. In his revolutionary *Les Demoiselles d'Avignon*, painted in 1907, the Spanish-born painter Pablo Picasso abandoned the use of the perspective systems that had prevailed for centuries; instead of using the illusion of depth to locate forms in space, he depicted a shifting structure of planes in indeterminate relationship to space. In Cubism, the artistic movement inaugurated by this painting, there was no clear distinction, as there had always been before, between solid forms and the space surrounding them. A sharp outline separating mass from space could dissolve; a dense shape could become weightless and transparent; a plane that defined the remoteness of the background could at the same time appear in the foreground. The very identity of objects was no longer stable: a book might become a table, a musical instrument could turn into a hand. Nothing was fixed and certain, including—perhaps above all—mean-

Wyndham Lewis's portrait of Eliot

Charles Lindbergh

1922
T.S. Eliot publishes The Waste Land

1927
Lindbergh flies across the Atlantic

ing itself; it was process, not answers, that concerned the artist.

THE BIRTH OF MODERN LITERATURE Just as the depiction of space in painting changed, so did the handling of time in the novel. Whereas earlier fiction had attempted to tell a sequential story, with one event giving rise to another in reasonably orderly progression, the Modernist novel that came into being shortly after the advent of Cubism was no longer concerned with depicting the forward movement of events within a definite time frame. Instead of showing cause and effect, it might present fragments of experience, their connection made clear only in the resolution of the work, or might depict past and present as flowing in and out of each other, existing not so much in linear, objective time — Newtonian time — as in the mind of a character.

The very concept of what constituted a mind, or a character, had changed. Increasingly, the idea of the unconscious — a realm of human exis-

tence that had been illuminated by the pioneering psychologists Sigmund Freud and Carl Jung — opened up an exciting new area of exploration for novelists, just as it did for such visual artists as the Surrealist painters, who were intent on portraying irrational, dream-like states on canvas. In the novel, too, dreams and submerged feelings, unconscious motivations, associations that were not necessarily logically connected, became the means through which character was revealed, rather than the depiction of conscious thoughts and intentions. In the past, character had been regarded as a fixed entity, something that might be affected by external events but was essentially a solid thing, like the mass of pre-Cubist art. Now it was seen as fluid, a matter of shadowy, fleeting images and perceptions, some of them rooted in that part of the mind Jung called "the collective unconscious." (In a sense, this conception of character is mirrored in the work of the Austrian-born philosopher Ludwig Wittgenstein, one of the most influential thinkers of the century. A

Campaign
poster for
Hitler and
Hindenburg

U.S.S. Virginia *and*
U.S.S. Tennessee
burning

1933
Hitler becomes Chancellor of Germany

1941
Japanese attack Pearl Harbor

central theme of his pioneering work with language is that its limitations include an absence of anything that could be called a fixed or definite inner language, which means there can be no fixed, essential inner self.)

Among the greatest innovators in fiction was the English novelist Virginia Woolf, whose poetic "stream-of-consciousness" style conveyed heightened states of feeling through the accumulation of impressions. Across the Channel, the Frenchman Marcel Proust created an epic novel of his "search for lost time," known in English as *Remembrance of Things Past*. In it he attempted to recapture certain intense moments from his past and triumph over the destructive forces of time and death through the act of memory and the power of art. Meanwhile, the Irishman James Joyce, who had fled his native country and, like many of the artists and writers of his day, settled in Paris, recreated Dublin and gave it a heroic grandeur in his allusive, often dream-like novel *Ulysses* (1922), which depicts a single day in the lives of two

men — the middle-aged Dublin Jew Leopold Bloom and the young Irish artist Stephen Daedalus — and recasts their experiences in terms of those of the ancient Greek hero. The American-born T. S. Eliot, whose haunting, fragmented poem *The Waste Land* depicting the bleakness of modern life was often cited as his generation's ultimate statement, said that *Ulysses* had "the importance of a scientific discovery."

One thing that differentiates Joyce from many other writers of his era, apart from the dazzling inventiveness of his language, is his love of the small, ordinary details of life, his rich and sensuous portrayal of the street life of Dublin. Much of the art of this century has become increasingly abstract — not just painting, where abstraction meant the eventual abandonment of even the distorted figures presented by Picasso, but poetry and fiction as well. The Czech-German writer Franz Kafka, for example, was a master at evoking the impersonal, menacing nature of the modern world in his fiction, without ever describing it in physical terms. In

Bomb blast
from Nagasaki

Mohandas
Gandhi

1945
Atomic bombs dropped on Hiroshima and Nagasaki

1947
India achieves independence

such works as *The Trial* (1925), he presents us with nightmarish situations in which a baffled, helpless human being, tormented by guilt for non-specific crimes he may or may not have committed, is at the mercy of a faceless bureaucracy that, for no understandable reason, is out to crush him.

It has been said that, when a society is in harmony with itself and the natural world, representational art is the natural outcome. When human beings are out of harmony with the world, they tend to turn away from the representation of people and nature in paintings and of ordinary human experience in poetry and fiction, and to use abstraction as a way of getting at some higher reality than the one they have turned their backs on. This is certainly true of many twentieth century artists, like T. S. Eliot and Kafka, although there were also artists who were very "alienated" without resorting to abstraction.

One of these was the American novelist Ernest Hemingway, whose characters have as bleak a view of human existence, and are as essentially alone, as any in literature; yet his fiction remains highly concrete. Rather than describing dream-like states or fleeting impressions in long poetic sentences, as Joyce or Virginia Woolf did, he wrote in short terse sentences that seemed to present "just the facts," while really choosing all his facts to contribute to the overall sense of aloneness and futility. Hemingway's characters might be seen as "existentialist" heroes, a term taken from the French philosophers known as existentialists, who argued that because the universe made no objective sense in itself, it was up to individual human beings to make sense of it by being true to a code of ethics that would make their actions meaningful.

SCIENCE AND PROGRESS
Interestingly, many of the artists who did not turn to abstraction were those who remained optimistic about what was happening around them. In particular, there were several groups of visual artists who believed that scientific progress was

*Crick and
Watson with
DNA strand*

*Workers
celebrating
in Beijing*

1949
Communist Revolution in China

1953
Crick and Watson discover DNA

going to eliminate all the ills of life, and that their role was to celebrate the glittering power of the machine as those in previous centuries had celebrated the glories of nature. Among these artist-enthusiasts were those associated with Futurism, a movement that began in Italy and that glorified modern urban structures and proclaimed the machine as the potential savior of humankind.

By the time World War II ended in 1945, however, there were few people left who would claim that technology was an unmixed blessing. The Nazi regime had harnessed technology to the most brutal and primitive impulses of mankind; rather than using it to save humans, Hitler's minions had employed it, with ruthless efficiency, to murder them. While genocide had been practiced before — on the Native American populations of North America, among others — it had never been so methodically carried out as it was in the Nazi concentration camps, where political dissidents, Gypsies, homosexuals, Slavs, and above all Jews had been killed with chemical gas

invented expressly for that purpose. Then the atomic bomb, an even more advanced method of destruction, was exploded over Japan. Although many diseases had been eradicated and many labor-saving devices had been invented to release people from drudgery, it was no longer possible to regard technological progress as a force for good alone. Its potential for evil and destruction had become frighteningly clear.

Many writers and artists struggled to come to terms with the threat to human life represented by the power of atomic weapons. While the American artist Jackson Pollock's abstract paintings don't address this issue directly — again, the only thing that could possibly be called their subject matter is the unconscious — there is nonetheless something about the chaos and energy of his work that seems unmistakably post-atomic; his explosions of paint, though not literally a depiction of the explosion of the bomb, suggest some of the power and terror that had been unleashed.

Even when science was not used for

Edmund Hillary and Tenzing Norgay

Sputnik I

1953
Tenzing Norgay and Edmund Hillary are the first
to reach the summit of Mount Everest

1957
Sputnik I goes into orbit

evil purposes, the dehumanizing effects of living in a mechanized world had begun to trouble many people. Were human beings not the masters but the slaves of technology? Was there a danger that they would become as mechanical and soulless, as devoid of feeling and conscience, as the vast machines they had created? Such questions became particularly urgent with the acceleration of technological progress that followed the War.

POLITICS AND PROGRESS The belief in social progress, too, grew less and less strong over the course of the modern era. The Depression that had afflicted the Western countries in the 1930s, leaving many homeless, hungry, and unemployed, had led many artists and intellectuals to place their faith in communism, which promised to create a workers' state in which no one would lack for the basic necessities or be treated as simply a tool in someone else's money-making schemes. Even the Stalinist purges in the 1930s and

the clear-sighted warnings of such writers as the English essayist and novelist George Orwell, a socialist whose innate honesty forced him to recognize that in actual practice the communist system was ruthlessly oppressive rather than conducive to a better life for all, had little effect on those who had seized on communism as the salvation of mankind.

But as the real nature of Soviet communism was finally exposed, it was impossible for people any longer to believe in its promises of an earthly paradise. Karl Marx, whose proposal of a system of state rather than private ownership had such an influence on twentieth century life, had been discredited except in certain parts of academia, where his theories still exert a powerful influence. In the world outside the university, however, disillusionment with communism had set in long before the dismantling of the communist bloc. Like the idea of salvation through technological progress that had enthralled so many people, the vision of social salvation through the elimination

*Independence
parade in
the Congo*

1960
17 African colonies achieve independence

of private property seemed bankrupt.

Perhaps partly because of this loss of faith in the idea of progress, there has come to be a renewed interest in non-Western cultures, particularly those whose traditions call for nature to be respected and served rather than conquered. Picasso had been strongly influenced by African carvings, as is evident in the jagged, elongated figures of the *Demoiselles*, and many other visual artists had taken their inspiration from the art of Africa or the Native American tribes or the Far East. Today there is a greater appreciation than ever of the world-view of ancient non-Western societies, even as the industrialized world continues to encroach on them. Rather than being dismissed as unsophisticated and "primitive," tribal cultures in particular are being hailed for their sense of the mysteries of nature and their rootedness in community. As a century of unprecedentedly rapid change draws to a close, admiration has grown for the durable wisdom of the pre-technological past.

Psychoanalysis

On the eve of the twentieth century, intellectuals and scientists were beginning to question whether all problems could be solved by the application of reason. Some even began to think about the enormous role that irrational behavior played in the history of civilization. One of these people was a Viennese neurologist named Sigmund Freud (**froid**) (1856–1939). Through his clinical studies of patients with psychiatric disorders, Freud came to believe that there were powerful drives and desires, which are not usually conscious, that control human behavior. These drives reside in a vast pool of the irrational, which Freud called the id, or the unconscious. The id does battle with the ego, or the individual, as it comes into contact with the rules, laws, and values of society at large, represented to the ego by what Freud called the superego. The superego acts as a conscience, attempting to control the irrational world of the id by repressing those desires and drives. This repression causes further conflict, often resulting in guilt, anxiety, or other psychological trauma. Psycho-analysis involves uncovering patterns of repression that go back to a person's earliest experience of life through hypnosis and the study of dreams. Freud's studies and theories brought to light ideas that shocked many people, particularly by challenging the concept of humans as rational beings. The following selection is an excerpt from his *History of the Psychoanalytic Movement* (1917). How does Freud envision the acceptance of his ideas?

THE INTERPRETATION OF DREAMS BECAME A SOLACE AND A support to me in those arduous first years of analysis, when I had to master the technique, clinical phenomena, and therapy of the neuroses [various mental or emotional disorders] all at the same time. At that period I was completely isolated and in the network of problems and accumulation of difficulties I often dreaded losing my bearings and also my confidence. There were often patients with whom an unaccountably long time elapsed before my hypothesis, that a neurosis was bound to become intelligible through analysis, proved true; but these patients' dreams, which might be regarded as analogues of their symptoms, almost always confirmed the hypothesis.

It was only my success in this direction that enabled me to persevere. The result is that I have acquired a habit of gauging the measure of a psychologist's understanding by his attitude to dream-interpretation; and I have observed with satisfaction that most of the opponents of psychoanalysis avoid this field altogether or else display remarkable clumsiness if they attempt to deal with it. Moreover, I soon saw the necessity of carrying out a self-analysis, and this I did with the help of a series of my own dreams which led me back through all the events of my childhood; and I am still of the opinion today that this kind of analysis may suffice for anyone who is a good dreamer and not too abnormal.

I think that by thus unrolling the story of the development of psychoanalysis I have shown what it is better than by a systematic description of it. I did not at first perceive the peculiar nature of what I had discovered. I unhesitatingly sacrificed my growing popularity as a doctor, and the increase in attendance during my consulting hours, by making a systematic enquiry into the sexual factors involved in the causation of my patients' neuroses; and this brought me a great many new facts which finally confirmed my conviction of the practical importance of the sexual factor. I innocently addressed a meeting of the Vienna Society for Psychiatry and Neurology, expecting that the material losses I had willingly undergone would be made up for by the interest and recognition of my colleagues. I treated my discoveries as ordinary contributions to science and hoped they would be received in the same spirit. But the silence which my communications met with, the void which formed itself about me, the hints that were conveyed to me, gradually made me realize that assertions on the part played by sexuality in the aetiology [the causes of a disease] of the neuroses cannot count upon meeting with the same kind of treatment as other communications. I understood that from now onwards I was one of those who have "disturbed the sleep of the world," as Hebbel [German dramatist] says, and that I could not reckon upon objectivity and tolerance....

I pictured the future as follows: — I should probably succeed in maintaining myself by means of the therapeutic success of the new procedure, but science would ignore me entirely during my lifetime; some decades later, someone else would infallibly come upon the same things—for which the time was not now ripe—would achieve recognition for them and bring me honor as a forerunner whose failure had been inevitable. Meanwhile, like Robinson Crusoe, I settled down as comfortably as possible on my desert island. When I look back to those lonely years, away from the pressures and confusions of today, it seems like a glorious heroic age. My "splendid isolation" was not without its advantages and charms. I did not have to read any publications, nor listen to any ill-informed opponents; I was not subject to influence from any quarter; there was nothing to hustle me…. Occasionally a colleague would make some reference to me in one of his publications; it would be very short and not at all flattering—words such as "eccentric," "extreme," or "very peculiar" would be used. It once happened that an assistant at the clinic in Vienna where I gave my University lectures asked me for permission to attend the course. He listened very attentively and said nothing; after the last lecture was over he offered to join me outside. As we walked away, he told me that with his chief's knowledge he had written a book combating my views; he regretted very much, however, that he had not first learnt more about them from my lectures, for in that case he would have written much of it differently. He had indeed enquired at the clinic whether he had not better first read *The Interpretation of Dreams*, but had been advised against doing so—it was not worth the trouble. He then himself compared the structure of my theory, so far as he now understood it, with that of the Catholic Church as regards its internal solidity. In the interests of the salvation of his soul, I shall assume that this remark implied a certain amount of appreciation. But he concluded by saying that it was too late to alter anything in his book, since it was already in print. Nor did my colleague think it necessary later to make any public avowal of his change of views on the subject of psychoanalysis; but preferred, in his capacity as a regular reviewer for a medical journal, to follow its development with flippant comments.

Whatever personal sensitiveness I possessed became blunted during those years, to my advantage. I was saved from becoming embittered, however, by a circumstance which is not always present to help lonely discoverers. Such people are as a rule tormented by the need to account for the lack of sympathy or the aversion of their contemporaries, and feel this attitude as a distressing contradiction of the security of their own sense of conviction. There was no need for me to feel so; for psychoanalytic theory enabled me to understand this attitude in my contemporaries and to see it as a necessary consequence of fundamental analytic premises. If it was true that the set of facts I had discovered were kept from the knowledge of patients themselves by internal resistances of an affective kind, then these resistances would be bound to appear in healthy people too, as soon as some external source confronted them with what was repressed. It was not surprising that they should be able to justify this rejection of my ideas on intellectual grounds though it was actually affective in origin. The same thing happened equally often with patients; the arguments they advanced were the same and were not precisely brilliant. In Falstaff's words, reasons are "as plenty as blackberries." The only difference was that with patients one was in a position to bring pressure to bear on them so as to induce them to get insight into their resistances and overcome them, whereas one had to do without this advantage in dealing with people who were ostensibly healthy. How to compel these healthy people to examine the matter in a cool and scientifically objective spirit was an unsolved problem which was best left to time to clear up. In the history of science one can clearly see that often the very proposition which has at first called out nothing but contradictions has later come to be accepted, although no new proofs in support of it have been brought forward.

THINKING CRITICALLY

1. *Recognizing Values* According to Freud, why did people reject his findings? Why did this not upset Freud?

2. *Making Inferences* Why did Freud's colleague not publicly recant his views after hearing Freud's lectures?

3. *Linking Past to Present* How important have Freud's theories become in today's world? Are they universally accepted?

WRITER'S PORTFOLIO

1. *Extending the Selection* Read the "Dream of July 23–24, 1895" from Section II of *The Interpretations of Dreams.* Write a summary of Freud's method of dream interpretation. Do you think it is foolproof?

2. *Examining Key Questions* According to Freud, what is the structure of the human personality?

The Theory of Relativity

In 1905, Albert Einstein (1879–1955), published a series of scientific papers that revolutionized the way we think of the universe and its physical laws and properties. Einstein's "Special Theory of Relativity" stated that time and space are not absolute concepts but are relative to the observer. An example Einstein used was of two trains traveling at different speeds on parallel tracks at the same time. A person traveling on one of the trains would not be aware of the overall speed of the two trains, but only of the relative speed of one to the other as the faster train eventually disappeared down the tracks. Einstein's theories were not only startling scientifically, but also intellectually. While most people have trouble understanding the Theory of Relativity, the idea that there are no absolutes or even a discernible reality in the universe strikes home. Here at last was the modern Newton. The following selection is a summary of Einstein's theory and its influence by the historian Paul Johnson. What was Einstein's reaction to the public furor over his theory?

THE MODERN WORLD BEGAN ON 29 MAY 1919 WHEN photographs of a solar eclipse, taken on the island of Principe off West Africa and at Sobral in Brazil, confirmed the truth of a new theory of the universe. It had been apparent for half a century that the Newtonian cosmology, based upon the straight lines of Euclidean geometry and Galileo's notions of absolute time, was in need of serious modification. It had stood for more than two hundred years. It was the framework within which the European Enlightenment, the Industrial Revolution, and the vast expansion of human knowledge, freedom and prosperity which characterized the nineteenth century, had taken place. But increasingly powerful telescopes were revealing anomalies. In particular, the motions of the planet Mercury deviated by forty-three seconds of arc a century from its predictable behavior under Newtonian laws of physics. Why?

In 1905, a twenty-six-year-old German Jew, Albert Einstein, then working in the Swiss patent office in Berne, had published a paper, "On the Electrodynamics of Moving Bodies," which became known as the Special Theory of Relativity. Einstein's observations on the way in which, in certain circumstances, lengths appeared to contract and clocks to slow down, are analogous to the effects of perspective in painting. In fact the discovery that space and time are relative rather than absolute terms of measurement is comparable, in its effect on our perception of the world, to the first use of perspective in art, which occurred in Greece in the two decades c. 500–480 B.C.

The originality of Einstein, amounting to a form of genius, and the curious elegance of his lines of argument, which colleagues compared to a kind of art, aroused growing, world-wide interest. In 1907 he published a demonstration that all mass has energy, encapsulated in the equation $E = mc^2$, which a later age saw as the starting point in the race for the A-bomb. Not even the onset of the European war prevented scientists from following his quest for an all-embracing General Theory of Relativity which would cover gravitational fields and provide a comprehensive revision of Newtonian physics. In 1915 news reached London that he had done it. The following spring, as the British were preparing their vast and catastrophic offensive on the Somme, the key paper was smuggled through the Netherlands and reached Cambridge, where it was received by Arthur Eddington, Professor of Astronomy and Secretary of the Royal Astronomical Society.

Eddington publicized Einstein's achievement in a 1918 paper for the Physical Society called "Gravitation and the Principle of Relativity." But it was of the essence of Einstein's methodology that he insisted his equations must be verified by empirical observation and he himself devised three specific tests for this purpose. The key one was that a ray of light just grazing the surface of the sun must be bent by 1.745 seconds of arc—twice the amount of gravitational deflection provided for by classical Newtonian theory. The experiment involved photographing a solar eclipse. The next was due on 29 May 1919. Before the end of the war, the Astronomer Royal, Sir Frank Dyson, had secured from a harassed government the promise of £1,000 to finance an expedition to take observations from Principe and Sobral....

Eddington's notebook records that on the morning of 29 May there was a tremendous thunderstorm in Principe. The clouds cleared just in time for the eclipse at 1:30 P.M. Eddington had only eight minutes in which to operate. "I did not see the eclipse, being too busy changing plates.... We took sixteen photographs." Thereafter, for six nights he developed the plates at the rate of two a night. On the evening of 3 June, having spent the whole day measuring the developed prints, he turned to his colleague [and informed him that] Einstein had been right....

From that point onward, Einstein was a global hero, in demand at every great university in the world, mobbed wherever he went, his wistful features familiar to hundreds of millions, the archetype of the abstracted natural philosopher. The impact of his theory was immediate, and cumulatively immeasurable. But it was to illustrate what Karl Popper was later to term "the law of unintended consequence." Innumerable books sought to explain clearly how the General Theory had altered the Newtonian concepts which, for ordinary men and women, formed their understanding of the world about them, and how it worked. Einstein himself summed it up thus: "The 'Principle of Relativity' in its widest sense is contained in the statement: The totality of physical phenomena is of such a character that it gives no basis for the introduction of the concept of 'absolute motion'; or, shorter but less precise: There is no absolute motion."

But for most people, to whom Newtonian physics, with their straight lines and right angles, were perfectly comprehensible, relativity never became more than a vague source of unease. It was grasped that absolute time and absolute length had been dethroned; that motion was curvilinear. All at once, nothing seemed certain in the movements of the spheres. "The world is out of joint," as Hamlet sadly observed. It was as though the spinning globe had been taken off its axis and cast adrift in a universe which no longer conformed to accustomed standards of measurement. At the beginning of the 1920s the belief began to circulate, for the first time at a popular level, that there were no longer any absolutes: of time and space, of good and evil, of knowledge, above all of value. Mistakenly but perhaps inevitably, relativity became confused with relativism.

No one was more distressed than Einstein by this public misapprehension. He was bewildered by the relentless publicity and error which his work seemed to promote. He wrote to his colleague Max Born on 9 September 1920: "Like the man in the fairy-tale who turned everything he touched into gold, so with me everything turns into a fuss in the newspapers." Einstein was not a practicing Jew, but he acknowledged a God. He believed passionately in absolute standards of right and wrong. His professional life was devoted to the quest not only for truth but for certitude. He insisted the world could be divided into subjective and objective spheres, and that one must be able to make precise statements about the objective portion. In the scientific (not the philosophical) sense he was a determinist. In the 1920s he found the indeterminacy principle of quantum mechanics not only unacceptable but abhorrent. For the rest of his life until his death in 1955 he sought to refute it by trying to anchor physics in a unified field theory. He wrote to Born: "You believe in a God who plays dice, and I in complete law and order in a world which objectively exists and which I, in a wildly speculative way, am trying to capture. I firmly *believe*, but I hope that someone will discover a more realistic way or rather a more tangible basis than it has been my lot to find." But Einstein failed to produce a unified theory, either in the 1920s or thereafter. He lived to see moral relativism, to him a disease, become a social pandemic, just as he lived to see his fatal equation bring into existence nuclear warfare. There were times, he said at the end of his life, when he wished he had been a simple watchmaker.

THINKING CRITICALLY

1. *Drawing Conclusions* Why did Einstein sometimes wish he had been a watchmaker? What is he saying about modern science?

2. *Recognizing Values* Why did so many people find the Theory of Relativity discomforting? Why did it become confused with relativism (the belief that there are no moral absolutes)?

3. *Linking Past to Present* The work of Einstein and his fellow atomic theorists were the first scientific theories which only trained scientists could understand. How has the growing complexity of science throughout this century affected science's place in society? in education?

WRITER'S PORTFOLIO

1. *Extending the Selection* Look up Werner Heisenberg's "Uncertainty Principle" and summarize it. Is it comparable to Einstein's theory?

2. *Examining Key Questions* Based on this reading, in what ways did Einstein's Theory of Relativity shape the twentieth century?

Post-Impressionism

While the Impressionist paintings of late nineteenth-century (see pages 483–485) differed from those of earlier, classical period in their structure and the brilliance of their often shimmering color, these pictures were still representational and realistic. A person in a portrait is recognizable; a landscape is a definite place; a still life depicts discernible objects. In the Post-Impressionist world, this realism began disappearing. The growing popularity of the camera, Freud's theories, and the influence of non-western art, all caused early twentieth century painters to become increasingly averse to being "imitators of nature." The five painters in this section each represent a significant early Post-Impressionist art movement: Fauvism, Cubism, Futurism, Surrealism (or fantasy), and pure Abstractionism. *The Roofs of Collioure*, by Henri Matisse (1869–1954), see page 557, a member of the Fauves (the "wild beasts," so-called because their first exhibit shocked the critics with its violent color and bold distortions), recalls Japanese prints with its sinuous lines, flat planes, and the merest hint of perspective. Pablo Picasso (1881–1973), generally considered the greatest and most versatile artist of the twentieth century, developed his Cubist style by trying to replace the representational painting with an intellectual concept of form and structure. In practice this meant superimposing multiple views of an object on one canvas. *Les Demoiselles d'Avignon*, which appears on page 557, reduces the natural forms of these five nudes to their basic geometric shapes. Umberto Boccioni (ŭm ber′tō bot chō′nē) (1882–1916), also known as a sculptor, was the major figure of the Futurist movement in Italy. He deplored the lure of Romanticism stressing instead the violence of the modern world and a celebration of the modern machine. Boccioni's *Riot in the Gallery*, which appears on page 558, typically emphasizes violent motion and vivid coloring. Wassily Kandinsky (1866–1944), an Abstractionist, founded a group of Munich artists who called themselves *Der Blaue Reiter* (the blue rider) and were influenced by the Fauves. In works such as

Painting with Green Center, which appears on page 558, the artist's imagination and intuition are expressed through geometric shapes rather than natural forms, and the abstract title is less descriptive of the painting than of the emotions the artist was expressing. The work of Giorgio de Chirico (jōr⁄jō dā kē⁄rē kō) (1888–1978) was a forerunner of the full-blown surrealism of the post-World War I period. *The Mystery and Melancholy of a Street*, is typical of his haunting perspective pictures of a lonely world. What traits are common to these five paintings?

Giorgio de Chirico, The Mystery and Melancholy of a Street *(1914)*

THINKING CRITICALLY

1. *Making Comparisons* What is the tone of each of these paintings? How has the artist manipulated color? line? perspective? light?

2. *Drawing Conclusions* The paintings in this section were all painted in the decade before World War I. Can you find any evidence of the artists' anticipation of that conflict?

3. *Linking Past and Present* Most of the Post-Impressionists were believers in "Art for Art's sake." Do you think that is the appropriate role for artists today?

WRITER'S PORTFOLIO

1. *Extending the Selection* Write a short narrative description of what you think is occurring in de Chirico's painting.

2. *Examining Key Questions* What were these artists trying to say about the relationship between the art of painting and realistic depiction?

World War I

World War I began with a tremendous wave of enthusiasm throughout the nations entering the war. Large numbers of young men joined up ready to fight, expecting a short, glorious war. Instead they were swept up in the most destructive war in history up until that time. Advances in technology — such as the machine gun and barbed wire — allowed the armies to create almost impregnable trench fortifications along the Western Front across France and Belgium. Behind these trenches, each side was able to inflict horrendous casualties on its attackers; a type of war memorably described as "eye-deep in hell." Many of the soldiers on both sides, but particularly the English, responded to this terrible slaughter by writing poetry which combined lyricism with anger and despair. Wilfred Owen (1893–1918) was probably the finest English war poet. "Anthem for a Doomed Youth" and "Dulce et Decorum Est" both display Owen's verbal mastery and his intense emotional response to the war. While Owen wrote in a traditional mode, using meter and rhyme, August Stramm (1874–1915), a German expressionistic poet, responded very differently to the war. Stramm's poems are far less emotional, but more expressive of the mechanistic, inhuman conflict of which he and Owen were a part. Stramm uses his words and sentence structure, not as we might in conversation, but in short, resonant expressions of horror. What is the tone of each of the following poems?

Wilfred Owen

Anthem for Doomed Youth

What passing-bells for these who die as cattle?
    —Only the monstrous anger of the guns.
    Only the stuttering rifles' rapid rattle
Can patter out their hasty orisons.
No mockeries now for them; no prayers nor bells;
    Nor any voice of mourning save the choirs,—

The shrill demented choirs of wailing shells;
        And bugles calling for them from sad shires.

What candles may be held to speed them all?
        Not in the hands of boys but in their eyes
Shall shine the holy glimmers of goodbyes.
        The pallor of girls' brows shall be their pall;
Their flowers the tenderness of patient minds,
And each slow dusk a drawing-down of blinds.

Dulce et Decorum Est

Bent double, like old beggars under sacks,
Knock-kneed, coughing like hags, we cursed through sludge,
Till on the haunting flares we turned our backs
And towards our distant rest began to trudge.
Men marched asleep. Many had lost their boots
But limped on, blood-shod. All went lame; all blind;
Drunk with fatigue; deaf even to the hoots
Of tired, outstripped Five-Nines[1] that dropped behind.

Gas! Gas! Quick, boys! — An ecstasy of fumbling,
Fitting the clumsy helmets just in time;
But someone still was yelling out and stumbling,
And flound'ring like a man in fire or lime…
Dim, through the misty panes and thick green light,
As under a green sea, I saw him drowning.

In all my dreams, before my helpless sight,
He plunges at me, guttering, choking, drowning.

If in some smothering dreams you too could pace
Behind the wagon that we flung him in,
And watch the white eyes writhing in his face,
His hanging face, like a devil's sick of sin;
If you could hear, at every jolt, the blood
Come gargling from the froth-corrupted lungs,
Obscene as cancer, bitter as the cud
Of vile, incurable sores on innocent tongues,—

---

1. **Five-Nines.** 5.9 inch caliber artillery shells

My friend, you would not tell with such high zest
To children ardent for some desperate glory,
The old Lie: Dulce et decorum est
Pro patria mori.[2]

August Stramm

Battlefield

Clod softness lulls iron off to sleep
bloods clot ooze patches
rusts crumble
fleshes slime
sucking ruts around decay
child eyes
blink
murder upon murder

Assault

From all corners fears yell pluck
scream
life
lashes
along
before
it
gasping death
the heavens shred
blindly horror butchers out wildly

Shells

Knowing stops
only sensing endures and deludes
deafness deafens ghastly wounds
rumbling fumbling burrowing screaming
shrieking whistling whizzing whirring
splintering crashing cracking crunching
cramping stamping

---

2. **Dulce et decorum est pro patria mori,** from the Roman poet Horace's odes, "It is sweet
   and honorable to die for one's country."

The sky stumps
the stars cinder
time undreads
Doggedness worlds shy space

War-Grave
Stakes implore crossed arms
writing falters the pale unknown
flowers impertinence dusts intimidate
faint light
runs with tears
glazes
forgetfulness

THINKING CRITICALLY

1. *Recognizing Values* Are Owen and Stramm expressing a similar attitude toward the war? Why or why not?

2. *Making Comparisons* Compare how Owen and Stramm express themselves. Which poems seem more appropriate to their subject matter? Which seem more impersonal? Which do you like better?

3. *Linking Past to Present* Are the attitudes toward war expressed in these poems similar to the attitudes toward war held by people today? Explain.

WRITER'S PORTFOLIO

1. *Extending the Selection* Write short summaries of the Stramm poems. Before you begin, determine how you think the poems should be punctuated.

2. *Examining Key Questions* Why do you think the experiences expressed by these poets would contribute to a general feeling of loss and the senselessness of life in the years following World War I?

Dadaism

In 1912, Marcel Duchamp (mär sel′ dY shäN′) (1887–1968) painted the second version of his *Nude Descending a Staircase*. This painting quickly grew famous because of its rejection by other Cubist artists exhibiting at the 1912 Salon des Indépendants show in Paris — they objected to its literary title and explicit subject — and the sensation it caused at the first major American exhibit of truly modern art, the 1913 Armory Show. Duchamp's painting was a structure of lines and shapes, giving the impression of form and movement, and which neatly anticipated the attitudes of Dadaism. This literary and artistic movement began in Zurich with the writer Tristan Tzara (tsä′rä) (1896–1963), who chose the word *dada* (French for a child's rocking horse) at random from an open dictionary. There are a wide variety of Dadaist works, from Hans Arp's collages and relief sculpture to Duchamp's mobiles and "found" sculpture to Man Ray's camera-less photographic images. Many of their works — like Tzara's poems composed of words cut from a newspaper, scattered on a table and picked up at random — were either fantastic or markedly, deliberately satirical. Chance, and hence a mockery of reason and logic were a key part of Dadaism. The following selection is from a lecture Tzara delivered in 1922. What would you say are the principles of Dadaism?

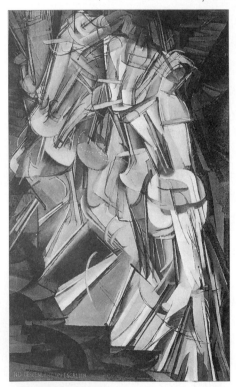

Marcel Duchamp, Nude Descending a Staircase, No. 2 *(1912)*

    I don't have to tell you that for the general public and for you, the refined public, a Dadaist is the equivalent of a leper. But that is only a manner of speaking. When these same people get close to us, they treat us with that remnant of elegance that comes from their old habit of belief in progress. At ten yards distance, hatred begins again. If you ask me why, I won't be able to tell you.

Another characteristic of Dada is the continuous breaking off of our friends. They are always breaking off and resigning. The first to tender his resignation from the Dada movement was myself. Everybody knows that Dada is nothing. I broke away from Dada and from myself as soon as I understood the implications of nothing....

These observations of everyday conditions have led us to a realization which constitutes our minimum basis of agreement, aside from the sympathy which binds us and which is inexplicable. It would not have been possible for us to found our agreement on principles. For everything is relative. What are the Beautiful, the Good, Art, Freedom? Words that have a different meaning for every individual. Words with the pretension of creating agreement among all, and that is why they are written with capital letters. Words which have not the moral value and objective force that people have grown accustomed to finding in them. Their meaning changes from one individual, one epoch, one country to the next. Men are different. It is diversity that makes life interesting. There is no common basis in men's minds. The unconscious is inexhaustible and uncontrollable. Its force surpasses us. It is as mysterious as the last particle of a brain cell. Even if we knew it, we could not reconstruct it....

We have had enough of the intelligent movements that have stretched beyond measure our credulity in the benefits of science. What we want now is spontaneity. Not because it is better or more beautiful than anything else. But because everything that issues freely from ourselves, without the intervention of speculative ideas, represents us. We must intensify this quantity of life that readily spends itself in every quarter. Art is not the most precious manifestation of life. Art has not the celestial and universal value that people like to attribute to it. Life is far more interesting. Dada knows the correct measure that should be given to art: with subtle, perfidious methods, Dada introduces it into daily life. And vice versa. In art, Dada reduces everything to an initial simplicity, growing always more relative. It mingles its caprices with the chaotic wind of creation and the barbaric dances of savage tribes. It wants logic reduced to a personal minimum, while literature in its view should be primarily intended for the individual who makes it. Words have a weight of their own and lend themselves to abstract construction. The absurd has no terrors for me, for from a more exalted point of view everything in life seems absurd to me. Only the elasticity of our conventions creates a bond between disparate acts. The Beautiful and the True in art do not exist; what interests me is the intensity of a personality transposed directly, clearly into the work; the man and his vitality; the angle from which he regards the elements and in what manner he knows how to gather sensation, emotion, into a lacework of words and sentiments.

Dada tries to find out what words mean before using them, from the point of view not of grammar but of representation. Objects and colors pass through the same filter. It is not the new technique that interests us, but the spirit. Why do you want us to be preoccupied with a pictorial, moral, poetic, literary, political or social renewal? We are well aware that these renewals of means are merely the successive cloaks of the various epochs of history, uninteresting questions of fashion and facade. We are well aware that people in the costumes of the Renaissance were pretty much the same as the people of today, and that Chuang-Tzu [Taoist philosopher] was just as Dada as we are. You are mistaken if you take Dada for a modern school, or even for a reaction against the schools of today. Several of my statements have struck you as old and natural, what better proof that you were Dadaist without knowing it, perhaps even before the birth of Dada.

THINKING CRITICALLY

1. *Making Comparisons* How does Tzara's lecture reflect Duchamp's painting style? What are both of them aiming at?

2. *Identifying Central Issues* Throughout his lecture, Tzara refuses to set forth any clear principles of Dadaism. What would you say are some of Dadaism's principles?

3. *Linking Past and Present* Can you find examples of Dada's negation of art and expansion of artistic boundaries in recent art?

WRITER'S PORTFOLIO

1. *Extending the Selection* Of the five Post-Impressionist artists discussed on pages 512–513, which seems to have influenced Duchamp the most and in what way?

2. *Examining Key Questions* What do Tzara's lecture and Duchamp's painting suggest about intellectual and artistic life after World War I?

Women and Literature

One of the major figures in modern literature was Virginia Woolf (1882–1941). Woolf's father was the writer and literary critic Leslie Stephen and she received an exceptional education. In 1912, she married Leonard Woolf and they began the Hogarth Press, a small publishing house which allowed them to publish works they admired and respected. Woolf's major concern, however, was her own writing, and she produced some of the finest, most experimental fiction of the time. Her attention focused on time in such a way that her writing sometimes seemed more like lyric poetry than fiction. Woolf perfected a narrative technique known as stream of consciousness, organizing her novels according to the way thoughts, feelings, perceptions, and memories tumble through the mind, rather than using a straight narrative chronology. In addition to fiction, Woolf wrote essays expressing her concern that women should be allowed, and indeed encouraged, to realize their potential artistically and professionally; her most famous essay, "A Room of One's Own," which is excerpted below, is about the artistic life of women. In this essay, Woolf acutely analyzes the social conditions that have kept women from realizing their artistic potential. Her writing has served to inspire readers, men as well as women, to see the world from a feminist point of view, a view that takes women into account as deserving of an equal chance in this world. What is the paradox Woolf presents about the historical place of women in society?

IT WAS DISAPPOINTING NOT TO HAVE BROUGHT BACK IN THE evening some important statement, some authentic fact. Women are poorer than men because—this or that. Perhaps now it would be better to give up seeking for the truth, and receiving on one's head an avalanche of opinion hot as lava, discolored as dish-water. It would be better to draw the curtains; to shut out distractions; to light the lamp; to narrow the enquiry and to ask the historian, who records not opinions but facts, to describe under what conditions women lived, not throughout the ages, but in England, say in the time of Elizabeth.

For it is a perennial puzzle why no woman wrote a word of that extraordinary literature when every other man, it seemed, was capable of song or sonnet. What were the conditions in which women lived, I asked myself; for fiction, imaginative work that it is, is not dropped like a pebble upon the ground, as science may be; fiction is like a spider's web, attached ever so lightly perhaps, but still attached to life at all four corners. Often the attachment is scarcely perceptible; Shakespeare's plays, for instance, seem to hang there complete by themselves. But when the web is pulled askew, hooked up at the edge, torn in the middle, one remembers that these webs are not spun in midair by incorporeal creatures, but are the work of suffering human beings, and are attached to grossly material things, like health and money and the houses we live in.

I went, therefore, to the shelf where the histories stand and took down one of the latest, Professor Trevelyan's *History of England*. Once more I looked up Women, found "position of," and turned to the pages indicated. "Wife-beating," I read, "was a recognized right of man, and was practiced without shame by high as well as low.... Similarly," the historian goes on, "the daughter who refused to marry the gentleman of her parents' choice was liable to be locked up, beaten, and flung about the room, without any shock being inflicted on public opinion. Marriage was not an affair of personal affection, but of family avarice, particularly in the 'chivalrous' upper classes.... Betrothal often took place while one or both of the parties was in the cradle, and marriage when they were scarcely out of the nurses' charge." That was about 1470, soon after Chaucer's time. The next reference to the position of women is some two hundred years later, in the time of the Stuarts. "It was still the exception for women of the upper and middle class to choose their own husbands, and when the husband had been assigned, he was lord and master, so far at least as law and custom could make him. Yet even so," Professor Trevelyan concludes, "neither Shakespeare's women nor those of authentic seventeenth-century memoirs, like the Verneys and the Hutchinsons, seem wanting in personality and character."... Certainly, if we consider it, Cleopatra [heroine of Shakespeare's *Antony and Cleopatra*] must have had a way with her; Lady Macbeth, one would suppose, had a will of her own; Rosalind [heroine of Shakespeare's *As You Like It*], one might conclude, was an attractive girl. Professor Trevelyan is speaking no more than the truth when he remarks that Shakespeare's women do not seem wanting in personality and character. Indeed, if woman had no existence save in the fiction written by men, one would imagine her a person of the utmost importance; very various; heroic and mean; splendid and sordid; infinitely beautiful and hideous in the extreme; as great as a man, some think even greater. But this is woman in fiction. In fact, as Professor Trevelyan points out, she was locked up, beaten, and flung about the room.

A very queer, composite being thus emerges. Imaginatively she is of the highest importance; practically she is completely insignificant. She pervades poetry from cover to cover; she is all but absent from history. She dominates the lives of kings and conquerors in fiction; in fact she was the slave of any boy whose parents forced a ring upon her finger. Some of the most inspired words, some of the most profound thoughts in literature fall from her lips; in real life she could hardly read, could scarcely spell, and was the property of her husband....

It would have been extremely odd had one of them suddenly written the plays of Shakespeare, I concluded, and I thought of that old gentleman, who is dead now, but was a bishop, I think, who declared that it was impossible for any woman, past, present, or to come, to have the genius of Shakespeare. He wrote to the papers about it. He also told a lady who applied to him for information that cats do not as a matter of fact go to heaven, though they have, he added, souls of a sort. How much thinking those old gentlemen used to save one! How the borders of ignorance shrank back at their approach! Cats do not go to heaven. Women cannot write the plays of Shakespeare.

Be that as it may, I could not help thinking, as I looked at the works of Shakespeare on the shelf, that the bishop was right at least in this; it would have been impossible, completely and entirely, for any woman to have written the plays of Shakespeare in the age of Shakespeare. Let me imagine, since facts are so hard to come by, what would have happened had Shakespeare had a wonderfully gifted sister, called Judith, let us say. Shakespeare himself went, very probably — his mother was an heiress — to the grammar school, where he may have learnt Latin — Ovid, Virgil, and Horace — and the elements of grammar and logic. He was, it is well known, a wild boy who poached rabbits, perhaps shot a deer, and had, rather sooner than he should have done, to marry a woman in the neighborhood, who bore him a child rather quicker than was right. That escapade sent him to seek his fortune in London. He had, it seemed, a taste for the theater; he began by holding horses at the stage door. Very soon he got work in the theater, became a successful actor, and lived at the hub of the universe, meeting everybody, knowing everybody, practicing his art on the boards, exercising his wits in the streets, and even getting access to the palace of the queen. Meanwhile his extraordinarily gifted sister, let us suppose, remained at home. She was as adventurous, as imaginative, as agog to see the world as he was. But she was not sent to school. She had no chance of learning grammar and logic, let alone of reading Horace and Virgil. She picked up a book now and then, one of her brother's perhaps, and read a few pages. But then her parents came in and told her to mend the stockings or mind the stew and not moon about with books and papers. They would have spoken sharply but kindly, for they were substantial people who knew the conditions of life for a woman and loved their daughter — indeed, more likely than not she was the apple of her father's eye. Perhaps she scribbled some pages up in an apple loft on the sly, but was careful to hide them or set fire to them. Soon, however, before she was out of her teens, she was to be betrothed to the son of a neighboring wool-stapler [seller of wool]. She cried out that marriage was hateful to her, and for that she was severely beaten by her father. Then he ceased to scold her. He begged her instead not to hurt him, not to shame him in this matter of her marriage. He would give her a chain of beads or a fine petticoat, he said; and there were tears in his eyes. How could she disobey him? How could she break his heart? The force of her own gift alone drove her to it. She made up a small parcel of her belongings, let herself down by a rope one summer's night and took the road to London. She was not seventeen. The birds that sang in the hedge were not more musical than she was. She had the quickest fancy, a gift like her brother's, for the tune of words. Like him, she had a taste for the theater. She stood at the stage door; she wanted to act, she said. Men laughed in her face. The manager — a fat, loose-lipped man — guffawed. He bellowed something about poodles dancing and women acting — no woman, he said, could possibly be an actress. He hinted — you can imagine what. She could get no training in her craft. Could she even seek her dinner in a tavern or roam the streets at midnight? Yet her genius was for fiction and lusted to feed abundantly upon the lives of men and women and the study of their ways. At last — for she was very young, oddly like Shakespeare the poet in her face, with the same grey eyes and rounded brows — at last Nick Green the actor-manager took pity on her; she found herself with child by that gentleman and so — who shall measure the heat and violence of the poet's heart when caught and tangled in a woman's body? — killed herself one winter's night and lies buried at some crossroads where the omnibuses now stop outside the Elephant and Castle.

That, more or less, is how the story would run, I think, if a woman in Shakespeare's day had had Shakespeare's genius. But for my part, I agree with the deceased bishop, if such he was — it is unthinkable that any woman in Shakespeare's day should have had Shakespeare's genius. For genius like Shakespeare's is not born among laboring, uneducated, servile people. It was not born in England among the Saxons and the Britons. It is not born today among the working classes. How, then, could it have been born among women whose work began, according to Professor Trevelyan, almost before they were out of the nursery, who were forced to it by their parents and held to it by all the power of law and custom? Yet genius of a sort must have existed among women as it must have existed among the working classes.... Indeed, I would venture to guess that Anon, who wrote so many poems without signing them, was often a woman. It was a woman Edward FitzGerald [poet and translator], I think, suggested who made the ballads and the folk songs, crooning them to her children, beguiling her spinning with them, or the length of the winter's night.

THINKING CRITICALLY

1. *Identifying Key Concepts* What point is Woolf trying to make through this hypothetical story of Shakespeare's sister?

2. *Recognizing Values* What values seem to be the most important to Woolf?

3. *Linking Past to Present* Compare the status of women today with that of women during Shakespeare's day.

WRITER'S PORTFOLIO

1. *Extending the Selection* Virginia Woolf is considered one of the finest English novelists. Research her life. Did she suffer from the same sort of societal discouragement Shakespeare's sister might have? Explain.

2. *Examining Key Questions* According to Woolf, what factors go into shaping an individual's personality?

Pacifism

Mohandas K. Gandhi (1869–1948), was the son of a middle-class Indian family. He studied law in London and upon receiving his degree, worked for an Indian law firm with offices in South Africa, where he defended his countrymen from the racist policies there. It was at this time that Gandhi began developing his ideas about non-violent or passive resistance in the face of unjust policies and laws. In the years after World War I, Gandhi lead the Indians in a non-violent revolt against British rule in India. Gandhi based his philosophy of non-violent resistance on the ancient Hindu concept of *ahimsa*, or reverence for life. Also the concept of *satyagraha*, or soul-force played an essential role in Gandhi's belief that it was only through love and non-violence that humans are truly capable of overcoming the opposition, no matter how brutal it might be. Gandhi lived his philosophy, wearing the clothes of a peasant, spinning his own cotton for his clothing every day, and fasting for long periods of time as part of his program of noncooperation with the British government. Although imprisoned many times, Gandhi held fast to his ideals and goals. He gathered an enormous following and gave the people of India a sense of purpose and the means to achieve independence, which they did in 1947. The following is an excerpt from *Hind Swaraj (Independent India)*, a dialogue Gandhi wrote to express his ideas about passive resistance. What are its four tenets?

EDITOR. Passive resistance is a method of securing rights by personal suffering; it is the reverse of resistance by arms. When I refuse to do a thing that is repugnant to my conscience, I use soul-force. For instance, the government of the day has passed a law which is applicable to me. I do not like it. If by using violence I force the government to repeal the law, I am employing what may be termed body-force. If I do not obey the law and accept the penalty for its breach, I use soul-force. It involves sacrifice of self.

Everybody admits that sacrifice of self is infinitely superior to sacrifice of others. Moreover, if this kind of force is used in a cause that is unjust, only the person using it suffers. He does not make others suffer for his mistakes. Men have before now done many things which were subsequently found to have been wrong. No man can claim that he is absolutely in the right or that a particular thing is wrong because he thinks so, but it is wrong for him so long as that is his deliberate judgment. It is therefore meet that he should not do that which he knows to be wrong, and suffer the consequence whatever it may be. This is the key to the use of soul-force.

READER. You would then disregard laws — this is rank disloyalty. We have always been considered a law-abiding nation. You seem to be going even beyond the extremists. They say that we must obey the laws that have been passed, but that if the laws be bad, we must drive out the lawgivers even by force.

EDITOR. Whether I go beyond them or whether I do not is a matter of no consequence to either of us. We simply want to find out what is right and to act accordingly. The real meaning of the statement that we are a law-abiding nation is that we are passive resisters. When we do not like certain laws, we do not break the heads of law-givers but we suffer and do not submit to the laws. That we should obey laws whether good or bad is a new-fangled notion. There was no such thing in former days. The people disregarded those laws they did not like and suffered the penalties for their breach. It is contrary to our manhood if we obey laws repugnant to our conscience. Such teaching is opposed to religion and means slavery. If the government were to ask us to go about without any clothing, should we do so? If I were a passive resister, I would say to them that I would have nothing to do with their law. But we have so forgotten ourselves and become so compliant that we do not mind any degrading law.....

READER. From what you say I deduce that passive resistance is a splendid weapon of the weak, but that when they are strong they may take up arms.

EDITOR. This is gross ignorance. Passive resistance, that is, soul-force, is matchless. It is superior to the force of arms. How, then, can it be considered only a weapon of the weak? Physical-force men are strangers to the courage that is requisite in a passive resister. Do you believe that a coward can ever disobey a law that he dislikes? Extremists are considered to be advocates of brute force. Why do they, then, talk about obeying laws? I do not blame them. They can say nothing else. When they succeed in driving out the English and they themselves become governors, they will want you and me to obey their laws. And that is a fitting thing for their constitution. But a passive resister will say he will not obey a law that is against his conscience, even though he may be blown to pieces at the mouth of a cannon.

What do you think? Wherein is courage required—in blowing others to pieces from behind a cannon, or with a smiling face to approach a cannon and be blown to pieces? Who is the true warrior—he who keeps death always as a bosom-friend, or he who controls the death of others? Believe me that a man devoid of courage and manhood can never be a passive resister.

This however, I will admit: that even a man weak in body is capable of offering this resistance.

After a great deal of experience it seems to me that those who want to become passive resisters for the service of the country have to observe perfect chastity, adopt poverty, follow truth, and cultivate fearlessness.

Chastity is one of the greatest disciplines without which the mind cannot attain requisite firmness. A man who is unchaste loses stamina, becomes emasculated and cowardly. He whose mind is given over to animal passions is not capable of any great effort. This can be proved by innumerable instances. What, then, is a married person to do is the question that arises naturally; and yet it need not. When a husband and wife gratify the passions, it is no less an animal indulgence on that account. Such an indulgence, except for perpetuating the race, is strictly prohibited. But a passive resister has to avoid even that very limited indulgence because he can have no desire for progeny. A married man, therefore, can observe perfect chastity.

Just as there is necessity for chastity, so is there for poverty. Pecuniary ambition and passive resistance cannot well go together. Those who have money are not expected to throw it away, but they *are* expected to be indifferent about it. They must be prepared to lose every penny rather than give up passive resistance.

Passive resistance has been described in the course of our discussion as truth-force. Truth, therefore, has necessarily to be followed and that at any cost. In this connection, academic questions such as whether a man may not lie in order to save a life, etc., arise, but these questions occur only to those who wish to justify lying. Those who want to follow truth every time are not placed in such a quandary; and if they are, they are still saved from a false position.

Passive resistance cannot proceed a step without fearlessness. Those alone can follow the path of passive resistance who are free from fear, whether as to their possessions, false honor, their relatives, the government, bodily injuries, or death.

These observances are not to be abandoned in the belief that they are difficult. Nature has implanted in the human breast ability to cope with any difficulty or suffering that may come to man unprovoked. These qualities are worth having, even for those who do not wish to serve the country. Let there be no mistake, as those who want to train themselves in the use of arms are also obliged to have these qualities more or less. Everybody does not become a warrior for the wish. A would-be warrior will have to observe chastity and to be satisfied with poverty as his lot. A warrior without fearlessness cannot be conceived of. It may be thought that he would not need to be exactly truthful, but that quality follows real fearlessness. When a man abandons truth, he does so owing to fear in some shape or form. The above four attributes, then, need not frighten anyone. It may be as well here to note that a physical-force man has to have many other useless qualities which a passive resister never needs. And you will find that whatever extra effort a swordsman needs is due to lack of fearlessness. If he is an embodiment of the latter, the sword will drop from his hand that very moment. He does not need its support. One who is free from hatred requires no sword.

THINKING CRITICALLY

1. *Identifying Central Issues* What does Gandhi mean by "soul-force"? What is its opposite?

2. *Recognizing Values* What must a passive resister do to be successful? What values must such a person hold?

3. *Linking Past to Present* Can you think of people who have followed Gandhi's example? What were their causes? Were they successful?

WRITER'S PORTFOLIO

1. *Extending the Selection* Pretend you are a follower of Gandhi's method. Write a letter to a newspaper explaining Gandhi's philosophy and your response to it.

2. *Examining Key Questions* Do you think passive-resistance is a powerful method of protest?

The Urban Image

It was not until the second-half of the nineteenth century that photography became a widely-used medium. With advances in technology—better lenses, smaller cameras, artificial lights, the use of paper instead of glass or metal for final impressions—photography found the potential to become a legitimate art form. In the United States, no one initially did more to achieve artistic status for photography than Alfred Stieglitz (1864–1946). As an engineering student in Germany, he had impulsively bought a camera, mastered it, and begun winning awards in Europe for his work. In 1902, he opened a gallery in New York City, the "291," which served as a headquarters for the development of photographic art in America.

Alfred Stieglitz, From the Shelton: The G.E. Building *(c. 1931–1932)*

Stieglitz's photographs of New York City show him at his technically most brilliant, carefully controlling the light and composition of his photographs, while recording the birth of the modern city. Berenice Abbott (1898–1991) was another American photographer who in 1929 began "the task of photographing not only the outward aspect of [New York City], but its very spirit." Abbott was concerned with capturing the structural and technical beauty of modern urban life. In 1926, the Hungarian photographer André Kertész (**an′drä kėr tezh′**) (1893–1985) settled in Paris; his city photographs often artfully, often wittily juxtapose people and man-made artifacts in order to comment on both. Henri Cartier-Bresson (**äNrē′ Kä tēā′-bresôn′**)

(b. 1908) is particularly noted for his ability to wait for the precise moment when subject, event, and form coalesce. His pictures of the city of Paris and its inhabitants show a remarkable eye for the ironic and artful photograph. Kertész and Cartier-Bresson were essentially people photographers, concentrating on motion and appearance, while Stieglitz and Abbot favored the composition and structure of the city and form. Do you think the photographers in this section regard the city as benign or malevolent?

Berenice Abbott, Exchange Place, New York *(c. 1934)*

Berenice Abbott, Nightview, New York *(1932)*

André Kertész, Shadows of the Eiffel Tower *(1929)*

Henri Cartier-Bresson, Quai Saint-Bernard *(1933)*

THINKING CRITICALLY

1. *Making Comparisons* Stieglitz and Abbott are Americans; Kertész and Cartier-Bresson are Europeans. What differences can you discern in their approach to the modern city?

2. *Drawing Conclusions* What appears to be the dominant attitude toward cities evident in these pictures? Whose picture best illustrates it? Whose picture least illustrates it?

3. *Linking Past and Present* How do you think these photographers would picture the city of today? Would Abbott's celebration of the sleek lines of architecture still be possible? What about Kertész's blending of people and the city?

WRITER'S PORTFOLIO

1. *Extending the Selection* Using one of the photographs in this section, write either a poem or a prose poem in praise of this "urban image."

2. *Examining Key Questions* If you were to judge by these pictures alone, what are a city's qualities of greatness?

The Holocaust

To those who served in World War I, it seemed impossible that war could grow more brutal. Yet that is just what happened during World War II. It is estimated that casualties for this war passed the fifty million mark, with more than sixty percent of these civilians. The most brutal event of all was the Nazi "final solution"; the attempt by the Germans to systematically annihilate the Jews and assorted other "undesirables" of Europe. More than six million people were killed in one of the most horrifying events of world history. Every Jew who could be identified was herded off to a concentration camp, where they were put to work until physically exhausted and then murdered. At Auschwitz alone, one of the principal concentration camps in Poland, more than three million men, women, and children were put to death between 1941 and 1945. In 1943, Primo Levi (1919–1987), an Italian Jew, had the misfortune to be sent to Auschwitz, but he survived until the Russians liberated the camp in 1945. In 1958, his book *If This Was a Man* told the story of his life at Auschwitz and how, in spite of the atrocities that he was forced to witness, he remained a man of compassion. In the following selection, Levi is chosen to help his friend Jean, who serves as the Pikolo or messenger-clerk for the German commander, bring back the soup to the camp. As they walk, Levi tries to recall a passage from Dante's *Divine Comedy* (see pages 210–214). Why does Levi start reciting Dante?

H<small>E CLIMBED OUT AND</small> I <small>FOLLOWED HIM, BLINKING IN THE</small> brightness of the day. It was warmish outside, the sun drew a faint smell of paint and tar from the greasy earth, which made me think of a holiday beach of my infancy. Pikolo gave me one of the two wooden poles, and we walked under a clear June sky.

I began to thank him, but he stopped me: it was not necessary. One could see the Carpathians covered in snow. I breathed in fresh air, I felt unusually light-hearted.

"Tu es fou de marcher si vite. On a le temps, tu sais." [You're crazy to walk so fast. We have time, you know.] The ration was collected half a mile away; one had to return with the pot weighing over a hundred pounds supported on the two poles. It was quite a tiring task, but it meant a pleasant walk there without a load, and the ever-welcome chance of going near the kitchens.

We slowed down. Pikolo was expert. He had chosen the path cleverly so that we would have to make a long detour, walking at least for an hour, without arousing suspicion. We spoke of our houses, of Strasbourg and Turin, of the books we had read, of what we had studied, of our mothers: how all mothers resemble each other! His mother too had scolded him for never knowing how much money he had in his pocket; his mother too would have been amazed if she had known that he had found his feet, that day by day he was finding his feet.

An SS man passed on a bicycle. It is Rudi, the *Blockführer*. Halt! Attention! Take off your beret! *"Sale brute, celui-là. Ein ganz gemeiner Hund."* [A dirty beast that one. A common dog.] Can he speak French and German with equal facility? Yes, he thinks indifferently in both languages. He spent a month in Liguria, he likes Italy, he would like to learn Italian. I would be pleased to teach him Italian: why not try? We can do it. Why not immediately, one thing is as good as another, the important thing is not to lose time, not to waste this hour.

Limentani from Rome walks by, dragging his feet, with a bowl hidden under his jacket. Pikolo listens carefully, picks up a few words of our conversation and repeats them smiling: *"Zup-pa, cam-po, acqua."* [Soup, field, water.]

Frenkl the spy passes. Quicken our pace, one never knows, he does evil for evil's sake.

...The canto of Ulysses. Who knows how or why it comes into my mind. But we have no time to change, this hour is already less than an hour. If Jean is intelligent he will understand. He *will* understand — today I feel capable of so much.

...Who is Dante? What is the Comedy? That curious sensation of novelty which one feels if one tries to explain briefly what is the Divine Comedy. How the Inferno is divided up, what are its punishments. Virgil is Reason, Beatrice is Theology.

Jean pays great attention, and I begin slowly and accurately:

Then of that age-old fire the loftier horn
Began to mutter and move, as a wavering flame

Wrestles against the wind and is over-worn;
And, like a speaking tongue vibrant to frame
Language, the tip of it flickering to and fro
Threw out a voice and answered: "When I came…"

Here I stop and try to translate. Disastrous — poor Dante and poor French! All the same, the experience seems to promise well: Jean admires the bizarre simile of the tongue and suggests the appropriate word to translate "age-old."

And after "When I came?" Nothing. A hole in my memory. "Before Aeneas ever named it so." Another hole. A fragment floats into my mind, not relevant: "…nor piety To my old father, not the wedded love That should have comforted Penelope…," is it correct?

"…So on the open sea I set forth."

Of this I am certain, I am sure, I can explain it to Pikolo, I can point out why "I set forth" is not "*je me mis*," it is much stronger and more audacious, it is a chain which has been broken, it is throwing oneself on the other side of a barrier, we know the impulse well. The open sea: Pikolo has travelled by sea, and knows what it means: it is when the horizon closes in on itself, straight ahead and simple, and there is nothing but the smell of the sea; sweet things, ferociously far away.

We have arrived at Kraftwerk, where the cable-laying Kommando works. Engineer Levi must be here. Here he is, one can only see his head above the trench. He waves to me, he is a brave man, I have never seen his morale low, he never speaks of eating.

"Open sea," "open sea," I know it rhymes with "left me": "…and that small band of comrades that had never left me," but I cannot remember if it comes before or after. And the journey as well, the foolhardy journey beyond the Pillars of Hercules, how sad, I have to tell it in prose — a sacrilege. I have only rescued two lines, but they are worth stopping for:

"…that none should prove so hardy
To venture the uncharted distances…"

"to venture": I had to come to realize that it is the same expression as before: "I set forth." But I say nothing to Jean, I am not sure that it is an important observation. How many things there are to say, and the sun is already high, midday is near. I am in a hurry, a terrible hurry.

Here, listen Pikolo, open your ears and your mind, you have to understand, for my sake:

"Think of your breed; for brutish ignorance
Your mettle was not made; you were made men,

To follow after knowledge and excellence."

As if I also was hearing it for the first time: like the blast of a trumpet, like the voice of God. For a moment I forget who I am and where I am.

Pikolo begs me to repeat it. How good Pikolo is, he is aware that it is doing me good. Or perhaps it is something more: perhaps, despite the wan translation and the pedestrian, rushed commentary, he has received the message, he has felt that it has to do with him, that it has to do with all men who toil, and with us in particular; and that it has to do with us two, who dare to reason of these things with the poles for the soup on our shoulders.

"My little speech made every one so keen…"

…and I try, but in vain, to explain how many things this "keen" means. There is another lacuna here, this time irreparable. "…the light kindles and grows Beneath the moon" or something like it; but before it?… Not an idea, *"keine Ahnung"* as they say here. Forgive me, Pikolo, I have forgotten at least four triplets.

"Ça ne fait rien, vas-y tout de même." [It doesn't matter, go ahead anyway.]

"…When at last hove up a mountain, grey
With distance, and so lofty and so steep,
I never had seen the like on any day."

Yes, yes, "so lofty and so steep," not "very steep," a consecutive proposition. And the mountains when one sees them in the distance… the mountains…oh, Pikolo, Pikolo, say something, speak, do not let me think of my mountains which used to show up against the dusk of evening as I returned by train from Milan to Turin!

Enough, one must go on, these are things that one thinks but does not say. Pikolo waits and looks at me.

I would give today's soup to know how to connect "the like on any day" to the last lines. I try to reconstruct it through the rhymes, I close my eyes, I bite my fingers—but it is no use, the rest is silence. Other verses dance in my head: "…The sodden ground belched wind…," no, it is something else. It is late, it is late, we have reached the kitchen, I must finish:

"And three times round she went in roaring smother
With all the waters; at the fourth the poop
Rose, and the prow went down, as pleased Another."

I keep Pikolo back, it is vitally necessary and urgent that he listen, that he understand this "as pleased Another" before it is too late;

tomorrow he or I might be dead, or we might never see each other again, I must tell him, I must explain to him about the Middle Ages, about the so human and so necessary and yet unexpected anachronism, but still more, something gigantic that I myself have only just seen, in a flash of intuition, perhaps the reason for our fate, for our being here today…

We are now in the soup queue, among the sordid, ragged crowd of soup-carriers from other Kommandos. Those just arrived press against our backs. *"Kraut und Rüben? Kraut und Rüben."* The official announcement is made that the soup today is of cabbages and turnips: *"Choux et navets. Kaposzta és répak."*

"And over our heads the hollow seas closed up."

THINKING CRITICALLY

1. *Making Inferences* What new significance does Dante's poem take on for Levi in Auschwitz?

2. *Recognizing Values* What is the importance of Dante's poetry and literature to Levi?

3. *Linking Past to Present* Primo Levi turned to literature to explain the horror that was the Holocaust. In what other ways has the Holocaust been remembered, commemorated, or explained?

WRITER'S PORTFOLIO

1. *Extending the Selection* Compare and contrast the meaning of the canto of Ulysses as Dante wrote it (see pages 213–214) and as Levi interprets it.

2. *Examining Key Questions* What does Dante provide to Levi in this darkest of times?

The Atomic Bomb

At 8:15 A.M. on August 6, 1945, a bomb nicknamed "Little Boy" slipped out of the bay of the B-29 bomber named the *Enola Gay*. 43 seconds later Hiroshima was engulfed in flame, a victim of the first atomic bomb attack in history. When Harry Truman had become president in April 1945, one of the greatest decisions facing him was whether or not to use the atomic bomb against Japan. A presidential advisory committee made up of scientists, politicians, and military leaders had recommended its use. Military leaders, in particular, feared the casualties of invading the Japanese home islands — 12,500 U.S. Marines and over 100,000 Japanese soldiers had died in the recent fighting on Okinawa. However, some felt that a weapon of such destructiveness should not be used against a civilian population, that only racism or a desire for vengeance for the Japanese attack on Pearl Harbor was involved in such a decision. Historians have also argued that the dropping of the bomb was intended to intimidate the Russians. Truman himself later recalled that from the moment he learned of the bomb's existence, he had "regarded the bomb as a military weapon and never had any doubt it should be used." And it was used, not only on Hiroshima, but also on Nagasaki, where a second atomic bomb was dropped three days later. The following day the Japanese sued for peace and World War II was over. However, casualties from the radiation of the two bombings continued to mount for five years and the Cold War settled in with its constant fear of nuclear warfare. The first of the following readings is a description of the bombing of Nagasaki from the *New York Times*. To what does the reporter compare the bomb blast?

WE HEARD THE PREARRANGED SIGNAL ON OUR RADIO, PUT ON our arc-welder's glasses, and watched tensely the maneuverings of the strike ship about half a mile in front of us.

"There she goes!" someone said.

Out of the belly of *The Great Artiste* [the bomber] what looked like a black object went downward.

Captain Bock swung around to get out of range; but even though we were turning away in the opposite direction, and despite the fact that it was broad daylight in our cabin, all of us became aware of a giant flash that broke through the dark barrier of our arc-welder's lenses and flooded our cabin with intense light.

We removed our glasses after the fire flash, but the light still lingered on, bluish-green light that illuminated the entire sky all around. A tremendous blast wave struck our ship and made it tremble from nose to tail. This was followed by four more blasts in rapid succession, each resounding like the boom of cannon fire hitting our plane from all directions.

Observers in the tail of our ship saw a giant ball of fire rise as though from the bowels of the earth, belching forth enormous white smoke-rings. Next they saw a giant pillar of purple fire, 10,000 feet high, shooting skyward with enormous speed.

By the time our ship had made another turn in the direction of the atomic explosion, the pillar of purple fire had reached the level of our altitude. Only about forty-five seconds had passed. Awestruck, we watched it shoot upward like a meteor coming from the earth instead of from outer space, becoming ever more alive as it climbed skyward through the white clouds. It was no longer smoke, or dust, or even a cloud of fire. It was a living thing, a new species of being, born before our incredulous eyes.

At one stage of its evolution, covering millions of years in terms of seconds, the entity assumed the form of a giant square totem pole, with its base about three miles long, tapering off to about a mile at the top. Its bottom was brown, its center was amber, its top white. But it was a living totem pole, carved with many grotesque masks grimacing at the earth.

Then, just when it appeared as if the thing had settled down into a state of permanence, there came shooting out of the top a giant mushroom that increased the height of the pillar to a total of 45,000 feet. The mushroom top was even more alive than the pillar, seething and boiling in a white fury of creamy foam, sizzling upward and then descending earthward, a thousand Old Faithful geysers rolled into one.

It kept struggling in an elemental fury, like a creature in the act of breaking the bonds that held it down. In a few seconds it had freed itself from its gigantic stem and floated upward with tremendous speed, its momentum carrying into the stratosphere to a height of about 60,000 feet.

But no sooner did this happen than another mushroom, smaller in size than the first one, began emerging out of the pillar. It was as though the decapitated monster were growing a new head.

As the first mushroom floated off into the blue, it changed its shape into a flower-like form, its giant petal curving downward, creamy white outside, rose-colored inside. It still retained that shape when we last gazed at it from a distance of about 200 miles.

The second reading is from an article by Henry Stimson (1867–1950), Secretary of War under Presidents Roosevelt and Truman. It was published in 1947 and defended the decision to use the atomic bomb. What does Stimson say was uppermost in the minds of U.S. officials?

As we understood it in July, there was a very strong possibility that the Japanese government might determine upon resistance to the end, in all the areas of the Far East under its control. In such an event the allies would be faced with the enormous task of destroying an armed force of five million men and five thousand suicide aircraft, belonging to a race [Stimson means the Japanese] which had already amply demonstrated its ability to fight literally to the death.

The strategic plans of our armed forces for the defeat of Japan, as they stood in July, had been prepared without reliance upon the atomic bomb, which had not yet been tested in New Mexico. We were planning an intensified sea and air blockade, and greatly intensified strategic air bombing through the summer and early fall, to be followed on November 1 by an invasion of [the Japanese home islands].... We estimated that if we should be forced to carry this plan to its conclusion, the major fighting would not end until the later part of 1946, at the earliest. I was informed that such operations might be expected to cost over a million casualties to American forces alone. Additional large losses might be expected among our allies, and, of course, if our campaign were successful and if we could judge by previous experience, enemy casualties would be much larger than our own....

In order to end the war in the shortest possible time and to avoid the enormous losses of human life which otherwise confronted us, I felt that we must use the emperor as our instrument to command and compel his people to cease fighting and to subject themselves to our authority through him, and that to accomplish this we must give him and his controlling advisors a compelling reason to accede to our demands. This furthermore must be of such a nature that his people could understand his decision. The bomb seemed to me to furnish a unique instrument for that purpose.

> The third reading is excerpts from an article by the American social critic Dwight MacDonald which appeared in the fall of 1945 and attacks the dropping of the atomic bomb. What does MacDonald say were the American public's reactions to the dropping of the bomb?

THE ATOMIC BOMB RENDERS ANTICLIMACTICAL EVEN THE ending of the greatest war in history. *The concepts "war" and "progress" are now obsolete.* Both suggest human aspirations, emotions, aims, consciousness. "The greatest achievement of organized science in history," said President Truman after the Hiroshima catastrophe — which it probably was, and so much the worse for organized science. *The futility of modern warfare should now be clear.* Must we not now conclude, with [French writer] Simone Weil, that the technical aspect of war today is the evil, regardless of political factors? Can one imagine that the Bomb could ever be used "in a good cause"? Do not such means instantly, of themselves, corrupt any cause?.... Perhaps only among men like soldiers and scientists, trained to think "objectively" — i.e., in terms of means, not ends — could such irresponsibility and moral callousness be found. In any case, it was undoubtedly the most magnificent scientific experiment in history, with cities as the laboratories and people as the guinea pigs.

The bomb produced two widespread and, from the standpoint of The Authorities, undesirable emotional reactions in this country: a feeling of guilt at "our" having done this to "them" and anxiety lest some future "they" do this to "us." Both feelings were heightened by the superhuman *scale* of The Bomb. The Authorities have therefore made valiant attempts to reduce the thing to a human context, where such concepts as Justice, Reason, Progress could be employed. Such moral defenses are offered as: the war was shortened and many lives, Japanese as well as American, saved; "we" had to invent and use The Bomb against "them" lest "they" invent and use it against "us"; the Japanese deserved it because they started the war, treated prisoners barbarously, etc., or because they refused to surrender. The flimsiness of these justifications is apparent; *any* atrocious action, absolutely *any* one, could be excused on such grounds.

> In the final reading, the American writer Paul Fussell emphasizes "the importance of experience, sheer vulgar experience, in influencing one's view about the first use of the bomb." What is Fussell's reaction to the dropping of the atomic bomb?

I WAS A 21-YEAR-OLD SECOND LIEUTENANT LEADING A RIFLE platoon. Although still officially in one piece, in the German war I had been wounded in the leg and back severely enough to be adjudged, after the war, 40 percent disabled. But even if my leg buckled whenever I jumped out of the back of a truck, my condition was held to be satisfactory for whatever lay ahead. When the bombs dropped and the news began to circulate that [the invasion of Japan] would not, after all, take place, that we would not be obliged to run up the beaches near Tokyo assault-firing while being mortared and shelled, for all the fake manliness of our facades we cried with relief and joy. We were going to live. We were going to grow up to adulthood after all.

THINKING CRITICALLY

1. *Recognizing Bias* Do any of these writers seem biased? If so, against whom?

2. *Making Inferences* Do any of the writers offer an alternative to dropping the bomb? Do you think their's was a better choice?

3. *Linking Past and Present* How does the dropping of the atomic bomb still haunt us? Do we still fear having it dropped on "us" as MacDonald intimates?

WRITER'S PORTFOLIO

1. *Extending the Selection* Do you think the United States should or should not have dropped the bomb? Use the evidence above to support your argument.

2. *Examining Key Questions* How do you think the atomic bomb helped to shape people's lives in the post-war era?

Mohawks in the Modern World

In 1949, Joseph Mitchell published his essay "Mohawks in High Steel" in the *New Yorker*. Mitchell was profiling the Caughnawagas (kä′nä wä′gəs), Canadian Mohawk Indians who came from a reservation on the banks of the St. Lawrence River near Montreal. During most of the nineteenth century, the Caughnawagas carried goods into, and furs out of, the Canadian wilds. As the fur trade declined, many became skilled timber-rafters, some reluctantly submitted to becoming farmers, and still others became itinerant peddlers. In 1886, technology provided a new career for many of the Caughnawaga men — one which continues to provide them a living still today: riveting together the narrow beams and girders that comprise the basic structure of many skyscrapers and bridges. In the following excerpts from Mitchell's essay, what is his attitude toward the Caughnawagas?

IN 1886, THE LIFE AT CAUGHNAWAGA CHANGED ABRUPTLY. IN the spring of that year, the Dominion Bridge Company began the construction of a cantilever railroad bridge across the St. Lawrence for the Canadian Pacific Railroad, crossing from the French-Canadian village of Lachine on the north shore to a point just below Caughnawaga village on the south shore. The D.B.C. is the biggest erector of iron and steel structures in Canada; it corresponds to the Bethlehem Steel Company in the United States. In obtaining the right to use reservation land for the bridge abutment, the Canadian Pacific and the D.B.C. promised that Caughnawagas would be employed on the job wherever possible.

"The records of the company for this bridge show that it was our understanding that we would employ these Indians as ordinary day laborers unloading materials," an official of the D.B.C. wrote recently in a letter. "They were dissatisfied with this arrangement and would come out on the bridge itself every chance they got. It was quite impossible to keep them off. As the work progressed, it became apparent to all concerned that these Indians were very odd in that they did not have any fear of heights. If not watched, they would climb up into the spans and walk around up there as cool and collected as the toughest of our riveters, most of whom at that period were old sailing-ship men especially picked for their experience in working aloft. These Indians were as agile as goats. They would walk a narrow beam high up in the air with nothing below them but the river, which is rough there and ugly to look down on, and it wouldn't mean any more to them than walking on the solid ground. They seemed immune to the noise of the riveting, which goes right through you and is often enough in itself to make newcomers to construction feel sick and dizzy. They were inquisitive about the riveting and were continually bothering our foremen by requesting that they be allowed to take a crack at it. This happens to be the most dangerous work in all construction, and the highest-paid. Men who want to do it are rare and men who can do it are even rarer, and in good construction years there are sometimes not enough of them to go around. We decided it would be mutually advantageous to see what these Indians could do, so we picked out some and gave them a little training, and it turned out that putting riveting tools in their hands was like putting ham with eggs. In other words, they were natural-born bridgemen...."

After the D.B.C. completed the Canadian Pacific Bridge, it began work on a jackknife bridge now known as the Soo Bridge, which crosses two canals and a river and connects the twin cities of Sault Ste. Marie, Ontario, and Sault Ste. Marie, Michigan. This job took two years. Old Mr. Jacobs, the patriarch of the band, says that the Caughnawaga riveting gangs went straight from the Canadian Pacific job to the Soo job and that each gang took along an apprentice. "The Indian boys turned the Soo Bridge into a college for themselves," he says. "The way they worked it, as soon as one apprentice was trained, they'd send back to the reservation for another one. By and by, there'd be enough men for a new Indian gang. When the new gang was organized, there'd be a shuffle-up—a couple of men from the old gangs would go into the new gang and a couple of the new men would go into the old gangs; the old would balance the new." This proliferation continued on subsequent jobs, and by 1907 there were over seventy skilled bridgemen in the Caughnawaga band. On August 27, 1907, during the erection of the Quebec Bridge, which crosses the St. Lawrence nine miles above Quebec

City, a span collapsed, killing ninety-six men, of whom thirty-five were Caughnawagas. In the band, this is always spoken of as "the disaster."

"People thought the disaster would scare the Indians away from high steel for good," Mr. Jacobs says. "Instead of which, the general effect it had, it made high steel much more interesting to them. It made them take pride in themselves that they could do such dangerous work. Up to then, the majority of them, they didn't consider it any more dangerous than timber-rafting. Also, it made them the most looked-up-to men on the reservation. The little boys in Caughnawaga used to look up to the men that went out with circuses in the summer and danced and war-whooped all over the States and came back to the reservation in the winter and holed up and sat by the stove and drank whiskey and bragged. That's what they wanted to do. Either that, or work on the timber rafts. After the disaster, they changed their minds — they all wanted to go into high steel...."

At present, there are eighty-three Caughnawagas in the Brooklyn local and forty-two in the Manhattan local. Less than a third of them work steadily in the city. They roam from coast to coast, usually by automobile, seeking rush jobs that offer unlimited overtime work at double pay. A gang may work in half a dozen widely separated cities in a single year.... Several foremen who have had years of experience with Caughnawagas believe that they roam because they can't help doing so, it is a passion, and that their search for overtime is only an excuse. A veteran foreman for the American Bridge Company says he has seen Caughnawagas leave jobs that offered all the overtime they could handle. When they are making up their minds to move on, he says, they become erratic. "Everything will be going along fine on a job," he says. "Good working conditions. Plenty of overtime. A nice city. Then the news will come over the grapevine about some big new job opening up somewhere; it might be a thousand miles away. That kind of news always causes a lot of talk, what we call water-bucket talk, but the Indians don't talk; they know what's in each other's mind. For a couple of days, they're tensed up and edgy. They look a little wild in the eyes. They've heard the call. Then, all of a sudden, they turn in their tools, and they're gone. Can't wait another minute. They'll quit at lunchtime, in the middle of the week. They won't even wait for their pay. Some other gang will collect their money and hold it until a postcard comes back telling where to send it."...

Occasionally, in a saloon or at a wedding or a wake, Caughnawagas become vivacious and talkative. Ordinarily, however, they are rather dour and don't talk much. There is only one person in the North Gowanus colony who has a reputation for garrulity. He is a man of fifty-four whose white name is Orvis Diabo and whose Indian name is O-ron-ia-ke-te, or He Carries the Sky.... Mr. Diabo started working in riveting gangs when he was nineteen and quit a year and a half ago. He had to quit because of crippling attacks of arthritis. He was a heater and worked on bridges and buildings in seventeen states. "I heated a million rivets," he says. "When they talk about the men that built this country, one of the men they mean is me...."

"An Indian high-steel man, when he first leaves the reservation to work in the States, the homesickness just about kills him. The first few years, he goes back as often as he can. Every time he finishes a job, unless he's thousands of miles away, he goes back. If he's working in New York, he drives up weekends, and it's a twelve-hour drive. After a while, he gets married and brings his wife down and starts a family, and he doesn't go back so often. Oh, he most likely takes the wife and children up for the summer, but he doesn't stay with them. After three or four days, the reservation gets on his nerves and he highballs it back to the States. He gets used to the States. The years go by. He gets to be my age, maybe a little older, maybe a little younger, and one fine morning he comes to the conclusion he's a little too damned stiff in the joints to be walking a naked beam five hundred feet in the air. Either that, or some foreman notices he hasn't got a sure step any longer and takes him aside and tells him a few home truths. He gives up high-steel work and he packs his belongings and he takes his money out of the bank or the postal savings, what little he's been able to squirrel away, and he goes on back to the reservation for good. And it's hard on him. He's used to danger, and reservation life is very slow; the biggest thing that ever happens is a funeral. He's used to jumping around from job to job, and reservation life boxes him in. He's used to having a drink, and it's against the law to traffic in liquor on the reservation; he has to buy a bottle in some French-Canadian town across the river and smuggle it in like a high-school boy, and that annoys the hell out of him.

"On the other hand there are things I look forward to.... One night, the last time I was home, the longhousers were having a festival. I decided I'd go up to the Catholic graveyard that's right below the longhouse and hide in the bushes and listen to the music.... They were singing Mohawk chants that came down from the old, old red-Indian times. I could hear men's voices and women's voices and children's voices. The Mohawk language, when it's sung, it's beautiful to hear. Oh, it takes your breath away. A feeling ran through me that made me tremble; I had to take a deep breath to quiet my heart, it was beating so fast. I felt very sad; at the same time, I felt very peaceful. I thought I was all alone in the graveyard, and then who loomed up out of the dark and sat down beside me but an old high-steel man I had been talking with in a store that afternoon, one of the soreheads, an old man that fights every improvement that's suggested on the reservation, whatever it is, on the grounds it isn't Indian — this isn't Indian, that isn't Indian. So he said to me, 'You're not alone up here. Look over there.' I looked where he pointed, and I saw a white shirt in among the bushes. And he said, 'Look over there,' and I saw a cigarette gleaming in the dark. 'The bushes are full of Catholics and Protestants,' he said. 'Every night there's a longhouse festival, they creep up here and listen to the singing. It draws them like flies.' So I said, 'The longhouse music is beautiful to hear, isn't it?' And he remarked it ought to be, it was the old Indian music. So I said the longhouse religion appealed to me. 'One of these days,' I said, 'I might possibly join.' I asked him how he felt about it. He said he was a Catholic and it was out of the question. 'If I was to join the longhouse,' he said, 'I'd be excommunicated, and I couldn't be buried in holy ground, and I'd burn in Hell.' I said to him, 'Hell isn't Indian.' It was the wrong thing to say. He didn't reply to me. He sat there awhile — I guess he was thinking it over — and then he got up and walked away."

THINKING CRITICALLY

1. *Making Inferences* Why did the Caughnawagas begin and continue working on "high steel"?

2. *Recognizing Values* How has being away from the reservation affected the Caughnawagas' sense of their heritage?

3. *Linking Past and Present* What factors in their traditional way of life would make the high-steel jobs appealing to the Mohawks?

WRITER'S PORTFOLIO

1. *Extending the Selection* Write a letter from a Mohawk bridgeman to his family back on the reservation, describing working on high steel.

2. *Examining Key Questions* How has the modern world undermined the traditional Mohawk beliefs and way of life?

Post-War Japan

The literature of modern Japan begins in 1854, with the opening of Japan to the West, and the resultant inrush of foreign influences. This influence increased markedly after 1905, with the Japanese victory in the Russo-Japanese War. One of the writers caught up in the intellectual and creative ferment of the early twentieth century was Yasunari Kawabata (1899–1972) who, in 1968, was the first Japanese writer to be awarded the Nobel Prize for Literature. Kawabata's parents had died when he was an infant and he was sent to grandparents to be raised, but both his grandmother and his sister died shortly thereafter and his grandfather died when he was sixteen. As a result of these losses, this lonely young man turned to writing. One of his first published works was the *Diary of a Sixteen-Year-Old* (1925), which chronicled his grandfather's last days. While in his twenties, Kawabata began writing short-short stories, little vignettes which he called *tanagokoro no shosetsu*, a term translated as "palm-of-the-hand" stories or "vest-pocket" stories. He once noted, "Most literary men write poetry when they are young, but I wrote these vignettes instead." By the time of his death, he had written over a hundred of these miniatures. Like the themes in his longer works, the recurrent motifs in these stories focus on human relationships, nature, change and loss. The following story, "Bamboo Leaves," was first published in 1950. Does the story end on a note of hope or loss?

Putting the bucket down beside the hollyhocks, Akiko pulled several leaves from the dwarf bamboo under the plum tree and dropped them into the water.

"Boats. Do you like them?"

The boy gazed intently down into the bucket. Then he looked up at Akiko and smiled.

"Akiko made you the nice boats," said his mother, "because you're such a good boy. Akiko will play with you if you're good."

He was the brother of Akiko's fiancé. She had come out into the garden because she had sensed that the mother wanted to be alone with her father. The boy was being troublesome, and she had brought him with her. He was her fiancé's youngest brother.

He churned at the leaves. "They're having a fight…." He was very pleased.

She wrung the kimono she had been washing and hung it out to dry.

The War was over, but her fiancé had not yet come back.

"Fight," said the boy, churning the water more violently. "Fight harder."

"You're splashing it all over yourself."

"But they won't move."

It was true that when he withdrew his hand they were quite still.

"We'll take them out to the river. That will keep them moving."

The boy gathered up the leaves. Akiko poured the water over the hollyhocks and took the bucket back to the kitchen.

She stood on a stone upriver and dropped the leaves in one by one.

He clapped with delight. "Mine is winning! Look, look!"

He ran downstream, not to lose track of the boat in the lead.

She threw the last ones in and started after him.

She must be careful that her left foot was full on the ground.

She had had infantile paralysis and her left heel did not touch the ground. It was narrow and tender and the arch was high. She had been unable to jump rope or to walk any distance. She had been resigned to not marrying, and then she had become engaged. Sure that determination could overcome physical defects, she tried more seriously than before to walk with her left heel on the ground. It blistered easily, but she persisted. Then came the defeat and she gave up. The scars from the blisters were still there, like very bad chilblains.

She was using her left heel for the first time in a very long while because the little boy was her fiancé's brother.

It was a narrow stream with weeds hanging over. Two or three of the boats caught in them.

Some ten paces ahead of her, the boy was looking after the boats, as if unaware of her approach. He paid no attention to her way of walking.

The hollow at the nape of his neck made her think of her fiancé. She wanted to take the boy in her arms.

The mother came out. She said good-by and led him off by the hand.

"Good-bye," he said calmly.

Either her fiancé was dead or the engagement had been canceled. It had probably been wartime sentimentality that had made him want to marry a cripple in the first place.

She did not go inside. She went instead to look at the house being put up next door. It was much the largest house in the neighborhood and everyone was watching it. Construction had been stopped during the war and weeds had grown high around the lumber; and then suddenly it was moving ahead once more. There were two nervous pine trees at the gate.

To Akiko it looked like a hard, unyielding sort of house. But it had very great numbers of windows. The parlor seemed almost completely encased in glass.

There had been speculation as to the sort of people who would move in, but no one knew for sure.

THINKING CRITICALLY

1. *Making Inferences* Why does Kawabata title his story "The Bamboo Leaves"? How do the bamboo leaves illuminate the events of the narrative?

2. *Drawing Conclusions* What is the tone of Kawabata's story and what details emphasize that tone? What single detail best suggests or implies Akiko's emotion?

3. *Linking Past and Present* Kawabata was a writer who preferred hinting at his characters' inner lives to writing character sketches. What western art form might you compare Kawabata's stories to?

WRITER'S PORTFOLIO

1. *Extending the Selection* Carefully reread the story and then write a continuation, in which you decide Akiko's fate.

2. *Examining Key Questions* What has shaped Akiko's personality? Is this because of personal or societal pressure?

Modern Fiction

Although subject to controversy when it was first published in 1952, *Invisible Man* by Ralph Ellison (1914–1994) won the National Book Award the following year and over the last forty years has become one of the classics of modern literature. It is one man's story of the numbing brutality of life in New York City and, although it is the story of the singular difficulties encountered by African Americans living in contemporary society, it is a story that anyone can understand. The following selection is from the prologue or introduction to the novel in which we meet the narrator and are given bits of his background and hints of his future. The most striking element of *Invisible Man* is the voice of the narrator himself. It is a voice that seems to have a life of its own, calling up a scene, filling in the details, venting emotional responses to people and situations. In fact, the style of *Invisible Man* has been compared to that of a jazz composition, the kind of composition in which the performer is very often the composer, but still creating new rhythms and motifs. Ellison's style is one of extraordinary vitality, filled with sonorous puns and sudden inspirations. In what sense is the narrator invisible?

I AM AN INVISIBLE MAN. NO, I AM NOT A SPOOK LIKE THOSE who haunted Edgar Allan Poe; nor am I one of your Hollywood-movie ectoplasms. I am a man of substance, of flesh and bone, fiber and liquids—and I might even be said to possess a mind. I am invisible, understand, simply because people refuse to see me. Like the bodiless head you see sometimes in circus sideshows, it is as though I have been surrounded by mirrors of hard, distorting glass. When they approach me they see only my surroundings, themselves, or figments of the imagination—indeed, everything and anything except me.

Nor is my invisibility exactly a matter of a bio-chemical accident to my epidermis. That invisibility to which I refer occurs because of a peculiar disposition of the eyes of those with whom I come in contact. A matter of the construction of their *inner* eyes, those eyes with which they look through their physical eyes upon reality. I am not complaining, nor am I protesting either. It is sometimes advantageous to be unseen, although it is most often rather wearing on the nerves. Then too, you're constantly being bumped against by those of poor vision. Or again, you often doubt if you really exist. You wonder whether you aren't simply a phantom in other people's minds. Say, a figure in a nightmare which the sleeper tries with all his strength to destroy. It's when you feel like this that, out of resentment, you begin to bump people back. And, let me confess, you feel that way most of the time. You ache with the need to convince yourself that you do exist in the real world, that you're a part of all the sound and anguish, and you strike out with your fists, you curse and you swear to make them recognize you. And, alas, it's seldom successful.

One night I accidentally bumped into a man, and perhaps because of the near darkness he saw me and called me an insulting name. I sprang at him, seized his coat lapels and demanded that he apologize. He was a tall blond man, and as my face came close to his he looked insolently out of his blue eyes and cursed me, his breath hot in my face as he struggled. I pulled his chin down sharp upon the crown of my head, butting him as I had seen the West Indians do, and I felt his flesh tear and the blood gush out, and I yelled, "Apologize! Apologize!" But he continued to curse and struggle, and I butted him again and again until he went down heavily, on his knees, profusely bleeding. I kicked him repeatedly, in a frenzy because he still uttered insults though his lips were frothy with blood. Oh yes, I kicked him! And in my outrage I got out my knife and prepared to slit his throat, right there beneath the lamplight in the deserted street, holding him in the collar with one hand, and opening the knife with my teeth—when it occurred to me that the man had not *seen* me, actually; that he, as far as he knew, was in the midst of a walking nightmare! And I stopped the blade, slicing the air as I pushed him away, letting him fall back to the street. I stared at him hard as the lights of a car stabbed through the darkness. He lay there, moaning on the asphalt; a man almost killed by a phantom. It unnerved me. I was both disgusted and ashamed. I was like a drunken man myself, wavering about on weakened legs. Then I was amused: Something in this man's thick head had sprung out and beaten him within an inch of his life. I began to laugh at this crazy discovery. Would he have awakened at the point of death? Would Death himself have freed him for wakeful living? But I didn't linger. I ran away into the dark, laughing so hard I feared I might rupture myself. The next day I saw his picture in the *Daily News*, beneath a caption stating that he had been "mugged." Poor fool, poor blind fool, I thought with sincere compassion, mugged by an invisible man!...

Now, aware of my invisibility, I live rent-free in a building rented strictly to whites, in a section of the basement that was shut off and forgotten during the nineteenth century....The point now is that I found a home—or a hole in the ground, as you will. Now don't jump to the conclusion that because I call my home a "hole" it is damp and cold like a grave; there are cold holes and warm holes. Mine is a warm hole. And remember, a bear retires to his hole for the winter and lives until spring; then he comes strolling out like the Easter chick breaking from its shell. I say all this to assure you that it is incorrect to assume that, because I'm invisible and live in a hole, I am dead. I am neither dead nor in a state of suspended animation. Call me Jack-the-Bear, for I am in a state of hibernation.

My hole is warm and full of light. Yes, *full* of light. I doubt if there is a brighter spot in all New York than this hole of mine, and I do not exclude Broadway. Or the Empire State Building on a photographer's dream night. But that is taking advantage of you. Those two spots are among the darkest of our whole civilization—pardon me, our whole culture (an important distinction, I've heard)—which might sound like a hoax, or a contradiction, but that (by contradiction, I mean) is how the world moves: not like an arrow, but a boomerang. (Beware of those who speak of the *spiral* of history; they are preparing a boomerang. Keep a steel helmet handy.) I know; I have been boomeranged across my head so much that I now can see the darkness of lightness. And I love light. Perhaps you'll think it strange that an invisible man should need light, desire light, love light. But maybe it is exactly because I *am* invisible. Light confirms my reality, gives birth to my form....

Since you never recognize me even when in closest contact with me, and since, no doubt, you'll hardly believe that I exist, it won't matter if you know that I tapped a power line leading into the building and ran it into my hole in the ground. Before that I lived in the darkness into which I was chased, but now I see. I've illuminated the blackness of my invisibility—and vice versa. And so I play the invisible music of my isolation. The last statement doesn't seem just right, does it? But it is; you hear this music simply because music is heard and seldom seen, except by musicians. Could this compulsion to put invisibility down in black and white be thus an urge to make music of invisibility? But I am an orator, a rabble rouser—Am? I *was*, and perhaps shall be again. Who knows? All sickness is not unto death, neither is invisibility.

I can hear you say, "What a horrible, irresponsible bastard!" And you're right. I leap to agree with you. I am one of the most irresponsible beings that ever lived. Irresponsibility is part of my invisibility; any way you face it, it is a denial. But to whom can I be responsible, and why should I be, when you refuse to see me? And wait until I reveal how truly irresponsible I am. Responsibility rests upon recognition, and recognition is a form of agreement. Take the man whom I almost killed: Who was responsible for that near murder—I? I don't think so, and I refuse it. I won't buy it. You can't give it to me. *He* bumped *me, he* insulted *me.* Shouldn't he, for his own personal safety, have recognized my hysteria, my "danger potential"? He, let us say, was lost in a dream world. But didn't *he* control that dream world—which, alas, is only too real!—and didn't *he* rule me out of it? And if he had yelled for a policeman, wouldn't I have been taken for the offending one? Yes, yes, yes! Let me agree with you, I was the irresponsible one; for I should have used my knife to protect the higher interests of society. Some day that kind of foolishness will cause us tragic trouble. All dreamers and sleepwalkers must pay the price, and even the invisible victim is responsible for the fate of all. But I shirked that responsibility; I became too snarled in the incompatible notions that buzzed within my brain. I was a coward...

But what did *I* do to be so blue? Bear with me.

THINKING CRITICALLY

1. *Identifying Assumptions* What assumptions does the narrator make about his relationship with other human beings?

2. *Making Inferences* Why did the narrator give up his apartment and life to live in his hole? Is he happy?

3. *Linking Past to Present* Are African-Americans less "invisible" today than in the early 1950s? Why or why not?

WRITER'S PORTFOLIO

1. *Extending the Selection* Are young people "invisible" today in a society dominated by adults? Why or why not?

2. *Examining Key Questions* What seems to have shaped the personality of Ellison's narrator?

Modern American Painting

The ideas of the Post-Impressionist artists had a decided effect on American artists of the post-World War II era as the American art scene became the most important and influential in the world. A major American painter who came to fame during the 1930s was Edward Hopper (1882–1967). His realistic scenes of commonplace subjects were heavily influenced by the Impressionists's concern with light. However, this was coupled with a deep-seated sense of realism. In his

Edward Hopper, Seven A.M. *(1948)*

painting *Seven A.M.* Hopper demonstrates his characteristic fascination with the effect of light on an anonymous, small-town storefront, one that echoes the mystery implicit in many of de Chirico's works. By the late 1940s, however, many American painters had rejected such realism for a style of painting known as Abstract Expressionism. One of the most influential of these post-war painters was Jackson Pollock (1912–1956). Born in Cody, Wyoming, Pollock had been influenced by Native American artists who poured sand onto a surface in order to create intricately patterned sand paintings. Abandoning his brushes, Pollock began to drip, pour, and splatter paint onto huge canvases laid on the floor rather than on an easel. These paintings were called "action paintings" and, indeed, these monumental works such as *Autumn Rhythm*, which appears on page 559, with its limited color palette and its sense of continuation far beyond the boundaries of the canvas, creates a sense of motion and perspective. Helen Frankenthaler (b. 1928) was the finest colorist of the Abstract Expressionists. Moreover, she even experimented with the nature of her paints. In her landmark work *Mountains and Sea*, which appears

Henri Matisse,
The Roofs of
Collioure *(1905)*

Pablo Picasso, Les Demoiselles d'Avignon
(June–July 1906)

Umberto Boccioni,
Riot in the Gallery
(1909)

Wassily Kandinsky, Painting with Green Center *(1913)*

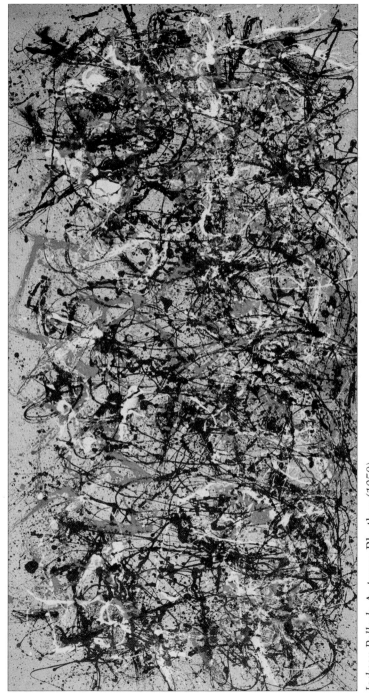

Jackson Pollock, Autumn Rhythm (1950)

Helen Frankenthaler, Mountains and Sea (1952)

on page 560, Frankenthaler reduced the texture of her paints by thinning them and applying them to an unprimed canvas, thus creating with oil paint an effect similar to that of watercolor. The Harlem-born painter Jacob Lawrence (b. 1917) was influenced by Matisse and his use of Japanese flat-plane painting. His painting *The Library III* shows the strong effect to which he puts this technique. Although he is sometimes categorized as a primitive painter and sometimes as a painter of social criticism, Lawrence's paintings demonstrate a sophisticated sense of rhythm and repetition. Which of these painters seems the most modern?

Jacob Lawrence, The Library III *(1960)*

THINKING CRITICALLY

1. *Making Inferences* Do you think these paintings have a message? What is each artist trying to say in their work?

2. *Drawing Conclusions* How important are the titles to understanding each of these paintings? Explain.

3. *Linking Past and Present* In a culture in which computers can generate images, are artists becoming unnecessary?

WRITER'S PORTFOLIO

1. *Extending the Selection* Write a letter to a friend describing your response to one of these paintings.

2. *Examining Key Questions* If a painting must have a subject, can that subject be the paint itself? Why or why not?

African Literature

As African colonies gained their independence, art and literature developed rapidly. Camara Laye was a novelist (1928–1980) who grew up in a tribal village in Guinea, West Africa, and received his education in France. In his novels, as in his life, Laye felt pulled in two directions — between the old ways of tribal Africa and the new ways of the West and between the problems caused by the old colonial government and the problems caused by the new regime. Out of this conflict Laye was able to create moving stories of his life and his country. In 1953, Laye published *The Dark Child*, excerpted below, a memoir of his childhood, which lovingly recalled his village life and family, particularly his father, a gifted metalsmith. What atmosphere pervades the workshop of Laye's father?

O F ALL THE DIFFERENT KINDS OF WORK MY FATHER ENGAGED in, none fascinated me so much as his skill with gold. No other occupation was so noble, no other needed such a delicate touch. And then, every time he worked in gold it was like a festival — indeed it was a festival — that broke the monotony of ordinary working days.

So if a woman, accompanied by a go-between, crossed the threshold of the workshop, I would follow her in at once. I knew what she wanted: she had brought some gold and wanted to ask my father to transform it into a trinket. The woman would have collected the gold in the placers of Siguiri, where, crouching over the river for months on end, she had patiently extracted grains of gold from the mud.

These women never came alone. They knew my father had other things to do than to make trinkets. And even when he had the time, they knew they were not the first to ask a favor of him, and that, consequently, they would not be served before others.

Generally they required the trinket for a certain date, either for the festival of Ramadan or the Tabaski [Islamic festivals] or some other family ceremony or dance.

Thereupon, to enhance their chance of being quickly served, and to more easily persuade my father to interrupt the work before him, they used to request the services of an official praise-singer, a go-between, arranging in advance the fee they were to pay him for his good offices.

The go-between installed himself in the workshop, tuned up his cora, which is our harp, and began to sing my father's praises. This was always a great event for me. I heard recalled the lofty deeds of my father's ancestors, and their names from the earliest times. As the couplets were reeled off it was like watching the growth of a great genealogical tree that spread its branches far and wide and flourished its boughs and twigs before my mind's eye. The harp played an accompaniment to this vast utterance of names, expanding it and punctuating it with notes that were now soft, now shrill.

I could sense my father's vanity was being inflamed, and I already knew that after having sipped this milk-and-honey he would lend a favorable ear to the woman's request. But I was not alone in my knowledge. The woman also had seen my father's eyes gleaming with contented pride. She held out her grains of gold as if the whole matter were settled. My father, took up his scales and weighed the gold....

Immediately all activity in the workshop almost came to a halt. During the whole time that the gold was being smelted, neither copper nor aluminium could be worked nearby, lest some particle of these base metals might fall into the container which held the gold. Only steel could be worked on such occasions, but the men, whose task that was, hurried to finish what they were doing, or left it abruptly to join the apprentices gathered around the forge. There were so many, and they crowded so around my father, that I, the smallest person present, had to come near the forge in order not to lose track of what was going on.

If he felt he had inadequate working space, my father had the apprentices stand well away from him. He merely raised his hand in a simple gesture: at that particular moment he would never utter a word, and no one else would, no one was allowed to utter a word. Even the go-between's voice was no longer to be raised in song. The silence was broken only by the panting of the bellows and by the faint hissing of the gold. But if my father never actually spoke, I know that he was forming words in his mind. I could tell from his lips, which kept moving, while, bending over the pot, he stirred the gold and charcoal with a bit of wood that kept bursting into flame, and had constantly to be replaced by a fresh one.

What words did my father utter? I do not know. At least I am not certain what they were. No one ever told me. But could they have been anything but incantations? On these occasions was he not invoking the genies of fire and gold, of fire and wind, of wind blown by the blast pipes of the forge, of fire born of wind, of gold married to fire? Was it not their assistance, their friendship, their espousal that he besought? Yes. Almost certainly he was invoking these genies, all of whom are equally indispensible for smelting gold.

The operation going on before my eyes was certainly the smelting of gold, yet something more than that: a magical operation that the guiding spirits could regard with favor or disfavor. That is why, all around my father, there was absolute silence and anxious expectancy....

By now the gold had been cooled in the hollow of the brick, and my father began to hammer and stretch it. This was the moment when his work as a goldsmith really began. I noticed that before embarking on it he never failed to stroke stealthily the little snake coiled up under the sheepskin. I can only assume that this was his way of gathering strength for what remained to be done, the most trying part of his task.

But was it not extraordinary and miraculous that on these occasions the little black serpent always coiled up under the sheepskin? He was not always there. He did not visit my father every day, but he was always present whenever there was gold to be worked. His presence was no surprise to me. After that evening when my father had spoken of the guiding spirit of his race I was no longer astonished. The snake was there intentionally. He knew what the future held. Did he tell my father? I think he most certainly did.

THINKING CRITICALLY

1. *Making Inferences* What kind of relationship does the narrator have with his father? How does he feel about his father?

2. *Recognizing Values* Why does the father so willingly agree to put his work aside to make gold trinkets?

3. *Linking Past to Present* Is flattery, such as that provided by the go-between, still a part of business? What forms does it take?

WRITER'S PORTFOLIO

1. *Extending the Selection* Write a description of one of your parents at work. Have your impressions changed as you grew older?

2. *Examining Key Questions* What factors have gone into shaping the personalities of Laye and his father?

The Meditative Landscape

Elizabeth Bishop (1911–1979) was one of the most exceptional American poets of the post-war era. She built on earlier poets's use of blank and free verse to develop a style of poetry that is both frank and simple in its language, while densely powerful in what it evokes. Bishop was raised by her grandparents in Nova Scotia and New England and began to write at an early age. She attended Vassar College and made the acquaintance of many people in the literary world, who encouraged her in her poetry. Bishop traveled extensively during her life, as well as living off and on in Brazil during the 1950s and 1960s. Her poems are extended meditations, which are dominated by her acute observations and active mind. The physical subjects of Bishop's poems are the catalyst for her consideration of inner realities and truths. Bishop was a very slow writer, who often worked on single poems for years. However, her perseverance and genius created intensely simple poems, where each word seems to be the absolute right choice. "Seascape" is from her first collection of poetry, *North and South* and the second poem is the title piece from her 1965 collection *Questions of Travel*. What is the setting of each poem?

Seascape

This celestial seascape, with white herons got up as angels,
flying as high as they want and as far as they want sidewise
in tiers and tiers of immaculate reflections;
the whole region, from the highest heron
down to the weightless mangrove island
with bright green leaves edged neatly with bird-droppings
like illumination in silver,
and down to the suggestively Gothic arches of the mangrove roots
and the beautiful pea-green back-pasture
where occasionally a fish jumps, like a wild-flower
in an ornamental spray of spray;

this cartoon by Raphael for a tapestry for a Pope:
it does look like heaven.
But a skeletal lighthouse standing there
in black and white clerical dress,
who lives on his nerves, thinks he knows better.
He thinks that hell rages below his iron feet,
that that is why the shallow water is so warm,
and he knows that heaven is not like this.
Heaven is not like flying or swimming,
but has something to do with blackness and a strong glare
and when it gets dark he will remember something
strongly worded to say on the subject.

Questions of Travel

There are too many waterfalls here; the crowded streams
hurry too rapidly down to the sea,
and the pressure of so many clouds on the mountaintops
makes them spill over the sides in soft slow-motion,
turning to waterfalls under our very eyes.
—For if those streaks, those mile-long, shiny, tearstains,
aren't waterfalls yet,
in a quick age or so, as ages go here,
they probably will be.
but if the streams and clouds keep travelling, travelling,
the mountains look like the hulls of capsized ships,
slime-hung and barnacled.

Think of the long trip home.
Should we have stayed at home and thought of here?
Where would we be today?
Is it right to be watching strangers in a play
in this strangest of theaters?
What childishness is it that while there's a breath of life
in our bodies, we are determined to rush
to see the sun the other way round?
The tiniest green hummingbird in the world?
To stare at some inexplicable old stonework,
inexplicable and impenetrable,

at any view,
instantly seen and always, always delightful?
Oh, must we dream our dreams
and have them, too?
And have we room
for one more folded sunset, still quite warm?

But surely it would have been a pity
not to have seen the trees along this road,
really exaggerated in their beauty,
not to have seen them gesturing
like noble pantomimists, robed in pink.
—Not to have had to stop for gas and heard
the sad, two-noted, wooden tune
of disparate wooden clogs
carelessly clacking over
a grease-stained filling-station floor.
(In another country the clogs would all be tested.
Each pair there would have identical pitch.)
—A pity not to have heard
the other, less primitive music of the fat brown bird
who sings above the broken gasoline pump
in a bamboo church of Jesuit baroque:
three towers, five silver crosses.
—Yes, a pity not to have pondered,
blurr'dly and inconclusively,
on what connection can exist for centuries
between the crudest wooden footwear
and, careful and finicky,
the whittled fantasies of wooden cages.
—Never to have studied history in
the weak calligraphy of songbirds' cages.
—And never to have had to listen to rain
so much like politicians' speeches:
two hours of unrelenting oratory
and then a sudden golden silence
in which the traveller takes a notebook, writes:

"Is it lack of imagination that makes us come
to imagined places, not just stay at home?

Or could Pascal have been not entirely right
about just sitting quietly in one's room?

Continent, city, country, society:
the choice is never wide and never free.
And here, or there… No. Should we have stayed at home,
wherever that may be?

THINKING CRITICALLY

1. *Making Comparisons* Compare and contrast the mood of the two poems. Which images contribute to these moods the most?

2. *Making Inferences* What is the message of these two poems? How does the language of the poems contribute to their meaning? What do they tell you about Bishop's world view?

3. *Linking Past to Present* Bishop was a very simple woman, who loved her friends and her work. Her image of the poet was that of a hard-working professional writer. Are the poets you hear about today more comparable to Bishop or to the Romantic poets (see pages 457–460)?

WRITER'S PORTFOLIO

1. *Extending the Selection* What is Bishop's attitude as a traveler? How do the images she presents evoke this attitude?

2. *Examining Key Questions* What do you think Bishop would say was the purpose of life?

EXAMINING KEY QUESTIONS

- *What shapes personality?*
- *Is there any purpose?*

Throughout this chapter, most selections have concluded with a writing project asking you to discuss how the art or literature you have examined provides answers to one of these key questions. The following writing projects will help you draw together what you have learned by examining how several selections illustrate these key questions.

- The question of what shapes one's personality has played throughout the intellectual and artistic movements of the twentieth century. How did Freud influence artists and thinkers? What events in this century had a profound effect on artists and thinkers? Explain.

- The twentieth century has been the most violent and destructive era in history. Human faith in reason and progress has been shattered by a series of events. How do you think the sense of loss and pessimism developed? What events most influenced it?

SPEAKING/LISTENING

- Read the poems included in this chapter aloud. How does hearing them aloud aid your understanding? What oral differences can you discern between the World War I poets and Elizabeth Bishop?

CRAFTING

- Create an Abstract Expressionist piece of art. Try to give your piece a sense of motion or action and make it express a heightened emotional response.

COLLECTING

- Collect a series of ten images which you think sum up the major events and ideas of the twentieth century. Present your images to the class and then with your classmates create a gallery of images.

Students at the Musee D'Orsay, Paris

The Humanities Today

The importance of the humanities has increased rather than diminished in recent years. There is a larger amount of art and scholarship produced today than at any time in world history, as well as a larger public audience and more public forums and money available to support these efforts. However, the arts are increasingly confronted with the challenge of bringing relevancy to media that in some cases are as old as civilization itself. A poet not only models his work after older poets, but must contend with them to succeed and find an audience. This is true for painters, sculptors, novelists, philosophers, etc. Yet, despite this challenge, it is the genius and brilliance of these older models that inspire us and so much of the best art actively incorporates the old in the creation of the new. The challenge will always be to understand the past and reiterate what is important and timeless. The other and equally important challenge to artists and scholars is to teach each new generation the importance of humanistic endeavor. As the modern world puts more and more stress on work and money, the time for contemplation in everyone's life shrinks. The desire to succeed, or in some people's case simply survive, is so great that the arts and learning seem superfluous and archaic. But they are not. The humanities teach us who we are, where we came from, and to question where we are going. The future of humanity resides in understanding our place in this world and the consequences of our lives and actions. The humanities are the history of this understanding, and they can express to you the absolute marvel which is human existence and civilization.

PORTFOLIO

Looking Back at Homer (1976)
Derek Walcott, "Sea Grapes"

Contemporary Landscape Painting (1984–1994)
April Gornik, *Crossing* and *Moving Storm*;
Joan Nelson, *Untitled (#368)* and *Untitled (#399)*

Post-modern Humanism (1994)
Vaclav Havel, speech of July 4, 1994

Looking Back at Homer

Awarded the Nobel Prize for Literature in 1992, Derek Walcott (b. 1930) is one of today's finest poets and playwrights. Born on St. Lucia in the West Indies, where he was educated and began a career in journalism, Walcott has exhibited throughout his poetry an exceptional ear for the rhythms and sounds of everyday Caribbean speech. Yet, he is also a learned poet, whose love and under-standing of English literature is present in all his poems. The principal theme of Walcott's poetry has been the conflict in his life between white and black and between the European tradition and the Caribbean heritage. He has struggled to build a bridge between these extremes and to celebrate this fusion of cultures. The following poem is the title poem from Walcott's 1976 collection Sea Grapes. In it he depicts a Caribbean beach which leads him to contemplation of Homer's Odyssey. With what image does the poem open?

Sea Grapes
That sail which leans on light,
tired of islands,
a schooner beating up the Caribbean

for home, could be Odysseus,
home-bound on the Aegean[1];
that father and husband's

longing, under gnarled sour grapes, is
like the adulterer hearing Nausicaa's[2] name
in every gull's outcry.

---

1. **Aegean.** The sea between Greece and Turkey
2. **Nausicaa** (nô si ⁄ kā ə). The princess who discovers Odysseus on the beach in Book 6 of the *Odyssey*. She falls in love with Odysseus, the "adulterer" of line 8.

This brings nobody peace. The ancient war
between obsession and responsibility
will never finish and has been the same

for the sea-wanderer or the one on shore
now wriggling on his sandals to walk home,
since Troy sighed its last flame,

and the blind giant's boulder heaved the trough
from whose groundswell the great hexameters[3] come
to the conclusions of exhausted surf.

The classics can console. But not enough.

_____

3. hexameters. The meter in which Homer composed the *Odyssey*.

THINKING CRITICALLY

1. *Making Inferences* What is the parallel Walcott is drawing between Odysseus and himself?

2. *Recognizing Values* What strengths and weaknesses does Walcott see in literature?

3. *Linking Past to Present* Walcott is drawing on Homer's *Odyssey* to give his poem more potency and meaning. Do you think it is a good thing for poets to make literary allusions? Why or why not?

WRITER'S PORTFOLIO

1. *Extending the Selection* What does Walcott mean by "the ancient war between obsession and responsibility"? How many different interpretations of this ambiguous phrase can you think of?

2. *Examining Key Questions* How important is Homer and classical literature to this poem by Walcott? Explain.

Contemporary Landscape Painting

The 1980s and 1990s have seen a revival of realistic landscape painting in the art world. A number of American artists have adapted this classical painting style to the modern consciousness. Two of the finest of these new painters are April Gornik and Joan Nelson. April Gornik's paintings are a type of psychological landscape, with the elements of nature giving vent to human emotion. Her paintings are reminiscent of the Romantics's glorification of the power and beauty of nature. Gornik has said that she finds in her paintings a way to speak about private truths. In her work's rich emotionality, there are

April Gornik, Crossing *(1984)*

April Gornik, Moving Storm *(1985)*

suggestions of both J. M. W. Turner and Caspar David Friedrich (see pages 455–456). Joan Nelson is a more austere painter. Her paintings are almost miniatures and she generally paints details rather than full landscapes. Nelson aims at capturing the essence of a picture by concentrating on small details. Her paintings are done on wood rather than canvas which gives them a dimensional texture and solidity. Moreover, Nelson also uses many nontraditional elements in her paints, such as wax, plaster, egg tempera, and varnish, to give them more physicality and heightened colors and glosses. Both painters are not aiming to recreate a natural scene, but rather to recreate the experience of viewing a landscape for the viewer. What is the subject of each of these paintings?

Joan Nelson,
Untitled (#368)
(1993)

Joan Nelson,
Untitled (#399)
(1994)

THINKING CRITICALLY

1. *Making Inferences* How would you describe the tone and the emotion of each painting? Which elements create these moods?

2. *Identifying Assumptions* What does each painter seem to be trying to express in her landscapes? Explain.

3. *Linking Past to Present* Why do you think that such a traditional form of painting still has interest for the late-twentieth century viewer?

WRITER'S PORTFOLIO

1. *Extending the Selection* Write a brief but detailed description of one of these landscapes. Build on what the painter has created, enlarging her vision.

2. *Examining Key Questions* How have the examples of older painters influenced April Gornik and Joan Nelson?

Post-modern Humanism

In 1989, the dissident playwright Vaclav Havel (1936–), who had spent many years in jail, became the first freely elected president of Czechoslovakia following the fall of the communist government. Months of mass demonstrations and widespread opposition had forced the long-time communist dictatorship to withdraw from power. Czechoslovakia was part of a revolution that swept Eastern Europe in the late 1980s, bringing down the communist regimes in countries including East Germany, Romania, Hungary, Bulgaria, and the Soviet Union. However, this victory for democracy came at a high price. A bloody war has engulfed the provinces of the former Yugoslavia, much of Eastern Europe is an economic and environmental ruin, and ethnic violence is on the rise. Even Czechoslovakia, the economically strongest nation in Eastern Europe, has undergone problems, dividing into two nations, the Czech Republic and Slovakia, in 1992. Yet, for all the problems, there is great hope for a new world order based on peace, mutual understanding, and economic stability, rather than the constant fear of nuclear war. On July 4, 1994, Havel delivered a speech at Independence Hall in Philadelphia, discussing the future of humanity. In the following excerpts from his speech, what is Havel proposing?

THERE ARE GOOD REASONS FOR SUGGESTING THAT THE MODERN age has ended. Many things indicate that we are going through a transitional period, when it seems that something is on the way out and something else is painfully being born. It is as if something were crumbling, decaying and exhausting itself, while something else, still indistinct, were arising from the rubble.

The distinguishing features of transitional periods are a mixing and blending of cultures and a plurality or parallelism of intellectual and spiritual worlds. These are periods when all consistent value systems collapse, when cultures distant in time and space are discovered or rediscovered. New meaning is gradually born from the encounter, or the intersection, of many different elements.

Today, this state of mind, or of the human world, is called post-modernism. For me, a symbol of that state is a Bedouin mounted on a camel and clad in traditional robes under which he is wearing jeans, with a transistor radio in his hands and an ad for Coca-Cola on the camel's back.

I am not ridiculing this, nor am I shedding an intellectual tear over the commercial expansion of the West that destroys alien cultures. I see it as a typical expression of this multicultural era, a signal that an amalgamation of cultures is taking place. I see it as proof that something is being born, that we are in a phase when one age is succeeding another, when everything is possible. Yes, everything is possible because our civilization does not have its own spirit, its own esthetic.

This is related to the crisis, or to the transformation, of science as the basis of the modern conception of the world. The dizzying development of science, with its unconditional faith in objective reality and complete dependency on general and rationally knowable laws, led to the birth of modern technological civilization. It is the first civilization that spans the entire globe and binds together all societies, submitting them to a common global destiny....

The world of our experiences seems chaotic, confusing. Experts can explain anything in the objective world to us, yet we understand our own lives less and less. We live in the post-modern world, where everything is possible and almost nothing is certain.

This state of affairs has its social and political consequences. The planetary civilization to which we all belong confronts us with global challenges. We stand helpless before them because our civilization has essentially globalized only the surface of our lives. But our inner self continues to have a life of its own. And the fewer answers the era of rational knowledge provides to the basic questions of human being, the more deeply it would seem that people, behind its back as it were, cling to the ancient certainties of their tribe....

In searching for the most natural source for the creation of a new world order, we usually look to an area that is the traditional foundation of modern justice and a great achievement of the modern age: to a set of values that were first declared in this building. I am referring to the respect for the unique human being and his or her liberties and inalienable rights, and the principle that all power derives from the people. I am referring to the fundamental ideas of modern democracy. Even these ideas are not enough. We must go farther and deeper.

Today, we are in a different place and facing a different situation, one to which classically modern solutions do not give a satisfactory response. After all, the very principle of inalienable human rights, conferred on man by the Creator, grew out of the typically modern notion that man — as a being capable of knowing nature and the world — was the pinnacle of creation and lord of the world.

This modern anthropocentrism inevitably meant that He who allegedly endowed man with his inalienable rights began to disappear from the world: He was so far beyond the grasp of modern science that He was gradually pushed in to a sphere of privacy of sorts, if not directly into a sphere of private fancy — that is, to a place where public obligations no longer apply. The existence of a higher authority than man himself simply began to get in the way of human aspirations.

The idea of human rights and freedoms must be an integral part of any meaningful world order. Yet I think it must be anchored in a different place, and in a different way, than has been the case so far.

Paradoxically, inspiration for the renewal of this lost integrity can once again be found in science. In a science that is new — post-modern — a science producing ideas that in a certain sense allow it to transcend its own limits. I will give two examples.

The "anthropic cosmological principle" brings us to an idea, perhaps as old as humanity itself; that we are not at all just an accidental anomaly, the microscopic caprice of a tiny particle whirling in the endless depths of the universe. Instead, we are mysteriously connected to the universe, we are mirrored in it, just as the entire evolution of the universe is mirrored in us.

The moment it begins to appear that we are deeply connected to the entire universe, science reaches the outer limits of its own powers.

With the "anthropic cosmological principle," science has found itself on the border between science and myth. In that, however, science has returned, in a roundabout way, to man, and offers him his lost integrity. It does so by anchoring him once more in the cosmos.

The second example is the "Gaia hypothesis." This theory brings together proof that the dense network of mutual interactions between the organic and inorganic portions of the Earth's surface form a single system, a kind of mega-organism, a living planet, Gaia, named after an ancient goddess recognizable as an archetype of the Earth Mother in perhaps all religions.

According to the Gaia hypothesis, we are parts of a greater whole. Our destiny is not dependent merely on what we do for ourselves but also on what we do for Gaia as a whole. If we endanger her, she will dispense with us in the interests of a higher value — life itself.

What makes the "anthropic principle" and the "Gaia hypothesis" so inspiring? One simple thing: Both remind us of what we have long suspected, of what we have long projected into our forgotten myths and what perhaps has always lain dormant within us as archetypes. That is, the awareness of our being anchored in the Earth and the universe, the awareness that we are not here alone nor for ourselves alone but that we are an integral part of higher, mysterious entities against whom it is not advisable to blaspheme.

This forgotten awareness is encoded in all religions. All cultures anticipate it in various forms. It is one of the things that form the basis of man's understanding of himself, of his place in the world and ultimately of the world as such....

It follows that, in today's multicultural world, the truly reliable path to peaceful co-existence and creative cooperation must start from what is at the root of all cultures and what lies infinitely deeper in human hearts and minds than political opinion, convictions, antipathies or sympathies: it must be rooted in self-transcendence.

The Declaration of Independence, adopted 218 years ago in this building, states that the Creator gave man the right to liberty. It seems man can realize that liberty only if he does not forget the One who endowed him with it.

THINKING CRITICALLY

1. *Recognizing Values* According to Havel, what was the modern conception of the place of humanity? What has replaced it?

2. *Understanding Assumptions* What does Havel say undermined the importance of God? What has this cost modern man?

3. *Linking Past to Present* Havel describes a Bedouin clad in both modern and ancient dress to explain his meaning. Find examples of this sort of multicultural juxtaposition in contemporary American life.

WRITER'S PORTFOLIO

1. *Extending the Selection* What is Havel's attitude towards modern science? What does it not provide to humans? Explain.

2. *Examining Key Questions* Is Havel suggesting a return to past ideals? Why or why not?

Abbasids (ab′bə sidz), second Arab dynasty (750–1258) of the Muslim caliphate. Following Muhammad's death, the title caliph (successor) was given to the spiritual and political leader of Islam. The Abbasid caliphs built a new capital, Baghdad, which became renowned under their leadership as a center of learning and culture.

Abstract Impressionism, twentieth-century art movement that stressed spontaneous application of paint to create large, highly decorated paintings that did not represent concrete images. Also known as action painting, Abstract Impressionism was the first important school of American painting to divorce itself from European influence (page 556).

action painting, see **Abstract Impressionism.**

adab (a′dab), an Islamic literary form in which etiquette, ethics, and belles-lettres are combined in a didactic, but entertaining prose essay. Adab was developed in the 700s by writers associated with the Abbasid court in Baghdad (page 137).

allegory (al ə gôr′ē), a narrative in verse or prose, in which characters, action, and setting represent abstract ideas — of moral, social, religious, or political significance — apart from the literal sense of the story.

alpha and omega, a phrase symbolizing Jesus and the Second Coming. In the Bible (Revelation 22:13) Jesus states, "I am Alpha and Omega"— the first and last letters of the Greek alphabet. Thus, Jesus spoke of himself as "the beginning and the end, the first and the last" (page 100).

Amarna (ä mär′nä), a revolutionary style of ancient Egyptian art dating from circa 1350 B.C. Associated with monotheistic worship of the sun, the style typically depicts the pharaoh, Amenhotep IV, in a relaxed pose that reveals his human, rather than divine, nature. The name derives from Tell el-Amarna, present-day site of Amenhotep's capital where most examples have been found (page 23).

Apocalypse (ə pok′ə lips), the final triumph of good over evil, specifically the symbolic vision of the end of the world and the triumph of Jesus described in the New Testament book of Revelation. By tradition, the author was St. John the Apostle, also known as St. John the Divine.

Apostles, the 12 disciples chosen by Jesus to preach the gospel. They include Peter, Andrew, James the Less, John, Philip, Bartholomew, Thomas, Matthew, Simon, Jude, James the Greater, and Judas Iscariot. While not part of the original 12, Matthias, Paul, and Barnabas are usually classed as Apostles.

Arianism (er′ē ə niz əm), a doctrine that held that Christ the Son was subordinate to God the Father because Christ was created by, and therefore came into being after, God. First taught in about 320 by Arius, an Alexandrian priest, the doctrine was condemned as heresy in 325 by the Council of Nicaea (page 102).

Ashanti (ə shan′tē), historic and present-day people and region of central Ghana in West Africa. In the late 1600s, an Ashanti leader, Osei Tutu, united various clans into a state with a highly developed army, which conquered and absorbed neighboring states. By the early 1800s, the Ashanti Empire included eastern Ivory Coast, much of modern-day Ghana, and western Togo. The Ashanti remain the largest and most powerful ethnic group in Ghana.

Aztec (az′tek), Native American people who in the 1400s developed a highly advanced civilization and empire in central and southern Mexico. Conquered in 1521 by Spanish invaders under Hernán Cortés, the Aztec capital, Tenochtitlán, stood on the site of present-day Mexico City.

Babylonian Captivity (bab ə lō′nē ən), sixth century B.C. exile of Jews in Babylonia. In 586 B.C., Babylonia, a city-state between the Tigris and Euphrates rivers, conquered Judea, the southern portion of ancient Israel, and took thousands of hostages. In 539 B.C., Babylonia was conquered by Persia, and captive Jews were freed. While most returned home, some remained to form a Jewish colony, which was the beginning of the Diaspora or scattering of Jews outside of Israel.

bard, an oral poet. The word entered English in the Middle Ages via Britain's Celtic peoples: the Irish, Scots, and Welsh. The profession, an entertainer who sings his own poems celebrating the exploits of heroes (not unlike today's folk singer), goes back at least as far as the ancient Greeks (page 40).

Benin (bə nēn′), historical kingdom and present-day country located between Togo and Nigeria on Africa's West Coast. Between the 1300s and mid-1600s, Benin, centered around the Niger River delta in present-day Nigeria, grew powerful through trade in copper, ivory, and slaves. Benin sculpture from this period ranks with the finest of African art.

blank verse, unrhymed poetry in iambic pentameter — lines of five units or feet, each foot with an unstressed syllable followed by a stressed one (page 565). Blank verse, popularized by English poets of the sixteenth century, reflects the natural, conversational rhythms of the English language.

Blaue Reiter, Der (dur blou′ə rī′tər), German Expressionist (see) art movement (1911–1914) characterized by both an ordered philosophical approach and chaotic, yet poetic spontaneity (page 512). The name derives from "The Blue Rider," a publication, by artists Wassily Kandinsky and Franz Marc, that announced artistic intentions.

Buddhism (bü′diz əm), religion based on the teachings of Buddha (c. 563–483 B.C.), a spiritual leader of northern India. Buddha, or the Enlightened One, taught that right living through a series of lifetimes will lead to the attainment of nirvana, a condition free from all desire and pain.

buttress (but′ris), a support built to strengthen a wall. In such buildings as Gothic cathedrals (page 196), the enormous weight of the roof, stone vaulting, and spires presses down on a wall, pushing it out. Exterior buttresses thrust against the wall in the opposite direction. (Buttress comes from a French word meaning "thrust against.") The resulting tension keeps the wall stable.

canto (kan′tō), literary term for the subdivisions of a narrative or epic poem. The cantos of a poem are approximately equivalent to the chapters of a book.

Cartesian (kär tē′zhən), having to do with the mathematical discoveries, scientific methods, and philosophy of René Descartes (1596–1650). Cartesian philosophy is grounded in universal doubt and the search for what is real and, therefore, true; only doubt cannot be doubted; thus, the proof of the reality of existence is the will for and ability to doubt, expressed in the famous dictum, "I think, therefore I am" (page 273).

communism, an economic, social, and political system based on common ownership of land and all means of production. Originating in the theories of German social philosopher Karl Marx (1818–1883), the modern concept of communism profoundly changed the course of the twentieth century, when such immense and populous nations as Russia and China adopted its basic tenets (page 472).

Confucianism (kən fyü′shə niz′əm), an ethical system based on the teachings of the Chinese philosopher Confucius (c. 551–470 B.C.) that stressed personal virtue, exemplary behavior, and reciprocity of duty between sovereign and subject, husband and wife, parent and child, brothers, and friends (page 290).

consubstantial (kän səb stan′chəl), the relationship, described in the Nicene Creed (see), between the three Persons of the Trinity, in which Father, Son, and Holy Ghost are of one and the same substance (page 102).

contrapposto (kōn trə pōs′tō), the counterpoising of limbs and masses in the composition of sculpture or painting. Traditional *contrapposto*, originating with ancient Greek sculpture, portrays the body at rest, standing, one leg forward, body weight carried primarily on the opposite leg (page 45).

Copernican (kə pėr′nə kən), of or having to do with the Polish astronomer Nicolaus Copernicus (1473–1543) or his system of astronomy, which explained how the earth might rotate on an axis and the planets revolve around the sun (page 269). Physics has since proven the Copernican system correct.

Counter Reformation, sixteenth-century reform movement within the Roman Catholic Church designed to counter the effects of the Reformation, an earlier movement that ultimately led to the establishment of Protestantism in much of northern Europe.

couplet (kup′lit), two successive lines of poetry, especially two that rhyme and have an identical meter or pattern of stressed and unstressed syllables.

Crucifixion, the putting to death of Jesus on the cross. While a common form of capital punishment throughout the ancient Roman world, crucifixion provided a particularly odious death, physically and emotionally; being nailed or tied to a cross was reserved for slaves and such political malcontents as the troublesome Jews of Judea.

Cubism (kyü′biz əm), early twentieth-century artistic style in which objects are represented by geometric forms, rather than by realistic details. Rejecting the sensual and emotional appeal of color, movement, atmosphere, and texture, the first Cubists — Pablo Picasso and Georges Braque — focused on the intellect, showing all sides of an object as the mind, not the eye, perceives it (page 512).

Dada (dä′ də), nihilistic art and literary movement (1916–1922) born in the disillusionment engendered by World War I. It rejected and ridiculed all standards and conventions (page 518), as Dadaists such as Tristan Tzara, Marcel Duchamp, and Man Ray stressed the absurd and unpredictable. Dada eventually metamorphosed into Surrealism.

Darwinism, theory of evolution through natural selection developed by Charles Darwin (1809–1882). According to Darwinist theory, natural selection results in the survival of some organisms, but not others. Among a number of slight variations, those best adapted to the environment survive, ultimately resulting in new, usually more complex species (page 479).

Der blaue Reiter *(see Blaue Reiter, Der)*

dharma (där′mə), moral and religious law as reflected in the teachings of Buddha, founder of Buddhism (page 326); also rules of duty and ethical conduct in Hinduism (see).

empiricism (em pir′ə siz əm), philosophical theory that all knowledge is based on experience. Empiricism is the outlook of most scientists, who attempt to answer questions through the acquisition of information gathered via the senses, rather than through the dictates of reason or authority, either religious or political.

epic, long narrative poem (originally handed down orally, later a literary form) that tells of the adventures and achievements of a great hero or band of heroes (pages 10, 40, 71, and 210). Usually written in a dignified, majestic style, epics often give expression to ethnic or national ideals.

Epicureanism (ep ə kyü rē′ə niz əm), principles of the ancient Greek philosopher Epicurus (c. 342–270 B.C.), who believed that pleasure, and hence the avoidance of pain, is the highest and only good. Real pleasure, however, is never indulgence, but is found in a life of prudence, honor, and justice (page 65).

Expressionism (ek spresh′ə niz əm), art and literary movement of the early 1900s in which nature or reality is distorted as a means of expressing inner reactions or visions of the artist (page 514).

Fauvism (fō′viz əm), style of Expressionist (see) painting developed in France in the early 1900s, characterized by the use of brilliant colors and bold, distorted designs (page 512). Critics of the day attacked the works as *fauves*, or wild beasts, a label that the artists, including Henri Matisse, cheerfully adopted.

foreshorten, the shortening of lines or objects in a drawing or painting to give the impression of depth and distance.

free verse, type of poetry "free" of fixed rhyme patterns, rhythms, or line lengths. The music of free verse is achieved through repetition and subtly patterned rhythm and through imagery and figurative language. Various forms of stanzaic organization link ideas and provide unity.

fresco (fres′kō), painting or design on walls or ceilings, executed in pigments mixed with water applied to fresh, lime plaster. The technique, appreciated for its clear, luminous colors and permanence, reached its height during the Italian Renaissance of the fifteenth and sixteenth centuries and was revived spectacularly by Mexican artist Diego Rivera in the twentieth century (pages 76, 208, and 251).

Futurism, early twentieth-century, Italian art movement, characterized by the sensation of motion. Glorifying the speed, energy, and, danger of the machine age, Futurists typically fragmented forms into multiple images and overlapped colors (page 512).

Good Shepherd, title for Jesus, based on the Parable of the Good Shepherd (Luke 15: 3–7) and John 10: 7–13. "I am the good shepherd; the good shepherd lays down his life for the sheep." In early Christian art, Jesus was often represented as the Good Shepherd with a lamb around his shoulders (page 100).

Gothic (goth′ik), architectural style (c. 1150–1500) of medieval Western Europe, characterized by verticality, lightness, and soaring spaces (page 196). Construction elements typically included pointed arches, ribbed vaulting (see), high, steep roofs, and flying buttresses (see), which allowed for great expanses of stained glass by reducing the amount of wall space needed for support. Revived in the nineteenth and twentieth centuries, Gothic style is still applied to a wide range of structures, from churches to skyscrapers.

griot (grē′ō), poet, troubadour, and historian of the African oral tradition. Performing a vital social function, griots committed to memory and passed to the next generation the literature and history of their peoples (page 360).

haiku (hī′kü), three-line, unrhymed poem constructed, in conformity with the original Japanese form, with 17 syllables: five in the first line; seven in the second; and five in the third (page 317). Classic haiku, linking nature to human nature, evokes the essence of a moment or mood by juxtaposing the concrete — a sight or sound in nature — with the abstract — a phrase suggesting an emotion.

Han (hän), Chinese dynasty (206 B.C.– A.D. 220) marked by the adoption of Confucianism (see) as the basis of the state, the introduction of Buddhism (see), and the extension of Chinese rule over Tibet, Manchuria, and present-day North Korea and northern Vietnam. During the Han Dynasty, the arts and sciences, particularly literature, flourished, and Chinese goods, including silk, were traded as far west as ancient Rome.

Heian (hā′än′), period of Japanese history (A.D. 794–1185) named for the capital, Heian-kyo, and characterized by the gradual naturalization of ideas and institutions borrowed from the Chinese. Meaning "capital of peace and tranquillity," Heian-kyo gradually become known simply as Kyoto, "capital city." Tokyo displaced Kyoto as Japan's capital in 1868.

heliocentric (hē lē ō sen′trik), having or representing the sun as the center. Copernicus advocated a heliocentric astronomical system — the planets revolving around the sun — as opposed to the Ptolemaic system (see), which held that Earth was the center of the universe (page 269).

Hijra (hi j′rə), also known *hegira*, flight of Muhammad from Mecca to Medina in A.D. 622. Muslims use a calendar reckoned from this date.

Hinduism (hin′dü iz əm), religious and social system of the vast majority of the people of India, characterized by an acceptance of the Vedas as the most sacred scriptures and a rigid caste system. The doctrine of karma (see) and moksha — continuing reincarnation until the soul, through spiritual perfection, enters a new level of existence — is a central belief. A synthesis of various ancient Indian religious and social elements and the religion of the Aryans, brought to the subcontinent in about 1700 B.C., Hinduism is unique among major world religions in that it is not identified with a single founder.

Holocaust (hol′ə kost), systematic annihilation of about six million Jews by German Nazis under Adolf Hitler during World War II (1939–1945). More than two-thirds of all the Jews in Europe, in addition to many Gypsies, gays, and Slavic and Polish civilians, were exterminated as undesirables (page 534).

icon, picture of Jesus, an angel, or a saint, venerated as sacred in the Eastern Orthodox Churches (page 208). Painted on wood or ivory according to rules established by church authorities, the icon's stylized image is intended to convey the heavenly glory of the subject portrayed.

illumination, in the Middle Ages, the decoration of pages of religious manuscripts and books, particularly Psalters and books of hours, with exquisite initial letters, margin designs, and appropriate miniature pictures in gold, silver, and brilliant colors (page 215).

imperialism (im pir′ē ə liz əm), policy of extending the rule of one country over other countries and colonies. The so-called Age of Imperialism flourished between the mid-nineteenth and twentieth centuries, when European nations colonized nearly all of Africa, much of Southeast Asia, and many islands in the South Pacific. Great Britain alone controlled about one quarter of the world's population and area.

Impressionism (im presh′ə niz əm), painting style, developed by French artists in the late 1800s, that presents an impression — what the eye sees in a glance — rather than what the painter knows or feels about the object or event pictured (page 483). Using strong, bright colors applied in dabs, the Impressionists conveyed an impression of light striking and reflecting from a surface, rather than photographically reproducing it.

Inca (ing′ ka), people of South America with a highly developed culture who ruled a large empire, primarily centered in present-day Ecuador, Peru, and Chile (pages 392 and 395). While the empire fell to Spaniards in the 1500s, the Inca language (Quechua) and certain customs have been retained by Native Americans in the Peruvian highlands.

Iroquois confederacy (ir′ə kwoi), powerful alliance of Native American tribes (c. 1570–1779) called the Five Nations (later Six Nations) or the *Ongwanonhsioni*, meaning "we long house builders" (page 406). Formerly living in present-day Quebec and Ontario, Canada, and New York State, the confederacy included the Mohawk, Oneida, Onondaga, Cayuga, Seneca, and later, the Tuscarora.

Judas (jü′dəs), Disciple who, for 30 pieces of silver, betrayed Jesus, later repented, and hanged himself. Iscariot, an epithet applied to Judas, has been interpreted in different ways: "man of Kerioth," a Judaean town; and a corruption of the Latin word for murderer, referring not to the betrayal, but to a radical, anti-Roman sect to which Judas may have belonged.

Kano (kä′nō), Japanese school of painting, flourishing from the fifteenth to the nineteenth century, led by seven generations of the Kano family (page 320). Transcending Chinese models, the Kano school developed the first thoroughly Japanese style of painting, characterized by sharp, bold technique and high moral symbolism.

karma (kär′mə), a concept, common to Buddhism and Hinduism, that all acts, words, and thoughts of one life determine destiny in future lives or incarnations (page 326). Karma, an impersonal law of moral cause and effect, is divorced from ideas of punishment or forgiveness of sin by a supreme being.

kouros (kür′os), ancient Greek statue of a naked, male youth (page 45). Although some *kouroi* represented the god Apollo, most depicted local heroes or athletes. The form may, thus, symbolize an ideal of physical perfection that humanity shares with the divine.

Kush, African kingdom (c. 2000 B.C.–A.D. 350) situated along the Nile River in what is now Sudan (page 350). In about 750 B.C., Kush conquered Egypt and held it until driven out by invading Assyrians in about 670 B.C. The same invasion forced the Kushites to move their own capital to the south where, away from the strong influence of Egypt, they developed a new and vital culture that flourished for over 1,000 years.

lyric poetry, rhymed or unrhymed poetic form, usually short, that expresses the emotion or state of mind of a single speaker. The sonnet is an example.

Manichaeanism (man′ə kē ən izəm), religion founded by Persian prophet Mani (c. A.D. 216–276), who taught that the universe is governed by two opposing forces—the light and the dark or the kingdom of God and spiritual enlightenment and the kingdom of Satan and material things (page 108). Trapped in this conflict, the soul, infused with divine light, yearns to escape the darkness of the body. While true escape is possible only through death, additional resources of light can be acquired through austerity, vegetarianism, and celibacy.

Mannerism (man′ə riz əm), European style of art, characterized by distortion of spatial relationships, curving elongated human figures, and disturbing, metallic colors and harsh lighting effects, that flourished (1520–1600) between the high Renaissance and baroque periods (page 267). The aims of such Mannerists as El Greco—style over form and imagination and invention over faithful reproduction of nature—deliberately contradicted the principles of the Renaissance.

Maya, Native American people who, between A.D. 350 and 800, created an advanced civilization in Central America and south Mexico. Outstanding astronomers and mathematicians, the Maya developed a calendar of great accuracy; produced an advanced form of writing; and devised architecture, painting, and sculpture of great sophistication (page 392). Mayan descendants continue to live in Mexico and Central America.

Mecca (mek′ ə), western Saudi Arabian city to which all Muslims face in prayer. Birthplace of Muhammad, Mecca, with its Great

Mosque enclosing the Kaaba, is the annual destination of millions of Islamic pilgrims making the *hajj*, or religious pilgrimage, required of all Muslims able to do so.

Medina (mə dē′ nə), western Saudi Arabian city — site of Muhammad's tomb — where the Prophet took refuge after the *hijra*, or forced flight, from Mecca, in A.D. 622.

Mihrab (mēr′əb), niche, chamber, or slab in a mosque that indicates the direction of Mecca, which all Muslims face in prayer (page 146).

mosaic (mō zā′ik), decoration, usually made of small pieces of stone or glass of different colors that are inlaid to form a picture or design on floors, walls, or ceilings. Widespread use of mosaics began in ancient Greece and spread to the Roman Empire, where the art form reached its peak in the magnificent decoration of such structures as the Hagia Sophia (completed A.D. 537) in Constantinople, the capital of the Byzantine Empire (pages 100 and 119).

Mughal (mō′gul), Muslim dynasty that ruled much of India from the early sixteenth to the mid-eighteenth century. Founded by Babar, a descendant of the Turkish conqueror Tamerlane and the Mongol ruler Genghis Khan (Mughal is a variant of Mongol), the dynasty established a highly stable, centralized government responsible for two centuries of order and a magnificent flowering of architecture — the Taj Mahal, for example — and art that successfully blended the culture of Persia with that of India (pages 160 and 164).

Neoplatonism (nē ō plā′tə niz əm), philosophy developed in the A.D. 200s by Plotinus in response to Stoics and skeptics. Based on Plato's theories, Neoplatonism structured all existence into a vast, ordered, hierarchical reality — from top to bottom: "The One," beyond being and unknowable; "Intellect," a realm of ideas, beyond time and space; "Soul," where the "Intellect" is linked to "Nature" — the dark realm of material bodies — and ultimately "Matter," a state of nonbeing. This last great Greek, pagan philosophy profoundly affected early Christian doctrine, particularly through the writings St. Augustine (page 239).

New Testament, second of the two principal divisions of the Bible, which contains the life and teachings of Jesus recorded by his fol-lowers, together with their experiences and teachings (page 95).

Nicene Creed (nī sēn′), formal statement of the chief tenets of Christian belief, based on arti-cles adopted at an A.D. 325 church council called by Byzantine Emperor Constantine at Nicaea, city in present-day Turkey, to settle disputes over the nature of the Trinity (page 102). The council concluded that God and Christ as God are of the same essence.

No **drama,** Japanese dramatic form, developed in the 1300s, that integrates mime, speech, singing, dancing, and instrumental music (page 314). Highly stylized — principal play-ers wear wooden masks and elaborate costumes — a typical *No* drama is short, his-torically themed, and tragic in mood.

octave (ok′tāv), the first eight lines of the 14-line Petrarchan sonnet (page 232). The octave states the proposition; the sestet, or final six lines, works out the resolution.

Old Testament, first of the two principal divi-sions of the Bible, which contains the religious and social laws of the Hebrews, a record of their history, their important literature, and writings of their prophets (page 90).

Olmec (ōl′mek), advanced agricultural culture of Native Americans living in southeastern Mexico from about 1200 to 100 B.C. The civilization developed a primitive form of hieroglyphic writing, a system for recording time, and sophisticated sculptural techniques (page 392).

Ottoman (ot′ə mən), nomadic, central Asian, and Turkish tribes that conquered the Byzantine Empire in the mid-1400s. At its height in the 1500s, the Muslim Ottoman Empire was the most powerful state in the world, controlling, from the capital, Constan-tinople (now Istanbul), much of Asia Minor and northern Africa and parts of southwest-ern Asia and southeastern Europe, including the Balkan states and Hungary. The empire declined through the eighteenth and nine-teenth centuries and collapsed during World War I.

parable (par′ə bəl), brief story used to teach some truth or moral lesson, most often applied to various lessons by Jesus (page 95). Christ's parables, such as The Good Samaritan, The Prodigal Son, and Dives and Lazarus, are among the most distinctive fea-tures of his teachings.

pathetic fallacy, a term used to signify the attribution of human traits, particularly emotions, to nonhuman objects.

perspective, technique of picturing objects on a flat surface to give the appearance of distance or depth. Aerial and linear perspective, the major methods employed in Western art, were understood by the ancient Greeks and Romans, but essentially forgotten until reformulated by the artists of Renaissance Italy (page 237). Rebelling against art as a mirror of reality, twentieth-century artists have largely dismissed the use of perspective.

philosophes (fil ə zəfz′), eighteenth-century, French philosophers, including Diderot, Rousseau, and Voltaire, who gave shape to the Enlightenment. Believing in progress and perfectibility, the *philosophes* insisted upon applying a rational, scientific approach to political, economic, social, and religious issues and divorcing all religious consideration from discussion of moral doctrine (page 436).

psychoanalysis (sī kō ə nal′ə sis), method of treating mental illness and the theories behind such treatment developed by Sigmund Freud at the turn of the twentieth century (page 504). Methodology includes examination by a trained physician of a person's mind to discover the unconscious desires, fears, and anxieties that produce mental and emotional disorders.

Ptolemaic (tol ə mā′ik), of or having to do with Ptolemy or his system of astronomy. A Greek astronomer who lived in Alexandria, Egypt, in the A.D. 100s, Ptolemy taught that the Earth was the fixed center of the universe with the sun, planets, and other heavenly bodies revolving around it. The Ptolemaic system dominated astronomy in Europe until the advent of the Copernican system (see), formulated in 1543 (page 269).

quatrain (kwot′rān), a verse stanza of four lines (page 232). This stanza, or group of lines set off to form a division in a poem, may take a variety of forms, depending upon line lengths and rhyme patterns.

Quran (kô rän′), sacred book of Islam and standard by which Muslims live (page 132). It consists of revelations of *Allah* (God in Arabic) to Muhammad.

Reformation (ref ər mā′shən), sixteenth-century religious movement that aimed at reform within the Roman Catholic Church, but led to Protestantism. It began on October 31, 1517, when Martin Luther, a monk and professor of theology, nailed his Ninety-Five Theses, or list of church abuses, to the door of a German church. Within forty years, most Northern European countries, which included about half the continental population, had officially abandoned the Catholic Church for various Protestant denominations.

relativity (rel ə tiv′ə tē), theory concerning matter, space, time, and motion, expressed in certain equations by Albert Einstein (page 508). According to his Special Theory of Relativity, if two systems are moving uniformly in relation to each other, it is impossible to determine anything about their motion except that it is relative, and the velocity of light is constant, independent of either the velocity of its source or an observer. Thus, it can be mathematically derived that mass and energy are interchangeable. Einstein's General Theory of Relativity is an extension of the special theory and deals with the equivalence of gravitational and inertial forces.

Romanesque (rō mə nesk′), medieval architectural style (A.D. 800–1100) primarily developed for church and monastic structures. While named for certain Roman features — the serial use of rounded arches — Romanesque developed in answer to specific needs of the age; in an era of universal faith, the monumental barrel vaults allowed for larger and larger church interiors and in a time of lawlessness, the massive, masonry exteriors provided safety and security (page 196).

rose window, enormous, stone-traceried, circular window over the central, west front portals and at the transept ends of a Gothic church (page 196). Typically, a rose window's stained glass depicted Biblical stories or lessons, designed to be "read," or interpreted, outward from the center.

Safavid (saf′ə vid), dynasty of kings that ruled Persia between 1501 and 1722. Founded by Ismail, leader of Turkish tribe that began invading Persia in the late 1400s, the dynasty was known for its patronage of the arts and architecture and for the beauty of its capital, Isfahan (page 166).

Sanskrit (san′skrit), ancient language of India that is usually divided into two historical periods: Vedic, lasting from approximately 1500 to 300 B.C., is the language of the *Vedas*, the oldest sacred scriptures of Hinduism (see); and classical Sanskrit, lasting from approximately 500 B.C. to A.D. 1000, is the language of important works of literature, including the epic poems the *Ramayana* and the *Mahabharata*.

Satyagraha (saht′ya grə ha), political and spiritual movement begun in 1919 by Mohandas Gandhi. To foster social change, including Indian independence from the British Empire, Gandhi, called the Mahatma (great soul), taught that truth, courage, and passive resistance was more effective than violence and that exemplary behavior was more important than achievement (page 526).

Second Coming, in Christian theology, the end of this world, the general resurrection of the dead, and the coming of Christ to judge the living and the dead as described in the New Testament, particularly in the last verses of the Book of Revelation.

sestet (ses tet′), last six lines of a Petrarchan sonnet. The sestet resolves the proposition laid out in the octave or first eight lines (page 232).

Shi'ite (shē īt′), member of the Islamic sect that believes that Muslim leadership passed from Muhammad through his daughter, Fatima, to his son-in-law, Ali. Because the majority of Shi'ites live in Iran, this division of Islam has been referred as a Persian variation.

Socratic method (sō krat′ik), use of a series of questions to lead a pupil into making logical conclusions. Socrates (c. 469–399 B.C.), a philosopher of ancient Greece, introduced the method to gain and demonstrate knowledge of universal truths (page 61).

sonnet (son′it), lyric poem of 14 lines in iambic pentameter. According to rhyme scheme, sonnets fall into either the Italian or English form (page 232). The Petrarchan sonnet (named for Italian poet Petrarch) is usually rhymed abba abba cde cde and forms a poem in two parts: an eight-line octave (see) and six-line sestet (see). The Shakespearean form (named for English poet Shakespeare) is usually rhymed *abab cdcd efef gg* and is presented in four parts: the central idea or theme is developed in three quatrains and concluded in a final couplet.

stele (stē′lē), upright slab or pillar of stone or terra cotta, bearing an inscription, sculptural design, or memorial (pages 15 and 350). The form is common to many cultures, from ancient Egypt, Greece, and the Maya of Mexico to cemeteries in modern America.

Stoicism (stō′ə siz əm), Greek school of philosophy founded by Zeno of Citium (Cyprus) in about 300 B.C. (page 65). The Stoics taught that all people contain within themselves reason. Reason connects the individual to humanity as well as to God — the Reason that governs the universe. Virtue — and through virtue, happiness — is found in reason, in freeing oneself from indulgence and passions, and in concentrating on duty and only that which can be controlled.

stream of consciousness, literary technique that records or recreates a character's flow of thought (page 521). Images, perceptions, and memories are presented by the author in a seemingly random, but in fact highly controlled, fashion to simulate the flow and workings of a human mind.

Sturm und Drang (shturm′unt dräng′), German literary movement of the late eighteenth century characterized by the rejection of neoclassical conventions, by strong nationalistic feelings, emotionalism, and spiritual restlessness. A forerunner of romanticism, *Sturm und Drang* (German for "storm and stress") drama and lyric poetry were revolutionary in their intensity, stress on subjectivity, and depiction of the unease of life, particularly the life of genius, in modern society (page 465).

Sufi (sü′fē), mystical Muslim sect and literary movement, originating in eighth-century Persia, that pursued insight into the Divine Being through ecstasy and contemplation. Sufi lyric poetry typically expresses, in highly developed symbols, the ecstasy of union between the soul and God. The name *Sufi*, Arabic for wool, symbolized the sect's rejection of worldly comfort: "The Sufi possesses nothing, desires nothing."

Sung (süng), also Song, Chinese dynasty (960–1279) marked by great urban expansion and a flowering of the arts, particularly in painting, ceramics, and philosophy.

Sunni (sun′ə), member of the majority division of Islam, which believes in the traditional part of Islamic law based on Muhammad's acts and sayings, as well as the Quran. The Sunni differ with the Shi'ite (see) primarily over legitimacy of Islamic leadership.

Surrealism (sə rē′ə liz əm), twentieth-century art and literary movement that attempted to show what took place in dreams in the subconscious mind (page 512). Such artists as René Magritte, Salvador Dali, and Max Ernst and the writer Jean Cocteau pictured a shocking, magical world of great and unexpected distortion that attempted to express human nature at a deeper, truer level.

T'ang (täng), also Tang, Chinese dynasty (A.D. 618–907) marked by physical expansion into central Asia, imperial favor of Buddhism, and the invention of the printing press. Called the golden age of Chinese civilization, T'ang dynasty China became a world center of the arts, literature, scholarship, and philosophy.

Taoism (tou′iz əm), Chinese philosophy and religion, derived by tradition from the teachings of Lao-tze, that developed between the fourth and second centuries B.C. Taoism teaches simplicity and humility as a way to peace and harmony.

terza rima (ter′tsä rē′mä), verse form, employed by Dante in the *Divine Comedy*, with a three-line stanza in which line two of each stanza rhymes with one and three of the next stanza: *aba, bcb, cdc,* and so on (page 210).

Torah (tōr′ ə), Hebrew name for the first five books of the Bible, believed by Orthodox Jews to have been handed down to Moses on Mount Sinai and then transferred by him to the Israelites. Torah can also refer to the entire body of Jewish law and tradition.

Trinity (trin′ə tē), fundamental Christian doctrine that the one God exists in three Divine Persons: God the Father, God the Son, and God the Holy Spirit. Most teachers of Christianity consider the Trinity a mystery, that is, a concept that cannot be fully comprehended by human intelligence.

trompe l'oeil (trônp lö′yə), in painting, a visual trick in which objects represented seem to be real (page 76). Trompe l'oeil, a French term literally meaning "deceives the eye," grew out of the development of one-point perspective (see) in the Renaissance.

troubadour (trü′bə dôr), poet-musicians of southern France in the eleventh, twelfth, and thirteenth centuries. Dealing mainly with chivalry and the tradition of courtly love, the short poetry of the troubadour was written and recited in a dialect — called Langue d'oc or Provence — that emerged from vulgate Latin in southern France and northern Italy.

ukiyo-e (ü′ki yo ye), seventeenth, eighteenth, and early nineteenth-century Japanese school of woodblock prints. Literally meaning "pictures of the floating world," the deceptively simple, two-dimensional prints often depict the ephemeral "floating world" of prostitutes, circus performers, and actors. Designed for the lower bourgeoisie, *ukiyo-e*, while shunned by Japanese intellectuals, greatly influenced such western artists as Whistler, Toulouse-Lautrec, and architect Frank Lloyd Wright (page 320).

vanishing point, in the technique of perspective (see), the point toward which receding parallel lines seem to converge (page 237).

vault, in architecture, an arched roof or ceiling (page 196). The barrel vault, characteristic of the Romanesque (see), is a continuous, unbroken, tunnel-like arch. Groined vaults, a characteristic of Gothic style (see), consist of two barrel vaults joined at right angles. When the meeting lines, or groins, are covered with reinforcing ribs, the system is referred to as ribbed vaulting.

winter count, pictorial symbol created to represent important events in a year in the life of a Native American tribe of the western plains (page 411). Each year, a winter count symbol was painted on the buffalo hide upon which was kept the narrative record of tribal history, which in some examples spans many generations.

Yoruba (yō′ru bə), historic and present-day people and region of West Africa. Today, the Yoruba inhabit southwestern Nigeria and parts of Benin and Togo (page 356). Before the eighteenth century, the Yoruba formed into powerful city-states, including the kingdoms of Ife and Oyo, that dominated the region. From the seventeenth through the nineteenth centuries, these states, with their unique urban culture, were weakened by continuous raiding by slave traders, who shipped many Yoruba to America.

Zulu (zü′lü), historic and present-day people of South Africa. Today, the Zulu inhabit part of the province of Natal in the Republic of South Africa. In the early nineteenth century, the Zulu under King Shaka conquered a large area of South Africa, which they held as Zululand, until subdued by the British in 1879 (page 377).

GLOSSARY

abhor (ab hôr'), v. regard with horror, disgust.

abide (ə bīd'), v. submit to, tolerate.

abjure (ab jur'), v. swear to give up, renounce.

ablaze (ə blāz'), adj. on fire, blazing.

abolish (ə bol'ish), v. do away with .

abound (ə bound'), v. be plentiful or numerous.

absolute (ab'sə lüt), adj. with no limits.

abstain (ab stān'), v. hold oneself back voluntarily, especially because of one's principles.

absurd (ab sėrd'), adj. plainly not true.

abundance (ə bun'dəns), n. an overflowing quantity or amount, great plenty.

abutment (ə but'mənt), n. a support for an arch or bridge.

accommodate (ə kom'ə dāt), v. have room for.

accordance (ə kôrd'ns), n. agreement, unity.

acquiesce (ak wē es'), v. give consent by keeping silent or not making objections, accept.

acquire (ə kwīr'), v. come into possession of.

adequate (ad'ə kwit), adj. sufficient.

adhere (ad hir'), v. stick fast, remain attached.

adjudge (ə juj'), v. decree or decide by law.

admonition (ad mə nish'ən), n. a gentle reproof.

adroit (ə droit'), adj. resourceful, clever.

adversary (ad'vər ser ē), n. person or group opposing or resisting another or others.

agile (aj'əl), adj. moving with speed or ease.

agitate (aj'ə tāt), v. disturb or upset very much.

agog (ə gog'), adj. full of expectation, eager.

allot (ə lot'), v. divide or distribute into shares.

alms (ämz), n. money or gifts freely given to help the poor, charity.

aloof (ə lüf'), adv. apart from, away from.

ambiguity (am bə gyü'ə tē), n. possibility of being understood in two or more ways.

amends (ə mendz'), n. something given or paid to make up for a wrong or an injury.

analogous (ə nal'ə gəs), adj. similar in certain qualities, circumstances, or uses; comparable.

analogue (an'l ôg), n. a similar thing.

analysis (ə nal'ə sis), n. a breaking up of anything complex into its various simple elements.

analytic (an l it'ik), adj. of analysis.

anathema (ə nath'ə mə), n. person or thing that has been cursed or is utterly detested.

ancestor (an'ses tər), n. person from whom one is descended.

anomaly (ə nom'ə lē), n. something that deviates from the rule or recognized standard.

apparent (ə par'ənt), adj. plain to see, evident.

arbitrary (är'bə trer ē), adj. based on one's own wishes, not going by rule or law.

archetype (är'kə tīp), n. an original model from which copies are made.

arduous (är'jü əs), adj. requiring much effort.

artificer (är tif'ə sər), n. a skilled workman.

ascend (ə send'), v. go up, rise, move upward.

ascertain (as ər tān'), v. find out for certain.

askew (ə skyü'), adv., adj. out of the proper position, turned the wrong way.

assent (ə sent'), v. express agreement, consent.

assertion (ə sėr'shən), n. a positive statement; an insisting on a right or claim.

assimilate (ə sim'ə lāt), v. take in and make part of oneself, absorb.

astute (ə stüt'), adj. shrewd, crafty.

avail (ə vāl'), v. be of use or value to, help.

avarice (av'ər is), n. too great a desire for money or property, greed for wealth.

averse (ə vėrs'), adj. opposed or unwilling.

avowal (ə vou'əl), n. a frank and open declaration, admission; acknowledgment.

banish (ban'ish), v. compel a person to leave a country by order of political authority, exile.

barbarous (bär'bər əs), adj. not civilized, cruel.

barnacled (bär'nə kəld), adj. covered with barnacles.

barrage (bə räzh'), n. barrier of artillery fire; a large number of words, blows, etc., coming quickly one after the other.

barred (bärd), v. put bars across, block.

barter (bär'tər), v. trade by exchanging goods or services for others, without using money.

battlement (bat'l mənt), n. a low wall for defense at the top of a tower or wall.

beacon (bē'kən), n. fire or light used as a signal.

befit (bi fit'), v. be suitable for, be proper for.

begotten (bē gôt'ən), v. fathered.

behoove (bi hüv'), v. be necessary for, be proper for.

beneficent (bə nef'ə sənt), adj. doing good.

bespatter (bi spat'ər), v. soil; slander.

bestow (bi stō'), v. give as a gift; make use of.

betrothal (bi trō'ŦHəl), n. a promise to marry.

bidding (bid'ing), n. command, order.

biennial (bī en'ē əl), adj. occurring every two years, event that occurs every two years.

bilious (bil'yəs), adj. greenish-yellow color.

blaspheme (bla sfēm'), v. speak about (God, sacred things, etc.) with abuse or contempt.

boisterous (boi'stər əs), adj. noisily cheerful, exuberant; rough and stormy.

bourgeois (bür zhwä'), n. person of the middle

class.

brand (brand), *n.* the quality or kind (of goods) as indicated by a mark, stamp, or label.

brandish (bran′dish), *v.* wave or shake threateningly; flourish.

briar (brī′ər), *n.* thorny or prickly bush.

callous (kal′əs), *adj.* unfeeling, insensitive.

calumny (kal′əm nē), *n.* a false statement made to injure someone's reputation.

capital (kap′ə təl), *n.* national or individual wealth as produced by industry.

caprice (kə prēs′), *n.* sudden change of mind without reason; whim.

capsize (kap sīz′), *v.* upset, overturn.

capstan (kap′stən), *n.* machine for lifting or pulling that revolves on an upright shaft, such as those used on ships to raise the anchor.

carnage (kär′nij), *n.* slaughter of a great number of people.

cascade (ka skād′), *v.* to flow in a rippling manner.

causeway (kôz′wā), *n.* a raised road or path, usually built across wet ground.

cavity (kav′ə tē), *n.* hollow place, hole.

cedar (sē′dər), *n.* evergreen tree of the pine family having fragrant, reddish wood.

celestial (sə les′chəl), *adj.* of the sky, heavens.

censor (sen′sər) *n.* examiner.

censure (sen′shər), *n.* expression of disapproval, criticism; penalty.

certitude (sėr′tə tüd), *n.* certainty, sureness.

chasm (kaz′əm), *n.* a deep opening in the earth.

chastisement (cha stīz′mənt), *n.* punishment; severe criticism or rebuke.

chastity (chas′tə tē), *n.* abstention from sexual intercourse; purity, virtue.

cinder (sin′dər), *n.* piece of wood or coal partly burned, but no longer flaming.

citadel (sit′ə dəl), *n.* a strongly fortified place.

civilization (siv ə lə zā′shən), *n.* the culture and ways of living of a people or nation.

clad (klad), *v.* clothed, covered.

cleanse (klenz), *v.* make clean, purify.

clemency (klem′ən sē), *n.* gentleness in the use of power or authority, mercy or leniency.

clergy (klėr′jē), *n.* persons ordained for religious work, ministers, priests, rabbis.

cleric (kler′ik), *n.* clergyman.

clinical (klin′ə kəl), *adj.* of or having to do with the study of disease by observation rather than by experiment or autopsy.

coffer (kô′fər), *n.* box, chest, or trunk, especially one used to hold money or other valuables.

combustion (kəm bus′chən), *n.* burning.

commence (kə mens′), *v.* make a start, begin.

commencement (kə mens′mənt), *n.* beginning.

commendation (kom ən dā′shən), *n.* praise, approval; recommendation.

commensurable (kə men′shər ə bəl), *adj.* measurable by the same standards or values.

commerce (kom′ərs), *n.* buying and selling between different places, business.

commodity (kə mod′ə tē), *n.* anything that is bought or sold.

commonwealth (kom′ən welth), *n.* a democratic state, republic.

compact (kom′pakt), *n.* agreement or contract.

compass (kum′pəs), *v.* plot, scheme.

compel (kəm pel′), *v.* drive or urge with force.

composite (kəm poz′it), *adj.* made up of various parts, compound.

composure (kəm pō′zhər), *n.* calmness, self-control.

compulsion (kəm pul′shən), *n.* an impulse that is hard to resist.

conception (kən sep′shən), *n.* thought, idea.

concernment (kən sėrn′mənt), *n.* importance, interest.

conduct (kon′dukt), *n.* way of acting, behavior.

confederacy (kən fed′ər ə sē), *n.* a union of countries, states, or tribes.

confederate (kən fed′ər it), *n.* a country, person, etc., joined with another.

congeal (kən jēl′), *v.* change from a liquid to a solid, thicken, stiffen.

conjecture (kən jek′chər), *n.* formation of an opinion without sufficient evidence for proof.

conjuration (kon jə rā′shən), *n.* an invoking by a sacred name.

conscience (kon′shəns), *n.* sense of right and wrong.

consolation (kon sə lā′shən), *n.* a comforting person, thing, or event.

consternation (kon stər nā′shən), *n.* great dismay.

constrain (kən strān′), *v.* force, compel.

constraint (kən strānt′), *n.* a holding back of natural feelings.

contagion (kən tā′jən), *n.* the spreading of disease by direct or indirect contact.

contagious (kən tā′jəs), *adj.* spreading by direct or indirect contact, catching.

contemptuous (kən temp′chü əs), *adj.* showing contempt, scornful.

contrary (kon′trer ē), *adj.* completely different.

contrivance (kən trī′vəns), *n.* invention, machine.

contrive (kən trīv′), *v.* plan with cleverness, invent, plot, scheme.

convene (kən vēn′), v. meet for some purpose.

coquettish (kō ket′ish), adj. acting in a manner to attract attention, flirtatious.

cornice (kôr′nis), n. an ornamental horizontal molding along the top of a wall or building.

corporate (kôr′pər it), adj. united, combined.

correspondence (kôr ə spon′dəns), n. a being in harmony, agreement.

corselet (kôrs′lit), n. armor for the upper part of the body.

cosmology (koz mol′ə jē), n. science or theory of the universe.

council (koun′səl), n. group of people called together to give advice or settle questions.

counterfeiter (koun′tər fit ər), n. someone who forges money, pictures, etc.

court (kôrt), n. residence of a sovereign.

covetous (kuv′ə təs), adj. desiring things that belong to others.

credulity (krə dü′lə tē), n. readiness to believe.

culture (kul′chər), n. behavior that is socially taught, rather than instinctive.

cumulative (kyü′myə lə tiv), adj. increasing or growing in amount, force, etc. by additions.

cunning (kun′ing), adj. sly, clever, skillful.

custom (kus′təm), n. usual action or practice.

damask (dam′əsk), n. a shiny, reversible linen, silk, or cotton fabric with woven designs.

day laborer (dā lā′bər ər), n. an unskilled or manual worker who is paid by the day.

debar (di bär′), v. bar out, shut out, prevent.

debauch (di bôch′), v. lead away from virtue.

decapitate (di kap′ə tāt), v. cut off the head of.

deed (dēd), n. thing done, act, performance.

defame (di fām′), v. attack the good name of.

degradation (deg rə dā′shən), n. a reduction of rank, character, or quality.

deign (dān), v. think fit, condescend.

deity (dē′ə tē), n. god or goddess.

dejection (di jek′shən), n. lowness of spirits.

delectable (di lek′tə bəl), adj. very pleasing.

demean (di mēn′), v. lower in quality or standing.

demented (di men′tid), adj. mentally ill, insane.

deportment (di pôrt′mənt), n. way a person acts.

deprecation (dep′rə kā shən), n. strong expression of disapproval.

derision (di rizh′ən), n. scornful laughter, ridicule.

derive (di rīv′), v. obtain from a source, get.

deter (di tėr′), v. discourage or prevent from acting or proceeding.

dictates (dik′tāts), n. commands, orders.

diffuse (di fyüz′), v. spread out, scatter widely.

dilemma (də lem′ə), n. situation requiring a choice between two unfavorable alternatives.

diligent (dil′ə jənt), adj. hard-working; careful.

din (din), n. continuing loud confused noise.

diplomatic (dip lō mat′ik), adj. having or showing skill in dealing with others, tactful.

disciple (də sī′pəl), n. believer in the thought and teaching of any leader, follower.

discourse (dis kôrs′), v. speak or write formally on some subject, talk, converse.

discrimination (dis krim′ə nā shən), n. the ability to make fine distinctions or notice differences.

dishevelment (də shev′əl mənt), n. disorder.

dispel (dis pel′), v. drive away, disperse.

dispensation (dis pən sā′shən), n. official permission to disregard a rule.

dissembler (di sem′blər), n. one who hides his true feelings, thoughts, and plans.

dissolution (dis′ə lü shən), n. the breaking up of an assembly by ending its session.

dissuade (di swād′), v. persuade not to do something, advise against.

distinction (dis tingk′shən), n. a distinguishing from others.

distortion (dis tôr′shən), n. a twisting out of shape, changing the normal appearance of.

docile (dos′əl), adj. easily managed or trained.

doctrine (dok′trən), n. what is taught as true by a church, nation, or group of persons, belief.

dole (dōl), n. money, food, etc. given in charity.

dominion (də min′yən), n. power or right of governing; a ruler's territory.

drawn (drôn), adj. made tense; strained.

dread (dred), v. fear greatly, feel terror about.

drudge (druj), n. person who does hard, tiresome, or disagreeable work.

dynasty (dī′nə stē), n. succession of rulers who belong to the same family.

ecclesiastical (i klē zē as′tə kəl), adj. of or having to do with the church.

edifice (ed′ə fis), n. a building, especially a large or impressive one.

effectual (ə fek′chü əl), adj. capable of producing the desired effect.

efficacy (ef′ə kə sē), n. power to produce the effect wanted.

effigy (ef′ə jē), n. image or statue.

electrodynamics (i lek trō dī nam′iks), n. branch of physics that deals with the nature and behavior of electric currents.

eloquence (el′ə kwəns), n. the art of using language so as to stir the feelings.

elude (i lüd′), v. avoid or escape from.

emasculate (i mas′kyə lāt), v. destroy the force of, weaken.

embalm (em bäm′), v. treat a dead body with chemicals to keep it from decaying.

embassy (em′bə sē), n. ambassador and staff of assistants.

emblem (em′bləm), n. object or representation that stands for a concept, quality, or idea.

encamped (en kamp′əd), v. living in a camp.

encapsulate (en kap′sə lāt), v. contain, sum up.

endowment (en dou′mənt), n. money or property given a person or institution to provide a permanent income; inborn ability or talent.

engrave (en grāv′), v. cut a design into a metal plate, block of wood, etc.; in printing, a print from such a plate or block.

enlighten (en lit′n), v. inform, instruct.

en masse (en mas′), adj. all together.

enmity (en′mə tē), n. hostility, hatred.

ennoble (en nō′bəl), v. dignify, make noble.

entreat (en trēt′), v. ask earnestly, beg.

epidemic (ep ə dem′ik), n. the rapid spread of a disease so that many people have it.

epidermis (ep ə dėr′mis), n. the outer protective layer of the skin.

epithet (ep′ə thet), n. a word or phrase expressing some quality or attribute.

epoch (ep′ək), n. a period of time, era, age.

erect (i rekt′), v. put up, build.

erratic (ə rat′ik), adj. not steady, uncertain.

escapade (es′kə pād), n. wild adventure.

essence (es′ns), n. that which makes a thing what it is, necessary part or parts.

esteem (e stēm′), v. have a good opinion of.

exceed (ek sēd′), v. be more, go beyond.

exert (eg zėrt′), v. put into use, make an effort.

exhort (eg zôrt′), v. urge strongly.

expediency (ek spē′dē ən sē), n. helping to bring about a desired result.

experimental (ek sper ə men′tl), adj. based on experiments; for testing or trying out.

exploit (ek sploit′), v. make unfair or selfish use of.

extent (ek stent′), n. size, space, length, amount or degree to which a thing extends.

exterminate (ek stėr′mə nāt), v. destroy completely.

fast (fast), v. go without food.

fathom (faтн′əm), n. unit of measure equal to six feet, for measuring the depth of water.

fay (fā), n. fairy.

fealty (fē′əl tē), n. loyalty owed, allegiance.

feat (fēt), n. a great deed, achievement.

feigner (fān′ir), n. one who puts on a false appearance or pretends.

felicity (fə lis′ə tē), n. good fortune.

felon (fel′ən), n. a criminal.

fetter (fet′ər), n. chain or shackle for the feet.

filial (fil′ē əl), adj. of a son or daughter.

firmament (fėr′mə mənt), n. the heavens, sky.

firm (ferm), adj. not yielding easily to pressure.

fleeting (flē′ting), adj. moving swiftly, rapidly.

flippant (flip′ənt), adj. smart or pert in speech or manner, not respectful.

floss (flôs), n. a shiny, untwisted silk thread.

foe (fō), n. enemy.

foment (fō ment′), v. stir up, instigate.

foretold (fôr′tōld), v. predicted.

fortify (fôr′tə fi), v. strengthen against attack.

fount (fount), n. fountain; source, origin.

frantic (fran′tik), adj. very much excited.

fraud (frôd), n. dishonest dealings, or person.

fray (frā), n. noisy quarrel, brawl.

frenzy (fren′zē), n. state of near madness.

frugal (frü′gəl), adj. avoiding waste, thrifty.

furl (fėrl), v. roll up, fold up.

furnish (fėr′nish), v. supply a room or house with furniture or equipment.

furrow (fėr′ō), n. a long, narrow groove or track cut in the earth by a plow.

futility (fyü til′ə tē), n. uselessness, ineffectiveness.

gable (gā′bəl), n. end of a ridged roof, with the three-cornered piece of wall that it covers.

garlanded (gär′lənd id), adj. decorated with wreaths or strings of flowers.

garment (gär′mənt), n. any article of clothing.

garrulity (gə rü′lə tē), n. talkativeness.

genocide (jen′ə sid), n. the extermination of a cultural or racial group.

germ (jerm), n. the beginning of anything.

glimmer (glim′ər), n. a faint light or idea.

gnaw (nô), v. wear away, trouble, torment.

gradation (grā dā′shən), n. a gradual change.

graft (graft), n. dishonest gains or profits made by a person through an official position.

gratify (grat′ə fi), v. give pleasure to; satisfy.

grave (grāv), adj. earnest, thoughtful, serious.

grieve (grēv), v. feel great sadness caused by trouble or loss.

grimace (grə mās′), n. a twisting of the face; an ugly or funny smile.

grovel (gruv′əl), v. abase or humble oneself.

guffaw (gu fô′), n. burst of loud laughter.

guile (gil), n. crafty deceit, cunning.

habitable (hab′ə tə bəl), adj. fit to live in.

habituate (hə bich′ü āt), v. accustom.

hag (hag), n. a very ugly old woman, especially one who is vicious or malicious.

halt (hôlt), v. stop for a time, order a stop.

harass (har′əs), v. trouble by repeated attacks.

harmony (här′mə nē), n. an orderly or pleasing

arrangement of parts, congruity.

heathen (hē′ᴛʜən), *n.* person who does not believe in the God or the Bible, that is, a non-Jew, non-Christian, or non-Muslim.

henchman (hench′mən), *n.* an obedient, unscrupulous follower.

hierophant (hī′ər ə fant), *n.* interpreter of sacred mysterious or religious knowledge.

hinder (hin′dər), *v.* keep back, hamper.

hitherto (hiᴛʜ ər tü′), *adv.* until now.

hoard (hôrd), *v.* save and store away.

homage (hom′ij), *n.* dutiful respect, reverence.

host (hōst), *n.* army of soldiers.

hostile (hos′tl), *adj.* opposed, unfriendly.

hotly (hot′lē), *adv.* fierily, violently.

hurl (hėrl), *v.* throw with much force, fling.

hypocrite (hip′ə krit), *n.* person who pretends to be very good or religious.

hypothesis (hī poth′ə sis), *n.* proposition assumed as a basis for reasoning.

ignoble (ig nō′bəl), *adj.* without honor.

illuminate (i lü′mə nāt), *v.* light up, brighten.

illustrious (i lus′trē əs), *adj.* very famous, great.

immersion (i mėr′zhən), *n.* dipping a person completely under water.

imminent (im′ə nənt), *adj.* about to occur.

immune (i myün′), *adj.* protected from disease, poison, etc.; free, exempt.

imperious (im pir′ē əs), *adj.* haughty, arrogant.

impertinent (im pėrt′n ənt), *adj.* rudely bold, impudent, insolent.

implement (im′plə mənt), *n.* tool, instrument.

implicit (im plis′it), *adj.* meant, but not clearly expressed or distinctly stated, implied.

impudent (im′pyə dənt), *adj.* rude, insolent.

inalienable (in ā′lyə nə bəl), *adj.* that cannot be given or taken away.

incantation (in kan tā′shən), *n.* set of words spoken as a magic charm.

incarnate (in kär′nāt), *adj.* embodied in flesh, especially in human form.

incite (in sīt′), *v.* stimulate to action, urge on.

incompatible (in kəm pat′ə bəl), *adj.* not able to live or act together peaceably.

incontrovertible (in kən trə ver′tə bəl), *adj.* that cannot be disputed or denied.

incorporeal (in kôr pôr′ē əl), *adj.* not made of any material substance, spiritual.

incredulous (in krej′ə ləs), *adj.* not ready to believe, doubting, skeptical.

inculcate (in kul′kāt), *v.* impress on the mind of another by frequent repetition.

incumbent (in kum′bənt), *adj.* resting on a person as a duty or obligation.

incur (in ker′), *v.* bring on oneself; cause.

indemnification (in dem nə fə kā′shən), *n.* a compensation for damage, loss, or hardship.

indispensable (in dis pen′sə bəl), *adj.* absolutely necessary.

indisputable (in dis pyü′tə bəl), *adj.* too evident to be disputed, certain.

indubitable (in dü′bə tə bəl), *adj.* too evident to be doubted, certain.

ineluctable (in i luk′tə bəl), *adj.* that cannot be escaped or avoided, inevitable.

inequality (in i kwol′ə tē), *n.* lack of equality; lack of evenness, regularity.

inexplicable (in ik splik′ə bəl), *adj.* that cannot be explained, understood.

infallible (in fal′ə bəl), *adj.* free from error.

infamy (in′fə mē), *n.* very bad reputation.

ingenious (in jē′nyəs), *adj.* skillful in making, cleverly planned.

inherent (in hir′ənt), *adj.* belonging to a person or thing as a permanent and essential quality.

inproscribable (in prō skrib′ə bəl), *adj.* not subject to prohibition, inalienable.

inquisitive (in kwiz′ə tiv), *adj.* questioning, curious.

insinuate (in sin′yü āt), *v.* suggest in an indirect way, hint.

insolence (in′sō ləns), *n.* bold rudeness, insulting behavior or speech.

instinct (in′stingkt), *n.* inborn tendency.

integrity (in teg′rə tē), *n.* honesty or sincerity.

intelligible (in tel′ə jə bəl), *adj.* capable of being understood, clear.

interstice (in ter′stis), *n.* a small or narrow space between things or parts, chink, crack.

intuition (in tü ish′ən), *n.* immediate perception or understanding of truths.

investigate (in ves′tə gāt), *v.* look into thoroughly.

inviolable (in vī′ə lə bəl), *adj.* must not be violated, sacred.

invocation (in və kā′shən), *n.* a calling upon in prayer.

juncture (jungk′chər), *n.* point of time.

justly (just′lē), *adv.* in a just or fair manner.

keenly (kēn′lē), *adv.* in a perceptive manner.

ken (ken), *n.* range of knowledge.

kin (kin), *n.* family, relatives.

kindle (kin′dl), *v.* stir up, arouse.

lamentable (lam′ən tə bəl), *adj.* to be regretted.

languid (lang′gwid), *adj.* without energy, weak.

lattice (lat′is), *n.* structure of crossed wood with open spaces between.

lavish (lav′ish), *adj.* extravagant, prodigal.

league (lēg), *n.* measure of distance, usually

about 3 miles.

lean (lēn), *adj.* spare, not fat.

leper (lep′ər), *n.* outcast; person with leprosy.

levity (lev′ə tē), *n.* lightness of mind.

libation (lī bā′shən), *n.* a pouring out of wine, water, etc., as an offering to a god.

linger (ling′gər), *v.* stay on, keep remaining.

litigious (lə tij′əs), *adj.* having the habit of bringing lawsuits.

loath (lōth), *adj.* unwilling, reluctant.

lofty (lôf′tē), *adj.* high, exalted, dignified.

luminous (lü′mə nəs), *adj.* shining with light.

magistrate (maj′ə strāt), *n.* governmental official who has power to enforce the law.

magnitude (mag′nə tüd), *n.* greatness of size.

mailed (māld), *adj.* covered or protected with armor made of metal rings or loops of chain.

majesty (maj′ə stē), *n.* royal dignity, noble appearance.

malefactor (mal′ə fak tər), *n.* criminal, evildoer.

malice (mal′is), *n.* active ill will, wish to hurt.

malign (mə lin′), *v.* speak ill of, slander.

malignant (mə lig′nənt), *adv.* very evil.

maneuver (mə nü′vər), *n.* agile or skillful movement made to elude or deceive.

manifestation (man ə fə stā′shən), *n.* an appearance to the eye or to the mind.

manifesto (man′ə fes tō), *n.* public declaration of intentions or motives.

manifold (man′ə fōld), *adj.* of many kinds.

masonry (mā′sn rē), *n.* stonewall or brickwork.

mast (mast), *n.* long pole rising from the keel of a sailing vessel to support the rigging.

mauve (mōv), *n.* a delicate, pale purple.

mechanics (mə kan′iks), *n.* branch of physics dealing with the action of forces on solids, liquids, and gases at rest or in motion.

medicinal herbs (mə dis′n əl erbz), *n.* herbs having value as medicine.

mentor (men′tər), *n.* wise and trusted advisor.

mere (mir), *adj.* nothing else than, only, simple.

methodology (meth ə dol′ə jē), *n.* system of procedures used in any field.

midst (midst), *n.* in the middle of.

might (mīt), *n.* great power, strength.

millet (mil′it), *n.* annual cereal grass, cultivated as a food grain and as fodder.

mingle (ming′gəl), *v.* combine, blend.

misogynist (mi soj′ə nist), *n,* hater of women.

mockery (mok′ər ē), *n.* ridicule, derision.

moor (mur), *v.* to secure a ship, anchor.

mortal (môr′tl), *adj.* sure to die sometime.

motivate (mō′tə vāt), *v.* give an incentive.

mourning (môr′ning), *n.* to show sorrow for a person's death.

multitudinous (mul tə tüd′n əs), *adj.* forming a great crowd, existing in great numbers.

munificent (myü nif′ə sənt), *adj.* bountiful.

neurosis (nu rō′sis), *n.* any of various mental or emotional disorders, characterized by depression, anxiety, compulsive behavior, etc.

neutralize (nü′trə līz), *v.* counterbalance.

notable (nō′tə bəl), *adj.* striking, remarkable.

notion (nō′shən), *n.* idea, understanding.

notoriety (nō tə rī′ə tē), *n.* bad or ill fame.

nurture (ner′chər), *v.* bring up, care for.

nymph (nimf), *n.* stage of life between egg and adulthood for insects.

objective (əb jek′tiv), *adj.* existing outside the mind as something actual, real.

oblation (o blā′shən), *n.* offering to a god.

oblige (ə blīj), *v.* bind by a promise, contract.

obliterate (ə blit′ə rāt), *v.* remove all traces of.

occult (ə kult′), *adj.* beyond the bounds of ordinary knowledge, supernatural.

odalisque (ō′də lisk), *n.* female slave in a harem, particularly that of a sultan of Turkey.

odoriferous (ō də rif′ər əs), *adj.* giving off an odor.

offering (ô′fər ing), *n.* the giving of something as an act of worship, gift as to a church.

omnibus (om′nə bus), *n.* bus.

opaque (ō pāk′), *adj.* not letting light through.

ordain (ôr dān′), *v.* order, establish as law.

ordeal (ôr dēl′), *n.* a severe test or experience.

ordinance (ôrd′n əns), *n.* rule, law, decree.

pall (pôl), 1 *n.* a dark, gloomy covering 2 *v.* become distasteful or tiresome.

pallor (pal′ər), *n.* lack of normal color.

panacea (pan ə sē ə), *n.* remedy for all diseases or ills, cure-all.

pandemic (pan dem′ik), *adj.* spread over an entire country, continent, or the whole world.

paradox (par′ə doks), *n.* statement that may be true but seems to say two opposite things.

paralogism (pa ral′ō jiz m), *n.* in logic, a reasoning false in form, in which the conclusion does not follow from the premise.

partisan (pär′tə zən), *n.* strong supporter of a person, party, or cause.

pasture (pas′chər), *n.* grassy field on which cattle, sheep, or horses can feed.

patent (pat′nt), *n.* an official government grant that gives a person or company sole rights to make, use, or sell a new invention.

patriarch (pā′trē ärk), *n.* father who is the ruler of a family or tribe; highly respected elder.

patrician (pə trish′ən), *n.* aristocrat or person of noble birth.

patronage (pā′trə nij), *n.* favor, encouragement, or support given by a patron.

pauper (pô′pər), *n.* a very poor person.

peculiar (pi kyü′lyər), *adj.* particular, distinctive.

pecuniary (pi kyü′nē er ē), *adj.* of or having to do with money.

perdition (pər dish′ən), *n.* hell; damnation.

perfidious (pər fid′ē əs), *adj.* deliberately faithless, treacherous.

perpetual (pər pech′ü əl), *adj.* lasting throughout life or for eternity.

perplexity (pər plek′sə tē), *n.* being puzzled, confused, bewildered.

persecution (per sə kyü′shən), *n.* oppression or period of systematic punishment.

piety (pi′ə tē), *n.* devotion to God and religion.

pinch (pinch), *n.* time of great need; emergency.

pinnacle (pin′ə kəl), *n.* the highest point.

pitch (pich), *n.* in music, the highness or lowness of a tone or sound.

pit (pit), *v.* set to fight or to compete.

plain (plān), *n.* flat stretch of land, prairie.

plebeian (pli bē′ən), *n.* one of the common people.

pliant (pli′ənt), *adj.* flexible, yielding.

plummet (plum′it), *v.* plunge, drop.

poach (pōch), *v.* to hunt without any right.

pommel (pum′əl), *n.* part of a saddle that sticks up at the front.

posit (poz′it), *v.* assume as a fact or principle.

potency (pōt′n sē), *n.* being powerful, strong.

prate (prāt), *v.* talk in a foolish way.

precipice (pres′ə pis), *n.* very steep rockface.

predecessor (pred′ə ses ər), *n.* thing that came before another.

prejudice (prej′ə dis), *v.* opinion formed without taking time and care to judge fairly.

premise (prem′is), *n.* in logic, a statement assumed to be true, used to draw a conclusion.

prescribe (pri skrīb′), *v.* lay down as a rule.

preside (pri zīd′), *v.* hold the place of authority.

pretence [pretense] (prē′tens), *n.* claim.

pretension (pri ten′shən), *n.* a showy display.

pretext (prē′tekst), *n.* misleading excuse.

prevail (pri vāl′), *v.* be the stongest.

procession (prə sesh′ən), *n.* an orderly moving forward.

procure (prə kyur′), *v.* obtain by care or effort.

prodigious (prə dij′əs), *adj.* very great, vast.

prodigy (prod′ə jē), *n.* person, especially a child, endowed with amazing brilliance.

profess (prə fes′), *v.* declare one's belief in.

profusion (prə fyü′zhən), *n.* great abundance.

progeny (proj′ə nē), *n.* children or offspring.

proletariat (prō lə ter′ē ət), *n.* the lowest economic class, includes unskilled labor.

proliferate (prō lif′ə rāt), *v.* multiply, spread.

prolific (prə lif′ik), *adj.* producing offspring abundantly.

prone (prōn), *adj.* inclined or disposed, liable.

propitious (prə pish′əs), *adj.* favorably inclined.

proprietorship (prə pri′ə tər ship), *n.* ownership.

prosperity (pro sper′ə tē), *n.* success.

prostrate (pros′trāt), *v.* lay down flat.

protuberance (prō tü′bər əns), *n.* part that sticks out, bulge.

providence (prov′ə dəns), *n.* God's care and help.

provision (prə vizh′ən), *n.* act of providing, preparation.

prow (prou), *n.* the front of a ship.

puerile (pyü′ər əl), *adj.* childish.

pyre (pīr), *n.* pile of wood for burning a dead body as a funeral rite.

quenche (kwench), *v.* stop, put out, drown out.

quiet (kwī′ət), *v.* make silent, hush.

rabble-rouser (rab′əl rou′zər), *n.* person who tries to stir up groups of people.

rafter (raf′tər), *n.* slanting beam of a roof.

rampart (ram′pärt), *n.* wide bank of earth built as a fortification.

rank (rank), *n.* position, grade, class.

rapier (rā′pē ər), *n.* long, light sword.

rapine (rap′ən), *n.* a robbing by force and carrying off, plundering.

ratio (rā′shē ō), *n.* relative magnitude.

rational (rash′ə nəl), *adj.* based on reasoning.

rattan (ra tan′), *n.* stems of various palms used for wickerwork, canes.

ravening (rav′ə ning), *adj.* greedy and hungry.

realm (relm), *n.* kingdom.

reap (rēp), *v.* cut grain or gather a crop.

reciprocal (ri sip′rə kəl), *adj.* in return, mutual.

recluse (rek′lüs), *n.* person who lives shut up or withdrawn from the world.

recompense (rek′əm pens), *n.* payment, reward.

recourse (rē′kôrs), *n.* a turning for help or protection.

recumbent (ri kum′bənt), *adj.* lying down.

refinement (ri fīn′mənt), *n.* improvement.

rekindle (rē kin′dl), *v.* ignite or arouse again.

relativistic (rel ə tə vis′tik), *adj.* of or having to do with relativity.

relinquish (ri ling′kwish), *v.* give up, release.

remnant (rem′nənt), *n.* a small part left.

render (ren′dər), *v.* give, do.

renown (ri noun′), *n.* a being widely celebrated or held in high repute, fame.

renunciation (ri nun sē ā′shən), *n.* a giving up of a right, title, possession, etc.

repel (ri pel′), *v.* drive away, reject, displease.

repellent (ri pel′ənt), *adj.* disagreeable, repugnant.

repent (ri pent′), *v.* feel sorry for having done wrong and seek forgiveness.

replenish (ri plen′ish), *v.* fill again, renew.

repugnant (ri pug′nənt), *adj.* disagreeable.

repulse (ri puls′), *v.* drive back, repel, reject.

requisite (rek′wə zit), *adj.* required by circumstances, necessary.

requite (ri kwīt′), *v.* pay back, reward.

resolve (ri zolv′), *n.* decide, determine.

resort (ri zôrt′), *v.* go or repair to.

retainer (ri tā′nər), *n.* person who serves a person of rank.

rhetorician (ret ə rish′ən), *n.* person skilled in, or a teacher of, rhetoric.

rigging (rig′ing), *n.* the arrangement of masts, sails, ropes, etc., on a ship.

righteous (rī′chəs), *adj.* virtuous, proper, just.

rite (rīt), *n.* a formal procedure or act in a religious or other ceremony.

ritual (rich′ü əl), *n.* form, system, or prescribed order of performing a ceremony or rite.

rugged (rug′id), *adj.* rough, sturdy, hardy.

Sabbath (sab′əth), *n.* day of the week — Sunday for most Christians — used for rest and worship.

sage (sāj), *adj.* showing wisdom or judgment.

salient (sā′lē ənt), *adj.* standing out, prominent.

salutary (sal′yə ter ē), *adj.* beneficial, healthy.

sate (sāt), *v.* satisfy fully.

scan (skan), *v.* look at closely, examine.

sceptic [skeptic] (skep′tik), *n.* person who questions the truth of theories or facts; doubter.

scorn (skôrn), *n.* a feeling of contempt.

scoundrel (skoun′drəl), *n.* a person without honor or principle.

scourge (skerj), *v.* whip, flog.

scurry (sker′ē), *v.* run quickly, hurry.

seal (sēl), *n.* thing that fastens; pledge.

sear (sēr), *v.* burn or char the surface of.

sect (sekt), *n.* a religious group separated from an established church.

seethe (sēᴛʜ), *v.* be excited, disturbed.

sepulcher (sep′əl kər), *n.* place of burial, tomb.

sequin (sē′kwən), *n.* spangle used to ornament clothing.

serene (sə rēn′), *adj.* peaceful, calm.

servile (ser′vəl), *adj.* like that of slaves; yielding through fear.

shaft (shaft), *n.* 1 stem, stalk, column; 2 ray or beam of light.

shire (shīr), *n.* county in Great Britain.

shod (shod), *v.* put shoes on a person or horse.

shrill (shril), *adj.* having a high pitch; piercing in sound.

shuttle (shut′l), *n.* device that carries the thread in weaving.

significance (sig nif′ə kəns), *n.* importance, consequence, meaning.

sinewy (sin′yü ē), *adj.* strong, tough, stringy.

sinuous (sin′yü əs), *adj.* having many curves.

smother (smuth′ər), *v.* suffocate; keep back.

social (sō′shəl), *adj.* concerned with human beings in their relations to each other.

sojourn (sō′jėrn), *v.* brief stay.

solace (sol′is), *n.* comfort, relief, consolation.

solar (sō′lər), *adj.* having to do with the sun.

solemn (sol′əm), *adj.* of a serious character.

sound (sound), *adj.* free from error, reliable.

sovereignty (sov′rən tē), *n.* supreme authority.

sow (sō), *v.* scatter seed on the ground, plant.

span (span), *n.* distance between the top of the thumb and the top of the little finger when the hand is spread out.

sparse (spärs), *adj.* thinly scattered, scanty.

specious (spē′shəs), *adj.* seeming desirable, reasonable, or probable, but not really so.

specter (spek′tər), *n.* phantom or ghost.

spherical (sfir′ə kəl), *adj.* spherical, round.

splendor (splen′dər), *n.* magnificent show.

spring (spring), *v.* arise, grow, burst forth.

spurious (spyúr′ē əs), *adj.* not genuine, false.

squire (skwīr), *n.* young man of noble family who attended a knight.

stamina (stam′ə nə), *n.* strength, endurance.

statute (stach′üt), *n.* law enacted by a legislative body.

steep (stēp), *adj.* having a sharp slope.

stifling (stī′fəl ing), *adj.* stopping the breath, smothering.

stratagem (strat′ə jəm), *n.* scheme or trick for deceiving an enemy.

strategic (strə tē′jik), *adj.* based on careful planning and management.

stratosphere (strat′ə sfir), *n.* region of the atmosphere.

stratum (strā′təm), *n.* layer of material.

stray (strā), *v.* lose one's way, wander.

subjugate (sub′jə gāt), *v.* subdue, conquer.

sublime (sə blīm′), *adj.* lofty or elevated in thought, feeling, etc.; noble, exalted

subsist (səb sist′), *v.* keep alive, live.

suffice (sə fīs′), *v.* be enough, sufficient.

summit (sum′it), *n.* the highest point, top.

sumptuous (sump′chü əs), *adj.* lavish, costly.

superfluous (su pėr′flù əs), *adj.* more than is

needed, unncessary.

suppliant (sup′lē ənt), *n*. person who asks humbly and earnestly.

supplication (sup′lṳ kā′shən), *n*. a humble prayer addressed to God or a deity.

supposition (sup′ə zish′ən), *n*. belief or opinion.

surpass (sər pas′), *v*. do better than, excel.

swathe (swoŦH), *v*. wrap up closely, envelop.

swoop (swüp), *v*. come down with a rush, descend in a sudden attack.

tartish (tärt′ish), *adj*. having a sour but agreeable taste.

teem (tēm), *v*. be full of, abound, swarm.

temperate (tem′pər it), *adj*. not hot and not cold.

tempered (tem′pərd), *adj*. treated so as to become hard but not too brittle, moderated.

tempest (tem′pist), *n*. violent disturbance.

thane (thān), *n*. in early English history, a man who ranked between an earl and an ordinary freeman. In Scottish history, a baron or lord.

thatch (thach), *n*. straw as roofing.

theologian (thē′ə lō′jən), *n*. an expert in religious doctrines.

thistle (this′əl), *n*. any of various composite plants with prickly stalks and leaves.

thither (thiŦH′ər), *adv*. to that place, there.

thong (thông), *n*. narrow strip of leather.

threshold (thresh′ōld), *n*. the bottom of a door frame; doorway.

throng (thrông), *v*. crowd, fill with a crowd.

tillage (til′ij), *n*. cultivation of land,.

timber (tim′bər), *n*. wooded land, forests.

toil (toil), *n*. hard work.

tolerance (tol′ər əns), *n*. a willingness to let other people do as they think best.

torrent (tôr′ənt), *n*. a violent, rushing stream of water; a heavy downpour.

totter (tot′ər), *v*. walk with unsteady steps.

tractable (trak′tə bəl), *adj*. easily controlled.

transfigure (tran sfig′yər), *v*. change in form or appearance; change so as to exalt.

transgress (trans gres′), *v*. break a law; sin.

translucence (tran slü′sens), *n*. something that lets light through without being transparent.

treachery (trech′er ē), *n*. a breaking of faith.

treatise (trē′tis), *n*. a formal and systematic book dealing with some subject.

trench (trench), *n*. a deep furrow, ditch.

tresses (tres′əs), *n*. long, flowing hair.

trifle (trī′fəl), *n*. thing of little value.

trinket (tring′kit), *n*. any small fancy article, bit of jewelry, or the like.

trodden (trod′n), *v*. stepped down upon heavily, trampled.

truant (trü′ənt), *n*. person who neglects duty.

trudge (truj), *v*. walk wearily or with effort.

tumult (tü′mult), *n*. uproar; violent disturbance.

unacquainted (un ə kwān′tid), *v*. not aware, informed, or knowledgeable.

unanimous (yü nan′ə məs), *adj*. in complete accord or agreement.

ungrounded (un groun′did), *adj*. without foundation, or reason.

unprecedented (un pres′ə den′tid), *adj*. having no precedent; never done before.

unstinted (un stint′id), *adj*. without limit.

untold (un tōld′), *adj*. too many to be counted.

valiant (val′yənt), *adj*. courageous.

vat (vat), *n*. a large container for liquids; a tank.

veil (vāl), *n*. piece of very thin material worn to protect or hide the face, or as an ornament.

venerate (ven′ə rāt′), *v*. regard with deep respect, revere.

veranda (və ran′də), *n*. a large porch or gallery along one or more sides of a house.

vex (veks), *v*. anger by trifles, annoy, provoke.

vial (vī′əl), *n*. a small bottle.

vicar (vik′ər), *n*. the minister of a parish in the Church of England.

vice (vīs), *n*. an immoral habit or tendency.

vicissitude (və sis′ə tüd), *n*. change in circumstances or fortune.

vigor (vig′ər), *n*. active strength; energy.

vile (vil), *adj*. very bad, evil.

vilify (vil′ə fī), *v*. speak evil of, slander.

vindictive (vin dik′tiv), *adj*. feeling or showing a strong tendency toward revenge.

vivacious (vī vā′shəs), *adj*. lively, sprightly.

void (void), *n*. an empty space, vacuum.

vow (vou), *n*. a solemn promise.

wage (wāj), *v*. carry on.

wield (wēld), *v*. hold and use, manage, control.

wistful (wist′fəl), *adj*. longing, yearning.

yoke (yōk), *n*. something that holds people in slavery or submission.

zealous (zel′əs), *adj*. full of zeal, eager.

ACKNOWLEDGMENTS

TEXTS

10 From *The Epic of Gilgamesh* translated by N. K. Sandars (Penguin Classics 1960, second revised edition 1972). Copyright © N. K. Sandars, 1960, 1964, 1972. Reprinted by permission of Penguin Books Ltd.

17 From "Judgement of the Dead" in *Ancient Egyptian Literature*, volume II by Miriam Lichtheim. Copyright © 1976 by The Regents of the University of California. Reprinted by permission.

18 From *Echoes of Egyptian Voices: An Anthology of Ancient Egyptian Poetry*, translated by John L. Foster. Copyright © 1992 by John L. Foster. Reprinted by permission of the University of Oklahoma Press.

20 From *Echoes of Egyptian Voices: An Anthology of Ancient Egyptian Poetry*, translated by John L. Foster. Copyright © 1992 by John L. Foster. Reprinted by permission of the University of Oklahoma Press.

26 Reprinted from *Love Songs of the New Kingdom* translated by John L. Foster. Copyright © 1969, 1970, 1971, 1972, 1973, 1974 by John L. Foster. By permission of the author and the University of Texas Press.

40 Reprinted from *The Iliad of Homer, the Wrath of Achilles*, Shortened and Translated by I. A. Richards, by permission of W. W. Norton & Company, Inc. Copyright © 1950 by W. W. Norton & Company, Inc. Copyright renewed 1978 by I. A. Richards.

49 From *Sappho and the Greek Lyric Poets* by Willis Barnstone, translator. Copyright © 1962, 1967, 1988 by Willis Barnstone. Reprinted by permission of Schocken Books, published by Pantheon Books, a division of Random House, Inc.

52 Excerpt from *The Presocratic Philosophers*, 2nd Edition by G. S. Kirk, J. E. Raven and M. Schofield. Copyright © Cambridge University Press 1957, 1983. Reprinted with the permission of Cambridge University Press.

55 From "Selection from Thucydides' History" translated by Gerald F. Else from *Classics in Translation Volume I: Greek Literature* edited by Paul MacKendrick and Herbert M. Howe. Copyright © 1952 by the Regents of the University of Wisconsin. Reprinted by permission of the University of Wisconsin Press.

61 Excerpts from *The Dialogues of Plato*, translated in English with analyses and introductions by B. Jowett, M.A. Reprinted by permission.

65 From *On the Nature of the Universe* by Lucretius, translated by R. E. Latham (Penguin Classics 1951). Copyright R. E. Latham, 1951. Reproduced by permission by Penguin Books Ltd.

69 From *Catullus* edited with introduction, translation and notes by G. P. Goold. Copyright © 1983 by G. P. Goold. Reprinted by permission of Gerald Duckworth and Company, Ltd.

71 From *The Aeneid of Virgil* by Allen Mandelbaum, Translation © 1971 by Allen Mandelbaum. Used by permission of Bantam Books, a division of Bantam Doubleday Dell Publishing Group.

90 and 95 From *The New English Bible*. Copyright © Oxford University Press and Cambridge University Press, 1961, 1970. Reprinted by permission.

108 From *Confessions* by Saint Augustine, translated by R. S. Pine-Coffin (Penguin Classics, 1961) Copyright © R. S. Pine-Coffin, 1961.

132 "Surah 1" from *Muhammad and the Quran* by Rafiq Zakaria (Penguin Books, 1991) Copyright © Rafiq Zakaria, 1991.

133 "Light" from *The Koran* translated by N. J. Dawood (Penguin Classics 1956, Fifth revised edition 1990) Copyright © N. J. Dawood, 1956, 1959, 1966, 1968, 1974, 1990.

137 From *The Life and Works of Jahiz*, translations of selected texts by Charles Pellat. Translated from the French by D. M. Hawke.

140 From *The Classical Heritage in Islam* by Franz Rosenthal, translated from the German by Emile and Jenny Marmorstein. Reprinted by permission of the University of California Press and Franz Rosenthal.

143 From *Andalusian Poems*. Translated by Christopher Middleton and Leticia Garza-Falcón. Copyright © 1993 by Christopher Middleton and Leticia Farza-Falcón. Reprinted by permission of David R. Godine, Publisher, Inc.

148 From *Rumi, Poet and Mystic (1207–1273)*. Selections from his writings translated from the Persian with Introduction and Notes by the late Reynold A. Nicholson (London, Allen and Unwin, 1968), Reprinted by permission of Unwin Hyman, an imprint of HarperCollins Publishers, Ltd.

154 From *Rose Garden of Sa'di*, translated by Edward Rehatsek and edited by W. A. Archer. (Allen & Unwin 1964). Reprinted by permission of Unwin Hyman, an imprint of Harper Collins Publishers, Ltd.

156 From *Ibn Khaldun, the Muqaddimah* translated from the Arabic by Franz Rosenthal. Copyright © 1967 by Princeton University Press. Reprinted by permission of Princeton University Press.

166 From *A Chronicle of the Carmelites in Persia and the Papal Mission of the XVIIth and XVIIIth Centuries*, compiled by H. G. Chick, London: Eyre and Spottiswoode.

180 "The Wanderer," translated by E. T. Donaldson, is reprinted from *The Norton Anthology of English Literature*, Sixth Edition, Volume 1, M. H. Abrams, General Editor. By permission of W. W. Norton & Company, Inc. Copyright © 1993, 1986, 1979, 1974, 1968, 1962 by W. W. Norton & Company, Inc.

182 From *A History of the English Church and People* by Bede, translated by Leo Sherley-Price (Penguin Classics 1955, Revised edition 1968) Copyright © Leo Sherley-Price, 1955, 1968.

188 Reprinted by permission of The Putnam Publishing Group from *Dark and Middle Ages Reader* by Harry E. Wedeck. Copyright © 1964 by Harry E. Wedeck.

192 From *The Letters of Abelard and Heloise* translated by Betty Radice (Penguin Classics, 1974) Copyright © Betty Radice, 1974.

202 Excerpt from *Dante Alighieri, La Vita Nuova* translated with an Introduction by Barbara Reynolds. Copyright © Barbara Reynolds, 1969. Reprinted by permission of David Higham Associates.

210 From *Dante Alighieri, The Divine Comedy* translated by Charles S. Singleton. Copyright © 1970 by Princeton University Press. Reprinted by permission of Princeton University Press.

234 "Francesco Petrarch" translated versions by T. G. Bergin and Morris Bishop from *Lyric Poetry of the Italian Renaissance*, an anthology with verse translations collected by L. R. Lind. Reprinted by permission.

234 From *A Book of Women Poets from Antiquity to Now* by Aliki and Willis Barnstone, editors. Copyright © 1980 by Schocken Books Inc. Reprinted by permission of Schocken Books, published by Pantheon Books, a division of Random House, Inc.

273 Excerpt from the first of Descartes' *Meditations*, a work first published in 1641. The translation is by Elizabeth S. Haldane and G. R. T. Ross and is reprinted with the permission of Cambridge University Press.

290 Reprinted with permission of Simon & Schuster and Unwin Hyman, an imprint of HarperCollins Publishers Limited from *The Analects of Confucius* by Arthur Waley, translator. Copyright © 1938 by George Allen & Unwin, Ltd.

291 From *Tao Te Ching* by Stephen Mitchell. Translation Copyright © 1988 by Stephen Mitchell. Reprinted by permission of HarperCollins Publishers, Inc.

293 From *Sources of Chinese Tradition* compiled by Wm. Theodore de Bary, Wing-tsit Chan and Burton Watson. Copyright © 1960 Columbia University Press. Reprinted by permission.

297 From *The Poetry of T'ao Ch'ien* translated by James Robert Hightower. Copyright © Oxford University Press 1970. Reprinted by permission of Oxford University Press.

298 From *The Poetry and Career of Li Po* by Arthur Waley. Copyright Allen and Unwin Ltd., 1956. Reprinted by permission of Unwin Hyman, an imprint of HarperCollins Publishers Limited.

299 "Watching the Reapers" from *Translations from the Chinese* by Arthur Waley. Copyright 1919 and renewed 1947 by Arthur Waley. Copyright 1947 and renewed 1969 by Alfred A. Knopf, Inc. Reprinted by permission of Alfred A. Knopf, Inc.

299 From *Sunflower Splendor: Three Thousand Years of Chinese Poetry* co-edited by Wu-chi Lu and Irving Yucheng Lo. Copyright © 1975 by Wu-chi Lu and Irving Lo. Reprinted by permission of Irving Lo.

301 From *The Life and Times of Po Chü-i* translated by Arthur Waley (Allen & Unwin 1949). Reprinted by permission of Unwin Hyman, an imprint of HarperCollins Publishers, Ltd.

306 From *The Pillow Book of Sei Shonagon* translated and edited by Ivan Morris. Copyright © 1967 by Ivan Morris. Reprinted by permission of Columbia University Press and Oxford University Press.

309 Reprinted from *The Tale of the Heike*, translated, with an Introduction, by Helen Craig McCullough with the permission of the publishers, Stanford University Press. © 1988 by the Board of Trustees of the Leland Stanford Junior University.

314 "Early Snow" from *The No Plays of Japan* edited and translated by Arthur Waley. Copyright 1922 by Arthur Waley. Used by permission of Grove/Atlantic, Inc.

317 From *Anthology of Japanese Literature*. Copyright © 1955 by Grove Press, Inc. Used by permission of Grove/Atlantic, Inc.

319 From *An Introduction to Haiku* by Harold G. Henderson. Copyright © 1958 by Harold G. Henderson. Used by permission of Doubleday, a division of Bantam Doubleday Dell Publishing Group, Inc.

326 From *Textual Sources for the Study of Hinduism* edited and translated by Wendy Doniger O'Flaherty with Daniel Gold, David Haberman and David Shulman. Copyright © Wendy Doniger O'Flaherty 1988. Originall published by Manchester University Press in 1988. Reprinted by permission of Manchester University Press.

330 From *The Bhagavad Gita* translated by Juan Mascaro (Penguin Classics, 1962). Copyright © Juan Mascaro, 1962.

333 Reprinted by permission of the publishers from *An Anthology of Sanskrit Court Poetry* translated by Daniel Ingalls, Cambridge, Mass.: Harvard University Press, Copyright © 1965 by the President and Fellows of Harvard College.

353 "How the World Changed" from *Liberian Folklore*, compiled by Doris Banks Henries. Copyright © 1966, Doris Banks Henries. Reprinted by permission of Macmillan Press Ltd.

354 From *African Folktales* selected and edited by Paul Radin. Copyright 1952 and renewed 1964 by Princeton University Press. Reprinted by permission of Princeton University Press.

360 From *Sundiata, An Epic of Old Mali* by D. T. Niane, translated by G. D. Pickett. Copyright © Longman Group Ltd. 1965. Reprinted by permission.

364 From *African Poetry, An Anthology of Traditional African Poems* compiled and edited by Ulli Beier. This selection © Cambridge University Press, 1966. Reprinted with the permission of Cambridge University Press and Ulli Beier.

368 Basil Davidson's "Mali in the Fourteenth Century," in *African Civilization Revisited: From Antiquity to Modern Times*, published by Africa World Press, 1991 Edition. All rights reserved. Reprinted by permission of the publisher.

373 Excerpt from *Equiano's Travels* Abridged and Edited by Paul Edwards. This Abridgement, Introduction, Appendix I, and Notes © Paul Edwards 1967. Reprinted by permission of Heinemann Publishers (Oxford) Limited.

377 From *Chaka: An Historical Romance* by Thomas Mofolo, translated from the original Sesuto by F. H. Dutton. Published for the International African Institute by Oxford University Press. Reprinted by permission.

395 Reprinted from *Royal Commentaries of the Incas and General History of Peru*, Part One by Garcilaso de la Vega, translated by Harold V. Livermore, Copyright © 1966. By permission of the University of Texas Press.

401 Selections from pp. 35–51 of Paul Zolbrod's *Diné Bahane: The Navajo Creation Story* (Albuquerque: University of New Mexico Press, 1984). Reprinted by permission.

406 From *Parker on the Iroquois* edited by William N. Fenton. Reprinted by permission of Syracuse University Press.

408 "Song" from *Cágaba* translated by Paul Radin from *Monotheism Among Primitive Peoples*. Reprinted by permission of Princeton University Press.

408 "Prayer." Neihardt, John G. *Black Elk Speaks: Being the Life Story of a Holy Man of the Oglala Sioux*. Lincoln: University of Nebraska Press, 1961.

408 Inca "Song" from *The Sacred Path*, edited by John Bierhorst. Copyright © 1983 by John Bierhorst. Reprinted by permission of Morrow Junior Books, a division of William Morrow & Company, Inc.

409 "Prayer to a Dead Buck" translated from the Navajo by W. W. Hill from *The Agricultural and Hunting Methods of the Navajo Indians*. Reprinted by permission of Yale University Press.

409 "Song" from *Under Mount Saint Elias: The History and Culture of the Yakutat Tlingit* translated by Frederica de Laguna. Reprinted by permission from the Smithsonian Institution Press.

412 Excerpt from "Ben Kindle's Winter Count" from Martha Warren Beckwith, "Mythology of the Oglala Sioux." Reproduced by permission of the American Folklore Society from *Journal of American Folklore 43,* October-December 1930. Not for further reproduction.

436 Sir Isaac Newton, *Mathematical Principles of Natural Philosophy and his System of the World,* translated by Andrew Motte (1729) and revised by Florian Cajori (Berkeley, Cal.: University of California Press, 1947), pp. xvii, xviii, 398–400. Used by permission.

440 From Jean Jacques Rousseau, *The Social Contract and Discourses* (1762, translated by G. D. H. Cole, Everyman's Library Edition, 1947). Reprinted by permission of Everyman's Library, David Campbell Publishers, Ltd.

445 "Jean Paul Marat: The Fall of Louis XVI" from Jean Paul Marat, "Le tyran puni," *Journal de la République Française, No. 105.* Wednesday, January 23, 1793. Reprinted in Jean Paul Marat, *Textes Choisis* edited by Lucien Scheler (Paris: Éditions de Minuit, 1945), pp. 165–8. Translated from the French by the editor. Reprinted by permission of the publisher.

461 von Clausewitz, Carl; *On War* Edited and Translated by Michael Howard and Peter Paret. Copyright © 1976 by Princeton University Press. Reprinted by permission of Princeton University Press.

465 "Autumn Feeling" and "On the Lake" by Johann Wolfgang von Goethe, translated by Christopher Middleton. Reprinted by permission of Suhrkamp Verlag.

466 "The Loreley" from *Monatshefte* (The University of Wisconsin Press) as appeared in *Heinrich Heine, Lyric Poems and Ballads,* translated by Ernest Feise (The University of Pittsburgh Press, 1961).

467 "The Silesian Weavers" is reprinted from *Heinrich Heine: Lyric Poems and Ballads,* Ernst Feise, translator, by permission of the University of Pittsburgh Press. © 1961, 1989 by University of Pittsburgh Press.

504 From *The Standard Edition of the Complete Psychological Works of Sigmund Freud* translated from the German under the general editorship of James Strachey, in collaboration with Anna Freud, assisted by Alix Strachey and Alan Tyson. Vol. XIV (1914–1916) *On the History of the Psycho-Analytic Movement* (London: The Hogarth Press and The Institute of Psycho-Analysis, 1957), pp. 20–24. Used by Permission of The Hogarth Press.

508 From *Modern Times: The World from the Twenties to the Eighties* by Paul Johnson. Copyright © 1983 by Paul Johnson. Reprinted by permission of HarperCollins Publishers, Inc.

514 "Dulce et Decorum Est" and "Anthem for Doomed Youth" by Wilfred Owen from *Collected Poems of Wilfred Owen.* Copyright © 1963 by Chatto & Windus, Ltd. Reprinted by permission of New Directions Publishing Corporation.

516 Poems from August Stramm, *Twenty Two Poems* translated by Patrick Bridgwater. Reprinted by permission of Patrick Bridgwater.

518 "Lecture on Dada" (1922) translated from the French by Robert Motherwell from *Dada Painters and Poets,* by Robert Motherwell, New York, 1951, pp. 246–51. Reprinted by permission.

521 Excerpts from *A Room of One's Own* by Virginia Woolf, Copyright © 1929 by Harcourt Brace & Company and renewed 1957 by Leonard Woolf, reprinted by permission of the publisher.

526 From *Hind Swaraj or Indian Rule* by M. K. Gandhi, Navajivan Publishing House, 1938. Reprinted by permission

534 From *Survival in Auschwitz* by Primo Levi, translated by Stuart Woolf, Translation Copyright © 1959 by The Orion Press, Inc., translation. Original copyright © 1958 by Giulio Einaudi editori S.p.A. Used by permission of Viking Penguin, a division of Penguin Books USA Inc.

539 "Report on the Bombing of Nagasaki" from *The New York Time.*, December 28, 1945. Copyright 1945 by The New York Times Company. Reprinted by permission.

543 Excerpt from *Thank God for the Atom Bomb* by Paul Fussell. Copyright © 1988 by Paul Fussell. Reprinted by permission of Simon & Schuster, Inc.

544 Specified excerpts from "Mohawks in High Steel" from *Up in the Old Hotel* by Joseph Mitchell. Reprinted by permission of Pantheon Books, a division of Random House, Inc. Originally published in the September 17, 1949 issue of *The New Yorker.*

549 "The Bamboo Leaves" from *Contemporary Japanese Literature* by Howard Hibbett, Editor. Copyright © 1977 by Alfred A. Knopf, Inc. Reprinted by permission of the publisher.

552 From *Invisible Man* by Ralph Ellison. Copyright © 1947, 1948, 1952 and renewed 1975, 1976, 1980 by Ralph Ellison. Reprinted by permission of Random House, Inc.

562 Excerpts from Chapter Two from *The Dark Child* by Camara Laye. Copyright 1954 and copyright renewed © 1982 by Camara Laye. Reprinted by permission of Hill and Wang, a division of Farrar, Straus & Giroux, Inc.

565 "Seascape" and "Questions of Travel" from *The Complete Poems 1927–1979* by Elizabeth Bishop. Copyright © 1979, 1983, by Alice Helen Methfessel. Reprinted by permission of Farrar, Straus & Giroux, Inc.

572 "Sea Grapes" from *Collected Poems* 1948–1984 by Derek Walcott. Copyright © 1986 by Derek Walcott. Reprinted by permission of Farrar, Straus & Giroux, Inc.

578 "The New Measure of Man" by Vaclav Havel from *The New York Times,* July 8, 1994. Copyright © 1994 by The New York Times Company. Reprinted by permission.

ILLUSTRATIONS

Unless otherwise acknowledged, all photographs are the property of Scott, Foresman and Company. Page abbreviations are as follows: (T) top, (C) center, (B) bottom, (L) left, (R) right.
BACK COVER © Stephen M. Mortensen

0-1 Copyright the British Museum **2** Hirmer Fotoarchiv, Munich **3L** Hirmer Fotoarchiv, Munich **3R** Neg.23277/Oriental Institute, The University of Chicago **4** Hirmer Fotoarchiv, Munich **5L** Hirmer Fotoarchiv, Munich **5R** Directorate General of Antiquities, Baghdad **6L** Hirmer Fotoarchiv, Munich **6R** Copyright the British Museum **7L** Hirmer Fotoarchiv, Munich **7R** The Metropolitan Museum of Art, Rogers Fund and Edward S.Harkness Gift, 1929 (29.3.3) **8L** Hirmer Fotoarchiv, Munich **8R** Hirmer Fotoarchiv, Munich **9L** UNESCO **9R** Neg. 23823, Oriental Institute, The University of Chicago

20 Ägyptisches Museum, Berlin 24 Harvard MFA Expedition/Courtesy, Museum of Fine Arts, Boston 25 Hirmer Fotoarchiv, Munich 30-31 Greek National Tourist Organization 32 Hirmer Fotoarchiv, Munich 33L Alison Frantz 33R Deutsches Archaologisches Institut, Athens 34L The Metropolitan Museum of Art, Fletcher Fund, 1956 (56.171.38) 34R Alinari/Art Resource, New York 35L The Metropolitan Museum of Art, Harris Brisbane Dick Fund, 1954 (54.3.3) 36L Copyright the British Museum 35R Alinari/Art Resource, New York 36R Alinari/Art Resource, New York 37L Hirmer Fotoarchiv, Munich 37R Copyright the British Museum 38R Musee National, Bardo 39L Alinari/Art Resource, New York 39R Copyright the British Museum 46L Nihatallah/Art Resource, New York 46C Hirmer Fotoarchiv, Munich 46R Scala/Art Resource, New York 47T Alinari/Art Resource, New York 47BL Alinari/Art Resource, New York 47BR Alinari/Art Resource, New York 76 The Metropolitan Museum of Art 77 Alinari/Art Resource, New York 80-81 Copyright the British Museum 82 The British Library 83L Erich Lessing/Art Resource, New York 83R The British Library 84L Erich Lessing/Art Resource, New York 84R Collection of The Israel Antiquities Authority. Photo,The Israel Museum, Jerusalem 85L The British Library 85R Collection Israel Museum, Jerusalem 86L Alinari/Art Resource, New York 86R Weidenfeld & Nicolson Archives 87L Bullaty and Lomeo 87R Alinari/Art Resource, New York 88L Hirmer Fotoarchiv, Munich 88R Hirmer Fotoarchiv, Munich 89L Kunsthistorisches Museum, Vienna 89R Giraudon/Art Resource, New York 101 Copyright the British Museum 113T Giraudon/Art Resource, New York 113B Ägyptisches Museum, Berlin/Staatliche Museen Preussischer Kulturbesitz 114T The Metropolitan Museum of Art, Rogers Fund, 1903 (03.14.5) 114B Erich Lessing/Art Resource, New York 115 Andre Held 116 ALLAndre Held 117 Turkish Press Broadcasting & Tourist Department 118 Hirmer Fotoarchiv, Munich 119 Hirmer Fotoarchiv, Munich 122-123 Shostal/SuperStock, Inc. 124 Spencer Collection/New York Public Library, Astor, Lenox and Tilden Foundations 125L The British Library 125R Freer Gallery of Art, The Smithsonian Institution, Wash., D.C. 126L American Numismatic Society 126R By courtesy of the Victoria & Albert Museum 127L The British Library 127R The British Library 128 Lekegian 129L Royal Asiatic Society Loan 5/The British Library 129R Edinburgh University Library 130L Hermitage, St.Petersburg 130R The Metropolitan Museum of Art, Anonymous Gift, 1950 (50.87) 131L The Metropolitan Museum of Art, Rogers Fund, 1938 (38.149.1) 131R Copyright the British Museum 146 Robert Frerck/Odyssey Productions, Chicago 147 Robert Frerck/Odyssey Productions, Chicago 149T Robert Frerck/Odyssey Productions, Chicago 149B Jean-Claude LeJeune 150 Robert Frerck/Odyssey Productions, Chicago 151 The Trustees of the Chester Beatty Library, Dublin 152 The British Library 164 By courtesy of the Victoria & Albert Museum 165 Courtesy of the Arthur M. Sackler Museum, Harvard University Museums, Private Collection 170-171 Alinari / Art Resource, New York 172 The British Library 173L Copyright the British Museum 173R Bibliotheque Nationale, Paris 174L Foto Marburg/Art Resource, New York 174R Pierpont Morgan Library 175L Museum fur Kunst und Kulturgeschichte Dortmund 175R Mansell Collection 176L Universitetets Oldsaksamling, Oslo 176R Bodleian Library, Oxford 177L Alinari/Art Resource, New York 177R The British Library 178L A.F.Kersting 178R Lambeth Palace Library 179L Giraudon/Art Resource, New York 179R National Portrait Gallery, London 186T Giraudon/Art Resource, New York 186B Phaidon Picture Archives 196 Foto Marburg/Art Resource, New York 197 Giraudon/Art Resource, New York 198B Ewing Galloway 199 Foto Marburg/Art Resource, New York 200 Foto Marburg/Art Resource, New York 208 Alinari/Art Resource, New York 215 Giraudon/Art Resource, New York 217TL Alinari/Art Resource, New York 217TR Alinari/Art Resource, New York 217B Erich Lessing/Art Resource, New York 218 Giraudon/Art Resource, New York 219 Erich Lessing/Art Resource, New York 220 Kunsthistorisches Museum, Vienna 222 Alinari/Art Resource, New York 224 Alinari/Art Resource, New York 225L North Wind Picture Archives 225R Library of Congress 226R Scala/Art Resource, New York 227L Alinari/Art Resource, New York 227R Albertina, Vienna 228R Alte Pinakothek, Munich 229L Prints Division/ New York Public Library, Astor, Lenox and Tilden Foundations 229R National Maritime Museum, Greenwich, England 230L Copyright the British Museum 230R Berg Collection/New York Public Library, Astor, Lenox and Tilden Foundations 231L National Library of Medicine, Bethesda, Maryland 231R John Freeman 237 Alinari/Art Resource, New York 239 Alinari/Art Resource, New York 243L Alinari/Art Resource, New York 243R Alinari/Art Resource, New York 244 Alinari/Art Resource, New York 251 Alinari/Art Resource, New York 253 Erich Lessing/Art Resource, New York 254 Scala/ Art Resource, New York 255 Matthias Grünewald, *The Small Crucifixion*, Samuel H. Kress Collection, ©1994 Board of Trustees, National Gallery of Art, Washington, D.C. 256 foto MAS 258 By permission of the American Geographical Society Collection, Univ. of Wisconsin, Milwaukee 260 John Carter Brown Library, Brown University 262 The National Gallery, London 263 Service Photographique de la Reunion des Musees Nationaux 267 El Greco, *Saint Martin and the Beggar*, Widener Collection, National Gallery of Art, Washington, D.C. 270 The British Library 271 The British Library 280 Bijutsu Shuppan-Sha, Tokyo 282 East Asian Library, Columbia Univ. 283L Jehangir Gazdar/Woodfin Camp & Associates 283R Sothebys 284L Cat.116445/Field Museum of Natural History, Chicago 284R Government of India Information Services, Washington, D.C. 285L By courtesy of the Victoria & Albert Museum 285R Eugene Fuller Memorial Collection/Seattle Art Museum 286L Copyright the British Museum 286R William Sturgis Bigelow Collection/ Courtesy, Museum of Fine Arts, Boston 287 Tokyo National Museum 288L National Palace Museum, Taipei, Taiwan, Republic of China 288R The British Library 289L The Granger Collection, New York 289R Eugene Fuller Memorial Collection/ Seattle Art Museum 304 National Palace Museum, Taipei, Taiwan, Republic of China 305 The Nelson-Atkins Museum of Art, Kansas City, Missouri, Purchase: Nelson Trust 46-51/2 320 Tokyo National Museum 321 Chinese and Japanese Special Fund/Courtesy, Museum of Fine Arts, Boston 322 Daitoku-Ji, Kyoto 323 Okumura

Masanobu, Japanese, 1668-1768, Perspective Picture of Cooling-off in the Evening at the Ryogoku Bridge, woodblock print, c.1735-40, 44.6 x 56.5 cm. Clarence Buckingham Collection, 1932.1355, photograph © 1994 The Art Institute of Chicago. All Rights Reserved. 324 The Nelson-Atkins Museum of Art, Kansas City, Missouri 336 Martin Hurlimann 337L National Museum, New Delhi 337R Martin Hurlimann 340-341 Werner Forman/Art Resource, New York 342T AP Service/National Museum, Athens 343L Werner Forman/Art Resource, New York 343R Reproduced by permission of the Trustees of The Wallace Collection 344 Basil Davidson 345L Copyright the British Museum 345R Bibliotheque Nationale, Paris 346L The University Museum, University of Pennsylvania 346R Photograph by Franko Khoury/National Museum of African Art, Eliot Elisofon Photographic Archives, Smithsonian Institution 347L The British Library 347R Werner Forman/Art Resource, New York 348 Museo Degli Argenti, Palazzo Pitti, Florence 349L Copyright the British Museum 349R The British Library 371 Buffalo Museum of Science 372 Phoebe A. Hearst Museum of Anthropology, The University of California at Berkeley 382-383 New York Public Library, Astor, Lenox and Tilden Foundations 384 Neg.315917/American Museum of Natural History 385 The Ohio Historical Society 386L Neg.322739/American Museum of Natural History 386R Neg.52185/Arizona State Museum, University of Arizona 387L Illinois Archaeological Survey 387R Lesley Newhart 388L Bodleian Library, Oxford 388R New York Public Library, Astor, Lenox and Tilden Foundations 389R Courtesy Onandaga Nation, Photo New York State Museum 390R Courtesy of: National Museum of the American Indian, Smithsonian Institution 391R Smithsonian Institution 392 Museo Nacional de Antropologia, Mexico City 393 Courtesy of: National Museum of the American Indian, Smithsonian Institution 399 Museo Nacional de Antropologia, Mexico City 400 Museo Nacional de Antropologia, Mexico City 411 From the Collection of The Detroit Institute of Art, Gift of Mr. and Mrs. Richard A. Pohrt 414 Werner Forman/Art Resource, New York 415 Denver Art Museum, Denver, Colorado 416 From the Collection of The Detroit Institute of Art, Gift of Mr. and Mrs. Richard A. Pohrt 421T Copyright the British Museum 421B The Museum for African Art. Photograph: Jerry L. Thompson 422 ColorPhoto Hans Hinz 423T Copyright the British Museum 423B Lee Boltin 424 Phoebe Hearst Museum of Anthropology, Courtesy University of California at Berkeley. Photo by Peter T. Furst 426 Hamburger Kunsthalle 428 Science Museum, London 429L Copyright the British Museum 430L Library of Congress 431L Musees de La Ville de Paris 432L Service Photographique de la Reunion des Musees Nationaux 432R Bettmann Archive 433L Windsor Castle, Royal Library, © Her Majesty Queen Elizabeth II 433R Staatliche Museen Preussischer Kulturbesitz 434L Library of Congress 434R Bettmann Archive 435L Culver Pictures 435R Edison National Historic Site/U. S. Dept. of the Interior, National Park Service 455 Staatliche Museen Preussischer Kulturbesitz 456 Museum of Art, Rhode Island School of Design, Providence, RI 476 Library of Congress 477 Brown Brothers 483 Courtauld Collection/Courtauld Institute Galleries, London 484 Mary Cassatt, American 1844-1926, The Bath, oil on canvas, 1891/92, 39-1/2 x 26 in., Robert A. Waller Fund, 1910.2, photograph courtesy of The Art Institute of Chicago. All Rights Reserved. 486 The Metropolitan Museum of Art, Gift of Thomas F. Ryan, 1910 (11.173.9) 487 Musee Rodin, Paris 488 Foto Marburg/Art Resource, New York 489 The National Gallery, London 490 Joseph M. W. Turner, Burning of the Houses of Parliament, Philadelphia Museum of Art, The John H. McFadden Collection 491 Erich Lessing/Art Resource, New York 492T Paul Cézanne, Mont Sainte-Victoire, Philadelphia Museum of Art, George W. Elkins Collection 492B Copyright Yale University Art Gallery B.A.1903, Bequest of Stephen Carlton Clark 494 Museo del Prado, Madrid. ©1995 Artists Rights Society, Inc. SPADEM, Paris 496 Bill Engdahl/Hedrich Blessing 497R Einstein Archives 498L Courtesy of the Harvard University Portrait Collection, Gift of Mrs. Stanley B. Resor 498R Ewing Galloway 499L UPI/Bettmann 499R Official U.S.Navy Photograph 500L The National Archives 500R AP/Wide World 501L Eastfoto/SOVFOTO 501R BBC Photo 502L The Mount Everest Foundation 502R Eastfoto/SOVFOTO 503 UPI/ Bettmann 513 Private Collection, Allan Mitchell Photograph 518 Philadelphia Museum of Art, Louise and Walter Arensberg Collection 530 Philadelphia Museum of Art, The Alfred Stieglitz Collection 531 ALL Berenice Abbott/ Commerce Graphics Ltd., Inc. 532T André Kertész, American, 1894-1985, Shadows of the Eiffel Tower (view looking down from tower to people underneath,) silver gelatin print, 1929. 16.5 x 21.9 cm, Julien Levy Collection, Special Photography Acquisition Fund, 1979.77, photograph © 1994, The Art Institute of Chicago. All Rights Reserved. 532B Henri Cartier-Bresson/ Magnum Photos 556 From the collection of Whitney Museum of American Art 557T © 1995 Succession H. Matisse, ARS, New York/Art Resource, New York 557B Picasso, Pablo. Les Demoiselles d'Avignon. (June-July 1907). Oil on canvas 8' x 7'8"(243.9 x 233.7 cm). The Museum of Modern Art, New York. Acquired through the Lillie P. Bliss Bequest. Photograph © 1995 The Museum of Modern Art, New York. © 1995 Artists Rights Society, Inc./SPADEM, Paris 558T Scala/Art Resource, New York 558B Vassily Kandinsky, French, born Russia, 1866-1944, Painting with Green Center, oil on canvas, 1913, 109.9 x 120.6 cm. Arthur Jerome Eddy Memorial Collection, 1931.510, photograph © 1994, The Art Institute of Chicago. All Rights Reserved. 559 The Metropolitan Museum of Art, George A. Hearn Fund, 1957 (57.92) 560 Helen Frankenthaler, Mountains and Sea, 1952. Oil on canvas, 7' 2 7/8" x 9' 9 1/4" Collection of the artist, on loan to the National Gallery of Art, Washington, D.C. 561 Collection of Citibank, N.A., Courtesy of the artist and Francine Seders Gallery, Seattle. 570-571 Grant LeDuc/Stock Boston 574 Photo: Zindman/Fremont/Edward Thorp Gallery 575 Photo: Zindman/Fremont/Edward Thorp Gallery 576 Robert Miller Gallery, New York 577 Robert Miller Gallery, New York

INDEX